GW00641076

MPSI
UNT
BRA
REF
ALLS
3 8B
4605

RY
R

SOLD

DIV.
Account

Researchers from all backgrounds often need to find the answers to apparently simple questions about the British electorate, such as: How did white-collar trade unionists vote in 1983? What is the proportion of council tenants in the electorate now compared with twenty years ago? Yet up to now there has been no single source which provides the answers. *The British Electorate 1963–1987* provides, for the first time, an authoritative reference guide to British voters and British elections. It is based on a wealth of statistical information collected over the past quarter century by the British Election Study research teams at the Universities of Oxford and Essex.

The information presented covers a wide range of topics including voting patterns, turnout, party membership, partisanship and attitudes on issues ranging from nationalisation to capital punishment, abortion and welfare benefits. There are also separate tables for groups within the electorate such as men and women, different generations, trade unionists, the unemployed and Conservative and Labour voters. Tables deal with the same groups for each election, allowing the reader to look up information for a specific election year, to compare any two elections between 1963 and 1987 or to trace trends across the whole period.

The authors present their information in a standard, easy to read format that is accessible to the non-technical user. *The British Electorate 1963–1987* will be of particular value to political and sociological researchers, academics and students of British government and politics, political journalists, pollsters, market researchers, industrialists and trade unionists. It will also be a source of fascinating material for the general reader interested in British politics.

The British Electorate 1963–1987

The British Electorate 1963–1987

*A compendium of data from
the British Election Studies*

Ivor Crewe
Neil Day and
Anthony Fox

CAMBRIDGE UNIVERSITY PRESS

Cambridge

New York   Port Chester   Melbourne   Sydney

Published by the Press Syndicate of the University of Cambridge
The Pitt Building, Trumpington Street, Cambridge CB2 1RP
40 West 20th Street, New York, NY 10011, USA
10 Stamford Road, Oakleigh, Melbourne 3166, Australia

© Cambridge University Press 1991

First published 1991

Printed in Great Britain by The Bath Press, Avon

British Library cataloguing in publication data

The British electorate 1963–1987: a compendium of data from
the British Election Studies.
1. Great Britain. Parliament. House of Commons. Members.
General elections, history. Voting behaviour of electorate
I. Crewe, Ivor   II. Day, Neil   III. Fox, Anthony D.

Library of Congress cataloguing in publication data

Crewe, Ivor.
The British electorate 1963–1987: a compendium of data from the
British election studies / Ivor Crewe, Neil Day, Anthony Fox.
   p.   cm.
ISBN 0-521-32197-2
1. Voting – Great Britain. 2. Elections – Great Britain. 3. Great
Britain – Politics and government – 1964–1979. 4. Great Britain –
Politics and government – 1979–   I. Day, Neil.
II. Fox, Anthony D.   III. Title.
JN956.C74   1991
324.941085–dc20   90-36080 CIP

ISBN 0 521 32197 2 hardback

HAMPSHIRE COUNTY LIBRARY

R
324.941
085

0 521 321 972

C002462085

GO

CONTENTS

PREFACE

The origins of this book go back a long way. In the late 1970s we worked together on the 1974 and 1979 British Election Studies, then located at the University of Essex. A major focus of research was change since the early and mid-1960s, especially in various dimensions of partisanship. The starting point for the analysis was usually a simple pairwise comparison or time-series of cross-tabulations. Yet the amount of work and checking required seemed out of proportion to the simplicity of what was produced. How much easier our task would have been had a basic portfolio of standard cross-tabulations been created for each election study. The addition of two election studies since then, it seems to us, has made the need more urgent still.

A common complaint about election studies is that 'the questions are always the same'. This book, we hope, will show why that is the strength, not the weakness, of election studies. Impressionistic assertions about the British voter are the stock in trade of political commentators. But we cannot establish trends over time and differences – or the absence of differences – between groups without rigorously controlled comparison; and the 'control' must consist of identically constructed measures based on identically or very similar worded questions over a series of studies. Indeed, our regret is that over the years too many of the questions and their accompanying answer categories have been needlessly altered or, when revisions were necessary, altered without an attempt to preserve continuity of measurement. The experience of compiling these tables has made us acutely aware of the potential for analysis that is lost even by small changes of question phrasing and of the responsibility that the directors of future election studies have for maintaining precise continuity, wherever possible, with the measures adopted in previous studies.

This book could not have been produced without the assistance and support of many others. We wish to thank the ESRC Data Archive at the University of Essex for providing the data and documentation, and most particularly its Assistant Director, Eric Roughley, for unflagging help and advice. We are grateful to the University of Manchester and the University of Essex who generously provided computing resources. Extensive assistance with the computing was provided by John Smith and Pat Thompson of the Research Support Unit, Faculty of Economics and Social Studies, University of Manchester; by Charles Malcolm-Brown and Mel Read of the Department of Government, University of Essex; and by Anne Hockey of the ESRC Data Archive, University of Essex. Athena Barrett and the Polytechnic of North London's Reprographic Department are thanked for their care in assembling and copying the final typescript. Finally, we owe a debt of gratitude to the principal investigators of the British Election Studies: David Butler of Nuffield College, Oxford and Donald Stokes of Princeton, who began the series; our former colleagues at Essex, Bo Särlvik, James Alt and David Robertson; and the co-directors of the 1983 and 1987 studies, Anthony Heath, Roger Jowell and John Curtice. They share in any merit this book has.

Ivor Crewe   Neil Day   Anthony Fox

INTRODUCTION:
HOW TO USE THIS BOOK

This book is purely a work of reference or what Americans call a 'data sourcebook'. It can be used to look up a frequency distribution (of the vote, or partisanship, or any of the other dependent variables) for the whole electorate or a sub-category of the electorate in one particular year. It can be used to examine change or stability across a set of elections; to compare two consecutive elections or two elections separated by a long period of time; or to compare groups within the electorate at one point in time or across time. Whatever uses readers may make of the book, no analyses or interpretations will be found here. However, readers may need guidance about the procedures and conventions adopted in the compilation of the tables, and this is offered in the notes that follow.

Selection of tables
In choosing which tables to include, we were constrained by a number of factors. The first was the availability of data over a sufficiently long or consecutive time-series. Our rule of thumb for the inclusion of a variable was that data on it should be available on at least three occasions, of which the most recent should be no further back than 1983. In practice the vast majority of tables extend up to 1987 and contain figures for at least four points in time. Where we have included tables without data for 1987 it is usually because we believe there is a good prospect of comparable data being collected in a future British Election Study.

The second factor is closely related. Occasionally we have had to exclude variables which are intrinsically interesting but for which the questions (or the answer categories) changed drastically over the period. A case in point is further education. Frequent changes of question-wording and coding frames make it impossible to classify respondents according to a consistent definition of any category of further education except for attendance at a university or polytechnic.

A third consideration was validity. We have excluded the very small number of variables whose accuracy we doubt. For example, election surveys consistently under-report non-voting: the proportion of the sample claiming to have voted is typically 10 to 15 percentage points above the official turnout figure, partly because some non-voters in the sample mistakenly claim to have voted but mainly because non-voters tend to be under-represented in the sample. We have therefore excluded non-voting as a dependent variable while retaining 'non-voters' as a category variable on the grounds that those who claim not to have voted are almost certainly telling the truth.

The final factor was the importance of the data. Our instinct has been inclusive rather than exclusive; being unable to predict what researchers might wish to explore we have erred on the side of generosity. But inevitably the limit on space has forced us to leave out those combinations of variables for which there was no evident substantive or theoretical benefit.

Table layout and conventions
Each table follows a standard format. The columns always represent different election study years, from 1963 to 1987. Thus, trends over time can be gauged by reading from left to right. The

1

figures for each year are based on the *cross-sectional* sample, not the panel sample, for that year. Occasionally questions were put to the panel sample but not the cross-sectional sample of the same year, for example, questions on nationalisation in 1970 and on big business power and trade union power in February 1974. Even though these questions were identically or very similarly worded to questions asked in preceding and following studies, we have excluded them from the tables because they were put only to the surviving members of a panel first interviewed some years earlier: they do not constitute a representative sample.

The *title* always consists of the dependent (or row) variable, followed by the independent (or category variable). Thus a table titled 'Vote by age' refers to a set of sub-tables giving the vote of each age group for the election study years 1963 to 1987. Each sub-table is headed by the sub-category of the population to which it applies: for example, the sub-table headed by 'Aged 25–34' shows the vote of 25- to 34-year-olds for each election study year.

Readers may reconstruct tables by converting the percentage figures back to raw numbers. The percentages are based on the *weighted* number of respondents. The total number of respondents, given in the 'N. of respondents' row, is the total weighted number, rounded to a whole number. Where the percentage base falls below twenty respondents the percentage figures are displayed in parentheses. The percentage figures are rounded to a single decimal point. The 'total' per cent figure has been rounded to exactly 100.0%.

Percentage figures of less than 0.5% are shown as '0.0'. This usually arises because the sample contained no respondents in the cell in question. A figure of 0.0% does not mean, of course, that the true measure of the population belonging in that cell is zero. A dash ('—') indicates either that the appropriate questions were not asked in that particular year or that the variable is unavailable because it is not applicable in that year, for example, membership of the post-1970 political generation among respondents interviewed in the 1960s.

'Single category' variables
Some tables provide data for only one category of a variable. In the case of dichotomous variables, for example, there is no need to show the percentages for both answer categories since one is always 100% minus the other. Thus the 'capital punishment' tables give only the percentages supporting capital punishment since the percentage opposed to capital punishment is always the former percentage subtracted from 100 per cent.

The number of respondents on which the percentage figures for single-category variables is based is not shown, but readers can obtain a close approximation by looking up the 'total N' for the same population sub-category in the same year in other tables with the standard format.

Missing data
The tables always exclude those respondents on whom information for any of the relevant variables is unavailable. This is usually because the respondent refused to answer the question, or replied 'don't know'. The proportion of respondents for whom data are missing is usually small and varies little from one study to the next. Readers may estimate the approximate number of such respondents by comparing the column Ns for the same population sub-category in the same year across dependent variables.

The representativeness of the samples and weighting
The data presented in this book are based on samples of the Great Britain electorate and are therefore subject to sampling error as well as the bias that can arise from non-response. A measure of the degree and direction of bias is provided by comparing the reported vote of the sample respondents with the actual share of the Great Britain vote obtained at the election by the parties.

Table 0.1 makes this comparison. It shows the over- and under-representation of voters for each party in the British Election Study samples for 1964 to 1987. There does not appear to be any serious partisan bias in the samples. The mean deviation between the parties' actual vote in the country and their reported vote in the samples is usually about one per cent. There is a tendency for the samples to over-represent Labour voters but by an average of only 1.5%. Liberal voters are consistently under-represented but, again, only marginally.

Table 0.1 *Difference between parties' shares of the vote in Great Britain and reported vote in the British Election Studies*

	1964	1966	1970	Feb. 1974	Oct. 1974	1979	1983	1987	Mean
Conservative	+0.1	−2.2	−0.6	−0.7	−0.7	+2.1	+1.2	+0.6	0.0
Labour	+2.1	+3.7	+0.6	+2.7	+2.3	−0.2	+1.0	−0.3	+1.5
Liberal*	−0.7	−0.4	−0.2	−0.7	−0.8	−0.3	−1.3	+0.4	−0.5
Other	−1.4	−1.1	+0.2	−1.3	−0.7	−1.6	−0.9	−0.7	−0.9
Mean error	1.1	1.9	0.4	1.4	1.1	1.1	1.1	0.5	1.1

*Including SDP and 'Alliance' in 1983 and 1987

Even though the partisan bias of the samples is slight, the data are weighted in order to make the interviewed sample socially and political representative of the electorate at the time. The weighting is accomplished by means of fractional counters, so that any weighting factor may be used which can be expressed in terms of a decimal number, a whole number, or a whole number plus a decimal number. The weight given to a case determines the extent to which it adds to the totals being collected. In cross-tabulations, for example, a case containing the weight 1.67 will result in 1.67 being added to the total number of respondents considered in building the table and the total number of respondents who occur in a specific cell of that table. To facilitate legibility all counts are rounded to the nearest whole number before being reported in tables. For the sake of accuracy, however, all statistics which are not dependent upon whole numbers are calculated on the basis of the accumulated fractional numbers. Owing to the mechanics of rounding, the reported number of respondents may vary from one statistical procedure to another. The extent of this rounding error, however, is exceedingly small and amounts to no more than a difference of a single case in a file of 3,000 original cases.

Chapter 1

VOTE

1. No general election was held in 1963 or 1969. For these two years the vote variable refers to vote intention, not actual vote.
2. In 1983 and 1987 the Liberal Party contested the election in electoral alliance with the SDP. In these two years Liberal voters include those voting for the SDP or the Alliance.

See also appendix E, p. 483 below.

Table 1.1 *Vote: all respondents (%)*

	1963	1964	1966	1969	1970	Feb. 1974	Oct. 1974	1979	1983	1987
Party voted for										
Conservative	37.0	41.9	38.7	56.3	45.7	38.1	36.0	47.0	44.7	43.9
Labour	49.5	47.0	52.6	31.2	44.6	40.7	42.5	37.6	29.3	31.2
Liberal	13.4	10.7	8.2	10.6	7.4	19.1	18.0	13.8	24.6	23.5
Other	0.1	0.4	0.5	2.0	2.4	2.1	3.5	1.6	1.4	1.4
Total	100.0	100.0	100.0	100.0	100.0	100.0	100.0	100.0	100.0	100.0
N. of respondents	1752	1578	1569	956	1461	2067	1955	1558	3205	3204

Table 1.2 *Vote by gender (%)*

Men										
	1963	1964	1966	1969	1970	Feb. 1974	Oct. 1974	1979	1983	1987
Party voted for										
Conservative	32.1	40.2	36.3	56.2	42.7	37.4	34.6	45.3	45.5	44.0
Labour	53.4	47.4	54.3	33.8	47.5	41.6	44.9	37.7	29.8	31.2
Liberal	14.2	11.7	8.7	8.0	7.0	17.5	15.6	14.7	23.4	23.5
Other	0.3	0.7	0.7	2.0	2.8	3.5	4.8	2.3	1.3	1.3
Total	100.0	100.0	100.0	100.0	100.0	100.0	100.0	100.0	100.0	100.0
N. of respondents	787	735	741	461	688	989	973	750	1494	1528

Women										
	1963	1964	1966	1969	1970	Feb. 1974	Oct. 1974	1979	1983	1987
Party voted for										
Conservative	41.0	43.1	40.9	56.4	48.3	38.6	37.4	48.5	44.9	44.2
Labour	46.3	46.5	50.9	28.7	42.0	39.8	40.0	37.5	27.7	30.9
Liberal	12.6	9.8	7.8	12.9	7.7	20.5	20.4	13.0	26.0	23.4
Other	0.0	0.6	0.4	2.0	2.0	1.1	2.2	1.0	1.4	1.4
Total	100.0	100.0	100.0	100.0	100.0	100.0	100.0	100.0	100.0	100.0
N. of respondents	965	843	829	495	773	1078	982	808	1711	1674

Table 1.3 *Vote by age (%)*

| | Aged under 25 | | | | | | | | | |
	1963	1964	1966	1969	1970	Feb. 1974	Oct. 1974	1979	1983	1987
Party voted for										
Conservative	28.4	40.0	39.0	52.5	36.9	24.9	24.2	39.7	43.2	36.3
Labour	64.2	51.4	55.8	30.7	52.1	41.8	51.5	40.5	31.6	40.5
Liberal	7.3	6.7	5.2	12.9	8.5	26.5	19.7	19.0	23.4	22.1
Other	0.0	2.0	0.0	4.0	2.6	6.9	4.5	0.8	1.8	1.1
Total	100.0	100.0	100.0	100.0	100.0	100.0	100.0	100.0	100.0	100.0
N. of respondents	109	96	96	101	194	189	198	121	404	366

| | Aged 25–34 | | | | | | | | | |
	1963	1964	1966	1969	1970	Feb. 1974	Oct. 1974	1979	1983	1987
Party voted for										
Conservative	31.5	40.1	30.9	63.8	43.1	32.6	30.3	44.6	41.7	38.2
Labour	51.6	47.5	58.3	24.6	47.6	40.7	40.3	36.6	27.9	36.0
Liberal	17.0	12.5	9.8	9.4	5.3	23.3	22.4	16.4	29.0	24.8
Other	0.0	0.0	1.0	2.2	4.0	3.4	7.1	2.4	1.5	1.0
Total	100.0	100.0	100.0	100.0	100.0	100.0	100.0	100.0	100.0	100.0
N. of respondents	289	242	256	138	221	386	380	336	568	575

| | Aged 35–44 | | | | | | | | | |
	1963	1964	1966	1969	1970	Feb. 1974	Oct. 1974	1979	1983	1987
Party voted for										
Conservative	32.6	31.3	35.8	56.2	40.9	37.2	34.7	47.3	45.9	44.3
Labour	52.6	52.1	54.5	26.5	46.0	41.9	43.2	38.1	26.0	27.8
Liberal	14.6	16.0	8.8	14.8	10.5	19.0	19.1	13.6	27.2	26.2
Other	0.3	0.6	0.9	2.5	2.6	2.0	2.9	1.1	0.9	1.7
Total	100.0	100.0	100.0	100.0	100.0	100.0	100.0	100.0	100.0	100.0
N. of respondents	371	347	326	162	253	358	340	273	610	637

| | Aged 45–54 | | | | | | | | | |
	1963	1964	1966	1969	1970	Feb. 1974	Oct. 1974	1979	1983	1987
Party voted for										
Conservative	34.0	43.9	37.4	52.2	42.3	37.6	34.8	44.2	43.1	49.5
Labour	51.2	45.5	51.1	36.0	47.4	42.7	45.5	39.0	29.4	29.9
Liberal	14.8	9.8	10.5	11.2	8.3	18.9	18.0	14.6	26.3	19.1
Other	0.0	0.8	0.9	0.6	2.0	0.8	1.7	2.3	1.2	1.5
Total	100.0	100.0	100.0	100.0	100.0	100.0	100.0	100.0	100.0	100.0
N. of respondents	365	324	339	161	253	386	356	308	540	506

Table 1.3 (*cont.*)

	Aged 55–64									
	1963	1964	1966	1969	1970	Feb. 1974	Oct. 1974	1979	1983	1987
Party voted for										
Conservative	45.9	49.0	46.2	59.8	51.9	38.9	41.5	47.8	45.6	44.3
Labour	42.9	42.5	48.1	31.1	42.0	42.4	39.9	39.6	30.0	28.7
Liberal	10.9	7.5	5.7	9.1	5.5	17.3	15.2	11.7	22.9	24.7
Other	0.3	1.1	0.0	0.0	0.6	1.5	3.5	0.9	1.5	2.2
Total	100.0	100.0	100.0	100.0	100.0	100.0	100.0	100.0	100.0	100.0
N. of respondents	303	295	289	164	268	342	316	230	507	524

	Aged 65–74									
	1963	1964	1966	1969	1970	Feb. 1974	Oct. 1974	1979	1983	1987
Party voted for										
Conservative	42.8	44.9	39.4	59.6	51.2	47.2	41.6	49.7	47.3	46.0
Labour	46.2	46.5	51.3	34.3	39.8	37.4	39.9	38.0	31.2	28.0
Liberal	11.1	8.6	9.4	4.0	5.7	14.0	16.9	10.2	20.1	25.3
Other	0.0	0.0	0.0	2.0	3.4	1.5	1.6	2.1	1.3	0.8
Total	100.0	100.0	100.0	100.0	100.0	100.0	100.0	100.0	100.0	100.0
N. of respondents	208	188	182	99	192	265	243	187	357	362

	Aged over 74									
	1963	1964	1966	1969	1970	Feb. 1974	Oct. 1974	1979	1983	1987
Party voted for										
Conservative	51.7	50.6	52.1	62.7	65.1	59.5	54.8	63.6	58.7	55.9
Labour	38.2	41.7	46.7	25.5	24.7	29.4	34.8	28.3	23.1	25.8
Liberal	10.1	7.7	1.2	9.8	8.9	9.5	8.7	8.1	16.7	17.8
Other	0.0	0.0	0.0	2.0	1.3	1.6	1.7	0.0	1.4	0.5
Total	100.0	100.0	100.0	100.0	100.0	100.0	100.0	100.0	100.0	100.0
N. of respondents	89	89	82	51	80	126	115	99	202	206

Table 1.4 *Vote by age and gender (%)*

	Men aged under 25									
	1963	1964	1966	1969	1970	Feb. 1974	Oct. 1974	1979	1983	1987
Party voted for										
Conservative	30.4	47.0	42.4	60.0	34.3	19.6	16.8	43.5	46.1	38.5
Labour	63.0	45.5	50.3	24.0	52.3	39.1	52.5	33.9	33.4	39.4
Liberal	6.5	5.8	7.2	12.0	11.4	28.3	22.8	22.6	18.8	20.9
Other	0.0	1.7	0.0	4.0	1.9	13.0	7.9	0.0	1.8	1.1
Total	100.0	100.0	100.0	100.0	100.0	100.0	100.0	100.0	100.0	100.0
N. of respondents	46	48	58	50	97	92	101	62	210	172

	Women aged under 25									
	1963	1964	1966	1969	1970	Feb. 1974	Oct. 1974	1979	1983	1987
Party voted for										
Conservative	27.0	32.9	33.7	45.1	39.4	29.9	32.0	35.6	40.1	34.3
Labour	65.1	57.2	64.2	37.3	51.9	44.3	50.5	47.5	29.6	41.5
Liberal	7.9	7.5	2.1	13.7	5.4	24.7	16.5	15.3	28.5	23.2
Other	0.0	2.3	0.0	3.9	3.3	1.0	1.0	1.7	1.9	1.0
Total	100.0	100.0	100.0	100.0	100.0	100.0	100.0	100.0	100.0	100.0
N. of respondents	63	48	38	51	96	97	97	59	194	194

	Men aged 25–44									
	1963	1964	1966	1969	1970	Feb. 1974	Oct. 1974	1979	1983	1987
Party voted for										
Conservative	25.7	33.0	30.3	58.7	40.6	34.3	32.6	42.8	44.2	40.4
Labour	58.7	50.0	60.5	29.0	48.8	44.1	43.4	37.2	26.6	32.3
Liberal	15.3	16.5	8.1	10.3	6.8	17.8	17.4	17.5	27.9	25.9
Other	0.3	0.4	1.0	1.9	3.7	3.7	6.6	2.5	1.3	1.4
Total	100.0	100.0	100.0	100.0	100.0	100.0	100.0	100.0	100.0	100.0
N. of respondents	300	267	272	155	233	376	362	285	550	591

	Women aged 25–44									
	1963	1964	1966	1969	1970	Feb. 1974	Oct. 1974	1979	1983	1987
Party voted for										
Conservative	37.5	36.5	36.5	60.7	43.1	35.3	32.1	48.5	43.5	42.4
Labour	46.7	50.3	52.4	22.1	44.8	38.3	39.9	37.3	27.1	31.1
Liberal	15.8	12.9	10.2	14.5	9.3	24.7	24.3	13.0	28.2	25.1
Other	0.0	0.3	0.9	2.8	2.9	1.6	3.6	1.2	1.2	1.4
Total	100.0	100.0	100.0	100.0	100.0	100.0	100.0	100.0	100.0	100.0
N. of respondents	360	322	310	145	241	368	358	324	628	621

Table 1.4 (*cont.*)

Men aged 45–64

	1963	1964	1966	1969	1970	Feb. 1974	Oct. 1974	1979	1983	1987
Party voted for										
Conservative	33.9	42.5	39.1	55.1	46.1	40.5	36.8	45.5	44.2	46.9
Labour	50.6	46.2	51.4	38.0	45.8	41.4	46.6	39.4	31.0	28.7
Liberal	15.2	10.2	8.7	6.3	6.5	16.7	13.5	12.6	23.6	22.8
Other	0.3	1.1	0.7	0.6	1.5	1.4	3.2	2.5	1.2	1.7
Total	100.0	100.0	100.0	100.0	100.0	100.0	100.0	100.0	100.0	100.0
N. of respondents	310	324	297	158	248	348	348	277	485	527

Women aged 45–64

	1963	1964	1966	1969	1970	Feb. 1974	Oct. 1974	1979	1983	1987
Party voted for										
Conservative	44.1	49.8	43.5	56.9	48.3	36.1	39.2	46.0	44.0	46.8
Labour	44.7	42.2	48.2	29.3	43.5	43.7	38.9	39.1	28.6	29.9
Liberal	11.2	7.2	7.9	13.8	7.1	19.5	20.1	14.2	25.6	21.0
Other	0.0	0.8	0.3	0.0	1.1	0.8	1.9	0.8	1.5	2.2
Total	100.0	100.0	100.0	100.0	100.0	100.0	100.0	100.0	100.0	100.0
N. of respondents	358	324	331	167	273	380	324	261	562	504

Men aged over 64

	1963	1964	1966	1969	1970	Feb. 1974	Oct. 1974	1979	1983	1987
Party voted for										
Conservative	43.1	47.2	39.9	60.7	46.2	48.5	45.9	51.2	51.4	51.1
Labour	44.7	45.6	49.2	33.9	44.4	37.7	39.6	37.6	30.7	27.3
Liberal	12.2	7.2	10.8	3.6	4.7	11.4	11.9	8.8	16.7	20.7
Other	0.0	0.0	0.0	1.8	4.7	2.4	2.5	2.4	1.2	0.9
Total	100.0	100.0	100.0	100.0	100.0	100.0	100.0	100.0	100.0	100.0
N. of respondents	123	125	114	56	109	167	159	125	243	227

Women aged over 64

	1963	1964	1966	1969	1970	Feb. 1974	Oct. 1974	1979	1983	1987
Party voted for										
Conservative	47.1	46.3	45.9	60.6	61.3	53.1	45.7	57.1	51.5	48.4
Labour	43.1	44.5	50.3	29.8	29.3	32.6	37.2	32.3	26.4	27.1
Liberal	9.8	9.2	3.7	7.4	7.9	13.4	16.1	9.9	20.6	23.9
Other	0.0	0.0	0.0	2.1	1.5	0.9	1.0	0.6	1.5	0.6
Total	100.0	100.0	100.0	100.0	100.0	100.0	100.0	100.0	100.0	100.0
N. of respondents	174	153	150	94	163	224	199	161	316	343

Table 1.5 *Vote by marital status (%)*

	Single									
	1963	1964	1966	1969	1970	Feb. 1974	Oct. 1974	1979	1983	1987
Party voted for										
Conservative	46.8	53.2	52.1	52.4	46.5	36.3	–	43.3	44.1	32.5
Labour	40.5	39.5	38.7	32.9	42.4	36.3	–	37.8	28.8	37.9
Liberal	12.7	6.1	7.9	11.0	8.1	23.0	–	16.7	24.3	22.7
Other	0.0	1.1	1.3	3.8	3.0	4.3	–	2.2	2.8	1.0
Total	100.0	100.0	100.0	100.0	100.0	100.0	–	100.0	100.0	100.0
N. of respondents	220	186	150	210	241	278	–	180	526	536

	Married									
	1963	1964	1966	1969	1970	Feb. 1974	Oct. 1974	1979	1983	1987
Party voted for										
Conservative	34.2	39.0	36.0	56.8	43.7	37.1	35.3	46.9	45.1	45.4
Labour	51.5	48.4	54.5	30.7	46.4	42.0	43.1	37.5	28.1	29.0
Liberal	14.1	12.0	8.9	11.0	7.7	19.0	18.1	16.7	24.3	23.9
Other	0.2	0.6	0.6	1.6	2.2	1.9	3.5	2.2	2.8	1.6
Total	100.0	100.0	100.0	100.0	100.0	100.0	100.0	100.0	100.0	100.0
N. of respondents	1315	1225	1235	629	1040	1546	1484	1134	2274	2233

	Divorced and separated									
	1963	1964	1966	1969	1970	Feb. 1974	Oct. 1974	1979	1983	1987
Party voted for										
Conservative	–	–	(50.0)	–	–	23.8	–	35.5	41.0	41.3
Labour	–	–	(42.9)	–	–	42.9	–	54.8	36.5	35.5
Liberal	–	–	(7.1)	–	–	28.6	–	9.7	21.9	22.5
Other	–	–	(0.0)	–	–	4.8	–	0.0	0.6	0.6
Total	–	–	(100.0)	–	–	100.0	–	100.0	100.0	100.0
N. of respondents	–	–	14	–	–	21	–	62	150	150

	Widowed									
	1963	1964	1966	1969	1970	Feb. 1974	Oct. 1974	1979	1983	1987
Party voted for										
Conservative	–	–	45.9	–	–	48.0	–	55.2	51.0	46.2
Labour	–	–	50.7	–	–	36.0	–	31.5	28.3	31.3
Liberal	–	–	3.4	–	–	14.2	–	12.7	18.9	21.8
Other	–	–	0.0	–	–	1.8	–	0.6	1.9	0.7
Total	–	–	100.0	–	–	100.0	–	100.0	100.0	100.0
N. of respondents	–	–	171	–	–	225	–	165	254	281

Table 1.6 *Vote by marital status and gender (%)*

Single men

	1963	1964	1966	1969	1970	Feb. 1974	Oct. 1974	1979	1983	1987
Party voted for										
Conservative	29.3	44.2	47.5	50.9	40.1	28.5	–	41.2	51.0	38.0
Labour	57.6	47.7	46.3	35.2	47.7	44.4	–	38.2	36.3	38.8
Liberal	13.1	7.0	3.8	10.2	8.2	20.8	–	18.6	10.2	22.5
Other	0.0	1.2	2.5	3.7	4.0	6.3	–	2.0	2.6	0.7
Total	100.0	100.0	100.0	100.0	100.0	100.0	–	100.0	100.0	100.0
N. of respondents	99	87	80	108	134	144	–	102	248	287

Single women

	1963	1964	1966	1969	1970	Feb. 1974	Oct. 1974	1979	1983	1987
Party voted for										
Conservative	61.2	60.6	57.7	53.9	54.4	44.8	–	46.2	53.7	39.0
Labour	26.4	33.3	29.6	30.4	35.8	27.6	–	37.2	31.3	36.8
Liberal	12.4	5.1	12.7	11.8	8.0	25.4	–	14.1	10.8	22.9
Other	0.0	1.0	0.0	3.9	1.8	2.2	–	2.6	4.1	1.3
Total	100.0	100.0	100.0	100.0	100.0	100.0	–	100.0	100.0	100.0
N. of respondents	121	99	70	102	107	134	–	78	196	248

Married men

	1963	1964	1966	1969	1970	Feb. 1974	Oct. 1974	1979	1983	1987
Party voted for										
Conservative	32.3	39.0	34.6	57.3	42.7	38.2	35.4	46.8	52.7	45.8
Labour	52.9	47.5	55.4	33.4	48.6	41.4	45.2	36.3	33.1	28.6
Liberal	14.5	12.8	9.6	7.7	6.6	17.3	15.1	14.5	12.9	24.1
Other	0.3	0.7	0.5	1.5	2.1	3.0	4.3	2.4	1.2	1.4
Total	100.0	100.0	100.0	100.0	100.0	100.0	100.0	100.0	100.0	100.0
N. of respondents	635	615	629	323	512	787	783	573	962	1128

Married women

	1963	1964	1966	1969	1970	Feb. 1974	Oct. 1974	1979	1983	1987
Party voted for										
Conservative	36.0	38.9	37.6	56.2	44.6	35.8	35.2	47.1	51.5	45.1
Labour	50.1	49.3	53.5	27.8	44.3	42.7	40.8	38.7	31.9	29.5
Liberal	13.8	11.3	8.2	14.4	8.8	20.7	21.4	13.2	15.5	23.7
Other	0.0	0.5	0.7	1.6	2.3	0.8	2.6	1.1	1.1	1.7
Total	100.0	100.0	100.0	100.0	100.0	100.0	100.0	100.0	100.0	100.0
N. of respondents	680	610	607	306	527	759	701	561	1007	1105

Table 1.6 (*cont.*)

Divorced men

	1963	1964	1966	1969	1970	Feb. 1974	Oct. 1974	1979	1983	1987
Party voted for										
Conservative	–	–	(0.0)	–	–	(40.0)	–	29.2	50.5	34.2
Labour	–	–	(0.0)	–	–	(20.0)	–	62.5	35.2	41.3
Liberal	–	–	(0.0)	–	–	(20.0)	–	8.3	12.5	22.7
Other	–	–	(0.0)	–	–	(20.0)	–	0.0	1.9	1.9
Total	–	–	(100.0)	–	–	(100.0)	–	100.0	100.0	100.0
N. of respondents	–	–	0	–	–	5	–	24	48	52

Divorced women

	1963	1964	1966	1969	1970	Feb. 1974	Oct. 1974	1979	1983	1987
Party voted for										
Conservative	–	–	(50.0)	–	–	(18.8)	–	39.5	43.3	45.1
Labour	–	–	(42.9)	–	–	(50.0)	–	50.0	44.2	32.5
Liberal	–	–	(7.1)	–	–	(31.3)	–	10.5	12.4	22.4
Other	–	–	(0.0)	–	–	(0.0)	–	0.0	0.0	0.0
Total	–	–	(100.0)	–	–	(100.0)	–	100.0	100.0	100.0
N. of respondents	–	–	14	–	–	16	–	38	86	98

Widowed men

	1963	1964	1966	1969	1970	Feb. 1974	Oct. 1974	1979	1983	1987
Party voted for										
Conservative	–	–	42.4	–	–	49.1	–	45.5	45.5	47.9
Labour	–	–	54.5	–	–	37.7	–	38.6	40.8	33.8
Liberal	–	–	3.0	–	–	11.3	–	13.6	13.8	16.5
Other	–	–	0.0	–	–	1.9	–	2.3	0.0	1.7
Total	–	–	100.0	–	–	100.0	–	100.0	100.0	100.0
N. of respondents	–	–	33	–	–	53	–	44	48	61

Widowed women

	1963	1964	1966	1969	1970	Feb. 1974	Oct. 1974	1979	1983	1987
Party voted for										
Conservative	–	–	46.4	–	–	47.7	–	58.7	57.4	45.7
Labour	–	–	50.0	–	–	35.5	–	28.9	27.8	30.6
Liberal	–	–	3.6	–	–	15.1	–	12.4	12.2	23.3
Other	–	–	0.0	–	–	1.7	–	0.0	2.5	0.4
Total	–	–	100.0	–	–	100.0	–	100.0	100.0	100.0
N. of respondents	–	–	138	–	–	172	–	121	188	220

Table 1.7 *Vote: new electors (%)*

	1963	1964	1966	1969	1970	Feb. 1974	Oct. 1974	1979	1983	1987
Party voted for										
Conservative	28.4	37.5	37.6	51.7	36.9	26.2	–	40.2	44.7	37.8
Labour	64.2	54.1	54.8	28.3	52.1	44.3	–	40.2	32.6	38.8
Liberal	7.3	6.9	7.5	15.0	8.5	27.9	–	18.5	20.7	21.3
Other	0.0	1.6	0.0	5.0	2.6	1.6	–	1.1	2.0	2.0
Total	100.0	100.0	100.0	100.0	100.0	100.0	–	100.0	100.0	100.0
N. of respondents	109	122	43	60	194	125	–	92	228	194

Table 1.8 *Vote by political generation (%)*

First voted 1918–1935

	1963	1964	1966	1969	1970	Feb. 1974	Oct. 1974	1979	1983	1987
Party voted for										
Conservative	43.3	47.2	44.0	58.2	52.7	46.7	43.2	54.9	55.6	53.2
Labour	44.6	43.3	49.4	33.8	39.0	38.3	40.2	34.1	24.3	26.8
Liberal	12.0	9.1	6.6	7.0	6.5	13.5	14.4	9.5	18.6	19.2
Other	0.1	0.5	0.0	1.0	1.8	1.5	2.2	1.5	1.4	0.8
Total	100.0	100.0	100.0	100.0	100.0	100.0	100.0	100.0	100.0	100.0
N. of respondents	749	670	607	267	465	520	465	264	388	241

First voted 1936–1950

	1963	1964	1966	1969	1970	Feb. 1974	Oct. 1974	1979	1983	1987
Party voted for										
Conservative	32.4	35.5	36.2	52.7	44.4	39.0	38.1	47.3	44.7	46.3
Labour	53.3	50.7	53.0	33.5	45.6	41.3	41.8	39.2	31.6	26.5
Liberal	14.1	12.9	9.5	12.7	8.1	18.6	17.5	13.0	22.3	25.6
Other	0.2	0.9	1.2	1.2	2.0	1.1	2.5	0.5	1.4	1.6
Total	100.0	100.0	100.0	100.0	100.0	100.0	100.0	100.0	100.0	100.0
N. of respondents	559	517	497	245	402	564	514	370	688	650

First voted 1951–1970

	1963	1964	1966	1969	1970	Feb. 1974	Oct. 1974	1979	1983	1987
Party voted for										
Conservative	31.2	39.6	34.0	56.1	39.9	34.1	31.4	46.3	45.1	46.3
Labour	54.3	48.9	56.4	28.7	49.1	41.4	43.6	37.1	27.3	29.7
Liberal	14.5	11.0	9.0	11.7	7.6	21.4	20.1	14.5	26.4	22.5
Other	0.0	0.5	0.6	3.4	3.3	3.1	4.9	2.1	1.2	1.6
Total	100.0	100.0	100.0	100.0	100.0	100.0	100.0	100.0	100.0	100.0
N. of respondents	414	369	454	383	559	833	821	712	1356	1276

Table 1.8 (*cont.*)

	First voted after 1970									
	1963	1964	1966	1969	1970	Feb. 1974	Oct. 1974	1979	1983	1987
Party voted for										
Conservative	–	–	–	–	–	23.2	25.2	37.7	39.2	37.7
Labour	–	–	–	–	–	43.2	48.1	42.0	29.4	37.0
Liberal	–	–	–	–	–	28.0	22.2	18.4	30.2	24.3
Other	–	–	–	–	–	5.6	4.4	1.9	1.2	1.1
Total	–	–	–	–	–	100.0	100.0	100.0	100.0	100.0
N. of respondents	–	–	–	–	–	125	135	207	538	1010

Table 1.9 *Vote by direction of partisanship (%)*

	Conservative identifiers									
	1963	1964	1966	1969	1970	Feb. 1974	Oct. 1974	1979	1983	1987
Party voted for										
Conservative	92.6	93.9	93.1	98.5	94.1	87.9	88.0	94.6	95.1	90.5
Labour	3.6	2.9	3.5	0.8	2.0	2.2	2.8	1.7	0.6	2.3
Liberal	3.8	2.9	3.2	0.6	2.3	9.3	6.9	3.2	4.0	7.0
Other	0.0	0.3	0.2	0.0	1.7	0.6	2.4	0.6	0.3	0.2
Total	100.0	100.0	100.0	100.0	100.0	100.0	100.0	100.0	100.0	100.0
N. of respondents	665	639	595	477	623	808	715	664	1314	1347

	Labour identifiers									
	1963	1964	1966	1969	1970	Feb. 1974	Oct. 1974	1979	1983	1987
Party voted for										
Conservative	1.9	1.9	1.4	9.2	3.8	2.6	1.7	5.2	4.8	4.6
Labour	96.1	95.5	95.9	83.5	92.9	87.5	91.6	86.6	81.5	84.6
Liberal	1.9	2.2	2.2	5.8	2.7	9.1	5.7	8.1	13.1	9.9
Other	0.1	0.5	0.5	1.5	0.6	0.9	1.0	0.2	0.6	0.8
Total	100.0	100.0	100.0	100.0	100.0	100.0	100.0	100.0	100.0	100.0
N. of respondents	854	698	763	327	650	894	825	620	1042	1048

	Liberal identifiers									
	1963	1964	1966	1969	1970	Feb. 1974	Oct. 1974	1979	1983	1987
Party voted for										
Conservative	4.1	18.7	17.3	12.0	26.8	12.4	13.0	19.5	12.0	13.5
Labour	2.1	15.9	28.9	9.8	13.7	8.1	7.8	8.7	3.3	5.5
Liberal	93.8	64.8	52.4	75.0	57.0	78.1	78.5	70.3	84.6	80.9
Other	0.0	0.5	1.3	3.3	2.5	1.4	0.7	1.5	0.1	0.4
Total	100.0	100.0	100.0	100.0	100.0	100.0	100.0	100.0	100.0	100.0
N. of respondents	195	194	156	92	119	283	307	195	642	565

Table 1.10 *Vote: non partisans (%)*

	Respondents with no party identification									
	1963	1964	1966	1969	1970	Feb. 1974	Oct. 1974	1979	1983	1987
Party voted for										
Conservative	25.0	23.5	29.0	57.1	45.2	31.6	31.9	54.2	47.0	41.9
Labour	46.9	49.9	47.7	22.9	29.5	34.2	38.3	27.1	16.9	19.1
Liberal	28.1	26.6	23.3	17.1	17.6	34.2	25.5	12.5	33.6	37.4
Other	0.0	0.0	0.0	2.9	7.7	0.0	4.3	6.3	2.6	1.6
Total	100.0	100.0	100.0	100.0	100.0	100.0	100.0	100.0	100.0	100.0
N. of respondents	32	38	48	35	48	38	47	48	110	120

Table 1.11 *Vote by strength and direction of partisanship (%)*

	Very strong Conservative identifiers									
	1963	1964	1966	1969	1970	Feb. 1974	Oct. 1974	1979	1983	1987
Party voted for										
Conservative	98.4	97.2	98.2	100.0	97.3	97.3	95.7	98.7	99.7	97.1
Labour	0.4	1.4	0.6	0.0	1.2	0.0	0.5	0.0	0.0	1.0
Liberal	1.2	0.9	1.1	0.0	0.0	2.3	3.3	0.6	0.0	1.9
Other	0.0	0.4	0.0	0.0	1.5	0.4	0.5	0.6	0.3	0.0
Total	100.0	100.0	100.0	100.0	100.0	100.0	100.0	100.0	100.0	100.0
N. of respondents	245	249	296	168	328	259	209	159	322	306

	Fairly strong Conservative identifiers									
	1963	1964	1966	1969	1970	Feb. 1974	Oct. 1974	1979	1983	1987
Party voted for										
Conservative	92.0	93.6	93.3	98.5	92.6	89.8	89.2	95.4	97.9	92.9
Labour	3.6	2.5	3.3	1.0	1.7	2.0	2.7	1.1	0.3	1.5
Liberal	4.3	3.5	2.9	0.5	3.6	7.8	6.0	2.9	1.5	5.3
Other	0.0	0.3	0.5	0.0	2.0	0.5	2.2	0.6	0.2	0.3
Total	100.0	100.0	100.0	100.0	100.0	100.0	100.0	100.0	100.0	100.0
N. of respondents	276	249	219	206	229	400	369	349	590	649

Table 1.11 (*cont.*)

Not very strong Conservative identifiers

	1963	1964	1966	1969	1970	Feb. 1974	Oct. 1974	1979	1983	1987
Party voted for										
Conservative	83.8	80.3	73.3	95.9	82.9	66.2	72.8	88.7	92.3	77.2
Labour	9.2	10.3	14.8	2.0	6.9	6.8	6.6	4.7	1.8	6.7
Liberal	7.0	9.4	11.9	2.0	8.9	25.7	14.0	6.0	5.2	16.0
Other	0.0	0.0	0.0	0.0	1.3	1.4	6.6	0.7	0.6	0.0
Total	100.0	100.0	100.0	100.0	100.0	100.0	100.0	100.0	100.0	100.0
N. of respondents	142	74	78	98	66	148	136	150	326	260

Very strong Liberal identifiers

	1963	1964	1966	1969	1970	Feb. 1974	Oct. 1974	1979	1983	1987
Party voted for										
Conservative	1.9	14.9	13.6	(5.9)	8.5	5.9	6.7	16.0	16.3	4.7
Labour	0.0	13.2	25.6	(11.8)	17.9	2.9	0.0	12.0	9.3	1.7
Liberal	98.1	71.9	57.1	(82.4)	71.2	88.2	93.3	72.0	74.4	93.5
Other	0.0	0.0	3.7	(0.0)	2.5	2.9	0.0	0.0	0.0	0.0
Total	100.0	100.0	100.0	(100.0)	100.0	100.0	100.0	100.0	100.0	100.0
N. of respondents	52	64	55	17	35	34	45	25	43	59

Fairly strong Liberal identifiers

	1963	1964	1966	1969	1970	Feb. 1974	Oct. 1974	1979	1983	1987
Party voted for										
Conservative	4.9	21.0	17.6	12.5	35.7	11.8	9.9	15.5	15.5	10.4
Labour	0.0	18.7	31.7	12.5	11.3	6.5	8.6	6.2	6.1	6.4
Liberal	95.1	59.2	50.7	75.0	50.9	80.4	80.9	75.3	78.4	83.2
Other	0.0	1.1	0.0	0.0	2.1	1.3	0.6	3.1	0.0	0.0
Total	100.0	100.0	100.0	100.0	100.0	100.0	100.0	100.0	100.0	100.0
N. of respondents	82	94	84	40	57	153	162	97	148	252

Not very strong Liberal identifiers

	1963	1964	1966	1969	1970	Feb. 1974	Oct. 1974	1979	1983	1987
Party voted for										
Conservative	5.0	19.4	(27.9)	14.3	31.7	15.6	21.4	26.4	29.2	17.6
Labour	6.7	13.7	(26.2)	5.7	13.5	12.5	10.2	11.1	4.9	5.2
Liberal	88.3	66.9	(45.9)	71.4	51.6	70.8	67.3	62.5	65.3	76.5
Other	0.0	0.0	(0.0)	8.6	3.2	1.0	1.0	0.0	0.7	0.7
Total	100.0	100.0	(100.0)	100.0	100.0	100.0	100.0	100.0	100.0	100.0
N. of respondents	60	37	17	35	27	96	98	72	144	267

Table 1.11 (*cont.*)

Very strong Labour identifiers

Party voted for	1963	1964	1966	1969	1970	Feb. 1974	Oct. 1974	1979	1983	1987
Conservative	0.6	1.3	0.3	1.9	1.2	0.0	0.0	1.7	1.6	1.8
Labour	99.1	97.8	99.0	95.2	97.6	96.7	98.7	96.0	95.7	94.5
Liberal	0.3	0.3	0.3	1.9	1.2	3.0	1.3	2.3	2.3	3.7
Other	0.0	0.6	0.5	1.0	0.0	0.3	0.0	0.0	0.3	0.0
Total	100.0	100.0	100.0	100.0	100.0	100.0	100.0	100.0	100.0	100.0
N. of respondents	321	358	398	104	318	367	312	176	304	272

Fairly strong Labour identifiers

Party voted for	1963	1964	1966	1969	1970	Feb. 1974	Oct. 1974	1979	1983	1987
Conservative	1.7	2.0	1.0	5.7	2.6	2.4	1.3	3.3	2.6	3.1
Labour	97.4	95.1	95.5	88.6	93.1	85.3	90.2	87.6	89.3	88.3
Liberal	0.6	2.9	3.2	4.9	3.9	11.0	7.0	8.7	7.9	7.7
Other	0.3	0.0	0.3	0.8	0.4	1.3	1.6	0.3	0.2	0.9
Total	100.0	100.0	100.0	100.0	100.0	100.0	100.0	100.0	100.0	100.0
N. of respondents	344	269	299	123	243	374	387	299	391	440

Not very strong Labour identifiers

Party voted for	1963	1964	1966	1969	1970	Feb. 1974	Oct. 1974	1979	1983	1987
Conservative	4.4	5.0	10.1	21.2	17.0	9.3	7.3	13.4	13.8	9.5
Labour	88.5	84.3	80.5	64.6	74.8	70.2	79.0	72.5	71.1	70.0
Liberal	7.1	9.1	7.9	11.1	4.8	19.2	12.1	14.1	13.3	18.9
Other	0.0	1.6	1.4	3.1	3.4	1.3	1.6	0.0	1.8	1.7
Total	100.0	100.0	100.0	100.0	100.0	100.0	100.0	100.0	100.0	100.0
N. of respondents	182	68	62	99	87	151	124	142	225	285

Table 1.12 *Vote by social class (%)*

	Professional and managerial classes									
	1963	1964	1966	1969	1970	Feb. 1974	Oct. 1974	1979	1983	1987
Party voted for										
Conservative	65.3	68.0	67.0	69.8	64.9	56.5	52.3	62.1	55.8	52.5
Labour	18.1	16.0	18.0	22.9	24.3	18.8	18.5	20.9	13.1	17.4
Liberal	16.6	14.9	14.6	7.3	7.8	22.7	25.8	15.5	30.3	28.4
Other	0.0	1.1	0.4	0.0	2.9	1.9	3.4	1.5	0.8	1.6
Total	100.0	100.0	100.0	100.0	100.0	100.0	100.0	100.0	100.0	100.0
N. of respondents	199	216	210	96	262	308	298	335	871	833

	Intermediate and routine non-manual classes									
	1963	1964	1966	1969	1970	Feb. 1974	Oct. 1974	1979	1983	1987
Party voted for										
Conservative	54.3	57.2	53.9	65.5	55.5	45.7	44.7	54.8	52.8	54.3
Labour	27.1	27.7	33.4	22.4	32.7	30.3	32.6	27.5	19.4	21.4
Liberal	18.6	14.2	11.8	10.3	9.8	22.6	19.5	15.8	26.3	22.7
Other	0.0	0.9	0.9	1.8	2.0	1.5	3.2	1.9	1.5	1.5
Total	100.0	100.0	100.0	100.0	100.0	100.0	100.0	100.0	100.0	100.0
N. of respondents	451	453	433	223	379	727	682	418	619	810

	Manual working class									
	1963	1964	1966	1969	1970	Feb. 1974	Oct. 1974	1979	1983	1987
Party voted for										
Conservative	23.7	26.3	24.9	48.2	34.4	24.6	23.5	35.5	34.5	34.0
Labour	65.1	65.6	69.5	40.6	57.1	57.0	58.2	50.7	42.6	43.7
Liberal	11.0	7.7	5.2	9.5	6.1	15.1	14.2	12.2	21.3	21.2
Other	0.2	0.4	0.5	1.7	2.4	3.3	4.1	1.6	1.7	1.1
Total	100.0	100.0	100.0	100.0	100.0	100.0	100.0	100.0	100.0	100.0
N. of respondents	995	861	900	409	763	921	873	744	1486	1418

Table 1.13 *Vote by occupational status (%)*

	Occupational status: class A/Registrar General Class I									
	1963	1964	1966	1969	1970	Feb. 1974	Oct. 1974	1979	1983	1987
Party voted for										
Conservative	68.7	71.7	75.4	70.4	73.2	68.0	58.0	64.4	52.6	51.6
Labour	14.5	16.1	13.7	14.8	14.6	12.5	9.8	15.4	11.3	11.9
Liberal	16.9	11.1	10.1	14.8	11.3	16.4	27.7	17.3	35.3	35.8
Other	0.0	1.1	0.8	0.0	1.0	3.1	4.5	2.9	0.8	0.8
Total	100.0	100.0	100.0	100.0	100.0	100.0	100.0	100.0	100.0	100.0
N. of respondents	83	92	104	27	90	128	112	104	140	128

	Occupational status: class B/Registrar General Class II									
	1963	1964	1966	1969	1970	Feb. 1974	Oct. 1974	1979	1983	1987
Party voted for										
Conservative	63.6	67.9	60.3	69.6	60.6	48.3	48.9	61.0	53.3	52.7
Labour	17.1	17.7	24.7	26.1	29.5	23.3	23.7	23.4	17.9	18.4
Liberal	19.3	13.5	15.0	4.3	6.0	27.2	24.7	14.7	27.1	27.1
Other	0.0	0.9	0.0	0.0	3.9	1.1	2.7	0.9	1.7	1.8
Total	100.0	100.0	100.0	100.0	100.0	100.0	100.0	100.0	100.0	100.0
N. of respondents	140	140	126	69	172	180	186	231	652	705

	Occupational status: class C1A/Registrar General Class III – non-manual									
	1963	1964	1966	1969	1970	Feb. 1974	Oct. 1974	1979	1983	1987
Party voted for										
Conservative	62.8	58.5	61.8	72.2	57.0	53.9	54.1	61.6	54.8	54.3
Labour	19.7	23.6	24.5	16.7	29.4	24.3	24.6	19.2	20.8	21.4
Liberal	17.2	17.1	12.8	8.9	10.6	20.1	18.3	16.9	23.0	22.7
Other	0.4	0.8	0.9	2.2	3.0	1.6	3.0	2.3	1.4	1.5
Total	100.0	100.0	100.0	100.0	100.0	100.0	100.0	100.0	100.0	100.0
N. of respondents	239	232	211	90	187	304	268	177	762	810

	Occupational status: class C1B/Registrar General Class III – manual									
	1963	1964	1966	1969	1970	Feb. 1974	Oct. 1974	1979	1983	1987
Party voted for										
Conservative	47.0	53.8	48.4	60.9	54.1	39.7	38.6	49.8	37.6	37.5
Labour	34.8	28.2	37.0	26.3	35.8	34.5	37.7	33.6	40.2	40.7
Liberal	18.3	17.1	13.9	11.3	9.0	24.3	20.3	14.9	20.7	20.3
Other	0.0	0.8	0.7	1.5	1.1	1.4	3.4	1.7	1.6	1.4
Total	100.0	100.0	100.0	100.0	100.0	100.0	100.0	100.0	100.0	100.0
N. of respondents	164	131	154	133	193	423	414	241	678	676

Table 1.13 (*cont.*)

	Occupational status: class C2/Registrar General Class IV									
	1963	1964	1966	1969	1970	Feb. 1974	Oct. 1974	1979	1983	1987
Party voted for										
Conservative	25.0	29.5	25.6	47.7	37.1	26.3	25.3	36.6	33.2	32.3
Labour	61.1	61.7	68.3	41.6	53.9	55.6	56.1	49.7	45.0	45.1
Liberal	13.7	8.6	5.4	8.9	6.1	15.6	14.7	11.8	22.6	21.8
Other	0.2	0.2	0.7	1.9	2.8	2.5	3.9	1.9	0.2	0.8
Total	100.0	100.0	100.0	100.0	100.0	100.0	100.0	100.0	100.0	100.0
N. of respondents	633	565	587	214	440	482	490	475	623	579

	Occupational status: class D/Registrar General Class V									
	1963	1964	1966	1969	1970	Feb. 1974	Oct. 1974	1979	1983	1987
Party voted for										
Conservative	20.7	25.0	24.3	48.7	30.7	22.8	21.1	33.5	25.3	25.3
Labour	72.2	68.2	70.0	39.5	61.4	58.5	60.8	52.4	52.2	51.7
Liberal	7.1	6.2	5.4	10.3	6.2	14.6	13.6	13.0	21.8	22.4
Other	0.0	0.7	0.3	1.5	1.8	4.1	4.4	1.1	0.6	0.6
Total	100.0	100.0	100.0	100.0	100.0	100.0	100.0	100.0	100.0	100.0
N. of respondents	396	352	360	195	323	439	383	269	198	163

Table 1.14 *Vote by class and gender (%)*

	Professional and managerial classes: men									
	1963	1964	1966	1969	1970	Feb. 1974	Oct. 1974	1979	1983	1987
Party voted for										
Conservative	58.2	64.9	67.3	69.4	61.2	56.2	51.6	57.5	57.4	55.8
Labour	20.4	17.1	20.0	22.2	25.3	18.5	19.8	24.6	12.5	15.1
Liberal	21.4	18.0	12.7	8.3	9.6	23.0	24.2	16.2	29.7	27.9
Other	0.0	0.0	0.0	0.0	4.0	2.2	4.4	1.7	0.4	1.2
Total	100.0	100.0	100.0	100.0	100.0	100.0	100.0	100.0	100.0	100.0
N. of respondents	98	111	110	72	134	178	182	179	448	490

Table 1.14 (*cont.*)

Professional and managerial classes: women

	1963	1964	1966	1969	1970	Feb. 1974	Oct. 1974	1979	1983	1987
Party voted for										
Conservative	71.2	73.0	66.1	70.8	68.8	56.9	53.4	67.3	54.1	48.0
Labour	12.8	17.2	19.8	25.0	23.4	19.2	16.4	16.7	13.7	20.5
Liberal	16.0	8.2	13.2	4.2	6.0	22.3	28.4	14.7	31.0	29.2
Other	0.0	1.6	0.8	0.0	1.8	1.5	1.7	1.3	1.2	2.3
Total	100.0	100.0	100.0	100.0	100.0	100.0	100.0	100.0	100.0	100.0
N. of respondents	125	122	121	24	128	130	116	156	423	343

Intermediate and routine non-manual classes: men

	1963	1964	1966	1969	1970	Feb. 1974	Oct. 1974	1979	1983	1987
Party voted for										
Conservative	50.0	55.7	53.1	76.5	55.2	52.2	49.6	58.6	52.3	48.0
Labour	30.0	26.2	34.3	17.6	32.3	27.3	32.5	22.9	20.1	18.9
Liberal	19.4	16.4	11.4	3.5	10.4	17.7	14.1	15.7	26.4	30.3
Other	0.6	1.6	1.1	2.4	2.0	2.8	3.8	2.9	1.1	2.8
Total	100.0	100.0	100.0	100.0	100.0	100.0	100.0	100.0	100.0	100.0
N. of respondents	180	183	175	85	156	249	234	140	174	172

Intermediate and routine non-manual classes: women

	1963	1964	1966	1969	1970	Feb. 1974	Oct. 1974	1979	1983	1987
Party voted for										
Conservative	61.4	57.5	59.3	58.7	55.7	42.3	42.2	52.9	53.0	56.0
Labour	22.4	24.3	25.4	25.4	32.9	31.8	32.6	29.9	19.1	22.1
Liberal	16.1	18.2	14.8	14.5	9.3	25.1	22.3	15.8	26.3	20.7
Other	0.0	0.0	0.5	1.4	2.1	0.8	2.9	1.4	1.6	1.2
Total	100.0	100.0	100.0	100.0	100.0	100.0	100.0	100.0	100.0	100.0
N. of respondents	223	181	190	138	224	478	448	278	445	638

Manual working class: men

	1963	1964	1966	1969	1970	Feb. 1974	Oct. 1974	1979	1983	1987
Party voted for										
Conservative	20.7	26.2	22.6	48.9	31.6	23.8	22.5	35.2	36.5	36.2
Labour	68.3	65.0	70.1	41.5	60.7	56.8	58.9	48.8	42.4	42.8
Liberal	10.8	8.3	6.7	8.2	4.9	14.8	13.1	13.6	19.3	19.8
Other	0.3	0.5	0.7	1.4	2.9	4.5	5.4	2.4	1.9	1.2
Total	100.0	100.0	100.0	100.0	100.0	100.0	100.0	100.0	100.0	100.0
N. of respondents	492	423	452	282	397	533	533	412	805	817

Table 1.14 *(cont.)*

	1963	1964	1966	1969	1970	Feb. 1974	Oct. 1974	1979	1983	1987
				Manual working class: women						
Party voted for										
Conservative	25.7	29.1	27.3	46.5	37.4	25.8	25.0	35.8	32.0	30.9
Labour	62.8	63.4	68.1	38.6	53.2	57.2	57.1	53.0	42.9	45.1
Liberal	11.5	7.3	4.2	12.6	7.5	15.5	15.9	10.5	23.6	23.0
Other	0.0	0.2	0.4	2.4	2.0	1.5	2.1	0.6	1.5	1.0
Total	100.0	100.0	100.0	100.0	100.0	100.0	100.0	100.0	100.0	100.0
N. of respondents	537	494	495	127	366	388	340	332	681	601

Table 1.15 *Vote by class and age (%)*

	1963	1964	1966	1969	1970	Feb. 1974	Oct. 1974	1979	1983	1987
				Professional and managerial classes: aged under 35						
Party voted for										
Conservative	59.6	55.3	56.9	51.6	47.3	49.4	37.2	56.5	49.2	45.4
Labour	28.8	23.6	21.4	38.7	41.7	22.2	25.6	25.0	15.2	24.5
Liberal	11.5	21.0	20.0	9.7	5.3	23.5	32.1	17.4	34.8	29.6
Other	0.0	0.0	1.7	0.0	5.6	4.9	5.1	1.1	0.8	0.5
Total	100.0	100.0	100.0	100.0	100.0	100.0	100.0	100.0	100.0	100.0
N. of respondents	52	50	47	31	75	81	78	92	256	216
				Intermediate and routine non-manual classes: aged under 35						
Party voted for										
Conservative	45.5	56.3	46.1	55.0	46.6	36.2	36.8	49.3	44.2	46.7
Labour	28.7	31.3	41.3	28.3	44.4	32.4	35.8	26.1	24.9	28.3
Liberal	25.7	11.6	10.5	13.3	7.1	28.6	21.2	21.8	28.6	24.3
Other	0.0	0.7	2.1	3.3	1.8	2.8	6.1	2.8	2.3	0.7
Total	100.0	100.0	100.0	100.0	100.0	100.0	100.0	100.0	100.0	100.0
N. of respondents	101	114	85	60	124	213	212	142	217	272

Table 1.15 (*cont.*)

Manual working class: aged under 35

	1963	1964	1966	1969	1970	Feb. 1974	Oct. 1974	1979	1983	1987
Party voted for										
Conservative	18.3	24.6	23.0	60.0	33.8	16.6	19.8	32.6	35.4	28.1
Labour	71.3	67.8	71.7	26.7	55.5	57.5	56.2	51.8	41.6	51.5
Liberal	10.4	6.9	5.3	10.5	7.2	19.4	17.1	13.5	21.1	19.1
Other	0.0	0.7	0.0	2.9	3.5	6.5	7.0	2.1	1.9	1.3
Total	100.0	100.0	100.0	100.0	100.0	100.0	100.0	100.0	100.0	100.0
N. of respondents	240	169	219	105	213	247	258	193	413	377

Professional and managerial classes: aged 35–54

	1963	1964	1966	1969	1970	Feb. 1974	Oct. 1974	1979	1983	1987
Party voted for										
Conservative	58.8	60.5	62.5	81.1	68.3	52.6	51.1	64.4	53.6	50.3
Labour	18.8	20.0	22.4	10.8	19.1	19.0	16.1	18.1	13.7	17.0
Liberal	22.4	17.2	15.1	8.1	10.8	27.7	29.2	16.1	32.5	30.7
Other	0.0	2.3	0.0	0.0	1.8	0.7	3.6	1.3	0.3	2.0
Total	100.0	100.0	100.0	100.0	100.0	100.0	100.0	100.0	100.0	100.0
N. of respondents	85	99	89	37	95	137	137	149	366	342

Intermediate and routine non-manual classes: aged 35–54

	1963	1964	1966	1969	1970	Feb. 1974	Oct. 1974	1979	1983	1987
Party voted for										
Conservative	49.8	52.2	51.1	68.1	53.8	43.7	41.5	53.8	52.9	55.3
Labour	31.0	30.4	34.3	18.1	29.7	33.8	33.8	29.0	17.5	20.1
Liberal	19.2	16.8	13.7	12.5	14.8	21.5	23.1	15.9	28.7	22.4
Other	0.0	0.6	0.9	1.4	1.8	1.1	1.5	1.4	0.9	2.3
Total	100.0	100.0	100.0	100.0	100.0	100.0	100.0	100.0	100.0	100.0
N. of respondents	203	205	218	72	128	284	260	145	223	304

Manual working class: aged 35–54

	1963	1964	1966	1969	1970	Feb. 1974	Oct. 1974	1979	1983	1987
Party voted for										
Conservative	20.8	22.3	21.3	41.3	27.1	24.4	21.1	31.2	33.5	38.4
Labour	67.8	67.5	71.6	43.8	63.6	60.7	67.0	54.0	42.6	42.3
Liberal	11.2	9.9	5.9	13.8	6.5	13.0	9.5	12.7	22.1	18.3
Other	0.2	0.3	1.2	1.3	2.8	1.9	2.4	2.2	1.7	1.0
Total	100.0	100.0	100.0	100.0	100.0	100.0	100.0	100.0	100.0	100.0
N. of respondents	438	360	356	160	279	308	294	276	516	482

Table 1.15 (*cont.*)

Professional and managerial classes: aged over 54

	1963	1964	1966	1969	1970	Feb. 1974	Oct. 1974	1979	1983	1987
Party voted for										
Conservative	80.0	88.7	78.8	80.0	75.5	71.3	68.3	63.8	65.9	61.1
Labour	8.3	4.3	10.5	16.0	15.8	13.8	15.9	21.3	9.8	12.2
Liberal	11.7	7.0	10.7	4.0	6.8	13.8	14.6	12.8	22.8	24.4
Other	0.0	0.0	0.0	0.0	1.9	1.1	1.2	2.1	1.6	2.2
Total	100.0	100.0	100.0	100.0	100.0	100.0	100.0	100.0	100.0	100.0
N. of respondents	60	67	74	25	91	87	82	94	246	270

Intermediate and routine non-manual classes: aged over 54

	1963	1964	1966	1969	1970	Feb. 1974	Oct. 1974	1979	1983	1987
Party voted for										
Conservative	67.4	65.3	63.8	76.1	65.9	57.3	56.5	61.8	63.5	61.7
Labour	19.6	20.5	26.7	14.9	24.2	23.6	27.8	27.5	15.2	15.2
Liberal	13.0	12.6	9.6	9.0	7.4	18.2	13.4	9.2	20.2	21.3
Other	0.0	1.6	0.0	0.0	2.5	0.9	2.4	1.5	1.1	1.7
Total	100.0	100.0	100.0	100.0	100.0	100.0	100.0	100.0	100.0	100.0
N. of respondents	138	134	130	67	127	225	209	131	178	230

Manual working class: aged over 54

	1963	1964	1966	1969	1970	Feb. 1974	Oct. 1974	1979	1983	1987
Party voted for										
Conservative	31.9	31.4	30.0	47.5	42.3	30.8	28.5	41.8	34.9	33.8
Labour	57.1	62.5	65.6	46.7	51.7	53.8	51.6	46.5	43.3	40.0
Liberal	10.6	5.8	4.4	5.0	4.9	13.2	16.5	10.9	20.4	25.0
Other	0.3	0.3	0.0	0.8	1.1	2.2	3.5	0.7	1.5	1.1
Total	100.0	100.0	100.0	100.0	100.0	100.0	100.0	100.0	100.0	100.0
N. of respondents	310	332	325	120	272	357	316	275	545	547

Table 1.16 *Vote by subjective social class (%)*

	'Spontaneous' middle class identification									
	1963	1964	1966	1969	1970	Feb. 1974	Oct. 1974	1979	1983	1987
Party voted for										
Conservative	65.0	65.2	65.5	61.5	56.3	53.4	49.8	60.1	58.5	57.8
Labour	17.5	17.9	22.2	23.1	27.7	26.2	25.9	22.8	17.1	18.4
Liberal	17.5	15.9	11.6	14.5	11.2	18.6	22.3	15.6	23.6	23.1
Other	0.0	1.0	0.7	0.9	4.8	1.8	1.9	1.5	0.9	0.7
Total	100.0	100.0	100.0	100.0	100.0	100.0	100.0	100.0	100.0	100.0
N. of respondents	314	231	266	117	105	328	309	263	661	540

	'Forced' middle class identification									
	1963	1964	1966	1969	1970	Feb. 1974	Oct. 1974	1979	1983	1987
Party voted for										
Conservative	64.2	69.8	66.1	75.3	70.1	58.6	56.1	69.7	61.5	60.3
Labour	17.0	18.5	21.6	15.5	19.9	17.4	20.5	13.8	9.8	14.2
Liberal	18.8	11.2	11.7	8.6	8.4	22.4	19.9	13.8	27.6	24.1
Other	0.0	0.5	0.5	0.6	1.6	1.6	3.6	2.7	1.1	1.4
Total	100.0	100.0	100.0	100.0	100.0	100.0	100.0	100.0	100.0	100.0
N. of respondents	165	217	197	174	128	384	337	261	661	564

	No class identification									
	1963	1964	1966	1969	1970	Feb. 1974	Oct. 1974	1979	1983	1987
Party voted for										
Conservative	50.0	54.8	47.0	52.6	57.2	50.0	44.9	58.7	54.8	48.9
Labour	30.0	27.8	36.7	31.6	34.3	25.6	30.6	28.3	20.3	17.9
Liberal	20.0	16.4	16.4	14.5	8.5	23.3	22.4	12.0	24.4	32.5
Other	0.0	1.0	0.0	1.3	0.0	1.1	2.0	1.1	0.5	0.8
Total	100.0	100.0	100.0	100.0	100.0	100.0	100.0	100.0	100.0	100.0
N. of respondents	90	80	53	174	55	90	98	92	196	126

	'Forced' working class identification									
	1963	1964	1966	1969	1970	Feb. 1974	Oct. 1974	1979	1983	1987
Party voted for										
Conservative	32.1	36.3	34.7	52.5	40.3	32.3	32.6	42.7	45.7	44.3
Labour	53.0	52.4	56.5	35.6	46.6	46.0	45.5	41.9	26.5	30.3
Liberal	14.9	10.5	8.5	9.7	10.4	19.2	17.9	13.4	26.0	23.5
Other	0.0	0.8	0.3	2.2	2.7	2.6	4.0	2.0	1.8	2.0
Total	100.0	100.0	100.0	100.0	100.0	100.0	100.0	100.0	100.0	100.0
N. of respondents	315	414	419	413	248	772	708	492	816	979

Table 1.16 (*cont.*)

'Spontaneous' working class identification

Party voted for	1963	1964	1966	1969	1970	Feb. 1974	Oct. 1974	1979	1983	1987
Conservative	21.7	24.7	20.3	44.3	26.8	18.8	17.1	28.4	26.8	26.4
Labour	68.6	66.7	74.1	41.5	65.9	62.5	65.4	57.3	48.1	50.3
Liberal	9.5	8.2	4.9	10.2	4.6	15.9	13.3	13.6	23.6	22.2
Other	0.2	0.4	0.6	4.0	2.7	2.8	4.2	0.7	1.6	1.2
Total	100.0	100.0	100.0	100.0	100.0	100.0	100.0	100.0	100.0	100.0
N. of respondents	856	615	622	176	175	496	503	450	1030	968

Table 1.17 *Vote by subjective and objective social class (%)*

Subjectively and objectively middle class										
Party voted for	1963	1964	1966	1969	1970	Feb. 1974	Oct. 1974	1979	1983	1987
Conservative	72.8	75.0	73.7	79.2	69.9	62.5	60.1	70.5	62.1	62.0
Labour	8.9	9.2	11.2	12.5	16.5	14.4	13.7	12.2	9.8	11.3
Liberal	18.3	15.1	14.5	8.3	8.7	20.7	23.0	14.9	27.4	25.5
Other	0.0	0.7	0.7	0.0	4.9	2.4	3.2	2.4	0.7	1.2
Total	100.0	100.0	100.0	100.0	100.0	100.0	100.0	100.0	100.0	100.0
N. of respondents	227	214	284	96	118	347	'313	295	762	764

Subjectively classless, objectively middle class										
Party voted for	1963	1964	1966	1969	1970	Feb. 1974	Oct. 1974	1979	1983	1987
Conservative	65.1	61.3	61.9	(47.4)	54.9	59.5	57.1	70.0	58.8	49.3
Labour	16.3	12.9	19.0	(36.8)	34.3	18.9	19.0	13.3	12.2	14.3
Liberal	18.6	22.6	19.0	(10.5)	10.8	21.6	21.4	16.7	28.3	35.1
Other	0.0	0.3	0.0	(5.3)	0.0	0.0	2.4	0.0	0.7	1.3
Total	100.0	100.0	100.0	(100.0)	100.0	100.0	100.0	100.0	100.0	100.0
N. of respondents	43	31	21	19	32	37	42	30	125	74

Table 1.17 (*cont.*)

Subjectively working class, objectively middle class

	1963	1964	1966	1969	1970	Feb. 1974	Oct. 1974	1979	1983	1987
Party voted for										
Conservative	41.0	44.9	45.1	66.2	47.0	43.0	42.2	47.1	40.9	45.5
Labour	41.4	39.2	43.6	25.4	37.5	32.9	33.2	34.2	29.1	27.5
Liberal	17.1	15.1	10.9	7.0	13.3	22.4	21.3	17.6	27.9	24.8
Other	0.4	0.8	0.4	1.4	2.3	1.8	3.3	1.1	2.1	2.1
Total	100.0	100.0	100.0	100.0	100.0	100.0	100.0	100.0	100.0	100.0
N. of respondents	192	219	237	71	63	228	211	187	840	799

Subjectively middle class, objectively working class

	1963	1964	1966	1969	1970	Feb. 1974	Oct. 1974	1979	1983	1987
Party voted for										
Conservative	42.4	45.1	50.3	67.8	59.4	48.4	46.8	56.7	54.4	52.6
Labour	38.6	41.8	42.9	22.6	30.4	30.1	31.6	26.4	25.5	29.0
Liberal	18.9	12.3	6.1	9.6	9.0	9.9	18.9	14.9	18.7	18.0
Other	0.0	0.8	0.7	0.0	1.2	1.6	2.7	1.9	1.4	0.4
Total	100.0	100.0	100.0	100.0	100.0	100.0	100.0	100.0	100.0	100.0
N. of respondents	232	158	147	115	103	322	297	208	280	272

Subjectively classless, objectively working class

	1963	1964	1966	1969	1970	Feb. 1974	Oct. 1974	1979	1983	1987
Party voted for										
Conservative	31.7	56.7	(38.9)	54.8	61.3	41.5	37.8	51.0	51.0	52.3
Labour	46.3	36.7	(55.6)	33.3	32.7	29.3	40.0	37.3	32.0	17.8
Liberal	22.0	6.7	(5.5)	11.9	6.0	26.8	20.0	9.8	17.0	29.9
Other	0.0	0.0	(0.0)	0.0	0.0	2.4	2.2	2.0	0.0	0.0
Total	100.0	100.0	(100.0)	100.0	100.0	100.0	100.0	100.0	100.0	100.0
N. of respondents	41	30	18	42	21	41	45	51	61	43

Subjectively and objectively working class

	1963	1964	1966	1969	1970	Feb. 1974	Oct. 1974	1979	1983	1987
Party voted for										
Conservative	19.8	23.5	19.8	46.0	32.5	22.6	22.1	33.1	29.6	28.4
Labour	70.7	69.1	74.7	41.8	57.6	57.3	58.4	52.9	47.1	48.5
Liberal	9.5	7.1	4.9	9.9	7.4	17.0	15.1	12.5	21.9	21.7
Other	0.1	0.3	0.5	2.3	2.5	3.1	4.3	1.5	1.5	1.4
Total	100.0	100.0	100.0	100.0	100.0	100.0	100.0	100.0	100.0	100.0
N. of respondents	920	770	791	385	343	981	945	726	925	1091

Table 1.18 *Vote by employment status (%)*

Self-employed with employees

	1963	1964	1966	1969	1970	Feb. 1974	Oct. 1974	1979	1983	1987
Party voted for										
Conservative	63.8	74.1	67.5	82.1	67.6	78.0	76.6	86.0	70.3	69.2
Labour	19.0	14.2	12.7	14.3	17.4	7.3	4.7	4.0	9.0	12.2
Liberal	17.2	11.7	19.8	3.6	10.3	13.4	12.5	8.0	19.4	17.4
Other	0.0	0.0	0.0	0.0	4.8	1.2	6.3	2.0	1.4	1.2
Total	100.0	100.0	100.0	100.0	100.0	100.0	100.0	100.0	100.0	100.0
N. of respondents	58	69	53	28	63	82	64	50	137	157

Self-employed, no employees

	1963	1964	1966	1969	1970	Feb. 1974	Oct. 1974	1979	1983	1987
Party voted for										
Conservative	47.8	(64.7)	49.6	82.6	66.6	56.9	57.7	70.0	67.0	53.9
Labour	30.4	(23.4)	38.8	4.3	18.6	25.0	15.5	15.0	15.3	22.9
Liberal	21.7	(12.0)	7.6	8.7	7.9	18.1	26.8	15.0	17.7	21.7
Other	0.0	(0.0)	4.0	4.3	6.9	0.0	0.0	0.0	0.0	1.6
Total	100.0	(100.0)	100.0	100.0	100.0	100.0	100.0	100.0	100.0	100.0
N. of respondents	23	17	28	23	27	72	71	60	114	135

Managers

	1963	1964	1966	1969	1970	Feb. 1974	Oct. 1974	1979	1983	1987
Party voted for										
Conservative	63.2	60.4	65.1	72.1	72.4	56.7	53.0	56.3	55.8	59.8
Labour	13.2	18.2	23.7	18.6	19.4	22.7	27.5	25.0	14.3	13.7
Liberal	23.7	20.0	11.2	7.0	5.1	19.3	18.1	15.6	29.0	24.9
Other	0.0	1.4	0.0	2.3	3.1	1.3	1.3	3.1	0.9	1.5
Total	100.0	100.0	100.0	100.0	100.0	100.0	100.0	100.0	100.0	100.0
N. of respondents	76	79	78	43	84	150	149	128	303	316

Foremen and supervisors

	1963	1964	1966	1969	1970	Feb. 1974	Oct. 1974	1979	1983	1987
Party voted for										
Conservative	39.6	42.2	39.5	57.1	38.5	47.0	40.8	53.5	44.0	45.0
Labour	38.5	44.7	52.2	31.7	53.1	33.7	42.7	31.0	26.1	28.2
Liberal	22.0	13.1	8.2	9.5	5.9	16.9	16.5	12.9	27.1	24.3
Other	0.0	0.0	0.0	1.6	2.4	2.4	0.0	2.6	2.7	2.4
Total	100.0	100.0	100.0	100.0	100.0	100.0	100.0	100.0	100.0	100.0
N. of respondents	91	99	91	63	95	83	103	155	187	197

Table 1.18 (cont.)

Rank and file employees

Party voted for	1963	1964	1966	1969	1970	Feb. 1974	Oct. 1974	1979	1983	1987
Conservative	30.6	37.2	32.4	52.7	39.0	31.8	29.8	38.7	41.2	40.2
Labour	57.2	51.5	59.5	35.9	52.4	45.5	47.5	44.4	33.3	34.9
Liberal	12.0	10.4	7.6	10.0	7.2	19.7	18.3	15.1	24.4	23.7
Other	0.2	0.8	0.6	1.4	1.3	2.9	4.3	1.8	1.1	1.2
Total	100.0	100.0	100.0	100.0	100.0	100.0	100.0	100.0	100.0	100.0
N. of respondents	880	798	807	571	767	1373	1290	773	2396	2271

Table 1.19 *Vote: unemployed (%)*

Party voted for	1963	1964	1966	1969	1970	Feb. 1974	Oct. 1974	1979	1983	1987
Conservative	(100.0)	(53.5)	(11.4)	(66.7)	55.8	10.5	21.4	42.3	22.5	18.1
Labour	(0.0)	(35.1)	(82.1)	(33.3)	33.2	65.8	60.7	42.3	52.0	62.0
Liberal	(0.0)	(11.4)	(6.5)	(0.0)	6.8	18.4	10.7	15.4	23.1	18.1
Other	(0.0)	(0.0)	(0.0)	(0.0)	4.3	5.3	7.1	0.0	2.4	1.8
Total	(100.0)	(100.0)	(100.0)	(100.0)	100.0	100.0	100.0	100.0	100.0	100.0
N. of respondents	3	11	12	9	34	38	28	26	191	164

Table 1.20 *Vote by class and employment status (%)*

Professional and managerial classes: self-employed

Party voted for	1963	1964	1966	1969	1970	Feb. 1974	Oct. 1974	1979	1983	1987
Conservative	76.7	84.2	66.7	85.7	74.8	73.9	67.5	86.1	69.2	61.0
Labour	6.7	10.5	7.4	9.5	14.2	6.5	2.5	8.3	10.3	14.0
Liberal	16.7	5.3	25.9	4.8	7.7	19.5	27.5	5.6	10.5	23.5
Other	0.0	0.0	0.0	0.0	3.3	0.0	2.5	0.0	0.0	1.5
Total	100.0	100.0	100.0	100.0	100.0	100.0	100.0	100.0	100.0	100.0
N. of respondents	30	37	27	21	26	46	40	36	117	136

Table 1.20 (*cont.*)

Professional and managerial classes: employees

	1963	1964	1966	1969	1970	Feb. 1974	Oct. 1974	1979	1983	1987
Party voted for										
Conservative	51.8	63.3	63.8	65.3	62.7	50.2	47.5	55.4	54.0	50.9
Labour	21.6	19.2	24.6	26.7	25.5	22.4	22.8	25.9	13.9	18.0
Liberal	20.7	17.5	11.5	8.0	9.4	24.7	26.0	17.0	31.3	29.5
Other	0.0	0.0	0.0	0.0	2.3	2.7	3.7	1.8	0.8	1.7
Total	100.0	100.0	100.0	100.0	100.0	100.0	100.0	100.0	100.0	100.0
N. of respondents	116	119	130	75	154	223	219	224	728	696

Intermediate and routine non-manual classes: self-employed

	1963	1964	1966	1969	1970	Feb. 1974	Oct. 1974	1979	1983	1987
Party voted for										
Conservative	50.0	65.7	70.3	77.3	63.6	68.6	72.5	65.9	73.9	80.0
Labour	26.3	17.1	13.5	9.1	18.7	14.0	13.0	11.4	13.0	6.7
Liberal	23.7	17.1	16.2	9.1	11.5	16.3	13.0	20.5	13.0	13.3
Other	0.0	0.0	0.0	4.5	6.3	1.2	1.4	2.3	0.0	0.0
Total	100.0	100.0	100.0	100.0	100.0	100.0	100.0	100.0	100.0	100.0
N. of respondents	38	36	37	22	50	86	69	44	23	30

Intermediate and routine non-manual classes: employees

	1963	1964	1966	1969	1970	Feb. 1974	Oct. 1974	1979	1983	1987
Party voted for										
Conservative	55.1	54.5	48.7	64.2	52.0	41.5	40.2	51.3	53.0	53.4
Labour	28.4	27.7	37.8	23.9	38.4	33.1	35.8	30.9	18.7	21.9
Liberal	16.1	16.6	12.6	10.4	8.7	23.7	20.9	15.9	26.9	23.0
Other	0.4	1.3	0.9	1.5	0.9	1.7	3.1	1.9	1.4	1.7
Total	100.0	100.0	100.0	100.0	100.0	100.0	100.0	100.0	100.0	100.0
N. of respondents	236	235	230	201	246	598	575	314	577	781

Manual working class: self-employed

	1963	1964	1966	1969	1970	Feb. 1974	Oct. 1974	1979	1983	1987
Party voted for										
Conservative	(36.4)	(54.5)	(35.3)	(87.5)	(66.8)	52.4	50.0	83.3	68.8	59.7
Labour	(54.5)	(27.3)	(58.8)	(12.5)	(20.9)	42.9	15.4	10.0	11.8	22.6
Liberal	(9.1)	(18.2)	(0.0)	(0.0)	(6.1)	4.8	26.9	6.7	17.2	16.1
Other	(0.0)	(0.0)	(5.9)	(0.0)	(6.1)	0.0	7.7	0.0	2.2	1.6
Total	(100.0)	(100.0)	(100.0)	(100.0)	(100.0)	100.0	100.0	100.0	100.0	100.0
N. of respondents	11	10	17	8	14	21	26	30	93	124

Table 1.20 (*cont.*)

Manual working class: employees

	1963	1964	1966	1969	1970	Feb. 1974	Oct. 1974	1979	1983	1987
Party voted for										
Conservative	21.8	28.6	24.6	47.4	31.5	25.3	22.7	32.6	33.4	31.6
Labour	65.9	62.5	69.3	41.1	61.5	56.0	59.2	51.7	43.2	45.7
Liberal	12.1	8.5	5.5	9.7	5.4	15.1	13.9	13.4	21.7	21.6
Other	0.1	0.5	0.5	1.7	1.7	3.6	4.2	2.3	1.7	1.0
Total	100.0	100.0	100.0	100.0	100.0	100.0	100.0	100.0	100.0	100.0
N. of respondents	678	602	612	401	545	775	740	515	1270	1294

Table 1.21 *Vote by trade union membership (%)*

Trade union members

	1963	1964	1966	1969	1970	Feb. 1974	Oct. 1974	1979	1983	1987
Party voted for										
Conservative	19.9	26.0	–	42.9	28.7	23.0	20.0	31.6	32.6	31.1
Labour	69.7	65.0	–	46.5	64.1	56.9	61.8	49.9	38.3	41.6
Liberal	9.8	8.4	–	9.2	5.1	17.1	14.2	15.9	27.5	25.2
Other	0.5	0.6	–	1.4	2.2	3.0	4.0	2.5	1.6	2.1
Total	100.0	100.0	–	100.0	100.0	100.0	100.0	100.0	100.0	100.0
N. of respondents	396	372	–	217	353	531	535	471	862	744

Respondent is married to a trade union member

	1963	1964	1966	1969	1970	Feb. 1974	Oct. 1974	1979	1983	1987
Party voted for										
Conservative	19.2	21.2	–	46.7	24.7	21.9	24.6	37.8	35.8	37.0
Labour	68.2	68.5	–	41.7	60.3	52.5	51.4	46.4	32.8	32.7
Liberal	12.5	10.3	–	11.7	9.3	24.2	20.5	14.2	30.9	29.3
Other	0.0	0.0	–	0.0	5.7	1.5	3.5	1.7	0.5	1.0
Total	100.0	100.0	–	100.0	100.0	100.0	100.0	100.0	100.0	100.0
N. of respondents	255	146	–	60	99	265	270	233	363	300

Table 1.21 (*cont.*)

	Neither respondent nor spouse belongs to a trade union									
	1963	1964	1966	1969	1970	Feb. 1974	Oct. 1974	1979	1983	1987
Party voted for										
Conservative	47.9	51.9	–	61.4	53.6	47.6	44.2	58.0	52.4	49.6
Labour	37.4	35.2	–	25.3	36.2	31.4	35.0	28.5	23.8	27.2
Liberal	14.8	12.1	–	10.9	8.0	18.8	18.1	12.5	22.4	22.1
Other	0.0	0.8	–	2.4	2.2	2.1	2.7	1.1	1.4	1.1
Total	100.0	100.0	–	100.0	100.0	100.0	100.0	100.0	100.0	100.0
N. of respondents	1076	961	–	679	1009	1274	1174	854	1966	2132

Table 1.22 *Vote by class and trade union membership (%)*

	Professional and managerial classes: trade union members									
	1963	1964	1966	1969	1970	Feb. 1974	Oct. 1974	1979	1983	1987
Party voted for										
Conservative	(42.1)	(45.2)	–	(35.3)	56.0	36.0	37.2	41.8	43.5	34.9
Labour	(36.8)	(35.1)	–	(64.7)	39.0	32.0	31.3	39.8	31.8	31.0
Liberal	(21.1)	(19.7)	–	(0.0)	2.5	29.3	29.2	16.3	22.9	29.8
Other	(0.0)	(0.0)	–	(0.0)	2.5	2.7	2.4	2.0	1.8	4.2
Total	(100.0)	(100.0)	–	(100.0)	100.0	100.0	100.0	100.0	100.0	100.0
N. of respondents	19	17	–	17	34	75	72	98	205	211

	Professional and managerial classes: non-members of unions									
	1963	1964	1966	1969	1970	Feb. 1974	Oct. 1974	1979	1983	1987
Party voted for										
Conservative	67.6	68.9	–	77.2	66.3	63.1	62.6	70.5	72.4	58.5
Labour	14.2	15.7	–	13.9	22.1	14.6	15.3	13.1	11.6	12.5
Liberal	18.1	14.3	–	8.9	8.6	20.6	20.6	15.2	14.8	28.3
Other	0.0	0.0	–	0.0	3.0	1.7	1.6	1.3	1.2	0.7
Total	100.0	100.0	–	100.0	100.0	100.0	100.0	100.0	100.0	100.0
N. of respondents	204	189	–	79	227	233	224	237	462	614

Table 1.22 (*cont.*)

Intermediate and routine non-manual classes: trade union members

	1963	1964	1966	1969	1970	Feb. 1974	Oct. 1974	1979	1983	1987
Party voted for										
Conservative	39.6	43.2	–	48.1	38.7	30.2	28.6	43.6	46.7	40.3
Labour	41.5	38.5	–	40.1	49.2	47.9	49.6	35.1	35.9	33.9
Liberal	17.0	16.5	–	11.7	10.6	20.8	20.8	20.2	15.2	24.3
Other	1.9	1.8	–	0.0	1.4	1.0	0.9	1.1	2.3	1.5
Total	100.0	100.0	–	100.0	100.0	100.0	100.0	100.0	100.0	100.0
N. of respondents	57	51	–	27	60	96	85	94	229	121

Intermediate and routine non-manual classes: non members of unions

	1963	1964	1966	1969	1970	Feb. 1974	Oct. 1974	1979	1983	1987
Party voted for										
Conservative	58.9	59.7	–	67.9	58.6	48.0	46.3	58.0	62.5	56.9
Labour	23.4	26.2	–	19.9	29.6	27.6	29.7	25.3	23.4	19.1
Liberal	17.7	14.1	–	10.2	9.6	22.8	22.4	14.5	12.5	22.4
Other	0.0	0.0	–	2.0	2.2	1.6	1.6	2.2	1.6	1.6
Total	100.0	100.0	–	100.0	100.0	100.0	100.0	100.0	100.0	100.0
N. of respondents	350	330	–	195	319	631	625	324	922	880

Manual working class: trade union members

	1963	1964	1966	1969	1970	Feb. 1974	Oct. 1974	1979	1983	1987
Party voted for										
Conservative	15.2	18.3	–	42.0	22.7	17.7	15.2	24.2	27.7	26.3
Labour	76.3	75.0	–	46.7	70.9	65.4	68.7	58.1	60.6	49.3
Liberal	8.2	6.4	–	9.5	4.1	13.1	12.6	14.4	10.2	23.2
Other	0.3	0.3	–	1.8	2.3	3.8	3.5	3.2	1.5	1.1
Total	100.0	100.0	–	100.0	100.0	100.0	100.0	100.0	100.0	100.0
N. of respondents	316	301	–	169	258	344	378	277	300	411

Manual working class: non-members of unions

	1963	1964	1966	1969	1970	Feb. 1974	Oct. 1974	1979	1983	1987
Party voted for										
Conservative	26.9	29.7	–	52.5	40.3	28.8	28.5	42.2	36.4	37.0
Labour	60.6	61.2	–	36.3	50.0	52.0	53.7	46.3	50.9	41.5
Liberal	12.5	9.1	–	9.6	7.2	16.3	15.1	10.9	11.4	20.4
Other	0.0	0.0	–	1.7	2.4	2.9	2.6	0.6	1.3	1.1
Total	100.0	100.0	–	100.0	100.0	100.0	100.0	100.0	100.0	100.0
N. of respondents	713	688	–	240	505	577	595	467	945	938

Table 1.23 *Vote by economic sector (%)*

	Works in private sector									
	1963	1964	1966	1969	1970	Feb. 1974	Oct. 1974	1979	1983	1987
Party voted for										
Conservative	–	–	–	–	–	–	34.1	44.8	46.6	44.2
Labour	–	–	–	–	–	–	45.3	38.8	29.3	31.7
Liberal	–	–	–	–	–	–	16.8	15.1	23.1	23.0
Other	–	–	–	–	–	–	3.8	1.3	1.0	1.1
Total	–	–	–	–	–	–	100.0	100.0	100.0	100.0
N. of respondents	–	–	–	–	–	–	880	615	1682	1797

	Works in public sector									
	1963	1964	1966	1969	1970	Feb. 1974	Oct. 1974	1979	1983	1987
Party voted for										
Conservative	–	–	–	–	–	–	27.6	38.3	37.9	39.7
Labour	–	–	–	–	–	–	48.8	42.7	31.7	33.6
Liberal	–	–	–	–	–	–	19.9	15.4	28.3	25.2
Other	–	–	–	–	–	–	3.8	3.6	2.1	1.5
Total	–	–	–	–	–	–	100.0	100.0	100.0	100.0
N. of respondents	–	–	–	–	–	–	453	389	1067	899

Table 1.24 *Vote by class and economic sector (%)*

	Professional and managerial classes: private sector									
	1963	1964	1966	1969	1970	Feb. 1974	Oct. 1974	1979	1983	1987
Party voted for										
Conservative	–	–	–	–	–	–	58.0	62.0	71.5	62.5
Labour	–	–	–	–	–	–	15.9	21.0	11.4	13.2
Liberal	–	–	–	–	–	–	21.6	17.0	16.1	23.4
Other	–	–	–	–	–	–	4.5	0.0	1.0	0.9
Total	–	–	–	–	–	–	100.0	100.0	100.0	100.0
N. of respondents	–	–	–	–	–	–	88	100	287	329

Table 1.24 (*cont.*)

Professional and managerial classes: public sector

	1963	1964	1966	1969	1970	Feb. 1974	Oct. 1974	1979	1983	1987
Party voted for										
Conservative	–	–	–	–	–	–	35.8	48.1	55.9	39.8
Labour	–	–	–	–	–	–	31.1	29.2	23.3	23.7
Liberal	–	–	–	–	–	–	31.1	18.9	19.1	33.9
Other	–	–	–	–	–	–	1.9	3.8	1.7	2.6
Total	–	–	–	–	–	–	100.0	100.0	100.0	100.0
N. of respondents	–	–	–	–	–	–	141	98	317	201

Intermediate and routine non-manual classes: private sector

	1963	1964	1966	1969	1970	Feb. 1974	Oct. 1974	1979	1983	1987
Party voted for										
Conservative	–	–	–	–	–	–	43.8	53.6	58.9	52.0
Labour	–	–	–	–	–	–	32.7	30.1	27.6	21.8
Liberal	–	–	–	–	–	–	21.0	14.8	11.9	24.7
Other	–	–	–	–	–	–	2.5	1.5	1.5	1.5
Total	–	–	–	–	–	–	100.0	100.0	100.0	100.0
N. of respondents	–	–	–	–	–	–	324	196	618	559

Intermediate and routine non-manual: public sector

	1963	1964	1966	1969	1970	Feb. 1974	Oct. 1974	1979	1983	1987
Party voted for										
Conservative	–	–	–	–	–	–	31.2	45.9	50.2	57.4
Labour	–	–	–	–	–	–	45.4	32.7	30.9	22.7
Liberal	–	–	–	–	–	–	20.6	18.4	15.8	18.9
Other	–	–	–	–	–	–	2.8	3.1	3.0	1.0
Total	–	–	–	–	–	–	100.0	100.0	100.0	100.0
N. of respondents	–	–	–	–	–	–	141	98	317	201

Manual working class: private sector

	1963	1964	1966	1969	1970	Feb. 1974	Oct. 1974	1979	1983	1987
Party voted for										
Conservative	–	–	–	–	–	–	22.6	34.1	37.7	32.5
Labour	–	–	–	–	–	–	59.8	49.7	51.3	44.5
Liberal	–	–	–	–	–	–	13.1	14.7	10.3	22.0
Other	–	–	–	–	–	–	4.5	1.6	0.8	1.0
Total	–	–	–	–	–	–	100.0	100.0	100.0	100.0
N. of respondents	–	–	–	–	–	–	465	320	563	899

Table 1.24 (*cont.*)

Manual working class: public sector

Party voted for	1963	1964	1966	1969	1970	Feb. 1974	Oct. 1974	1979	1983	1987
Conservative	–	–	–	–	–	–	20.9	29.0	24.3	28.5
Labour	–	–	–	–	–	–	60.2	55.2	60.4	49.6
Liberal	–	–	–	–	–	–	13.9	12.0	12.6	21.2
Other	–	–	–	–	–	–	5.0	3.8	2.7	0.8
Total	–	–	–	–	–	–	100.0	100.0	100.0	100.0
N. of respondents	–	–	–	–	–	–	201	183	272	357

Table 1.25 *Vote by housing (%)*

Owner occupiers

Party voted for	1963	1964	1966	1969	1970	Feb. 1974	Oct. 1974	1979	1983	1987
Conservative	49.8	55.8	–	62.1	53.3	50.0	46.7	56.3	53.3	51.2
Labour	33.2	29.9	–	25.7	36.2	27.7	29.6	26.7	19.0	22.7
Liberal	16.9	13.9	–	11.3	8.0	21.1	21.4	15.5	26.8	24.7
Other	0.1	0.4	–	0.9	2.4	1.2	2.4	1.6	0.9	1.4
Total	100.0	100.0	–	100.0	100.0	100.0	100.0	100.0	100.0	100.0
N. of respondents	741	736	–	443	762	1100	1062	903	2131	2287

Council tenants

Party voted for	1963	1964	1966	1969	1970	Feb. 1974	Oct. 1974	1979	1983	1987
Conservative	25.0	22.1	–	47.3	31.2	17.4	17.8	27.6	23.3	21.5
Labour	67.3	70.2	–	39.6	59.8	63.6	65.3	59.6	55.0	58.3
Liberal	7.8	7.0	–	9.5	6.6	14.9	11.9	10.7	20.3	18.8
Other	0.0	0.7	–	3.6	2.3	4.1	5.0	2.0	1.5	1.3
Total	100.0	100.0	–	100.0	100.0	100.0	100.0	100.0	100.0	100.0
N. of respondents	501	441	–	275	396	632	580	456	797	641

Table 1.25 (*cont.*)

	Private tenants									
	1963	1964	1966	1969	1970	Feb. 1974	Oct. 1974	1979	1983	1987
Party voted for										
Conservative	29.7	38.1	–	56.1	43.4	34.3	33.6	45.9	43.4	37.3
Labour	57.0	54.0	–	31.6	47.1	42.6	43.3	38.9	27.1	35.4
Liberal	13.1	7.0	–	10.4	6.9	21.1	18.5	14.0	28.2	26.7
Other	0.2	1.0	–	1.9	2.6	2.1	4.7	1.3	1.2	0.6
Total	100.0	100.0	–	100.0	100.0	100.0	100.0	100.0	100.0	100.0
N. of respondents	428	334	–	212	275	289	298	157	147	161

Table 1.26 *Vote by school leaving age (%)*

	Left school aged under 15									
	1963	1964	1966	1969	1970	Feb. 1974	Oct. 1974	1979	1983	1987
Party voted for										
Conservative	30.3	34.7	32.0	51.5	40.4	36.4	32.9	41.4	40.3	38.1
Labour	57.5	55.1	60.4	35.5	51.2	47.5	49.1	46.2	36.0	35.6
Liberal	12.1	9.9	7.1	11.5	6.7	14.7	15.6	11.3	21.9	25.2
Other	0.2	0.4	0.4	1.4	1.7	1.4	2.4	1.1	1.9	1.1
Total	100.0	100.0	100.0	100.0	100.0	100.0	100.0	100.0	100.0	100.0
N. of respondents	1061	929	892	425	643	914	844	539	949	764

	Left school aged 15									
	1963	1964	1966	1969	1970	Feb. 1974	Oct. 1974	1979	1983	1987
Party voted for										
Conservative	38.2	41.3	36.3	62.8	41.8	29.6	29.5	40.8	42.6	45.1
Labour	47.3	46.9	55.8	26.1	46.8	46.6	50.7	43.6	32.9	33.8
Liberal	14.6	10.1	7.0	8.1	7.0	20.6	15.0	13.4	23.4	19.3
Other	0.0	1.6	0.9	3.0	4.4	3.1	4.7	2.1	1.1	1.9
Total	100.0	100.0	100.0	100.0	100.0	100.0	100.0	100.0	100.0	100.0
N. of respondents	364	325	327	234	333	577	552	424	817	771

Table 1.26 (*cont.*)

Left school aged 16

Party voted for	1963	1964	1966	1969	1970	Feb. 1974	Oct. 1974	1979	1983	1987
Conservative	53.0	57.3	55.6	62.6	55.6	46.7	49.6	55.6	47.4	42.6
Labour	31.5	31.6	34.1	23.1	37.9	28.4	26.1	28.5	25.1	34.6
Liberal	15.5	11.2	10.3	12.1	5.8	22.8	20.6	15.2	26.1	21.4
Other	0.0	0.0	0.0	2.2	0.7	2.1	3.7	0.7	1.4	1.4
Total	100.0	100.0	100.0	100.0	100.0	100.0	100.0	100.0	100.0	100.0
N. of respondents	168	167	180	91	148	285	272	302	749	753

Left school aged 17

Party voted for	1963	1964	1966	1969	1970	Feb. 1974	Oct. 1974	1979	1983	1987
Conservative	71.0	78.2	63.9	63.0	63.8	57.7	51.9	63.9	54.3	59.5
Labour	10.5	9.2	21.4	31.5	27.7	17.5	19.1	19.4	16.8	16.8
Liberal	18.4	11.1	12.3	3.7	7.7	19.7	22.9	14.8	27.9	23.4
Other	0.0	1.5	2.4	1.9	0.9	5.1	6.1	1.9	1.0	0.3
Total	100.0	100.0	100.0	100.0	100.0	100.0	100.0	100.0	100.0	100.0
N. of respondents	76	66	76	54	96	137	131	108	277	269

Left school aged over 17

Party voted for	1963	1964	1966	1969	1970	Feb. 1974	Oct. 1974	1979	1983	1987
Conservative	57.1	61.8	58.8	53.8	54.3	46.9	39.9	53.3	51.6	50.4
Labour	28.6	16.7	24.0	34.6	30.1	17.2	20.3	23.1	17.6	24.2
Liberal	14.3	21.5	17.2	9.6	11.9	33.8	36.2	20.1	29.9	24.5
Other	0.0	0.0	0.0	1.9	3.8	2.1	3.6	3.6	0.8	0.9
Total	100.0	100.0	100.0	100.0	100.0	100.0	100.0	100.0	100.0	100.0
N. of respondents	77	81	78	52	95	145	138	169	407	322

Table 1.27 Vote: university or polytechnic educated (%)

Party voted for	1963	1964	1966	1969	1970	Feb. 1974	Oct. 1974	1979	1983	1987
Conservative	56.0	45.8	–	50.0	47.7	–	–	–	43.9	–
Labour	32.0	25.5	–	41.2	33.1	–	–	–	17.3	–
Liberal	12.0	28.7	–	5.9	17.4	–	–	–	37.9	–
Other	0.0	0.0	–	2.9	1.8	–	–	–	0.9	–
Total	100.0	100.0	–	100.0	100.0	–	–	–	100.0	–
N. of respondents	25	32	–	34	48	–	–	–	343	–

Table 1.28 *Vote by type of school attended (%)*

	Non-selective state school									
	1963	1964	1966	1969	1970	Feb. 1974	Oct. 1974	1979	1983	1987
Party voted for										
Conservative	31.7	35.5	32.6	54.6	41.2	32.3	32.0	40.8	41.2	39.8
Labour	55.4	54.0	59.7	33.3	49.7	46.9	49.4	45.5	32.8	34.4
Liberal	12.8	9.8	7.1	10.1	6.8	18.9	16.3	12.8	24.7	24.3
Other	0.1	0.7	0.6	2.0	2.3	1.9	2.3	1.0	1.3	1.4
Total	100.0	100.0	100.0	100.0	100.0	100.0	100.0	100.0	100.0	100.0
N. of respondents	1386	1215	1207	736	1102	1429	1420	924	2180	1967

	Selective state school									
	1963	1964	1966	1969	1970	Feb. 1974	Oct. 1974	1979	1983	1987
Party voted for										
Conservative	53.8	60.0	57.9	54.4	52.9	48.3	48.0	48.5	52.6	49.2
Labour	30.9	26.7	29.6	28.2	33.6	25.6	27.3	31.2	18.1	21.3
Liberal	14.9	13.4	11.6	14.8	10.1	21.8	20.9	17.3	27.5	27.7
Other	0.4	0.0	0.9	2.7	3.3	4.3	3.8	3.0	1.8	1.8
Total	100.0	100.0	100.0	100.0	100.0	100.0	100.0	100.0	100.0	100.0
N. of respondents	249	237	205	149	237	422	418	398	673	603

	Private school									
	1963	1964	1966	1969	1970	Feb. 1974	Oct. 1974	1979	1983	1987
Party voted for										
Conservative	73.8	74.9	67.2	87.5	82.1	72.2	72.0	70.0	75.9	65.8
Labour	12.5	11.8	21.0	8.3	10.5	13.5	13.7	15.5	5.8	14.1
Liberal	13.8	12.1	11.8	4.2	5.6	13.5	13.1	12.7	18.4	19.4
Other	0.0	1.2	0.0	0.0	1.8	0.8	1.2	1.9	0.0	0.6
Total	100.0	100.0	100.0	100.0	100.0	100.0	100.0	100.0	100.0	100.0
N. of respondents	80	84	94	48	81	126	115	84	133	158

Table 1.29 *Vote by religion (%)*

Anglicans

Party voted for	1963	1964	1966	1969	1970	Feb. 1974	Oct. 1974	1979	1983	1987
Conservative	40.1	45.2	42.2	61.1	50.8	–	43.8	54.9	52.3	53.1
Labour	46.9	44.3	50.3	28.4	41.6	–	35.2	30.6	22.6	24.1
Liberal	13.0	9.7	6.9	9.9	6.5	–	20.4	14.4	24.8	22.5
Other	0.0	0.7	0.5	0.5	1.1	–	0.6	0.0	0.3	0.4
Total	100.0	100.0	100.0	100.0	100.0	–	100.0	100.0	100.0	100.0
N. of respondents	1120	1018	998	566	873	–	819	506	1478	1349

Non-conformists

Party voted for	1963	1964	1966	1969	1970	Feb. 1974	Oct. 1974	1979	1983	1987
Conservative	24.1	31.5	28.3	43.4	37.8	–	33.6	48.0	41.7	34.2
Labour	55.1	53.1	60.1	37.7	43.1	–	32.8	31.0	27.3	31.8
Liberal	20.9	15.5	11.0	15.1	12.0	–	32.1	21.0	29.7	31.7
Other	0.0	0.0	0.7	3.8	7.0	–	1.5	0.0	1.4	2.2
Total	100.0	100.0	100.0	100.0	100.0	–	100.0	100.0	100.0	100.0
N. of respondents	158	151	150	106	213	–	131	100	212	169

Roman Catholics

Party voted for	1963	1964	1966	1969	1970	Feb. 1974	Oct. 1974	1979	1983	1987
Conservative	23.2	26.3	25.5	49.0	31.3	–	26.0	49.4	34.4	34.5
Labour	64.9	64.6	70.5	36.5	62.3	–	60.4	42.5	43.3	46.2
Liberal	11.9	9.1	4.0	11.5	5.8	–	11.2	8.1	21.0	18.7
Other	0.0	0.0	0.0	3.1	0.6	–	2.4	0.0	1.2	0.6
Total	100.0	100.0	100.0	100.0	100.0	–	100.0	100.0	100.0	100.0
N. of respondents	151	120	139	96	150	–	169	160	373	323

No religious affiliation

Party voted for	1963	1964	1966	1969	1970	Feb. 1974	Oct. 1974	1979	1983	1987
Conservative	28.3	26.9	31.7	36.6	29.1	–	30.1	41.7	42.4	37.1
Labour	56.6	50.3	55.0	48.8	61.3	–	50.7	42.8	30.3	36.4
Liberal	13.2	20.8	13.3	9.8	7.4	–	14.8	12.6	25.4	25.1
Other	1.9	2.0	0.0	4.9	2.2	–	4.4	2.9	2.0	1.4
Total	100.0	100.0	100.0	100.0	100.0	–	100.0	100.0	100.0	100.0
N. of respondents	53	49	50	41	64	–	641	626	779	970

Table 1.30 *Vote by religiosity (%)*

| | Attend church regularly | | | | | | | | | |
	1963	1964	1966	1969	1970	Feb. 1974	Oct. 1974	1979	1983	1987
Party voted for										
Conservative	44.8	47.3	42.3	57.6	43.2	–	–	49.3	46.6	46.5
Labour	38.1	38.6	47.5	27.3	42.0	–	–	32.5	24.1	26.9
Liberal	17.1	13.8	8.7	12.2	10.4	–	–	16.8	27.2	24.3
Other	0.0	0.3	1.6	2.9	4.4	–	–	1.4	2.1	2.2
Total	100.0	100.0	100.0	100.0	100.0	–	–	100.0	100.0	100.0
N. of respondents	375	345	319	172	268	–	–	292	486	466

| | Attend church occasionally | | | | | | | | | |
	1963	1964	1966	1969	1970	Feb. 1974	Oct. 1974	1979	1983	1987
Party voted for										
Conservative	41.5	43.0	41.0	62.0	56.4	–	–	54.0	53.1	48.5
Labour	45.0	43.5	47.9	26.0	35.4	–	–	30.5	21.4	28.6
Liberal	13.4	12.6	10.8	10.4	6.1	–	–	14.8	24.6	22.0
Other	0.2	0.9	0.3	1.6	2.2	–	–	0.7	0.9	0.9
Total	100.0	100.0	100.0	100.0	100.0	–	–	100.0	100.0	100.0
N. of respondents	545	476	494	250	378	–	–	413	490	447

| | Attend church only rarely | | | | | | | | | |
	1963	1964	1966	1969	1970	Feb. 1974	Oct. 1974	1979	1983	1987
Party voted for										
Conservative	30.6	40.0	37.1	54.8	46.5	–	–	44.6	39.9	48.5
Labour	57.2	51.3	56.5	32.6	44.7	–	–	40.7	32.2	28.6
Liberal	12.2	8.1	6.4	11.1	6.8	–	–	13.1	27.0	22.0
Other	0.0	0.6	0.0	1.5	1.9	–	–	1.6	0.9	0.9
Total	100.0	100.0	100.0	100.0	100.0	–	–	100.0	100.0	100.0
N. of respondents	395	363	388	270	403	–	–	567	862	835

| | Never attend church | | | | | | | | | |
	1963	1964	1966	1969	1970	Feb. 1974	Oct. 1974	1979	1983	1987
Party voted for										
Conservative	30.9	38.3	33.9	54.6	36.2	–	–	36.9	41.5	44.5
Labour	58.6	55.1	60.0	35.4	54.4	–	–	48.3	35.1	31.2
Liberal	10.6	6.2	5.5	7.9	7.8	–	–	11.4	22.4	23.0
Other	0.0	0.3	0.6	2.2	1.7	–	–	3.4	1.0	1.2
Total	100.0	100.0	100.0	100.0	100.0	–	–	100.0	100.0	100.0
N. of respondents	379	336	309	229	346	–	–	263	862	814

Table 1.31 *Vote by region (%)*

	Scotland					Feb. 1974	Oct. 1974			
	1963	1964	1966	1969	1970	1974	1974	1979	1983	1987
Party voted for										
Conservative	40.6	42.0	36.5	59.4	41.3	35.5	23.8	37.4	23.6	29.0
Labour	50.9	53.0	50.6	25.0	44.9	41.1	39.8	39.0	44.1	38.0
Liberal	8.0	4.3	11.7	7.3	7.6	4.1	5.0	11.4	22.0	22.9
Other	0.6	0.7	1.1	8.3	6.3	19.3	31.5	12.2	10.2	10.1
Total	100.0	100.0	100.0	100.0	100.0	100.0	100.0	100.0	100.0	100.0
N. of respondents	175	158	136	96	156	197	181	123	291	286

	Wales					Feb. 1974	Oct. 1974			
	1963	1964	1966	1969	1970	1974	1974	1979	1983	1987
Party voted for										
Conservative	18.4	27.0	25.9	37.2	28.2	24.3	17.5	20.4	33.5	22.2
Labour	64.4	54.0	55.7	27.9	39.6	55.0	59.6	62.4	40.7	54.6
Liberal	17.2	14.2	10.0	16.3	11.0	15.3	17.5	12.9	22.0	17.8
Other	0.0	4.8	8.5	18.6	21.2	5.4	5.3	4.3	3.8	5.4
Total	100.0	100.0	100.0	100.0	100.0	100.0	100.0	100.0	100.0	100.0
N. of respondents	87	66	80	43	84	111	114	93	177	172

	The North					Feb. 1974	Oct. 1974			
	1963	1964	1966	1969	1970	1974	1974	1979	1983	1987
Party voted for										
Conservative	33.9	36.5	35.5	50.7	42.8	36.9	34.9	45.0	39.7	37.3
Labour	53.8	50.7	57.0	38.1	49.1	47.1	46.6	41.5	37.0	44.6
Liberal	12.3	12.6	7.4	10.8	8.1	15.8	18.5	13.5	23.4	18.1
Other	0.0	0.3	0.0	0.4	0.0	0.2	0.0	0.0	0.0	0.0
Total	100.0	100.0	100.0	100.0	100.0	100.0	100.0	100.0	100.0	100.0
N. of respondents	496	456	416	268	421	601	556	431	859	856

	The Midlands					Feb. 1974	Oct. 1974			
	1963	1964	1966	1969	1970	1974	1974	1979	1983	1987
Party voted for										
Conservative	35.2	43.9	39.4	58.7	49.5	39.9	38.1	45.6	49.8	45.4
Labour	52.7	51.5	56.6	28.1	44.5	45.5	48.8	41.8	28.5	27.8
Liberal	12.1	4.6	4.0	12.6	5.6	14.6	14.8	12.2	21.5	26.6
Other	0.0	0.0	0.0	0.6	0.4	0.0	0.3	0.4	0.2	0.2
Total	100.0	100.0	100.0	100.0	100.0	100.0	100.0	100.0	100.0	100.0
N. of respondents	315	279	308	167	249	323	324	263	480	532

Table 1.31 (*cont.*)

Greater London

	1963	1964	1966	1969	1970	Feb. 1974	Oct. 1974	1979	1983	1987
Party voted for										
Conservative	35.8	44.4	36.7	57.6	47.0	37.1	42.0	46.8	46.4	51.8
Labour	46.3	43.7	52.7	31.8	48.5	41.8	43.6	40.5	27.6	28.3
Liberal	17.9	11.0	10.6	10.0	4.5	20.7	13.3	10.8	25.5	19.3
Other	0.0	0.9	0.0	0.6	0.0	0.4	1.1	1.9	0.6	0.6
Total	100.0	100.0	100.0	100.0	100.0	100.0	100.0	100.0	100.0	100.0
N. of respondents	268	227	235	170	225	237	188	158	385	370

The South

	1963	1964	1966	1969	1970	Feb. 1974	Oct. 1974	1979	1983	1987
Party voted for										
Conservative	45.5	47.4	46.1	62.7	51.9	41.8	42.4	56.9	55.5	54.7
Labour	40.1	37.6	44.6	27.8	37.2	28.3	32.3	25.9	15.6	16.0
Liberal	14.1	14.5	9.3	9.4	8.9	29.8	24.8	16.7	28.6	29.1
Other	0.2	0.5	0.0	0.0	2.0	0.2	0.5	0.4	0.3	0.2
Total	100.0	100.0	100.0	100.0	100.0	100.0	100.0	100.0	100.0	100.0
N. of respondents	411	396	395	212	326	601	592	490	1019	987

Table 1.32 *Preferred party of non-voters (%)*

	1964	1966	1969	1970	Feb. 1974	Oct. 1974	1979	1983	1987
Party preferred									
Conservative	40.3	33.7	–	40.2	26.2	30.6	–	40.3	40.5
Labour	40.8	41.6	–	37.5	37.9	39.0	–	27.0	27.8
Liberal	9.5	8.4	–	10.9	18.3	18.8	–	20.2	16.7
Other	0.9	1.3	–	0.9	2.4	3.2	–	2.0	1.9
None	1.5	5.7	–	5.0	8.3	4.9	–	} 10.4	} 13.1
Don't know	7.1	9.2	–	5.6	6.9	3.5	–		
Total	100.0	100.0	–	100.0	100.0	100.0	–	100.0	100.0
N. of respondents	191	294	–	341	290	346	–	647	528

Chapter 2

PARTY IDENTIFICATION

1. Strength and direction of partisanship excludes respondents who identified with the Scottish Nationalists, Plaid Cymru or other small parties; respondents who had no party identification; and respondents who identified with one of the main parties but were unable to say how strongly.
2. In 1983 and 1987 the Liberal Party contested the election in an electoral alliance with the SDP. In these two years identification with the Liberal party includes those who said they identified with the SDP or the Alliance.

See also appendix E, p. 472 on the construction of, the strength and direction of partisanship variable.

Table 2.1 *Strength and direction of partisanship: all respondents (%)*

	1963	1964	1966	1969	1970	Feb. 1974	Oct. 1974	1979	1983	1987
Conservative										
very strong	13.6	19.9	18.4	17.1	21.5	12.3	10.2	10.0	11.5	10.3
fairly strong	16.2	16.7	14.7	21.7	16.7	18.9	19.7	22.7	21.4	22.4
not very strong	9.8	5.3	6.0	11.1	6.2	8.6	8.8	11.6	14.3	10.6
Liberal										
very strong	3.0	3.9	3.6	1.8	2.2	1.6	2.1	1.8	1.7	2.0
fairly strong	4.9	6.1	5.7	4.5	4.5	7.5	8.7	6.3	6.7	8.4
not very strong	3.8	2.9	1.5	4.4	1.9	5.3	5.6	5.3	6.3	10.0
Labour										
very strong	17.5	22.4	24.2	11.1	21.1	17.6	15.7	11.4	10.7	9.4
fairly strong	19.8	16.9	19.9	14.4	18.0	18.8	20.8	20.3	15.4	15.6
not very strong	11.4	5.9	6.1	13.8	7.9	9.3	8.4	10.7	12.1	11.3
Total	100.0	100.0	100.0	100.0	100.0	100.0	100.0	100.0	100.0	100.0
N. of respondents	1872	1708	1770	980	1696	2272	2165	1708	3427	3192

Table 2.2 *Strength and direction of partisanship by gender (%)*

Men										
	1963	1964	1966	1969	1970	Feb. 1974	Oct. 1974	1979	1983	1987
Conservative										
very strong	12.7	17.0	16.3	16.4	20.3	11.2	8.3	9.2	9.0	9.3
fairly strong	12.4	15.7	13.2	21.1	15.7	19.3	20.8	22.5	20.6	22.3
not very strong	10.0	4.9	5.7	11.0	6.5	9.0	8.9	12.7	14.0	10.3
Liberal										
very strong	4.1	4.4	3.3	1.5	2.0	1.5	1.9	2.0	2.2	2.0
fairly strong	4.5	6.9	6.7	3.2	3.1	6.6	7.6	6.2	8.5	8.5
not very strong	3.9	3.1	1.7	3.2	2.0	5.1	5.3	4.6	8.3	9.1
Labour										
very strong	21.4	24.6	25.3	14.9	23.8	17.6	16.5	12.2	11.5	10.4
fairly strong	20.3	17.0	21.6	13.6	18.2	20.3	21.5	20.9	14.6	15.8
not very strong	10.6	6.4	6.1	15.1	8.4	9.5	9.3	9.7	11.2	12.2
Total	100.0	100.0	100.0	100.0	100.0	100.0	100.0	100.0	100.0	100.0
N. of respondents	837	772	825	464	790	1065	1066	818	1625	1536

Table 2.2 (*cont.*)

	Women									
	1963	1964	1966	1969	1970	Feb. 1974	Oct. 1974	1979	1983	1987
Conservative										
very strong	14.3	22.2	20.2	17.8	22.5	13.3	12.0	10.8	12.1	11.3
fairly strong	19.3	17.5	15.9	22.3	17.6	18.5	18.7	22.8	19.2	22.4
not very strong	9.6	5.7	6.2	11.2	6.0	8.3	8.7	10.6	12.7	11.0
Liberal										
very strong	2.1	3.6	3.9	2.1	2.3	1.7	2.4	1.6	2.4	2.0
fairly strong	5.1	5.4	4.9	5.6	5.6	8.3	9.8	6.4	9.4	8.4
not very strong	3.8	2.7	1.3	5.4	1.8	5.6	5.9	5.8	10.5	10.8
Labour										
very strong	14.4	20.6	23.2	7.8	18.8	17.7	14.8	10.6	8.5	8.4
fairly strong	19.3	16.7	18.4	15.1	17.8	17.6	20.1	19.8	14.0	15.3
not very strong	12.1	5.6	6.0	12.6	7.4	9.1	7.6	11.7	11.2	10.5
Total	100.0	100.0	100.0	100.0	100.0	100.0	100.0	100.0	100.0	100.0
N. of respondents	1035	936	945	516	906	1207	1099	890	1801	1656

Table 2.3 *Strength and direction of partisanship by age (%)*

	Aged under 25									
	1963	1964	1966	1969	1970	Feb. 1974	Oct. 1974	1979	1983	1987
Conservative										
very strong	7.9	10.9	10.3	11.2	6.6	4.1	2.8	4.1	3.7	2.9
fairly strong	10.5	22.7	20.8	19.4	20.0	14.1	16.3	18.6	19.6	15.8
not very strong	12.3	8.5	3.7	19.4	11.3	7.3	10.2	11.7	19.2	14.6
Liberal										
very strong	0.0	2.1	1.8	1.0	1.1	0.9	2.4	2.1	1.4	0.5
fairly strong	2.6	2.9	3.1	3.1	2.6	10.9	10.2	8.3	5.1	7.5
not very strong	5.3	1.6	2.2	7.1	3.0	9.5	8.5	8.3	11.7	11.0
Labour										
very strong	15.8	21.1	14.6	3.1	13.0	15.5	11.0	6.9	5.2	6.0
fairly strong	28.1	23.2	31.0	20.4	27.9	22.7	26.0	20.7	15.2	20.6
not very strong	17.5	6.0	12.5	15.3	14.4	15.0	12.6	19.3	18.9	21.1
Total	100.0	100.0	100.0	100.0	100.0	100.0	100.0	100.0	100.0	100.0
N. of respondents	114	100	130	98	238	220	246	145	483	381

Table 2.3 (*cont.*)

	1963	1964	1966	1969	1970	Feb. 1974	Oct. 1974	1979	1983	1987
Aged 25–34										
Conservative										
very strong	6.8	14.0	12.1	8.5	15.9	8.6	6.6	6.6	5.6	5.0
fairly strong	18.1	17.1	13.3	33.3	17.3	16.9	17.7	20.9	18.6	19.9
not very strong	12.9	8.2	7.4	11.3	8.4	8.8	10.4	15.9	17.5	12.5
Liberal										
very strong	1.3	1.9	2.4	0.0	0.3	1.7	1.4	2.4	1.9	1.2
fairly strong	5.5	8.2	5.0	4.3	5.3	8.1	10.4	6.1	9.0	8.2
not very strong	5.2	4.2	1.6	5.0	2.1	9.5	6.4	5.8	11.1	12.4
Labour										
very strong	12.9	16.4	22.3	7.1	17.7	12.2	10.9	7.4	8.2	7.9
fairly strong	21.3	20.0	27.0	17.7	22.0	21.5	24.6	20.4	13.8	18.4
not very strong	16.1	9.9	8.9	12.8	11.2	12.6	11.6	14.6	14.3	14.4
Total	100.0	100.0	100.0	100.0	100.0	100.0	100.0	100.0	100.0	100.0
N. of respondents	310	277	294	141	268	419	423	378	651	568
Aged 35–44										
Conservative										
very strong	9.0	12.4	17.0	20.1	16.3	10.7	6.6	10.5	10.3	9.6
fairly strong	15.9	15.8	12.2	20.7	17.5	21.6	21.8	22.7	20.3	22.0
not very strong	9.5	6.7	5.7	8.5	6.0	8.6	8.0	11.2	14.9	10.4
Liberal										
very strong	2.0	4.9	4.0	0.6	2.2	1.6	2.4	1.3	2.4	1.9
fairly strong	5.6	7.1	8.1	6.1	5.3	5.2	8.5	6.1	11.6	10.0
not very strong	5.4	3.0	0.8	6.2	3.5	4.9	6.4	5.8	8.2	12.2
Labour										
very strong	17.9	21.2	23.1	9.1	22.8	16.1	14.1	8.3	7.3	6.3
fairly strong	25.1	23.1	23.4	13.4	18.2	20.0	23.1	24.3	14.3	17.3
not very strong	9.7	5.7	5.8	15.2	8.3	11.2	9.0	9.9	10.7	10.3
Total	100.0	100.0	100.0	100.0	100.0	100.0	100.0	100.0	100.0	100.0
N. of respondents	391	368	344	164	289	384	376	313	623	635

Table 2.3 (*cont.*)

	Aged 45–54									
	1963	1964	1966	1969	1970	Feb. 1974	Oct. 1974	1979	1983	1987
Conservative										
very strong	11.8	19.8	16.3	13.3	23.3	9.4	7.0	8.2	10.0	12.0
fairly strong	15.2	16.6	16.7	17.9	13.5	21.5	22.1	23.1	21.7	25.2
not very strong	10.0	5.0	5.9	11.6	5.0	8.2	9.1	10.8	10.7	12.5
Liberal										
very strong	3.6	3.5	3.2	2.9	2.5	1.7	1.0	1.6	2.6	3.0
fairly strong	5.9	6.2	5.3	6.4	4.6	9.2	8.3	5.1	10.5	7.6
not very strong	3.1	3.5	2.4	1.7	1.3	4.6	5.2	4.7	10.3	8.4
Labour										
very strong	19.0	24.5	25.3	15.0	24.2	18.1	18.2	14.9	11.1	9.7
fairly strong	20.1	15.3	19.0	16.8	19.5	19.6	18.8	22.2	14.7	12.4
not very strong	11.3	5.7	6.0	14.5	6.1	7.7	10.2	9.5	8.3	9.1
Total	100.0	100.0	100.0	100.0	100.0	100.0	100.0	100.0	100.0	100.0
N. of respondents	389	346	373	173	286	414	384	316	542	479

	Aged 55–64									
	1963	1964	1966	1969	1970	Feb. 1974	Oct. 1974	1979	1983	1987
Conservative										
very strong	22.2	28.7	22.9	21.3	27.6	14.0	13.6	13.2	13.3	12.0
fairly strong	15.5	16.7	15.0	23.6	17.3	17.7	21.0	22.3	19.4	26.9
not very strong	8.5	3.1	6.4	9.0	4.0	9.7	7.7	9.1	8.2	7.4
Liberal										
very strong	3.6	3.7	4.1	1.7	3.9	1.3	2.7	0.8	3.0	1.9
fairly strong	4.0	5.4	5.7	3.9	3.3	7.8	7.7	9.1	10.0	9.4
not very strong	2.7	2.3	2.0	4.5	0.6	3.5	5.3	4.1	8.7	7.7
Labour										
very strong	19.5	24.4	25.5	13.5	22.9	22.0	17.5	13.6	11.5	11.6
fairly strong	16.1	13.1	15.5	10.7	14.3	18.8	20.1	20.2	17.2	14.7
not very strong	7.9	2.6	2.9	11.8	6.1	5.1	4.4	7.4	8.7	8.5
Total	100.0	100.0	100.0	100.0	100.0	100.0	100.0	100.0	100.0	100.0
N. of respondents	329	309	319	178	312	372	338	242	519	514

Table 2.3 (*cont.*)

Aged 65–74

	1963	1964	1966	1969	1970	Feb. 1974	Oct. 1974	1979	1983	1987
Conservative										
very strong	19.2	24.6	23.9	27.6	33.1	22.3	18.4	13.1	18.2	15.5
fairly strong	18.8	16.2	12.7	20.4	14.4	18.5	19.1	27.1	19.3	23.2
not very strong	8.0	3.6	6.4	9.2	2.8	7.9	6.7	9.0	8.5	6.3
Liberal										
very strong	5.4	5.7	5.5	4.1	1.8	2.1	2.6	2.5	2.4	3.0
fairly strong	3.6	5.1	7.4	2.0	5.9	6.2	9.0	5.0	6.8	9.6
not very strong	1.8	1.0	0.6	4.1	1.3	1.7	3.0	6.0	8.2	6.9
Labour										
very strong	18.3	25.9	28.2	20.4	27.8	21.9	22.1	15.6	16.0	15.9
fairly strong	13.8	11.1	12.3	8.2	10.0	14.0	15.7	15.6	12.5	12.0
not very strong	11.2	6.8	3.0	4.1	2.7	5.5	3.4	6.0	8.2	7.5
Total	100.0	100.0	100.0	100.0	100.0	100.0	100.0	100.0	100.0	100.0
N. of respondents	224	202	201	98	207	292	267	199	385	357

Aged over 74

	1963	1964	1966	1969	1970	Feb. 1974	Oct. 1974	1979	1983	1987
Conservative										
very strong	25.0	35.1	34.5	27.6	41.5	23.8	28.2	20.5	25.0	21.7
fairly strong	19.8	13.9	14.9	20.4	16.6	21.9	18.5	25.0	20.4	23.8
not very strong	5.2	0.9	3.4	9.2	6.0	9.3	8.9	8.9	9.8	9.7
Liberal										
very strong	6.3	5.7	4.9	4.1	4.0	2.0	4.0	1.8	3.4	2.9
fairly strong	3.1	3.2	1.3	2.0	4.8	3.3	4.8	5.4	8.1	4.5
not very strong	3.1	3.4	0.0	4.1	1.0	2.6	2.4	0.9	3.9	8.6
Labour										
very strong	17.7	24.5	29.7	20.4	17.0	19.9	20.2	17.0	15.2	12.0
fairly strong	10.4	8.1	5.4	8.2	5.4	9.9	9.7	12.5	9.2	9.2
not very strong	9.4	5.1	5.8	4.1	3.8	7.3	3.2	8.0	5.1	7.6
Total	100.0	100.0	100.0	100.0	100.0	100.0	100.0	100.0	100.0	100.0
N. of respondents	96	105	106	51	90	151	124	112	209	236

Table 2.4 *Strength and direction of partisanship by age and gender (%)*

	Men aged under 25									
	1963	1964	1966	1969	1970	Feb. 1974	Oct. 1974	1979	1983	1987
Conservative										
very strong	10.6	9.9	12.8	14.6	7.0	3.9	0.8	4.4	2.6	2.1
fairly strong	10.6	27.5	21.9	18.8	18.7	12.6	16.4	17.6	21.8	16.7
not very strong	10.6	9.7	4.3	25.0	12.5	7.8	10.7	14.7	20.2	16.7
Liberal										
very strong	0.0	3.4	0.0	2.1	0.0	1.0	3.3	2.9	2.4	0.0
fairly strong	2.1	1.7	3.3	4.2	2.6	9.7	12.3	8.8	4.3	7.5
not very strong	2.1	0.0	1.4	4.2	3.4	10.7	7.4	4.4	9.3	9.2
Labour										
very strong	21.3	17.6	12.2	4.2	17.6	13.6	10.7	7.4	6.1	6.2
fairly strong	27.7	25.4	30.8	12.5	24.5	28.2	28.7	19.1	16.7	19.8
not very strong	14.9	4.7	13.3	14.6	13.7	12.6	9.7	20.6	16.8	21.9
Total	100.0	100.0	100.0	100.0	100.0	100.0	100.0	100.0	100.0	100.0
N. of respondents	47	47	74	48	117	103	122	68	253	193

	Women aged under 25									
	1963	1964	1966	1969	1970	Feb. 1974	Oct. 1974	1979	1983	1987
Conservative										
very strong	6.0	11.8	7.1	8.0	6.2	4.3	4.8	3.9	4.9	3.8
fairly strong	10.4	18.6	19.3	20.0	21.2	15.4	16.1	19.5	17.2	14.8
not very strong	13.4	7.5	2.8	14.0	10.2	6.8	9.7	9.1	18.2	12.5
Liberal										
very strong	0.0	2.4	4.2	0.0	2.2	0.9	1.6	1.3	0.4	1.0
fairly strong	3.0	3.9	2.8	2.0	2.6	12.0	8.1	7.8	5.9	7.5
not very strong	7.5	3.0	3.4	10.0	2.7	8.5	9.7	11.7	14.3	12.9
Labour										
very strong	11.9	24.2	17.7	2.0	8.6	17.1	11.3	6.5	4.3	5.8
fairly strong	28.4	21.4	31.2	28.0	31.2	17.9	23.4	22.1	13.5	21.4
not very strong	19.4	7.1	11.5	16.0	15.1	17.1	15.3	18.2	21.3	20.2
Total	100.0	100.0	100.0	100.0	100.0	100.0	100.0	100.0	100.0	100.0
N. of respondents	67	53	57	50	121	117	124	77	231	188

Table 2.4 (*cont.*)

Men aged 25–44										
	1963	1964	1966	1969	1970	Feb. 1974	Oct. 1974	1979	1983	1987
Conservative										
very strong	8.0	9.9	10.9	14.3	15.6	9.4	6.4	8.6	7.5	7.9
fairly strong	10.2	16.4	10.8	24.7	16.8	18.8	19.3	19.6	19.8	19.7
not very strong	12.1	6.3	6.1	8.4	7.2	8.9	9.7	15.8	16.7	10.4
Liberal										
very strong	2.9	3.9	2.6	0.6	1.7	1.5	2.0	1.8	2.3	1.7
fairly strong	3.8	9.3	7.6	5.2	3.0	5.4	7.9	6.3	10.6	9.4
not very strong	6.1	3.7	1.8	5.2	3.1	6.4	6.7	6.8	8.6	11.4
Labour										
very strong	20.4	21.8	24.1	11.7	23.2	14.1	12.1	8.3	9.2	8.2
fairly strong	24.6	20.7	28.8	16.2	19.8	23.2	23.8	22.6	12.8	17.0
not very strong	11.8	8.0	7.2	13.6	9.6	12.3	12.1	10.1	12.5	14.3
Total	100.0	100.0	100.0	100.0	100.0	100.0	100.0	100.0	100.0	100.0
N. of respondents	313	290	293	154	276	405	404	336	600	595

Women aged 25–44										
	1963	1964	1966	1969	1970	Feb. 1974	Oct. 1974	1979	1983	1987
Conservative										
very strong	8.0	15.7	17.9	15.2	16.5	9.8	6.5	8.6	8.2	6.8
fairly strong	22.2	16.2	14.3	28.5	18.0	19.6	20.0	19.6	19.1	22.5
not very strong	10.1	8.3	6.8	11.3	7.1	8.5	8.9	15.8	15.9	12.4
Liberal										
very strong	0.8	3.4	3.8	0.0	0.9	1.8	1.8	1.8	2.0	1.5
fairly strong	7.0	6.1	5.9	5.3	7.4	8.0	11.1	6.3	10.0	8.8
not very strong	4.6	3.4	0.6	6.0	2.5	8.3	6.1	6.8	10.7	13.2
Labour										
very strong	11.9	17.0	21.6	4.6	17.5	14.1	12.8	8.3	6.5	6.0
fairly strong	22.4	22.7	21.9	14.6	20.2	18.3	24.1	22.6	15.1	18.7
not very strong	13.1	7.2	7.2	14.6	9.8	11.6	8.6	10.1	12.6	10.2
Total	100.0	100.0	100.0	100.0	100.0	100.0	100.0	100.0	100.0	100.0
N. of respondents	388	355	344	151	281	398	395	336	674	605

Table 2.4 (*cont.*)

	Men aged 45–64									
	1963	1964	1966	1969	1970	Feb. 1974	Oct. 1974	1979	1983	1987
Conservative										
very strong	15.2	21.9	18.3	17.2	25.8	10.3	7.1	8.3	9.5	10.4
fairly strong	11.9	12.1	13.5	22.5	13.7	21.7	25.4	24.1	22.2	27.1
not very strong	8.6	4.0	5.6	9.5	4.2	9.5	7.7	11.5	9.9	9.2
Liberal										
very strong	4.8	3.9	2.9	1.8	2.8	1.1	0.8	1.8	2.2	2.6
fairly strong	6.0	6.3	6.0	0.6	2.6	7.3	6.6	6.1	9.8	7.8
not very strong	3.3	3.8	2.1	1.8	0.7	4.3	4.4	2.9	7.4	8.6
Labour										
very strong	20.8	28.7	29.0	17.8	24.9	21.8	19.4	14.4	13.4	10.6
fairly strong	19.3	14.5	17.0	14.2	18.3	18.2	20.2	22.3	16.5	14.4
not very strong	10.1	4.9	5.6	14.7	7.0	5.7	8.5	8.6	9.0	9.2
Total	100.0	100.0	100.0	100.0	100.0	100.0	100.0	100.0	100.0	100.0
N. of respondents	336	308	332	169	282	368	366	278	509	499

	Women aged 45–64									
	1963	1964	1966	1969	1970	Feb. 1974	Oct. 1974	1979	1983	1987
Conservative										
very strong	17.8	25.9	18.3	17.6	25.3	12.7	13.2	12.5	13.6	13.6
fairly strong	18.3	20.6	13.5	19.2	17.1	17.9	17.7	21.4	19.0	25.3
not very strong	9.9	4.2	5.6	11.0	4.7	8.4	9.3	8.6	9.1	10.5
Liberal										
very strong	2.6	3.4	2.9	2.7	3.5	1.9	2.9	0.7	3.3	2.2
fairly strong	4.2	5.4	6.0	9.3	5.2	9.6	9.6	7.5	10.7	9.1
not very strong	2.6	2.2	2.1	4.4	1.2	3.8	6.2	6.1	11.5	7.5
Labour										
very strong	17.8	20.6	29.0	11.0	22.3	18.4	16.3	14.3	9.4	10.9
fairly strong	17.3	14.0	17.0	13.2	15.4	20.1	18.5	20.4	15.4	12.6
not very strong	9.4	3.6	5.6	11.5	5.3	7.2	6.5	8.6	8.0	8.3
Total	100.0	100.0	100.0	100.0	100.0	100.0	100.0	100.0	100.0	100.0
N. of respondents	382	347	332	182	317	418	356	280	552	494

Table 2.4 (*cont.*)

	Men aged over 64									
	1963	1964	1966	1969	1970	Feb. 1974	Oct. 1974	1979	1983	1987
Conservative										
very strong	18.2	24.2	25.4	30.9	32.0	20.9	19.3	14.8	17.9	16.0
fairly strong	18.2	17.8	13.2	14.5	14.8	19.8	18.1	28.1	18.5	24.1
not very strong	8.3	2.4	6.0	7.3	3.6	8.8	8.8	6.7	9.4	6.3
Liberal										
very strong	6.8	6.9	8.2	1.8	3.0	2.7	2.9	2.2	2.1	3.0
fairly strong	3.8	4.7	8.2	5.5	4.9	5.5	5.8	5.2	5.4	8.9
not very strong	1.5	1.7	1.0	3.6	1.5	0.5	2.3	3.0	8.4	5.1
Labour										
very strong	25.0	23.8	26.2	30.9	28.6	19.8	25.1	20.0	17.7	19.8
fairly strong	9.8	11.6	11.2	1.8	7.8	14.3	13.5	14.8	13.3	11.8
not very strong	8.3	7.0	0.6	3.6	3.8	7.7	4.1	5.2	7.4	5.1
Total	100.0	100.0	100.0	100.0	100.0	100.0	100.0	100.0	100.0	100.0
N. of respondents	132	126	126	55	114	182	171	135	258	236

	Women aged over 64									
	1963	1964	1966	1969	1970	Feb. 1974	Oct. 1974	1979	1983	1987
Conservative										
very strong	22.9	30.9	29.1	33.0	38.0	24.1	23.2	16.5	22.7	19.3
fairly strong	19.7	13.8	13.7	19.1	15.3	19.5	19.5	25.0	20.6	22.7
not very strong	6.4	2.9	5.0	9.6	3.9	8.0	6.4	10.8	8.5	8.4
Liberal										
very strong	4.8	4.9	3.3	6.4	2.1	1.5	3.2	2.3	3.3	3.1
fairly strong	3.2	4.3	3.3	0.0	6.0	5.0	9.1	5.1	8.6	7.0
not very strong	2.7	2.0	0.0	3.2	1.1	3.1	3.2	5.1	5.4	9.2
Labour										
very strong	13.3	26.6	30.4	11.7	22.0	22.2	18.6	13.1	14.2	10.9
fairly strong	14.9	9.1	9.0	11.7	9.2	11.5	14.1	14.2	9.8	10.4
not very strong	12.2	5.6	6.2	5.3	2.5	5.0	2.7	8.0	6.9	9.0
Total	100.0	100.0	100.0	100.0	100.0	100.0	100.0	100.0	100.0	100.0
N. of respondents	188	181	181	94	184	261	220	176	336	357

Table 2.5 *Strength and direction of partisanship by marital status (%)*

	Single									
	1963	1964	1966	1969	1970	Feb. 1974	Oct. 1974	1979	1983	1987
Conservative										
very strong	13.2	23.3	22.9	12.9	15.1	10.5	–	6.1	6.2	7.0
fairly strong	17.6	21.3	15.8	19.1	20.6	17.9	–	20.8	19.9	18.7
not very strong	15.0	7.0	7.9	14.8	8.6	9.8	–	15.7	18.4	10.2
Liberal										
very strong	1.7	3.5	2.0	1.9	0.8	2.0	–	1.0	2.4	1.0
fairly strong	5.6	3.8	3.6	4.8	5.5	9.5	–	7.6	6.9	9.4
not very strong	6.0	2.4	1.5	6.7	3.8	6.1	–	7.6	9.7	11.9
Labour										
very strong	11.6	17.1	17.4	3.3	14.2	13.9	–	8.1	5.5	9.2
fairly strong	17.2	17.2	20.1	17.3	21.3	18.6	–	19.3	15.7	17.2
not very strong	12.0	4.5	8.8	19.1	10.2	11.8	–	13.7	15.4	15.5
Total	100.0	100.0	100.0	100.0	100.0	100.0	100.0	100.0	100.0	100.0
N. of respondents	233	199	192	209	292	296	–	197	598	560

	Married									
	1963	1964	1966	1969	1970	Feb. 1974	Oct. 1974	1979	1983	1987
Conservative										
very strong	12.2	18.5	16.5	17.0	21.4	11.7	8.9	10.2	11.0	10.8
fairly strong	15.6	15.3	14.5	22.8	15.9	19.1	21.0	22.9	20.0	23.4
not very strong	9.6	5.4	5.9	10.1	6.0	8.1	8.1	11.2	12.7	11.1
Liberal										
very strong	3.0	3.9	3.9	1.8	2.3	1.4	1.5	1.7	2.3	2.1
fairly strong	5.2	6.8	6.4	4.6	4.3	7.9	9.1	6.4	9.7	8.3
not very strong	3.8	3.2	1.8	3.5	1.5	5.6	5.0	5.4	9.9	9.9
Labour										
very strong	18.3	23.3	24.4	13.2	22.4	17.7	16.0	10.8	10.4	8.4
fairly strong	20.9	17.4	20.6	14.1	18.3	19.5	22.0	21.2	13.7	15.6
not very strong	11.5	6.1	6.1	12.9	7.8	9.1	8.3	10.3	10.3	10.4
Total	100.0	100.0	100.0	100.0	100.0	100.0	100.0	100.0	100.0	100.0
N. of respondents	1408	1316	1364	653	1205	1680	1753	1238	2403	2179

Table 2.5 (*cont.*)

Divorced and separated

	1963	1964	1966	1969	1970	Feb. 1974	Oct. 1974	1979	1983	1987
Conservative										
very strong	–	–	(47.1)	–	–	0.0	–	7.1	9.8	8.7
fairly strong	–	–	(6.9)	–	–	12.5	–	12.9	19.0	19.3
not very strong	–	–	(0.0)	–	–	16.7	–	7.1	7.3	8.4
Liberal										
very strong	–	–	(0.0)	–	–	0.0	–	1.4	2.8	2.6
fairly strong	–	–	(13.8)	–	–	4.2	–	1.4	8.5	10.9
not very strong	–	–	(0.0)	–	–	8.3	–	2.9	9.0	7.1
Labour										
very strong	–	–	(15.5)	–	–	16.7	–	20.0	11.5	12.6
fairly strong	–	–	(10.9)	–	–	25.0	–	25.7	18.8	16.2
not very strong	–	–	(5.7)	–	–	16.7	–	21.4	13.2	14.3
Total	–	–	(100.0)	–	–	100.0	–	100.0	100.0	100.0
N. of respondents	–	–	17	–	–	24	–	70	147	152

Widowed

	1963	1964	1966	1969	1970	Feb. 1974	Oct. 1974	1979	1983	1987
Conservative										
very strong	–	–	24.8	–	–	19.5	–	14.2	17.8	13.9
fairly strong	–	–	15.6	–	–	19.1	–	27.9	19.5	23.1
not very strong	–	–	5.5	–	–	9.9	–	11.1	10.6	9.2
Liberal										
very strong	–	–	4.0	–	–	2.6	–	3.2	2.1	2.6
fairly strong	–	–	2.4	–	–	2.9	–	6.3	8.1	6.1
not very strong	–	–	0.0	–	–	2.6	–	3.2	4.9	8.8
Labour										
very strong	–	–	29.2	–	–	21.7	–	13.2	14.3	15.4
fairly strong	–	–	15.1	–	–	14.7	–	14.7	13.6	12.0
not very strong	–	–	3.5	–	–	7.0	–	6.3	9.1	8.9
Total	–	–	100.0	–	–	100.0	–	100.0	100.0	100.0
N. of respondents	–	–	195	–	–	272	–	190	277	299

Table 2.6 *Strength and direction of partisanship by marital status and gender (%)*

	Single men									
	1963	1964	1966	1969	1970	Feb. 1974	Oct. 1974	1979	1983	1987
Conservative										
very strong	–	–	19.9	8.7	10.7	7.5	–	4.5	2.9	5.0
fairly strong	–	–	11.7	19.2	20.1	15.7	–	19.8	21.3	19.8
not very strong	–	–	7.5	16.3	9.7	10.7	–	16.2	18.8	11.4
Liberal										
very strong	–	–	0.8	1.9	0.5	1.3	–	1.8	3.0	0.6
fairly strong	–	–	1.6	4.8	5.4	7.5	–	8.1	6.4	9.5
not very strong	–	–	1.0	3.8	4.9	5.7	–	6.3	9.8	10.0
Labour										
very strong	–	–	20.3	5.8	17.2	13.8	–	9.0	5.6	10.2
fairly strong	–	–	28.3	16.3	20.5	25.2	–	20.7	17.0	17.6
not very strong	–	–	8.8	23.1	11.0	12.6	–	13.5	15.2	15.9
Total	–	–	100.0	100.0	100.0	100.0	–	100.0	100.0	100.0
N. of respondents	–	–	98	104	160	159	–	111	347	317

	Single women									
	1963	1964	1966	1969	1970	Feb. 1974	Oct. 1974	1979	1983	1987
Conservative										
very strong	–	–	26.0	17.1	20.5	13.9	–	8.1	10.6	9.6
fairly strong	–	–	20.0	19.0	21.1	20.4	–	22.1	17.8	17.3
not very strong	–	–	8.3	13.3	7.3	8.8	–	15.1	17.8	8.5
Liberal										
very strong	–	–	3.2	1.9	1.1	2.9	–	0.0	1.6	1.6
fairly strong	–	–	5.7	4.8	5.6	11.7	–	7.0	7.5	9.2
not very strong	–	–	2.0	9.5	2.5	6.6	–	9.3	9.7	14.3
Labour										
very strong	–	–	14.4	1.0	10.6	13.9	–	7.0	5.3	7.9
fairly strong	–	–	11.5	18.1	22.2	10.9	–	17.4	14.0	16.7
not very strong	–	–	8.8	15.2	9.1	10.9	–	14.0	15.6	14.9
Total	–	–	100.0	100.0	100.0	100.0	–	100.0	100.0	100.0
N. of respondents	–	–	94	105	132	137	–	86	251	243

Table 2.6 (*cont.*)

Married men

	1963	1964	1966	1969	1970	Feb. 1974	Oct. 1974	1979	1983	1987
Conservative										
very strong	–	–	15.6	18.4	21.8	11.1	–	9.9	10.5	10.5
fairly strong	–	–	13.3	21.1	14.8	19.5	–	23.2	20.8	23.1
not very strong	–	–	5.3	10.0	5.6	8.9	–	12.8	12.8	10.0
Liberal										
very strong	–	–	3.7	1.5	2.1	1.3	–	1.9	2.0	2.3
fairly strong	–	–	7.6	2.7	2.5	6.8	–	6.1	9.3	8.3
not very strong	–	–	2.0	3.0	1.1	5.4	–	4.8	8.2	9.3
Labour										
very strong	–	–	26.0	17.5	26.1	18.3	–	11.5	12.6	10.0
fairly strong	–	–	20.7	12.7	18.2	19.5	–	20.8	13.3	14.8
not very strong	–	–	5.9	13.0	7.8	9.3	–	9.1	10.5	11.6
Total	–	–	100.0	100.0	100.0	100.0	–	100.0	100.0	100.0
N. of respondents	–	–	687	331	584	841	–	626	1162	1104

Married women

	1963	1964	1966	1969	1970	Feb. 1974	Oct. 1974	1979	1983	1987
Conservative										
very strong	–	–	17.4	15.5	21.1	12.3	–	10.5	11.4	11.1
fairly strong	–	–	15.7	24.5	17.1	18.7	–	22.5	19.2	23.7
not very strong	–	–	6.5	10.2	6.4	7.3	–	9.6	12.6	12.2
Liberal										
very strong	–	–	4.0	2.2	2.5	1.4	–	1.5	2.6	1.8
fairly strong	–	–	5.2	6.5	6.0	9.1	–	6.7	10.0	8.4
not very strong	–	–	1.6	4.0	1.9	5.8	–	6.0	11.6	10.5
Labour										
very strong	–	–	22.9	8.7	19.0	17.0	–	10.1	8.3	6.7
fairly strong	–	–	20.5	15.5	18.4	19.4	–	21.6	14.2	16.4
not very strong	–	–	6.2	12.7	7.6	8.9	–	11.4	10.1	9.2
Total	–	–	100.0	100.0	100.0	100.0	–	100.0	100.0	100.0
N. of respondents	–	–	677	322	621	839	–	612	1240	1075

Table 2.6 (*cont.*)

Divorced men

	1963	1964	1966	1969	1970	Feb. 1974	Oct. 1974	1979	1983	1987
Conservative										
very strong	–	–	(50.0)	–	–	(0.4)	–	7.7	13.0	5.6
fairly strong	–	–	(0.0)	–	–	(14.3)	–	15.4	19.7	21.4
not very strong	–	–	(0.0)	–	–	(28.6)	–	3.8	12.2	11.5
Liberal										
very strong	–	–	(0.0)	–	–	(0.0)	–	0.0	5.4	2.2
fairly strong	–	–	(0.0)	–	–	(0.0)	–	0.0	5.7	10.2
not very strong	–	–	(0.0)	–	–	(0.0)	–	3.8	7.2	3.4
Labour										
very strong	–	–	(0.0)	–	–	(14.3)	–	23.1	9.2	8.8
fairly strong	–	–	(0.0)	–	–	(28.6)	–	34.6	20.7	21.8
not very strong	–	–	(50.0)	–	–	(14.3)	–	11.5	6.8	15.1
Total	–	–	(100.0)	–	–	(100.0)	–	100.0	100.0	100.0
N. of respondents	–	–	2	–	–	7	–	26	56	54

Divorced women

	1963	1964	1966	1969	1970	Feb. 1974	Oct. 1974	1979	1983	1987
Conservative										
very strong	–	–	(40.0)	–	–	(0.0)	–	6.8	7.8	10.5
fairly strong	–	–	(6.7)	–	–	(11.8)	–	11.4	18.6	18.1
not very strong	–	–	(0.0)	–	–	(11.8)	–	9.1	4.4	6.7
Liberal										
very strong	–	–	(0.0)	–	–	(0.0)	–	2.3	1.2	2.8
fairly strong	–	–	(13.3)	–	–	(5.9)	–	2.3	10.2	11.3
not very strong	–	–	(0.0)	–	–	(11.8)	–	2.3	10.1	9.1
Labour										
very strong	–	–	(26.7)	–	–	(17.6)	–	18.2	13.0	14.7
fairly strong	–	–	(13.3)	–	–	(23.5)	–	20.5	17.6	13.0
not very strong	–	–	(0.0)	–	–	(17.6)	–	27.3	17.2	13.9
Total	–	–	(100.0)	–	–	(100.0)	–	100.0	100.0	100.0
N. of respondents	–	–	15	–	–	17	–	44	91	98

Table 2.6 (*cont.*)

Widowed men

	1963	1964	1966	1969	1970	Feb. 1974	Oct. 1974	1979	1983	1987
Conservative										
very strong	–	–	14.5	–	–	24.1	–	12.2	10.1	13.6
fairly strong	–	–	18.1	–	–	27.6	–	24.5	13.5	21.1
not very strong	–	–	9.6	–	–	3.4	–	10.2	8.7	8.1
Liberal										
very strong	–	–	3.8	–	–	5.2	–	4.1	0.0	3.1
fairly strong	–	–	3.8	–	–	1.7	–	6.1	8.7	4.9
not very strong	–	–	0.0	–	–	0.0	–	0.0	5.2	6.6
Labour										
very strong	–	–	0.0	–	–	17.2	–	18.4	25.9	20.8
fairly strong	–	–	20.5	–	–	17.2	–	18.4	21.1	19.9
not very strong	–	–	29.6	–	–	3.4	–	6.1	6.8	1.7
Total	–	–	100.0	–	–	100.0	–	100.0	100.0	100.0
N. of respondents	–	–	37	–	–	58	–	49	58	61

Widowed women

	1963	1964	1966	1969	1970	Feb. 1974	Oct. 1974	1979	1983	1987
Conservative										
very strong	–	–	27.1	–	–	18.2	–	14.9	19.8	13.9
fairly strong	–	–	15.0	–	–	16.8	–	29.1	21.1	23.6
not very strong	–	–	4.5	–	–	11.7	–	11.3	11.1	9.4
Liberal										
very strong	–	–	4.0	–	–	1.9	–	2.8	2.7	2.5
fairly strong	–	–	2.0	–	–	3.3	–	6.4	7.9	6.4
not very strong	–	–	0.0	–	–	3.3	–	4.3	4.9	9.4
Labour										
very strong	–	–	29.1	–	–	22.9	–	11.3	11.2	14.0
fairly strong	–	–	13.8	–	–	14.0	–	13.5	11.6	10.0
not very strong	–	–	4.4	–	–	7.9	–	6.4	9.8	10.7
Total	–	–	100.0	–	–	100.0	–	100.0	100.0	100.0
N. of respondents	–	–	158	–	–	214	–	141	219	239

Table 2.7 *Strength and direction of partisanship: new electors (%)*

	1963	1964	1966	1969	1970	Feb. 1974	Oct. 1974	1979	1983	1987
Conservative										
very strong	7.9	11.7	10.4	8.9	6.6	2.7	–	4.7	3.5	3.5
fairly strong	10.5	20.0	15.6	21.4	20.0	14.7	–	19.8	20.1	13.2
not very strong	12.3	8.0	5.2	17.9	11.3	6.7	–	12.3	21.0	15.0
Liberal										
very strong	0.0	2.2	1.3	1.8	1.1	0.0	–	0.9	1.8	1.0
fairly strong	2.6	3.0	6.5	3.6	2.6	12.0	–	8.5	4.0	7.2
not very strong	5.3	1.8	1.3	12.5	3.0	9.3	–	10.4	10.6	13.4
Labour										
very strong	15.8	22.3	10.4	5.4	13.0	14.7	–	8.5	4.4	2.5
fairly strong	28.1	23.2	37.6	12.5	27.9	16.0	–	17.0	14.5	21.4
not very strong	17.5	7.7	11.7	16.1	14.4	24.0	–	17.9	20.0	22.9
Total	100.0	100.0	100.0	100.0	100.0	100.0	–	100.0	100.0	100.0
N. of respondents	114	132	62	56	238	75	–	106	266	198

Table 2.8 *Strength and direction of partisanship by political generation (%)*

First voted 1918–1935										
	1963	1964	1966	1969	1970	Feb. 1974	Oct. 1974	1979	1983	1987
Conservative										
very strong	19.9	27.3	24.0	25.3	32.1	19.5	18.7	15.9	22.6	20.6
fairly strong	16.7	16.0	14.6	20.3	14.5	18.8	19.7	27.0	19.8	23.6
not very strong	8.4	3.6	6.0	8.7	3.8	9.7	6.1	9.0	9.3	9.6
Liberal										
very strong	4.1	4.4	4.1	2.7	3.2	2.1	3.0	2.1	2.2	3.3
fairly strong	4.3	5.7	5.8	3.0	4.5	5.2	7.5	4.8	7.3	5.4
not very strong	3.1	2.6	1.4	4.0	1.1	2.4	3.9	4.5	6.8	8.3
Labour										
very strong	17.8	23.4	27.1	17.7	24.6	21.6	21.7	15.9	14.2	12.1
fairly strong	15.8	11.9	13.3	10.0	11.8	14.9	15.2	14.2	10.7	8.5
not very strong	10.0	5.1	3.8	8.3	4.5	5.9	4.1	6.6	7.0	8.6
Total	100.0	100.0	100.0	100.0	100.0	100.0	100.0	100.0	100.0	100.0
N. of respondents	810	720	681	300	525	579	507	289	411	268

Table 2.8 (*cont.*)

First voted 1936–1950

	1963	1964	1966	1969	1970	Feb. 1974	Oct. 1974	1979	1983	1987
Conservative										
very strong	9.2	14.7	17.2	15.1	20.9	12.3	10.0	10.9	13.9	13.4
fairly strong	15.8	15.6	14.2	18.5	17.2	20.4	21.8	23.3	19.6	26.0
not very strong	9.5	5.3	5.3	10.4	5.7	7.8	9.5	8.3	8.3	6.5
Liberal										
very strong	2.6	4.4	4.2	1.9	2.5	1.5	1.8	1.6	3.2	2.6
fairly strong	5.6	6.5	5.6	6.2	4.7	8.9	8.2	8.5	9.3	9.7
not very strong	4.1	3.2	1.6	3.1	2.4	4.3	4.9	4.4	8.3	7.4
Labour										
very strong	19.7	24.7	25.4	12.7	22.5	20.7	17.5	15.2	13.3	14.1
fairly strong	23.5	20.7	21.1	15.8	18.6	18.4	19.1	19.6	16.0	13.2
not very strong	10.0	4.9	5.4	16.2	5.6	5.8	7.3	8.3	8.2	7.1
Total	100.0	100.0	100.0	100.0	100.0	100.0	100.0	100.0	100.0	100.0
N. of respondents	588	551	545	259	461	604	550	387	661	641

First voted 1951–1970

	1963	1964	1966	1969	1970	Feb. 1974	Oct. 1974	1979	1983	1987
Conservative										
very strong	7.3	13.5	12.0	11.5	12.9	8.6	6.3	9.2	9.7	11.1
fairly strong	16.1	18.6	15.3	24.7	17.8	18.9	19.2	22.0	20.7	23.6
not very strong	12.7	8.5	6.5	13.1	8.6	8.8	9.0	13.6	14.0	11.0
Liberal										
very strong	0.9	2.2	2.1	0.8	1.3	1.4	1.6	1.7	2.2	2.0
fairly strong	4.8	6.5	5.9	4.3	4.3	7.3	9.3	5.6	10.7	8.9
not very strong	5.2	3.2	1.6	5.9	2.0	7.6	6.4	5.5	9.5	9.9
Labour										
very strong	13.9	17.4	19.3	6.2	17.9	13.8	12.7	8.9	8.9	8.4
fairly strong	22.7	21.4	27.4	18.0	22.7	21.3	24.0	22.4	14.1	15.3
not very strong	16.4	8.6	10.0	15.5	12.4	12.3	11.3	11.2	10.3	9.8
Total	100.0	100.0	100.0	100.0	100.0	100.0	100.0	100.0	100.0	100.0
N. of respondents	440	409	527	373	663	907	920	786	1401	1250

Table 2.8 (*cont.*)

					First voted after 1970					
	1963	1964	1966	1969	1970	Feb. 1974	Oct. 1974	1979	1983	1987
Conservative										
very strong	–	–	–	–	–	5.4	2.4	4.5	4.4	4.5
fairly strong	–	–	–	–	–	12.9	17.0	18.5	18.4	18.4
not very strong	–	–	–	–	–	7.5	10.9	12.8	16.8	12.9
Liberal										
very strong	–	–	–	–	–	1.4	3.6	2.1	1.8	1.2
fairly strong	–	–	–	–	–	10.9	11.5	7.0	8.1	7.9
not very strong	–	–	–	–	–	8.2	9.1	7.0	11.8	12.0
Labour										
very strong	–	–	–	–	–	15.0	9.1	7.8	7.7	7.1
fairly strong	–	–	–	–	–	23.1	26.7	22.2	15.3	19.3
not very strong	–	–	–	–	–	15.6	9.7	18.1	15.6	16.6
Total	–	–	–	–	–	100.0	100.0	100.0	100.0	100.0
N. of respondents	–	–	–	–	–	147	165	243	634	1011

Table 2.9 *Strength and direction of partisanship: non-voters (%)*

						Feb.	Oct.			
	1963	1964	1966	1969	1970	1974	1974	1979	1983	1987
Conservative										
very strong	–	14.4	11.5	–	11.2	7.3	3.3	5.0	7.5	5.8
fairly strong	–	20.1	15.4	–	18.6	10.5	18.7	17.4	13.3	16.6
not very strong	–	9.2	9.7	–	12.4	16.6	14.7	17.4	22.0	19.0
Liberal										
very strong	–	2.2	3.8	–	0.6	0.8	0.3	2.3	1.4	0.8
fairly strong	–	5.4	6.4	–	6.1	5.3	8.7	4.1	4.8	4.7
not very strong	–	5.7	3.6	–	1.4	8.1	7.0	8.3	9.6	12.4
Labour										
very strong	–	13.1	11.6	–	13.5	13.4	9.0	7.8	5.8	6.6
fairly strong	–	10.4	20.3	–	20.5	18.6	20.3	19.7	11.8	14.8
not very strong	–	19.5	17.7	–	15.6	19.4	18.0	17.9	23.7	19.3
Total	–	100.0	100.0	–	100.0	100.0	100.0	100.0	100.0	100.0
N. of respondents	–	170	252	–	291	247	300	218	531	380

Table 2.10 *Strength and direction of partisanship by vote (%)*

	Conservative voters									
	1963	1964	1966	1969	1970	Feb. 1974	Oct. 1974	1979	1983	1987
Conservative										
very strong	37.8	47.0	49.3	33.2	49.6	32.9	29.3	22.7	24.4	24.3
fairly strong	39.8	36.1	34.7	40.1	33.0	46.8	48.2	48.1	43.9	49.3
not very strong	18.7	9.2	9.7	18.6	8.6	12.8	14.6	19.2	22.8	16.5
Liberal										
very strong	0.2	1.5	1.3	0.2	0.5	0.3	0.4	0.6	0.6	0.2
fairly strong	0.6	3.1	2.5	1.0	3.2	2.3	2.3	2.2	1.7	2.1
not very strong	0.5	1.1	0.8	1.0	1.3	2.0	3.1	2.7	3.2	3.8
Labour										
very strong	0.3	0.7	0.2	0.4	0.6	0.0	0.0	0.4	0.4	0.4
fairly strong	0.9	0.9	0.5	1.4	1.0	1.2	0.7	1.4	0.7	1.1
not very strong	1.3	0.5	1.1	4.2	2.3	1.8	1.3	2.7	2.4	2.2
Total	100.0	100.0	100.0	100.0	100.0	100.0	100.0	100.0	100.0	100.0
N. of respondents	638	646	590	506	643	767	682	693	1319	1222

	Labour voters									
	1963	1964	1966	1969	1970	Feb. 1974	Oct. 1974	1979	1983	1987
Conservative										
very strong	0.1	0.6	0.2	0.0	0.6	0.0	0.1	0.0	0.0	0.3
fairly strong	1.2	0.9	0.9	0.7	0.6	1.0	1.3	0.7	0.2	1.1
not very strong	1.5	1.1	1.5	0.7	0.7	1.2	1.1	1.2	0.7	1.9
Liberal										
very strong	0.0	1.2	1.8	0.7	1.0	0.1	0.0	0.5	0.5	0.1
fairly strong	0.0	2.5	3.3	1.8	1.0	1.2	1.8	1.1	1.0	1.8
not very strong	0.5	0.7	0.6	0.7	0.6	1.5	1.3	1.4	0.8	1.5
Labour										
very strong	37.8	49.1	49.5	34.7	49.2	43.2	38.5	30.1	35.2	28.4
fairly strong	39.8	35.9	35.9	38.2	35.9	38.9	43.7	46.6	42.2	42.8
not very strong	19.1	8.1	6.3	22.5	10.3	12.9	12.3	18.3	19.4	22.0
Total	100.0	100.0	100.0	100.0	100.0	100.0	100.0	100.0	100.0	100.0
N. of respondents	842	713	795	285	630	821	799	562	828	906

Table 2.10 (*cont.*)

Liberal voters

	1963	1964	1966	1969	1970	Feb. 1974	Oct. 1974	1979	1983	1987
Conservative										
very strong	1.3	1.8	2.9	0.0	0.0	1.6	2.1	0.5	0.3	0.0
fairly strong	5.4	5.5	5.5	1.1	8.3	8.2	6.6	4.9	3.3	14.9
not very strong	4.5	4.4	8.0	2.2	5.9	10.1	5.7	4.4	3.6	0.0
Liberal										
very strong	22.9	28.7	26.9	15.4	24.9	8.0	12.6	8.7	8.7	0.0
fairly strong	35.0	34.8	36.7	33.0	29.4	32.6	39.3	35.4	34.7	0.0
not very strong	23.8	15.4	6.8	27.5	13.9	18.0	19.8	21.8	30.6	15.1
Labour										
very strong	0.4	0.7	0.9	2.2	3.9	2.9	1.2	1.9	1.5	0.0
fairly strong	0.9	4.9	8.2	6.6	9.5	10.9	8.1	12.6	9.0	32.4
not very strong	5.8	3.9	4.2	12.1	4.2	7.7	4.5	9.7	8.3	37.6
Total	100.0	100.0	100.0	100.0	100.0	100.0	100.0	100.0	100.0	100.0
N. of respondents	223	159	116	91	100	377	333	206	705	648

Voters for other parties

	1963	1964	1966	1969	1970	Feb. 1974	Oct. 1974	1979	1983	1987
Conservative										
very strong	(0.0)	(20.6)	(0.0)	(0.0)	(28.8)	5.9	(3.6)	(12.5)	(10.8)	(0.0)
fairly strong	(0.0)	(12.7)	(15.9)	(0.0)	(27.1)	11.8	(28.6)	(25.0)	(9.0)	(14.9)
not very strong	(0.0)	(0.0)	(0.0)	(0.0)	(5.0)	11.8	(32.1)	(12.5)	(16.7)	(0.0)
Liberal										
very strong	(0.0)	(0.0)	(29.0)	(0.0)	(5.0)	5.9	(0.0)	(0.0)	(0.0)	(0.0)
fairly strong	(0.0)	(15.9)	(0.0)	(0.0)	(7.1)	11.8	(3.6)	(37.5)	(0.0)	(0.0)
not very strong	(0.0)	(0.0)	(0.0)	(37.5)	(5.0)	5.9	(3.6)	(0.0)	(8.4)	(15.1)
Labour										
very strong	(0.0)	(33.2)	(27.5)	(12.5)	(0.0)	5.9	(0.0)	(0.0)	(9.7)	(0.0)
fairly strong	(100.0)	(0.0)	(14.5)	(12.5)	(5.0)	29.4	(21.4)	(12.5)	(8.4)	(32.4)
not very strong	(0.0)	(17.5)	(13.0)	(37.5)	(17.1)	11.8	(7.1)	(0.0)	(37.1)	(37.6)
Total	(100.0)	(100.0)	(100.0)	(100.0)	(100.0)	100.0	(100.0)	(100.0)	(100.0)	(100.0)
N. of respondents	1	6	7	8	17	28	8	11	13	13

Table 2.11 *Strength and direction of partisanship by social class (%)*

	Professional and managerial classes									
	1963	1964	1966	1969	1970	Feb. 1974	Oct. 1974	1979	1983	1987
Conservative										
very strong	24.3	36.9	35.1	22.2	35.7	17.8	11.9	15.3	13.3	13.5
fairly strong	25.7	26.3	23.4	30.3	20.9	28.8	27.5	29.1	26.5	28.0
not very strong	18.0	7.6	13.1	9.1	8.0	12.5	14.7	15.5	15.7	10.6
Liberal										
very strong	2.3	5.8	4.6	1.0	2.4	2.2	2.8	1.4	3.1	3.4
fairly strong	7.2	7.8	6.7	4.0	5.6	10.6	12.5	7.1	12.2	10.6
not very strong	5.9	2.2	1.6	4.0	1.9	6.9	9.2	7.6	11.5	12.7
Labour										
very strong	4.1	6.4	5.8	7.1	8.8	7.2	5.8	5.1	5.2	4.8
fairly strong	6.8	5.7	6.0	12.1	10.1	8.8	9.8	11.0	7.2	9.1
not very strong	5.9	1.3	3.8	10.1	6.7	5.3	5.8	7.9	5.3	7.2
Total	100.0	100.0	100.0	100.0	100.0	100.0	100.0	100.0	100.0	100.0
N. of respondents	222	218	229	99	278	320	327	354	930	823

	Intermediate and routine non-manual classes									
	1963	1964	1966	1969	1970	Feb. 1974	Oct. 1974	1979	1983	1987
Conservative										
very strong	20.0	26.4	25.0	23.5	25.2	15.7	12.0	11.7	12.7	12.6
fairly strong	21.6	22.3	19.4	23.5	19.7	24.8	25.7	28.0	22.7	29.5
not very strong	15.1	7.7	8.0	12.6	8.7	8.2	9.1	13.2	13.9	12.0
Liberal										
very strong	5.1	4.4	6.3	1.3	2.9	2.2	2.3	2.6	2.1	1.3
fairly strong	7.3	7.3	5.3	4.3	6.9	9.0	9.6	7.6	9.1	7.7
not very strong	4.9	4.0	2.0	5.7	3.1	6.3	6.8	6.5	9.8	11.2
Labour										
very strong	6.7	9.9	12.0	6.1	10.5	11.0	10.8	6.3	7.9	5.0
fairly strong	11.0	13.5	15.8	10.0	16.1	14.7	17.4	15.4	11.2	12.3
not very strong	8.4	4.5	6.3	13.0	7.0	8.2	6.3	8.7	10.6	8.5
Total	100.0	100.0	100.0	100.0	100.0	100.0	100.0	100.0	100.0	100.0
N. of respondents	491	483	488	230	434	782	748	461	677	787

Table 2.11 (*cont.*)

	Manual working class									
	1963	1964	1966	1969	1970	Feb. 1974	Oct. 1974	1979	1983	1987
Conservative										
very strong	8.0	11.9	11.7	11.9	15.1	8.3	6.9	6.7	5.9	7.1
fairly strong	12.0	11.6	10.3	17.4	14.4	11.0	13.6	17.3	10.8	15.7
not very strong	5.9	3.8	3.6	9.7	4.8	7.2	6.3	8.4	10.6	10.3
Liberal										
very strong	2.0	3.2	2.2	1.7	1.8	0.9	1.7	1.4	1.7	1.7
fairly strong	3.5	4.9	5.8	4.1	2.8	5.8	6.9	5.7	6.5	7.4
not very strong	3.1	2.3	1.3	3.6	1.5	4.1	3.5	3.9	7.3	7.8
Labour										
very strong	25.0	32.9	33.4	18.9	29.4	25.5	22.6	16.0	16.8	14.5
fairly strong	26.7	21.6	25.1	16.2	21.3	25.8	27.5	27.5	23.6	20.4
not very strong	13.8	7.9	6.6	16.5	8.9	11.4	11.0	13.0	16.8	15.2
Total	100.0	100.0	100.0	100.0	100.0	100.0	100.0	100.0	100.0	100.0
N. of respondents	1046	941	1022	413	918	1030	978	830	1739	1421

Table 2.12 *Strength and direction of partisanship by occupational status (%)*

	Occupational status class A/Registrar General Class I									
	1963	1964	1966	1969	1970	Feb. 1974	Oct. 1974	1979	1983	1987
Conservative										
very strong	26.7	35.2	43.1	21.4	37.0	19.2	13.1	9.7	12.5	12.1
fairly strong	25.6	31.3	19.6	28.6	23.9	36.9	32.8	28.3	33.1	25.8
not very strong	21.7	7.5	16.2	14.3	9.7	10.8	18.9	22.1	14.7	14.9
Liberal										
very strong	2.2	6.8	1.7	0.0	3.6	1.5	2.5	0.9	3.7	4.9
fairly strong	4.4	3.3	4.7	3.6	4.9	10.0	11.5	9.7	13.9	12.6
not very strong	6.1	3.5	0.8	10.7	2.7	10.0	8.2	10.6	12.5	11.5
Labour										
very strong	2.2	6.6	4.4	3.6	3.9	2.3	3.3	4.4	3.7	3.9
fairly strong	7.8	5.7	6.6	7.1	7.9	4.6	4.9	5.3	2.9	8.7
not very strong	3.3	0.0	2.9	10.7	6.3	4.6	4.9	8.8	2.9	5.6
Total	100.0	100.0	100.0	100.0	100.0	100.0	100.0	100.0	100.0	100.0
N. of respondents	90	79	96	28	94	130	122	113	141	127

Table 2.12 (*cont.*)

Occupational status class B/Registrar General Class II

	1963	1964	1966	1969	1970	Feb. 1974	Oct. 1974	1979	1983	1987
Conservative										
very strong	22.3	37.9	29.3	22.5	35.0	16.8	11.2	17.8	13.7	13.8
fairly strong	25.5	23.4	26.1	31.0	19.3	23.2	24.4	29.5	28.4	28.4
not very strong	17.8	7.6	10.8	7.0	7.0	13.7	12.2	12.4	15.2	9.8
Liberal										
very strong	3.2	5.2	6.8	1.4	1.8	2.6	2.9	1.7	2.8	3.2
fairly strong	8.3	10.4	8.1	4.2	6.0	11.1	13.2	5.8	11.8	10.2
not very strong	6.4	1.4	2.1	1.4	1.4	4.7	9.8	6.2	10.2	12.9
Labour										
very strong	4.5	6.3	6.9	8.5	11.4	10.5	7.3	5.4	5.2	5.0
fairly strong	7.0	5.7	5.5	14.1	11.2	11.6	12.7	13.7	6.9	9.2
not very strong	5.1	2.1	4.4	9.9	6.9	5.8	6.3	7.5	5.9	7.4
Total	100.0	100.0	100.0	100.0	100.0	100.0	100.0	100.0	100.0	100.0
N. of respondents	157	139	133	71	184	190	205	241	757	696

Occupational status class C1A/Registrar General Class III – non manual

	1963	1964	1966	1969	1970	Feb. 1974	Oct. 1974	1979	1983	1987
Conservative										
very strong	24.1	29.7	25.6	32.2	28.8	16.2	14.9	12.8	14.5	12.6
fairly strong	24.9	22.4	21.9	24.4	18.2	31.1	29.5	34.4	19.5	29.5
not very strong	15.7	9.2	10.4	11.1	8.1	10.4	10.5	16.9	14.8	12.0
Liberal										
very strong	6.1	4.7	6.2	2.2	2.8	1.8	1.0	3.6	2.3	1.3
fairly strong	6.5	7.9	4.0	1.1	9.2	8.2	10.8	4.6	11.7	7.7
not very strong	3.8	4.2	1.9	6.7	3.2	6.4	7.5	4.6	11.8	11.2
Labour										
very strong	2.7	8.6	10.3	4.4	7.3	7.3	8.1	5.1	5.3	5.0
fairly strong	9.2	10.6	14.4	8.9	14.4	11.3	12.5	10.8	10.9	12.3
not very strong	6.9	2.6	5.2	8.9	8.1	7.3	5.1	7.2	9.2	8.5
Total	100.0	100.0	100.0	100.0	100.0	100.0	100.0	100.0	100.0	100.0
N. of respondents	261	319	250	90	201	328	295	195	642	787

Table 2.12 (*cont.*)

	Occupational status class C1B/Registrar General Class III – manual									
	1963	1964	1966	1969	1970	Feb. 1974	Oct. 1974	1979	1983	1987
Conservative										
very strong	16.9	19.9	24.4	17.9	22.1	15.4	10.2	10.9	8.7	8.2
fairly strong	22.6	22.1	16.7	22.9	21.0	20.3	23.2	23.3	17.5	17.9
not very strong	11.3	5.0	5.4	13.6	9.3	6.6	8.2	10.5	12.7	9.2
Liberal										
very strong	4.0	3.7	6.4	0.7	3.0	2.4	3.1	1.9	1.0	1.1
fairly strong	9.0	6.1	6.6	6.4	4.9	9.5	8.8	9.8	5.8	6.6
not very strong	4.0	3.6	2.0	5.0	3.0	6.2	6.4	7.9	7.8	8.0
Labour										
very strong	11.9	12.5	13.8	7.1	13.3	13.7	12.6	7.1	14.0	12.5
fairly strong	13.6	19.1	17.2	10.7	17.5	17.2	20.5	18.8	19.2	20.4
not very strong	6.8	8.0	7.4	15.7	6.0	8.8	7.1	9.8	13.4	16.1
Total	100.0	100.0	100.0	100.0	100.0	100.0	100.0	100.0	100.0	100.0
N. of respondents	177	164	237	140	233	454	453	266	830	649

	Occupational status class C2/Registrar General Class IV									
	1963	1964	1966	1969	1970	Feb. 1974	Oct. 1974	1979	1983	1987
Conservative										
very strong	8.3	13.1	10.4	10.6	15.5	9.0	7.2	7.6	6.5	5.6
fairly strong	12.5	12.2	9.9	16.7	15.8	12.1	15.0	17.4	11.9	14.7
not very strong	5.6	3.9	4.4	11.6	5.1	6.8	6.5	8.8	8.6	11.9
Liberal										
very strong	2.4	2.5	2.7	0.9	1.2	0.5	1.6	1.1	2.7	2.1
fairly strong	4.4	5.0	5.8	3.7	3.4	6.8	6.9	5.0	7.5	8.4
not very strong	4.0	2.5	1.3	3.7	1.5	4.2	3.8	4.2	8.5	7.9
Labour										
very strong	22.6	30.1	31.6	18.5	26.0	24.5	20.8	16.3	17.6	14.9
fairly strong	25.1	22.2	26.3	15.7	21.4	24.4	27.1	26.0	20.7	20.6
not very strong	15.2	8.5	7.6	18.5	10.2	11.7	11.0	13.6	16.1	14.0
Total	100.0	100.0	100.0	100.0	100.0	100.0	100.0	100.0	100.0	100.0
N. of respondents	665	634	576	216	521	546	553	523	603	594

Table 2.12 (*cont.*)

	1963	1964	1966	1969	1970	Feb. 1974	Oct. 1974	1979	1983	1987
				Occupational status class D/Registrar General Class V						
Conservative										
very strong	7.0	9.5	13.4	13.2	14.7	7.6	6.4	5.2	4.0	8.1
fairly strong	9.2	10.4	10.8	18.3	12.4	9.7	11.8	17.3	9.9	10.6
not very strong	7.2	3.4	2.6	7.6	4.5	7.6	6.1	7.8	12.9	8.8
Liberal										
very strong	1.4	4.7	1.6	2.5	2.5	1.2	1.9	2.0	2.5	2.2
fairly strong	2.4	4.7	5.8	4.6	2.0	4.8	6.8	6.8	6.9	7.4
not very strong	2.4	1.9	1.4	3.6	1.4	3.9	3.1	3.3	7.4	7.0
Labour										
very strong	28.7	38.5	35.7	19.3	34.0	26.7	24.9	15.6	12.9	20.4
fairly strong	27.2	20.3	23.6	16.8	21.2	27.5	28.0	30.0	22.8	19.5
not very strong	14.5	6.6	5.2	14.2	7.3	11.0	11.1	12.1	20.8	16.0
Total	100.0	100.0	100.0	100.0	100.0	100.0	100.0	100.0	100.0	100.0
N. of respondents	415	314	446	197	397	484	425	307	202	178

Table 2.13 *Strength and direction of partisanship by class and gender (%)*

	1963	1964	1966	1969	1970	Feb. 1974	Oct. 1974	1979	1983	1987
				Professional and managerial classes: men						
Conservative										
very strong	20.4	32.4	29.6	24.7	33.9	19.0	10.6	13.9	13.5	13.9
fairly strong	20.4	23.1	22.2	28.8	19.2	26.6	27.6	25.1	29.0	29.3
not very strong	24.1	10.2	15.5	9.6	9.3	12.0	15.6	18.2	17.0	10.8
Liberal										
very strong	0.9	7.4	4.7	1.4	2.0	2.7	2.5	1.1	2.6	3.6
fairly strong	8.3	10.4	7.4	2.7	5.5	9.8	11.6	8.0	12.4	10.9
not very strong	9.3	3.7	1.0	5.5	2.4	8.2	9.0	6.4	9.4	11.4
Labour										
very strong	4.6	6.5	5.2	8.2	9.6	7.6	5.5	7.5	6.1	5.3
fairly strong	7.4	5.6	9.0	11.0	10.0	8.7	10.6	11.2	5.5	7.2
not very strong	4.6	0.9	5.3	8.2	8.0	5.4	7.0	8.6	4.4	7.7
Total	100.0	100.0	100.0	100.0	100.0	100.0	100.0	100.0	100.0	100.0
N. of respondents	108	108	116	73	141	184	199	187	458	486

Table 2.13 (*cont.*)

| Professional and managerial classes: women | | | | | | | | | |
| | | | | | Feb. | Oct. | | | |
	1963	1964	1966	1969	1970	1974	1974	1979	1983	1987
Conservative										
very strong	27.7	41.8	40.7	15.4	37.5	16.2	14.1	16.8	13.6	13.0
fairly strong	31.3	29.1	24.4	34.6	22.6	31.6	27.3	33.5	29.2	26.2
not very strong	12.5	4.5	10.5	7.7	6.6	13.2	13.3	12.6	13.1	10.3
Liberal										
very strong	3.6	4.5	4.6	0.0	2.8	1.5	3.1	1.8	3.2	3.2
fairly strong	5.4	5.5	5.9	7.7	5.7	11.8	14.1	6.0	11.7	10.2
not very strong	2.7	0.9	2.1	0.0	1.3	5.1	9.4	9.0	11.7	14.6
Labour										
very strong	3.6	6.4	6.5	3.8	8.1	6.6	6.3	2.4	3.7	4.1
fairly strong	6.3	5.5	2.9	15.4	10.2	8.8	8.6	10.8	7.1	11.9
not very strong	7.0	1.8	2.3	15.4	5.3	5.1	3.9	7.2	6.7	6.4
Total	100.0	100.0	100.0	100.0	100.0	100.0	100.0	100.0	100.0	100.0
N. of respondents	112	110	113	26	137	136	128	167	435	338

| Intermediate and routine non-manual classes: men | | | | | | | | | |
| | | | | | Feb. | Oct. | | | |
	1963	1964	1966	1969	1970	1974	1974	1979	1983	1987
Conservative										
very strong	20.5	22.5	26.3	31.0	26.7	14.3	11.2	10.3	9.4	11.5
fairly strong	18.4	23.0	16.8	24.1	18.5	30.8	32.0	34.0	23.4	29.4
not very strong	15.3	5.7	7.3	13.8	8.8	9.4	8.8	15.4	14.1	8.0
Liberal										
very strong	8.4	5.7	6.1	1.1	3.6	1.5	1.2	3.8	3.1	1.7
fairly strong	5.8	5.7	4.9	1.1	3.8	8.3	9.6	6.4	13.5	10.4
not very strong	4.7	3.8	3.8	2.3	5.0	6.0	5.2	5.1	10.4	13.0
Labour										
very strong	6.8	11.0	13.1	6.9	11.7	7.1	10.8	5.8	8.3	6.2
fairly strong	10.5	16.3	15.6	8.0	14.7	13.2	16.0	12.2	8.3	11.0
not very strong	9.5	6.2	6.1	11.6	7.2	9.4	5.2	7.1	9.4	8.9
Total	100.0	100.0	100.0	100.0	100.0	100.0	100.0	100.0	100.0	100.0
N. of respondents	190	209	195	87	171	266	250	156	192	172

Table 2.13 (*cont.*)

Intermediate and routine non-manual classes: women

	1963	1964	1966	1969	1970	Feb. 1974	Oct. 1974	1979	1983	1987
Conservative										
very strong	19.8	29.0	24.2	18.9	24.2	16.5	12.4	12.5	16.7	13.0
fairly strong	23.5	21.4	21.1	23.1	20.5	21.7	22.5	24.9	17.8	29.5
not very strong	15.0	9.4	8.5	11.9	8.7	7.6	9.2	12.1	15.1	13.1
Liberal										
very strong	3.1	3.3	6.5	1.4	2.4	2.5	2.8	2.0	2.0	1.1
fairly strong	8.2	8.3	5.5	6.3	8.9	9.3	9.6	8.2	10.9	6.9
not very strong	5.1	4.3	0.7	7.7	1.9	0.9	7.6	7.2	12.4	10.7
Labour										
very strong	6.5	9.4	11.3	5.6	9.8	13.0	10.8	6.6	4.0	4.6
fairly strong	11.3	11.6	15.9	11.2	16.9	15.5	18.2	17.0	12.0	12.6
not very strong	7.5	3.3	6.4	14.0	6.8	13.0	6.8	9.5	9.1	8.5
Total	100.0	100.0	100.0	100.0	100.0	100.0	100.0	100.0	100.0	100.0
N. of respondents	293	276	292	143	264	516	498	305	450	615

Manual working class: men

	1963	1964	1966	1969	1970	Feb. 1974	Oct. 1974	1979	1983	1987
Conservative										
very strong	7.9	10.1	9.5	10.6	14.0	7.7	6.1	7.0	6.7	6.1
fairly strong	8.6	10.6	9.9	18.4	13.8	11.4	14.3	17.0	15.5	16.9
not very strong	5.3	3.4	2.9	10.3	4.9	7.4	6.3	9.8	11.4	10.5
Liberal										
very strong	2.8	3.2	2.0	1.1	1.4	1.0	1.9	1.5	1.5	1.2
fairly strong	3.5	6.3	7.2	3.5	1.8	4.5	5.3	5.5	5.7	6.6
not very strong	2.8	2.5	1.1	2.8	0.9	3.4	3.6	3.9	7.1	7.1
Labour										
very strong	29.7	35.6	34.6	19.9	32.5	26.2	23.1	16.2	15.9	14.8
fairly strong	26.7	20.3	26.7	16.0	21.7	27.5	27.9	27.9	20.9	21.3
not very strong	12.8	8.1	6.1	17.4	9.0	10.8	11.6	11.1	15.3	15.5
Total	100.0	100.0	100.0	100.0	100.0	100.0	100.0	100.0	100.0	100.0
N. of respondents	509	444	511	282	476	581	588	458	891	819

Table 2.13 (*cont.*)

Manual working class: women

	1963	1964	1966	1969	1970	Feb. 1974	Oct. 1974	1979	1983	1987
Conservative										
very strong	8.1	13.3	13.9	14.5	16.3	9.1	7.9	6.5	7.9	8.5
fairly strong	15.3	12.5	10.6	15.3	15.0	10.5	12.6	17.7	13.3	14.0
not very strong	6.4	4.0	4.3	8.4	4.8	6.9	6.4	6.7	10.9	10.0
Liberal										
very strong	1.3	3.4	2.5	3.1	2.1	0.7	1.5	1.3	2.3	2.3
fairly strong	3.6	3.8	4.4	5.3	3.8	7.6	9.2	5.9	7.5	8.5
not very strong	3.2	2.2	1.6	5.3	2.1	4.9	3.3	3.8	9.1	8.8
Labour										
very strong	20.4	30.2	32.2	16.8	26.2	24.7	21.8	15.9	14.2	14.0
fairly strong	26.8	22.7	23.6	16.8	20.9	23.6	26.9	26.9	19.4	19.1
not very strong	14.7	8.0	7.0	14.5	8.8	12.0	10.3	15.3	15.3	14.7
Total	100.0	100.0	100.0	100.0	100.0	100.0	100.0	100.0	100.0	100.0
N. of respondents	529	503	512	131	442	449	390	372	744	602

Table 2.14 *Strength and direction of partisanship by class and age (%)*

Professional and managerial classes aged under 35

	1963	1964	1966	1969	1970	Feb. 1974	Oct. 1974	1979	1983	1987
Conservative										
very strong	16.7	25.7	20.5	9.1	21.7	12.5	8.2	8.9	6.7	5.1
fairly strong	23.3	18.6	24.7	27.3	19.7	21.6	20.0	28.7	22.9	23.1
not very strong	25.0	18.8	19.6	9.1	9.8	19.3	14.1	18.8	19.3	15.3
Liberal										
very strong	0.0	6.7	0.0	0.0	0.0	1.1	0.0	2.0	1.7	1.9
fairly strong	3.3	11.0	6.7	6.1	3.2	9.2	12.9	5.9	13.0	8.8
not very strong	8.3	0.0	0.0	6.1	4.3	10.2	12.9	7.9	13.5	17.6
Labour										
very strong	6.7	7.8	14.1	9.1	11.3	8.0	4.7	4.0	6.8	5.6
fairly strong	8.3	7.3	10.8	21.2	15.5	13.6	18.8	10.9	9.1	13.0
not very strong	8.3	4.1	3.5	12.2	14.5	4.5	8.2	12.9	6.9	9.7
Total	100.0	100.0	100.0	100.0	100.0	100.0	100.0	100.0	100.0	100.0
N. of respondents	60	46	45	33	80	88	85	101	286	216

Table 2.14 (*cont.*)

	Intermediate and routine non-manual classes aged under 35									
	1963	1964	1966	1969	1970	Feb. 1974	Oct. 1974	1979	1983	1987
Conservative										
very strong	13.6	16.1	16.4	15.5	13.2	9.0	6.9	6.3	6.6	5.3
fairly strong	20.9	30.5	23.9	27.6	22.2	20.6	22.7	26.6	22.5	26.3
not very strong	19.1	8.1	5.5	12.1	12.4	8.2	13.0	15.2	18.6	12.0
Liberal										
very strong	0.9	2.2	5.7	0.0	0.0	3.0	1.6	3.2	1.2	0.4
fairly strong	9.1	8.1	2.6	0.0	3.8	11.2	10.5	7.6	6.2	7.5
not very strong	8.2	3.2	1.7	8.6	3.5	10.7	7.3	10.1	11.5	13.2
Labour										
very strong	0.9	8.2	12.6	3.4	9.6	9.0	7.7	3.2	5.2	4.1
fairly strong	10.0	21.4	21.6	17.2	25.3	15.9	21.1	15.2	12.2	16.5
not very strong	17.3	2.2	9.9	15.5	10.0	12.4	9.3	12.7	16.0	14.7
Total	100.0	100.0	100.0	100.0	100.0	100.0	100.0	100.0	100.0	100.0
N. of respondents	110	128	107	58	147	233	247	158	359	266

	Manual working class aged under 35									
	1963	1964	1966	1969	1970	Feb. 1974	Oct. 1974	1979	1983	1987
Conservative										
very strong	1.6	8.2	8.2	7.0	7.9	4.7	3.3	4.3	1.3	2.1
fairly strong	12.4	10.8	10.9	23.2	16.6	9.8	12.9	11.7	9.8	11.7
not very strong	7.2	6.2	4.3	17.2	8.0	3.6	5.9	12.1	17.1	14.4
Liberal										
very strong	1.2	1.2	1.3	0.0	1.3	0.0	2.3	1.7	1.6	0.8
fairly strong	3.2	4.6	4.5	6.1	4.0	6.5	9.2	6.9	3.9	5.6
not very strong	3.2	4.6	2.2	6.1	1.5	8.3	4.6	3.9	8.8	8.5
Labour										
very strong	20.9	26.6	24.1	7.1	19.9	18.5	16.2	10.4	9.9	10.6
fairly strong	31.7	23.8	33.3	18.2	27.0	32.2	30.7	29.4	21.8	22.6
not very strong	18.5	14.0	11.3	15.2	13.8	16.3	14.9	19.5	25.8	23.7
Total	100.0	100.0	100.0	100.0	100.0	100.0	100.0	100.0	100.0	100.0
N. of respondents	249	198	269	99	274	276	303	231	449	376

Table 2.14 (*cont.*)

	Professional and managerial classes aged 35–54									
	1963	1964	1966	1969	1970	Feb. 1974	Oct. 1974	1979	1983	1987
Conservative										
very strong	20.0	32.8	31.0	28.2	31.5	14.9	7.9	12.5	12.3	13.9
fairly strong	26.7	24.4	23.4	30.8	24.5	31.2	31.8	31.6	29.4	25.2
not very strong	14.4	4.8	11.6	10.3	7.0	9.2	15.9	17.1	13.7	11.5
Liberal										
very strong	2.2	7.6	6.3	0.0	3.8	2.8	4.6	2.0	3.7	4.8
fairly strong	8.9	8.4	7.2	5.1	8.7	10.6	10.6	5.9	14.2	11.5
not very strong	7.8	4.6	0.9	5.1	1.7	7.8	10.6	7.9	11.8	13.3
Labour										
very strong	4.4	7.3	5.0	2.6	8.8	5.7	5.3	2.6	4.1	5.2
fairly strong	8.9	8.9	7.3	5.1	11.0	9.2	7.3	12.5	6.2	8.2
not very strong	6.7	1.0	7.4	12.8	2.9	8.5	6.0	7.9	4.6	6.4
Total	100.0	100.0	100.0	100.0	100.0	100.0	100.0	100.0	100.0	100.0
N. of respondents	90	101	96	39	99	141	151	152	322	330

	Intermediate and routine non-manual classes aged 35–54									
	1963	1964	1966	1969	1970	Feb. 1974	Oct. 1974	1979	1983	1987
Conservative										
very strong	15.2	23.3	21.4	29.1	25.3	12.8	8.3	14.0	12.3	9.9
fairly strong	20.5	19.2	21.4	21.5	18.5	26.2	27.3	29.3	22.5	33.0
not very strong	17.9	10.7	6.0	11.4	7.8	8.4	7.6	10.8	14.4	12.9
Liberal										
very strong	5.4	4.3	5.5	1.3	2.7	2.0	1.8	1.9	2.6	1.0
fairly strong	7.1	6.5	7.5	5.1	9.7	9.4	10.4	6.4	10.3	8.5
not very strong	4.9	4.6	3.0	6.3	3.9	5.4	8.3	6.4	10.2	11.6
Labour										
very strong	7.6	11.2	11.8	6.3	9.9	11.7	11.2	8.9	6.1	4.1
fairly strong	14.3	14.0	18.9	8.9	13.8	15.4	18.0	15.9	11.2	11.2
not very strong	7.1	6.1	4.6	10.1	8.3	8.7	7.2	6.4	10.5	7.8
Total	100.0	100.0	100.0	100.0	100.0	100.0	100.0	100.0	100.0	100.0
N. of respondents	224	216	228	79	145	298	278	157	375	294

Table 2.14 (cont.)

Manual working class aged 35–54

	1963	1964	1966	1969	1970	Feb. 1974	Oct. 1974	1979	1983	1987
Conservative										
very strong	6.3	7.8	10.1	9.0	13.6	6.1	5.2	5.2	5.0	8.9
fairly strong	10.5	12.1	8.4	16.2	11.8	13.1	12.9	16.0	11.1	16.5
not very strong	5.0	3.4	4.3	6.6	4.1	7.6	6.1	7.8	10.1	10.1
Liberal										
very strong	1.8	3.4	1.7	3.0	1.4	0.8	0.3	1.0	1.2	1.5
fairly strong	4.4	5.9	6.1	4.7	1.7	4.4	5.5	5.2	9.6	7.2
not very strong	3.4	2.3	1.0	3.0	1.9	2.9	1.5	3.6	5.3	8.2
Labour										
very strong	26.5	33.3	36.1	19.2	34.2	26.5	25.5	16.9	18.2	11.6
fairly strong	29.5	25.1	25.9	19.2	23.0	28.2	30.1	32.2	26.3	22.8
not very strong	12.7	6.8	6.3	19.2	8.2	10.5	12.9	12.1	13.2	13.1
Total	100.0	100.0	100.0	100.0	100.0	100.0	100.0	100.0	100.0	100.0
N. of respondents	457	389	391	167	324	344	326	307	433	473

Professional and managerial classes aged over 54

	1963	1964	1966	1969	1970	Feb. 1974	Oct. 1974	1979	1983	1987
Conservative										
very strong	35.7	50.2	74.1	32.0	51.6	28.1	22.2	25.7	23.7	14.9
fairly strong	27.1	34.1	22.6	36.0	18.4	32.6	27.8	25.7	27.0	50.9
not very strong	17.1	4.1	11.3	8.0	6.5	10.1	12.2	10.0	13.3	4.6
Liberal										
very strong	4.3	2.6	5.1	4.0	3.1	2.2	2.2	0.0	4.0	2.3
fairly strong	7.1	4.9	6.2	0.0	4.5	12.4	15.6	9.9	8.1	8.6
not very strong	1.4	0.0	3.2	0.0	0.0	2.2	3.3	6.9	8.6	6.0
Labour										
very strong	1.4	4.1	2.4	8.0	7.0	9.0	7.8	9.9	4.8	3.1
fairly strong	2.9	0.0	2.1	8.0	4.9	3.4	5.6	8.9	6.4	5.4
not very strong	2.9	0.0	0.0	4.0	4.1	0.0	3.3	3.0	4.1	4.3
Total	100.0	100.0	100.0	100.0	100.0	100.0	100.0	100.0	100.0	100.0
N. of respondents	70	70	88	25	98	89	90	101	214	350

Table 2.14 (*cont.*)

	Intermediate non-manual classes aged over 54									
	1963	1964	1966	1969	1970	Feb. 1974	Oct. 1974	1979	1983	1987
Conservative										
very strong	32.2	40.8	37.1	30.0	38.4	25.6	22.1	15.2	19.1	25.6
fairly strong	23.5	19.3	13.4	24.3	18.2	26.8	27.0	28.3	23.4	28.7
not very strong	8.1	2.6	12.3	12.9	5.9	8.1	6.8	13.1	8.7	10.3
Liberal										
very strong	8.1	6.5	8.1	2.9	6.2	1.6	3.6	2.8	2.5	2.7
fairly strong	6.0	7.9	3.9	7.1	6.8	6.5	7.7	9.0	10.9	6.7
not very strong	2.7	3.9	0.7	4.3	1.9	3.3	4.5	2.8	7.4	8.5
Labour										
very strong	9.4	9.5	12.0	7.1	11.7	12.2	14.0	6.9	12.4	6.7
fairly strong	6.7	5.5	7.2	4.3	8.4	12.6	12.6	15.2	10.1	8.5
not very strong	3.4	4.1	5.3	7.1	2.5	3.3	1.8	6.9	5.4	2.2
Total	100.0	100.0	100.0	100.0	100.0	100.0	100.0	100.0	100.0	100.0
N. of respondents	149	139	150	70	138	246	222	145	294	223

	Manual working class aged over 54									
	1963	1964	1966	1969	1970	Feb. 1974	Oct. 1974	1979	1983	1987
Conservative										
very strong	15.1	18.3	16.1	20.6	22.9	12.8	11.3	10.3	10.6	8.8
fairly strong	13.9	11.4	11.8	15.1	14.8	10.3	15.1	23.3	11.2	17.7
not very strong	6.0	2.9	2.4	7.9	2.9	9.3	6.7	6.2	5.9	7.6
Liberal										
very strong	3.0	4.2	3.5	1.6	2.5	1.5	2.6	1.7	2.3	2.5
fairly strong	2.7	4.1	6.4	2.4	2.9	6.3	6.1	5.1	5.8	8.8
not very strong	2.4	1.1	1.1	3.2	1.0	2.0	4.3	4.1	7.4	7.1
Labour										
very strong	25.9	35.8	37.4	31.0	32.9	29.8	25.8	19.5	20.7	19.6
fairly strong	19.3	16.5	18.0	9.5	14.7	19.5	22.3	20.9	23.1	16.6
not very strong	11.7	5.7	3.4	8.7	5.5	8.5	5.8	8.9	13.0	11.2
Total	100.0	100.0	100.0	100.0	100.0	100.0	100.0	100.0	100.0	100.0
N. of respondents	332	361	362	126	320	400	345	292	564	565

Table 2.15 *Strength and direction of partisanship by subjective social class (%)*

	1963	1964	1966	1969	1970	Feb. 1974	Oct. 1974	1979	1983	1987
\'Spontaneous\' middle class identification										
Conservative										
very strong	29.2	33.7	33.6	16.9	31.5	19.1	16.7	18.1	17.4	18.3
fairly strong	25.4	27.5	24.2	29.0	18.7	28.9	27.2	27.2	28.7	27.1
not very strong	12.8	7.0	8.3	10.5	5.2	7.9	9.9	13.4	12.4	10.5
Liberal										
very strong	3.8	5.6	4.3	4.0	2.1	0.8	1.5	2.3	2.1	3.0
fairly strong	7.0	6.5	7.8	4.8	6.5	9.0	9.6	6.7	10.1	9.9
not very strong	3.8	3.0	0.9	6.5	2.0	3.9	8.2	3.4	9.5	10.2
Labour										
very strong	4.1	4.5	9.1	5.6	13.7	9.6	7.3	5.7	4.8	4.6
fairly strong	7.6	9.4	8.6	8.9	17.0	11.8	14.0	14.4	8.9	9.8
not very strong	6.4	2.9	3.2	13.7	3.3	9.0	5.6	8.7	6.1	6.6
Total	100.0	100.0	100.0	100.0	100.0	100.0	100.0	100.0	100.0	100.0
N. of respondents	343	254	304	124	119	356	342	298	716	530
\'Forced\' middle class identification										
Conservative										
very strong	24.4	33.6	28.0	26.1	37.9	21.6	16.9	13.1	14.1	16.8
fairly strong	25.6	25.4	21.6	28.3	24.0	28.3	27.8	40.5	29.0	34.3
not very strong	16.7	9.7	13.9	16.1	6.0	11.0	11.6	15.3	17.8	12.9
Liberal										
very strong	5.0	3.7	6.0	0.6	0.8	2.6	2.9	0.7	2.8	1.4
fairly strong	5.6	7.7	6.5	3.9	5.3	9.6	10.6	5.8	9.8	10.1
not very strong	6.1	5.7	2.7	3.9	4.3	7.0	7.1	8.0	11.5	10.4
Labour										
very strong	2.2	6.1	6.2	3.9	11.9	6.7	6.6	4.7	2.9	4.6
fairly strong	7.2	4.0	10.1	7.2	6.2	8.2	10.8	5.6	6.7	5.5
not very strong	7.2	4.1	5.0	10.0	3.7	5.0	5.6	6.2	5.5	4.1
Total	100.0	100.0	100.0	100.0	100.0	100.0	100.0	100.0	100.0	100.0
N. of respondents	180	229	224	180	137	417	378	274	493	567

Table 2.15 (*cont.*)

	No class identification									
	1963	1964	1966	1969	1970	Feb. 1974	Oct. 1974	1979	1983	1987
Conservative										
very strong	11.2	26.7	23.8	17.6	29.4	14.6	11.0	10.5	11.7	12.2
fairly strong	25.5	19.1	12.5	21.6	27.0	21.9	25.7	33.7	22.8	23.9
not very strong	13.3	7.8	7.7	9.5	2.0	12.5	13.8	11.6	19.7	14.1
Liberal										
very strong	3.1	9.1	7.1	2.7	4.1	2.1	2.8	0.0	2.1	2.3
fairly strong	7.1	11.6	6.8	5.4	0.0	10.4	11.0	4.2	11.8	12.1
not very strong	8.2	4.0	7.3	5.4	0.0	7.3	3.7	5.3	11.1	11.5
Labour										
very strong	12.2	12.8	15.4	6.8	12.2	15.6	11.0	10.5	6.4	5.0
fairly strong	11.2	5.3	12.0	16.2	11.8	11.5	11.0	10.5	5.8	8.5
not very strong	8.2	3.7	7.5	14.9	13.5	4.2	10.1	13.7	8.7	10.3
Total	100.0	100.0	100.0	100.0	100.0	100.0	100.0	100.0	100.0	100.0
N. of respondents	98	85	56	74	54	96	109	95	201	130

	'Forced' working class identification									
	1963	1964	1966	1969	1970	Feb. 1974	Oct. 1974	1979	1983	1987
Conservative										
very strong	9.4	16.8	16.4	17.1	18.5	8.8	7.9	7.8	9.1	8.0
fairly strong	14.8	14.3	15.0	18.3	15.7	17.2	19.8	19.6	19.6	22.2
not very strong	10.9	5.4	5.6	9.2	6.8	9.6	8.9	12.0	15.2	11.7
Liberal										
very strong	4.2	3.9	4.1	3.6	2.7	1.5	2.4	2.8	2.1	1.8
fairly strong	4.5	7.4	4.5	4.3	5.7	7.0	8.6	6.2	8.8	8.6
not very strong	3.6	2.1	1.8	1.9	1.1	5.7	5.6	5.8	10.4	12.0
Labour										
very strong	16.6	22.5	23.5	13.5	20.9	18.5	17.1	9.8	8.8	6.9
fairly strong	19.9	17.6	21.5	17.6	18.7	21.6	21.7	23.2	14.7	15.0
not very strong	16.0	10.0	7.7	14.5	9.9	10.2	7.9	12.9	11.4	13.8
Total	100.0	100.0	100.0	100.0	100.0	100.0	100.0	100.0	100.0	100.0
N. of respondents	331	451	467	415	311	856	783	552	857	943

Table 2.15 (*cont.*)

	| ‘Spontaneous’ working class identification									
	1963	1964	1966	1969	1970	Feb. 1974	Oct. 1974	1979	1983	1987
Conservative										
very strong	7.3	10.7	9.3	8.6	7.6	6.0	4.5	5.7	5.9	4.1
fairly strong	10.5	10.9	8.3	18.2	15.9	7.3	8.3	11.2	9.5	13.4
not very strong	6.3	2.9	2.6	11.8	6.3	5.1	5.1	8.0	9.0	7.8
Liberal										
very strong	1.9	2.8	2.0	1.1	1.7	1.3	1.4	1.0	2.4	1.8
fairly strong	3.6	3.7	5.2	4.8	4.6	5.1	6.7	7.0	7.7	6.2
not very strong	3.1	2.2	0.9	4.8	1.2	4.0	3.3	4.3	7.6	7.6
Labour										
very strong	26.6	36.2	37.8	18.2	34.6	30.3	25.9	20.4	17.7	17.6
fairly strong	27.7	25.0	27.5	17.1	21.2	28.5	32.4	30.9	22.5	25.6
not very strong	12.9	5.4	6.3	15.5	7.0	12.2	12.5	11.5	17.7	15.8
Total	100.0	100.0	100.0	100.0	100.0	100.0	100.0	100.0	100.0	100.0
N. of respondents	905	660	704	187	206	547	553	489	1110	996

Table 2.16 *Strength and direction of partisanship by subjective and objective class (%)*

	| Subjectively and objectively middle class									
	1963	1964	1966	1969	1970	Feb. 1974	Oct. 1974	1979	1983	1987
Conservative										
very strong	31.4	41.9	39.0	30.0	49.3	21.5	16.0	18.1	18.0	17.9
fairly strong	27.1	29.4	26.8	31.0	16.4	33.8	31.8	35.9	34.5	33.6
not very strong	17.0	8.5	12.6	10.0	6.1	11.2	12.9	15.9	16.3	11.5
Liberal										
very strong	4.2	4.2	5.6	2.0	1.9	1.9	2.6	1.9	1.7	2.5
fairly strong	6.9	6.6	7.3	3.0	6.1	10.1	11.2	5.4	8.2	10.4
not very strong	5.2	3.6	1.0	6.0	2.9	6.3	9.2	6.7	7.1	11.8
Labour										
very strong	0.3	2.9	4.5	3.0	6.9	3.8	2.9	1.9	3.6	2.4
fairly strong	3.6	2.6	2.1	6.0	8.5	7.1	9.7	7.3	6.4	5.9
not very strong	4.2	0.3	1.1	9.0	2.0	4.4	3.7	7.0	4.2	4.0
Total	100.0	100.0	100.0	100.0	100.0	100.0	100.0	100.0	100.0	100.0
N. of respondents	306	261	163	100	119	367	349	315	730	748

Table 2.16 (*cont.*)

	Subjectively classless, objectively middle class									
	1963	1964	1966	1969	1970	Feb. 1974	Oct. 1974	1979	1983	1987
Conservative										
very strong	11.4	31.1	30.2	20.0	31.3	13.2	8.9	6.7	16.5	12.6
fairly strong	31.4	27.0	22.6	20.0	25.9	23.7	28.9	50.0	28.0	24.9
not very strong	25.7	8.0	13.0	5.0	3.8	15.8	22.2	16.7	20.8	15.6
Liberal										
very strong	5.7	8.1	5.7	5.0	3.8	2.6	2.2	0.0	1.7	3.9
fairly strong	11.4	19.3	5.4	5.0	0.0	13.2	8.9	0.0	10.4	10.4
not very strong	5.7	0.0	2.4	5.0	0.0	5.3	6.7	10.0	8.7	14.5
Labour										
very strong	0.0	3.7	6.1	5.0	11.9	13.2	6.7	3.3	2.7	3.8
fairly strong	2.9	2.7	10.0	20.0	10.9	5.3	6.7	6.7	2.5	9.2
not very strong	5.7	0.0	4.6	15.0	12.4	7.8	8.9	6.7	8.8	5.1
Total	100.0	100.0	100.0	100.0	100.0	100.0	100.0	100.0	100.0	100.0
N. of respondents	35	30	44	20	28	38	45	30	117	77

	Subjectively classless, objectively working class									
	1963	1964	1966	1969	1970	Feb. 1974	Oct. 1974	1979	1983	1987
Conservative										
very strong	7.0	24.4	16.3	18.4	24.8	15.9	7.7	12.1	7.6	12.4
fairly strong	22.8	16.1	13.9	13.2	31.0	22.7	28.8	25.9	21.5	24.8
not very strong	7.0	8.3	6.0	10.5	0.0	9.1	7.7	10.3	22.1	15.9
Liberal										
very strong	1.8	10.4	4.5	2.6	0.0	0.0	1.9	0.0	0.0	0.0
fairly strong	5.3	6.1	5.5	5.3	0.0	11.4	9.6	6.9	6.2	17.0
not very strong	8.8	4.1	2.5	5.3	0.0	6.8	1.9	3.4	3.5	5.1
Labour										
very strong	21.1	17.3	22.1	10.5	13.8	13.6	13.5	10.3	17.6	9.1
fairly strong	15.8	7.3	20.7	18.4	14.2	18.2	17.3	12.1	14.2	4.9
not very strong	10.5	6.1	8.4	15.8	16.2	2.3	11.5	19.0	7.4	10.9
Total	100.0	100.0	100.0	100.0	100.0	100.0	100.0	100.0	100.0	100.0
N. of respondents	57	51	54	38	23	44	52	58	55	41

Table 2.16 (*cont.*)

	Subjectively and objectively working class									
	1963	1964	1966	1969	1970	Feb. 1974	Oct. 1974	1979	1983	1987
Conservative										
very strong	7.1	11.5	8.3	12.2	12.5	7.0	5.2	6.1	5.9	4.3
fairly strong	10.3	10.9	6.8	16.2	16.5	10.5	13.5	14.5	12.2	12.9
not very strong	6.2	3.8	2.0	9.1	6.7	7.2	6.5	8.3	11.0	9.2
Liberal										
very strong	2.0	2.6	1.6	1.3	1.7	1.2	2.2	1.7	1.6	1.8
fairly strong	3.8	4.2	5.6	5.1	3.6	6.3	6.8	6.3	4.5	7.1
not very strong	3.1	2.2	1.0	3.8	1.1	4.6	4.2	5.0	5.1	8.2
Labour										
very strong	26.1	33.6	39.3	19.0	28.7	25.4	22.2	15.4	17.6	15.9
fairly strong	26.7	23.0	29.1	16.3	20.4	26.5	28.9	29.8	24.5	23.5
not very strong	14.6	8.0	6.3	17.0	8.8	11.4	10.5	12.8	17.6	17.0
Total	100.0	100.0	100.0	100.0	100.0	100.0	100.0	100.0	100.0	100.0
N. of respondents	996	897	613	395	422	1087	1045	805	975	1091

	Subjectively working class, objectively middle class									
	1963	1964	1966	1969	1970	Feb. 1974	Oct. 1974	1979	1983	1987
Conservative										
very strong	19.5	19.9	18.5	24.6	20.4	10.7	10.1	9.8	9.8	8.4
fairly strong	22.6	18.3	19.2	24.6	15.7	25.1	23.2	20.6	17.8	24.9
not very strong	9.7	4.9	7.4	11.6	7.8	11.1	10.5	16.2	14.4	10.7
Liberal										
very strong	4.1	6.2	5.2	0.0	6.0	2.1	0.9	2.9	1.7	1.9
fairly strong	6.7	9.2	2.8	1.4	12.7	7.8	13.2	8.3	8.7	7.7
not very strong	4.1	2.4	0.0	4.3	1.6	7.4	7.5	5.9	6.5	12.0
Labour										
very strong	8.7	17.0	24.4	10.1	11.6	11.5	13.2	10.3	11.6	7.5
fairly strong	13.8	18.0	16.2	14.5	15.8	15.2	14.0	17.2	15.3	15.2
not very strong	10.8	4.2	6.4	8.7	8.5	9.1	7.5	8.8	14.2	11.7
Total	100.0	100.0	100.0	100.0	100.0	100.0	100.0	100.0	100.0	100.0
N. of respondents	195	169	181	69	77	243	228	204	793	776

Table 2.16 (*cont.*)

						Feb.	Oct.			
	1963	1964	1966	1969	1970	1974	1974	1979	1983	1987

Subjectively middle class, objectively working class

	1963	1964	1966	1969	1970	Feb. 1974	Oct. 1974	1979	1983	1987
Conservative										
very strong	12.9	22.2	25.8	15.8	23.0	20.7	16.3	12.4	16.5	16.6
fairly strong	20.2	22.2	22.4	29.2	26.6	22.9	24.8	31.8	24.2	25.3
not very strong	16.0	7.8	3.4	15.8	4.6	6.2	8.2	10.7	14.6	13.0
Liberal										
very strong	4.9	5.5	3.1	1.7	1.0	2.0	2.1	1.3	0.7	1.4
fairly strong	4.9	8.5	8.2	3.3	3.9	8.5	9.4	7.7	4.9	7.6
not very strong	4.9	4.6	0.8	4.2	3.9	4.8	5.4	4.7	7.5	6.9
Labour										
very strong	9.2	8.5	14.3	7.5	17.5	12.2	11.5	9.4	6.5	9.7
fairly strong	18.4	13.3	16.1	8.3	14.2	13.6	15.1	13.3	13.6	10.5
not very strong	8.6	7.5	5.8	14.2	5.3	9.1	7.3	8.6	11.5	9.0
Total	100.0	100.0	100.0	100.0	100.0	100.0	100.0	100.0	100.0	100.0
N. of respondents	163	198	134	120	125	353	331	233	306	277

Table 2.17 *Strength and direction of partisanship by employment status (%)*

Self-employed with employees

	1963	1964	1966	1969	1970	Feb. 1974	Oct. 1974	1979	1983	1987
Conservative										
very strong	28.6	39.2	37.7	33.3	43.6	29.1	25.4	23.6	19.6	24.5
fairly strong	15.7	21.2	22.5	33.3	20.7	40.7	38.8	45.5	36.7	30.1
not very strong	25.7	7.6	5.9	7.4	5.5	9.3	17.9	13.2	16.6	13.0
Liberal										
very strong	5.7	4.2	10.0	0.0	3.8	2.3	0.0	0.0	2.9	2.0
fairly strong	7.1	9.9	9.6	3.7	6.8	2.3	6.0	3.6	4.7	7.7
not very strong	1.4	2.9	3.5	7.4	1.8	4.7	3.0	5.5	6.4	9.3
Labour										
very strong	5.7	8.2	4.5	7.4	7.4	2.3	3.0	1.8	4.8	1.9
fairly strong	10.0	5.4	6.4	3.7	6.9	5.8	3.0	0.0	2.8	7.0
not very strong	0.0	1.5	0.0	3.7	3.4	3.5	3.0	1.8	5.5	4.6
Total	100.0	100.0	100.0	100.0	100.0	100.0	100.0	100.0	100.0	100.0
N. of respondents	70	79	63	27	62	86	67	55	149	154

Table 2.17 (*cont.*)

	Self-employed, no employees									
	1963	1964	1966	1969	1970	Feb. 1974	Oct. 1974	1979	1983	1987
Conservative										
very strong	18.2	26.1	26.6	34.8	26.0	18.8	14.9	20.0	19.3	12.1
fairly strong	18.2	33.0	16.9	34.8	24.0	30.0	30.0	35.4	29.3	29.0
not very strong	9.1	5.3	8.8	13.0	15.5	13.8	12.6	13.8	16.4	11.1
Liberal										
very strong	0.0	0.0	7.8	0.0	0.0	2.5	3.4	1.5	2.6	1.3
fairly strong	13.6	0.0	3.1	0.0	7.0	7.5	10.3	6.2	6.8	6.7
not very strong	9.1	14.9	5.9	8.7	7.0	3.8	5.7	6.2	7.6	10.2
Labour										
very strong	13.6	4.3	17.8	0.0	4.2	8.8	5.7	1.5	4.4	5.4
fairly strong	13.6	10.6	9.4	4.3	7.7	10.0	11.5	10.8	9.3	10.7
not very strong	4.5	5.9	3.8	4.3	8.6	5.0	5.7	4.6	4.3	13.4
Total	100.0	100.0	100.0	100.0	100.0	100.0	100.0	100.0	100.0	100.0
N. of respondents	22	19	32	23	25	86	87	65	119	134

	Managers									
	1963	1964	1966	1969	1970	Feb. 1974	Oct. 1974	1979	1983	1987
Conservative										
very strong	22.2	33.8	32.3	44.2	7.4	16.1	13.6	16.9	14.6	16.0
fairly strong	23.5	26.7	20.6	16.3	17.4	32.9	27.8	27.2	27.5	33.2
not very strong	19.8	3.5	16.7	9.3	45.4	10.3	10.5	11.8	15.4	11.4
Liberal										
very strong	7.4	7.7	4.4	0.0	0.9	2.6	3.7	0.7	3.0	3.8
fairly strong	7.4	6.6	5.6	4.7	6.8	7.7	11.1	6.6	12.0	8.5
not very strong	6.2	5.1	0.0	0.0	0.9	4.5	7.4	5.1	8.8	10.7
Labour										
very strong	2.5	8.1	4.2	4.7	10.3	11.6	8.0	12.5	5.7	3.4
fairly strong	4.9	6.1	10.5	11.6	5.0	8.4	11.7	11.8	8.0	6.8
not very strong	6.2	2.5	5.5	9.3	5.9	5.8	6.2	7.4	5.0	6.2
Total	100.0	100.0	100.0	100.0	100.0	100.0	100.0	100.0	100.0	100.0
N. of respondents	81	79	86	43	97	155	162	136	514	309

Table 2.17 (*cont.*)

Foremen and supervisors

	1963	1964	1966	1969	1970	Feb. 1974	Oct. 1974	1979	1983	1987
Conservative										
very strong	16.3	21.0	11.6	13.6	19.9	12.2	14.3	12.0	10.9	12.4
fairly strong	14.4	11.3	20.6	25.8	18.6	25.6	21.4	26.9	20.0	23.2
not very strong	6.7	3.2	9.1	9.1	0.8	5.6	4.5	14.3	12.4	10.6
Liberal										
very strong	4.8	4.1	4.2	1.5	2.7	1.1	0.0	2.3	1.9	1.1
fairly strong	7.7	9.2	3.8	3.0	3.3	7.8	10.7	5.7	10.4	8.2
not very strong	6.7	2.9	0.0	4.5	1.9	6.7	4.5	3.4	8.5	9.1
Labour										
very strong	19.2	17.9	22.4	12.1	25.1	13.3	12.5	10.9	10.3	10.9
fairly strong	7.7	22.6	19.5	12.1	20.3	15.6	25.0	16.0	12.7	13.2
not very strong	16.3	7.9	8.7	18.2	7.5	12.2	7.1	8.6	13.0	11.3
Total	100.0	100.0	100.0	100.0	100.0	100.0	100.0	100.0	100.0	100.0
N. of respondents	104	105	100	66	110	90	112	175	418	194

Rank and file employees

	1963	1964	1966	1969	1970	Feb. 1974	Oct. 1974	1979	1983	1987
Conservative										
very strong	10.4	14.6	15.2	13.7	5.7	10.4	7.6	6.5	8.5	8.2
fairly strong	14.2	16.2	11.8	19.7	15.6	15.4	17.5	18.5	16.9	20.4
not very strong	8.9	5.9	4.8	10.8	16.1	8.5	8.0	10.5	12.9	10.6
Liberal										
very strong	2.3	4.2	2.7	1.7	2.2	1.4	2.1	2.0	2.0	1.9
fairly strong	4.3	6.2	6.4	4.5	3.6	7.8	8.5	7.6	8.8	8.4
not very strong	3.9	2.4	1.9	4.3	1.8	5.5	5.7	6.0	10.3	10.1
Labour										
very strong	21.4	25.3	26.7	14.9	25.1	18.7	18.0	12.0	10.7	10.9
fairly strong	23.1	18.3	24.1	14.9	20.5	21.8	23.0	24.6	17.1	17.3
not very strong	11.4	6.9	6.4	15.4	9.4	10.4	9.5	12.4	12.8	12.3
Total	100.0	100.0	100.0	100.0	100.0	100.0	100.0	100.0	100.0	100.0
N. of respondents	929	848	913	583	913	1496	1414	850	1835	2260

Table 2.18 *Strength and direction of partisanship: unemployed (%)*

	1963	1964	1966	1969	1970	Feb. 1974	Oct. 1974	1979	1983	1987
Conservative										
very strong	(66.7)	(48.0)	(0.0)	(8.3)	23.3	4.7	2.7	3.1	4.0	2.3
fairly strong	(0.0)	(10.2)	(11.4)	(25.0)	21.9	7.0	13.5	12.5	8.3	9.9
not very strong	(33.3)	(7.9)	(0.0)	(16.7)	8.4	0.0	13.5	6.3	9.1	5.5
Liberal										
very strong	(0.0)	(10.2)	(0.0)	(0.0)	2.4	4.7	5.4	3.1	2.0	2.9
fairly strong	(0.0)	(0.0)	(6.5)	(0.0)	6.5	4.7	9.1	6.3	7.8	5.6
not very strong	(0.0)	(0.0)	(0.0)	(8.3)	0.0	2.3	2.7	3.1	8.7	7.3
Labour										
very strong	(0.0)	(15.7)	(57.7)	(16.7)	23.5	32.2	18.9	18.8	19.0	17.0
fairly strong	(0.0)	(7.9)	(24.4)	(25.0)	10.5	30.2	29.7	31.3	21.3	31.9
not very strong	(0.0)	(0.0)	(0.0)	(0.0)	3.5	9.3	5.4	15.6	19.7	17.7
Total	(100.0)	(100.0)	(100.0)	(100.0)	100.0	100.0	100.0	100.0	100.0	100.0
N. of respondents	3	13	12	12	35	43	37	32	204	179

Table 2.19 *Strength and direction of partisanship by class and employment status (%)*

	Professional and managerial classes: self employed									
	1963	1964	1966	1969	1970	Feb. 1974	Oct. 1974	1979	1983	1987
Conservative										
very strong	25.7	43.1	36.9	38.1	33.0	31.9	16.7	17.9	20.3	20.3
fairly strong	22.9	26.5	22.1	38.1	38.8	36.2	40.5	43.6	33.3	28.3
not very strong	34.3	7.6	11.2	4.8	6.5	8.5	14.3	23.1	15.4	13.0
Liberal										
very strong	2.9	2.5	11.2	0.0	4.3	6.4	2.4	0.0	2.4	2.9
fairly strong	8.6	6.9	9.1	4.8	0.0	4.3	16.7	2.6	7.3	10.1
not very strong	0.0	4.9	3.6	4.8	0.0	2.1	0.0	5.1	8.1	10.9
Labour										
very strong	0.0	8.6	6.0	9.5	7.6	2.1	2.4	0.0	5.7	2.2
fairly strong	5.7	0.0	0.0	0.0	9.8	4.3	2.4	2.6	3.3	8.0
not very strong	0.0	0.0	0.0	0.0	0.0	4.3	4.8	5.1	4.1	4.3
Total	100.0	100.0	100.0	100.0	100.0	100.0	100.0	100.0	100.0	100.0
N. of respondents	35	41	33	21	26	47	42	39	123	138

Table 2.19 (*cont.*)

Professional and managerial classes: employees

	1963	1964	1966	1969	1970	Feb. 1974	Oct. 1974	1979	1983	1987
Conservative										
very strong	20.4	30.5	26.6	17.9	36.0	12.9	10.7	13.1	12.1	12.1
fairly strong	23.1	26.1	24.2	28.2	17.4	26.7	23.0	25.4	28.4	28.0
not very strong	14.8	9.2	16.5	10.3	7.4	13.4	15.5	15.7	15.3	10.1
Liberal										
very strong	0.0	8.3	3.4	1.3	2.3	1.7	3.3	1.3	2.9	3.5
fairly strong	8.3	10.0	7.5	3.8	7.9	11.6	11.5	7.6	12.8	10.7
not very strong	10.2	1.6	0.7	3.8	2.1	8.6	11.0	7.6	10.7	13.1
Labour										
very strong	6.5	4.7	5.0	6.4	10.1	9.1	6.5	7.2	4.9	5.4
fairly strong	9.3	7.5	10.0	15.4	9.9	9.9	11.5	13.1	6.9	9.3
not very strong	7.4	2.1	6.2	12.8	6.9	6.0	7.0	8.9	5.9	7.7
Total	100.0	100.0	100.0	100.0	100.0	100.0	100.0	100.0	100.0	100.0
N. of respondents	108	101	112	78	162	232	244	236	750	685

Intermediate and routine non-manual classes: self-employed

	1963	1964	1966	1969	1970	Feb. 1974	Oct. 1974	1979	1983	1987
Conservative										
very strong	23.4	31.3	38.5	30.0	42.0	21.3	23.4	18.0	19.2	39.4
fairly strong	12.8	24.6	20.1	25.0	16.4	39.4	36.4	38.0	26.9	33.3
not very strong	17.0	5.8	4.8	20.0	8.2	11.7	14.3	16.0	19.2	6.1
Liberal										
very strong	6.4	4.6	9.6	0.0	2.7	1.1	0.0	2.0	3.8	0.0
fairly strong	6.4	10.3	7.2	0.0	12.7	5.3	5.2	6.0	7.7	3.0
not very strong	6.4	4.2	4.3	15.0	2.5	6.4	5.2	8.0	7.7	9.1
Labour										
very strong	12.8	4.0	4.3	0.0	5.5	5.3	3.9	2.0	0.0	0.0
fairly strong	14.9	12.7	11.2	5.0	3.7	7.4	7.8	8.0	7.7	6.1
not very strong	0.0	2.4	0.0	5.0	6.3	2.1	3.9	2.0	7.7	3.0
Total	100.0	100.0	100.0	100.0	100.0	100.0	100.0	100.0	100.0	100.0
N. of respondents	47	50	42	20	46	94	77	50	26	33

Table 2.19 (*cont.*)

Intermediate and routine non-manual classes: employees

	1963	1964	1966	1969	1970	Feb. 1974	Oct. 1974	1979	1983	1987
Conservative										
very strong	17.4	22.6	21.8	22.9	20.5	13.7	10.0	11.0	14.5	11.5
fairly strong	21.9	22.3	17.4	23.3	20.5	22.6	23.5	26.1	19.5	29.4
not very strong	15.8	8.1	8.1	11.9	8.2	8.0	8.3	11.9	15.0	12.2
Liberal										
very strong	5.1	4.5	4.9	1.4	3.1	2.3	2.5	3.2	2.4	1.3
fairly strong	6.4	6.1	4.4	4.8	4.2	9.7	10.8	8.1	12.0	7.8
not very strong	5.5	4.0	2.4	4.8	3.8	6.2	7.2	6.4	11.8	11.3
Labour										
very strong	5.8	11.0	13.9	6.7	13.1	11.9	11.9	7.2	4.9	5.2
fairly strong	11.3	15.8	19.6	10.5	18.1	16.1	18.9	16.2	11.3	12.6
not very strong	10.9	5.5	7.5	13.8	8.5	9.5	6.8	9.9	8.7	8.7
Total	100.0	100.0	100.0	100.0	100.0	100.0	100.0	100.0	100.0	100.0
N. of respondents	311	330	326	210	292	641	629	345	595	755

Manual working class: self-employed

	1963	1964	1966	1969	1970	Feb. 1974	Oct. 1974	1979	1983	1987
Conservative										
very strong	(33.3)	(42.6)	(20.7)	(33.3)	(37.9)	20.8	14.3	32.3	18.2	12.1
fairly strong	(11.1)	(0.0)	(20.2)	(44.4)	(6.3)	20.8	20.0	38.7	37.4	29.3
not very strong	(0.0)	(14.7)	(4.3)	(0.0)	(12.6)	12.5	17.1	6.5	13.1	12.9
Liberal										
very strong	(0.0)	(0.0)	(5.9)	(0.0)	(0.0)	0.0	5.7	0.0	2.0	0.9
fairly strong	(22.2)	(0.0)	(5.3)	(0.0)	(0.0)	4.2	5.7	6.5	3.0	5.2
not very strong	(0.0)	(14.7)	(5.9)	(0.0)	(12.6)	0.0	8.6	3.2	7.1	8.6
Labour										
very strong	(11.1)	(11.8)	(19.1)	(0.0)	(7.6)	12.5	8.6	3.2	5.1	6.0
fairly strong	(11.1)	(0.0)	(12.2)	(11.1)	(13.9)	16.7	14.3	6.5	9.1	10.3
not very strong	(11.1)	(16.2)	(6.4)	(11.1)	(9.1)	12.5	5.7	3.2	5.1	14.7
Total	(100.0)	(100.0)	(100.0)	(100.0)	(100.0)	100.0	100.0	100.0	100.0	100.0
N. of respondents	9	7	19	9	14	24	35	31	99	116

Table 2.19 (*cont.*)

Manual working class: employees

	1963	1964	1966	1969	1970	Feb. 1974	Oct. 1974	1979	1983	1987
Conservative										
very strong	8.1	10.9	11.7	11.4	14.2	8.4	6.8	5.2	6.8	6.7
fairly strong	10.5	11.7	9.4	16.8	13.8	11.0	14.0	15.8	13.6	14.4
not very strong	5.9	3.4	3.4	9.9	3.7	7.6	5.4	9.0	11.3	10.0
Liberal										
very strong	2.3	3.7	1.9	1.7	1.7	0.8	1.5	1.4	1.7	1.8
fairly strong	3.6	6.2	6.7	4.2	2.6	5.5	6.7	6.6	6.8	7.7
not very strong	2.9	2.1	1.3	3.7	0.7	4.2	3.2	4.2	8.3	7.7
Labour										
very strong	28.2	33.3	33.2	19.3	31.9	24.7	23.3	16.5	15.3	15.3
fairly strong	26.2	20.8	26.3	16.3	21.8	26.1	27.8	28.4	20.7	21.3
not very strong	12.4	7.9	6.1	16.6	9.6	11.7	11.3	13.0	15.5	15.2
Total	100.0	100.0	100.0	100.0	100.0	100.0	100.0	100.0	100.0	100.0
N. of respondents	695	597	660	404	667	857	808	577	1402	1304

Table 2.20 *Strength and direction of partisanship by trade union membership (%)*

Trade union members

	1963	1964	1966	1969	1970	Feb. 1974	Oct. 1974	1979	1983	1987
Conservative										
very strong	7.0	10.4	–	7.3	9.6	3.9	3.5	4.3	5.0	4.4
fairly strong	8.5	10.3	–	17.7	14.7	13.1	13.5	15.5	14.9	17.1
not very strong	6.5	3.6	–	10.0	4.9	6.5	6.7	9.8	11.2	9.6
Liberal										
very strong	1.9	3.7	–	0.0	1.1	0.5	0.7	1.6	2.5	1.5
fairly strong	3.6	5.7	–	2.7	2.3	5.7	5.8	8.0	10.2	10.0
not very strong	3.1	2.3	–	3.2	0.9	6.2	4.7	4.1	8.4	10.5
Labour										
very strong	30.7	33.8	–	20.9	32.1	25.0	28.5	13.9	12.8	12.0
fairly strong	25.6	23.1	–	20.0	24.1	27.8	25.1	29.2	20.5	20.7
not very strong	13.0	7.0	–	18.2	10.2	11.3	11.5	13.7	14.6	14.2
Total	100.0	100.0	–	100.0	100.0	100.0	100.0	100.0	100.0	100.0
N. of respondents	414	413	–	220	420	565	531	511	834	715

Table 2.20 (*cont.*)

					Respondents married to members of trade unions					
	1963	1964	1966	1969	1970	Feb. 1974	Oct. 1974	1979	1983	1987
Conservative										
very strong	5.2	11.9	–	9.7	11.4	8.1	7.9	8.2	8.3	7.4
fairly strong	11.8	12.4	–	21.0	14.3	12.7	12.6	22.4	14.1	19.3
not very strong	6.6	4.0	–	9.6	5.9	6.7	6.4	5.1	12.6	12.4
Liberal										
very strong	1.8	2.2	–	0.0	1.6	1.4	1.6	1.6	2.5	2.7
fairly strong	5.5	5.2	–	6.5	6.1	9.9	8.3	5.1	13.7	7.4
not very strong	2.2	2.6	–	1.6	2.4	5.7	5.3	7.1	13.3	11.7
Labour										
very strong	20.3	31.5	–	9.7	27.0	21.2	24.0	12.9	9.0	6.2
fairly strong	32.5	23.3	–	22.6	25.9	23.7	23.9	27.1	16.7	22.8
not very strong	14.0	6.9	–	19.4	5.3	10.6	10.0	10.6	9.8	10.1
Total	100.0	100.0	–	100.0	100.0	100.0	100.0	100.0	100.0	100.0
N. of respondents	271	160	–	62	118	238	229	255	378	299

					Neither respondent nor spouse belongs to a trade union					
	1963	1964	1966	1969	1970	Feb. 1974	Oct. 1974	1979	1983	1987
Conservative										
very strong	18.0	25.7	–	20.9	26.8	16.5	16.7	13.6	13.5	12.6
fairly strong	20.1	19.5	–	23.1	17.7	22.4	22.0	26.6	22.9	24.4
not very strong	11.7	6.2	–	11.6	6.7	9.8	10.0	14.3	14.3	10.7
Liberal										
very strong	3.7	4.6	–	2.6	2.6	2.0	2.3	1.9	2.2	2.0
fairly strong	5.3	6.5	–	4.9	5.1	7.7	7.4	5.7	7.7	8.1
not very strong	4.4	3.2	–	5.0	2.2	4.9	4.8	5.4	9.2	9.6
Labour										
very strong	12.1	15.0	–	8.2	16.6	14.0	14.1	9.6	8.8	9.0
fairly strong	14.4	13.9	–	11.9	15.0	14.4	14.1	13.7	11.3	12.9
not very strong	10.2	5.4	–	11.9	7.3	8.2	8.5	9.1	10.1	10.6
Total	100.0	100.0	–	100.0	100.0	100.0	100.0	100.0	100.0	100.0
N. of respondents	1158	1032	–	698	1158	1424	1462	942	2126	2157

Table 2.21 *Strength and direction of partisanship by class and trade union membership (%)*

| | Professional and managerial classes: trade union members | | | | | | | | | |
	1963	1964	1966	1969	1970	Feb. 1974	Oct. 1974	1979	1983	1987
Conservative										
very strong	9.5	28.2	–	(0.0)	21.0	7.7	7.2	6.3	6.2	6.2
fairly strong	38.1	20.4	–	(21.1)	23.4	19.2	19.0	23.2	25.4	20.0
not very strong	14.3	4.1	–	(5.3)	6.0	12.8	12.0	15.8	14.2	7.5
Liberal										
very strong	0.0	15.5	–	(15.8)	0.0	1.3	1.1	1.1	2.4	2.1
fairly strong	4.8	12.7	–	(0.0)	5.5	12.8	13.0	9.5	10.2	11.6
not very strong	4.8	3.3	–	(0.0)	0.0	12.8	12.8	1.1	5.6	17.0
Labour										
very strong	9.5	11.8	–	(21.1)	20.2	15.4	16.1	10.5	13.3	9.9
fairly strong	4.8	4.1	–	(36.8)	21.6	12.8	13.6	17.9	13.4	14.5
not very strong	14.3	0.0	–	(15.8)	2.2	5.1	5.1	14.7	9.4	11.1
Total	100.0	100.0	–	(100.0)	100.0	100.0	100.0	100.0	100.0	100.0
N. of respondents	21	25	–	19	38	78	73	95	207	207

| | Professional and managerial classes: non-members of trade unions | | | | | | | | | |
	1963	1964	1966	1969	1970	Feb. 1974	Oct. 1974	1979	1983	1987
Conservative										
very strong	25.8	37.4	–	27.5	38.0	21.1	20.0	18.5	18.3	15.9
fairly strong	24.4	26.6	–	32.5	20.5	31.8	31.2	31.3	31.4	30.7
not very strong	18.4	7.9	–	10.0	8.3	12.4	14.3	15.4	19.0	11.7
Liberal										
very strong	2.5	4.8	–	1.2	2.8	2.5	2.4	1.5	1.5	3.9
fairly strong	7.5	7.5	–	5.0	5.6	9.9	9.8	6.2	7.5	10.3
not very strong	6.0	2.1	–	5.0	2.2	5.0	4.3	10.0	8.7	11.3
Labour										
very strong	3.5	5.9	–	3.8	7.0	4.5	4.9	3.1	3.0	3.1
fairly strong	7.0	6.2	–	6.3	8.3	7.4	8.3	8.5	6.0	7.1
not very strong	5.0	1.6	–	8.8	7.4	5.4	4.8	5.4	4.5	5.9
Total	100.0	100.0	–	100.0	100.0	100.0	100.0	100.0	100.0	100.0
N. of respondents	222	185	–	80	240	242	254	259	709	609

Table 2.21 (*cont.*)

Intermediate and routine non-manual classes: trade union members

	1963	1964	1966	1969	1970	Feb. 1974	Oct. 1974	1979	1983	1987
Conservative										
very strong	12.3	13.0	–	11.1	6.1	2.8	2.9	7.5	6.8	4.4
fairly strong	9.2	12.8	–	18.5	21.5	21.7	22.0	21.5	19.1	26.5
not very strong	10.8	10.7	–	14.8	13.2	2.8	3.2	12.1	13.8	8.7
Liberal										
very strong	3.1	2.1	–	0.2	4.5	0.0	0.0	3.7	2.1	1.8
fairly strong	9.2	4.7	–	3.7	1.3	7.5	7.8	9.3	9.0	8.2
not very strong	7.7	4.9	–	3.7	4.8	10.4	8.2	8.4	6.7	10.5
Labour										
very strong	13.8	22.3	–	7.4	15.2	15.1	14.6	7.5	7.4	8.3
fairly strong	15.4	24.1	–	11.1	22.7	25.5	27.3	18.7	19.4	17.4
not very strong	18.5	5.5	–	29.6	10.8	14.2	14.0	11.2	15.8	14.3
Total	100.0	100.0	–	100.0	100.0	100.0	100.0	100.0	100.0	100.0
N. of respondents	65	84	–	27	66	106	98	107	260	113

Intermediate and routine non-manual classes: non-members of trade unions

	1963	1964	1966	1969	1970	Feb. 1974	Oct. 1974	1979	1983	1987
Conservative										
very strong	21.0	29.1	–	25.1	28.6	17.8	16.6	13.0	15.3	13.9
fairly strong	23.3	24.5	–	24.1	19.4	25.3	26.2	29.9	25.7	30.2
not very strong	15.7	7.4	–	12.3	7.9	9.0	9.0	13.6	15.2	12.6
Liberal										
very strong	5.5	5.1	–	1.5	2.6	2.5	2.7	2.3	1.6	1.2
fairly strong	7.1	7.7	–	4.4	7.9	9.2	8.9	7.1	6.8	7.6
not very strong	4.5	3.7	–	5.9	2.8	5.6	5.5	5.9	5.8	11.4
Labour										
very strong	5.7	7.4	–	5.9	9.7	10.4	12.3	5.9	8.8	4.5
fairly strong	10.2	10.6	–	9.9	14.9	13.0	12.0	14.4	10.4	11.2
not very strong	6.9	4.5	–	10.8	6.3	7.2	6.8	7.9	10.4	7.5
Total	100.0	100.0	–	100.0	100.0	100.0	100.0	100.0	100.0	100.0
N. of respondents	426	381	–	203	369	676	650	354	517	668

Table 2.21 (*cont.*)

Manual working class: trade union members

	1963	1964	1966	1969	1970	Feb. 1974	Oct. 1974	1979	1983	1987
Conservative										
very strong	5.8	8.9	–	7.1	8.8	3.6	3.0	2.6	4.1	3.4
fairly strong	6.5	9.1	–	16.5	12.4	8.8	9.0	11.1	9.1	12.9
not very strong	5.2	1.4	–	9.4	3.1	6.1	6.4	7.2	9.8	11.0
Liberal										
very strong	1.8	3.4	–	17.1	0.5	0.6	0.6	1.0	1.1	1.0
fairly strong	2.5	4.6	–	2.9	1.8	3.3	3.6	7.2	3.8	9.7
not very strong	2.2	1.3	–	3.5	0.3	3.6	3.3	3.6	3.2	7.1
Labour										
very strong	35.4	39.2	–	23.5	37.4	29.8	32.0	17.3	19.4	14.2
fairly strong	28.6	24.4	–	20.0	24.5	32.5	32.3	35.8	29.8	24.9
not very strong	12.0	7.8	–	17.1	11.2	11.8	9.8	14.3	19.8	15.7
Total	100.0	100.0	–	100.0	100.0	100.0	100.0	100.0	100.0	100.0
N. of respondents	325	285	–	170	313	363	360	307	362	395

Manual working class: non-members of trade unions

	1963	1964	1966	1969	1970	Feb. 1974	Oct. 1974	1979	1983	1987
Conservative										
very strong	9.3	13.4	–	15.2	18.4	10.9	9.8	9.2	7.4	8.5
fairly strong	14.7	12.5	–	18.1	15.4	12.1	12.6	21.0	12.3	16.7
not very strong	6.3	4.9	–	9.9	5.7	7.8	8.5	9.2	11.8	10.0
Liberal										
very strong	2.1	3.0	–	2.9	2.4	1.0	1.0	1.7	1.1	1.9
fairly strong	4.1	5.1	–	4.9	3.3	7.2	6.3	4.8	5.6	6.6
not very strong	3.4	2.8	–	3.7	2.1	4.3	4.5	4.0	7.2	8.0
Labour										
very strong	20.2	30.0	–	15.6	25.3	23.3	25.4	15.3	16.5	14.7
fairly strong	25.5	20.4	–	13.6	19.6	22.2	21.0	22.6	21.9	18.6
not very strong	14.4	8.0	–	16.0	7.7	11.1	10.9	12.2	16.3	15.1
Total	100.0	100.0	–	100.0	100.0	100.0	100.0	100.0	100.0	100.0
N. of respondents	702	647	–	243	605	667	618	523	691	1021

Table 2.22 *Strength and direction of partisanship by economic sector (%)*

	Works in private sector									
	1963	1964	1966	1969	1970	Feb. 1974	Oct. 1974	1979	1983	1987
Conservative										
very strong	–	–	–	–	–	–	7.8	8.2	11.2	9.9
fairly strong	–	–	–	–	–	–	20.5	22.4	20.5	21.9
not very strong	–	–	–	–	–	–	8.9	10.9	15.2	11.3
Liberal										
very strong	–	–	–	–	–	–	2.3	2.2	1.0	1.9
fairly strong	–	–	–	–	–	–	7.5	6.5	6.4	8.0
not very strong	–	–	–	–	–	–	6.1	6.2	6.2	9.7
Labour										
very strong	–	–	–	–	–	–	15.6	11.3	10.4	9.5
fairly strong	–	–	–	–	–	–	22.2	21.1	15.8	16.1
not very strong	–	–	–	–	–	–	9.1	11.1	13.3	11.6
Total	–	–	–	–	–	–	100.0	100.0	100.0	100.0
N. of respondents	–	–	–	–	–	–	982	691	1724	1790

	Works in public sector									
	1963	1964	1966	1969	1970	Feb. 1974	Oct. 1974	1979	1983	1987
Conservative										
very strong	–	–	–	–	–	–	7.8	7.4	9.4	8.2
fairly strong	–	–	–	–	–	–	14.1	17.1	19.6	21.7
not very strong	–	–	–	–	–	–	7.0	12.4	11.9	9.7
Liberal										
very strong	–	–	–	–	–	–	1.8	1.4	2.2	1.9
fairly strong	–	–	–	–	–	–	10.7	8.6	7.9	8.9
not very strong	–	–	–	–	–	–	5.7	4.5	6.6	11.2
Labour										
very strong	–	–	–	–	–	–	19.3	12.4	13.3	11.3
fairly strong	–	–	–	–	–	–	23.2	24.5	16.9	15.7
not very strong	–	–	–	–	–	–	10.5	11.7	12.0	11.3
Total	–	–	–	–	–	–	100.0	100.0	100.0	100.0
N. of respondents	–	–	–	–	–	–	488	420	1000	890

Table 2.23 *Strength and direction of partisanship by class and economic sector (%)*

	Professional and managerial classes: private sector									
	1963	1964	1966	1969	1970	Feb. 1974	Oct. 1974	1979	1983	1987
Conservative										
very strong	–	–	–	–	–	–	10.4	13.8	17.3	15.4
fairly strong	–	–	–	–	–	–	32.3	31.2	31.0	33.3
not very strong	–	–	–	–	–	–	19.8	16.5	20.8	10.8
Liberal										
very strong	–	–	–	–	–	–	3.1	0.9	1.3	3.7
fairly strong	–	–	–	–	–	–	6.3	6.4	7.7	7.4
not very strong	–	–	–	–	–	–	13.5	9.2	6.4	12.3
Labour										
very strong	–	–	–	–	–	–	2.1	5.5	2.6	3.4
fairly strong	–	–	–	–	–	–	6.3	9.2	7.2	6.3
not very strong	–	–	–	–	–	–	6.3	7.3	5.6	7.4
Total	–	–	–	–	–	–	100.0	100.0	100.0	100.0
N. of respondents	–	–	–	–	–	–	96	109	319	327

	Professional and managerial classes: public sector									
	1963	1964	1966	1969	1970	Feb. 1974	Oct. 1974	1979	1983	1987
Conservative										
very strong	–	–	–	–	–	–	6.6	10.1	11.8	8.5
fairly strong	–	–	–	–	–	–	14.0	21.1	29.5	23.2
not very strong	–	–	–	–	–	–	15.7	16.5	14.1	9.8
Liberal										
very strong	–	–	–	–	–	–	4.2	1.8	2.3	3.1
fairly strong	–	–	–	–	–	–	14.0	10.1	9.8	11.9
not very strong	–	–	–	–	–	–	10.7	6.4	7.9	15.1
Labour										
very strong	–	–	–	–	–	–	10.7	7.3	8.7	7.6
fairly strong	–	–	–	–	–	–	17.4	16.5	8.9	12.2
not very strong	–	–	–	–	–	–	6.6	10.1	6.9	8.5
Total	–	–	–	–	–	–	100.0	100.0	100.0	100.0
N. of respondents	–	–	–	–	–	–	121	109	340	327

Table 2.23 (*cont.*)

Intermediate and routine non-manual classes: private sector

	1963	1964	1966	1969	1970	Feb. 1974	Oct. 1974	1979	1983	1987
Conservative										
very strong	–	–	–	–	–	–	9.2	10.0	13.2	11.0
fairly strong	–	–	–	–	–	–	26.6	28.1	23.3	29.7
not very strong	–	–	–	–	–	–	8.4	12.2	15.6	13.2
Liberal										
very strong	–	–	–	–	–	–	3.4	4.1	1.0	1.4
fairly strong	–	–	–	–	–	–	10.9	7.2	6.7	8.3
not very strong	–	–	–	–	–	–	7.0	5.4	6.7	11.0
Labour										
very strong	–	–	–	–	–	–	10.4	6.3	9.1	4.9
fairly strong	–	–	–	–	–	–	18.2	15.8	11.8	12.3
not very strong	–	–	–	–	–	–	5.9	10.9	12.5	8.1
Total	–	–	–	–	–	–	100.0	100.0	100.0	100.0
N. of respondents	–	–	–	–	–	–	357	221	716	541

Intermediate and routine non-manual classes: public sector

	1963	1964	1966	1969	1970	Feb. 1974	Oct. 1974	1979	1983	1987
Conservative										
very strong	–	–	–	–	–	–	7.8	11.5	10.7	13.1
fairly strong	–	–	–	–	–	–	19.0	21.1	18.8	28.0
not very strong	–	–	–	–	–	–	5.2	12.5	13.7	9.9
Liberal										
very strong	–	–	–	–	–	–	1.3	1.1	2.9	1.0
fairly strong	–	–	–	–	–	–	13.1	8.7	9.0	6.7
not very strong	–	–	–	–	–	–	7.2	7.7	6.5	12.1
Labour										
very strong	–	–	–	–	–	–	16.3	9.6	9.8	5.9
fairly strong	–	–	–	–	–	–	17.6	18.3	16.2	13.1
not very strong	–	–	–	–	–	–	12.4	9.6	12.4	10.2
Total	–	–	–	–	–	–	100.0	100.0	100.0	100.0
N. of respondents	–	–	–	–	–	–	153	104	364	197

Table 2.23 (*cont.*)

Manual working class: private sector

	1963	1964	1966	1969	1970	Feb. 1974	Oct. 1974	1979	1983	1987
Conservative										
very strong	–	–	–	–	–	–	6.3	5.5	6.4	7.1
fairly strong	–	–	–	–	–	–	14.3	16.3	12.3	13.5
not very strong	–	–	–	–	–	–	7.0	8.3	12.3	10.3
Liberal										
very strong	–	–	–	–	–	–	1.5	1.4	0.9	1.6
fairly strong	–	–	–	–	–	–	5.5	6.1	5.4	8.0
not very strong	–	–	–	–	–	–	4.2	5.8	5.7	8.0
Labour										
very strong	–	–	–	–	–	–	21.7	16.1	15.4	14.3
fairly strong	–	–	–	–	–	–	27.9	28.0	24.1	21.9
not very strong	–	–	–	–	–	–	11.6	12.5	17.6	15.3
Total	–	–	–	–	–	–	100.0	100.0	100.0	100.0
N. of respondents	–	–	–	–	–	–	526	361	681	912

Manual working class: public sector

	1963	1964	1966	1969	1970	Feb. 1974	Oct. 1974	1979	1983	1987
Conservative										
very strong	–	–	–	–	–	–	8.1	3.9	5.2	5.5
fairly strong	–	–	–	–	–	–	11.0	13.2	9.3	15.6
not very strong	–	–	–	–	–	–	3.3	10.2	7.4	9.5
Liberal										
very strong	–	–	–	–	–	–	1.0	1.5	1.4	1.3
fairly strong	–	–	–	–	–	–	7.1	7.8	4.1	7.6
not very strong	–	–	–	–	–	–	1.9	2.0	5.0	7.2
Labour										
very strong	–	–	–	–	–	–	25.7	16.6	23.2	17.9
fairly strong	–	–	–	–	–	–	31.0	31.2	26.9	20.8
not very strong	–	–	–	–	–	–	11.0	13.7	17.6	14.7
Total	–	–	–	–	–	–	100.0	100.0	100.0	100.0
N. of respondents	–	–	–	–	–	–	210	205	293	357

Table 2.24 *Strength and direction of partisanship by housing (%)*

	Owner occupiers									
	1963	1964	1966	1969	1970	Feb. 1974	Oct. 1974	1979	1983	1987
Conservative										
very strong	18.0	27.0	–	20.2	26.7	15.1	13.4	13.2	12.7	12.1
fairly strong	21.4	21.0	–	23.8	18.7	26.1	25.0	28.2	24.3	26.7
not very strong	13.3	6.8	–	13.1	6.8	10.0	11.2	13.3	15.8	11.7
Liberal										
very strong	4.2	4.5	–	2.7	2.5	1.6	2.2	1.7	2.3	1.9
fairly strong	5.9	8.0	–	5.3	5.3	9.2	10.0	6.4	10.5	8.7
not very strong	4.5	3.4	–	4.7	2.2	6.2	7.5	6.4	10.2	11.3
Labour										
very strong	10.0	14.7	–	7.3	15.0	9.9	10.2	6.3	6.0	5.6
fairly strong	13.3	10.3	–	13.6	15.5	14.5	14.2	15.2	9.6	12.5
not very strong	9.4	4.2	–	9.3	6.2	7.4	6.4	9.2	8.5	9.4
Total	100.0	100.0	–	100.0	100.0	100.0	100.0	100.0	100.0	100.0
N. of respondents	807	778	–	450	857	1199	1162	963	2251	2240

	Council tenants									
	1963	1964	1966	1969	1970	Feb. 1974	Oct. 1974	1979	1983	1987
Conservative										
very strong	10.0	10.7	–	9.5	12.6	6.6	5.2	5.3	5.0	4.3
fairly strong	9.3	9.2	–	19.5	11.8	8.2	10.6	11.6	9.3	9.8
not very strong	5.5	3.3	–	9.1	4.8	5.4	3.6	5.9	6.8	6.8
Liberal										
very strong	1.5	3.8	–	0.7	2.1	1.6	2.1	1.8	2.3	1.5
fairly strong	2.6	3.9	–	3.6	2.9	5.1	5.7	5.5	5.6	6.8
not very strong	3.0	1.7	–	4.4	2.1	3.8	3.3	3.0	7.3	7.2
Labour										
very strong	27.2	34.4	–	15.3	30.5	29.9	26.0	21.1	19.6	20.7
fairly strong	26.3	24.9	–	15.6	22.8	27.6	31.7	30.8	26.0	25.7
not very strong	14.6	8.2	–	22.2	10.4	11.6	11.8	15.0	18.1	17.1
Total	100.0	100.0	–	100.0	100.0	100.0	100.0	100.0	100.0	100.0
N. of respondents	529	483	–	275	487	680	634	507	873	674

Table 2.24 (*cont.*)

Private tenants

	1963	1964	1966	1969	1970	Feb. 1974	Oct. 1974	1979	1983	1987
Conservative										
very strong	10.2	16.5	–	19.1	19.3	12.0	8.5	8.6	13.1	9.3
fairly strong	14.9	18.2	–	21.3	16.3	14.4	18.9	20.9	14.5	19.5
not very strong	8.6	4.9	–	9.1	7.1	9.6	10.5	16.6	12.1	11.8
Liberal										
very strong	2.0	1.9	–	1.7	1.4	1.5	2.0	2.1	3.3	3.9
fairly strong	5.5	4.9	–	3.0	5.2	6.0	9.9	8.0	11.4	11.2
not very strong	3.8	3.6	–	3.9	0.3	5.1	3.7	5.3	10.8	6.8
Labour										
very strong	19.7	23.6	–	13.5	24.4	22.2	15.3	10.7	14.5	9.8
fairly strong	23.3	20.1	–	14.3	18.1	18.3	22.6	18.7	10.7	16.0
not very strong	12.0	6.4	–	13.9	7.9	11.0	8.6	9.1	9.5	11.7
Total	100.0	100.0	–	100.0	100.0	100.0	100.0	100.0	100.0	100.0
N. of respondents	451	366	–	230	317	334	354	187	160	164

Table 2.25 *Strength and direction of partisanship by school leaving age (%)*

Left school aged under 15

	1963	1964	1966	1969	1970	Feb. 1974	Oct. 1974	1979	1983	1987
Conservative										
very strong	11.5	17.0	16.6	15.8	21.1	12.6	11.3	9.2	12.7	10.5
fairly strong	13.8	13.4	12.4	19.9	13.9	15.9	18.6	20.9	15.8	20.6
not very strong	6.9	3.7	3.5	9.0	4.9	9.1	5.9	8.6	8.4	7.5
Liberal										
very strong	3.0	4.1	3.5	1.6	2.6	1.4	2.2	1.2	2.2	2.3
fairly strong	4.6	6.1	5.5	5.4	3.2	5.9	7.4	6.2	9.6	7.4
not very strong	3.4	2.4	1.3	4.1	1.5	2.9	4.0	3.5	8.3	8.7
Labour										
very strong	21.8	28.2	31.0	15.8	27.4	23.2	22.3	18.8	16.3	16.6
fairly strong	23.5	18.4	21.5	15.4	18.4	20.9	21.2	22.5	16.9	16.2
not very strong	11.6	6.6	4.6	12.9	7.0	8.0	7.0	9.2	9.9	10.2
Total	100.0	100.0	100.0	100.0	100.0	100.0	100.0	100.0	100.0	100.0
N. of respondents	1132	1002	990	442	758	1020	918	579	947	785

Table 2.25 (*cont.*)

| | Left school aged 15 | | | | | | | | | |
	1963	1964	1966	1969	1970	Feb. 1974	Oct. 1974	1979	1983	1987
Conservative										
very strong	14.1	17.2	13.0	13.1	13.3	9.4	7.3	7.0	8.6	10.0
fairly strong	13.6	19.8	17.0	26.2	21.4	17.7	16.7	18.6	18.2	21.4
not very strong	14.9	7.3	6.9	14.0	7.3	5.5	8.1	12.0	13.4	10.6
Liberal										
very strong	2.6	2.7	2.7	0.4	0.9	1.1	1.6	1.8	1.8	1.4
fairly strong	5.4	3.2	4.6	3.0	5.0	7.0	9.2	6.8	8.1	8.2
not very strong	3.6	4.0	1.7	3.5	0.9	6.3	4.3	5.4	7.4	7.9
Labour										
very strong	14.9	19.5	21.0	4.8	17.5	17.1	13.2	9.6	10.4	9.2
fairly strong	18.5	20.1	22.6	15.7	23.9	23.3	27.6	26.1	17.4	18.4
not very strong	12.6	6.1	10.5	19.2	9.8	12.5	12.1	12.6	14.8	12.9
Total	100.0	100.0	100.0	100.0	100.0	100.0	100.0	100.0	100.0	100.0
N. of respondents	390	364	393	229	408	631	630	499	873	748

| | Left school aged 16 | | | | | | | | | |
	1963	1964	1966	1969	1970	Feb. 1974	Oct. 1974	1979	1983	1987
Conservative										
very strong	20.0	25.7	24.2	23.1	27.3	16.3	11.6	14.8	9.2	7.9
fairly strong	25.1	22.8	20.9	19.8	17.5	23.9	25.9	26.1	19.4	22.4
not very strong	10.9	8.5	7.3	14.3	6.5	8.8	14.6	11.8	19.0	11.2
Liberal										
very strong	4.0	4.0	5.2	3.3	0.7	0.3	2.0	1.8	2.0	1.0
fairly strong	5.1	9.7	6.7	4.4	6.6	10.8	8.6	5.5	6.5	7.8
not very strong	5.1	2.6	2.9	5.5	3.0	6.9	7.0	7.6	11.6	10.3
Labour										
very strong	7.4	9.1	10.9	3.3	14.7	9.5	8.3	5.8	4.8	6.6
fairly strong	12.0	11.1	15.2	12.1	14.0	13.1	15.3	14.5	13.7	17.8
not very strong	10.3	6.5	6.7	14.3	9.7	10.5	6.6	12.1	13.8	15.0
Total	100.0	100.0	100.0	100.0	100.0	100.0	100.0	100.0	100.0	100.0
N. of respondents	175	172	195	91	164	306	301	330	823	746

Table 2.25 (*cont.*)

Left school aged 17

	1963	1964	1966	1969	1970	Feb. 1974	Oct. 1974	1979	1983	1987
Conservative										
very strong	20.7	42.5	31.6	17.9	27.7	17.2	13.2	15.7	12.7	17.4
fairly strong	35.4	26.8	16.0	25.0	25.3	30.3	29.4	32.2	27.9	29.8
not very strong	17.1	10.6	15.3	14.3	9.9	13.1	8.8	16.5	14.5	11.5
Liberal										
very strong	4.9	4.5	4.4	0.0	1.7	5.5	4.4	0.9	2.4	1.9
fairly strong	6.1	4.2	8.8	3.6	2.5	6.9	10.3	6.1	9.8	5.5
not very strong	4.9	5.4	1.8	7.1	3.3	6.9	9.6	4.3	12.5	11.6
Labour										
very strong	0.0	2.7	8.2	5.4	7.9	5.5	8.1	6.1	5.9	5.2
fairly strong	3.7	3.4	7.7	8.9	12.1	9.0	10.3	10.4	9.1	8.5
not very strong	7.3	0.0	6.1	17.9	9.7	5.5	5.9	7.8	5.1	8.7
Total	100.0	100.0	100.0	100.0	100.0	100.0	100.0	100.0	100.0	100.0
N. of respondents	82	67	87	56	102	145	136	115	294	270

Left school aged over 17

	1963	1964	1966	1969	1970	Feb. 1974	Oct. 1974	1979	1983	1987
Conservative										
very strong	17.4	32.8	36.5	14.0	22.1	10.9	9.2	8.2	11.5	12.2
fairly strong	25.6	20.8	13.6	24.6	19.1	23.1	19.6	27.1	28.2	22.4
not very strong	16.3	5.2	16.1	12.3	11.5	12.8	17.8	17.1	12.9	16.1
Liberal										
very strong	1.2	6.7	5.7	1.8	4.3	3.8	2.5	4.1	4.2	2.1
fairly strong	4.7	13.2	5.3	3.5	6.4	14.1	13.5	7.6	14.1	9.3
not very strong	7.0	3.2	0.0	3.5	4.4	12.8	14.1	7.6	10.1	13.1
Labour										
very strong	10.5	10.7	8.8	8.8	9.4	9.0	4.9	5.3	6.4	4.3
fairly strong	7.0	7.4	12.2	21.1	15.2	8.3	11.0	14.1	6.2	11.8
not very strong	10.5	0.0	1.9	10.5	7.5	5.1	7.4	8.8	6.5	8.8
Total	100.0	100.0	100.0	100.0	100.0	100.0	100.0	100.0	100.0	100.0
N. of respondents	86	85	85	57	104	156	163	170	425	311

Table 2.26 *Strength and direction of partisanship: university or polytechnic educated (%)*

	1963	1964	1966	1969	1970	Feb. 1974	Oct. 1974	1979	1983	1987
Conservative										
very strong	20.0	21.6	–	17.9	16.9	–	–	6.5	9.6	–
fairly strong	20.0	13.1	–	15.4	19.8	–	–	18.5	22.7	–
not very strong	16.7	8.2	–	10.3	13.0	–	–	21.7	15.2	–
Liberal										
very strong	0.0	9.9	–	2.6	1.7	–	–	1.1	3.7	–
fairly strong	3.3	17.8	–	2.6	7.3	–	–	9.8	15.7	–
not very strong	6.7	9.3	–	7.7	3.4	–	–	10.9	13.1	–
Labour										
very strong	10.0	12.0	–	10.3	13.6	–	–	4.3	6.1	–
fairly strong	6.7	8.2	–	17.9	16.7	–	–	17.4	9.0	–
not very strong	16.7	0.0	–	15.4	7.7	–	–	9.8	4.8	–
Total	100.0	100.0	–	100.0	100.0	–	–	100.0	100.0	–
N. of respondents	30	34	–	39	51	–	–	92	324	–

Table 2.27 *Strength and direction of partisanship by type of school attended (%)*

	Non-selective state school									
	1963	1964	1966	1969	1970	Feb. 1974	Oct. 1974	1979	1983	1987
Conservative										
very strong	11.4	16.4	15.3	16.7	18.7	10.5	10.2	7.5	9.5	7.4
fairly strong	14.2	14.9	13.2	20.1	15.3	15.7	16.1	20.2	18.4	21.1
not very strong	8.3	4.8	4.0	11.0	5.8	7.9	7.8	9.1	14.3	10.5
Liberal										
very strong	2.9	3.8	3.4	1.6	2.2	1.3	1.5	1.7	1.6	1.6
fairly strong	4.8	5.9	5.3	4.4	4.0	7.1	7.8	6.1	6.7	8.3
not very strong	3.6	2.8	1.6	4.1	1.7	5.0	4.1	4.9	6.1	10.3
Labour										
very strong	20.1	25.9	27.9	12.2	24.2	20.0	22.1	13.9	11.7	10.4
fairly strong	22.5	19.0	22.7	14.3	20.5	22.6	20.7	24.4	17.6	17.6
not very strong	12.2	6.6	6.5	14.6	7.7	10.0	9.8	12.1	14.2	12.7
Total	100.0	100.0	100.0	100.0	100.0	100.0	100.0	100.0	100.0	100.0
N. of respondents	1485	1324	1362	748	1300	1587	1590	1040	2207	1999

Table 2.27 (*cont.*)

	Selective state school									
	1963	1964	1966	1969	1970	Feb. 1974	Oct. 1974	1979	1983	1987
Conservative										
very strong	18.3	30.5	23.8	15.2	22.3	14.3	13.0	9.7	14.8	13.9
fairly strong	24.3	22.1	22.6	25.0	22.1	28.0	29.4	24.8	29.3	25.9
not very strong	14.8	7.0	14.0	9.8	8.6	9.5	9.4	14.9	14.6	9.7
Liberal										
very strong	3.8	4.4	5.5	3.0	2.1	3.0	3.0	1.7	2.3	3.4
fairly strong	4.9	6.6	4.2	4.9	6.7	9.5	9.6	9.0	7.6	11.3
not very strong	4.9	3.1	2.0	6.1	2.7	7.3	7.4	5.8	7.1	11.4
Labour										
very strong	8.4	10.5	10.5	3.7	12.6	10.2	10.3	7.8	7.9	5.9
fairly strong	11.0	11.1	12.4	18.9	11.8	10.7	10.5	16.7	9.7	11.4
not very strong	9.5	4.6	5.0	13.4	11.0	7.5	7.5	9.7	6.7	7.2
Total	100.0	100.0	100.0	100.0	100.0	100.0	100.0	100.0	100.0	100.0
N. of respondents	263	249	244	164	266	440	435	424	613	567

	Private school									
	1963	1964	1966	1969	1970	Feb. 1974	Oct. 1974	1979	1983	1987
Conservative										
very strong	33.7	39.8	43.2	27.7	52.1	27.6	25.3	22.5	33.0	25.3
fairly strong	27.9	24.0	14.2	40.4	24.9	35.8	36.2	30.2	36.9	29.4
not very strong	19.8	11.7	13.2	19.1	6.8	10.4	12.3	16.7	13.8	10.8
Liberal										
very strong	2.3	3.3	3.2	0.0	2.0	2.2	2.4	2.3	0.0	2.5
fairly strong	4.7	5.7	8.4	2.1	2.0	6.0	6.0	3.2	5.8	10.2
not very strong	1.2	2.8	0.0	2.1	3.1	3.0	2.8	5.9	6.6	8.4
Labour										
very strong	3.5	8.4	10.8	6.4	4.3	5.2	6.0	5.4	0.8	3.9
fairly strong	1.2	4.3	3.7	0.0	3.7	3.7	4.2	8.0	1.6	6.3
not very strong	5.8	0.0	3.3	2.1	1.0	6.0	4.7	5.9	1.5	3.2
Total	100.0	100.0	100.0	100.0	100.0	100.0	100.0	100.0	100.0	100.0
N. of respondents	86	86	98	47	84	134	125	222	127	158

Table 2.28 *Strength and direction of partisanship by religion (%)*

| | Anglicans | | | | | | | | | |
	1963	1964	1966	1969	1970	Feb. 1974	Oct. 1974	1979	1983	1987
Conservative										
very strong	15.5	22.6	21.6	18.7	25.2	–	14.8	14.4	13.8	12.9
fairly strong	18.1	17.2	15.4	23.2	17.6	–	21.8	28.2	23.1	27.9
not very strong	9.6	5.4	6.2	11.4	5.8	–	9.7	10.7	12.5	11.0
Liberal										
very strong	2.4	3.8	3.0	1.2	1.7	–	1.3	1.3	2.3	1.4
fairly strong	5.2	5.2	4.9	3.5	3.3	–	9.8	6.0	9.1	8.7
not very strong	3.4	2.6	1.3	3.7	1.5	–	6.0	4.7	9.9	9.2
Labour										
very strong	17.0	22.4	24.0	10.4	19.6	–	13.0	9.7	8.0	7.9
fairly strong	18.5	15.4	18.5	14.6	18.1	–	16.8	15.8	11.8	12.6
not very strong	10.3	5.4	5.1	13.1	7.3	–	6.9	9.1	9.4	8.5
Total	100.0	100.0	100.0	100.0	100.0	–	100.0	100.0	100.0	100.0
N. of respondents	1203	1103	1135	594	1037	–	922	549	1582	1373

| | Non-conformists | | | | | | | | | |
	1963	1964	1966	1969	1970	Feb. 1974	Oct. 1974	1979	1983	1987
Conservative										
very strong	9.2	9.1	8.6	10.4	14.3	–	9.6	9.1	9.5	7.6
fairly strong	8.0	16.6	13.7	17.9	18.2	–	16.2	27.3	18.8	17.1
not very strong	10.3	4.7	4.1	9.4	6.0	–	8.1	7.3	13.8	9.3
Liberal										
very strong	7.5	4.7	8.0	4.7	6.0	–	5.9	1.8	3.7	4.6
fairly strong	6.9	11.1	8.6	7.5	11.0	–	15.4	8.2	13.9	11.3
not very strong	4.6	6.4	1.6	9.4	2.3	–	8.1	10.0	8.5	15.6
Labour										
very strong	17.2	23.9	30.2	12.3	23.6	–	11.8	10.9	10.2	9.7
fairly strong	23.6	19.8	20.7	14.2	13.3	–	21.3	16.4	12.1	16.4
not very strong	12.6	3.7	4.6	14.2	5.3	–	3.7	9.1	9.4	8.4
Total	100.0	100.0	100.0	100.0	100.0	–	100.0	100.0	100.0	100.0
N. of respondents	174	163	172	106	231	–	136	110	215	167

Table 2.28 (*cont.*)

Roman Catholics

	1963	1964	1966	1969	1970	Feb. 1974	Oct. 1974	1979	1983	1987
Conservative										
very strong	7.6	8.5	13.6	15.5	14.4	–	5.2	9.8	8.2	6.8
fairly strong	11.4	12.7	8.7	18.6	8.9	–	16.6	19.6	13.0	17.7
not very strong	6.3	3.3	1.7	11.3	6.3	–	5.7	12.3	11.2	11.1
Liberal										
very strong	2.5	2.2	0.6	1.0	0.5	–	3.6	1.8	2.0	1.8
fairly strong	1.9	9.0	5.9	4.1	3.5	–	5.2	5.5	6.4	5.4
not very strong	4.4	2.1	1.3	4.1	2.7	–	5.2	3.7	7.8	8.4
Labour										
very strong	24.7	28.4	26.2	14.4	26.1	–	22.8	11.7	12.2	13.0
fairly strong	22.2	24.6	33.4	15.5	28.3	–	24.4	23.3	22.4	21.5
not very strong	19.0	9.3	8.6	15.5	9.3	–	11.4	12.3	16.8	14.3
Total	100.0	100.0	100.0	100.0	100.0	–	100.0	100.0	100.0	100.0
N. of respondents	158	129	145	106	119	–	193	163	397	311

No religious affiliation

	1963	1964	1966	1969	1970	Feb. 1974	Oct. 1974	1979	1983	1987
Conservative										
very strong	6.9	14.8	8.5	13.2	8.9	–	6.3	7.1	7.0	6.7
fairly strong	8.6	9.5	9.7	7.9	12.0	–	16.4	18.9	18.4	17.7
not very strong	19.0	9.3	7.0	7.9	2.4	–	8.6	12.5	16.2	11.0
Liberal										
very strong	0.0	5.7	0.0	0.0	2.4	–	1.8	1.6	1.7	1.9
fairly strong	3.4	7.5	8.3	5.3	6.9	–	8.1	6.3	8.8	9.2
not very strong	5.2	3.7	3.5	2.6	4.2	–	4.7	5.6	9.6	10.7
Labour										
very strong	27.6	24.7	27.5	15.8	29.5	–	17.0	13.1	10.4	10.8
fairly strong	17.2	22.9	18.4	31.6	20.4	–	26.1	23.6	14.5	17.6
not very strong	12.1	2.0	17.2	15.8	13.3	–	11.0	11.3	13.4	14.4
Total	100.0	100.0	100.0	100.0	100.0	–	100.0	100.0	100.0	100.0
N. of respondents	58	51	52	38	71	–	725	702	853	977

Table 2.29 *Strength and direction of partisanship by religiosity (%)*

| | Attend church regularly | | | | | | | | | |
	1963	1964	1966	1969	1970	Feb. 1974	Oct. 1974	1979	1983	1987
Conservative										
very strong	17.7	20.6	20.1	22.6	23.5	–	–	11.3	16.9	13.6
fairly strong	18.7	20.2	15.2	25.4	16.3	–	–	23.7	24.0	23.9
not very strong	11.5	6.1	6.0	7.9	5.4	–	–	12.7	13.1	10.3
Liberal										
very strong	3.5	5.5	6.9	2.3	2.6	–	–	2.7	2.4	2.2
fairly strong	6.5	10.4	7.6	4.0	7.4	–	–	6.3	8.9	9.1
not very strong	5.0	2.2	1.9	6.8	3.8	–	–	6.3	7.2	11.2
Labour										
very strong	13.0	16.2	19.1	9.0	16.5	–	–	6.3	9.5	8.5
fairly strong	17.0	13.9	17.6	11.9	17.5	–	–	22.7	10.9	13.6
not very strong	7.2	5.0	5.5	10.2	6.9	–	–	8.0	7.1	7.6
Total	100.0	100.0	100.0	100.0	100.0	–	–	100.0	100.0	100.0
N. of respondents	401	359	356	177	296	–	–	300	462	436

| | Attend church occasionally | | | | | | | | | |
	1963	1964	1966	1969	1970	Feb. 1974	Oct. 1974	1979	1983	1987
Conservative										
very strong	13.7	20.8	20.0	18.3	27.0	–	–	10.8	15.4	15.3
fairly strong	20.9	18.5	17.4	22.5	21.1	–	–	30.0	24.5	27.9
not very strong	8.2	5.8	5.7	14.5	5.8	–	–	12.3	15.0	9.0
Liberal										
very strong	2.4	4.0	3.9	2.3	2.4	–	–	0.9	1.6	2.8
fairly strong	5.6	5.6	6.5	3.8	3.9	–	–	7.6	8.3	9.6
not very strong	4.2	3.6	1.3	4.6	2.2	–	–	4.0	7.1	7.2
Labour										
very strong	13.6	20.2	23.2	8.0	14.3	–	–	9.4	7.5	4.4
fairly strong	19.5	16.9	17.9	11.8	16.7	–	–	13.9	11.6	16.4
not very strong	12.0	4.7	4.1	14.1	6.6	–	–	11.0	9.1	7.3
Total	100.0	100.0	100.0	100.0	100.0	–	–	100.0	100.0	100.0
N. of respondents	575	507	534	262	425	–	–	446	713	428

Table 2.29 (*cont.*)

	Attend church rarely									
	1963	1964	1966	1969	1970	Feb. 1974	Oct. 1974	1979	1983	1987
Conservative										
very strong	11.2	17.6	19.0	15.1	19.3	–	–	9.1	11.2	12.5
fairly strong	14.2	15.7	12.0	22.8	16.8	–	–	20.6	21.9	24.8
not very strong	7.7	3.5	4.5	9.9	6.6	–	–	11.5	13.0	10.3
Liberal										
very strong	3.5	3.7	1.8	1.1	2.0	–	–	2.2	0.7	1.3
fairly strong	4.9	4.6	4.1	5.5	4.0	–	–	5.3	5.5	8.7
not very strong	3.5	3.0	2.0	3.7	1.2	–	–	6.6	6.3	10.0
Labour										
very strong	20.9	24.5	26.5	9.6	21.3	–	–	12.1	10.6	8.1
fairly strong	22.1	20.1	23.7	15.8	20.0	–	–	22.6	20.2	12.8
not very strong	12.1	7.3	6.3	16.5	8.8	–	–	10.0	10.7	11.6
Total	100.0	100.0	100.0	100.0	100.0	–	–	100.0	100.0	100.0
N. of respondents	430	402	438	272	488	–	–	637	299	434

	Never attend church									
	1963	1964	1966	1969	1970	Feb. 1974	Oct. 1974	1979	1983	1987
Conservative										
very strong	12.7	20.8	15.3	15.0	18.3	–	–	8.9	9.1	9.1
fairly strong	10.7	12.5	13.6	19.2	13.1	–	–	15.5	18.9	22.9
not very strong	11.2	5.6	7.7	11.5	7.6	–	–	9.2	11.6	11.9
Liberal										
very strong	3.2	2.4	2.8	2.1	1.7	–	–	1.3	1.8	1.9
fairly strong	2.5	4.1	3.9	3.4	3.3	–	–	6.9	5.0	6.4
not very strong	2.0	2.2	0.8	3.4	0.6	–	–	3.3	5.8	9.6
Labour										
very strong	22.6	29.2	27.2	16.7	30.3	–	–	17.5	13.3	10.8
fairly strong	20.9	15.7	20.7	15.4	17.1	–	–	23.4	19.0	15.3
not very strong	14.2	7.6	8.1	13.2	8.0	–	–	13.9	15.4	12.1
Total	100.0	100.0	100.0	100.0	100.0	–	–	100.0	100.0	100.0
N. of respondents	402	374	378	234	410	–	–	303	902	850

Table 2.30 *Strength and direction of partisanship by region (%)*

	Scotland									
	1963	1964	1966	1969	1970	Feb. 1974	Oct. 1974	1979	1983	1987
Conservative										
very strong	14.0	18.3	15.2	19.1	19.9	8.6	7.5	6.5	5.8	7.6
fairly strong	19.6	20.3	16.0	29.8	19.0	23.0	23.3	21.8	15.1	18.5
not very strong	8.9	4.0	6.4	12.8	8.8	7.5	10.1	10.5	10.3	5.8
Liberal										
very strong	1.7	1.8	3.5	1.1	1.6	2.1	1.3	1.6	1.3	2.9
fairly strong	3.4	4.0	7.9	3.2	1.8	3.7	4.4	11.3	6.4	8.4
not very strong	1.1	0.8	1.1	3.2	1.8	4.8	3.1	4.8	7.7	9.1
Labour										
very strong	16.2	21.8	24.4	10.6	24.1	18.2	17.6	13.7	15.1	11.3
fairly strong	23.5	18.9	19.8	7.4	13.6	20.9	24.5	19.4	23.8	17.5
not very strong	11.7	10.2	5.6	12.8	9.3	11.2	8.2	10.5	14.5	18.9
Total	100.0	100.0	100.0	100.0	100.0	100.0	100.0	100.0	100.0	100.0
N. of respondents	179	169	152	94	161	187	159	124	281	265

	Wales									
	1963	1964	1966	1969	1970	Feb. 1974	Oct. 1974	1979	1983	1987
Conservative										
very strong	8.8	14.6	9.6	7.3	13.6	7.4	5.9	4.4	4.2	10.6
fairly strong	8.8	7.5	9.7	19.5	15.1	11.5	11.0	10.0	16.8	6.7
not very strong	5.5	7.2	10.2	9.8	8.9	8.2	4.2	8.9	12.1	8.9
Liberal										
very strong	2.2	1.5	6.2	4.9	2.7	0.0	4.2	0.0	1.6	1.7
fairly strong	7.7	11.3	6.0	9.8	5.4	3.3	3.4	6.7	7.9	9.5
not very strong	3.3	1.5	0.0	14.6	4.9	4.1	3.4	4.4	9.5	7.3
Labour										
very strong	27.5	38.6	40.0	12.2	29.9	32.0	28.8	25.6	18.4	15.6
fairly strong	24.2	16.4	12.0	4.9	12.5	25.4	34.7	25.6	14.7	24.0
not very strong	12.1	1.5	6.3	17.1	7.0	8.2	4.2	14.4	14.7	15.6
Total	100.0	100.0	100.0	100.0	100.0	100.0	100.0	100.0	100.0	100.0
N. of respondents	91	66	83	41	75	122	118	90	184	166

Table 2.30 (*cont.*)

The North

	1963	1964	1966	1969	1970	Feb. 1974	Oct. 1974	1979	1983	1987
Conservative										
very strong	10.7	16.9	16.1	13.4	22.7	10.9	9.8	9.0	8.7	7.5
fairly strong	14.8	14.6	15.4	19.9	11.3	16.9	17.1	20.7	16.0	18.6
not very strong	9.8	5.7	5.6	10.9	5.5	8.2	9.0	11.7	12.9	9.5
Liberal										
very strong	3.1	3.4	3.4	1.8	3.1	0.9	0.9	1.3	1.1	2.2
fairly strong	4.2	5.3	5.4	2.9	4.0	7.0	8.6	4.8	10.2	5.5
not very strong	4.1	3.8	2.3	3.3	1.7	5.7	6.9	6.1	8.0	8.3
Labour										
very strong	20.8	24.1	24.8	14.5	24.3	20.0	16.4	14.6	12.3	13.3
fairly strong	21.0	21.3	21.3	16.3	20.7	21.0	21.8	21.7	17.9	20.7
not very strong	11.4	5.1	5.8	17.0	6.6	9.4	9.5	10.2	12.8	14.3
Total	100.0	100.0	100.0	100.0	100.0	100.0	100.0	100.0	100.0	100.0
N. of respondents	542	494	487	276	507	681	642	479	920	870

The Midlands

	1963	1964	1966	1969	1970	Feb. 1974	Oct. 1974	1979	1983	1987
Conservative										
very strong	10.4	19.0	18.3	11.2	18.2	14.7	10.5	8.8	10.7	8.9
fairly strong	18.0	16.0	14.1	29.4	18.9	16.0	20.5	23.9	19.9	22.7
not very strong	8.8	5.5	4.3	10.6	3.9	10.9	7.8	8.8	12.8	11.5
Liberal										
very strong	1.5	3.8	1.8	1.2	1.0	1.4	0.8	1.1	2.2	1.4
fairly strong	6.1	4.9	4.9	6.5	4.0	5.7	7.0	6.0	8.1	7.8
not very strong	3.0	2.4	0.5	5.3	2.2	3.5	4.3	3.5	9.0	11.6
Labour										
very strong	18.6	23.9	26.2	10.0	20.0	16.0	18.6	9.1	8.8	9.1
fairly strong	22.6	19.6	22.7	17.6	21.2	20.9	20.8	24.2	13.5	16.4
not very strong	11.0	5.0	7.1	8.2	10.7	10.9	9.7	14.7	15.1	10.6
Total	100.0	100.0	100.0	100.0	100.0	100.0	100.0	100.0	100.0	100.0
N. of respondents	328	312	342	170	305	368	371	285	528	545

Table 2.30 (*cont.*)

Greater London

	1963	1964	1966	1969	1970	Feb. 1974	Oct. 1974	1979	1983	1987
Conservative										
very strong	13.5	23.9	18.5	23.1	20.6	13.3	7.5	8.9	10.7	13.5
fairly strong	14.2	13.9	13.3	15.4	17.4	18.5	21.2	22.6	18.6	23.4
not very strong	11.5	5.4	5.2	8.8	7.0	10.0	8.5	12.1	12.8	11.4
Liberal										
very strong	4.9	5.1	3.5	0.5	2.2	2.4	3.3	2.6	1.6	1.9
fairly strong	5.2	7.0	4.8	6.0	4.6	7.2	5.7	5.3	8.2	9.0
not very strong	4.2	1.7	2.3	2.2	0.6	2.8	6.1	4.2	11.2	6.7
Labour										
very strong	13.2	20.1	20.2	12.1	19.6	20.1	19.3	11.6	9.8	8.0
fairly strong	20.8	14.7	23.4	14.3	19.0	16.1	21.2	21.6	14.5	14.4
not very strong	12.5	8.2	8.8	17.6	9.0	9.6	7.1	11.1	12.6	11.9
Total	100.0	100.0	100.0	100.0	100.0	100.0	100.0	100.0	100.0	100.0
N. of respondents	288	245	265	182	271	249	212	190	427	371

The South

	1963	1964	1966	1969	1970	Feb. 1974	Oct. 1974	1979	1983	1987
Conservative										
very strong	21.4	23.2	23.7	22.6	25.4	14.1	12.5	13.7	14.6	13.1
fairly strong	18.2	21.3	15.5	20.3	21.1	22.9	22.0	26.1	25.3	28.9
not very strong	9.5	5.0	7.2	13.4	7.0	7.7	9.8	13.5	15.0	12.5
Liberal										
very strong	3.3	5.3	5.0	3.2	2.0	2.3	3.5	2.6	4.1	1.8
fairly strong	4.5	7.4	6.4	3.2	6.5	10.8	12.8	7.0	9.6	11.0
not very strong	5.2	4.0	1.5	5.5	2.3	7.2	5.9	6.1	10.7	12.6
Labour										
very strong	14.0	18.3	21.1	6.9	15.9	12.5	9.4	6.7	5.7	4.9
fairly strong	13.1	10.2	15.4	14.3	13.9	14.7	16.3	15.9	9.1	9.0
not very strong	10.8	5.3	4.1	10.6	6.0	7.8	7.8	8.3	6.0	6.2
Total	100.0	100.0	100.0	100.0	100.0	100.0	100.0	100.0	100.0	100.0
N. of respondents	444	421	440	217	377	665	663	540	1085	975

Table 2.31 *Non-partisanship: all respondents (%)*

	1963	1964	1966	1969	1970	Feb. 1974	Oct. 1974	1979	1983	1987
Per cent non-partisan:	5.3	3.8	5.1	7.8	5.5	3.6	3.9	5.6	5.0	6.2

Table 2.32 *Non-partisanship by gender (%)*

	1963	1964	1966	1969	1970	Feb. 1974	Oct. 1974	1979	1983	1987
Per cent non-partisan:										
Men	5.3	4.0	5.6	8.1	6.0	3.3	3.9	6.0	4.9	5.8
Women	5.4	3.7	4.6	7.5	5.0	3.7	4.0	5.2	5.5	6.6

Table 2.33 *Non-partisanship by age (%)*

	1963	1964	1966	1969	1970	Feb. 1974	Oct. 1974	1979	1983	1987
Per cent non-partisan:										
Aged under 25	7.1	5.7	5.2	10.8	8.2	3.9	5.4	11.6	8.1	10.6
Aged 25–34	4.8	6.2	9.3	9.0	8.1	4.3	5.2	7.1	5.3	7.2
Aged 35–44	5.8	2.9	6.2	7.3	6.1	4.9	3.6	2.8	5.3	6.5
Aged 45–54	3.9	4.0	1.6	4.9	3.4	3.5	3.3	6.2	4.3	5.2
Aged 55–64	5.5	4.3	4.7	3.3	3.1	2.4	2.9	4.3	3.6	3.5
Aged 65–74	4.2	1.5	4.8	5.8	2.6	2.3	2.9	2.4	3.9	4.9
Aged over 74	6.7	1.1	1.9	5.5	6.1	1.9	4.6	6.4	6.5	5.2

Table 2.34 *Non-partisanship by age and gender (%)*

	1963	1964	1966	1969	1970	Feb. 1974	Oct. 1974	1979	1983	1987
Per cent non-partisan:										
Men under 25	4.0	2.5	4.1	12.7	8.9	1.9	3.9	11.7	6.7	10.8
Women under 25	9.2	8.4	6.5	8.9	7.5	5.6	6.8	11.5	9.6	10.3
Men 25–44	6.5	5.3	8.5	7.7	7.2	4.7	4.9	5.1	5.5	5.7
Women 25–44	4.4	3.6	6.9	8.5	6.9	4.5	3.9	5.3	5.1	8.2
Men 45–64	3.7	3.6	3.7	3.4	3.9	3.1	2.4	6.4	4.3	4.1
Women 45–64	5.4	4.6	2.4	4.7	2.6	2.8	3.8	4.4	3.7	4.5
Men over 64	5.7	2.5	4.0	6.7	3.6	1.6	3.9	4.8	2.8	5.3
Women over 64	4.5	0.5	3.7	5.1	3.8	2.6	3.1	3.3	6.3	4.7

Table 2.35 *Non-partisanship by marital status (%)*

	1963	1964	1966	1969	1970	Feb. 1974	Oct. 1974	1979	1983	1987
Per cent non-partisan:										
Single	7.1	4.5	7.4	13.5	6.4	6.3	–	9.2	6.6	8.9
Married	5.0	4.1	5.1	5.9	5.3	3.1	3.7	5.0	4.7	5.5
Divorced or separated	–	–	0.0	–	–	7.4	–	7.9	5.1	6.4
Widowed	–	–	3.6	–	–	3.2	–	4.5	6.9	5.5

Table 2.36 *Non-partisanship by marital status and gender (%)*

	1963	1964	1966	1969	1970	Feb. 1974	Oct. 1974	1979	1983	1987
Per cent non-partisan:										
Single men	7.9	5.6	8.5	14.6	7.5	4.8	–	9.0	6.8	10.0
Single women	6.3	3.5	5.9	12.3	4.9	8.1	–	9.5	6.5	7.4
Married men	5.2	4.1	5.2	5.9	5.5	3.1	3.7	5.3	4.6	4.6
Married women	4.9	4.0	5.1	5.8	5.2	3.0	3.7	4.8	5.8	6.6
Divorced or separated men	–	–	–	–	–	0.0	–	10.3	6.7	6.4
Divorced or separated women	–	–	–	–	–	10.0	–	6.4	5.0	6.4
Widowed men	–	–	–	–	–	3.3	–	5.8	4.9	4.6
Widowed women	–	–	–	–	–	3.2	–	4.1	7.1	5.7

Table 2.37 *Non-partisanship: new electors (%)*

	1963	1964	1966	1969	1970	Feb. 1974	Oct. 1974	1979	1983	1987
Per cent non-partisan:										
New electors	7.1	7.7	4.9	10.9	8.2	6.3	–	13.1	8.8	13.2

Table 2.38 *Non-partisanship by political generation (%)*

	1963	1964	1966	1969	1970	Feb. 1974	Oct. 1974	1979	1983	1987
Per cent non-partisan:										
First voted 1918–1935	4.6	3.4	3.6	4.8	3.5	1.5	3.6	3.9	5.4	5.2
First voted 1936–1950	5.4	2.7	2.5	4.7	3.5	3.3	2.8	4.7	3.7	4.2
First voted 1951–1970	6.3	6.1	9.0	10.9	7.5	4.3	4.3	5.2	4.8	5.3
First voted after 1970	–	–	–	–	–	6.3	6.7	10.0	6.2	8.7

Table 2.39 *Non-partisanship: non-voters (%)*

	1963	1964	1966	1969	1970	Feb. 1974	Oct. 1974	1979	1983	1987
Per cent non-partisan:										
Non-voters	–	12.9	14.2	–	13.0	12.3	9.9	17.0	10.5	17.0

Table 2.40 *Non-partisanship by vote (%)*

	1963	1964	1966	1969	1970	Feb. 1974	Oct. 1974	1979	1983	1987
Per cent non-partisan:										
Conservative voters	1.2	1.3	2.3	3.8	3.3	1.5	2.1	3.6	3.6	3.6
Labour voters	1.7	2.4	2.8	2.7	2.2	1.6	2.2	2.2	2.1	2.3
Liberal voters	3.9	5.6	8.7	6.2	7.8	3.3	3.4	2.8	4.8	6.2
Voters for other parties	0.0	0.0	0.0	11.1	17.7	0.0	6.9	27.3	20.6	12.6

Table 2.41 *Non-partisanship by social class (%)*

	1963	1964	1966	1969	1970	Feb. 1974	Oct. 1974	1979	1983	1987
Per cent non-partisan:										
Professional and managerial	3.5	5.5	4.5	3.8	4.7	3.3	3.5	3.3	4.0	4.7
Intermediate and routine non-manual	7.3	5.3	4.6	7.9	5.2	3.7	3.8	4.7	5.2	5.8
Manual working class	4.8	2.9	5.3	8.4	5.6	3.5	4.1	6.9	6.0	7.5

Table 2.42 *Non-partisanship by occupational status (%)*

	1963	1964	1966	1969	1970	Feb. 1974	Oct. 1974	1979	1983	1987
Per cent non-partisan:										
Class A/RG I	5.3	7.6	6.1	3.4	5.9	2.3	2.4	4.2	4.2	4.1
Class B/RG II	3.1	4.3	3.2	4.0	4.0	4.0	4.2	2.8	4.0	4.8
Class C1A/RG III	5.8	5.8	3.9	7.2	5.3	2.9	4.2	5.7	5.2	5.8
Class C1B/RG III manual	7.3	4.2	5.3	8.3	5.1	4.2	3.6	4.0	7.1	8.1
Class C2/RG IV	5.9	3.6	7.1	7.7	5.8	3.7	4.0	7.1	6.1	7.2
Class D/RG V	4.5	1.4	3.0	9.1	5.3	3.2	4.3	6.7	4.9	5.9

Table 2.43 *Non-partisanship by class and gender (%)*

	1963	1964	1966	1969	1970	Feb. 1974	Oct. 1974	1979	1983	1987
Per cent non-partisan:										
Professional and managerial										
Men	5.3	7.5	6.3	5.1	6.6	2.6	3.8	3.9	4.8	4.5
Women	2.3	2.8	3.8	0.0	2.9	4.2	3.0	3.1	3.1	4.9
Intermediate & routine non-manual										
Men	7.5	5.6	4.8	5.3	5.5	3.6	4.6	4.5	3.5	4.8
Women	7.0	5.2	4.5	9.4	5.0	3.7	3.5	5.0	5.9	6.1
Manual working class										
Men	5.0	4.2	5.3	8.5	5.9	3.3	3.4	6.4	5.8	6.8
Women	4.7	2.3	5.2	7.0	5.1	3.6	5.1	7.4	6.2	8.4

Table 2.44 *Non-partisanship by class and age (%)*

	1963	1964	1966	1969	1970	Feb. 1974	Oct. 1974	1979	1983	1987
Per cent non-partisan:										
Aged under 35:										
Professional and managerial	0.0	11.8	7.2	0.0	8.0	2.2	2.5	4.7	4.6	4.7
Intermediate and routine non-manual	6.7	5.3	8.3	9.2	7.0	4.5	4.3	7.6	7.7	7.9
Manual working	6.3	5.3	8.2	13.8	9.0	3.8	4.7	10.5	11.3	12.4
Aged 35–54:										
Professional and managerial	6.3	3.1	6.2	4.9	4.4	4.7	2.6	2.6	3.5	4.3
Intermediate and routine non-manual	5.9	4.4	3.5	5.9	4.1	4.5	2.4	3.7	3.9	4.6
Manual working	4.0	3.0	3.5	4.0	4.8	3.6	4.4	5.8	6.4	7.7
Aged over 54:										
Professional and managerial	2.8	4.5	0.9	3.7	2.1	1.1	1.1	2.9	4.0	5.1
Intermediate and routine non-manual	8.6	4.3	3.6	4.1	4.5	2.0	5.1	2.7	3.5	4.7
Manual working	4.3	1.4	5.0	3.8	2.6	2.9	3.1	5.2	3.6	3.8

Table 2.45 *Non-partisanship by subjective social class (%)*

	1963	1964	1966	1969	1970	Feb. 1974	Oct. 1974	1979	1983	1987
Per cent non-partisan:										
'Spontaneous' middle-class	2.8	3.2	2.8	4.5	4.7	1.9	4.2	2.3	2.6	2.6
'Forced' middle class	5.7	4.1	6.3	4.7	4.0	2.1	4.3	4.2	5.7	4.9
No class identification	15.5	7.4	9.8	12.6	12.0	9.4	7.6	9.0	10.1	15.4
'Forced' working class	6.5	4.0	7.1	9.0	5.8	4.7	3.9	7.4	6.7	8.6
'Spontaneous' working class	4.4	3.3	3.9	7.8	2.5	2.8	2.8	5.6	4.4	5.0

Table 2.46 *Non-partisanship by subjective and objective class (%)*

	1963	1964	1966	1969	1970	Feb. 1974	Oct. 1974	1979	1983	1987
Per cent non-partisan:										
Objectively middle class										
Subjectively middle class	3.2	3.7	3.5	3.8	4.5	1.9	4.6	2.2	3.4	3.8
Classless	4.3	4.8	3.1	4.8	14.6	9.5	4.3	3.1	6.9	9.7
Working class	7.6	6.7	5.3	8.0	5.1	4.0	2.6	7.2	5.3	6.1
Objectively working class										
Subjectively middle class	4.8	4.5	4.4	4.7	4.7	2.5	4.3	4.5	5.7	3.5
Classless	7.7	6.7	7.0	14.9	5.8	10.2	8.8	9.4	15.8	26.5
Working class	6.3	7.5	8.0	8.8	4.3	3.8	3.6	6.5	5.1	7.5

Table 2.47 *Non-partisanship by employment status (%)*

	1963	1964	1966	1969	1970	Feb. 1974	Oct. 1974	1979	1983	1987
Per cent non-partisan:										
Self-employed with employees	5.3	2.8	1.3	9.7	3.6	3.4	5.7	5.2	3.1	3.5
Self-employed, no employees	15.4	6.0	0.0	0.0	11.6	1.2	1.1	5.7	4.5	6.3
Managers	9.0	2.2	4.9	8.5	5.2	1.9	4.1	4.2	4.1	5.3
Foremen and supervisors	5.5	4.7	9.9	5.7	2.8	5.3	5.8	6.4	6.3	6.4
Rank and file workers	5.3	4.3	4.9	8.0	6.0	3.9	3.7	5.5	5.3	6.6

Table 2.48 *Non-partisanship: unemployed (%)*

	1963	1964	1966	1969	1970	Feb. 1974	Oct. 1974	1979	1983	1987
Per cent non-partisan:										
Unemployed	0.0	0.0	6.1	7.7	6.1	2.3	7.5	11.1	6.1	8.5

Table 2.49 *Non-partisanship by class and employment status (%)*

	1963	1964	1966	1969	1970	Feb. 1974	Oct. 1974	1979	1983	1987
Per cent non-partisan:										
Self-employed:										
Professional and managerial	4.2	4.4	4.0	4.3	8.0	4.1	2.3	2.5	2.0	2.6
Intermediate and routine non-manual	6.3	6.2	5.8	9.1	6.9	2.1	3.8	5.7	4.3	8.1
Manual working class	0.2	0.0	2.3	0.0	9.0	0.0	2.8	8.6	0.0	5.9
Employees:										
Professional and managerial	3.8	4.0	3.2	3.7	4.5	3.7	3.9	3.3	4.3	5.1
Intermediate and routine non-manual	3.7	3.6	3.5	7.2	3.8	3.9	3.5	4.4	5.1	5.7
Manual working class	5.8	5.3	4.9	8.6	3.8	3.9	4.3	7.1	6.1	7.6

Table 2.50 *Non-partisanship by trade union membership (%)*

	1963	1964	1966	1969	1970	Feb. 1974	Oct. 1974	1979	1983	1987
Per cent non-partisan:										
Respondent is a union member	3.5	4.0	–	9.4	5.2	3.9	–	5.7	4.5	4.9
Married to a union member	3.5	4.5	–	6.1	4.9	1.7	–	5.6	5.1	7.7
Neither is a union member	6.2	3.7	–	7.4	5.6	3.8	–	5.6	5.5	6.4

Table 2.51 *Non-partisanship by class and trade union membership (%)*

	1963	1964	1966	1969	1970	Feb. 1974	Oct. 1974	1979	1983	1987
Per cent non-partisan:										
Respondent is a union member:										
Professional and managerial	4.5	7.4	–	0.0	5.0	3.7	–	5.0	2.9	2.8
Intermediate and routine non-manual	5.7	8.7	–	10.0	8.3	3.6	–	4.5	6.5	5.4
Manual working class	4.1	3.7	–	9.9	7.1	4.0	–	6.4	6.2	5.8
Respondent is not a union member:										
Professional and managerial	3.4	6.6	–	4.8	7.7	3.2	–	2.6	5.6	5.3
Intermediate and routine non-manual	8.3	7.5	–	7.6	7.3	3.7	–	4.8	5.2	5.9
Manual working class	9.3	5.5	–	7.3	7.8	3.2	–	7.2	5.0	8.1

Table 2.52 *Non-partisanship by economic sector (%)*

	1963	1964	1966	1969	1970	Feb. 1974	Oct. 1974	1979	1983	1987
Per cent non-partisan:										
Works in:										
Private sector	–	–	–	–	–	–	3.3	4.3	3.9	6.2
Public sector	–	–	–	–	–	–	4.1	6.6	5.9	6.3

Table 2.53 *Non-partisanship by class and economic sector (%)*

	1963	1964	1966	1969	1970	Feb. 1974	Oct. 1974	1979	1983	1987
Per cent non-partisan:										
Professional and managerial										
Private sector	–	–	–	–	–	–	6.7	2.7	3.8	4.7
Public sector	–	–	–	–	–	–	2.4	5.2	4.6	5.5
Intermediate and routine non-manual										
Private sector	–	–	–	–	–	–	4.0	4.7	5.0	5.4
Public sector	–	–	–	–	–	–	3.7	5.5	5.4	5.7
Manual working class										
Private sector	–	–	–	–	–	–	3.7	8.8	6.0	7.5
Public sector	–	–	–	–	–	–	3.7	3.3	6.1	7.2

Table 2.54 *Non-partisanship by housing (%)*

	1963	1964	1966	1969	1970	Feb. 1974	Oct. 1974	1979	1983	1987
Per cent non-partisan:										
Owner occupiers	4.6	4.3	–	7.2	4.4	3.8	3.6	4.5	4.9	6.0
Council tenants	5.5	3.1	–	8.9	6.0	3.0	4.5	6.8	5.4	6.4
Private tenants	5.6	3.7	–	7.6	6.8	4.0	4.0	7.0	6.8	4.4

Table 2.55 *Non-partisanship by school leaving age (%)*

	1963	1964	1966	1969	1970	Feb. 1974	Oct. 1974	1979	1983	1987
Per cent non-partisan:										
Left school										
Under 15	5.4	3.4	4.3	5.5	3.3	3.0	3.4	5.1	4.4	5.4
At 15	5.5	4.6	7.3	14.4	10.1	4.1	4.7	6.4	5.5	7.5
At 16	3.8	2.8	5.7	4.1	2.8	4.1	3.5	5.7	7.8	7.8
At 17	3.5	4.2	1.6	3.4	6.8	0.7	4.9	3.3	2.9	2.5
18 or over	5.5	6.0	6.0	8.1	5.9	6.5	3.6	6.6	3.0	6.2

Table 2.56 *Non-partisanship: educated at university or polytechnic (%)*

	1963	1964	1966	1969	1970	Feb. 1974	Oct. 1974	1979	1983	1987
Per cent non-partisan:										
University or polytechnic educated	6.3	13.5	–	4.9	7.7	–	–	–	4.0	–

Table 2.57 *Non-partisanship by type of school attended (%)*

	1963	1964	1966	1969	1970	Feb. 1974	Oct. 1974	1979	1983	1987
Per cent non-partisan:										
Non-selective state school	5.5	3.9	5.6	8.2	5.3	3.6	3.6	6.7	5.6	5.7
Selective state school	4.0	4.0	3.7	6.8	5.1	3.7	4.0	4.1	3.6	4.6
Private school	4.4	0.9	2.4	2.1	1.4	3.6	3.5	3.4	3.9	2.8

Table 2.58 *Non-partisanship by religion (%)*

	1963	1964	1966	1969	1970	Feb. 1974	Oct. 1974	1979	1983	1987
Per cent non-partisan:										
Anglicans	4.9	2.9	3.9	6.0	5.4	–	3.2	3.5	3.7	4.3
Non-conformists	3.3	4.0	4.1	10.2	6.2	–	2.8	2.7	3.9	4.2
Roman Catholics	5.9	4.2	8.1	8.5	4.7	–	5.4	7.3	3.3	6.1
No religious affiliation	6.5	4.3	10.1	24.0	7.5	–	4.4	7.0	7.5	8.3

Table 2.59 *Non-partisanship by religiosity (%)*

	1963	1964	1966	1969	1970	Feb. 1974	Oct. 1974	1979	1983	1987
Per cent non-partisan:										
Attends church										
Regularly	4.5	4.6	6.3	5.9	2.9	–	–	4.1	5.3	7.6
Occasionally	4.4	2.9	4.5	6.4	5.1	–	–	4.5	3.7	4.9
Rarely	5.1	3.5	5.3	8.3	6.1	–	–	5.6	3.5	3.9
Never	7.5	4.7	4.2	7.5	6.4	–	–	8.4	4.9	4.6

Table 2.60 *Non-partisanship by region (%)*

	1963	1964	1966	1969	1970	Feb. 1974	Oct. 1974	1979	1983	1987
Per cent non-partisan:										
Scotland	5.3	4.6	8.6	6.0	7.6	4.1	5.9	5.3	7.5	9.9
Wales	7.1	2.1	3.5	10.9	9.6	1.6	1.7	5.2	4.4	5.0
The North	4.9	4.0	4.5	8.9	3.8	4.3	4.7	3.4	4.1	4.2
The Midlands	5.4	3.6	6.5	7.0	6.0	3.1	3.9	8.6	7.2	5.5
Greater London	5.9	5.1	4.5	8.0	6.3	4.2	4.1	7.3	6.5	7.0
The South	5.1	2.9	4.1	6.8	4.9	2.9	3.1	5.4	4.2	7.1

Chapter 3

PARTY MEMBERSHIP

1. Questions on party membership were not asked in 1966, 1970, February 1974 and 1979.
2. The category 'member of a political party' excludes members of political organisations other than parties and those who belong to the Labour Party solely through paying the political levy to their trade union. It includes members of parties other than the Conservative Party and Labour Party.

See appendix E, p. 473 on the construction of the party membership variable.

Table 3.1 *Party membership: all respondents (%)*

	1963	1964	1966	1969	1970	Feb. 1974	Oct. 1974	1979	1983	1987
All parties	9.4	10.0	–	6.2	–	–	6.8	–	6.5	5.8
Conservative Party	5.3	7.0	–	3.9	–	–	4.4	–	4.1	3.8
Labour Party	3.4	2.1	–	1.0	–	–	1.3	–	1.3	1.2

Table 3.2 *Party membership by gender (%)*

	1963	1964	1966	1969	1970	Feb. 1974	Oct. 1974	1979	1983	1987
Men										
All parties	9.2	12.3	–	5.7	–	–	7.7	–	7.3	5.6
Conservative Party	4.8	8.9	–	3.4	–	–	4.7	–	4.5	3.7
Labour Party	3.7	2.4	–	1.3	–	–	1.5	–	1.5	1.2
Women										
All parties	8.2	9.3	–	6.8	–	–	5.9	–	5.7	5.8
Conservative Party	5.3	6.9	–	4.4	–	–	4.2	–	3.8	2.8
Labour Party	2.1	1.4	–	0.7	–	–	1.1	–	1.1	0.9

Table 3.3 *Party membership by age (%)*

	1963	1964	1966	1969	1970	Feb. 1974	Oct. 1974	1979	1983	1987
Aged under 25										
All parties	0.8	3.9	–	3.6	–	–	1.8	–	1.6	2.5
Conservative Party	0.3	1.9	–	1.8	–	–	0.4	–	0.7	0.8
Labour Party	0.3	0.3	–	0.9	–	–	0.0	–	0.5	0.4
Aged 25–34										
All parties	3.9	6.3	–	3.7	–	–	4.0	–	3.7	2.8
Conservative Party	2.1	4.1	–	1.2	–	–	1.7	–	1.7	0.9
Labour Party	1.6	1.2	–	0.6	–	–	1.3	–	0.9	0.6
Aged 35–44										
All parties	7.2	7.6	–	7.1	–	–	7.2	–	5.6	4.5
Conservative Party	3.7	4.1	–	4.9	–	–	4.2	–	2.8	1.9
Labour Party	2.8	1.7	–	1.1	–	–	1.5	–	1.7	0.9
Aged 45–54										
All parties	9.1	13.1	–	7.0	–	–	8.1	–	9.3	5.5
Conservative Party	5.8	8.2	–	4.3	–	–	4.9	–	5.7	2.8
Labour Party	3.0	3.8	–	2.2	–	–	1.7	–	1.4	0.7
Aged 55–64										
All parties	14.9	15.0	–	7.7	–	–	8.3	–	8.4	8.5
Conservative Party	11.5	10.8	–	6.0	–	–	6.6	–	5.4	5.2
Labour Party	2.8	2.7	–	1.1	–	–	1.1	–	1.3	1.2
Aged 65–74										
All parties	11.9	15.5	–	9.4	–	–	11.0	–	10.3	11.1
Conservative Party	8.7	10.2	–	5.7	–	–	8.2	–	8.9	8.4
Labour Party	2.3	2.7	–	0.9	–	–	2.5	–	0.5	0.6
Aged 74										
All parties	9.5	9.5	–	12.1	–	–	9.0	–	9.2	9.5
Conservative Party	6.5	6.3	–	6.9	–	–	8.2	–	6.7	6.5
Labour Party	0.0	0.0	–	0.0	–	–	0.0	–	2.1	1.0

Table 3.4 *Party membership by age and gender (%)*

	1963	1964	1966	1969	1970	Feb. 1974	Oct. 1974	1979	1983	1987
Men aged under 25										
All parties	2.0	6.9	–	5.3	–	–	3.6	–	1.7	2.9
Conservative Party	0.7	2.9	–	1.8	–	–	0.7	–	0.7	1.0
Labour Party	0.6	0.7	–	1.8	–	–	0.0	–	0.3	0.6
Women aged under 25										
All parties	0.0	1.3	–	1.8	–	–	0.0	–	1.5	1.6
Conservative Party	0.0	0.8	–	1.8	–	–	0.0	–	0.8	0.8
Labour Party	0.0	0.0	–	0.0	–	–	0.0	–	0.7	0.2
Men aged 25–44										
All parties	6.7	8.6	–	5.1	–	–	5.7	–	5.6	3.3
Conservative Party	3.7	4.0	–	2.8	–	–	2.6	–	3.1	2.1
Labour Party	1.8	2.2	–	1.1	–	–	1.5	–	1.5	0.2
Women aged 25–44										
All parties	4.9	5.9	–	5.9	–	–	5.2	–	3.7	4.0
Conservative Party	2.9	2.8	–	3.6	–	–	3.1	–	1.5	1.9
Labour Party	1.1	1.4	–	0.6	–	–	1.2	–	1.7	0.7
Men aged 45–64										
All parties	11.7	15.6	–	6.2	–	–	9.8	–	9.9	7.4
Conservative Party	8.3	10.7	–	4.5	–	–	6.5	–	5.4	4.3
Labour Party	2.7	3.0	–	1.7	–	–	1.8	–	2.0	1.1
Women aged 45–64										
All parties	11.9	12.7	–	8.4	–	–	6.5	–	7.9	7.2
Conservative Party	8.8	9.1	–	5.8	–	–	5.0	–	5.6	5.5
Labour Party	1.9	1.8	–	1.6	–	–	1.0	–	0.8	0.7
Men aged over 64										
All parties	11.3	14.6	–	11.3	–	–	11.5	–	11.6	11.4
Conservative Party	7.6	8.3	–	6.5	–	–	9.3	–	9.7	9.6
Labour Party	1.3	1.6	–	1.6	–	–	1.6	–	1.5	1.1
Women aged over 64										
All parties	11.0	12.6	–	9.8	–	–	9.4	–	8.7	9.9
Conservative Party	8.1	8.9	–	5.9	–	–	7.3	–	7.0	7.0
Labour Party	0.7	0.4	–	0.0	–	–	1.7	–	0.7	0.2

Table 3.5 *Party membership by marital status (%)*

	1963	1964	1966	1969	1970	Feb. 1974	Oct. 1974	1979	1983	1987
Single										
All parties	5.2	10.2	–	4.6	–	–	–	–	2.8	4.5
Conservative Party	2.7	6.4	–	2.7	–	–	–	–	1.6	3.2
Labour Party	1.5	1.1	–	0.4	–	–	–	–	0.7	0.4
Married										
All parties	9.2	11.2	–	6.8	–	–	–	–	7.2	6.3
Conservative Party	5.4	7.9	–	4.2	–	–	–	–	4.6	3.9
Labour Party	3.8	2.8	–	1.3	–	–	–	–	1.5	1.3

Table 3.6 *Party membership: new electors (%)*

	1963	1964	1966	1969	1970	Feb. 1974	Oct. 1974	1979	1983	1987
New electors										
All parties	0.8	7.3	–	6.0	–	–	–	–	1.9	0.7
Conservative Party	0.3	3.0	–	3.0	–	–	–	–	1.3	0.3
Labour Party	0.3	2.8	–	1.5	–	–	–	–	0.3	0.1

Table 3.7 *Party membership by political generation (%)*

	1963	1964	1966	1969	1970	Feb. 1974	Oct. 1974	1979	1983	1987
First voted 1918–1935										
All parties	11.9	14.5	–	7.9	–	–	9.9	–	10.4	9.0
Conservative Party	7.4	9.9	–	5.1	–	–	7.9	–	8.5	8.0
Labour Party	1.9	2.3	–	0.9	–	–	1.5	–	1.3	0.6
First voted 1936–1950										
All parties	8.5	9.5	–	7.2	–	–	8.4	–	8.6	10.6
Conservative Party	5.6	5.7	–	5.0	–	–	5.7	–	6.0	6.2
Labour Party	1.9	1.9	–	1.4	–	–	1.6	–	1.1	1.1
First voted 1951–1970										
All parties	3.1	5.8	–	4.5	–	–	5.2	–	6.7	5.4
Conservative Party	1.9	3.8	–	2.3	–	–	2.7	–	4.0	3.2
Labour Party	0.8	1.1	–	0.9	–	–	1.3	–	1.3	1.0
First voted after 1970										
All parties	–	–	–	–	–	–	2.3	–	2.7	2.6
Conservative Party	–	–	–	–	–	–	0.6	–	0.6	0.5
Labour Party	–	–	–	–	–	–	1.3	–	1.7	1.7

Table 3.8 *Party membership: non-voters (%)*

	1963	1964	1966	1969	1970	Feb. 1974	Oct. 1974	1979	1983	1987
All parties	–	4.5	–	–	–	–	2.0	–	3.1	1.5
Conservative Party	–	3.5	–	–	–	–	1.2	–	2.6	1.0
Labour Party	–	0.5	–	–	–	–	0.6	–	0.1	0.5

Table 3.9 *Party membership by vote (%)*

	1963	1964	1966	1969	1970	Feb. 1974	Oct. 1974	1979	1983	1987
Conservative voters										
All parties	15.2	18.0	–	8.2	–	–	13.7	–	9.8	9.8
Conservative Party	14.7	17.4	–	8.1	–	–	13.7	–	9.8	9.8
Labour Party	0.0	0.0	–	0.0	–	–	0.0	–	0.0	0.0
Labour voters										
All parties	5.8	5.9	–	4.4	–	–	3.3	–	5.5	4.6
Conservative Party	0.2	0.3	–	0.0	–	–	0.0	–	0.0	0.0
Labour Party	5.2	5.1	–	3.4	–	–	3.1	–	5.3	4.6
Liberal voters										
All parties	5.6	9.8	–	6.1	–	–	6.0	–	5.0	3.2
Conservative Party	0.8	3.0	–	0.0	–	–	1.1	–	0.4	0.1
Labour Party	0.4	0.0	–	0.0	–	–	0.6	–	0.1	0.1
Voters for other parties										
All parties	(50.0)	(18.6)	–	15.8	–	–	10.1	–	4.3	2.3
Conservative Party	(0.0)	(10.0)	–	0.0	–	–	1.4	–	0.0	0.0
Labour Party	(0.0)	(0.0)	–	0.0	–	–	0.0	–	0.0	0.0

Table 3.10 *Party membership by strength and direction of partisanship (%)*

	1963	1964	1966	1969	1970	Feb. 1974	Oct. 1974	1979	1983	1987
Very strong Conservative identifiers										
All parties	20.1	21.7	–	13.3	–	–	19.1	–	21.7	23.4
Conservative Party	20.1	21.7	–	13.3	–	–	18.6	–	21.7	23.4
Labour Party	0.0	0.0	–	0.0	–	–	0.0	–	0.0	0.0
Fairly strong Conservative identifiers										
All parties	13.2	14.1	–	7.1	–	–	12.9	–	8.2	7.0
Conservative Party	13.2	14.1	–	6.6	–	–	12.6	–	8.2	7.0
Labour Party	0.0	0.0	–	0.0	–	–	0.2	–	0.0	0.0
Not very strong Conservative identifiers										
All parties	7.2	8.7	–	6.5	–	–	3.2	–	2.6	2.1
Conservative Party	7.2	8.7	–	6.5	–	–	3.2	–	2.6	2.1
Labour Party	0.0	0.0	–	0.0	–	–	0.0	–	0.0	0.0
Very strong Liberal identifiers										
All parties	10.7	18.9	–	16.7	–	–	15.6	–	25.0	25.4
Conservative Party	1.8	3.0	–	0.0	–	–	0.0	–	0.0	0.0
Labour Party	0.0	0.0	–	0.0	–	–	0.0	–	0.0	0.0
Fairly strong Liberal identifiers										
All parties	6.6	3.8	–	7.0	–	–	3.2	–	5.8	3.3
Conservative Party	0.0	1.0	–	0.0	–	–	1.0	–	1.0	0.0
Labour Party	0.0	0.0	–	0.0	–	–	0.0	–	0.0	0.0
Not very strong Liberal identifiers										
All parties	2.8	11.1	–	4.8	–	–	3.3	–	1.9	0.3
Conservative Party	1.4	8.3	–	0.0	–	–	0.8	–	1.5	0.3
Labour Party	0.0	0.0	–	0.0	–	–	0.0	–	0.0	0.0
Very strong Labour identifiers										
All parties	9.8	8.4	–	7.4	–	–	6.5	–	9.4	10.7
Conservative Party	0.0	0.0	–	0.0	–	–	0.0	–	0.0	0.0
Labour Party	9.2	7.8	–	7.4	–	–	6.5	–	9.4	10.7

Table 3.10 (*cont.*)

	1963	1964	1966	1969	1970	Feb. 1974	Oct. 1974	1979	1983	1987
Fairly strong Labour identifiers										
All parties	3.3	3.7	–	2.9	–	–	1.3	–	2.5	2.6
Conservative Party	0.3	0.0	–	0.1	–	–	0.0	–	0.0	0.0
Labour Party	3.0	2.8	–	2.1	–	–	1.3	–	2.5	2.6
Not very strong Labour identifiers										
All parties	3.3	2.9	–	0.0	–	–	0.5	–	0.5	0.5
Conservative Party	0.5	1.0	–	0.0	–	–	0.0	–	0.0	0.0
Labour Party	2.8	1.0	–	0.0	–	–	0.0	–	0.5	0.0

Table 3.11 *Party membership by social class (%)*

	1963	1964	1966	1969	1970	Feb. 1974	Oct. 1974	1979	1983	1987
Professional and managerial classes										
All parties	19.3	26.1	–	15.9	–	–	14.7	–	12.5	10.5
Conservative Party	13.5	19.5	–	11.3	–	–	10.8	–	9.6	7.4
Labour Party	2.3	1.8	–	1.9	–	–	1.7	–	0.8	0.6
Intermediate and routine non-manual classes										
All parties	10.1	12.0	–	7.4	–	–	7.3	–	6.8	6.3
Conservative Party	7.2	8.0	–	5.5	–	–	5.1	–	4.2	4.0
Labour Party	0.9	1.1	–	1.2	–	–	1.1	–	0.5	0.2
Manual working class										
All parties	6.3	5.9	–	2.3	–	–	4.0	–	3.0	2.8
Conservative Party	2.0	2.3	–	1.1	–	–	2.0	–	1.5	1.2
Labour Party	3.4	5.5	–	0.6	–	–	1.3	–	1.5	1.2

Chapter 4

THE ELECTORAL DECISION

1. Questions on the electoral decision were not asked in 1963 or 1969 because no general election was held in those two years.
2. In 1983 and 1987 the Liberal Party contested the election in an electoral alliance with the SDP. In these two years wavering towards the Liberal Party includes those who said that they wavered towards the SDP or the Alliance.
3. Respondents who thought of voting for two or more parties other than the one they eventually voted for are coded as 'other'.

See Appendix E, pp. 485 and 499 on the construction of the campaign wavering and time of voting decision variables.

Table 4.1   Campaign wavering: all respondents
Table 4.2   Campaign wavering by gender
Table 4.3   Campaign wavering by age
Table 4.4   Campaign wavering by marital status
Table 4.5   Campaign wavering: new electors
Table 4.6   Campaign wavering by vote
Table 4.7   Campaign wavering by strength and direction of partisanship
Table 4.8   Campaign wavering: non-partisans
Table 4.9   Campaign wavering by social class
Table 4.10 Campaign wavering by employment status
Table 4.11 Campaign wavering: unemployed
Table 4.12 Campaign wavering by region
Table 4.13 Time of voting decision: all respondents
Table 4.14 Time of voting decision by gender
Table 4.15 Time of voting decision by age
Table 4.16 Time of voting decision by marital status
Table 4.17 Time of voting decision: new electors
Table 4.18 Time of voting decision by vote
Table 4.19 Time of voting decision by strength and direction of partisanship
Table 4.20 Time of voting decision: non-partisans
Table 4.21 Time of voting decision by social class
Table 4.22 Time of voting decision by employment status
Table 4.23 Time of voting decision: unemployed
Table 4.24 Time of voting decision by region

Table 4.1 *Campaign wavering: all respondents (%)*

	1964	1966	1969	1970	Feb. 1974	Oct. 1974	1979	1983	1987
Considered voting for									
Conservative Party	4.8	3.3	–	4.3	4.9	5.3	8.6	6.2	6.9
Labour Party	3.5	3.5	–	3.0	4.2	3.6	6.1	4.7	5.3
Liberal Party	15.1	13.9	–	12.0	13.9	10.5	12.7	13.1	13.4
Other party	1.1	1.7	–	1.7	1.6	1.8	2.9	0.9	1.3
No other party	75.5	77.6	–	79.0	75.4	78.9	69.6	75.0	73.1
Total	100.0	100.0	–	100.0	100.0	100.0	100.0	100.0	100.0
N. of respondents	1547	1502	–	1423	2061	1784	1594	3138	3146

Table 4.2 *Campaign wavering by gender (%)*

Men									
	1964	1966	1969	1970	Feb. 1974	Oct. 1974	1979	1983	1987
Considered voting for									
Conservative Party	4.9	3.8	–	4.3	4.4	4.6	8.7	5.4	6.9
Labour Party	3.6	3.9	–	3.5	4.3	3.6	5.1	4.7	6.1
Liberal Party	16.5	15.1	–	11.7	12.0	9.0	12.5	13.0	11.2
Other party	1.7	1.7	–	2.3	2.0	1.8	3.8	1.2	1.2
No other party	73.3	75.5	–	78.2	77.3	80.9	68.8	75.7	74.6
Total	100.0	100.0	–	100.0	100.0	100.0	100.0	100.0	100.0
N. of respondents	719	709	–	674	988	885	767	1461	1496

Women									
	1964	1966	1969	1970	Feb. 1974	Oct. 1974	1979	1983	1987
Considered voting for									
Conservative Party	4.7	2.8	–	4.3	5.4	5.9	8.5	7.0	7.0
Labour Party	3.4	3.3	–	2.6	4.2	3.6	6.2	4.7	4.6
Liberal Party	14.0	12.8	–	12.2	15.6	11.9	12.9	13.2	15.3
Other party	0.6	1.8	–	1.2	1.2	1.8	2.1	0.7	1.4
No other party	77.3	79.4	–	79.7	73.6	76.9	70.4	74.4	71.7
Total	100.0	100.0	–	100.0	100.0	100.0	100.0	100.0	100.0
N. of respondents	828	793	–	749	1073	899	827	1676	1630

Table 4.3 *Campaign wavering by age*

	Aged under 25								
	1964	1966	1969	1970	Feb. 1974	Oct. 1974	1979	1983	1987
Considered voting for									
Conservative Party	6.5	1.9	–	6.7	4.2	4.4	12.3	8.7	6.8
Labour Party	6.5	5.2	–	6.9	7.9	4.4	12.3	6.1	6.9
Liberal Party	19.4	15.9	–	19.7	15.3	13.8	18.9	15.7	17.1
Other party	1.0	2.6	–	4.3	1.1	3.3	3.3	2.2	2.4
No other party	66.7	74.4	–	62.3	71.6	74.0	53.3	67.4	66.8
Total	100.0	100.0	–	100.0	100.0	100.0	100.0	100.0	100.0
N. of respondents	93	93	–	188	190	181	122	386	360

	Aged 25–34								
	1964	1966	1969	1970	Feb. 1974	Oct. 1974	1979	1983	1987
Considered voting for									
Conservative Party	6.3	5.6	–	5.7	7.3	7.4	9.1	8.1	9.0
Labour Party	6.2	7.2	–	4.1	3.7	4.8	8.5	5.8	6.2
Liberal Party	19.2	16.8	–	12.0	17.6	12.2	18.4	14.6	15.2
Other party	2.1	3.0	–	1.8	2.9	3.4	2.6	0.5	1.4
No other party	66.3	67.3	–	76.4	68.5	72.2	61.4	71.0	68.3
Total	100.0	100.0	–	100.0	100.0	100.0	100.0	100.0	100.0
N. of respondents	239	245	–	215	381	352	342	554	565

	Aged 35–44								
	1964	1966	1969	1970	Feb. 1974	Oct. 1974	1979	1983	1987
Considered voting for									
Conservative Party	7.3	3.2	–	6.0	4.7	6.8	11.5	8.6	7.7
Labour Party	2.9	2.4	–	3.0	5.8	4.5	4.3	5.1	6.3
Liberal Party	17.0	18.6	–	11.5	13.9	11.3	11.8	13.0	14.9
Other party	1.5	1.7	–	2.9	2.8	1.9	3.9	1.2	1.5
No other party	71.3	74.0	–	76.6	72.7	75.5	68.5	72.2	69.7
Total	100.0	100.0	–	100.0	100.0	100.0	100.0	100.0	100.0
N. of respondents	342	310	–	248	359	310	279	603	624

	Aged 45–54								
	1964	1966	1969	1970	Feb. 1974	Oct. 1974	1979	1983	1987
Considered voting for									
Conservative Party	4.4	3.5	–	2.4	5.0	5.9	8.4	7.3	6.4
Labour Party	4.4	4.1	–	3.7	3.4	2.8	6.1	3.6	4.0
Liberal Party	17.4	13.0	–	11.9	13.9	6.5	7.7	12.6	11.5
Other party	1.6	1.7	–	0.8	1.6	1.2	3.2	1.1	1.8
No other party	72.2	77.6	–	81.2	76.1	83.5	74.6	75.5	76.3
Total	100.0	100.0	–	100.0	100.0	100.0	100.0	100.0	100.0
N. of respondents	316	323	–	247	380	321	311	534	493

Table 4.3 (*cont.*)

	Aged 55–64								
	1964	1966	1969	1970	Feb. 1974	Oct. 1974	1979	1983	1987
Considered voting for									
Conservative Party	3.5	1.9	–	2.5	4.7	4.8	7.9	3.0	6.1
Labour Party	2.1	1.7	–	1.6	5.0	2.1	5.0	4.6	5.3
Liberal Party	12.5	12.3	–	13.8	12.6	13.1	10.0	13.8	13.3
Other party	0.3	1.5	–	0.4	0.0	0.7	2.9	0.8	0.6
No other party	81.5	82.7	–	81.7	77.8	79.3	74.1	77.8	74.7
Total	100.0	100.0	–	100.0	100.0	100.0	100.0	100.0	100.0
N. of respondents	267	279	–	262	348	290	239	497	518

	Aged 65–74								
	1964	1966	1969	1970	Feb. 1974	Oct. 1974	1979	1983	1987
Considered voting for									
Conservative Party	0.5	3.9	–	4.1	3.8	1.4	5.9	2.3	5.0
Labour Party	1.1	1.6	–	0.0	1.1	2.8	4.3	3.3	3.9
Liberal Party	9.3	8.6	–	5.6	12.8	8.3	14.9	10.6	8.3
Other party	0.0	0.6	–	0.5	1.1	0.9	1.6	0.0	0.8
No other party	89.0	85.4	–	89.9	81.1	86.7	73.4	83.9	82.0
Total	100.0	100.0	–	100.0	100.0	100.0	100.0	100.0	100.0
N. of respondents	182	174	–	185	265	218	188	350	357

	Aged over 74								
	1964	1966	1969	1970	Feb. 1974	Oct. 1974	1979	1983	1987
Considered voting for									
Conservative Party	2.3	0.0	–	1.8	0.0	2.8	2.8	2.0	5.0
Labour Party	1.1	3.2	–	1.1	1.6	3.8	2.8	3.1	2.3
Liberal Party	5.7	4.9	–	2.9	7.1	4.7	7.5	8.6	9.7
Other party	0.0	0.0	–	1.1	0.8	0.0	1.9	0.0	0.5
No other party	90.8	91.9	–	93.0	90.5	88.7	85.0	86.4	82.5
Total	100.0	100.0	–	100.0	100.0	100.0	100.0	100.0	100.0
N. of respondents	87	79	–	78	126	106	107	198	203

Table 4.4 *Campaign wavering by marital status (%)*

	Single								
	1964	1966	1969	1970	Feb. 1974	Oct. 1974	1979	1983	1987
Considered voting for									
Conservative Party	4.4	4.3	–	5.1	4.0	–	13.2	8.1	6.2
Labour Party	2.2	6.6	–	5.8	6.8	–	9.9	5.8	5.3
Liberal Party	18.3	14.8	–	19.0	12.9	–	12.6	14.5	16.3
Other party	0.5	3.5	–	2.1	1.1	–	5.5	1.8	0.0
No other party	74.5	70.8	–	68.0	75.2	–	58.8	69.7	72.3
Total	100.0	100.0	–	100.0	100.0	–	100.0	100.0	100.0
N. of respondents	180	143	–	235	278	–	182	507	528

	Married								
	1964	1966	1969	1970	Feb. 1974	Oct. 1974	1979	1983	1987
Considered voting for									
Conservative Party	5.1	3.5	–	4.7	5.1	5.5	8.7	6.1	7.1
Labour Party	3.8	3.4	–	2.7	3.8	4.0	5.6	4.6	5.2
Liberal Party	15.3	14.5	–	10.7	14.3	10.4	13.0	12.9	12.7
Other party	1.3	1.7	–	1.6	1.7	1.7	2.0	0.8	1.1
No other party	74.4	77.0	–	80.3	75.0	78.4	70.7	75.6	73.8
Total	100.0	100.0	–	100.0	100.0	100.0	100.0	100.0	100.0
N. of respondents	1200	1181	–	1014	1539	1360	1158	2237	2193

	Divorced and separated								
	1964	1966	1969	1970	Feb. 1974	Oct. 1974	1979	1983	1987
Considered voting for									
Conservative Party	–	(0.0)	–	–	(10.0)	–	4.7	8.7	9.1
Labour Party	–	(0.0)	–	–	(5.0)	–	7.8	5.5	8.5
Liberal Party	–	(17.9)	–	–	(20.0)	–	12.5	15.8	15.2
Other party	–	(0.0)	–	–	(0.0)	–	4.7	1.3	1.3
No other party	–	(82.1)	–	–	(65.0)	–	70.3	68.6	65.9
Total	–	(100.0)	–	–	(100.0)	–	100.0	100.0	100.0
N. of respondents	–	11	–	–	20	–	64	146	147

	Widowed								
	1964	1966	1969	1970	Feb. 1974	Oct. 1974	1979	1983	1987
Considered voting for									
Conservative Party	–	0.7	–	–	4.0	–	5.3	1.9	5.5
Labour Party	–	2.5	–	–	3.6	–	5.9	3.2	4.3
Liberal Party	–	9.1	–	–	11.6	–	12.4	10.4	12.0
Other party	–	0.5	–	–	1.8	–	5.9	0.0	1.0
No other party	–	87.3	–	–	79.0	–	70.6	84.5	77.1
Total	–	100.0	–	–	100.0	–	100.0	100.0	100.0
N. of respondents	–	166	–	–	224	–	170	247	277

Table 4.5 *Campaign wavering: new electors (%)*

	1964	1966	1969	1970	Feb. 1974	Oct. 1974	1979	1983	1987
Considered voting for									
Conservative Party	7.5	1.9	–	6.7	6.5	–	12.9	9.8	6.6
Labour Party	5.0	5.8	–	6.9	9.7	–	14.0	4.6	6.9
Liberal Party	17.5	13.4	–	19.7	12.9	–	16.1	18.6	18.6
Other party	1.7	3.8	–	4.3	1.6	–	3.2	2.6	3.5
No other party	68.3	75.1	–	62.3	69.4	–	53.8	64.3	64.4
Total	100.0	100.0	–	100.0	100.0	–	100.0	100.0	100.0
N. of respondents	120	42	–	188	62	–	93	218	190

Table 4.6 *Campaign wavering by vote (%)*

Conservative voters									
	1964	1966	1969	1970	Feb. 1974	Oct. 1974	1979	1983	1987
Considered voting for									
Conservative Party	–	–	–	–	–	–	–	–	–
Labour Party	4.4	4.6	–	2.8	3.7	4.3	6.6	2.8	3.7
Liberal Party	18.9	15.7	–	13.1	19.4	15.1	15.0	16.4	16.4
Other party	0.5	1.1	–	1.0	1.0	0.9	2.6	0.4	0.3
No other party	76.2	78.6	–	83.1	75.9	79.7	75.7	80.4	79.6
Total	100.0	100.0	–	100.0	100.0	100.0	100.0	100.0	100.0
N. of respondents	655	603	–	654	783	655	731	1423	1395

Labour voters									
	1964	1966	1969	1970	Feb. 1974	Oct. 1974	1979	1983	1987
Considered voting for									
Conservative Party	5.3	3.7	–	5.7	6.2	3.9	13.7	7.2	7.9
Labour Party	–	–	–	–	–	–	–	–	–
Liberal Party	15.2	14.9	–	13.6	15.9	10.9	14.4	19.3	19.0
Other party	1.5	2.3	–	2.2	2.5	2.6	2.1	1.9	2.7
No other party	78.0	79.1	–	78.5	75.4	82.6	69.8	71.7	70.4
Total	100.0	100.0	–	100.0	100.0	100.0	100.0	100.0	100.0
N. of respondents	730	768	–	634	837	770	584	903	984

Table 4.6 (*cont.*)

	Liberal voters								
	1964	1966	1969	1970	Feb. 1974	Oct. 1974	1979	1983	1987
Considered voting for									
Conservative Party	21.6	15.8	–	21.4	11.0	18.1	22.5	16.5	18.5
Labour Party	15.4	18.9	–	19.7	12.8	9.5	21.6	13.0	14.7
Liberal Party	–	–	–	–	–	–	–	–	–
Other party	1.9	0.9	–	0.8	1.0	1.6	2.8	1.0	1.4
No other party	61.1	64.4	–	58.1	75.1	70.7	53.1	69.5	65.4
Total	100.0	100.0	–	100.0	100.0	100.0	100.0	100.0	100.0
N. of respondents	163	128	–	106	390	304	213	770	726

	Voters for other parties								
	1964	1966	1969	1970	Feb. 1974	Oct. 1974	1979	1983	1987
Considered voting for									
Conservative Party	–	–	–	7.3	8.7	16.4	12.0	8.9	14.3
Labour Party	–	–	–	10.2	15.2	7.3	4.0	20.9	21.7
Liberal Party	–	–	–	0.0	0.0	7.3	24.0	7.2	9.5
Other party	–	–	–	7.9	0.0	1.8	0.0	0.0	2.4
No other party	–	–	–	74.7	76.1	67.3	60.0	63.0	52.2
Total	–	–	–	100.0	100.0	100.0	100.0	100.0	100.0
N. of respondents	–	–	–	29	46	55	25	41	41

Table 4.7 *Campaign wavering by strength and direction of partisanship (%)*

	Very strong Conservative identifiers								
	1964	1966	1969	1970	Feb. 1974	Oct. 1974	1979	1983	1987
Considered voting for									
Conservative Party	0.6	1.1	–	0.9	0.4	2.6	1.3	0.6	1.6
Labour Party	1.0	0.8	–	0.3	0.4	1.0	1.3	0.6	0.0
Liberal Party	8.7	5.2	–	4.6	6.9	4.7	5.6	4.2	5.2
Other party	0.0	0.6	–	1.0	0.8	0.5	1.3	0.0	0.0
No other party	89.6	92.4	–	93.2	91.5	91.1	90.6	94.5	93.2
Total	100.0	100.0	–	100.0	100.0	100.0	100.0	100.0	100.0
N. of respondents	309	293	–	321	259	191	160	310	304

Table 4.7 (*cont.*)

| | | | | | Feb. | Oct. | | | |
| | 1964 | 1966 | 1969 | 1970 | 1974 | 1974 | 1979 | 1983 | 1987 |

Fairly strong Conservative identifiers

	1964	1966	1969	1970	Feb. 1974	Oct. 1974	1979	1983	1987
Considered voting for									
Conservative Party	4.1	2.7	–	3.6	4.5	5.7	4.3	2.5	4.8
Labour Party	5.3	4.8	–	2.5	2.0	1.7	4.0	1.7	0.8
Liberal Party	22.9	16.7	–	15.2	18.1	13.1	13.2	11.7	14.4
Other party	0.0	1.1	–	0.8	1.3	1.4	1.4	0.2	0.5
No other party	67.8	74.7	–	78.0	74.1	78.0	77.1	83.9	79.6
Total	100.0	100.0	–	100.0	100.0	100.0	100.0	100.0	100.0
N. of respondents	245	214	–	227	898	350	349	589	641

Not very strong Conservative identifiers

	1964	1966	1969	1970	Feb. 1974	Oct. 1974	1979	1983	1987
Considered voting for									
Conservative Party	11.1	5.5	–	7.9	8.9	10.6	7.5	5.2	12.6
Labour Party	9.7	12.5	–	6.2	4.1	8.1	10.7	3.1	5.5
Liberal Party	22.2	23.1	–	23.0	24.7	17.1	20.8	23.5	15.2
Other party	2.8	2.1	–	3.0	2.1	0.8	5.7	0.6	0.4
No other party	54.2	56.8	–	59.9	60.3	63.4	55.3	67.6	66.3
Total	100.0	100.0	–	100.0	100.0	100.0	100.0	100.0	100.0
N. of respondents	72	78	–	65	146	123	159	327	257

Very strong Liberal identifiers

	1964	1966	1969	1970	Feb. 1974	Oct. 1974	1979	1983	1987
Considered voting for									
Conservative Party	4.8	5.8	–	6.6	8.8	5.9	8.0	4.3	4.9
Labour Party	4.8	3.6	–	7.7	0.0	0.0	4.0	1.4	7.2
Liberal Party	14.3	35.9	–	21.4	2.9	5.4	12.0	7.1	1.8
Other party	0.0	0.0	–	2.5	0.0	0.0	4.0	1.4	0.0
No other party	76.2	54.8	–	61.9	88.2	88.2	72.0	85.7	86.0
Total	100.0	100.0	–	100.0	100.0	100.0	100.0	100.0	100.0
N. of respondents	62	52	–	35	34	34	25	70	56

Fairly strong Liberal identifiers

	1964	1966	1969	1970	Feb. 1974	Oct. 1974	1979	1983	1987
Considered voting for									
Conservative Party	14.3	8.7	–	16.7	8.5	7.2	11.2	11.2	9.6
Labour Party	5.5	9.2	–	8.6	5.9	5.8	13.3	5.2	9.3
Liberal Party	27.5	30.0	–	23.7	7.8	10.1	12.2	7.1	10.5
Other party	3.3	0.0	–	0.0	0.0	0.7	5.1	0.4	1.2
No other party	49.5	52.1	–	51.0	77.8	76.3	58.2	76.2	69.5
Total	100.0	100.0	–	100.0	100.0	100.0	100.0	100.0	100.0
N. of respondents	91	84	–	55	153	139	98	269	249

Table 4.7 (*cont.*)

	Not very strong Liberal identifiers								
	1964	1966	1969	1970	Feb. 1974	Oct. 1974	1979	1983	1987
Considered voting for									
Conservative Party	13.5	(10.5)	–	17.4	7.4	18.6	23.9	18.1	13.1
Labour Party	24.3	(10.5)	–	7.5	8.5	7.0	7.0	7.9	9.7
Liberal Party	21.6	(32.0)	–	31.5	17.0	19.8	15.5	11.8	13.2
Other party	0.0	(0.0)	–	3.2	0.0	2.3	0.0	0.0	1.2
No other party	40.5	(47.1)	–	40.4	67.0	52.3	53.5	62.2	62.9
Total	100.0	(100.0)	–	100.0	100.0	100.0	100.0	100.0	100.0
N. of respondents	37	(17)	–	27	94	86	71	254	257

	Very strong Labour identifiers								
	1964	1966	1969	1970	Feb. 1974	Oct. 1974	1979	1983	1987
Considered voting for									
Conservative Party	2.3	0.3	–	1.4	2.5	1.0	2.8	1.3	0.7
Labour Party	0.6	0.3	–	1.2	1.4	0.7	1.7	1.3	3.4
Liberal Party	6.6	7.8	–	5.5	5.5	3.8	7.3	11.3	7.8
Other party	0.9	2.3	–	1.5	0.8	0.7	2.3	1.0	1.8
No other party	89.7	89.3	–	90.5	89.9	93.8	85.9	85.1	86.3
Total	100.0	100.0	–	100.0	100.0	100.0	100.0	100.0	100.0
N. of respondents	351	371	–	312	366	288	177	309	269

	Fairly strong Labour identifiers								
	1964	1966	1969	1970	Feb. 1974	Oct. 1974	1979	1983	1987
Considered voting for									
Conservative Party	5.7	3.8	–	4.7	4.3	4.7	11.2	5.5	4.7
Labour Party	1.9	2.7	–	4.1	5.9	4.7	5.3	7.6	6.3
Liberal Party	17.1	14.6	–	17.4	18.5	10.5	14.5	18.6	19.7
Other party	1.9	3.0	–	1.5	3.2	2.5	2.3	1.7	2.1
No other party	73.4	75.9	–	72.3	68.0	77.7	66.7	66.7	67.2
Total	100.0	100.0	–	100.0	100.0	100.0	100.0	100.0	100.0
N. of respondents	263	278	–	233	372	363	303	420	435

	Not very strong Labour identifiers								
	1964	1966	1969	1970	Feb. 1974	Oct. 1974	1979	1983	1987
Considered voting for									
Conservative Party	10.8	9.2	–	14.1	9.3	1.8	16.9	11.8	13.4
Labour Party	7.7	9.2	–	5.2	14.6	7.3	14.1	11.0	11.1
Liberal Party	21.5	7.6	–	17.7	21.9	18.2	15.5	17.1	15.7
Other party	1.5	0.0	–	1.5	3.3	6.4	2.1	1.6	1.4
No other party	58.5	74.1	–	61.5	51.0	66.4	51.4	58.5	58.4
Total	100.0	100.0	–	100.0	100.0	100.0	100.0	100.0	100.0
N. of respondents	66	58	–	84	151	110	142	246	277

Table 4.8 *Campaign wavering: non-partisans (%)*

	Respondents with no party identification								
	1964	1966	1969	1970	Feb. 1974	Oct. 1974	1979	1983	1987
Considered voting for									
Conservative Party	0.0	4.0	–	13.5	6.8	17.9	11.3	11.0	7.5
Labour Party	2.1	8.9	–	5.4	9.1	12.5	7.6	7.3	7.2
Liberal Party	19.1	10.7	–	21.6	15.9	8.9	15.5	15.6	15.7
Other party	2.1	8.7	–	2.7	4.5	3.6	1.7	1.8	3.2
No other party	76.6	67.7	–	56.8	63.6	57.1	63.9	64.2	66.4
Total	100.0	100.0	–	100.0	100.0	100.0	100.0	100.0	100.0
N. of respondents	47	43	–	37	44	56	108	109	197

Table 4.9 *Campaign wavering by social class (%)*

	Professional and managerial classes								
	1964	1966	1969	1970	Feb. 1974	Oct. 1974	1979	1983	1987
Considered voting for									
Conservative Party	2.2	5.1	–	3.4	5.8	7.3	9.1	7.5	7.7
Labour Party	4.0	6.5	–	3.6	2.9	3.6	3.5	5.1	5.7
Liberal Party	19.6	19.7	–	15.6	14.3	14.2	16.7	12.0	13.2
Other party	0.4	1.8	–	2.0	0.6	1.5	3.5	0.7	1.7
No other party	73.8	66.9	–	75.5	76.3	73.4	67.3	74.6	71.7
Total	100.0	100.0	–	100.0	100.0	100.0	100.0	100.0	100.0
N. of respondents	225	205	–	258	308	274	342	855	817

	Intermediate and routine non-manual classes								
	1964	1966	1969	1970	Feb. 1974	Oct. 1974	1979	1983	1987
Considered voting for									
Conservative Party	6.4	4.1	–	4.0	5.4	5.6	7.2	7.4	7.4
Labour Party	3.4	5.0	–	4.5	4.0	4.0	7.0	4.7	4.6
Liberal Party	16.2	14.2	–	12.2	16.3	12.2	12.9	17.0	14.7
Other party	1.1	2.0	–	1.4	1.8	1.8	2.6	0.5	1.0
No other party	72.8	74.6	–	77.9	72.5	76.3	70.3	70.4	72.4
Total	100.0	100.0	–	100.0	100.0	100.0	100.0	100.0	100.0
N. of respondents	357	416	–	370	723	621	428	612	793

Table 4.9 (*cont.*)

| | Manual working class | | | | | | | | |
	1964	1966	1969	1970	Feb. 1974	Oct. 1974	1979	1983	1987
Considered voting for									
Conservative Party	4.8	2.5	–	4.6	4.7	4.3	9.5	4.8	6.5
Labour Party	3.2	2.1	–	2.2	4.5	3.4	6.3	4.7	5.5
Liberal Party	13.4	12.5	–	10.7	12.1	8.0	11.5	12.4	12.3
Other party	1.2	1.4	–	1.9	1.7	1.9	2.8	1.2	1.2
No other party	77.4	81.5	–	80.6	77.0	82.5	70.0	76.9	74.6
Total	100.0	100.0	–	100.0	100.0	100.0	100.0	100.0	100.0
N. of respondents	902	856	–	740	918	800	759	1452	1395

Table 4.10 *Campaign wavering by employment status (%)*

| | Self-employed with employees | | | | | | | | |
	1964	1966	1969	1970	Feb. 1974	Oct. 1974	1979	1983	1987
Considered voting for									
Conservative Party	4.0	5.1	–	1.8	3.7	1.8	1.9	8.3	5.9
Labour Party	4.5	0.0	–	4.9	2.4	1.8	5.8	2.4	3.6
Liberal Party	7.7	11.8	–	9.9	14.6	8.8	11.5	16.0	13.9
Other party	0.0	0.0	–	1.4	1.2	0.0	5.8	0.7	0.0
No other party	83.8	83.0	–	82.0	78.0	87.7	75.0	72.6	76.5
Total	100.0	100.0	–	100.0	100.0	100.0	100.0	100.0	100.0
N. of respondents	51	52	–	62	82	57	52	132	155
	Self-employed, no employees								
	1964	1966	1969	1970	Feb. 1974	Oct. 1974	1979	1983	1987
Considered voting for									
Conservative Party	0.0	8.5	–	0.0	5.6	3.1	5.1	4.9	9.1
Labour Party	0.0	4.0	–	0.0	1.4	4.6	5.1	1.7	4.4
Liberal Party	15.3	26.6	–	4.7	13.9	6.2	13.6	10.1	9.7
Other party	0.0	0.0	–	0.0	0.0	0.0	1.7	0.9	1.3
No other party	84.7	60.9	–	95.3	79.2	86.2	74.6	82.4	75.5
Total	100.0	100.0	–	100.0	100.0	100.0	100.0	100.0	100.0
N. of respondents	14	25	–	26	72	65	59	111	135

Table 4.10 (*cont.*)

	Managers								
	1964	1966	1969	1970	Feb. 1974	Oct. 1974	1979	1983	1987
Considered voting for									
Conservative Party	12.8	2.8	–	3.3	6.1	6.1	7.6	9.2	6.8
Labour Party	4.1	3.9	–	3.1	2.7	3.8	5.3	6.5	6.5
Liberal Party	22.1	17.1	–	13.6	13.5	9.8	12.9	12.7	10.4
Other party	0.0	4.2	–	1.0	0.7	1.5	3.8	0.0	2.6
No other party	61.0	71.9	–	79.0	77.0	78.8	70.5	71.7	73.6
Total	100.0	100.0	–	100.0	100.0	100.0	100.0	100.0	100.0
N. of respondents	56	76	–	83	148	132	132	496	311

	Foremen and supervisors								
	1964	1966	1969	1970	Feb. 1974	Oct. 1974	1979	1983	1987
Considered voting for									
Conservative Party	4.7	7.1	–	7.3	8.4	6.2	8.0	4.6	6.8
Labour Party	5.9	4.9	–	1.8	1.2	2.1	6.8	5.6	3.8
Liberal Party	17.7	14.8	–	16.8	14.5	7.2	13.0	13.1	10.1
Other party	1.4	3.9	–	3.2	0.0	0.0	1.9	1.7	0.5
No other party	70.2	69.4	–	71.0	75.9	84.5	70.4	75.0	78.9
Total	100.0	100.0	–	100.0	100.0	100.0	100.0	100.0	100.0
N. of respondents	69	86	–	93	83	97	169	383	191

	Rank and file employees								
	1964	1966	1969	1970	Feb. 1974	Oct. 1974	1979	1983	1987
Considered voting for									
Conservative Party	3.6	3.3	–	4.2	5.1	5.3	10.4	5.4	7.1
Labour Party	3.2	4.0	–	3.2	4.8	4.0	5.7	4.8	5.4
Liberal Party	13.1	14.8	–	11.2	13.7	10.7	13.1	13.5	14.0
Other party	2.2	1.8	–	1.9	2.1	2.2	3.3	1.0	1.2
No other party	77.9	76.2	–	79.6	74.3	77.7	67.5	75.3	72.4
Total	100.0	100.0	–	100.0	100.0	100.0	100.0	100.0	100.0
N. of respondents	564	771	–	745	1368	1186	787	1660	2228

Table 4.11 *Campaign wavering: unemployed (%)*

	1964	1966	1969	1970	Feb. 1974	Oct. 1974	1979	1983	1987
Considered voting for									
Conservative Party	(0.0)	(0.0)	–	0.0	2.6	3.8	7.4	8.6	5.5
Labour Party	(12.3)	(0.0)	–	0.0	7.9	3.8	11.1	4.2	4.7
Liberal Party	(12.3)	(0.0)	–	15.0	18.4	19.2	14.8	13.1	15.6
Other party	(0.0)	(0.0)	–	0.0	0.0	7.7	3.7	1.0	2.9
No other party	(75.3)	(100.0)	–	85.0	71.1	65.4	63.0	73.1	71.4
Total	100.0	100.0	–	100.0	100.0	100.0	100.0	100.0	100.0
N. of respondents	8	10	–	32	38	26	27	187	163

Table 4.12 *Campaign wavering by region (%)*

Scotland	1964	1966	1969	1970	Feb. 1974	Oct. 1974	1979	1983	1987
Considered voting for									
Conservative Party	7.1	0.7	–	2.9	2.6	5.6	9.6	5.0	6.8
Labour Party	1.9	3.1	–	5.5	4.1	3.9	5.6	5.7	7.2
Liberal Party	16.1	15.6	–	5.5	8.7	6.2	16.8	12.3	12.5
Other party	1.9	6.8	–	6.1	10.7	9.6	8.0	5.7	9.3
No other party	72.9	73.7	–	80.0	74.0	74.7	60.0	71.4	64.2
Total	100.0	100.0	–	100.0	100.0	100.0	100.0	100.0	100.0
N. of respondents	154	134	–	155	195	178	125	288	268

Wales	1964	1966	1969	1970	Feb. 1974	Oct. 1974	1979	1983	1987
Considered voting for									
Conservative Party	3.3	6.5	–	6.6	3.6	8.6	9.8	4.5	7.1
Labour Party	3.3	1.5	–	1.5	5.4	5.4	6.5	1.1	5.4
Liberal Party	3.3	10.8	–	3.5	9.9	2.2	3.3	10.7	12.5
Other party	9.8	6.8	–	2.3	5.4	3.2	6.5	2.2	1.6
No other party	80.3	74.3	–	86.0	75.7	80.6	73.9	81.5	73.4
Total	100.0	100.0	–	100.0	100.0	100.0	100.0	100.0	100.0
N. of respondents	61	65	–	81	111	93	92	173	171

Table 4.12 (*cont.*)

The North

	1964	1966	1969	1970	Feb. 1974	Oct. 1974	1979	1983	1987
Considered voting for									
Conservative Party	4.3	3.4	–	3.8	6.4	5.9	8.1	7.3	7.3
Labour Party	2.7	2.4	–	4.0	5.2	2.7	7.6	4.0	5.3
Liberal Party	12.3	13.5	–	13.9	15.2	11.7	12.1	14.7	14.4
Other party	0.4	0.4	–	1.1	0.0	1.1	3.1	0.2	0.4
No other party	80.3	80.3	–	77.2	73.2	78.6	69.1	73.9	72.6
Total	100.0	100.0	–	100.0	100.0	100.0	100.0	100.0	100.0
N. of respondents	447	401	–	417	598	523	447	841	842

The Midlands

	1964	1966	1969	1970	Feb. 1974	Oct. 1974	1979	1983	1987
Considered voting for									
Conservative Party	5.0	3.2	–	3.3	4.7	5.8	12.5	5.4	7.7
Labour Party	3.6	3.3	–	3.5	4.7	4.8	3.8	4.6	6.2
Liberal Party	16.9	15.6	–	13.0	16.8	13.8	13.2	12.2	11.9
Other party	0.7	2.6	–	0.3	0.0	0.6	1.9	0.4	0.6
No other party	73.7	75.4	–	79.8	73.9	74.9	68.7	77.4	73.6
Total	100.0	100.0	–	100.0	100.0	100.0	100.0	100.0	100.0
N. of respondents	278	304	–	246	322	311	265	468	525

Greater London

	1964	1966	1969	1970	Feb. 1974	Oct. 1974	1979	1983	1987
Considered voting for									
Conservative Party	5.5	3.9	–	6.0	6.4	2.5	7.9	6.5	6.5
Labour Party	6.6	5.8	–	2.0	2.6	1.9	4.2	5.9	4.2
Liberal Party	18.4	13.0	–	13.4	9.4	12.3	12.1	14.3	14.8
Other party	0.4	0.0	–	0.5	1.7	0.6	4.2	0.6	0.3
No other party	69.1	77.3	–	78.1	79.9	82.7	71.5	72.6	74.2
Total	100.0	100.0	–	100.0	100.0	100.0	100.0	100.0	100.0
N. of respondents	232	223	–	210	234	162	165	375	369

The South

	1964	1966	1969	1970	Feb. 1974	Oct. 1974	1979	1983	1987
Considered voting for									
Conservative Party	3.9	3.2	–	4.8	4.0	4.4	6.8	6.3	6.3
Labour Party	2.7	4.2	–	1.2	3.5	3.9	6.8	5.3	4.7
Liberal Party	16.7	13.4	–	13.0	15.2	9.7	14.0	12.4	13.1
Other party	0.9	0.7	–	1.9	0.3	0.6	0.8	0.3	0.6
No other party	75.8	78.5	–	79.1	77.0	81.4	71.6	75.7	75.3
Total	100.0	100.0	–	100.0	100.0	100.0	100.0	100.0	100.0
N. of respondents	375	376	–	315	600	517	500	993	971

Table 4.13 *Time of voting decision: all respondents (%)*

	1964	1966	1969	1970	Feb. 1974	Oct. 1974	1979	1983	1987
A long time ago	78.2	77.0	–	69.8	63.5	60.2	57.4	60.1	62.2
Over the last year or two	10.7	11.7	–	18.3	13.8	17.7	14.6	18.1	17.1
During the campaign	11.1	11.3	–	11.9	22.7	22.0	28.0	21.8	20.7
Total	100.0	100.0	–	100.0	100.0	100.0	100.0	100.0	100.0
N. of respondents	1156	1526	–	1416	2069	2006	1594	3292	3270

Table 4.14 *Time of voting decision by gender (%)*

Men									
	1964	1966	1969	1970	Feb. 1974	Oct. 1974	1979	1983	1987
A long time ago	78.8	77.0	–	69.4	64.6	62.4	58.6	61.3	63.6
Over the last year or two	10.0	12.3	–	20.9	15.1	17.1	15.4	18.9	17.5
During the campaign	11.2	10.7	–	9.8	20.3	20.5	26.0	19.8	18.9
Total	100.0	100.0	–	100.0	100.0	100.0	100.0	100.0	100.0
N. of respondents	526	721	–	671	987	1001	768	1542	1560
Women									
	1964	1966	1969	1970	Feb. 1974	Oct. 1974	1979	1983	1987
A long time ago	77.6	77.0	–	70.2	62.5	58.2	56.3	59.1	61.0
Over the last year or two	11.2	11.1	–	16.1	12.7	18.4	13.8	17.3	16.6
During the campaign	11.1	11.9	–	13.8	24.9	23.6	29.9	23.6	22.4
Total	100.0	100.0	–	100.0	100.0	100.0	100.0	100.0	100.0
N. of respondents	631	805	–	746	1082	1005	826	1750	1710

Table 4.15 *Time of voting decision by age (%)*

Aged under 25									
	1964	1966	1969	1970	Feb. 1974	Oct. 1974	1979	1983	1987
A long time ago	56.9	42.0	–	21.2	38.9	43.5	31.1	42.1	40.0
Over the last year or two	29.1	39.4	–	50.1	25.8	30.0	14.8	22.9	22.1
During the campaign	14.0	18.6	–	28.6	35.3	26.5	54.1	35.0	37.8
Total	100.0	100.0	–	100.0	100.0	100.0	100.0	100.0	100.0
N. of respondents	59	95	–	184	190	200	122	409	370

Table 4.15 (*cont.*)

Aged 25–34

	1964	1966	1969	1970	Feb. 1974	Oct. 1974	1979	1983	1987
A long time ago	68.2	70.0	–	60.4	48.4	49.7	43.7	50.4	56.4
Over the last year or two	15.4	12.3	–	22.8	18.2	21.0	19.2	21.4	19.3
During the campaign	16.4	17.7	–	16.9	33.3	29.3	37.0	28.2	24.2
Total	100.0	100.0	–	100.0	100.0	100.0	100.0	100.0	100.0
N. of respondents	185	250	–	213	384	386	343	578	575

Aged 35–44

	1964	1966	1969	1970	Feb. 1974	Oct. 1974	1979	1983	1987
A long time ago	74.5	71.2	–	70.9	62.5	56.6	59.2	55.3	55.1
Over the last year or two	11.2	13.3	–	15.1	13.8	17.2	13.8	19.3	19.6
During the campaign	14.4	15.5	–	14.0	23.7	26.1	27.0	25.4	25.3
Total	100.0	100.0	–	100.0	100.0	100.0	100.0	100.0	100.0
N. of respondents	279	315	–	248	355	348	282	625	644

Aged 45–54

	1964	1966	1969	1970	Feb. 1974	Oct. 1974	1979	1983	1987
A long time ago	83.6	83.2	–	79.1	67.9	63.6	59.6	63.9	69.4
Over the last year or two	8.2	9.8	–	13.6	12.4	17.9	14.7	19.0	15.7
During the campaign	8.2	7.0	–	7.3	19.7	18.5	25.6	17.0	14.9
Total	100.0	100.0	–	100.0	100.0	100.0	100.0	100.0	100.0
N. of respondents	246	331	–	246	386	368	312	562	525

Aged 55–64

	1964	1966	1969	1970	Feb. 1974	Oct. 1974	1979	1983	1987
A long time ago	85.2	85.2	–	84.8	71.1	68.9	66.5	67.7	70.1
Over the last year or two	7.9	7.4	–	10.2	9.9	12.6	12.3	16.2	16.3
During the campaign	6.9	7.4	–	5.0	18.4	18.5	21.1	16.2	13.6
Total	100.0	100.0	–	100.0	100.0	100.0	100.0	100.0	100.0
N. of respondents	214	276	–	263	343	325	236	523	538

Table 4.15 (*cont.*)

Aged 65–74

	1964	1966	1969	1970	Feb. 1974	Oct. 1974	1979	1983	1987
A long time ago	81.6	83.3	–	85.1	76.3	70.9	70.9	75.7	74.9
Over the last year or two	7.4	7.8	–	9.5	10.9	14.7	13.8	12.2	11.7
During the campaign	11.0	8.8	–	5.4	12.8	14.3	15.3	12.1	13.3
Total	100.0	100.0	–	100.0	100.0	100.0	100.0	100.0	100.0
N. of respondents	130	179	–	183	266	251	189	370	382

Aged over 74

	1964	1966	1969	1970	Feb. 1974	Oct. 1974	1979	1983	1987
A long time ago	97.5	95.3	–	90.4	86.6	76.2	77.9	78.6	78.4
Over the last year or two	0.0	1.4	–	4.9	3.9	7.4	5.8	9.7	9.2
During the campaign	2.5	3.4	–	4.8	9.4	16.4	16.3	11.8	12.4
Total	100.0	100.0	–	100.0	100.0	100.0	100.0	100.0	100.0
N. of respondents	44	80	–	78	127	122	104	207	208

Table 4.16 *Time of voting decision by marital status (%)*

Single

	1964	1966	1969	1970	Feb. 1974	Oct. 1974	1979	1983	1987
A long time ago	77.0	66.3	–	43.5	52.5	–	47.8	48.1	52.2
Over the last year or two	11.2	18.0	–	37.0	16.9	–	13.2	21.1	19.4
During the campaign	11.8	15.7	–	19.5	30.6	–	39.0	30.8	28.4
Total	100.0	100.0	–	100.0	100.0	–	100.0	100.0	100.0
N. of respondents	119	145	–	228	278	–	182	540	544

Married

	1964	1966	1969	1970	Feb. 1974	Oct. 1974	1979	1983	1987
A long time ago	76.9	76.6	–	73.4	63.7	60.7	57.4	60.9	63.7
Over the last year or two	11.4	11.8	–	15.7	14.2	17.3	15.2	18.3	16.9
During the campaign	11.7	11.6	–	10.9	22.2	21.9	27.4	20.8	19.4
Total	100.0	100.0	–	100.0	100.0	100.0	100.0	100.0	100.0
N. of respondents	926	1199	–	1014	1544	1522	1163	2336	2285

Table 4.16 (*cont.*)

| | Divorced and separated | | | | | | | | |
	1964	1966	1969	1970	Feb. 1974	Oct. 1974	1979	1983	1987
A long time ago	–	(74.0)	–	–	61.9	–	59.4	65.3	61.2
Over the last year or two	–	(17.9)	–	–	4.8	–	10.9	15.5	15.5
During the campaign	–	(8.1)	–	–	33.3	–	29.7	19.2	23.4
Total	–	(100.0)	–	–	100.0	–	100.0	100.0	100.0
N. of respondents	–	12	–	–	21	–	64	152	153

| | Widowed | | | | | | | | |
	1964	1966	1969	1970	Feb. 1974	Oct. 1974	1979	1983	1987
A long time ago	–	89.0	–	–	76.1	–	68.0	74.8	69.2
Over the last year or two	–	5.2	–	–	8.4	–	11.2	11.2	14.8
During the campaign	–	5.9	–	–	15.5	–	20.7	14.1	16.0
Total	–	100.0	–	–	100.0	–	100.0	100.0	100.0
N. of respondents	–	168	–	–	226	–	169	262	285

Table 4.17 *Time of voting decision: new electors (%)*

	1964	1966	1969	1970	Feb. 1974	Oct. 1974	1979	1983	1987
A long time ago	63.0	33.5	–	21.2	25.8	–	30.1	37.4	34.7
Over the last year or two	24.5	37.2	–	50.1	29.0	–	14.0	24.1	22.2
During the campaign	12.5	29.3	–	28.6	45.2	–	55.9	38.5	43.1
Total	100.0	100.0	–	100.0	100.0	–	100.0	100.0	100.0
N. of respondents	81	41	–	184	62	–	108	93	229

Table 4.18 *Time of voting decision by vote (%)*

| | Conservative voters | | | | | | | | |
	1964	1966	1969	1970	Feb. 1974	Oct. 1974	1979	1983	1987
A long time ago	81.0	81.1	–	71.6	72.7	65.8	62.9	66.9	70.6
Over the last year or two	6.9	8.8	–	19.3	10.8	14.2	15.8	18.0	15.2
During the campaign	12.1	10.2	–	9.1	16.4	19.4	21.2	15.1	14.2
Total	100.0	100.0	–	100.0	100.0	100.0	100.0	100.0	100.0
N. of respondents	450	590	–	651	785	702	726	1447	1402

Table 4.18 (*cont.*)

Labour voters

	1964	1966	1969	1970	Feb. 1974	Oct. 1974	1979	1983	1987
A long time ago	81.7	79.2	–	74.0	70.6	68.7	59.5	75.8	70.2
Over the last year or two	11.5	12.0	–	15.3	11.0	14.4	13.2	9.2	12.0
During the campaign	6.9	8.8	–	10.7	18.4	16.9	27.3	15.0	17.8
Total	100.0	100.0	–	100.0	100.0	100.0	100.0	100.0	100.0
N. of respondents	527	807	–	633	838	828	583	919	985

Liberal voters

	1964	1966	1969	1970	Feb. 1974	Oct. 1974	1979	1983	1987
A long time ago	53.4	44.3	–	40.8	32.7	36.9	36.8	31.4	37.1
Over the last year or two	20.0	23.0	–	25.6	24.9	31.3	13.2	28.5	27.1
During the campaign	26.6	32.7	–	33.6	42.4	31.8	50.0	40.1	35.9
Total	100.0	100.0	–	100.0	100.0	100.0	100.0	100.0	100.0
N. of respondents	105	127	–	103	394	352	212	790	748

Voters for other parties

	1964	1966	1969	1970	Feb. 1974	Oct. 1974	1979	1983	1987
A long time ago	–	–	–	40.5	42.6	34.8	48.0	61.0	59.8
Over the last year or two	–	–	–	36.5	23.4	21.7	12.0	12.9	10.9
During the campaign	–	–	–	23.1	34.0	41.5	40.0	26.1	29.4
Total	–	–	–	100.0	100.0	100.0	100.0	100.0	100.0
N. of respondents	–	–	–	29	47	69	25	43	44

Table 4.19 *Time of voting decision by strength and direction of partisanship (%)*

Very strong Conservative identifiers

	1964	1966	1969	1970	Feb. 1974	Oct. 1974	1979	1983	1987
A long time ago	90.0	90.7	–	89.6	91.5	87.1	90.0	94.3	93.0
Over the last year or two	4.1	4.2	–	7.7	3.9	3.8	3.8	5.0	4.4
During the campaign	5.9	5.1	–	2.7	4.7	9.0	6.3	0.6	2.6
Total	100.0	100.0	–	100.0	100.0	100.0	100.0	100.0	100.0
N. of respondents	227	293	–	319	258	210	160	318	306

Table 4.19 (*cont.*)

Fairly strong Conservative identifiers

	1964	1966	1969	1970	Feb. 1974	Oct. 1974	1979	1983	1987
A long time ago	74.3	75.6	–	69.9	69.3	61.4	67.1	71.9	74.1
Over the last year or two	8.8	12.3	–	21.1	12.3	18.4	16.7	16.4	13.8
During the campaign	16.9	12.0	–	9.1	18.3	20.3	16.1	11.8	12.2
Total	100.0	100.0	–	100.0	100.0	100.0	100.0	100.0	100.0
N. of respondents	173	213	–	225	398	370	347	604	648

Not very strong Conservative identifiers

	1964	1966	1969	1970	Feb. 1974	Oct. 1974	1979	1983	1987
A long time ago	61.1	59.5	–	28.6	35.8	32.9	39.6	41.7	42.0
Over the last year or two	19.5	15.4	–	37.5	23.6	21.9	23.9	26.2	27.6
During the campaign	19.5	25.1	–	33.9	40.5	45.2	36.5	32.1	30.4
Total	100.0	100.0	–	100.0	100.0	100.0	100.0	100.0	100.0
N. of respondents	61	73	–	63	148	146	159	336	264

Very strong Liberal identifiers

	1964	1966	1969	1970	Feb. 1974	Oct. 1974	1979	1983	1987
A long time ago	61.3	58.7	–	65.7	79.4	68.9	72.0	69.0	82.0
Over the last year or two	18.7	14.2	–	18.7	8.8	15.6	8.0	14.1	9.8
During the campaign	20.0	27.1	–	15.6	11.8	15.6	20.0	16.9	8.2
Total	100.0	100.0	–	100.0	100.0	100.0	100.0	100.0	100.0
N. of respondents	41	47	–	34	34	45	25	71	60

Fairly strong Liberal identifiers

	1964	1966	1969	1970	Feb. 1974	Oct. 1974	1979	1983	1987
A long time ago	44.6	59.0	–	42.4	44.8	43.8	44.9	44.6	49.5
Over the last year or two	19.3	18.5	–	36.6	27.3	30.9	20.4	32.1	25.5
During the campaign	36.1	22.5	–	21.0	27.9	25.3	34.7	23.2	25.0
Total	100.0	100.0	–	100.0	100.0	100.0	100.0	100.0	100.0
N. of respondents	61	79	–	52	154	162	98	280	252

Table 4.19 (*cont.*)

	1964	1966	1969	1970	Feb. 1974	Oct. 1974	1979	1983	1987
Not very strong Liberal identifiers									
A long time ago	61.2	(42.7)	–	28.9	23.2	19.0	31.0	23.5	30.9
Over the last year or two	24.7	(36.0)	–	25.7	25.3	29.0	23.9	29.9	29.0
During the campaign	14.1	(21.3)	–	45.4	51.6	52.0	45.1	46.6	40.1
Total	100.0	(100.0)	–	100.0	100.0	100.0	100.0	100.0	100.0
N. of respondents	30	16	–	27	95	100	71	268	269
Very strong Labour identifiers									
A long time ago	89.6	90.4	–	88.8	89.1	88.1	78.5	90.2	88.7
Over the last year or two	7.6	7.2	–	8.1	3.5	7.4	6.8	4.8	5.0
During the campaign	2.8	2.3	–	3.1	7.4	4.5	14.7	5.1	6.3
Total	100.0	100.0	–	100.0	100.0	100.0	100.0	100.0	100.0
N. of respondents	258	390	–	314	367	312	177	315	272
Fairly strong Labour identifiers									
A long time ago	83.8	74.9	–	62.5	61.9	63.0	54.3	66.6	67.1
Over the last year or two	7.0	15.0	–	24.5	14.7	18.5	16.2	14.4	14.2
During the campaign	9.2	10.1	–	12.9	23.3	18.5	29.5	19.0	18.8
Total	100.0	100.0	–	100.0	100.0	100.0	100.0	100.0	100.0
N. of respondents	206	295	–	235	373	389	302	431	435
Not very strong Labour identifiers									
A long time ago	57.6	49.4	–	39.5	25.0	36.7	31.9	40.5	46.6
Over the last year or two	27.9	27.2	–	31.5	27.0	27.3	12.8	18.1	23.1
During the campaign	14.5	23.3	–	29.0	48.0	35.9	55.3	41.3	30.3
Total	100.0	100.0	–	100.0	100.0	100.0	100.0	100.0	100.0
N. of respondents	49	61	–	83	152	128	141	259	289

Table 4.20 *Time of voting decision: non partisans (%)*

	Respondents with no party identification								
	1964	1966	1969	1970	1974	Feb. 1974	Oct. 1979	1983	1987
A long time ago	46.9	30.4	–	20.0	18.4	33.3	26.8	22.9	24.3
Over the last year or two	37.1	17.0	–	32.5	13.2	16.7	8.9	34.6	32.6
During the campaign	16.0	52.6	–	47.5	68.4	50.0	64.3	42.6	43.1
Total	100.0	100.0	–	100.0	100.0	100.0	100.0	100.0	100.0
N. of respondents	28	47	–	43	38	54	56	130	187

Table 4.21 *Time of voting decision by social class (%)*

	Professional and managerial classes								
	1964	1966	1969	1970	1974	Feb. 1974	Oct. 1979	1983	1987
A long time ago	73.3	70.1	–	69.6	62.1	52.9	60.9	58.0	61.6
Over the last year or two	9.2	11.6	–	17.6	15.5	20.0	14.9	20.0	18.6
During the campaign	17.5	18.3	–	12.9	22.3	27.1	24.2	22.1	19.7
Total	100.0	100.0	–	100.0	100.0	100.0	100.0	100.0	100.0
N. of respondents	154	207	–	253	309	310	343	902	859
	Intermediate and routine non-manual classes								
	1964	1966	1969	1970	1974	Feb. 1974	Oct. 1979	1983	1987
A long time ago	74.4	73.8	–	65.8	60.1	53.7	55.3	56.1	60.4
Over the last year or two	11.7	13.8	–	19.2	14.5	20.3	14.7	17.8	16.2
During the campaign	13.9	12.4	–	15.1	25.4	26.0	30.0	26.1	23.5
Total	100.0	100.0	–	100.0	100.0	100.0	100.0	100.0	100.0
N. of respondents	319	418	–	371	725	696	430	635	831
	Manual working class								
	1964	1966	1969	1970	1974	Feb. 1974	Oct. 1979	1983	1987
A long time ago	81.5	80.1	–	71.2	66.2	66.6	57.0	62.5	63.2
Over the last year or two	10.2	10.8	–	18.9	12.8	15.6	14.6	17.6	16.7
During the campaign	8.2	9.1	–	9.9	21.0	17.7	28.4	20.0	20.2
Total	100.0	100.0	–	100.0	100.0	100.0	100.0	100.0	100.0
N. of respondents	646	875	–	739	921	896	760	1523	984

Table 4.22 *Time of voting decision by employment status (%)*

Self-employed with employees									
	1964	1966	1969	1970	Feb. 1974	Oct. 1974	1979	1983	1987
A long time ago	83.5	77.4	–	75.0	75.6	65.6	71.2	71.7	69.0
Over the last year or two	2.3	11.6	–	21.6	9.8	6.3	9.6	13.8	15.2
During the campaign	14.2	11.0	–	3.3	14.6	28.1	19.2	14.5	15.8
Total	100.0	100.0	–	100.0	100.0	100.0	100.0	100.0	100.0
N. of respondents	49	53	–	60	82	64	52	140	156

Self-employed, no employees									
	1964	1966	1969	1970	Feb. 1974	Oct. 1974	1979	1983	1987
A long time ago	(84.7)	78.4	–	51.3	70.8	64.5	70.0	69.9	60.0
Over the last year or two	(0.0)	9.1	–	33.8	9.7	17.1	6.7	17.9	16.2
During the campaign	(15.3)	12.5	–	14.9	19.4	18.4	23.3	12.2	23.8
Total	(100.0)	100.0	–	100.0	100.0	100.0	100.0	100.0	100.0
N. of respondents	14	23	–	26	72	76	60	116	142

Managers									
	1964	1966	1969	1970	Feb. 1974	Oct. 1974	1979	1983	1987
A long time ago	64.0	79.5	–	77.7	62.4	56.2	65.9	58.4	66.9
Over the last year or two	18.2	13.7	–	13.3	14.8	22.2	14.4	20.9	19.3
During the campaign	17.8	6.8	–	9.0	22.8	21.6	19.7	20.7	13.9
Total	100.0	100.0	–	100.0	100.0	100.0	100.0	100.0	100.0
N. of respondents	55	78	–	83	149	153	132	518	324

Foremen and supervisors									
	1964	1966	1969	1970	Feb. 1974	Oct. 1974	1979	1983	1987
A long time ago	76.1	75.5	–	73.8	62.2	64.2	53.1	62.5	66.8
Over the last year or two	11.2	11.9	–	17.8	14.6	18.3	16.0	19.9	17.8
During the campaign	12.7	12.7	–	8.4	23.2	17.4	30.9	17.6	15.4
Total	100.0	100.0	–	100.0	100.0	100.0	100.0	100.0	100.0
N. of respondents	74	89	–	93	82	109	162	399	204

Rank and file employees									
	1964	1966	1969	1970	Feb. 1974	Oct. 1974	1979	1983	1987
A long time ago	78.3	76.1	–	68.3	61.6	59.3	53.6	58.8	60.7
Over the last year or two	11.4	12.5	–	18.6	14.5	18.2	16.6	17.0	16.8
During the campaign	10.3	11.3	–	13.0	23.9	22.5	29.8	24.2	22.4
Total	100.0	100.0	–	100.0	100.0	100.0	100.0	100.0	100.0
N. of respondents	575	787	–	745	1375	1315	791	1744	2315

Table 4.23 *Time of voting decision: unemployed (%)*

	1964	1966	1969	1970	Feb. 1974	Oct. 1974	1979	1983	1987
A long time ago	(87.7)	(75.6)	–	72.6	71.1	59.3	50.0	53.5	61.4
Over the last year or two	(12.3)	(24.4)	–	15.0	7.9	22.2	17.9	22.0	14.7
During the campaign	(0.0)	(0.0)	–	12.4	21.1	18.5	32.1	24.4	23.8
Total	(100.0)	(100.0)	–	100.0	100.0	100.0	100.0	100.0	100.0
N. of respondents	8	12	–	32	38	27	28	194	166

Table 4.24 *Time of voting decision by region (%)*

Scotland	1964	1966	1969	1970	Feb. 1974	Oct. 1974	1979	1983	1987
A long time ago	76.3	77.3	–	62.9	58.2	58.6	54.0	64.1	58.3
Over the last year or two	4.9	7.1	–	19.4	20.4	14.0	10.5	14.0	18.9
During the campaign	18.8	15.6	–	17.7	21.4	27.4	35.5	21.9	22.8
Total	100.0	100.0	–	100.0	100.0	100.0	100.0	100.0	100.0
N. of respondents	102	130	–	155	196	186	124	298	291

Wales	1964	1966	1969	1970	Feb. 1974	Oct. 1974	1979	1983	1987
A long time ago	78.7	76.4	–	63.2	69.1	65.2	62.8	65.4	67.6
Over the last year or two	8.8	12.6	–	25.4	10.9	15.7	11.7	14.4	13.3
During the campaign	12.5	11.0	–	11.4	20.0	19.1	25.5	20.2	19.1
Total	100.0	100.0	–	100.0	100.0	100.0	100.0	100.0	100.0
N. of respondents	46	72	–	81	110	115	94	182	175

The North	1964	1966	1969	1970	Feb. 1974	Oct. 1974	1979	1983	1987
A long time ago	77.6	75.8	–	72.4	61.7	57.4	55.4	58.4	64.5
Over the last year or two	10.3	12.2	–	16.0	14.9	20.0	16.5	17.4	13.8
During the campaign	12.1	12.0	–	11.6	23.4	23.6	28.1	24.2	21.7
Total	100.0	100.0	–	100.0	100.0	100.0	100.0	100.0	100.0
N. of respondents	322	409	–	414	603	571	442	881	865

Table 4.24 (*cont.*)

The Midlands

	1964	1966	1969	1970	Feb. 1974	Oct. 1974	1979	1983	1987
A long time ago	81.1	77.5	–	63.9	62.4	62.9	53.3	61.3	60.6
Over the last year or two	10.4	12.6	–	25.2	11.2	15.5	15.6	17.8	18.6
During the campaign	8.5	9.9	–	10.9	26.4	21.6	31.1	20.8	20.8
Total	100.0	100.0	–	100.0	100.0	100.0	100.0	100.0	100.0
N. of respondents	225	296	–	241	322	329	270	499	547

Greater London

	1964	1966	1969	1970	Feb. 1974	Oct. 1974	1979	1983	1987
A long time ago	76.3	73.9	–	67.2	69.6	63.5	58.8	57.6	61.6
Over the last year or two	13.8	13.7	–	20.8	12.7	14.6	15.8	18.8	21.1
During the campaign	9.9	12.4	–	12.0	17.7	21.9	25.5	23.5	17.3
Total	100.0	100.0	–	100.0	100.0	100.0	100.0	100.0	100.0
N. of respondents	159	234	–	209	237	192	165	397	378

The South

	1964	1966	1969	1970	Feb. 1974	Oct. 1974	1979	1983	1987
A long time ago	78.2	79.8	–	77.6	64.2	59.9	60.7	59.9	61.5
Over the last year or two	11.9	10.5	–	12.2	13.0	19.4	13.4	20.3	17.6
During the campaign	10.0	9.7	–	10.2	22.8	20.7	25.9	19.9	20.9
Total	100.0	100.0	–	100.0	100.0	100.0	100.0	100.0	100.0
N. of respondents	302	384	–	316	601	613	499	1035	1014

Chapter 5

INTEREST IN ELECTIONS

1.   The question on interest in politics was not asked in 1983 or 1987. Its wording refers to 'interest in the recent campaign' in 1964, 1966 and 1970 and to 'interest in politics' in 1963, 1969, February 1974, October 1974 and 1979.
2.   The question on caring about the election result was not asked in 1979.
3.   Because of variations in the question wording and answer categories for the political interest variable, readers should interpret comparisons over time with care. The question in 1964, 1966 and 1970 refers to interest in the campaign; later surveys to interest in politics. The answer category 'none at all' was added to the question in February 1974, October 1974 and 1979. For purposes of comparison with earlier surveys it has been combined with the 'not much' category.

See Appendix E, p. 486 on the construction of the variables in this chapter.

Table 5.1 *Interest in politics: all respondents (%)*

	1963	1964	1966	1969	1970	Feb. 1974	Oct. 1974	1979
Interest in politics								
A great deal	15.8	34.0	31.4	–	37.8	17.1	19.2	12.9
Some	37.2	35.9	35.6	–	33.6	45.4	46.1	47.6
Not much or none	47.0	30.1	33.0	–	28.6	37.5	34.6	39.4
Total	100.0	100.0	100.0	–	100.0	100.0	100.0	100.0
N. of respondents	1998	1793	1891	–	1838	2435	2342	1877

Table 5.2 *Interest in politics by gender (%)*

Men								
	1963	1964	1966	1969	1970	Feb. 1974	Oct. 1974	1979
Interest in politics								
A great deal	23.6	40.0	35.4	–	41.9	21.1	23.8	17.1
Some	43.6	36.1	34.5	–	33.7	49.8	48.0	50.8
Not much or none	32.8	24.0	30.1	–	24.5	29.2	28.2	32.2
Total	100.0	100.0	100.0	–	100.0	100.0	100.0	100.0
N. of respondents	895	811	889	–	866	1159	1167	908

Women								
	1963	1964	1966	1969	1970	Feb. 1974	Oct. 1974	1979
Interest in politics								
A great deal	9.4	29.1	27.9	–	34.1	13.5	14.6	9.1
Some	32.1	35.8	36.6	–	33.6	41.5	44.3	44.7
Not much or none	58.6	35.1	35.5	–	32.3	45.1	41.1	46.2
Total	100.0	100.0	100.0	–	100.0	100.0	100.0	100.0
N. of respondents	1103	982	1002	–	972	1276	1175	969

Table 5.3 *Interest in politics by age (%)*

	Aged under 25							
	1963	1964	1966	1969	1970	Feb. 1974	Oct. 1974	1979
Interest in politics								
A great deal	8.8	28.1	27.2	–	25.2	8.5	9.5	8.1
Some	33.1	44.2	40.4	–	42.2	45.2	45.1	46.8
Not much or none	58.1	27.8	32.3	–	32.6	46.4	45.4	45.1
Total	100.0	100.0	100.0	–	100.0	100.0	100.0	100.0
N. of respondents	148	108	141	–	268	248	275	174

	Aged 25–34							
	1963	1964	1966	1969	1970	Feb. 1974	Oct. 1974	1979
Interest in politics								
A great deal	13.0	32.6	25.9	–	34.3	12.9	13.2	11.7
Some	44.4	38.3	39.7	–	38.8	49.9	52.6	50.2
Not much or none	42.6	29.1	34.4	–	26.8	37.2	34.2	38.0
Total	100.0	100.0	100.0	–	100.0	100.0	100.0	100.0
N. of respondents	331	297	331	–	297	465	477	426

	Aged 35–44							
	1963	1964	1966	1969	1970	Feb. 1974	Oct. 1974	1979
Interest in politics								
A great deal	16.7	33.6	30.3	–	36.7	14.3	16.0	11.2
Some	42.6	39.4	40.0	–	30.5	46.4	46.4	52.1
Not much or none	40.7	27.1	29.7	–	32.9	39.3	37.6	36.7
Total	100.0	100.0	100.0	–	100.0	100.0	100.0	100.0
N. of respondents	418	381	370	–	313	422	401	330

	Aged 45–54							
	1963	1964	1966	1969	1970	Feb. 1974	Oct. 1974	1979
Interest in politics								
A great deal	15.5	34.9	30.6	–	42.0	20.6	24.4	13.1
Some	35.5	34.0	38.8	–	31.5	46.0	46.8	48.4
Not much or none	49.0	31.2	30.6	–	26.4	33.3	28.7	38.5
Total	100.0	100.0	100.0	–	100.0	100.0	100.0	100.0
N. of respondents	406	357	384	–	298	441	410	343

Table 5.3 (*cont.*)

	Aged 55–64							
	1963	1964	1966	1969	1970	Feb. 1974	Oct. 1974	1979
Interest in politics								
A great deal	19.1	36.9	36.5	–	41.4	19.6	23.8	16.3
Some	40.2	35.0	33.3	–	31.2	47.3	47.8	49.8
Not much or none	40.7	28.1	30.2	–	27.4	33.1	28.5	33.8
Total	100.0	100.0	100.0	–	100.0	100.0	100.0	100.0
N. of respondents	351	331	338	–	331	387	361	263

	Aged 65–74							
	1963	1964	1966	1969	1970	Feb. 1974	Oct. 1974	1979
Interest in politics								
A great deal	21.0	34.1	38.5	–	47.9	23.2	27.3	16.7
Some	23.9	29.1	23.1	–	28.0	40.4	38.5	43.5
Not much or none	55.0	36.8	38.5	–	24.1	36.4	34.1	39.7
Total	100.0	100.0	100.0	–	100.0	100.0	100.0	100.0
N. of respondents	238	207	213	–	218	302	275	209

	Aged over 74							
	1963	1964	1966	1969	1970	Feb. 1974	Oct. 1974	1979
Interest in politics								
A great deal	7.8	32.8	29.8	–	38.5	22.8	24.4	15.1
Some	25.2	31.5	23.0	–	33.1	32.9	35.1	28.6
Not much or none	70.0	35.7	47.3	–	28.3	44.3	40.4	56.3
Total	100.0	100.0	100.0	–	100.0	100.0	100.0	100.0
N. of respondents	103	110	109	–	100	149	131	126

Table 5.4 *Interest in politics by age and gender (%)*

	Men aged under 24							
	1963	1964	1966	1969	1970	Feb. 1974	Oct. 1974	1979
Interest in politics								
A great deal	13.3	31.3	28.7	–	30.1	12.5	11.4	13.3
Some	41.7	45.8	38.1	–	42.6	49.2	48.6	49.4
Not much or none	45.0	22.9	33.2	–	27.3	38.3	40.0	37.3
Total	100.0	100.0	100.0	–	100.0	100.0	100.0	100.0
N. of respondents	60	49	78	–	134	120	140	83

	Women aged under 24							
	1963	1964	1966	1969	1970	Feb. 1974	Oct. 1974	1979
Interest in politics								
A great deal	5.7	25.4	25.4	–	20.4	4.7	7.4	3.3
Some	27.3	42.4	43.2	–	41.7	41.4	41.5	44.4
Not much or none	67.0	32.2	31.3	–	37.9	53.9	51.1	52.2
Total	100.0	100.0	100.0	–	100.0	100.0	100.0	100.0
N. of respondents	88	59	63	–	134	128	135	90

	Men aged 25–44							
	1963	1964	1966	1969	1970	Feb. 1974	Oct. 1974	1979
Interest in politics								
A great deal	23.8	38.3	35.8	–	42.0	18.1	20.0	16.0
Some	50.1	39.9	36.7	–	32.4	53.3	52.3	54.9
Not much or none	26.1	21.8	27.5	–	25.6	28.6	27.7	29.1
Total	100.0	100.0	100.0	–	100.0	100.0	100.0	100.0
N. of respondents	341	308	325	–	304	454	455	368

	Women aged 25–44							
	1963	1964	1966	1969	1970	Feb. 1974	Oct. 1974	1979
Interest in politics								
A great deal	7.8	28.8	21.6	–	29.2	8.8	8.5	7.2
Some	37.7	38.0	42.7	–	36.6	43.0	47.0	47.4
Not much or none	54.4	33.2	35.7	–	34.2	48.1	44.4	45.4
Total	100.0	100.0	100.0	–	100.0	100.0	100.0	100.0
N. of respondents	408	371	376	–	307	430	423	388

Table 5.4 (*cont.*)

Men aged 45–64

	1963	1964	1966	1969	1970	Feb. 1974	Oct. 1974	1979
Interest in politics								
A great deal	24.5	43.4	36.1	–	44.8	24.3	28.9	17.0
Some	43.9	34.4	36.1	–	33.6	49.4	47.2	53.3
Not much or none	31.6	22.2	27.8	–	21.6	26.3	24.0	29.7
Total	100.0	100.0	100.0	–	100.0	100.0	100.0	100.0
N. of respondents	351	320	353	–	301	391	388	306

Women aged 45–64

	1963	1964	1966	1969	1970	Feb. 1974	Oct. 1974	1979
Interest in politics								
A great deal	10.8	29.1	30.7	–	38.9	16.5	19.3	12.0
Some	32.3	34.5	36.4	–	29.3	44.2	47.3	44.7
Not much or none	56.9	36.4	32.9	–	31.8	39.4	33.4	43.3
Total	100.0	100.0	100.0	–	100.0	100.0	100.0	100.0
N. of respondents	406	368	369	–	328	437	383	300

Men aged over 64

	1963	1964	1966	1969	1970	Feb. 1974	Oct. 1974	1979
Interest in politics								
A great deal	25.4	37.3	36.0	–	47.1	27.4	31.5	22.3
Some	27.5	28.4	22.8	–	28.4	41.9	39.3	35.8
Not much or none	47.2	34.3	41.2	–	24.5	30.6	29.2	41.9
Total	100.0	100.0	100.0	–	100.0	100.0	100.0	100.0
N. of respondents	142	134	131	–	122	186	178	148

Women aged over 64

	1963	1964	1966	1969	1970	Feb. 1974	Oct. 1974	1979
Interest in politics								
A great deal	11.1	31.5	35.2	–	43.6	20.0	22.4	11.2
Some	22.1	31.4	23.3	–	30.3	35.1	36.0	39.6
Not much or none	66.8	53.0	41.6	–	26.0	44.9	41.7	49.2
Total	100.0	100.0	100.0	–	100.0	100.0	100.0	100.0
N. of respondents	199	185	191	–	196	265	228	187

Table 5.5 *Interest in politics by marital status (%)*

| | Single | | | | | | | |
	1963	1964	1966	1969	1970	Feb. 1974	Oct. 1974	1979
Interest in politics								
A great deal	15.4	30.8	29.0	–	33.3	14.1	–	11.0
Some	35.9	38.3	36.9	–	39.0	44.0	–	46.7
Not much or none	48.6	30.8	34.1	–	27.7	41.9	–	42.3
Total	100.0	100.0	100.0	–	100.0	100.0	–	100.0
N. of respondents	250	214	212	–	323	341	–	227
	Married							
	1963	1964	1966	1969	1970	Feb. 1974	Oct. 1974	1979
Interest in politics								
A great deal	16.6	35.4	31.1	–	38.6	17.4	19.6	14.5
Some	39.1	35.7	36.6	–	33.1	47.3	47.6	48.8
Not much or none	44.3	28.9	32.3	–	28.3	35.3	32.8	36.8
Total	100.0	100.0	100.0	–	100.0	100.0	100.0	100.0
N. of respondents	1498	1380	1454	–	1296	1785	1749	1333

Table 5.6 *Interest in politics: new electors (%)*

	1963	1964	1966	1969	1970	Feb. 1974	Oct. 1974	1979
Interest in politics								
A great deal	8.6	31.2	25.0	–	25.2	3.5	–	8.5
Some	32.0	39.8	38.0	–	42.2	47.1	–	46.5
Not much or none	59.4	29.0	37.0	–	32.6	49.4	–	45.0
Total	100.0	100.0	100.0	–	100.0	100.0	–	100.0
N. of respondents	128	145	67	–	268	85	–	129

Table 5.7 *Interest in politics: non-voters (%)*

	1963	1964	1966	1969	1970	Feb. 1974	Oct. 1974	1979
Interest in politics								
A great deal	–	19.2	16.2	–	22.9	8.6	11.6	6.9
Some	–	29.8	27.6	–	31.4	34.1	36.0	31.9
Not much or none	–	51.1	56.2	–	45.6	57.2	52.3	61.2
Total	–	100.0	100.0	–	100.0	100.0	100.0	100.0
N. of respondents	–	200	301	–	340	290	344	276

Table 5.8 *Interest in politics by vote (%)*

Conservative voters							
	1963	1964	1966	1969	1970	Feb. 1974	Oct. 1974	1979
Interest in politics								
A great deal	17.3	34.8	32.8	–	48.8	20.7	22.7	13.7
Some	43.2	39.3	37.7	–	32.6	52.4	53.3	52.1
Not much or none	39.5	25.9	29.5	–	18.6	27.0	24.0	34.2
Total	100.0	100.0	100.0	–	100.0	100.0	100.0	100.0
N. of respondents	648	654	606	–	666	779	696	729

Labour voters							
	1963	1964	1966	1969	1970	Feb. 1974	Oct. 1974	1979
Interest in politics								
A great deal	16.8	38.7	36.7	–	36.7	18.6	20.5	14.9
Some	34.9	35.1	36.8	–	35.3	44.3	43.7	48.4
Not much or none	48.3	26.2	26.5	–	27.9	37.1	35.8	36.7
Total	100.0	100.0	100.0	–	100.0	100.0	100.0	100.0
N. of respondents	865	732	822	–	649	838	824	583

Liberal voters							
	1963	1964	1966	1969	1970	Feb. 1974	Oct. 1974	1979
Interest in politics								
A great deal	15.8	29.2	27.0	–	23.3	14.8	17.4	13.1
Some	37.2	38.1	38.5	–	36.3	45.3	49.0	54.2
Not much or none	47.0	32.7	34.5	–	40.4	39.9	33.6	32.7
Total	100.0	100.0	100.0	–	100.0	100.0	100.0	100.0
N. of respondents	234	164	127	–	108	393	351	214

Voters for other parties							
	1963	1964	1966	1969	1970	Feb. 1974	Oct. 1974	1979
Interest in politics								
A great deal	(100.0)	(55.7)	(21.8)	–	42.8	17.0	17.6	20.0
Some	(0.0)	(8.2)	(58.6)	–	32.1	34.0	39.7	28.0
Not much or none	(0.0)	(36.1)	(19.5)	–	25.1	49.0	42.7	52.0
Total	(100.0)	(100.0)	(100.0)	–	100.0	100.0	100.0	100.0
N. of respondents	2	10	9	–	35	47	68	25

Table 5.9 *Interest in politics by strength and direction of partisanship (%)*

| | Very strong Conservative identifiers | | | | | | | |
	1963	1964	1966	1969	1970	Feb. 1974	Oct. 1974	1979
Interest in politics								
A great deal	23.6	44.9	40.0	–	63.8	34.4	38.0	30.0
Some	45.3	33.0	34.5	–	22.1	48.9	42.6	49.4
Not much or none	31.1	22.1	25.5	–	14.1	16.7	19.4	20.6
Total	100.0	100.0	100.0	–	100.0	100.0	100.0	100.00
N. of respondents	254	336	324	–	363	276	216	171

| | Fairly strong Conservative identifiers | | | | | | | |
	1963	1964	1966	1969	1970	Feb. 1974	Oct. 1974	1979
Interest in politics								
A great deal	14.2	23.4	27.3	–	36.7	12.4	17.6	10.6
Some	44.6	46.3	37.8	–	43.4	58.5	57.9	59.4
Not much or none	41.3	30.3	34.9	–	20.0	29.1	24.4	30.0
Total	100.0	100.0	100.0	–	100.0	100.0	100.0	100.0
N. of respondents	303	283	258	–	283	426	425	387

| | Not very strong Conservative identifiers | | | | | | | |
	1963	1964	1966	1969	1970	Feb. 1974	Oct. 1974	1979
Interest in politics								
A great deal	8.8	17.7	18.1	–	22.6	9.8	11.6	5.6
Some	34.1	38.7	38.5	–	39.5	44.6	47.1	44.1
Not much or none	57.1	43.6	43.3	–	37.9	45.6	41.3	50.3
Total	100.0	100.0	100.0	–	100.0	100.0	100.0	100.0
N. of respondents	182	91	106	–	106	193	189	197

| | Very strong Liberal identifiers | | | | | | | |
	1963	1964	1966	1969	1970	Feb. 1974	Oct. 1974	1979
Interest in politics								
A great deal	37.5	43.8	35.4	–	34.1	30.6	28.3	30.0
Some	28.6	29.1	30.2	–	36.8	52.8	37.0	40.0
Not much or none	33.9	27.2	34.4	–	29.2	16.7	34.7	30.0
Total	100.0	100.0	100.0	–	100.0	100.0	100.0	100.0
N. of respondents	56	64	64	–	37	36	46	30

Table 5.9 (*cont.*)

	Fairly strong Liberal identifiers							
	1963	1964	1966	1969	1970	Feb. 1974	Oct. 1974	1979
Interest in politics								
A great deal	12.1	30.2	18.8	–	27.1	15.3	15.3	11.1
Some	40.7	38.9	40.8	–	42.0	47.6	55.0	58.3
Not much or none	47.3	30.9	40.4	–	30.9	37.1	29.6	30.6
Total	100.0	100.0	100.0	–	100.0	100.0	100.0	100.0
N. of respondents	91	102	101	–	76	170	189	108

	Not very strong Liberal identifers							
	1963	1964	1966	1969	1970	Feb. 1974	Oct. 1974	1979
Interest in politics								
A great deal	5.6	26.9	16.3	–	29.9	6.7	16.5	5.6
Some	43.1	35.0	39.6	–	32.6	40.0	39.7	46.7
Not much or none	51.4	38.1	44.1	–	37.5	53.3	43.8	47.8
Total	100.0	100.0	100.0	–	100.0	100.0	100.0	100.0
N. of respondents	72	49	27	–	32	120	121	90

	Very strong Labour identifiers							
	1963	1964	1966	1969	1970	Feb. 1974	Oct. 1974	1979
Interest in politics								
A great deal	26.9	50.1	47.7	–	44.3	26.3	30.5	28.0
Some	35.5	30.0	33.0	–	27.7	40.1	38.2	43.0
Not much or none	37.6	19.9	19.3	–	28.0	33.6	31.4	29.0
Total	100.0	100.0	100.0	–	100.0	100.0	100.0	100.0
N. of respondents	327	380	426	–	359	399	338	193

	Fairly strong Labour identifiers							
	1963	1964	1966	1969	1970	Feb. 1974	Oct. 1974	1979
Interest in politics								
A great deal	10.0	25.9	24.1	–	25.2	12.7	13.3	6.9
Some	43.0	42.7	43.6	–	41.5	45.0	47.4	49.0
Not much or none	47.0	31.4	32.3	–	33.3	42.2	39.3	44.1
Total	100.0	100.0	100.0	–	100.0	100.0	100.0	100.0
N. of respondents	370	282	352	–	304	424	443	347

Table 5.9 (*cont.*)

	Not very strong Labour identifiers							
	1963	1964	1966	1969	1970	Feb. 1974	Oct. 1974	1979
Interest in politics								
A great deal	8.9	20.6	15.8	–	19.5	10.0	11.0	10.5
Some	23.8	31.6	29.1	–	39.4	39.5	37.6	38.1
Not much or none	67.3	47.8	55.1	–	41.1	50.5	51.3	51.4
Total	100.0	100.0	100.0	–	100.0	100.0	100.0	100.0
N. of respondents	214	99	108	–	132	210	181	181

Table 5.10 *Interest in politics by social class (%)*

	Professional and managerial classes							
	1963	1964	1966	1969	1970	Feb. 1974	Oct. 1974	1979
Interest in politics								
A great deal	24.2	40.5	39.2	–	56.5	26.3	28.5	20.5
Some	45.7	42.6	36.4	–	30.5	54.7	52.8	57.3
Not much or none	30.1	16.9	24.5	–	13.0	19.0	18.7	22.2
Total	100.0	100.0	100.0	–	100.0	100.0	100.0	100.0
N. of respondents	256	231	242	–	299	342	354	293

	Intermediate and routine non-manual classes							
	1963	1964	1966	1969	1970	Feb. 1974	Oct. 1974	1979
Interest in politics								
A great deal	15.7	34.4	29.3	–	41.7	17.5	19.0	12.8
Some	38.6	37.0	37.9	–	34.9	47.7	49.9	51.7
Not much or none	45.8	28.6	32.7	–	23.4	34.7	31.1	35.5
Total	100.0	100.0	100.0	–	100.0	100.0	100.0	100.0
N. of respondents	472	513	522	–	467	832	805	437

	Manual working class							
	1963	1964	1966	1969	1970	Feb. 1974	Oct. 1974	1979
Interest in politics								
A great deal	14.3	31.8	30.2	–	30.9	13.6	16.0	11.4
Some	35.7	34.1	35.0	–	34.6	42.4	42.3	44.6
Not much or none	50.0	34.1	34.8	–	34.5	44.0	41.8	43.9
Total	100.0	100.0	100.0	–	100.0	100.0	100.0	100.0
N. of respondents	1159	990	1093	–	990	1110	1060	708

Table 5.11 *Interest in politics by school leaving age (%)*

	Left school aged under 15							
	1963	1964	1966	1969	1970	Feb. 1974	Oct. 1974	1979
Interest in politics								
A great deal	13.8	32.1	33.0	–	37.2	17.1	20.7	12.8
Some	35.7	33.7	32.8	–	31.7	41.8	42.3	42.2
Not much or none	50.5	34.3	34.3	–	31.0	41.1	37.1	45.0
Total	100.0	100.0	100.0	–	100.0	100.0	100.0	100.0
N. of respondents	1207	1045	1046	–	795	1065	968	625

	Left school aged 15							
	1963	1964	1966	1969	1970	Feb. 1974	Oct. 1974	1979
Interest in politics								
A great deal	14.8	31.7	24.2	–	26.9	12.4	13.5	9.5
Some	34.3	38.3	39.8	–	38.0	47.3	45.6	46.9
Not much or none	51.0	30.0	36.0	–	35.1	40.3	41.0	43.6
Total	100.0	100.0	100.0	–	100.0	100.0	100.0	100.0
N. of respondents	420	382	428	–	464	695	691	546

	Left school aged 16							
	1963	1964	1966	1969	1970	Feb. 1974	Oct. 1974	1979
Interest in politics								
A great deal	17.5	37.2	33.4	–	46.6	21.9	20.4	13.1
Some	48.6	42.7	37.5	–	37.7	46.5	52.1	51.5
Not much or none	33.9	20.1	29.0	–	15.7	31.6	27.5	35.4
Total	100.0	100.0	100.0	–	100.0	100.0	100.0	100.0
N. of respondents	183	182	210	–	174	329	334	368

	Left school aged 17							
	1963	1964	1966	1969	1970	Feb. 1974	Oct. 1974	1979
Interest in politics								
A great deal	27.1	40.8	30.5	–	51.8	26.3	31.0	23.8
Some	41.2	41.7	44.5	–	30.6	50.0	52.3	53.2
Not much or none	31.8	17.5	25.0	–	17.6	23.7	16.8	23.0
Total	100.0	100.0	100.0	–	100.0	100.0	100.0	100.0
N. of respondents	85	73	90	–	110	156	155	126

Table 5.11 (*cont.*)

| | Left school aged 18 or over | | | | | | | |
	1963	1964	1966	1969	1970	Feb. 1974	Oct. 1974	1979
Interest in politics								
A great deal	33.0	53.4	42.4	–	55.1	18.4	20.9	17.4
Some	47.3	35.6	40.6	–	32.7	55.7	54.2	57.1
Not much or none	19.8	11.0	17.0	–	12.2	25.9	24.8	25.5
Total	100.0	100.0	100.0	–	100.0	100.0	100.0	100.0
N. of respondents	91	90	92	–	116	174	177	184

Table 5.12 *Interest in politics: university or polytechnic educated* (%)

	1963	1964	1966	1969	1970	Feb. 1974	Oct. 1974	1979
Interest in politics								
A great deal	33.3	55.4	–	–	69.3	–	–	–
Some	48.1	31.5	–	–	20.0	–	–	–
Not much or none	18.5	13.1	–	–	10.8	–	–	–
Total	100.0	100.0	–	–	100.0	–	–	–
N. of respondents	27	41	–	–	59	–	–	–

Table 5.13 *Interest in politics by region* (%)

| | Scotland | | | | | | | |
	1963	1964	1966	1969	1970	Feb. 1974	Oct. 1974	1979
Interest in politics								
A great deal	18.8	38.9	29.2	–	41.3	13.3	15.5	17.5
Some	35.1	29.9	35.7	–	28.4	40.8	41.5	39.9
Not much or none	46.1	31.1	35.1	–	30.3	45.9	43.0	42.7
Total	100.0	100.0	100.0	–	100.0	100.0	100.0	100.0
N. of respondents	191	177	169	–	179	233	207	143

| | Wales | | | | | | | |
	1963	1964	1966	1969	1970	Feb. 1974	Oct. 1974	1979
Interest in politics								
A great deal	20.2	43.1	38.3	–	31.1	12.3	17.6	14.6
Some	35.4	31.9	34.6	–	38.3	48.5	48.1	44.7
Not much or none	44.4	25.0	27.1	–	30.6	39.2	34.4	40.8
Total	100.0	100.0	100.0	–	100.0	100.0	100.0	100.0
N. of respondents	99	72	88	–	96	130	131	103

Table 5.13 (*cont.*)

The North

	1963	1964	1966	1969	1970	Feb. 1974	Oct. 1974	1979
Interest in politics								
A great deal	14.2	29.6	28.2	–	36.6	18.5	19.2	10.0
Some	36.1	36.7	34.7	–	34.1	44.1	44.7	51.7
Not much or none	49.7	33.8	37.2	–	29.3	37.4	36.2	38.3
Total	100.0	100.0	100.0	–	100.0	100.0	100.0	100.0
N. of respondents	571	521	515	–	531	725	683	509

The Midlands

	1963	1964	1966	1969	1970	Feb. 1974	Oct. 1974	1979
Interest in politics								
A great deal	12.3	34.3	29.7	–	33.8	14.7	17.0	13.4
Some	39.3	36.7	37.5	–	37.5	45.4	47.6	43.3
Not much or none	48.4	28.9	32.8	–	28.7	39.9	35.5	43.3
Total	100.0	100.0	100.0	–	100.0	100.0	100.0	100.0
N. of respondents	351	332	375	–	337	381	389	328

Greater London

	1963	1964	1966	1969	1970	Feb. 1974	Oct. 1974	1979
Interest in politics								
A great deal	17.5	36.7	31.1	–	39.8	20.1	25.1	13.2
Some	40.4	36.7	32.6	–	30.5	44.7	48.0	45.8
Not much or none	42.1	26.7	36.3	–	29.7	35.2	26.8	41.0
Total	100.0	100.0	100.0	–	100.0	100.0	100.0	100.0
N. of respondents	311	259	278	–	294	264	227	212

The South

	1963	1964	1966	1969	1970	Feb. 1974	Oct. 1974	1979
Interest in politics								
A great deal	16.7	33.7	36.0	–	41.2	17.9	20.0	13.7
Some	36.1	36.7	37.1	–	33.3	48.0	47.1	49.7
Not much or none	47.2	25.6	26.9	–	25.5	34.0	32.9	36.6
Total	100.0	100.0	100.0	–	100.0	100.0	100.0	100.0
N. of respondents	475	432	466	–	400	705	705	582

Table 5.14 *Care which party wins: all respondents (%)*

	1963	1964	1966	1969	1970	Feb. 1974	Oct. 1974	1979	1983	1987
All respondents	66.7	68.9	71.7	68.0	69.5	67.6	68.9	–	74.7	76.8

Table 5.15 *Care which party wins by gender (%)*

	1963	1964	1966	1969	1970	Feb. 1974	Oct. 1974	1979	1983	1987
Men	71.5	71.3	72.2	71.7	71.8	70.6	69.7	–	76.7	78.6
Women	62.7	67.0	71.3	64.6	67.5	67.7	68.0	–	72.9	75.4

Table 5.16 *Care which party wins by age (%)*

	1963	1964	1966	1969	1970	Feb. 1974	Oct. 1974	1979	1983	1987
Aged under 25	53.5	60.6	68.3	55.1	60.2	61.9	59.5	–	61.6	66.0
Aged 25–34	61.2	66.4	68.2	74.5	66.1	68.9	66.5	–	71.7	76.1
Aged 35–44	69.8	72.3	73.0	70.6	66.2	67.0	69.8	–	80.5	80.9
Aged 45–54	67.6	68.1	74.2	72.1	72.3	70.7	73.4	–	78.3	79.2
Aged 55–64	73.1	73.6	75.4	75.0	75.6	72.5	69.7	–	78.5	79.5
Aged 65–74	68.0	68.8	69.4	74.5	77.2	73.5	73.0	–	76.2	78.0
Aged over 74	61.0	60.8	67.2	63.6	72.0	64.9	68.1	–	76.0	74.0

Table 5.17 *Care which party wins by age and gender (%)*

	1963	1964	1966	1969	1970	Feb. 1974	Oct. 1974	1979	1983	1987
Men under 25	66.1	59.3	66.0	53.6	63.3	59.2	61.2	–	68.3	64.3
Women under 25	44.6	61.7	71.1	56.9	57.1	64.6	57.8	–	54.4	67.8
Men 25–44	69.3	68.9	68.8	77.1	68.9	69.6	68.9	–	76.2	80.2
Women 25–44	63.3	70.4	72.4	67.5	63.5	66.4	67.1	–	75.8	76.9
Men 45–64	73.7	75.2	76.7	76.3	77.4	73.4	73.6	–	80.6	80.8
Women 45–64	67.0	66.8	72.9	71.1	70.9	70.0	69.8	–	76.4	77.9
Men over 64	73.8	71.4	71.6	75.0	75.7	75.0	69.6	–	78.5	82.0
Women over 64	60.0	62.2	66.5	68.3	75.6	67.4	72.8	–	74.3	72.6

Table 5.18 *Care which party wins by marital status (%)*

	1963	1964	1966	1969	1970	Feb. 1974	Oct. 1974	1979	1983	1987
Single	59.8	63.1	64.2	55.6	63.1	63.5	–	–	65.8	67.2
Married	67.9	70.3	73.3	73.6	70.3	70.7	69.4	–	77.3	79.2
Divorced or separated	–	–	79.3	–	–	51.9	–	–	71.0	73.5
Widowed	–	–	67.6	–	–	67.3	–	–	73.6	75.9

Table 5.19 *Care which party wins: new electors (%)*

	1963	1964	1966	1969	1970	Feb. 1974	Oct. 1974	1979	1983	1987
New electors	54.7	61.5	67.6	55.6	60.2	60.7	–	–	57.9	61.0

Table 5.20 *Care which party wins: non-voters (%)*

	1963	1964	1966	1969	1970	Feb. 1974	Oct. 1974	1979	1983	1987
Non-voters	–	44.1	48.1	–	50.6	39.1	25.8	–	46.1	48.5

Table 5.21 *Care which party wins by vote (%)*

	1963	1964	1966	1969	1970	Feb. 1974	Oct. 1974	1979	1983	1987
Voted for										
Conservative Party	80.1	77.2	75.6	83.6	84.6	80.4	79.4	–	89.5	90.6
Labour Party	67.8	73.4	80.3	64.6	70.5	73.6	78.5	–	75.5	75.2
Liberal Party	61.2	54.3	59.2	44.9	48.0	62.7	61.3	–	72.7	76.2
Other party voters	(50.0)	(45.4)	(46.0)	(42.1)	44.7	46.7	52.9	–	50.5	46.4

Table 5.22 *Care which party wins by strength and direction of partisanship (%)*

	1963	1964	1966	1969	1970	Feb. 1974	Oct. 1974	1979	1983	1987
Conservative identifiers										
Very strong	91.3	91.6	91.3	94.6	96.2	95.7	92.2	–	97.2	96.8
Fairly strong	76.3	68.6	66.8	85.4	82.9	78.1	75.9	–	91.1	91.8
Not very strong	52.3	47.8	35.5	62.3	40.7	53.2	53.2	–	69.4	74.5
Liberal identifiers										
Very strong	91.1	68.5	75.1	66.7	66.1	77.1	82.6	–	89.7	87.5
Fairly strong	62.9	53.7	52.7	50.0	61.8	61.7	61.9	–	78.5	77.4
Not very strong	35.7	36.4	29.6	41.5	25.3	44.4	48.3	–	62.7	49.9
Labour identifiers										
Very strong	83.2	86.5	93.2	78.7	85.3	87.7	87.3	–	85.2	90.5
Fairly strong	68.9	68.7	71.5	65.9	59.3	68.2	72.7	–	70.7	88.2
Not very strong	38.8	22.6	44.3	48.1	27.3	38.9	49.4	–	47.0	66.1

Table 5.23 *Care which party wins: non-partisans (%)*

	1963	1964	1966	1969	1970	Feb. 1974	Oct. 1974	1979	1983	1987
No party identification	19.8	25.7	26.2	21.1	24.3	29.9	20.5	–	45.9	46.8

Table 5.24 *Care which party wins by social class (%)*

	1963	1964	1966	1969	1970	Feb. 1974	Oct. 1974	1979	1983	1987
Professional and managerial classes	81.3	76.5	68.8	84.5	79.5	78.2	70.3	–	85.2	87.6
Intermediate and routine non-manual	69.1	68.4	72.4	69.8	68.5	70.6	71.2	–	77.0	81.7
Manual working class	63.0	67.2	72.2	65.2	67.2	65.6	66.4	–	68.3	68.1

Table 5.25 *Care which party wins: unemployed (%)*

	1963	1964	1966	1969	1970	Feb. 1974	Oct. 1974	1979	1983	1987
Unemployed	52.6	81.9	89.3	61.5	76.7	69.6	59.5	–	64.3	69.4

Table 5.26 *Care which party wins by school leaving age (%)*

	1963	1964	1966	1969	1970	Feb. 1974	Oct. 1974	1979	1983	1987
Left school aged										
Under 15	65.4	68.0	72.8	69.3	71.2	68.3	69.7	–	72.1	74.0
At 15	62.0	69.3	68.2	61.3	63.8	67.9	66.7	–	74.9	76.1
At 16	75.7	69.8	75.1	78.9	71.2	71.2	69.6	–	69.5	71.3
At 17	79.8	78.0	76.2	75.0	73.8	76.9	74.2	–	84.8	85.3
18 or over	78.9	71.7	67.9	79.4	71.9	69.9	66.7	–	84.9	86.2

Table 5.27 *Care which party wins: university or polytechnic educated (%)*

	1963	1964	1966	1969	1970	Feb. 1974	Oct. 1974	1979	1983	1987
Attended university or polytechnic	66.7	60.8	–	76.2	79.8	71.8	68.7	–	84.6	–

Table 5.28 *Care which party wins by region (%)*

	1963	1964	1966	1969	1970	Feb. 1974	Oct. 1974	1979	1983	1987
Scotland	64.4	67.7	74.2	72.4	73.3	64.9	63.8	–	76.4	76.6
Wales	63.2	65.5	65.7	64.0	51.4	77.1	76.2	–	72.2	74.2
The North	63.7	70.7	71.4	66.6	68.3	66.2	67.5	–	72.1	74.1
The Midlands	66.4	69.0	70.7	67.4	68.3	67.1	66.2	–	72.5	74.6
Greater London	70.8	68.1	71.9	69.9	68.9	77.8	75.3	–	74.3	76.7
The South	69.2	66.4	73.0	67.6	75.4	69.8	69.7	–	81.0	80.3

Chapter 6

PARTY IMAGE

1. The questions on the extremism of the Conservative and Labour parties and on whether these parties are good for one or for all classes were first asked in February 1974 and thereafter except for 1979.
2. The question on whether the Liberals are closer to the Conservatives or to Labour was first asked in February 1974 and thereafter at every election.

See Appendix E, pp. 495, 497 and 498 on the construction of these variables.

Table 6.1 *Perceived difference between the parties: all respondents (%)*

	1963	1964	1966	1969	1970	Feb. 1974	Oct. 1974	1979	1983	1987
Perceived difference between the parties										
A great deal	39.5	48.0	43.7	30.9	33.0	33.8	39.5	47.6	83.6	84.6
Some	22.6	24.6	27.0	23.4	28.4	30.3	30.4	30.1	10.2	10.8
Not much or none	37.9	27.4	29.3	45.8	38.5	35.9	30.1	22.3	6.3	4.6
Total	100.0	100.0	100.0	100.0	100.0	100.0	100.0	100.0	100.0	100.0
N. of respondents	1809	1699	1804	1053	1780	2391	2332	1826	3893	3776

Table 6.2 *Perceived difference between the parties by gender (%)*

	Men									
	1963	1964	1966	1969	1970	Feb. 1974	Oct. 1974	1979	1983	1987
Perceived difference between the parties										
A great deal	41.3	50.7	44.0	33.8	35.3	35.3	41.4	50.2	85.1	86.1
Some	21.8	21.0	25.6	23.4	26.7	27.8	29.7	27.3	9.0	9.6
Not much or none	36.9	28.4	30.4	42.9	38.0	36.8	28.9	22.5	5.9	4.3
Total	100.0	100.0	100.0	100.0	100.0	100.0	100.0	100.0	100.0	100.0
N. of respondents	854	791	861	518	844	1146	1162	886	1851	1821
	Women									
	1963	1964	1966	1969	1970	Feb. 1974	Oct. 1974	1979	1983	1987
Perceived difference between the parties										
A great deal	37.9	45.6	43.4	28.0	31.0	32.4	37.6	45.1	82.2	83.3
Some	23.2	27.8	28.3	23.4	30.0	32.6	31.1	32.8	11.2	11.9
Not much or none	38.8	26.6	28.3	48.6	39.0	35.0	31.3	22.1	6.6	4.8
Total	100.0	100.0	100.0	100.0	100.0	100.0	100.0	100.0	100.0	100.0
N. of respondents	955	909	943	535	936	1245	1170	940	2041	1955

Table 6.3 *Perceived difference between the parties by age (%)*

	Aged under 25									
	1963	1964	1966	1969	1970	Feb. 1974	Oct. 1974	1979	1983	1987
Perceived difference between the parties										
A great deal	30.9	42.9	38.9	22.9	24.5	27.3	33.8	41.6	76.6	77.3
Some	33.3	32.2	30.5	28.4	34.1	38.4	39.7	33.1	16.7	16.2
Not much or none	35.7	24.9	30.6	48.6	41.5	34.3	26.5	25.3	6.6	6.5
Total	100.0	100.0	100.0	100.0	100.0	100.0	100.0	100.0	100.0	100.0
N. of respondents	126	101	137	109	260	242	275	166	541	479

Table 6.3 (*cont.*)

Aged 25–34

	1963	1964	1966	1969	1970	Feb. 1974	Oct. 1974	1979	1983	1987
Perceived difference between the parties										
A great deal	36.0	48.9	36.0	28.0	23.6	33.3	39.0	41.9	83.5	85.3
Some	24.0	28.2	32.7	28.6	33.7	32.8	34.6	34.7	11.0	11.2
Not much or none	40.0	22.9	31.3	43.5	42.7	33.9	26.4	23.4	5.5	3.5
Total	100.0	100.0	100.0	100.0	100.0	100.0	100.0	100.0	100.0	100.0
N. of respondents	300	287	317	161	287	460	477	415	735	677

Aged 35–44

	1963	1964	1966	1969	1970	Feb. 1974	Oct. 1974	1979	1983	1987
Perceived difference between the parties										
A great deal	43.6	51.2	45.4	30.9	30.4	34.6	38.9	51.4	87.1	86.1
Some	22.7	25.9	30.7	20.1	27.8	31.5	30.2	29.5	9.0	10.1
Not much or none	33.7	22.9	23.8	49.1	41.8	33.9	30.9	19.1	4.0	3.8
Total	100.0	100.0	100.0	100.0	100.0	100.0	100.0	100.0	100.0	100.0
N. of respondents	392	368	357	175	307	413	401	319	710	749

Aged 45–54

	1963	1964	1966	1969	1970	Feb. 1974	Oct. 1974	1979	1983	1987
Perceived difference between the parties										
A great deal	39.3	46.5	45.5	29.1	37.9	36.1	38.0	46.0	86.8	87.1
Some	23.8	24.7	23.2	24.7	24.9	28.7	33.6	31.6	7.8	8.9
Not much or none	36.9	28.8	31.3	46.2	37.2	35.2	28.4	22.4	5.5	3.9
Total	100.0	100.0	100.0	100.0	100.0	100.0	100.0	100.0	100.0	100.0
N. of respondents	366	343	374	182	292	435	405	335	622	573

Aged 55–64

	1963	1964	1966	1969	1970	Feb. 1974	Oct. 1974	1979	1983	1987
Perceived difference between the parties										
A great deal	44.2	51.3	44.9	38.9	38.9	32.0	42.5	50.6	84.9	87.3
Some	21.2	21.7	25.4	20.6	23.8	24.6	23.1	25.7	8.2	9.1
Not much or none	34.6	27.0	29.7	40.6	37.3	43.4	34.4	23.7	6.9	3.6
Total	100.0	100.0	100.0	100.0	100.0	100.0	100.0	100.0	100.0	100.0
N. of respondents	321	316	325	175	324	378	355	257	591	592

Table 6.3 (*cont.*)

Aged 65–74

	1963	1964	1966	1969	1970	Feb. 1974	Oct. 1974	1979	1983	1987
Perceived difference between the parties										
A great deal	35.3	41.6	48.5	40.6	40.2	39.2	45.2	55.3	82.3	83.4
Some	18.1	20.4	21.5	14.9	25.1	25.3	21.9	25.7	9.5	10.4
Not much or none	46.5	38.0	30.0	44.6	34.7	35.5	33.0	18.9	8.3	6.2
Total	100.0	100.0	100.0	100.0	100.0	100.0	100.0	100.0	100.0	100.0
N. of respondents	215	193	195	101	210	296	279	206	436	417

Aged over 74

	1963	1964	1966	1969	1970	Feb. 1974	Oct. 1974	1979	1983	1987
Perceived difference between the parties										
A great deal	38.8	45.4	49.4	41.5	43.6	31.5	39.7	49.6	79.5	82.5
Some	11.8	18.7	19.7	22.6	30.7	33.6	23.7	25.2	9.2	10.5
Not much or none	49.4	35.9	30.9	35.8	25.7	35.0	36.6	25.2	11.3	7.0
Total	100.0	100.0	100.0	100.0	100.0	100.0	100.0	100.0	100.0	100.0
N. of respondents	85	91	95	55	89	143	131	119	239	255

Table 6.4 *Perceived difference between the parties by marital status (%)*

Single

	1963	1964	1966	1969	1970	Feb. 1974	Oct. 1974	1979	1983	1987
Perceived difference between the parties										
A great deal	35.2	50.5	36.3	33.9	32.1	27.8	–	39.5	79.7	81.2
Some	25.7	20.5	35.3	27.6	31.2	32.2	–	35.5	14.6	14.7
Not much or none	39.1	27.0	28.5	48.6	36.7	34.0	–	25.0	5.7	4.1
Total	100.0	100.0	100.0	100.0	100.0	100.0	–	100.0	100.0	100.0
N. of respondents	230	199	198	243	312	335	–	220	676	682

Married

	1963	1964	1966	1969	1970	Feb. 1974	Oct. 1974	1979	1983	1987
Perceived difference between the parties										
A great deal	40.7	48.2	44.4	33.4	32.2	35.5	41.5	49.1	84.8	86.0
Some	22.6	25.3	26.5	21.5	28.0	28.9	28.4	30.2	9.3	9.4
Not much or none	36.6	26.5	29.1	45.1	39.8	35.5	30.1	20.7	5.9	4.5
Total	100.0	100.0	100.0	100.0	100.0	100.0	100.0	100.0	100.0	100.0
N. of respondents	1367	1327	1401	688	1265	1759	1748	1323	2725	2577

Table 6.4 (*cont.*)

| | Divorced and separated | | | | | | | | | |
	1963	1964	1966	1969	1970	Feb. 1974	Oct. 1974	1979	1983	1987
Perceived difference between the parties										
A great deal	–	–	(18.4)	–	–	33.3	–	47.4	82.4	83.1
Some	–	–	(5.7)	–	–	22.2	–	27.6	11.2	13.1
Not much or none	–	–	(29.9)	–	–	44.4	–	25.0	6.4	3.8
Total	–	–	(100.0)	–	–	100.0	–	100.0	100.0	100.0
N. of respondents	–	–	9	–	–	76	–	76	176	183

| | Widowed | | | | | | | | | |
	1963	1964	1966	1969	1970	Feb. 1974	Oct. 1974	1979	1983	1987
Perceived difference between the parties										
A great deal	–	–	46.7	–	–	30.0	–	46.5	82.1	82.0
Some	–	–	20.5	–	–	30.4	–	25.4	7.5	12.0
Not much or none	–	–	32.7	–	–	39.6	–	28.1	10.4	6.0
Total	–	–	100.0	–	–	100.0	–	100.0	100.0	100.0
N. of respondents	–	–	189	–	–	270	–	185	314	333

Table 6.5 *Perceived difference between the parties: new electors (%)*

	1963	1964	1966	1969	1970	Feb. 1974	Oct. 1974	1979	1983	1987
Perceived difference between the parties										
A great deal	29.7	16.1	32.0	23.1	24.5	22.6	–	43.4	71.5	75.0
Some	34.2	29.9	32.0	27.7	34.1	41.7	–	30.3	21.3	19.1
Not much or none	36.0	24.0	35.9	49.2	41.5	35.7	–	26.2	7.2	5.9
Total	100.0	100.0	100.0	100.0	100.0	100.0	–	100.0	100.0	100.0
N. of respondents	111	126	65	65	260	84	–	122	297	269

Table 6.6 *Perceived difference between the parties: non voters (%)*

	1963	1964	1966	1969	1970	Feb. 1974	Oct. 1974	1979	1983	1987
Perceived difference between the parties										
A great deal	–	42.2	33.4	–	25.9	23.4	28.2	35.6	70.7	75.5
Some	–	22.3	27.4	–	24.3	30.9	28.8	33.2	16.2	15.5
Not much or none	–	35.5	39.2	–	49.8	45.7	42.9	31.2	13.1	9.0
Total	–	100.0	100.0	–	100.0	100.0	100.0	100.0	100.0	100.0
N. of respondents	–	175	276	–	325	282	340	250	626	515

Table 6.7 *Perceived difference between the parties by vote (%)*

	Conservative voters									
	1963	1964	1966	1969	1970	Feb. 1974	Oct. 1974	1979	1983	1987
Perceived difference between the parties										
A great deal	42.5	51.6	43.2	38.8	43.0	40.9	46.3	54.0	90.2	89.1
Some	23.5	24.5	29.3	27.4	29.8	30.2	29.2	31.5	7.5	8.9
Not much or none	33.9	23.9	27.4	33.8	27.2	29.1	24.5	14.5	2.3	2.0
Total	100.0	100.0	100.0	100.0	100.0	100.0	100.0	100.0	100.0	100.0
N. of respondents	595	621	578	515	650	771	695	717	1443	1405

	Labour voters									
	1963	1964	1966	1969	1970	Feb. 1974	Oct. 1974	1979	1983	1987
Perceived difference between the parties										
A great deal	42.0	48.3	50.0	28.6	31.0	34.3	42.5	49.9	79.0	81.7
Some	21.2	24.2	24.5	18.0	27.0	29.5	30.6	26.3	11.4	12.1
Not much or none	36.9	27.5	25.5	53.4	42.0	36.2	26.9	23.8	9.6	6.3
Total	100.0	100.0	100.0	100.0	100.0	100.0	100.0	100.0	100.0	100.0
N. of respondents	784	702	788	283	634	814	818	571	905	979

	Liberal voters									
	1963	1964	1966	1969	1970	Feb. 1974	Oct. 1974	1979	1983	1987
Perceived difference between the parties										
A great deal	38.4	42.4	34.1	16.0	17.6	27.8	35.2	40.4	89.0	87.4
Some	26.5	30.3	30.3	20.0	37.3	35.0	33.0	36.1	7.6	9.0
Not much or none	35.2	27.3	35.7	64.0	45.1	37.3	31.8	23.6	3.3	3.6
Total	100.0	100.0	100.0	100.0	100.0	100.0	100.0	100.0	100.0	100.0
N. of respondents	219	165	129	100	106	389	349	208	786	747

	Voters for other parties									
	1963	1964	1966	1969	1970	Feb. 1974	Oct. 1974	1979	1983	1987
Perceived difference between the parties										
A great deal	(0.0)	(39.1)	(33.3)	(22.2)	14.8	25.5	25.4	25.0	66.9	82.6
Some	(0.0)	(20.7)	(43.7)	(16.7)	31.8	23.4	39.8	16.7	15.2	6.5
Not much or none	(100.0)	(40.2)	(23.0)	(61.1)	53.4	51.1	35.8	58.3	18.0	11.0
Total	(100.0)	(100.0)	(100.0)	(100.0)	100.0	100.0	100.0	100.0	100.0	100.0
N. of respondents	2	9	9	18	34	47	67	24	42	44

Table 6.8 *Perceived difference between the parties by strength and direction of partisanship (%)*

	Very strong Conservative identifiers									
	1963	1964	1966	1969	1970	Feb. 1974	Oct. 1974	1979	1983	1987
Perceived difference between the parties										
A great deal	54.7	65.3	54.4	57.7	58.7	59.0	67.6	76.9	91.6	93.8
Some	21.4	19.1	27.2	22.7	24.8	23.2	19.0	19.5	5.6	5.0
Not much or none	23.9	15.6	18.3	19.6	16.5	17.7	13.4	3.6	2.8	1.2
Total	100.0	100.0	100.0	100.0	100.0	100.0	100.0	100.0	100.0	100.0
N. of respondents	243	317	302	163	355	271	216	169	357	325

	Fairly strong Conservative identifiers									
	1963	1964	1966	1969	1970	Feb. 1974	Oct. 1974	1979	1983	1987
Perceived difference between the parties										
A great deal	38.0	40.3	33.8	33.5	33.8	33.6	40.4	54.3	90.5	89.3
Some	25.0	29.7	33.8	32.0	33.3	34.8	34.4	32.6	6.9	8.6
Not much or none	37.0	30.0	32.4	34.5	32.9	31.5	25.2	13.1	2.7	2.1
Total	100.0	100.0	100.0	100.0	100.0	100.0	100.0	100.0	100.0	100.0
N. of respondents	276	271	251	203	277	422	421	383	671	713

	Not very strong Conservative identifiers									
	1963	1964	1966	1969	1970	Feb. 1974	Oct. 1974	1979	1983	1987
Perceived difference between the parties										
A great deal	30.8	38.8	23.9	22.9	11.7	18.5	30.0	40.5	82.9	84.8
Some	22.6	29.3	27.8	27.6	40.5	32.3	36.3	33.7	11.7	13.0
Not much or none	46.5	31.9	48.3	49.5	47.8	49.2	33.7	25.8	5.4	2.1
Total	100.0	100.0	100.0	100.0	100.0	100.0	100.0	100.0	100.0	100.0
N. of respondents	159	83	100	105	99	189	190	190	445	338

	Very strong Liberal identifiers									
	1963	1964	1966	1969	1970	Feb. 1974	Oct. 1974	1979	1983	1987
Perceived difference between the parties										
A great deal	44.1	51.9	49.2	(35.3)	27.2	47.2	41.3	51.7	87.2	88.3
Some	26.4	17.9	28.5	(11.8)	31.3	25.0	23.9	24.1	7.7	8.2
Not much or none	24.5	30.2	22.3	(52.9)	41.5	27.8	34.8	24.1	5.1	3.5
Total	100.0	100.0	100.0	(100.0)	100.0	100.0	100.0	100.0	100.0	100.0
N. of respondents	53	65	64	17	36	36	46	29	78	63

Table 6.8 (*cont.*)

Fairly strong Liberal identifiers

	1963	1964	1966	1969	1970	Feb. 1974	Oct. 1974	1979	1983	1987
Perceived difference between the parties										
A great deal	36.9	40.3	27.4	38.6	20.8	27.2	34.4	38.7	91.8	85.9
Some	33.3	29.5	29.9	18.2	32.8	36.1	31.7	37.7	6.6	10.7
Not much or none	29.8	30.3	42.7	43.2	46.5	36.7	33.9	23.6	1.6	3.3
Total	100.0	100.0	100.0	100.0	100.0	100.0	100.0	100.0	100.0	100.0
N. of respondents	84	97	101	44	76	169	189	106	305	268

Not very strong Liberal identifiers

	1963	1964	1966	1969	1970	Feb. 1974	Oct. 1974	1979	1983	1987
Perceived difference between the parties										
A great deal	27.0	41.2	29.3	9.3	5.6	22.9	25.8	29.9	87.1	89.0
Some	27.0	35.6	18.5	20.9	41.4	33.1	37.5	44.8	8.5	7.3
Not much or none	46.0	23.3	52.1	69.8	52.9	44.1	36.7	25.3	4.4	3.7
Total	100.0	100.0	100.0	100.0	100.0	100.0	100.0	100.0	100.0	100.0
N. of respondents	63	49	26	43	30	118	120	87	318	318

Very strong Labour identifiers

	1963	1964	1966	1969	1970	Feb. 1974	Oct. 1974	1979	1983	1987
Perceived difference between the parties										
A great deal	54.6	58.1	66.1	37.7	40.1	45.6	56.1	64.7	84.0	83.9
Some	20.7	19.5	18.2	19.8	27.4	27.7	24.8	20.0	8.4	9.5
Not much or none	24.7	22.4	15.7	42.5	32.5	26.7	19.1	15.3	7.6	6.6
Total	100.0	100.0	100.0	100.0	100.0	100.0	100.0	100.0	100.0	100.0
N. of respondents	304	368	414	106	350	386	335	190	344	295

Fairly strong Labour identifiers

	1963	1964	1966	1969	1970	Feb. 1974	Oct. 1974	1979	1983	1987
Perceived difference between the parties										
A great deal	38.3	40.2	38.9	20.6	20.1	30.4	35.4	42.2	79.0	84.0
Some	21.7	30.6	31.6	22.1	29.0	31.3	32.7	32.3	12.8	11.3
Not much or none	40.0	29.2	29.5	57.3	50.8	38.3	31.8	25.5	8.1	4.7
Total	100.0	100.0	100.0	100.0	100.0	100.0	100.0	100.0	100.0	100.0
N. of respondents	345	268	338	131	297	415	443	341	491	495

Table 6.8 (*cont.*)

	Not very strong Labour identifiers									
	1963	1964	1966	1969	1970	Feb. 1974	Oct. 1974	1979	1983	1987
Perceived difference between the parties										
A great deal	21.8	29.0	21.7	20.3	21.0	18.0	28.2	34.3	69.8	75.2
Some	24.6	23.0	28.0	14.8	20.8	28.8	29.4	31.4	15.1	15.8
Not much or none	53.6	48.0	50.3	64.8	58.1	53.2	42.4	34.3	15.1	9.0
Total	100.0	100.0	100.0	100.0	100.0	100.0	100.0	100.0	100.0	100.0
N. of respondents	179	93	94	128	127	205	177	175	378	353

Table 6.9 *Perceived difference between the parties by social class (%)*

	Professional and managerial classes									
	1963	1964	1966	1969	1970	Feb. 1974	Oct. 1974	1979	1983	1987
Perceived difference between the parties										
A great deal	45.7	44.4	37.8	32.1	37.1	41.6	40.8	51.1	90.2	91.2
Some	27.2	32.4	32.9	34.0	32.5	31.3	36.5	35.1	7.5	7.4
Not much or none	27.2	23.1	29.3	34.0	30.4	27.1	22.7	3.9	2.3	1.4
Total	100.0	100.0	100.0	100.0	100.0	100.0	100.0	100.0	100.0	100.0
N. of respondents	243	210	236	106	292	339	353	368	1011	970

	Intermediate and routine non-manual classes									
	1963	1964	1966	1969	1970	Feb. 1974	Oct. 1974	1979	1983	1987
Perceived difference between the parties										
A great deal	41.0	47.6	40.5	32.1	30.6	37.3	42.6	47.7	87.9	85.8
Some	18.9	25.3	29.3	23.9	31.3	31.3	32.0	32.8	9.0	11.1
Not much or none	40.1	27.1	30.2	44.0	38.1	31.4	25.4	19.6	3.1	3.2
Total	100.0	100.0	100.0	100.0	100.0	100.0	100.0	100.0	100.0	100.0
N. of respondents	429	500	496	243	461	821	806	491	736	944

	Manual working class									
	1963	1964	1966	1969	1970	Feb. 1974	Oct. 1974	1979	1983	1987
Perceived difference between the parties										
A great deal	37.5	48.9	46.8	31.3	32.3	29.5	38.4	45.8	78.3	80.6
Some	23.6	22.1	24.4	17.7	26.1	28.4	26.2	27.0	12.0	12.5
Not much or none	38.9	29.1	28.8	51.0	41.6	42.1	35.4	27.2	9.7	6.8
Total	100.0	100.0	100.0	100.0	100.0	100.0	100.0	100.0	100.0	100.0
N. of respondents	1042	926	1040	453	953	1084	1052	890	1863	1677

Table 6.10 *Perceived difference between the parties by school leaving age (%)*

	Left school aged under 15									
	1963	1964	1966	1969	1970	Feb. 1974	Oct. 1974	1979	1983	1987
Perceived difference between the parties										
A great deal	38.9	47.4	48.8	33.6	35.0	31.2	40.1	49.3	80.5	80.2
Some	21.4	22.7	22.7	19.6	25.0	26.3	24.6	26.2	9.5	12.7
Not much or none	39.7	29.9	28.4	46.8	40.0	42.4	35.3	24.5	10.0	7.1
Total	100.0	100.0	100.0	100.0	100.0	100.0	100.0	100.0	100.0	100.0
N. of respondents	1084	992	993	455	774	1037	965	603	1143	900

	Left school aged 15									
	1963	1964	1966	1969	1970	Feb. 1974	Oct. 1974	1979	1983	1987
Perceived difference between the parties										
A great deal	37.5	48.4	39.7	26.8	26.1	33.9	37.0	44.3	85.0	83.9
Some	24.1	26.6	29.2	21.8	29.7	31.4	33.2	29.7	9.9	11.1
Not much or none	38.3	24.9	31.0	51.3	44.2	34.7	29.7	26.0	5.1	5.0
Total	100.0	100.0	100.0	100.0	100.0	100.0	100.0	100.0	100.0	100.0
N. of respondents	373	371	413	261	445	681	683	535	991	906

	Left school aged 16									
	1963	1964	1966	1969	1970	Feb. 1974	Oct. 1974	1979	1983	1987
Perceived difference between the parties										
A great deal	47.7	46.8	35.5	35.0	36.8	38.8	45.3	51.0	79.5	83.2
Some	19.9	25.7	32.5	31.0	30.6	34.2	33.0	31.0	13.6	12.6
Not much or none	32.4	27.5	31.9	34.0	32.7	27.1	21.6	18.0	6.9	4.2
Total	100.0	100.0	100.0	100.0	100.0	100.0	100.0	100.0	100.0	100.0
N. of respondents	176	170	202	100	173	325	333	355	940	897

	Left school aged 17									
	1963	1964	1966	1969	1970	Feb. 1974	Oct. 1974	1979	1983	1987
Perceived difference between the parties										
A great deal	33.8	42.7	23.0	27.9	34.8	34.8	43.2	43.4	91.6	89.2
Some	36.4	38.0	48.8	26.2	37.8	33.5	33.5	40.2	7.0	7.2
Not much or none	29.9	19.4	28.2	45.9	27.4	31.6	23.2	16.4	1.4	3.6
Total	100.0	100.0	100.0	100.0	100.0	100.0	100.0	100.0	100.0	100.0
N. of respondents	77	66	86	61	110	155	155	122	328	306

Table 6.10 (*cont.*)

| | Left school aged 18 or over | | | | | | | | | |
	1963	1964	1966	1969	1970	Feb. 1974	Oct. 1974	1979	1983	1987
Perceived difference between the parties										
A great deal	41.4	57.0	43.0	24.6	30.1	38.4	31.5	48.1	90.8	88.9
Some	26.4	26.3	27.9	35.4	40.4	40.7	44.4	36.8	7.5	8.5
Not much or none	32.2	16.7	29.1	40.0	29.4	20.9	24.2	15.1	1.7	2.7
Total	100.0	100.0	100.0	100.0	100.0	100.0	100.0	100.0	100.0	100.0
N. of respondents	87	88	87	65	114	177	178	185	480	377

Table 6.11 *Perceived difference between the parties: university or polytechnic educated (%)*

	1963	1964	1966	1969	1970	Feb. 1974	Oct. 1974	1979	1983	1987
Perceived difference between the parties										
A great deal	40.0	46.0	–	31.8	31.6	–	–	–	88.9	–
Some	32.0	23.8	–	40.9	49.3	–	–	–	8.5	–
Not much or none	28.0	30.2	–	27.3	19.1	–	–	–	2.6	–
Total	100.0	100.0	–	100.0	100.0	–	–	–	100.0	–
N. of respondents	25	37	–	44	58	–	–	–	407	–

Table 6.12 *Perceived difference between the parties by region (%)*

| | Scotland | | | | | | | | | |
	1963	1964	1966	1969	1970	Feb. 1974	Oct. 1974	1979	1983	1987
Perceived difference between the parties										
A great deal	38.6	53.8	43.2	37.3	33.5	28.9	36.8	42.7	77.6	81.9
Some	18.1	18.9	30.3	24.5	25.5	30.3	31.3	27.3	12.4	10.8
Not much or none	43.3	27.2	26.5	38.2	41.0	40.8	31.8	30.1	10.1	7.2
Total	100.0	100.0	100.0	100.0	100.0	100.0	100.0	100.0	100.0	100.0
N. of respondents	171	169	163	102	173	228	201	143	351	346

Table 6.12 (*cont.*)

Wales

	1963	1964	1966	1969	1970	Feb. 1974	Oct. 1974	1979	1983	1987
Perceived difference between the parties										
A great deal	50.6	39.1	43.2	32.0	31.0	39.1	38.9	51.5	87.5	81.5
Some	11.2	29.0	26.8	24.0	24.1	31.3	35.1	25.3	6.3	11.8
Not much or none	38.2	31.9	30.0	44.0	45.0	29.7	26.0	23.2	6.3	6.6
Total	100.0	100.0	100.0	100.0	100.0	100.0	100.0	100.0	100.0	100.0
N. of respondents	89	68	87	50	94	128	131	99	202	196

The North

	1963	1964	1966	1969	1970	Feb. 1974	Oct. 1974	1979	1983	1987
Perceived difference between the parties										
A great deal	40.0	48.7	45.6	27.8	33.0	34.7	36.9	49.3	82.6	82.5
Some	20.2	25.1	26.1	25.8	27.3	29.4	28.7	31.2	9.8	12.3
Not much or none	39.8	26.3	28.3	46.4	39.7	35.9	34.4	19.5	7.6	5.2
Total	100.0	100.0	100.0	100.0	100.0	100.0	100.0	100.0	100.0	100.0
N. of respondents	520	495	484	291	520	708	677	493	1049	980

The Midlands

	1963	1964	1966	1969	1970	Feb. 1974	Oct. 1974	1979	1983	1987
Perceived difference between the parties										
A great deal	36.6	49.8	44.0	30.5	29.9	32.5	42.3	48.8	82.3	85.3
Some	25.6	25.2	25.4	23.0	31.9	28.3	30.8	26.9	11.3	9.7
Not much or none	37.9	24.9	30.6	46.5	38.2	39.2	26.9	24.4	6.3	5.0
Total	100.0	100.0	100.0	100.0	100.0	100.0	100.0	100.0	100.0	100.0
N. of respondents	317	309	365	187	319	375	390	320	621	635

Greater London

	1963	1964	1966	1969	1970	Feb. 1974	Oct. 1974	1979	1983	1987
Perceived difference between the parties										
A great deal	35.2	47.5	39.7	26.6	31.0	33.8	44.2	43.6	81.2	83.9
Some	27.8	25.5	26.0	20.3	28.0	28.5	31.4	34.2	14.2	12.1
Not much or none	36.9	27.0	34.3	53.1	41.0	37.6	24.3	22.3	4.6	4.0
Total	100.0	100.0	100.0	100.0	100.0	100.0	100.0	100.0	100.0	100.0
N. of respondents	306	282	264	192	286	263	226	202	486	451

Table 6.12 (*cont.*)

| | The South | | | | | | | | | |
	1963	1964	1966	1969	1970	Feb. 1974	Oct. 1974	1979	1983	1987
Perceived difference between the parties										
A great deal	44.8	44.6	44.1	35.5	37.3	39.1	39.7	47.5	87.2	87.8
Some	22.2	24.7	28.6	22.5	29.9	32.9	30.4	31.1	8.2	9.3
Not much or none	33.0	30.8	27.3	42.0	32.8	32.9	29.8	21.4	4.6	2.8
Total	100.0	100.0	100.0	100.0	100.0	100.0	100.0	100.0	100.0	100.0
N. of respondents	406	376	440	231	388	689	707	569	1184	1166

Table 6.13 *Extremism of the Conservative and Labour parties: all respondents (%)*

	Feb. 1974	Oct. 1974	1979	1983	1987
All respondents perceiving extremism in					
Conservative Party	44.9	47.5	–	54.7	54.0
Labour Party	44.0	54.6	–	57.4	57.2

Table 6.14 *Extremism of the Conservative and Labour parties by gender (%)*

	Feb. 1974	Oct. 1974	1979	1983	1987
Men perceiving extremism in					
Conservative Party	47.1	49.4	–	55.8	56.8
Labour Party	46.3	59.3	–	62.1	57.3
Women perceiving extremism in					
Conservative Party	42.8	45.5	–	53.6	51.4
Labour Party	41.9	49.5	–	52.9	56.8

Table 6.15 *Extremism of the Conservative and Labour parties by age (%)*

	Feb. 1974	Oct. 1974	1979	1983	1987
Aged under 25 perceiving extremism in					
Conservative Party	49.7	57.3	–	46.1	53.0
Labour Party	39.4	54.4	–	53.3	46.7
Aged 25–34					
Conservative Party	50.5	50.6	–	55.7	54.8
Labour Party	42.6	57.5	–	54.7	55.0
Aged 35–44					
Conservative Party	47.4	47.3	–	56.6	57.2
Labour Party	46.5	50.8	–	62.4	62.0
Aged 45–54					
Conservative Party	45.3	46.5	–	58.3	55.5
Labour Party	46.2	54.1	–	56.3	59.6
Aged 55–64					
Conservative Party	45.2	44.5	–	60.9	53.9
Labour Party	38.7	55.2	–	60.0	58.6
Aged 65–74					
Conservative Party	36.6	46.0	–	51.8	55.7
Labour Party	46.5	53.2	–	56.1	60.2
Aged over 74					
Conservative Party	27.0	31.3	–	44.9	39.0
Labour Party	52.0	59.6	–	61.0	55.1

Table 6.16 *Extremism of the Conservative and Labour parties: new electors (%)*

	Feb. 1974	Oct. 1974	1979	1983	1987
New electors perceiving extremism in					
Conservative Party	55.1	–	–	43.1	47.5
Labour Party	42.3	–	–	54.1	47.5

Table 6.17 Extremism of the Conservative and Labour parties by political generation (%)

	Feb. 1974	Oct. 1974	1979	1983	1987
First voted 1918–1935 perceiving extremism in					
Conservative Party	35.7	42.3	–	45.1	39.8
Labour Party	44.8	54.2	–	60.1	55.5
First voted 1936–1950					
Conservative Party	46.3	45.5	–	60.1	55.0
Labour Party	44.1	55.2	–	57.8	60.7
First voted 1951–1970					
Conservative Party	48.9	50.3	–	57.2	56.0
Labour Party	43.6	53.8	–	59.2	60.3
First voted after 1970					
Conservative Party	55.1	57.3	–	53.6	54.3
Labour Party	39.8	56.3	–	52.7	51.7

Table 6.18 *Extremism of the Conservative and Labour parties: non-voters (%)*

	Feb. 1974	Oct. 1974	1979	1983	1987
Non-voters perceiving extremism in					
Conservative Party	48.2	47.6	–	48.0	49.3
Labour Party	38.4	55.1	–	48.1	51.5

Table 6.19 *Extremism of the Conservative and Labour parties by vote (%)*

	Feb. 1974	Oct. 1974	1979	1983	1987
Conservative voters perceiving extremism in					
Conservative Party	19.6	20.0	–	31.6	26.1
Labour Party	67.4	75.8	–	75.0	75.3
Labour voters					
Conservative Party	68.5	70.8	–	77.7	80.5
Labour Party	21.2	31.1	–	28.6	24.2
Liberal voters					
Conservative Party	47.6	50.5	–	74.4	73.2
Labour Party	48.9	66.6	–	67.1	59.0
Voters for other parties					
Conservative Party	64.9	50.0	–	59.1	72.4
Labour Party	44.1	45.8	–	34.0	54.5

Table 6.20 *Extremism of the Conservative and Labour parties by strength and direction of partisanship (%)*

	Feb. 1974	Oct. 1974	1979	1983	1987
Very strong Conservative identifiers perceiving extremism in					
Conservative Party	12.8	15.3	–	31.2	24.9
Labour Party	78.9	77.7	–	80.3	84.9
Fairly strong Conservative identifiers					
Conservative Party	18.9	21.3	–	31.9	27.5
Labour Party	61.4	73.6	–	75.7	74.5
Not very strong Conservative identifiers					
Conservative Party	37.3	19.0	–	30.9	35.4
Labour Party	60.4	75.3	–	65.5	67.5
Very strong Liberal identifiers					
Conservative Party	44.1	53.8	–	79.2	84.5
Labour Party	49.4	61.9	–	67.2	68.4
Fairly strong Liberal identifiers					
Conservative Party	41.2	53.8	–	76.7	69.9
Labour Party	55.2	67.1	–	71.1	71.0
Not very strong Liberal identifiers					
Conservative Party	48.9	44.2	–	68.1	67.0
Labour Party	54.8	64.8	–	68.0	67.7
Very strong Labour identifiers					
Conservative Party	71.2	71.6	–	82.2	85.3
Labour Party	15.7	29.8	–	26.2	21.4

Table 6.20 (*cont.*)

	Feb. 1974	Oct. 1974	1979	1983	1987
Fairly strong Labour identifiers					
Conservative Party	70.2	72.0	–	74.0	79.5
Labour Party	22.3	31.8	–	31.7	26.2
Not very strong Labour identifiers					
Conservative Party	57.2	69.7	–	62.9	64.5
Labour Party	24.2	36.9	–	38.1	34.5

Table 6.21 *Extremism of the Conservative and Labour parties: non-partisans (%)*

	Feb. 1974	Oct. 1974	1979	1983	1987
Respondents with no party identification perceiving extremism in					
Conservative Party	40.7	50.0	–	48.8	38.3
Labour Party	47.3	58.3	–	47.1	57.1

Table 6.22 *Extremism of the Conservative and Labour parties by political generation and partisanship (%)*

	Feb. 1974	Oct. 1974	1979	1983	1987
Conservative identifiers: first voted 1918–1935 perceiving extremism in					
Conservative Party	17.4	16.3	–	26.2	16.5
Labour Party	69.4	75.0	–	79.2	71.4
Labour identifiers: first voted 1918–1935					
Conservative Party	58.5	69.4	–	64.1	70.5
Labour Party	15.1	29.9	–	32.0	24.6
Conservative identifiers: first voted 1936–1950					
Conservative Party	22.4	20.1	–	34.5	26.5
Labour Party	67.3	77.6	–	73.1	77.4
Labour identifiers: first voted 1936–1950					
Conservative Party	73.5	69.2	–	79.5	80.6
Labour Party	21.4	30.3	–	30.8	27.9
Conservative identifiers: first voted 1951–1970					
Conservative Party	21.7	19.1	–	31.5	32.7
Labour Party	63.7	71.8	–	77.8	79.2
Labour identifiers: first voted 1951–1970					
Conservative Party	69.8	74.1	–	76.2	80.7
Labour Party	21.2	34.4	–	29.3	28.5
Conservative identifiers: first voted after 1970					
Conservative Party	28.6	25.6	–	29.3	29.9
Labour Party	60.0	81.0	–	64.9	68.8
Labour identifiers: first voted after 1970					
Conservative Party	68.8	69.4	–	70.7	71.4
Labour Party	24.2	33.3	–	33.7	27.1

Table 6.23 *Extremism of the Conservative and Labour parties by social class (%)*

	Feb. 1974	Oct. 1974	1979	1983	1987
Professional and managerial classes perceiving extremism in					
Conservative Party	27.5	33.6	–	50.4	53.9
Labour Party	63.4	76.8	–	70.9	65.8
Intermediate and routine non-manual classes					
Conservative Party	39.3	40.9	–	50.0	49.1
Labour Party	51.2	57.6	–	64.6	65.8
Manual working class					
Conservative Party	54.9	57.1	–	59.2	56.7
Labour Party	32.6	44.5	–	46.7	48.0

Table 6.24 *Extremism of the Conservative and Labour parties by employment status (%)*

	Feb. 1974	Oct. 1974	1979	1983	1987
Self-employed with employees perceiving extremism in					
Conservative Party	19.8	20.6	–	46.1	43.4
Labour Party	67.1	78.8	–	73.8	73.8
Self-employed, no employees					
Conservative Party	32.9	29.1	–	44.9	58.1
Labour Party	49.3	69.4	–	68.6	64.4
Managers					
Conservative Party	36.2	39.6	–	49.4	50.7
Labour Party	70.0	69.6	–	70.9	70.0
Foremen and supervisors					
Conservative Party	38.8	49.5	–	58.5	53.8
Labour Party	47.4	55.4	–	59.7	61.3
Rank and file employees					
Conservative Party	49.6	50.8	–	55.6	54.7
Labour Party	40.0	51.1	–	51.9	54.1

Table 6.25 *Extremism of the Conservative and Labour parties: unemployed (%)*

	Feb. 1974	Oct. 1974	1979	1983	1987
Unemployed perceiving extremism in					
Conservative Party	60.6	56.3	–	60.8	64.6
Labour Party	35.1	58.8	–	44.5	41.8

Table 6.26 *Extremism of the Conservative and Labour parties by trade union membership (%)*

	Feb. 1974	Oct. 1974	1979	1983
Respondent is a trade union member perceiving extremism in				
Conservative Party	59.1	54.3	–	65.2
Labour Party	35.0	46.6	–	53.7
Respondent is married to a trade union member				
Conservative Party	54.4	57.2	–	60.6
Labour Party	35.1	48.4	–	52.5
Neither respondent nor spouse belongs to a trade union				
Conservative Party	37.2	36.6	–	49.0
Labour Party	49.6	56.6	–	59.9

Table 6.27 *Extremism of the Conservative and Labour parties by region (%)*

	Feb. 1974	Oct. 1974	1979	1983	1987
Scotland perceiving extremism in					
Conservative Party	42.1	50.0	–	60.6	60.8
Labour Party	42.0	53.3	–	47.4	52.6
Wales					
Conservative Party	51.5	58.3	–	54.8	66.5
Labour Party	30.5	48.3	–	46.5	43.4
The North					
Conservative Party	48.2	48.6	–	58.4	57.1
Labour Party	39.4	53.1	–	54.0	50.3
The Midlands					
Conservative Party	45.3	42.9	–	51.3	48.4
Labour Party	46.6	50.9	–	56.3	57.7
Greater London					
Conservative Party	46.2	47.0	–	60.2	58.1
Labour Party	49.5	55.0	–	60.6	58.1
The South					
Conservative Party	40.5	46.2	–	49.0	48.9
Labour Party	48.9	59.4	–	64.5	65.9

Table 6.28 *Whether Conservative and Labour parties benefit a single class: all respondents (%)*

	Feb. 1974	Oct. 1974	1979	1983	1987
All respondents agreeing					
Conservative Party	65.2	65.3	–	62.1	62.1
Labour Party	45.3	50.4	–	61.4	64.4

Table 6.29 *Whether Conservative and Labour parties benefit a single class by gender (%)*

	Feb. 1974	Oct. 1974	1979	1983	1987
Men agreeing					
Conservative Party	67.0	65.7	–	62.8	62.5
Labour Party	45.9	52.3	–	64.4	66.5
Women agreeing					
Conservative Party	63.6	64.8	–	61.4	62.0
Labour Party	44.8	48.5	–	58.8	62.3

Table 6.30 *Whether Conservative and Labour parties benefit a single class by age (%)*

	Feb. 1974	Oct. 1974	1979	1983	1987
Aged under 25 agreeing					
Conservative Party	80.6	77.7	–	67.5	72.8
Labour Party	36.8	47.2	–	56.8	54.8
Aged 25–34					
Conservative Party	67.4	69.4	–	66.3	69.3
Labour Party	44.5	52.8	–	61.7	61.4
Aged 35–44					
Conservative Party	67.3	63.5	–	61.2	60.4
Labour Party	45.0	51.5	–	63.4	65.0
Aged 45–54					
Conservative Party	64.1	68.1	–	62.2	55.4
Labour Party	47.1	50.1	–	62.2	69.4
Aged 55–64					
Conservative Party	65.6	60.6	–	61.2	57.2
Labour Party	42.3	50.3	–	63.2	68.4
Aged 65–74					
Conservative Party	55.6	60.0	–	57.1	63.6
Labour Party	51.1	48.5	–	60.1	67.8
Aged over 74					
Conservative Party	45.2	46.9	–	49.9	51.5
Labour Party	56.9	53.6	–	63.4	64.8

Table 6.31 *Whether Conservative and Labour parties benefit a single class: new electors (%)*

	Feb. 1974	Oct. 1974	1979	1983	1987
New electors agreeing					
Conservative Party	77.2	–	–	67.2	73.6
Labour Party	36.7	–	–	53.9	54.5

Table 6.32 *Whether Conservative and Labour parties benefit a single class by political generation (%)*

	Feb. 1974	Oct. 1974	1979	1983	1987
First voted 1918–1935 agreeing					
Conservative Party	56.3	57.7	–	52.2	53.5
Labour Party	48.6	49.3	–	63.2	63.4
First voted 1936–1950					
Conservative Party	63.8	64.6	–	60.8	55.8
Labour Party	45.8	50.9	–	61.6	68.6
First voted 1951–1970					
Conservative Party	68.7	68.2	–	61.5	57.5
Labour Party	44.5	51.5	–	62.8	67.1
First voted after 1970					
Conservative Party	77.2	76.5	–	68.9	70.5
Labour Party	36.7	47.1	–	60.8	59.1

Table 6.33 *Whether Conservative and Labour parties benefit a single class: non-voters (%)*

	Feb. 1974	Oct. 1974	1979	1983	1987
Did not vote agreeing					
Conservative Party	75.7	69.8	–	61.0	67.8
Labour Party	45.6	50.3	–	54.8	60.6

Table 6.34 *Whether Conservative and Labour parties benefit a single class by vote (%)*

	Feb. 1974	Oct. 1974	1979	1983	1987
Conservative voters agreeing					
Conservative Party	27.6	27.1	–	21.9	21.8
Labour Party	73.0	79.1	–	82.8	85.9
Labour voters					
Conservative Party	91.7	93.0	–	96.1	95.9
Labour Party	20.2	22.2	–	28.9	32.6
Liberal voters					
Conservative Party	72.3	71.9	–	88.0	86.8
Labour Party	49.6	60.5	–	70.8	72.6
Voters for other parties					
Conservative Party	86.4	80.6	–	86.7	86.1
Labour Party	31.0	58.1	–	49.1	73.0

Table 6.35 *Whether Conservative and Labour parties benefit a single class by strength and direction of partisanship (%)*

	Feb. 1974	Oct. 1974	1979	1983	1987
Very strong Conservative identifiers agreeing					
Conservative Party	17.8	17.2	–	9.6	10.7
Labour Party	79.2	82.9	–	89.3	91.4
Fairly strong Conservative identifiers					
Conservative Party	29.4	26.5	–	21.1	22.4
Labour Party	72.8	77.2	–	82.6	86.0
Not very strong Conservative identifiers					
Conservative Party	50.6	40.8	–	36.8	38.3
Labour Party	63.7	75.7	–	74.4	81.2
Very strong Liberal identifiers					
Conservative Party	69.7	75.0	–	87.5	91.1
Labour Party	55.9	65.9	–	70.0	87.3
Fairly strong Liberal identifiers					
Conservative Party	72.2	80.6	–	84.8	83.1
Labour Party	48.6	60.6	–	77.0	73.6
Not very strong Liberal identifiers					
Conservative Party	74.0	65.8	–	82.1	80.3
Labour Party	52.5	57.8	–	72.6	71.4
Very strong Labour identifiers					
Conservative Party	94.3	97.2	–	96.5	95.9
Labour Party	17.3	17.6	–	23.4	26.8
Fairly strong Labour identifiers					
Conservative Party	91.8	90.4	–	96.9	95.2
Labour Party	20.2	21.9	–	31.8	34.8
Not very strong Labour identifiers					
Conservative Party	86.5	88.7	–	90.1	91.9
Labour Party	30.1	38.2	–	40.8	41.7

Table 6.36 *Whether Conservative and Labour parties benefit a single class: non-partisans (%)*

	Feb. 1974	Oct. 1974	1979	1983	1987
Respondents with no party identification agreeing					
Conservative Party	65.6	80.3	–	55.7	74.3
Labour Party	48.3	60.5	–	67.9	68.3

Table 6.37 *Whether Conservative and Labour parties benefit a single class by political generation and partisanship (%)*

	Feb. 1974	Oct. 1974	1979	1983	1987
Conservative identifiers: first voted 1918–1935 agreeing					
Conservative Party	23.6	24.7	–	16.9	28.0
Labour Party	73.7	75.4	–	84.2	88.6
Labour identifiers: first voted 1918–1935					
Conservative Party	87.7	88.5	–	92.1	87.8
Labour Party	22.4	22.6	–	28.6	33.8
Conservative identifiers: first voted 1936–1950					
Conservative Party	29.3	26.0	–	18.5	19.9
Labour Party	72.8	78.0	–	81.9	88.4
Labour identifiers: first voted 1936–1950					
Conservative Party	94.1	94.8	–	95.9	98.1
Labour Party	20.3	21.8	–	32.8	36.6
Conservative identifiers: first voted 1951–1970					
Conservative Party	33.2	29.4	–	22.3	19.0
Labour Party	72.3	82.7	–	83.4	87.1
Labour identifiers: first voted 1951–1970					
Conservative Party	91.9	92.8	–	93.9	91.4
Labour Party	22.0	24.6	–	32.1	37.0
Conservative identifiers: first voted after 1970					
Conservative Party	57.6	28.9	–	29.1	31.4
Labour Party	64.7	69.6	–	81.2	82.0
Labour identifiers: first voted after 1970					
Conservative Party	94.6	94.4	–	95.6	95.7
Labour Party	16.2	24.7	–	36.8	31.9

Table 6.38 *Whether Conservative and Labour parties benefit a single class by social class (%)*

	Feb. 1974	Oct. 1974	1979	1983	1987
Professional and managerial classes agreeing					
Conservative Party	49.8	47.7	–	49.6	53.9
Labour Party	61.5	72.5	–	74.9	74.2
Intermediate and routine non-manual classes					
Conservative Party	59.5	60.3	–	60.1	54.8
Labour Party	52.2	54.1	–	69.8	70.0
Manual working class					
Conservative Party	74.5	75.0	–	70.8	70.4
Labour Party	35.3	40.0	–	51.7	56.5

Table 6.39 *Whether Conservative and Labour parties benefit a single class by employment status (%)*

	Feb. 1974	Oct. 1974	1979	1983	1987
Self-employed with employees agreeing					
Conservative Party	33.7	36.8	–	35.8	37.1
Labour Party	71.1	74.6	–	84.7	76.0
Self-employed, no employees					
Conservative Party	54.1	48.3	–	48.0	53.8
Labour Party	58.1	83.5	–	82.3	72.7
Managers					
Conservative Party	53.3	51.8	–	49.6	46.3
Labour Party	63.9	62.2	–	73.9	80.0
Foremen and supervisors					
Conservative Party	60.9	64.7	–	65.1	61.2
Labour Party	46.0	50.5	–	62.0	66.0
Rank and file employees					
Conservative Party	69.5	69.8	–	66.6	66.0
Labour Party	41.9	47.0	–	57.5	61.6

Table 6.40 *Whether Conservative and Labour parties benefit a single class: unemployed (%)*

	Feb. 1974	Oct. 1974	1979	1983	1987
Unemployed agreeing					
Conservative Party	86.0	69.4	–	75.1	81.6
Labour Party	16.7	46.2	–	45.5	43.9

Table 6.41 *Whether Conservative and Labour parties benefit a single class by trade union membership (%)*

	Feb. 1974	Oct. 1974	1979	1983	1987
Respondent is a trade union member agreeing					
Conservative Party	73.8	75.6	–	74.2	71.9
Labour Party	36.4	42.4	–	56.3	60.2
Respondent is married to a trade union member					
Conservative Party	70.0	70.8	–	67.6	64.2
Labour Party	36.6	43.7	–	56.2	65.1
Neither respondent nor spouse belongs to a trade union					
Conservative Party	58.5	58.7	–	56.0	58.7
Labour Party	51.0	60.3	–	64.7	65.5

Table 6.42 *Whether Conservative and Labour parties benefit a single class by region (%)*

	Feb. 1974	Oct. 1974	1979	1983	1987
Scotland agreeing					
Conservative Party	66.4	68.8	–	74.0	72.8
Labour Party	39.8	51.6	–	47.4	52.1
Wales					
Conservative Party	70.8	77.5	–	65.9	75.5
Labour Party	29.2	29.6	–	44.4	48.9
The North					
Conservative Party	66.7	65.4	–	67.1	68.7
Labour Party	41.3	46.5	–	56.8	60.1
The Midlands					
Conservative Party	66.1	62.7	–	63.4	61.4
Labour Party	46.1	49.5	–	60.3	62.7
Greater London					
Conservative Party	68.4	70.5	–	61.3	56.6
Labour Party	50.4	48.6	–	63.4	67.3
The South					
Conservative Party	60.8	61.7	–	52.7	53.8
Labour Party	52.4	58.8	–	73.2	74.2

Table 6.43 *Whether the Liberal Party is perceived as closer to the Conservatives or to Labour: all respondents (%)*

	Feb. 1974	Oct. 1974	1979	1983	1987
Liberal Party is closer to the					
Conservative Party	63.2	59.9	46.4	53.0	53.7
Labour Party	17.3	16.9	44.5	34.0	36.5
Neither	19.5	23.2	9.1	13.0	9.8
Total	100.0	100.0	100.0	100.0	100.0
N. of respondents	2450	2335	1727	3537	3288

Table 6.44 *Whether the Liberal Party is perceived as closer to the Conservatives or to Labour: new electors (%)*

	Feb. 1974	Oct. 1974	1979	1983	1987
Liberal Party is closer to the					
Conservative Party	52.4	–	40.2	41.8	53.5
Labour Party	27.4	–	48.2	51.1	39.8
Neither	20.2	–	11.6	7.1	6.7
Total	100.0	–	100.0	100.0	100.0
N. of respondents	168	–	112	247	213

Table 6.45 *Whether the Liberal Party is perceived as closer to the Conservatives or to Labour by political generation (%)*

	First voted 1918–1935				
	Feb. 1974	Oct. 1974	1979	1983	1987
Liberal Party is closer to the					
Conservative Party	64.8	57.7	45.3	53.1	51.4
Labour Party	15.8	16.4	43.9	30.9	36.4
Neither	19.4	25.8	10.7	16.0	12.2
Total	100.0	100.0	100.0	100.0	100.0
N. of respondents	602	542	289	407	251

	First voted 1936–1950				
	Feb. 1974	Oct. 1974	1979	1983	1987
Liberal Party is closer to the					
Conservative Party	65.3	61.0	47.9	55.2	56.6
Labour Party	16.3	17.6	43.6	29.6	32.7
Neither	18.4	21.4	8.5	15.3	10.7
Total	100.0	100.0	100.0	100.0	100.0
N. of respondents	640	579	388	743	678

	First voted 1951–1970				
	Feb. 1974	Oct. 1974	1979	1983	1987
Liberal Party is closer to the					
Conservative Party	63.4	61.3	48.0	54.9	56.6
Labour Party	17.2	16.4	43.7	32.0	33.3
Neither	19.4	22.3	8.2	13.1	10.0
Total	100.0	100.0	100.0	100.0	100.0
N. of respondents	998	999	791	1469	1301

	First voted after 1970				
	Feb. 1974	Oct. 1974	1979	1983	1987
Liberal Party is closer to the					
Conservative Party	52.4	59.1	40.0	50.7	48.8
Labour Party	27.4	17.2	48.6	38.6	42.8
Neither	20.2	23.7	11.4	10.6	8.4
Total	100.0	100.0	100.0	100.0	100.0
N. of respondents	168	186	255	664	1058

Table 6.46 *Whether the Liberal Party is perceived as closer to the Conservatives or to Labour by vote (%)*

	Conservative voters				
	Feb. 1974	Oct. 1974	1979	1983	1987
Liberal Party is closer to the					
Conservative Party	75.8	69.0	63.6	63.2	63.1
Labour Party	8.9	10.9	28.3	24.6	29.2
Neither	15.3	20.1	8.1	12.2	7.7
Total	100.0	100.0	100.0	100.0	100.0
N. of respondents	785	691	681	1338	1325

	Labour voters				
	Feb. 1974	Oct. 1974	1979	1983	1987
Liberal Party is closer to the					
Conservative Party	58.9	57.9	32.6	46.4	45.3
Labour Party	22.8	21.9	58.2	43.9	46.3
Neither	18.3	20.2	9.2	9.7	8.3
Total	100.0	100.0	100.0	100.0	100.0
N. of respondents	835	821	543	819	875

	Liberal voters				
	Feb. 1974	Oct. 1974	1979	1983	1987
Liberal Party is closer to the					
Conservative Party	57.7	54.0	38.4	46.3	47.8
Labour Party	20.5	17.9	52.7	34.3	37.2
Neither	21.8	28.0	8.9	19.4	15.0
Total	100.0	100.0	100.0	100.0	100.0
N. of respondents	395	346	203	731	704

	Voters for other parties				
	Feb. 1974	Oct. 1974	1979	1983	1987
Liberal Party is closer to the					
Conservative Party	72.3	62.3	40.0	42.6	41.7
Labour Party	10.6	11.6	40.0	46.2	44.3
Neither	17.0	26.1	20.0	11.6	14.0
Total	100.0	100.0	100.0	100.0	100.0
N. of respondents	47	51	25	35	36

Table 6.47 *Whether the Liberal Party is perceived as closer to the Conservatives or to Labour by strength and direction of partisanship (%)*

	Very strong Conservative identifiers				
	Feb. 1974	Oct. 1974	1979	1983	1987
Liberal Party is closer to the					
Conservative Party	78.5	65.6	64.0	61.5	55.1
Labour Party	8.2	10.1	25.5	24.2	34.3
Neither	13.3	24.3	10.6	14.3	10.6
Total	100.0	100.0	100.0	100.0	100.0
N. of respondents	279	218	161	335	300
	Fairly strong Conservative identifiers				
	Feb. 1974	Oct. 1974	1979	1983	1987
Liberal Party is closer to the					
Conservative Party	76.2	69.2	65.7	68.1	66.7
Labour Party	7.9	11.7	27.5	21.7	26.9
Neither	15.9	19.1	6.8	10.2	6.4
Total	100.0	100.0	100.0	100.0	100.0
N. of respondents	428	419	367	630	647
	Not very strong Conservative identifiers				
	Feb. 1974	Oct. 1974	1979	1983	1987
Liberal Party is closer to the					
Conservative Party	76.5	72.1	62.2	60.8	63.3
Labour Party	10.2	9.5	29.7	27.7	28.9
Neither	13.3	18.4	8.1	11.5	7.8
Total	100.0	100.0	100.0	100.0	100.0
N. of respondents	196	190	185	393	296
	Very strong Liberal identifiers				
	Feb. 1974	Oct. 1974	1979	1983	1987
Liberal Party is closer to the					
Conservative Party	55.5	47.7	24.1	38.0	27.1
Labour Party	5.5	20.5	65.5	42.3	47.4
Neither	38.9	31.8	10.3	19.7	25.5
Total	100.0	100.0	100.0	100.0	100.0
N. of respondents	36	44	29	71	58

Table 6.47 (*cont.*)

	Fairly strong Liberal identifiers				
	Feb. 1974	Oct. 1974	1979	1983	1987
Liberal Party is closer to the					
Conservative Party	57.6	51.3	46.1	49.0	47.7
Labour Party	16.5	20.1	46.1	32.0	37.5
Neither	25.9	28.6	7.8	19.0	14.8
Total	100.0	100.0	100.0	100.0	100.0
N. of respondents	170	189	102	294	252

	Not very strong Liberal identifiers				
	Feb. 1974	Oct. 1974	1979	1983	1987
Liberal Party is closer to the					
Conservative Party	52.9	64.1	51.9	49.0	52.1
Labour Party	22.3	15.4	38.3	34.3	34.9
Neither	24.8	20.5	9.9	16.8	13.0
Total	100.0	100.0	100.0	100.0	100.0
N. of respondents	121	117	81	286	289

	Very strong Labour identifiers				
	Feb. 1974	Oct. 1974	1979	1983	1987
Liberal Party is closer to the					
Conservative Party	59.8	58.2	24.7	48.8	52.0
Labour Party	25.4	22.4	66.1	43.8	41.2
Neither	14.8	19.4	9.2	7.4	6.8
Total	100.0	100.0	100.0	100.0	100.0
N. of respondents	398	335	174	324	262

	Fairly strong Labour identifiers				
	Feb. 1974	Oct. 1974	1979	1983	1987
Liberal Party is closer to the					
Conservative Party	53.2	55.6	29.8	44.5	42.6
Labour Party	27.1	23.9	62.3	45.8	47.1
Neither	19.8	20.5	7.9	9.7	10.3
Total	100.0	100.0	100.0	100.0	100.0
N. of respondents	425	444	329	445	444

Table 6.47 (*cont.*)

	Not very strong Labour identifiers				
	Feb. 1974	Oct. 1974	1979	1983	1987
Liberal Party is closer to the					
Conservative Party	55.5	53.3	33.7	41.5	43.7
Labour Party	23.2	16.5	55.0	48.0	49.9
Neither	21.3	30.2	11.2	10.5	6.5
Total	100.0	100.0	100.0	100.0	100.0
N. of respondents	211	182	169	323	289

Table 6.48 *Whether the Liberal Party is perceived as closer to the Conservatives or to Labour by political generation and partisanship (%)*

	Conservative identifiers: first voted 1918–1935				
	Feb. 1974	Oct. 1974	1979	1983	1987
Liberal Party is closer to the					
Conservative Party	73.4	67.4	64.4	61.6	55.6
Labour Party	8.6	8.9	25.5	21.9	33.9
Neither	18.0	23.7	10.1	16.5	10.5
Total	100.0	100.0	100.0	100.0	100.0
N. of respondents	278	224	149	205	124

	Labour identifiers: first voted 1918–1935				
	Feb. 1974	Oct. 1974	1979	1983	1987
Liberal Party is closer to the					
Conservative Party	61.5	51.2	20.8	43.8	42.2
Labour Party	23.8	24.6	68.8	46.8	48.4
Neither	14.8	24.2	10.4	9.4	9.4
Total	100.0	100.0	100.0	100.0	100.0
N. of respondents	244	207	96	115	64

	Conservative identifiers: first voted 1936–1950				
	Feb. 1974	Oct. 1974	1979	1983	1987
Liberal Party is closer to the					
Conservative Party	78.9	66.8	65.1	62.3	61.7
Labour Party	9.1	11.7	28.9	22.7	31.8
Neither	12.0	21.5	5.9	15.1	6.6
Total	100.0	100.0	100.0	100.0	100.0
N. of respondents	242	223	152	291	274

Table 6.48 (*cont.*)

	Labour identifiers: first voted 1936–1950				
	Feb. 1974	Oct. 1974	1979	1983	1987
Liberal Party is closer to the					
Conservative Party	57.9	58.8	35.0	51.3	53.2
Labour Party	24.2	22.6	53.5	39.0	33.7
Neither	17.9	18.5	11.5	9.8	13.2
Total	100.0	100.0	100.0	100.0	100.0
N. of respondents	273	243	157	256	190

	Conservative identifiers: first voted 1951–1970				
	Feb. 1974	Oct. 1974	1979	1983	1987
Liberal Party is closer to the					
Conservative Party	80.9	71.7	63.6	68.2	67.0
Labour Party	6.4	11.1	28.6	20.7	26.2
Neither	12.7	17.1	7.8	11.1	6.8
Total	100.0	100.0	100.0	100.0	100.0
N. of respondents	330	315	332	600	512

	Labour identifiers: first voted 1951–1970				
	Feb. 1974	Oct. 1974	1979	1983	1987
Liberal Party is closer to the					
Conservative Party	53.7	57.3	30.8	45.3	48.8
Labour Party	25.9	20.2	61.5	44.9	43.9
Neither	20.3	22.5	7.7	9.8	7.4
Total	100.0	100.0	100.0	100.0	100.0
N. of respondents	428	436	312	441	367

	Conservative identifiers: first voted after 1970				
	Feb. 1974	Oct. 1974	1979	1983	1987
Liberal Party is closer to the					
Conservative Party	63.2	71.4	67.5	62.6	60.8
Labour Party	21.1	10.2	23.8	29.4	30.5
Neither	15.8	18.4	8.8	8.0	8.6
Total	100.0	100.0	100.0	100.0	100.0
N. of respondents	38	49	80	231	324

Table 6.48 (*cont.*)

	Labour identifiers: first voted after 1970				
	Feb. 1974	Oct. 1974	1979	1983	1987
Liberal Party is closer to the					
Conservative Party	50.6	55.4	24.5	44.0	38.6
Labour Party	34.2	21.6	67.3	46.0	54.9
Neither	15.2	23.0	8.2	9.9	6.5
Total	100.0	100.0	100.0	100.0	100.0
N. of respondents	79	74	110	235	368

Table 6.49 *Whether the Liberal Party is perceived as closer to the Conservatives or to Labour by social class (%)*

	Professional and managerial classes				
	Feb. 1974	Oct. 1974	1979	1983	1987
Liberal Party is closer to the					
Conservative Party	72.1	64.7	55.7	56.3	52.0
Labour Party	10.5	13.1	36.2	26.9	37.1
Neither	17.4	22.2	8.1	16.2	10.9
Total	100.0	100.0	100.0	100.0	100.0
N. of respondents	344	351	359	947	893
	Intermediate and routine non-manual classes				
	Feb. 1974	Oct. 1974	1979	1983	1987
Liberal Party is closer to the					
Conservative Party	66.4	61.3	49.0	57.1	56.7
Labour Party	14.8	16.4	41.5	30.0	33.3
Neither	18.8	22.4	9.4	13.0	10.0
Total	100.0	100.0	100.0	100.0	100.0
N. of respondents	836	800	467	671	822
	Manual-working class				
	Feb. 1974	Oct. 1974	1979	1983	1987
Liberal Party is closer to the					
Conservative Party	59.6	58.2	40.9	49.7	53.6
Labour Party	20.8	17.8	50.2	39.4	36.9
Neither	19.6	24.0	8.9	10.9	9.5
Total	100.0	100.0	100.0	100.0	100.0
N. of respondents	1120	1063	843	1673	1445

Table 6.50 *Whether the Liberal Party is perceived as closer to the Conservatives or to Labour by region (%)*

	Scotland				
	Feb. 1974	Oct. 1974	1979	1983	1987
Liberal Party is closer to the					
Conservative Party	67.1	60.4	48.9	57.1	57.7
Labour Party	15.4	14.5	43.7	32.8	34.2
Neither	17.5	25.1	7.4	10.2	8.1
Total	100.0	100.0	100.0	100.0	100.0
N. of respondents	234	207	135	320	298
	Wales				
	Feb. 1974	Oct. 1974	1979	1983	1987
Liberal Party is closer to the					
Conservative Party	58.8	50.0	40.2	49.2	56.0
Labour Party	19.8	23.8	52.2	35.7	35.7
Neither	21.4	26.2	7.6	15.1	8.2
Total	100.0	100.0	100.0	100.0	100.0
N. of respondents	131	130	92	179	169
	The North				
	Feb. 1974	Oct. 1974	1979	1983	1987
Liberal Party is closer to the					
Conservative Party	62.0	61.0	45.8	51.7	52.2
Labour Party	19.1	17.3	45.6	38.2	38.7
Neither	18.9	21.8	8.6	10.2	9.2
Total	100.0	100.0	100.0	100.0	100.0
N. of respondents	729	684	476	961	854
	The Midlands				
	Feb. 1974	Oct. 1974	1979	1983	1987
Liberal Party is closer to the					
Conservative Party	64.2	61.8	39.1	52.6	52.4
Labour Party	17.8	14.6	50.7	36.2	38.4
Neither	18.0	23.6	10.2	11.2	9.2
Total	100.0	100.0	100.0	100.0	100.0
N. of respondents	388	390	294	570	570

Table 6.50 (*cont.*)

	Greater London				
	Feb. 1974	Oct. 1974	1979	1983	1987
Liberal Party is closer to the					
Conservative Party	64.5	62.4	45.7	50.0	54.6
Labour Party	17.0	14.6	46.8	32.5	35.5
Neither	18.5	23.0	7.5	17.5	9.9
Total	100.0	100.0	100.0	100.0	100.0
N. of respondents	265	226	186	420	398
	The South				
	Feb. 1974	Oct. 1974	1979	1983	1987
Liberal Party is closer to the					
Conservative Party	62.9	58.7	51.5	55.2	53.7
Labour Party	15.4	17.9	38.2	29.7	34.6
Neither	21.8	23.4	10.3	15.2	11.7
Total	100.0	100.0	100.0	100.0	100.0
N. of respondents	703	698	544	1085	1035

Chapter 7

THE ECONOMY

1. The party complexion of the government referred to in the question was Conservative in February 1974, 1983 and 1987 and Labour in October 1974 and 1979.

2. The February 1974, October 1974 and 1983 questions refer to 'rising prices', the 1987 question to 'inflation'. The strongest category of importance in February and October 1974 is 'the most important single thing', while in 1979 and 1983 it is 'extremely important'. These categories are treated as equivalent for the purposes of comparison.

See Appendix E, pp. 489 and 498 on the construction of the variables on the economy.

Table 7.1 *Perceived standard of living: all respondents (%)*

	Feb. 1974	Oct. 1974	1979	1983
Income over the last year or so has				
Fallen behind prices	–	52.3	61.4	49.8
Kept up with prices	–	42.2	32.1	41.6
Risen more than prices	–	5.5	6.5	8.6
Total	–	100.0	100.0	100.0
Income in the next year or so will				
Fall behind prices	47.4	57.2	59.8	46.7
Keep up with prices	45.9	38.7	34.3	44.5
Rise more than prices	6.7	4.1	5.9	8.8
Total	100.0	100.0	100.0	100.0

Table 7.2 *Perceived standard of living by gender (%)*

	Men			
	Feb. 1974	Oct. 1974	1979	1983
Income over the last year or so has				
Fallen behind prices	–	51.2	59.5	50.0
Kept up with prices	–	41.2	33.4	39.7
Risen more than prices	–	7.7	7.1	10.3
Total	–	100.0	100.0	100.0
Income in the next year or so will				
Fall behind prices	47.5	54.2	60.6	47.0
Keep up with prices	44.2	40.4	32.1	42.3
Rise more than prices	8.3	5.4	7.3	10.7
Total	100.0	100.0	100.0	100.0

Table 7.2 (*cont.*)

	Women			
	Feb. 1974	Oct. 1974	1979	1983
Income over the last year or so has				
Fallen behind prices	–	53.4	63.2	49.7
Kept up with prices	–	43.2	30.9	43.2
Risen more than prices	–	3.4	5.9	7.1
Total	–	100.0	100.0	100.0
Income in the next year or so will				
Fall behind prices	47.3	60.3	58.4	46.5
Keep up with prices	47.5	36.9	37.0	46.5
Rise more than prices	5.2	2.8	4.7	7.0
Total	100.0	100.0	100.0	100.0

Table 7.3 *Perceived standard of living by age (%)*

	Aged under 25			
	Feb. 1974	Oct. 1974	1979	1983
Per cent whose income has, in the last year or so,				
Fallen behind prices	–	45.0	50.6	41.4
Kept up with prices	–	45.8	40.7	50.3
Risen more than prices	–	9.2	8.6	8.3
Total	–	100.0	100.0	100.0
Per cent whose income will, in the next year or so,				
Fall behind prices	43.5	50.6	51.3	38.4
Keep up with prices	45.7	41.7	40.7	49.9
Rise more than prices	10.9	7.7	8.0	11.7
Total	100.0	100.0	100.0	100.0
	Aged 25–34			
	Feb. 1974	Oct. 1974	1979	1983
Per cent whose income has, in the last year or so,				
Fallen behind prices	–	46.3	60.1	45.1
Kept up with prices	–	44.4	31.3	42.3
Risen more than prices	–	9.3	8.6	12.6
Total	–	100.0	100.0	100.0
Per cent whose income will, in the next year or so,				
Fall behind prices	46.9	50.0	51.8	40.4
Keep up with prices	42.6	42.4	40.2	47.3
Rise more than prices	10.5	7.6	7.9	12.3
Total	100.0	100.0	100.0	100.0

Table 7.3 (*cont.*)

	Aged 35–44			
	Feb. 1974	Oct. 1974	1979	1983
Per cent whose income has, in the last year or so,				
Fallen behind prices	–	54.5	58.5	45.4
Kept up with prices	–	38.9	32.9	43.1
Risen more than prices	–	6.6	8.6	11.6
Total	–	100.0	100.0	100.0
Per cent whose income will, in the next year or so,				
Fall behind prices	46.2	56.2	59.3	40.8
Keep up with prices	45.7	40.2	37.1	48.0
Rise more than prices	8.1	3.6	3.6	11.2
Total	100.0	100.0	100.0	100.0

	Aged 45-54			
	Feb. 1974	Oct. 1974	1979	1983
Per cent whose income has, in the last year or so,				
Fallen behind prices	–	50.0	59.9	50.4
Kept up with prices	–	45.9	35.4	41.7
Risen more than prices	–	4.1	4.7	7.8
Total	–	100.0	100.0	100.0
Per cent whose income will, in the next year or so,				
Fall behind prices	44.8	55.1	57.4	46.2
Keep up with prices	51.2	42.2	40.0	44.8
Rise more than prices	4.0	2.6	2.6	9.0
Total	100.0	100.0	100.0	100.0

	Aged 55–64			
	Feb. 1974	Oct. 1974	1979	1983
Per cent whose income has, in the last year or so,				
Fallen behind prices	–	53.2	66.1	58.6
Kept up with prices	–	44.5	29.6	35.6
Risen more than prices	–	2.2	4.3	5.7
Total	–	100.0	100.0	100.0
Per cent whose income will, in the next year or so,				
Fall behind prices	51.4	61.3	63.3	56.7
Keep up with prices	45.4	36.6	34.5	38.4
Rise more than prices	3.2	2.1	2.2	4.9
Total	100.0	100.0	100.0	100.0

Table 7.3 (*cont.*)

	Aged 65–74			
	Feb. 1974	Oct. 1974	1979	1983
Per cent whose income has, in the last year or so,				
Fallen behind prices	–	67.3	68.6	62.2
Kept up with prices	–	30.5	26.5	34.8
Risen more than prices	–	2.2	4.9	3.0
Total	–	100.0	100.0	100.0
Per cent whose income will, in the next year or so,				
Fall behind prices	54.5	74.7	77.2	63.7
Keep up with prices	42.2	24.5	22.2	33.3
Rise more than prices	3.3	0.8	0.6	2.9
Total	100.0	100.0	100.0	100.0

	Aged over 74			
	Feb. 1974	Oct. 1974	1979	1983
Per cent whose income has, in the last year or so,				
Fallen behind prices	–	54.8	69.6	49.8
Kept up with prices	–	44.4	27.8	42.8
Risen more than prices	–	0.8	2.6	7.4
Total	–	100.0	100.0	100.0
Per cent whose income will, in the next year or so,				
Fall behind prices	44.3	62.2	62.7	48.0
Keep up with prices	49.2	36.9	36.0	48.0
Rise more than prices	6.6	0.9	1.2	3.9
Total	100.0	100.0	100.0	100.0

Table 7.4 *Perceived standard of living by vote (%)*

	Conservative voters			
	Feb. 1974	Oct. 1974	1979	1983
Per cent whose income has, in the last year or so,				
Fallen behind prices	–	52.5	60.3	35.7
Kept up with prices	–	42.3	34.1	53.6
Risen more than prices	–	5.2	5.5	10.8
Total	–	100.0	100.0	100.0
Per cent whose income will, in the next year or so,				
Fall behind prices	46.4	60.6	48.6	30.2
Keep up with prices	46.0	36.1	44.1	58.1
Rise more than prices	7.7	3.3	7.4	11.7
Total	100.0	100.0	100.0	100.0

Table 7.4 (*cont.*)

	Labour voters			
	Feb. 1974	Oct. 1974	1979	1983
Per cent whose income has, in the last year or so,				
Fallen behind prices	–	49.3	59.0	66.4
Kept up with prices	–	44.9	33.6	28.8
Risen more than prices	–	5.8	7.4	4.8
Total	–	100.0	100.0	100.0
Per cent whose income will, in the next year or so,				
Fall behind prices	43.2	52.0	72.0	66.6
Keep up with prices	52.0	43.3	23.5	27.3
Rise more than prices	4.8	4.7	4.4	6.1
Total	100.0	100.0	100.0	100.0

	Liberal voters			
	Feb. 1974	Oct. 1974	1979	1983
Per cent whose income has, in the last year or so,				
Fallen behind prices	–	53.4	61.7	54.5
Kept up with prices	–	40.8	32.5	36.0
Risen more than prices	–	5.8	5.7	9.5
Total	–	100.0	100.0	100.0
Per cent whose income will, in the next year or so,				
Fall behind prices	49.1	56.5	55.2	52.0
Keep up with prices	43.1	39.2	39.0	40.7
Rise more than prices	7.8	4.3	5.7	7.3
Total	100.0	100.0	100.0	100.0

	Voters for other parties			
	Feb. 1974	Oct. 1974	1979	1983
Per cent whose income has, in the last year or so,				
Fallen behind prices	–	55.1	79.8	46.1
Kept up with prices	–	36.2	25.0	42.0
Risen more than prices	–	8.7	4.2	11.9
Total	–	100.0	100.0	100.0
Per cent whose income will, in the next year or so,				
Fall behind prices	56.1	65.0	60.5	48.6
Keep up with prices	36.6	30.0	32.2	37.8
Rise more than prices	7.3	5.0	7.2	13.6
Total	100.0	100.0	100.0	100.0

Table 7.5 *Perceived standard of living by strength and direction of partisanship (%)*

	Very strong Conservative identifiers			
	Feb. 1974	Oct. 1974	1979	1983
Per cent whose income has, in the last year or so,				
Fallen behind prices	–	59.3	59.3	38.7
Kept up with prices	–	37.5	36.5	51.2
Risen more than prices	–	3.2	4.2	10.1
Total	–	100.0	100.0	100.0
Per cent whose income will, in the next year or so,				
Fall behind prices	44.6	68.3	48.0	31.0
Keep up with prices	48.1	30.2	45.0	56.2
Rise more than prices	7.4	1.5	7.1	12.8
Total	100.0	100.0	100.0	100.0

	Fairly strong Conservative identifiers			
	Feb. 1974	Oct. 1974	1979	1983
Per cent whose income has, in the last year or so,				
Fallen behind prices	–	50.5	60.5	32.8
Kept up with prices	–	43.3	34.2	55.1
Risen more than prices	–	6.3	5.3	12.1
Total	–	100.0	100.0	100.0
Per cent whose income will, in the next year or so,				
Fall behind prices	47.6	58.2	49.2	27.5
Keep up with prices	44.9	38.7	44.1	59.8
Rise more than prices	7.5	3.0	6.7	12.7
Total	100.0	100.0	100.0	100.0

	Not very strong Conservative identifiers			
	Feb. 1974	Oct. 1974	1979	1983
Per cent whose income has, in the last year or so,				
Fallen behind prices	–	51.9	60.4	38.8
Kept up with prices	–	40.6	29.7	51.6
Risen more than prices	–	7.5	9.9	9.5
Total	–	100.0	100.0	100.0
Per cent whose income will, in the next year or so,				
Fall behind prices	49.2	56.5	48.5	32.7
Keep up with prices	43.5	35.0	43.7	57.0
Rise more than prices	7.3	8.5	7.7	10.3
Total	100.0	100.0	100.0	100.0

Table 7.5 (*cont.*)

	Very strong Liberal identifiers			
	Feb. 1974	Oct. 1974	1979	1983
Per cent whose income has, in the last year or so,				
Fallen behind prices	–	67.4	53.3	54.5
Kept up with prices	–	30.4	40.0	29.9
Risen more than prices	–	2.2	6.7	15.6
Total	–	100.0	100.0	100.0
Per cent whose income will, in the next year or so,				
Fall behind prices	61.8	68.2	57.4	56.3
Keep up with prices	35.3	27.3	36.2	33.8
Rise more than prices	2.9	4.5	6.4	9.9
Total	100.0	100.0	100.0	100.0
	Fairly strong Liberal identifiers			
	Feb. 1974	Oct. 1974	1979	1983
Per cent whose income has, in the last year or so,				
Fallen behind prices	–	51.9	68.3	53.8
Kept up with prices	–	44.3	29.8	38.2
Risen more than prices	–	3.8	1.9	8.0
Total	–	100.0	100.0	100.0
Per cent whose income will, in the next year or so,				
Fall behind prices	51.6	54.6	54.3	52.5
Keep up with prices	41.4	41.4	39.4	42.3
Rise more than prices	7.0	4.0	6.3	5.3
Total	100.0	100.0	100.0	100.0
	Not very strong Liberal identifiers			
	Feb. 1974	Oct. 1974	1979	1983
Per cent whose income has, in the last year or so,				
Fallen behind prices	–	51.7	60.5	50.2
Kept up with prices	–	39.0	32.6	41.5
Risen more than prices	–	9.3	7.0	8.3
Total	–	100.0	100.0	100.0
Per cent whose income will, in the next year or so,				
Fall behind prices	49.1	59.5	55.0	46.0
Keep up with prices	43.0	36.9	38.7	46.7
Rise more than prices	7.9	3.6	6.3	7.3
Total	100.0	100.0	100.0	100.0

Table 7.5 (*cont.*)

	Very strong Labour identifiers			
	Feb. 1974	Oct. 1974	1979	1983
Per cent whose income has, in the last year or so,				
Fallen behind prices	–	54.8	56.3	75.7
Kept up with prices	–	40.6	36.8	20.7
Risen more than prices	–	4.5	6.8	3.6
Total	–	100.0	100.0	100.0
Per cent whose income will, in the next year or so,				
Fall behind prices	41.8	53.2	76.3	73.7
Keep up with prices	51.9	42.3	22.3	21.1
Rise more than prices	6.3	4.5	1.4	5.1
Total	100.0	100.0	100.0	100.0

	Fairly strong Labour identifiers			
	Feb. 1974	Oct. 1974	1979	1983
Per cent whose income has, in the last year or so,				
Fallen behind prices	–	45.1	57.3	52.4
Kept up with prices	–	49.0	34.9	33.0
Risen more than prices	–	5.9	7.8	4.6
Total	–	100.0	100.0	100.0
Per cent whose income will, in the next year or so,				
Fall behind prices	44.2	50.1	71.2	63.9
Keep up with prices	49.9	46.1	23.4	30.9
Rise more than prices	5.9	3.8	5.5	5.2
Total	100.0	100.0	100.0	100.0

	Not very strong Labour identifiers			
	Feb. 1974	Oct. 1974	1979	1983
Per cent whose income has, in the last year or so,				
Fallen behind prices	–	55.2	67.4	57.0
Kept up with prices	–	39.1	25.8	35.7
Risen more than prices	–	5.7	6.7	7.3
Total	–	100.0	100.0	100.0
Per cent whose income will, in the next year or so,				
Fall behind prices	50.5	63.0	71.6	56.5
Keep up with prices	42.4	32.7	24.7	35.9
Rise more than prices	7.1	4.2	3.6	7.6
Total	100.0	100.0	100.0	100.0

Table 7.6 *Perceived standard of living: non-partisans (%)*

	Respondents with no party identification			
	Feb. 1974	Oct. 1974	1979	1983
Per cent whose income has, in the last year or so,				
Fallen behind prices	–	51.7	71.3	50.0
Kept up with prices	–	42.5	22.8	40.7
Risen more than prices	–	5.7	5.9	9.3
Total	–	100.0	100.0	100.0
Per cent whose income will, in the next year or so,				
Fall behind prices	50.7	56.0	60.2	44.2
Keep up with prices	42.0	40.0	32.5	46.9
Rise more than prices	7.2	4.0	7.2	8.9
Total	100.0	100.0	100.0	100.0

Table 7.7 *Perceived standard of living by occupational status (%)*

	Occupational status: class A/ Registrar General Class I			
	Feb. 1974	Oct. 1974	1979	1983
Per cent whose income has, in the last year or so,				
Fallen behind prices	–	57.0	52.1	30.7
Kept up with prices	–	31.3	35.9	47.3
Risen more than prices	–	11.7	12.0	22.0
Total	–	100.0	100.0	100.0
Per cent whose income will, in the next year or so,				
Fall behind prices	44.6	56.1	–	24.5
Keep up with prices	39.2	39.0	–	57.8
Rise more than prices	16.2	4.9	–	17.7
Total	100.0	100.0	–	100.0

	Occupational status: class B/ Registrar General Class II			
	Feb. 1974	Oct. 1974	1979	1983
Per cent whose income has, in the last year or so,				
Fallen behind prices	–	52.5	61.6	40.0
Kept up with prices	–	39.2	32.8	46.0
Risen more than prices	–	8.3	5.6	14.0
Total	–	100.0	100.0	100.0
Per cent whose income will, in the next year or so,				
Fall behind prices	51.0	51.7	–	36.8
Keep up with prices	41.8	39.5	–	48.8
Rise more than prices	7.1	8.8	–	14.5
Total	100.0	100.0	–	100.0

Table 7.7 (*cont.*)

	Occupational status: class C1A/ Registrar General Class III – non-manual			
	Feb. 1974	Oct. 1974	1979	1983
Per cent whose income has, in the last year or so,				
Fallen behind prices	–	54.9	55.8	45.7
Kept up with prices	–	37.2	36.4	46.3
Risen more than prices	–	7.9	7.8	8.0
Total	–	100.0	100.0	100.0
Per cent whose income will, in the next year or so,				
Fall behind prices	44.7	59.7	–	41.4
Keep up with prices	47.1	35.7	–	52.1
Rise more than prices	8.2	4.6	–	6.4
Total	100.0	100.0	–	100.0

	Occupational status: class C1B/ Registrar General Class III – manual			
	Feb. 1974	Oct. 1974	1979	1983
Per cent whose income has, in the last year or so,				
Fallen behind prices	–	52.1	61.6	56.6
Kept up with prices	–	44.5	33.0	36.6
Risen more than prices	–	3.4	5.4	6.8
Total	–	100.0	100.0	100.0
Per cent whose income will, in the next year or so,				
Fall behind prices	46.2	57.0	–	51.4
Keep up with prices	47.1	40.4	–	40.8
Rise more than prices	6.8	2.7	–	7.9
Total	100.0	100.0	–	100.0

	Occupational status: class C2/ Registrar General Class IV			
	Feb. 1974	Oct. 1974	1979	1983
Per cent whose income has, in the last year or so,				
Fallen behind prices	–	46.9	61.0	57.7
Kept up with prices	–	46.9	32.5	38.4
Risen more than prices	–	6.2	6.6	4.0
Total	–	100.0	100.0	100.0
Per cent whose income will, in the next year or so,				
Fall behind prices	45.9	54.3	–	57.6
Keep up with prices	49.7	41.3	–	37.1
Rise more than prices	4.3	4.4	–	5.3
Total	100.0	100.0	–	100.0

Table 7.7 (*cont.*)

	Occupational status: class D/ Registrar General Class V			
	Feb. 1974	Oct. 1974	1979	1983
Per cent whose income has, in the last year or so,				
Fallen behind prices	–	54.7	68.3	60.3
Kept up with prices	–	42.7	26.9	35.6
Risen more than prices	–	2.6	4.8	4.1
Total	–	100.0	100.0	100.0
Per cent whose income will, in the next year or so,				
Fall behind prices	48.3	58.8	–	59.7
Keep up with prices	46.3	39.0	–	34.0
Rise more than prices	5.4	2.2	–	6.3
Total	100.0	100.0	–	100.0

Table 7.8 *Perceived standard of living by employment status (%)*

	Self-employed with employees			
	Feb. 1974	Oct. 1974	1979	1983
Per cent whose income has, in the last year or so,				
Fallen behind prices	–	58.1	52.7	31.6
Kept up with prices	–	31.1	36.4	51.3
Risen more than prices	–	10.8	10.9	17.1
Total	–	100.0	100.0	100.0
Per cent whose income will, in the next year or so,				
Fall behind prices	41.2	55.1	48.4	22.9
Keep up with prices	45.9	40.6	39.7	54.4
Rise more than prices	12.9	4.3	12.0	22.7
Total	100.0	100.0	100.0	100.0
	Self-employed, no employees			
	Feb. 1974	Oct. 1974	1979	1983
Per cent whose income has, in the last year or so,				
Fallen behind prices	–	63.2	56.3	39.8
Kept up with prices	–	31.0	36.6	54.0
Risen more than prices	–	5.7	7.0	6.1
Total	–	100.0	100.0	100.0
Per cent whose income will, in the next year or so,				
Fall behind prices	43.2	63.8	48.0	30.8
Keep up with prices	51.4	32.5	39.5	53.9
Rise more than prices	5.4	3.8	12.5	15.3
Total	100.0	100.0	100.0	100.0

Table 7.8 (*cont.*)

	Managers			
	Feb. 1974	Oct. 1974	1979	1983
Per cent whose income has, in the last year or so,				
Fallen behind prices	–	53.2	57.9	39.3
Kept up with prices	–	38.0	33.8	44.4
Risen more than prices	–	8.8	8.3	16.2
Total	–	100.0	100.0	100.0
Per cent whose income will, in the next year or so,				
Fall behind prices	48.1	55.4	42.0	36.3
Keep up with prices	40.4	37.3	48.1	50.3
Rise more than prices	11.5	7.2	9.9	13.4
Total	100.0	100.0	100.0	100.0

	Foremen and supervisors			
	Feb. 1974	Oct. 1974	1979	1983
Per cent whose income has, in the last year or so,				
Fallen behind prices	–	45.9	55.5	49.4
Kept up with prices	–	50.8	36.1	41.0
Risen more than prices	–	4.2	8.4	9.6
Total	–	100.0	100.0	100.0
Per cent whose income will, in the next year or so,				
Fall behind prices	40.9	52.7	57.5	47.7
Keep up with prices	55.9	45.5	35.0	44.8
Rise more than prices	3.2	1.8	7.4	7.5
Total	100.0	100.0	100.0	100.0

	Rank and file employees			
	Feb. 1974	Oct. 1974	1979	1983
Per cent whose income has, in the last year or so,				
Fallen behind prices	–	50.5	61.9	52.4
Kept up with prices	–	44.2	32.9	41.1
Risen more than prices	–	5.4	5.3	6.5
Total	–	100.0	100.0	100.0
Per cent whose income will, in the next year or so,				
Fall behind prices	47.5	55.9	59.2	49.7
Keep up with prices	46.1	40.3	34.7	43.6
Rise more than prices	6.4	3.8	6.0	6.7
Total	100.0	100.0	100.0	100.0

Table 7.9 *Perceived standard of living: unemployed (%)*

	Feb. 1974	Oct. 1974	1979	1983
Per cent whose income has, in the last year or so,				
Fallen behind prices	–	68.3	73.7	74.9
Kept up with prices	–	24.4	23.7	21.0
Risen more than prices	–	7.3	2.6	4.2
Total	–	100.0	100.0	100.0
Per cent whose income will, in the next year or so,				
Fall behind prices	41.5	57.1	64.0	68.4
Keep up with prices	53.7	31.4	32.8	23.5
Rise more than prices	4.9	11.4	3.2	8.0
Total	100.0	100.0	100.0	100.0

Table 7.10 *Perceived standard of living by class and employment status (%)*

	Self-employed: professional and managerial classes			
	Feb. 1974	Oct. 1974	1979	1983
Per cent whose income has, in the last year or so,				
Fallen behind prices	–	61.9	55.3	38.3
Kept up with prices	–	23.8	34.2	47.7
Risen more than prices	–	14.3	10.5	14.1
Total	–	100.0	100.0	100.0
Per cent whose income will, in the next year or so,				
Fall behind prices	40.0	54.1	47.1	31.7
Keep up with prices	36.7	43.2	41.2	50.0
Rise more than prices	11.3	2.7	11.8	18.3
Total	100.0	100.0	100.0	100.0
	Employees: professional and managerial classes			
	Feb. 1974	Oct. 1974	1979	1983
Per cent whose income has, in the last year or so,				
Fallen behind prices	–	52.1	57.5	38.3
Kept up with prices	–	38.6	34.4	45.9
Risen more than prices	–	9.3	8.1	15.9
Total	–	100.0	100.0	100.0
Per cent whose income will, in the next year or so,				
Fall behind prices	50.4	53.6	55.3	34.9
Keep up with prices	38.8	38.5	35.9	50.5
Rise more than prices	10.7	7.9	8.9	14.7
Total	100.0	100.0	100.0	100.0

Table 7.10 (*cont.*)

	Self-employed: intermediate and routine non-manual classes			
	Feb. 1974	Oct. 1974	1979	1983
Per cent whose income has, in the last year or so,				
Fallen behind prices	–	70.0	50.0	27.6
Kept up with prices	–	26.3	38.5	65.5
Risen more than prices	–	3.8	11.8	6.9
Total	–	100.0	100.0	100.0
Per cent whose income will, in the next year or so,				
Fall behind prices	41.8	67.1	48.0	20.0
Keep up with prices	50.5	31.6	36.0	64.0
Rise more than prices	7.7	1.3	16.0	16.0
Total	100.0	100.0	100.0	100.0

	Employees: intermediate and routine non-manual classes			
	Feb. 1974	Oct. 1974	1979	1983
Per cent whose income has, in the last year or so,				
Fallen behind prices	–	50.8	58.2	45.6
Kept up with prices	–	43.4	35.7	46.0
Risen more than prices	–	5.7	6.0	8.4
Total	–	100.0	100.0	100.0
Per cent whose income will, in the next year or so,				
Fall behind prices	46.5	56.7	55.0	41.1
Keep up with prices	45.8	39.5	40.1	52.8
Rise more than prices	7.7	3.8	5.0	6.2
Total	100.0	100.0	100.0	100.0

	Self-employed: manual working class			
	Feb. 1974	Oct. 1974	1979	1983
Per cent whose income has, in the last year or so,				
Fallen behind prices	–	41.0	61.1	35.5
Kept up with prices	–	48.7	36.1	56.4
Risen more than prices	–	10.3	2.8	8.2
Total	–	100.0	100.0	100.0
Per cent whose income will, in the next year or so,				
Fall behind prices	47.8	48.5	50.0	27.0
Keep up with prices	43.5	39.4	43.3	54.0
Rise more than prices	8.7	12.1	6.7	19.0
Total	100.0	100.0	100.0	100.0

Table 7.10 (*cont.*)

| | Employees: manual working class | | | |
	Feb. 1974	Oct. 1974	1979	1983
Per cent whose income has, in the last year or so,				
Fallen behind prices	–	49.1	62.8	56.9
Kept up with prices	–	46.4	31.8	37.6
Risen more than prices	–	4.5	5.4	5.5
Total	–	100.0	100.0	100.0
Per cent whose income will, in the next year or so,				
Fall behind prices	46.9	55.5	63.3	54.6
Keep up with prices	48.3	41.6	31.2	39.4
Rise more than prices	4.8	2.8	5.5	6.0
Total	100.0	100.0	100.0	100.0

Table 7.11 *Perceived standard of living by economic sector (%)*

| | Works in private sector | | | |
	Feb. 1974	Oct. 1974	1979	1983
Per cent whose income has, in the last year or so,				
Fallen behind prices	–	49.0	58.0	51.9
Kept up with prices	–	43.8	34.6	39.5
Risen more than prices	–	7.2	7.4	8.6
Total	–	100.0	100.0	100.0
Per cent whose income will, in the next year or so,				
Fall behind prices	–	54.0	59.3	46.9
Keep up with prices	–	41.3	34.0	44.4
Rise more than prices	–	4.7	6.7	8.7
Total	–	100.0	100.0	100.0

| | Works in public sector | | | |
	Feb. 1974	Oct. 1974	1979	1983
Per cent whose income has, in the last year or so,				
Fallen behind prices	–	50.3	66.0	50.3
Kept up with prices	–	45.2	30.5	41.3
Risen more than prices	–	4.5	3.5	8.3
Total	–	100.0	100.0	100.0
Per cent whose income will, in the next year or so,				
Fall behind prices	–	56.6	60.7	51.1
Keep up with prices	–	39.4	34.8	41.7
Rise more than prices	–	4.1	4.4	7.2
Total	–	100.0	100.0	100.0

Table 7.12 *Perceived standard of living by class and economic sector (%)*

	Professional and managerial classes: private sector			
	Feb. 1974	Oct. 1974	1979	1983
Per cent whose income has, in the last year or so,				
Fallen behind prices	–	44.1	47.8	37.9
Kept up with prices	–	41.2	39.8	44.1
Risen more than prices	–	14.7	12.4	18.0
Total	–	100.0	100.0	100.0
Per cent whose income will, in the next year or so,				
Fall behind prices	–	51.5	45.5	29.6
Keep up with prices	–	35.6	42.7	51.7
Rise more than prices	–	12.9	11.8	18.7
Total	–	100.0	100.0	100.0

	Professional and managerial classes: public sector			
	Feb. 1974	Oct. 1974	1979	1983
Per cent whose income has, in the last year or so,				
Fallen behind prices	–	58.6	69.5	39.6
Kept up with prices	–	34.4	27.1	47.2
Risen more than prices	–	7.0	3.4	13.3
Total	–	100.0	100.0	100.0
Per cent whose income will, in the next year or so,				
Fall behind prices	–	53.2	64.0	41.7
Keep up with prices	–	41.1	30.6	48.1
Rise more than prices	–	5.6	5.4	10.2
Total	–	100.0	100.0	100.0

	Intermediate and routine non-manual classes: private sector			
	Feb. 1974	Oct. 1974	1979	1983
Per cent whose income has, in the last year or so,				
Fallen behind prices	–	48.7	57.1	45.4
Kept up with prices	–	43.9	35.9	46.7
Risen more than prices	–	7.4	6.9	7.9
Total	–	100.0	100.0	100.0
Per cent whose income will, in the next year or so,				
Fall behind prices	–	52.9	55.1	41.6
Keep up with prices	–	41.8	40.7	46.7
Rise more than prices	–	5.3	4.2	6.7
Total	–	100.0	100.0	100.0

Table 7.12 (*cont.*)

	Intermediate and routine non-manual classes: public sector			
	Feb. 1974	Oct. 1974	1979	1983
Per cent whose income has, in the last year or so,				
Fallen behind prices	–	51.2	59.1	49.3
Kept up with prices	–	45.2	37.4	43.3
Risen more than prices	–	3.6	3.5	7.4
Total	–	100.0	100.0	100.0
Per cent whose income will, in the next year or so,				
Fall behind prices	–	61.9	56.9	44.7
Keep up with prices	–	36.1	37.6	51.9
Rise more than prices	–	1.9	5.5	3.4
Total	–	100.0	100.0	100.0

	Manual working class: private sector			
	Feb. 1974	Oct. 1974	1979	1983
Per cent whose income has, in the last year or so,				
Fallen behind prices	–	49.8	61.4	59.8
Kept up with prices	–	44.5	32.4	34.6
Risen more than prices	–	5.7	6.2	5.6
Total	–	100.0	100.0	100.0
Per cent whose income will, in the next year or so,				
Fall behind prices	–	55.1	66.0	55.2
Keep up with prices	–	42.1	27.4	38.9
Rise more than prices	–	2.9	6.6	5.9
Total	–	100.0	100.0	100.0

	Manual working class: public sector			
	Feb. 1974	Oct. 1974	1979	1983
Per cent whose income has, in the last year or so,				
Fallen behind prices	–	44.3	67.4	57.2
Kept up with prices	–	51.8	29.0	37.8
Risen more than prices	–	3.9	3.6	5.0
Total	–	100.0	100.0	100.0
Per cent whose income will, in the next year or so,				
Fall behind prices	–	54.8	61.1	59.0
Keep up with prices	–	41.0	35.6	34.5
Rise more than prices	–	4.3	3.4	6.5
Total	–	100.0	100.0	100.0

Table 7.13 *Government's handling of inflation: all respondents (%)*

	Feb. 1974	Oct. 1974	1979	1983	1987
Government handled inflation					
Very well	4.5	7.6	13.0	35.6	15.9
Fairly well	29.3	40.6	48.5	44.1	49.8
Not very well	36.0	37.1	28.1	14.0	24.6
Not at all well	30.2	14.6	10.5	6.3	9.7
Total	100.0	100.0	100.0	100.0	100.0
N. of respondents	2398	2288	1860	3876	3378

Table 7.14 *Government's handling of inflation by gender (%)*

	Men				
	Feb. 1974	Oct. 1974	1979	1983	1987
Government handled inflation					
Very well	4.5	8.4	15.4	42.0	19.1
Fairly well	28.0	43.1	50.1	42.4	49.9
Not very well	36.2	34.2	24.4	10.3	22.5
Not at all well	31.3	14.3	10.1	5.3	8.5
Total	100.0	100.0	100.0	100.0	100.0
N. of respondents	1150	1148	902	1854	1634
	Women				
	Feb. 1974	Oct. 1974	1979	1983	1987
Government handled inflation					
Very well	4.5	6.9	10.6	30.2	13.2
Fairly well	30.4	38.2	47.0	45.6	49.8
Not very well	35.8	39.9	31.5	17.2	26.4
Not at all well	29.2	15.0	10.9	6.9	10.6
Total	100.0	100.0	100.0	100.0	100.0
N. of respondents	1248	1140	958	2022	1743

Table 7.15 *Government's handling of inflation by age (%)*

	Aged under 25				
	Feb. 1974	Oct. 1974	1979	1983	1987
Government handled inflation					
Very well	2.0	6.4	12.4	28.3	14.6
Fairly well	27.5	48.3	55.3	50.6	53.5
Not very well	39.3	36.3	25.3	16.9	24.5
Not at all well	31.1	9.0	7.1	4.2	7.4
Total	100.0	100.0	100.0	100.0	100.0
N. of respondents	244	267	170	543	428
	Aged 25–34				
	Feb. 1974	Oct. 1974	1979	1983	1987
Government handled inflation					
Very well	2.2	6.8	12.8	33.8	20.2
Fairly well	29.2	45.5	54.0	50.1	52.8
Not very well	39.0	34.7	25.6	11.0	20.4
Not at all well	29.6	13.0	7.6	5.0	6.5
Total	100.0	100.0	100.0	100.0	100.0
N. of respondents	459	470	422	737	604
	Aged 35–44				
	Feb. 1974	Oct. 1974	1979	1983	1987
Government handled inflation					
Very well	4.6	6.4	12.2	35.6	16.9
Fairly well	26.1	41.4	50.5	45.7	52.7
Not very well	36.0	37.1	28.9	14.0	21.6
Not at all well	33.3	15.1	8.5	4.8	8.8
Total	100.0	100.0	100.0	100.0	100.0
N. of respondents	414	391	329	711	676
	Aged 45–54				
	Feb. 1974	Oct. 1974	1979	1983	1987
Government handled inflation					
Very well	4.8	7.5	14.2	38.9	15.7
Fairly well	25.8	36.2	52.8	39.3	52.2
Not very well	39.3	41.7	25.4	14.5	22.8
Not at all well	30.1	14.6	7.7	7.3	9.3
Total	100.0	100.0	100.0	100.0	100.0
N. of respondents	438	398	339	626	521

Table 7.15 (*cont.*)

	Aged 55–64				
	Feb. 1974	Oct. 1974	1979	1983	1987
Government handled inflation					
Very well	4.2	9.2	13.4	38.2	15.4
Fairly well	29.0	34.9	42.5	40.6	47.0
Not very well	37.1	40.9	33.0	13.9	25.9
Not at all well	29.8	15.0	11.1	7.3	11.7
Total	100.0	100.0	100.0	100.0	100.0
N. of respondents	383	347	261	581	544

	Aged 65–74				
	Feb. 1974	Oct. 1974	1979	1983	1987
Government handled inflation					
Very well	7.4	8.3	13.4	39.9	14.1
Fairly well	33.4	40.1	37.8	39.4	41.1
Not very well	29.7	32.1	30.5	12.5	31.8
Not at all well	29.4	19.5	18.2	8.2	13.0
Total	100.0	100.0	100.0	100.0	100.0
N. of respondents	296	277	209	430	378

	Aged over 74				
	Feb. 1974	Oct. 1974	1979	1983	1987
Government handled inflation					
Very well	8.5	11.7	12.2	39.7	10.8
Fairly well	47.2	34.4	34.1	35.4	40.8
Not very well	20.4	33.6	30.1	16.5	34.4
Not at all well	23.9	20.3	23.6	8.4	14.0
Total	100.0	100.0	100.0	100.0	100.0
N. of respondents	164	138	130	248	227

Table 7.16 *Government's handling of inflation by marital status and gender (%)*

	Single men				
	Feb. 1974	Oct. 1974	1979	1983	1987
Government handled inflation					
Very well	3.3	–	20.8	33.5	–
Fairly well	27.5	–	52.8	49.9	–
Not very well	38.5	–	16.8	11.9	–
Not at all well	30.8	–	9.6	4.7	–
Total	100.0	–	100.0	100.0	–
N. of respondents	182	–	125	388	–

	Single women				
	Feb. 1974	Oct. 1974	1979	1983	1987
Government handled inflation					
Very well	6.0	–	7.2	25.2	–
Fairly well	36.2	–	46.4	52.8	–
Not very well	38.3	–	34.0	17.8	–
Not at all well	19.5	–	12.4	4.2	–
Total	100.0	–	100.0	100.0	–
N. of respondents	149	–	97	284	–

	Married men				
	Feb. 1974	Oct. 1974	1979	1983	1987
Government handled inflation					
Very well	4.4	8.5	14.5	45.1	–
Fairly well	27.6	42.6	49.9	40.1	–
Not very well	36.2	34.6	25.6	9.5	–
Not at all well	31.8	14.3	10.1	5.2	–
Total	100.0	100.0	100.0	100.0	–
N. of respondents	900	899	684	1334	–

	Married women				
	Feb. 1974	Oct. 1974	1979	1983	1987
Government handled inflation					
Very well	3.9	7.0	11.7	31.3	–
Fairly well	29.1	39.6	48.7	45.2	–
Not very well	36.3	40.2	30.6	16.3	–
Not at all well	30.7	13.2	9.0	7.2	–
Total	100.0	100.0	100.0	100.0	–
N. of respondents	870	816	657	1384	–

Table 7.16 (*cont.*)

	Divorced and separated men				
	Feb. 1974	Oct. 1974	1979	1983	1987
Government handled inflation					
Very well	(12.5)	–	16.1	38.1	–
Fairly well	(25.0)	–	51.6	43.6	–
Not very well	(25.0)	–	19.4	10.4	–
Not at all well	(37.5)	–	12.9	7.9	–
Total	(100.0)	–	100.0	100.0	–
N. of respondents	8	–	31	64	–

	Divorced and separated women				
	Feb. 1974	Oct. 1974	1979	1983	1987
Government handled inflation					
Very well	(5.3)	–	14.3	24.3	–
Fairly well	(26.3)	–	40.8	43.5	–
Not very well	(42.1)	–	34.7	27.2	–
Not at all well	(26.3)	–	10.2	5.0	–
Total	(100.0)	–	100.0	100.0	–
N. of respondents	19	–	49	114	–

	Widowed men				
	Feb. 1974	Oct. 1974	1979	1983	1987
Government handled inflation					
Very well	8.3	–	17.6	31.4	–
Fairly well	36.7	–	43.1	45.0	–
Not very well	30.0	–	27.5	14.6	–
Not at all well	25.0	–	11.8	9.0	–
Total	100.0	–	100.0	100.0	–
N. of respondents	60	–	51	66	–

	Widowed women				
	Feb. 1974	Oct. 1974	1979	1983	1987
Government handled inflation					
Very well	5.7	–	6.2	32.8	–
Fairly well	32.4	–	40.7	40.8	–
Not very well	31.4	–	33.8	16.7	–
Not at all well	30.5	–	19.3	9.7	–
Total	100.0	–	100.0	100.0	–
N. of respondents	210	–	145	240	–

Table 7.17 *Government's handling of inflation: new electors (%)*

	Feb. 1974	Oct. 1974	1979	1983	1987
Government handled inflation					
Very well	2.4	4.4	15.5	32.9	18.4
Fairly well	31.0	46.7	53.2	49.2	53.0
Not very well	41.5	41.8	23.7	13.2	21.5
Not at all well	26.2	7.1	7.6	4.7	7.1
Total	100.0	100.0	100.0	100.0	100.0
N. of respondents	84	182	278	717	1101

Table 7.18 *Government's handling of inflation by political generation (%)*

	First voted 1918–1935				
	Feb. 1974	Oct. 1974	1979	1983	1987
Government handled inflation					
Very well	5.9	9.8	12.6	40.5	11.1
Fairly well	35.5	37.7	34.6	37.8	40.2
Not very well	29.6	33.7	32.0	13.6	33.8
Not at all well	28.9	18.8	20.7	8.1	14.9
Total	100.0	100.0	100.0	100.0	100.0
N. of respondents	577	528	309	458	230

	First voted 1936–1950				
	Feb. 1974	Oct. 1974	1979	1983	1987
Government handled inflation					
Very well	5.0	7.8	12.9	38.1	14.5
Fairly well	27.4	35.5	45.0	40.1	44.0
Not very well	37.0	41.9	31.1	14.1	29.6
Not at all well	30.6	14.8	10.9	7.7	12.0
Total	100.0	100.0	100.0	100.0	100.0
N. of respondents	635	566	411	793	683

	First voted 1951–1970				
	Feb. 1974	Oct. 1974	1979	1983	1987
Government handled inflation					
Very well	3.1	6.9	12.3	36.8	15.9
Fairly well	27.3	44.3	53.7	43.8	51.8
Not very well	38.2	35.3	26.5	13.6	22.9
Not at all well	31.4	13.5	7.5	5.8	9.4
Total	100.0	100.0	100.0	100.0	100.0
N. of respondents	985	989	854	1601	1336

Table 7.18 (*cont.*)

	First voted after 1970				
	Feb. 1974	Oct. 1974	1979	1983	1987
Government handled inflation					
Very well	2.4	4.4	15.5	32.9	18.4
Fairly well	31.0	46.7	53.2	49.2	53.0
Not very well	40.5	41.8	23.7	13.2	21.5
Not at all well	26.2	7.1	7.6	4.7	7.1
Total	100.0	100.0	100.0	100.0	100.0
N. of respondents	84	182	278	717	1101

Table 7.19 *Government's handling of inflation by vote (%)*

	Conservative voters				
	Feb. 1974	Oct. 1974	1979	1983	1987
Government handled inflation					
Very well	11.0	1.5	5.0	56.5	29.6
Fairly well	56.8	19.6	38.7	40.1	58.2
Not very well	26.5	51.6	40.0	3.0	10.0
Not at all well	5.7	27.3	16.4	0.4	2.2
Total	100.0	100.0	100.0	100.0	100.0
N. of respondents	771	684	727	1432	1252

	Labour voters				
	Feb. 1974	Oct. 1974	1979	1983	1987
Government handled inflation					
Very well	0.8	16.0	25.5	15.4	3.7
Fairly well	7.4	61.1	59.2	41.9	36.5
Not very well	40.5	20.6	12.4	25.8	38.1
Not at all well	51.3	2.3	2.9	16.9	21.6
Total	100.0	100.0	100.0	100.0	100.0
N. of respondents	828	800	581	895	866

	Liberal voters				
	Feb. 1974	Oct. 1974	1979	1983	1987
Government handled inflation					
Very well	1.6	3.2	12.3	22.5	10.7
Fairly well	24.4	40.2	53.8	51.6	50.3
Not very well	45.1	41.3	25.5	20.7	30.5
Not at all well	29.0	15.3	8.5	5.1	8.5
Total	100.0	100.0	100.0	100.0	100.0
N. of respondents	386	346	212	275	703

Table 7.19 (*cont.*)

	Voters for other parties				
	Feb. 1974	Oct. 1974	1979	1983	1987
Government handled inflation					
Very well	0.0	3.1	12.0	32.7	4.7
Fairly well	12.8	34.4	52.0	45.5	47.3
Not very well	51.1	46.9	24.0	16.4	36.0
Not at all well	36.2	15.6	12.0	5.5	12.0
Total	100.0	100.0	100.0	100.0	100.0
N. of respondents	47	64	25	92	40

Table 7.20 *Government's handling of inflation by strength and direction of partisanship (%)*

	Very strong Conservative identifiers				
	Feb. 1974	Oct. 1974	1979	1983	1987
Government handled inflation					
Very well	17.1	2.8	1.8	71.5	41.4
Fairly well	64.0	10.3	29.6	26.3	47.4
Not very well	15.3	46.0	39.6	2.3	9.0
Not at all well	3.6	40.8	29.0	0.0	2.1
Total	100.0	100.0	100.0	100.0	100.0
N. of respondents	275	213	169	354	286
	Fairly strong Conservative identifiers				
	Feb. 1974	Oct. 1974	1979	1983	1987
Government handled inflation					
Very well	9.3	1.0	5.2	56.4	29.1
Fairly well	55.8	21.0	38.2	41.0	59.6
Not very well	29.7	53.5	42.6	2.1	9.6
Not at all well	5.2	24.6	14.0	0.4	1.7
Total	100.0	100.0	100.0	100.0	100.0
N. of respondents	421	415	387	668	647
	Not very strong Conservative identifiers				
	Feb. 1974	Oct. 1974	1979	1983	1987
Government handled inflation					
Very well	3.7	4.3	9.3	40.7	16.2
Fairly well	44.7	26.1	44.8	52.1	66.4
Not very well	37.4	48.9	32.5	6.5	15.4
Not at all well	14.2	20.7	13.4	0.7	1.9
Total	100.0	100.0	100.0	100.0	100.0
N. of respondents	190	184	194	447	303

Table 7.20 (*cont.*)

	Very strong Liberal identifiers				
	Feb. 1974	Oct. 1974	1979	1983	1987
Government handled inflation					
Very well	5.7	8.7	23.3	27.6	8.0
Fairly well	20.0	23.9	50.0	28.9	54.5
Not very well	45.7	43.5	16.7	27.6	20.6
Not at all well	28.6	23.9	10.0	15.8	16.9
Total	100.0	100.0	100.0	100.0	100.0
N. of respondents	35	46	30	76	61

	Fairly strong Liberal identifiers				
	Feb. 1974	Oct. 1974	1979	1983	1987
Government handled inflation					
Very well	0.0	2.2	10.3	35.1	10.8
Fairly well	27.1	42.9	53.3	47.5	51.9
Not very well	49.4	42.9	28.0	14.4	28.5
Not at all well	23.5	12.1	8.4	3.0	8.8
Total	100.0	100.0	100.0	100.0	100.0
N. of respondents	166	182	107	305	255

	Not very strong Liberal identifiers				
	Feb. 1974	Oct. 1974	1979	1983	1987
Government handled inflation					
Very well	0.8	2.5	4.5	26.0	13.1
Fairly well	28.0	42.9	51.7	53.7	54.6
Not very well	45.8	41.2	39.3	16.4	25.2
Not at all well	25.4	13.4	4.5	3.9	7.0
Total	100.0	100.0	100.0	100.0	100.0
N. of respondents	118	119	89	311	293

	Very strong Labour identifiers				
	Feb. 1974	Oct. 1974	1979	1983	1987
Government handled inflation					
Very well	1.0	27.2	37.8	16.0	4.3
Fairly well	4.8	56.3	47.2	35.3	24.6
Not very well	30.6	15.0	10.9	25.5	36.6
Not at all well	63.5	1.5	4.1	23.1	34.5
Total	100.0	100.0	100.0	100.0	100.0
N. of respondents	392	327	193	337	261

Table 7.20 (*cont.*)

	Fairly strong Labour identifiers				
	Feb. 1974	Oct. 1974	1979	1983	1987
Government handled inflation					
Very well	1.0	8.5	17.5	16.6	3.6
Fairly well	9.5	64.1	68.2	46.0	40.0
Not very well	46.5	24.3	12.2	24.8	40.7
Not at all well	43.0	3.2	2.0	12.5	15.7
Total	100.0	100.0	100.0	100.0	100.0
N. of respondents	419	437	343	487	442

	Not very strong Labour identifiers				
	Feb. 1974	Oct. 1974	1979	1983	1987
Government handled inflation					
Very well	0.5	5.1	17.8	18.0	6.2
Fairly well	12.6	51.4	55.0	49.2	42.3
Not very well	44.4	37.1	20.6	24.6	36.4
Not at all well	42.5	6.3	6.7	8.2	15.0
Total	100.0	100.0	100.0	100.0	100.0
N. of respondents	207	175	180	378	312

Table 7.21 *Government's handling of inflation: non-partisans (%)*

	Feb. 1974	Oct. 1974	1979	1983	1987
Government handled inflation					
Very well	2.6	5.9	5.2	26.2	13.3
Fairly well	18.4	37.6	45.4	53.6	50.9
Not very well	34.2	37.6	34.0	15.8	27.9
Not at all well	44.7	18.8	15.5	4.4	7.9
Total	100.0	100.0	100.0	100.0	100.0
N. of respondents	76	85	97	183	178

Table 7.22 *Government's handling of inflation by social class (%)*

	Professional and managerial classes				
	Feb. 1974	Oct. 1974	1979	1983	1987
Government handled inflation					
Very well	6.8	2.9	11.5	45.1	24.1
Fairly well	40.6	30.3	50.9	44.3	57.5
Not very well	34.7	47.4	29.5	7.8	13.3
Not at all well	17.9	19.4	8.0	2.7	5.0
Total	100.0	100.0	100.0	100.0	100.0
N. of respondents	340	346	373	908	872
	Intermediate and routine non-manual classes				
	Feb. 1974	Oct. 1974	1979	1983	1987
Government handled inflation					
Very well	4.2	6.0	11.4	39.4	16.7
Fairly well	35.2	38.3	45.8	44.0	55.1
Not very well	36.4	39.5	31.6	13.4	21.8
Not at all well	24.2	16.2	11.2	3.1	6.3
Total	100.0	100.0	100.0	100.0	100.0
N. of respondents	818	788	500	731	860
	Manual working class				
	Feb. 1974	Oct. 1974	1979	1983	1987
Government handled inflation					
Very well	3.9	9.9	14.5	29.5	10.4
Fairly well	20.9	46.4	49.0	44.0	42.6
Not very well	36.3	32.3	26.0	17.2	33.3
Not at all well	38.9	11.3	10.5	9.3	13.8
Total	100.0	100.0	100.0	100.0	100.0
N. of respondents	1093	1036	911	1858	1493

Table 7.23 *Government's handling of inflation by employment status (%)*

	Self-employed with employees				
	Feb. 1974	Oct. 1974	1979	1983	1987
Government handled inflation					
Very well	13.6	2.9	6.9	59.9	27.3
Fairly well	47.7	21.7	27.6	34.3	51.1
Not very well	26.1	40.6	39.7	3.9	16.4
Not at all well	12.5	34.8	25.9	1.9	4.8
Total	100.0	100.0	100.0	100.0	100.0
N. of respondents	88	69	58	152	150

Table 7.23 (*cont.*)

	Self-employed, no employees				
	Feb. 1974	Oct. 1974	1979	1983	1987
Government handled inflation					
Very well	2.5	3.3	9.9	39.9	18.6
Fairly well	46.9	34.1	45.1	46.7	60.0
Not very well	28.4	41.8	33.8	10.3	15.5
Not at all well	22.2	20.9	11.3	3.0	5.9
Total	100.0	100.0	100.0	100.0	100.0
N. of respondents	81	91	71	114	148

	Managers				
	Feb. 1974	Oct. 1974	1979	1983	1987
Government handled inflation					
Very well	6.7	4.6	13.7	49.5	28.9
Fairly well	32.1	32.4	54.1	41.3	56.5
Not very well	40.6	44.5	26.0	6.8	10.8
Not at all well	20.6	18.5	6.2	2.5	3.8
Total	100.0	100.0	100.0	100.0	100.0
N. of respondents	165	173	146	285	312

	Foremen and supervisors				
	Feb. 1974	Oct. 1974	1979	1983	1987
Government handled inflation					
Very well	6.4	6.7	15.1	40.3	16.2
Fairly well	39.4	42.0	46.9	40.2	50.0
Not very well	30.9	38.7	25.5	13.4	25.4
Not at all well	23.4	12.6	12.5	6.1	8.4
Total	100.0	100.0	100.0	100.0	100.0
N. of respondents	94	119	192	222	213

	Rank and file employees				
	Feb. 1974	Oct. 1974	1979	1983	1987
Government handled inflation					
Very well	3.5	8.1	15.0	29.8	13.4
Fairly well	26.2	43.5	50.1	46.5	48.4
Not very well	37.3	35.7	26.7	16.6	27.5
Not at all well	33.1	12.6	8.2	7.1	10.7
Total	100.0	100.0	100.0	100.0	100.0
N. of respondents	1593	1498	926	2470	2424

Table 7.24 *Government's handling of inflation: unemployed (%)*

	Feb. 1974	Oct. 1974	1979	1983	1987
Government handled inflation					
Very well	2.2	4.9	7.9	22.3	18.6
Fairly well	15.2	43.9	57.9	47.0	48.1
Not very well	37.0	29.3	21.1	18.9	19.4
Not at all well	45.7	22.0	13.2	11.8	13.9
Total	100.0	100.0	100.0	100.0	100.0
N. of respondents	46	41	38	236	185

Table 7.25 *Government's handling of inflation by economic sector (%)*

	Works in private sector				
	Feb. 1974	Oct. 1974	1979	1983	1987
Government handled inflation					
Very well	–	7.4	14.5	34.2	15.5
Fairly well	–	41.3	48.2	44.1	47.6
Not very well	–	37.8	27.6	14.7	26.9
Not at all well	–	13.6	9.7	7.0	10.0
Total	–	100.0	100.0	100.0	100.0
N. of respondents	–	1046	753	2087	1914

	Works in public sector				
	Feb. 1974	Oct. 1974	1979	1983	1987
Government handled inflation					
Very well	–	8.9	14.8	35.3	14.7
Fairly well	–	44.9	53.6	45.1	52.3
Not very well	–	34.6	24.1	14.0	23.7
Not at all well	–	11.6	7.6	5.6	9.3
Total	–	100.0	100.0	100.0	100.0
N. of respondents	–	517	461	1247	945

Table 7.26 *Government's handling of inflation by trade union membership (%)*

	Trade union members				
	Feb. 1974	Oct. 1974	1979	1983	1987
Government handled inflation					
Very well	2.4	5.1	14.3	34.1	14.7
Fairly well	18.9	51.5	54.5	45.4	52.9
Not very well	38.2	37.3	23.7	14.4	23.5
Not at all well	40.5	6.1	7.5	6.1	8.9
Total	100.0	100.0	100.0	100.0	100.0
N. of respondents	618	598	561	1037	774
	Respondent is married to a trade union member				
	Feb. 1974	Oct. 1974	1979	1983	1987
Government handled inflation					
Very well	3.4	4.1	14.6	33.1	12.8
Fairly well	21.6	52.5	51.1	42.2	48.6
Not very well	40.1	35.3	26.6	17.0	29.5
Not at all well	34.9	8.1	7.7	7.7	9.1
Total	100.0	100.0	100.0	100.0	100.0
N. of respondents	292	285	274	423	329
	Neither respondent nor spouse belongs to a trade union				
	Feb. 1974	Oct. 1974	1979	1983	1987
Government handled inflation					
Very well	5.6	4.3	11.8	37.1	17.0
Fairly well	35.1	26.1	44.5	44.0	49.0
Not very well	34.3	48.9	30.8	13.1	24.1
Not at all well	25.1	20.7	12.9	5.8	10.0
Total	100.0	100.0	100.0	100.0	100.0
N. of respondents	1488	1405	1025	2416	2275

Table 7.27 *Importance of inflation issue: all respondents (%)*

	Feb. 1974	Oct. 1974	1979	1983	1987
Government's handling of inflation was					
Extremely important	31.9	32.5	41.3	51.7	–
Fairly important	49.4	53.8	38.6	37.6	–
Not very important	18.6	13.7	20.2	10.7	–
Total	100.0	100.0	100.0	100.0	–
N. of respondents	2401	2274	1844	3938	–

Table 7.28 *Importance of inflation issue by gender (%)*

	Men				
	Feb. 1974	Oct. 1974	1979	1983	1987
Government's handling of inflation was					
Extremely important	29.7	29.3	38.6	49.8	–
Fairly important	49.3	56.0	41.4	39.4	–
Not very important	21.1	14.7	20.0	10.9	–
Total	100.0	100.0	100.0	100.0	–
N. of respondents	1143	1139	894	1868	–
	Women				
	Feb. 1974	Oct. 1974	1979	1983	1987
Government's handling of inflation was					
Extremely important	34.0	35.7	43.8	53.5	–
Fairly important	49.6	51.5	35.9	36.0	–
Not very important	16.4	12.8	20.3	10.5	–
Total	100.0	100.0	100.0	100.0	–
N. of respondents	1258	1135	950	2071	–

Table 7.29 *Importance of inflation issue by age (%)*

	Aged under 25				
	Feb. 1974	Oct. 1974	1979	1983	1987
Government's handling of inflation was					
Extremely important	20.4	25.7	28.4	40.9	–
Fairly important	55.9	58.2	41.4	46.1	–
Not very important	23.7	16.1	30.2	13.1	–
Total	100.0	100.0	100.0	100.0	–
N. of respondents	245	261	162	557	–
	Aged 25–34				
	Feb. 1974	Oct. 1974	1979	1983	1987
Government's handling of inflation was					
Extremely important	32.1	28.3	35.8	47.8	–
Fairly important	48.1	58.3	44.3	40.6	–
Not very important	19.8	13.4	19.9	11.7	–
Total	100.0	100.0	100.0	100.0	–
N. of respondents	455	470	422	743	–

Table 7.29 (*cont.*)

	Aged 35–44				
	Feb. 1974	Oct. 1974	1979	1983	1987
Government's handling of inflation was					
Extremely important	30.8	28.6	39.7	51.5	–
Fairly important	52.7	57.5	38.8	38.1	–
Not very important	16.5	13.9	21.5	10.4	–
Total	100.0	100.0	100.0	100.0	–
N. of respondents	412	388	325	714	–
	Aged 45–54				
	Feb. 1974	Oct. 1974	1979	1983	1987
Government's handling of inflation was					
Extremely important	30.8	30.9	38.8	55.8	–
Fairly important	51.5	57.7	42.4	33.5	–
Not very important	17.8	11.4	18.8	10.7	–
Total	100.0	100.0	100.0	100.0	–
N. of respondents	439	395	335	633	–
	Aged 55–64				
	Feb. 1974	Oct. 1974	1979	1983	1987
Government's handling of inflation was					
Extremely important	38.0	38.2	48.9	56.3	–
Fairly important	45.7	48.3	34.4	35.8	–
Not very important	16.3	13.5	16.8	7.9	–
Total	100.0	100.0	100.0	100.0	–
N. of respondents	387	348	262	593	–
	Aged 65–74				
	Feb. 1974	Oct. 1974	1979	1983	1987
Government's handling of inflation was					
Extremely important	40.2	43.5	56.0	59.2	–
Fairly important	43.6	43.5	30.1	31.3	–
Not very important	16.2	13.0	13.9	9.4	–
Total	100.0	100.0	100.0	100.0	–
N. of respondents	295	276	209	440	–

Table 7.29 (*cont.*)

	Aged over 74				
	Feb. 1974	Oct. 1974	1979	1983	1987
Government's handling of inflation was					
Extremely important	24.1	40.5	47.5	55.4	–
Fairly important	49.7	42.9	26.2	32.6	–
Not very important	26.2	16.7	26.2	12.0	–
Total	100.0	100.0	100.0	100.0	–
N. of respondents	145	126	122	241	–

Table 7.30 *Importance of inflation issue by marital status and gender (%)*

	Single men				
	Feb. 1974	Oct. 1974	1979	1983	1987
Government's handling of inflation was					
Extremely important	18.9	–	31.7	43.1	–
Fairly important	56.1	–	40.7	44.2	–
Not very important	25.0	–	27.6	12.7	–
Total	100.0	–	100.0	100.0	–
N. of respondents	180	–	123	397	–

	Single women				
	Feb. 1974	Oct. 1974	1979	1983	1987
Government's handling of inflation was					
Extremely important	22.7	–	29.9	42.2	–
Fairly important	53.2	–	45.4	45.3	–
Not very important	24.0	–	24.7	12.5	–
Total	100.0	–	100.0	100.0	–
N. of respondents	154	–	97	297	–

	Married men				
	Feb. 1974	Oct. 1974	1979	1983	1987
Government's handling of inflation was					
Extremely important	31.9	30.0	40.0	51.2	–
Fairly important	47.8	56.3	41.3	38.5	–
Not very important	20.4	13.8	18.7	10.3	–
Total	100.0	100.0	100.0	100.0	–
N. of respondents	894	921	678	1342	–

Table 7.30 (*cont.*)

	Married women				
	Feb. 1974	Oct. 1974	1979	1983	1987
Government's handling of inflation was					
Extremely important	35.7	37.1	44.3	55.1	–
Fairly important	49.8	51.8	36.7	35.3	–
Not very important	14.5	11.1	19.0	9.6	–
Total	100.0	100.0	100.0	100.0	–
N. of respondents	374	840	652	1403	–
	Divorced and separated men				
	Feb. 1974	Oct. 1974	1979	1983	1987
Government's handling of inflation was					
Extremely important	(12.5)	–	35.5	54.0	–
Fairly important	(37.5)	–	45.2	36.7	–
Not very important	(50.0)	–	19.4	9.3	–
Total	(100.0)	–	100.0	100.0	–
N. of respondents	8	–	31	63	–
	Divorced and separated women				
	Feb. 1974	Oct. 1974	1979	1983	1987
Government's handling of inflation was					
Extremely important	(52.9)	–	54.2	59.3	–
Fairly important	(29.4)	–	35.4	29.8	–
Not very important	(17.6)	–	10.4	10.9	–
Total	(100.0)	–	100.0	100.0	–
N. of respondents	17	–	48	117	–
	Widowed men				
	Feb. 1974	Oct. 1974	1979	1983	1987
Government's handling of inflation was					
Extremely important	31.1	–	43.1	56.9	–
Fairly important	52.5	–	39.2	31.1	–
Not very important	16.4	–	17.6	11.9	–
Total	100.0	–	100.0	100.0	–
N. of respondents	61	–	51	64	–

Table 7.30 (*cont.*)

	Widowed women				
	Feb. 1974	Oct. 1974	1979	1983	1987
Government's handling of inflation was					
Extremely important	33.8	–	49.0	55.6	–
Fairly important	47.9	–	26.6	31.8	–
Not very important	18.3	–	24.5	12.6	–
Total	100.0	–	100.0	100.0	–
N. of respondents	213	–	143	253	–

Table 7.31 *Importance of inflation issue: new electors (%)*

	Feb. 1974	Oct. 1974	1979	1983	1987
Government's handling of inflation was					
Extremely important	19.4	–	25.6	39.2	–
Fairly important	56.4	–	41.3	46.7	–
Not very important	24.2	–	33.1	14.1	–
Total	100.0	–	100.0	100.0	–
N. of respondents	165	–	121	309	–

Table 7.32 *Importance of inflation issue by political generation (%)*

	First voted 1918–1935				
	Feb. 1974	Oct. 1974	1979	1983	1987
Government's handling of inflation was					
Extremely important	37.7	41.6	54.2	57.8	–
Fairly important	44.6	44.8	27.6	32.3	–
Not very important	17.6	13.5	18.2	9.9	–
Total	100.0	100.0	100.0	100.0	–
N. of respondents	578	524	308	473	–

Table 7.32 (*cont.*)

	First voted 1936–1950				
	Feb. 1974	Oct. 1974	1979	1983	1987
Government's handling of inflation was					
Extremely important	32.4	33.2	46.0	56.6	–
Fairly important	50.3	54.8	35.4	34.8	–
Not very important	17.2	12.0	18.6	8.6	–
Total	100.0	100.0	100.0	100.0	–
N. of respondents	638	566	413	811	–

	First voted 1951–1970				
	Feb. 1974	Oct. 1974	1979	1983	1987
Government's handling of inflation was					
Extremely important	30.8	29.1	37.2	52.8	–
Fairly important	50.7	57.7	42.9	37.0	–
Not very important	18.5	13.2	19.9	10.1	–
Total	100.0	100.0	100.0	100.0	–
N. of respondents	980	984	844	1613	–

	First voted after 1970				
	Feb. 1974	Oct. 1974	1979	1983	1987
Government's handling of inflation was					
Extremely important	19.4	22.7	32.1	45.5	–
Fairly important	56.4	58.5	42.1	41.5	–
Not very important	24.2	18.8	25.8	13.1	–
Total	100.0	100.0	100.0	100.0	–
N. of respondents	165	176	271	724	–

Table 7.33 *Importance of inflation issue by vote (%)*

	Conservative voters				
	Feb. 1974	Oct. 1974	1979	1983	1987
Government's handling of inflation was					
Extremely important	21.0	27.8	34.0	57.5	–
Fairly important	50.8	55.3	42.0	36.8	–
Not very important	28.2	16.8	24.1	5.7	–
Total	100.0	100.0	100.0	100.0	–
N. of respondents	776	683	727	1449	–

Table 7.33 (*cont.*)

	Labour voters				
	Feb. 1974	Oct. 1974	1979	1983	1987
Government's handling of inflation was					
Extremely important	44.0	36.1	52.7	50.9	–
Fairly important	47.6	54.0	33.9	34.6	–
Not very important	8.5	10.0	13.5	14.5	–
Total	100.0	100.0	100.0	100.0	–
N. of respondents	828	804	579	915	–

	Liberal voters				
	Feb. 1974	Oct. 1974	1979	1983	1987
Government's handling of inflation was					
Extremely important	29.4	32.3	36.4	41.5	–
Fairly important	50.9	52.7	43.5	45.1	–
Not very important	19.7	15.0	20.1	13.4	–
Total	100.0	100.0	100.0	100.0	–
N. of respondents	391	347	214	793	–

	Voters for other parties				
	Feb. 1974	Oct. 1974	1979	1983	1987
Government's handling of inflation was					
Extremely important	21.3	20.0	36.0	54.3	–
Fairly important	61.7	56.9	32.0	33.1	–
Not very important	17.0	23.1	32.0	12.6	–
Total	100.0	100.0	100.0	100.0	–
N. of respondents	47	65	25	43	–

Table 7.34 *Importance of inflation issue by strength and direction of partisanship (%)*

	Very strong Conservative identifiers				
	Feb. 1974	Oct. 1974	1979	1983	1987
Government's handling of inflation was					
Extremely important	24.4	31.3	41.2	65.9	–
Fairly important	46.2	52.3	32.9	30.2	–
Not very important	29.5	16.4	25.9	3.9	–
Total	100.0	100.0	100.0	100.0	–
N. of respondents	275	214	170	358	–

Table 7.34 (*cont.*)

	Fairly strong Conservative identifiers				
	Feb. 1974	Oct. 1974	1979	1983	1987
Government's handling of inflation was					
Extremely important	21.8	28.3	30.8	57.0	–
Fairly important	54.5	57.5	48.7	36.4	–
Not very important	23.7	14.3	20.5	6.7	–
Total	100.0	100.0	100.0	100.0	–
N. of respondents	426	414	386	674	–

	Not very strong Conservative identifiers				
	Feb. 1974	Oct. 1974	1979	1983	1987
Government's handling of inflation was					
Extremely important	24.9	26.3	32.3	51.1	–
Fairly important	49.2	52.5	38.5	40.5	–
Not very important	25.9	21.2	29.2	8.4	–
Total	100.0	100.0	100.0	100.0	–
N. of respondents	189	179	195	452	–

	Very strong Liberal identifiers				
	Feb. 1974	Oct. 1974	1979	1983	1987
Government's handling of inflation was					
Extremely important	27.8	45.7	30.0	53.8	–
Fairly important	44.4	34.8	43.3	34.6	–
Not very important	27.8	19.6	26.7	11.5	–
Total	100.0	100.0	100.0	100.0	–
N. of respondents	36	46	30	78	–

	Fairly strong Liberal identifiers				
	Feb. 1974	Oct. 1974	1979	1983	1987
Government's handling of inflation was					
Extremely important	30.4	31.1	50.0	41.2	–
Fairly important	53.0	55.7	33.0	50.0	–
Not very important	16.7	13.1	17.0	8.8	–
Total	100.0	100.0	100.0	100.0	–
N. of respondents	168	183	106	306	–

Table 7.34 (*cont.*)

	Not very strong Liberal identifiers				
	Feb. 1974	Oct. 1974	1979	1983	1987
Government's handling of inflation was					
Extremely important	21.7	30.8	28.9	45.9	–
Fairly important	54.2	52.5	38.9	39.1	–
Not very important	24.2	16.7	32.2	15.0	–
Total	100.0	100.0	100.0	100.0	–
N. of respondents	120	120	90	320	–

	Very strong Labour identifiers				
	Feb. 1974	Oct. 1974	1979	1983	1987
Government's handling of inflation was					
Extremely important	46.8	42.8	65.8	53.9	–
Fairly important	45.0	47.4	21.8	29.7	–
Not very important	8.1	9.8	12.4	16.3	–
Total	100.0	100.0	100.0	100.0	–
N. of respondents	393	327	193	343	–

	Fairly strong Labour identifiers				
	Feb. 1974	Oct. 1974	1979	1983	1987
Government's handling of inflation was					
Extremely important	42.7	35.0	49.0	52.5	–
Fairly important	50.1	56.8	41.7	34.9	–
Not very important	7.2	8.2	9.3	12.5	–
Total	100.0	100.0	100.0	100.0	–
N. of respondents	419	437	345	495	–

	Not very strong Labour identifiers				
	Feb. 1974	Oct. 1974	1979	1983	1987
Government's handling of inflation was					
Extremely important	34.5	33.7	38.6	45.2	–
Fairly important	48.8	54.1	38.0	42.9	–
Not very important	16.7	12.2	23.4	11.9	–
Total	100.0	100.0	100.0	100.0	–
N. of respondents	203	172	171	385	–

Table 7.35 *Importance of inflation issue by social class (%)*

	Professional and managerial classes				
	Feb. 1974	Oct. 1974	1979	1983	1987
Government's handling of inflation was					
Extremely important	17.0	21.7	27.9	48.6	–
Fairly important	51.3	57.7	45.8	41.4	–
Not very important	31.7	20.6	26.3	10.0	–
Total	100.0	100.0	100.0	100.0	–
N. of respondents	341	345	373	1014	–
	Intermediate and routine non-manual classes				
	Feb. 1974	Oct. 1974	1979	1983	1987
Government's handling of inflation was					
Extremely important	31.0	32.4	37.0	52.8	–
Fairly important	50.8	54.1	40.7	38.6	–
Not very important	18.1	13.5	22.3	8.6	–
Total	100.0	100.0	100.0	100.0	–
N. of respondents	828	780	494	744	–
	Manual working class				
	Feb. 1974	Oct. 1974	1979	1983	1987
Government's handling of inflation was					
Extremely important	38.1	36.4	49.2	53.6	–
Fairly important	47.9	52.6	35.1	34.9	–
Not very important	14.1	11.0	15.7	11.5	–
Total	100.0	100.0	100.0	100.0	–
N. of respondents	1088	1030	900	1888	–

Table 7.36 *Importance of inflation issue by employment status (%)*

	Self-employed with employees				
	Feb. 1974	Oct. 1974	1979	1983	1987
Government's handling of inflation was					
Extremely important	19.1	30.0	27.6	53.7	–
Fairly important	50.6	50.0	36.2	41.1	–
Not very important	30.3	20.0	36.2	5.1	–
Total	100.0	100.0	100.0	100.0	–
N. of respondents	89	70	58	162	–

Table 7.36 (*cont.*)

	Self-employed, no employees				
	Feb. 1974	Oct. 1974	1979	1983	1987
Government's handling of inflation was					
Extremely important	22.0	38.9	29.2	58.1	–
Fairly important	51.2	46.7	44.4	32.9	–
Not very important	26.8	14.4	26.4	9.0	–
Total	100.0	100.0	100.0	100.0	–
N. of respondents	82	90	72	133	–

	Managers				
	Feb. 1974	Oct. 1974	1979	1983	1987
Government's handling of inflation was					
Extremely important	26.1	26.7	28.8	52.3	–
Fairly important	44.8	54.1	45.2	39.9	–
Not very important	29.1	19.2	26.0	7.9	–
Total	100.0	100.0	100.0	100.0	–
N. of respondents	165	172	146	385	–

	Foremen and supervisors				
	Feb. 1974	Oct. 1974	1979	1983	1987
Government's handling of inflation was					
Extremely important	27.6	30.5	38.2	54.8	–
Fairly important	51.0	56.8	45.5	35.7	–
Not very important	21.4	12.7	16.2	9.5	–
Total	100.0	100.0	100.0	100.0	–
N. of respondents	98	118	191	231	–

	Rank and file employees				
	Feb. 1974	Oct. 1974	1979	1983	1987
Government's handling of inflation was					
Extremely important	34.2	31.9	43.5	52.0	–
Fairly important	49.5	54.7	38.1	36.9	–
Not very important	16.3	13.4	18.4	11.0	–
Total	100.0	100.0	100.0	100.0	–
N. of respondents	1591	1487	914	2569	–

Table 7.37 *Importance of inflation issue: unemployed (%)*

	Feb. 1974	Oct. 1974	1979	1983	1987
Government's handling of inflation was					
Extremely important	41.3	33.3	45.9	45.3	–
Fairly important	43.5	56.4	40.5	38.0	–
Not very important	15.2	10.3	13.5	16.7	–
Total	100.0	100.0	100.0	100.0	–
N. of respondents	46	39	37	240	–

Table 7.38 *Importance of inflation issue by class and employment (%)*

	Professional and managerial classes: self-employed				
	Feb. 1974	Oct. 1974	1979	1983	1987
Government's handling of inflation was					
Extremely important	6.4	23.8	28.2	51.1	–
Fairly important	55.3	45.2	35.9	38.3	–
Not very important	38.3	31.0	35.9	10.5	–
Total	100.0	100.0	100.0	100.0	–
N. of respondents	47	42	39	133	–

	Professional and managerial classes: employees				
	Feb. 1974	Oct. 1974	1979	1983	1987
Government's handling of inflation was					
Extremely important	19.4	20.0	27.2	48.5	–
Fairly important	49.0	58.5	49.6	41.8	–
Not very important	31.6	21.5	23.2	9.7	–
Total	100.0	100.0	100.0	100.0	–
N. of respondents	253	260	250	852	–

	Intermediate and routine non-manual classes: self-employed				
	Feb. 1974	Oct. 1974	1979	1983	1987
Government's handling of inflation was					
Extremely important	26.3	36.7	25.5	69.0	–
Fairly important	48.5	46.8	38.2	31.0	–
Not very important	25.3	16.5	36.4	0.0	–
Total	100.0	100.0	100.0	100.0	–
N. of respondents	99	79	55	29	–

Table 7.38 (*cont.*)

	Intermediate and routine non-manual classes: employees				
	Feb. 1974	Oct. 1974	1979	1983	1987
Government's handling of inflation was					
Extremely important	32.3	31.1	38.2	52.4	–
Fairly important	50.7	55.1	40.9	39.2	–
Not very important	17.1	13.8	20.9	8.4	–
Total	100.0	100.0	100.0	100.0	–
N. of respondents	679	653	369	689	–

	Manual working class: self employed				
	Feb. 1974	Oct. 1974	1979	1983	1987
Government's handling of inflation was					
Extremely important	25.0	43.6	33.3	55.3	–
Fairly important	50.0	53.8	50.0	40.4	–
Not very important	25.0	2.6	16.7	4.4	–
Total	100.0	100.0	100.0	100.0	–
N. of respondents	24	39	36	114	–

	Manual working class: employees				
	Feb. 1974	Oct. 1974	1979	1983	1987
Government's handling of inflation was					
Extremely important	37.2	35.0	48.0	54.0	–
Fairly important	48.3	53.2	35.8	34.6	–
Not very important	14.5	11.8	16.2	11.4	–
Total	100.0	100.0	100.0	100.0	–
N. of respondents	911	856	629	1618	–

Table 7.39 *Importance of inflation issue by trade union membership (%)*

	Trade union members				
	Feb. 1974	Oct. 1974	1979	1983	1987
Government's handling of inflation was					
Extremely important	34.6	35.4	39.7	48.2	–
Fairly important	51.2	50.4	41:0	40.0	–
Not very important	14.2	14.2	19.2	11.8	–
Total	100.0	100.0	100.0	100.0	–
N. of respondents	613	540	551	1044	–
	Respondent is married to a trade union member				
	Feb. 1974	Oct. 1974	1979	1983	1987
Government's handling of inflation was					
Extremely important	40.2	40.5	44.0	50.5	–
Fairly important	47.6	48.0	41.4	39.9	–
Not very important	12.2	11.5	14.7	9.6	–
Total	100.0	100.0	100.0	100.0	–
N. of respondents	296	269	273	432	–
	Neither respondent nor spouse belongs to a trade union				
	Feb. 1974	Oct. 1974	1979	1983	1987
Government's handling of inflation was					
Extremely important	29.2	29.4	41.4	53.3	–
Fairly important	49.1	48.7	36.5	36.3	–
Not very important	21.7	21.9	22.2	10.4	–
Total	100.0	100.0	100.0	100.0	–
N. of respondents	1492	1545	1020	2446	–

Chapter 8

BUSINESS, TRADE UNIONS AND STRIKE

1. The pair of questions on big business and trade union power in the 1987 study has five answer categories whereas in all previous studies it has two. For the purposes of comparability, the 1987 categories 'far too much power' and 'too much power' are combined into 'too much power'.

See Appendix E, pp. 485, 494 and 499 on the construction of these industrial relations variables.

Table 8.1 *Perceptions of business and trade union power: all respondents (%)*

	1963	1964	1966	1969	1970	Feb. 1974	Oct. 1974	1979	1983	1987
Business and trade union power										
Only trade unions have too much	20.7	24.6	27.3	33.7	35.9	–	31.9	32.2	23.4	34.0
Neither has too much	9.3	10.6	9.6	10.6	9.4	–	6.6	7.5	8.4	34.3
Both have too much	42.8	37.8	44.1	37.9	37.2	–	49.0	48.9	49.9	11.4
Only business has too much	27.2	27.0	19.0	17.8	17.5	–	12.5	11.4	18.4	20.3
Total	100.0	100.0	100.0	100.0	100.0	–	100.0	100.0	100.0	100.0
Total unions have too much power	63.5	62.4	71.4	71.6	73.1	–	80.9	81.1	73.3	45.4
Total business has too much power	70.0	64.8	63.1	55.7	54.7	–	61.5	60.3	68.3	31.7
N. of respondents	1503	1367	1512	867	1457	–	2124	1650	3380	3353

Table 8.2 *Perceptions of business and trade union power by gender (%)*

Men										
	1963	1964	1966	1969	1970	Feb. 1974	Oct. 1974	1979	1983	1987
Business and trade union power										
Only trade unions have too much	18.1	21.5	26.7	36.8	37.3	–	29.5	29.2	20.6	29.1
Neither has too much	9.6	11.7	10.5	9.8	11.2	–	6.7	8.3	9.4	35.2
Both have too much	38.2	35.5	41.5	33.8	32.1	–	49.4	48.5	48.4	10.9
Only business has too much	34.1	31.3	21.3	19.7	19.5	–	14.4	14.0	21.6	24.8
Total	100.0	100.0	100.0	100.0	100.0	–	100.0	100.0	100.0	100.0
Total unions have too much power	56.3	57.0	68.2	70.6	69.4	–	78.9	77.7	69.0	40.0
Total business has too much power	72.3	66.8	62.8	53.5	51.6	–	63.8	62.5	70.0	35.7
N. of respondents	790	728	807	468	769	–	1123	840	1695	1637

Table 8.2 (*cont.*)

	Women									
	1963	1964	1966	1969	1970	Feb. 1974	Oct. 1974	1979	1983	1987
Business and trade union power										
Only trade unions have too much	23.6	28.1	28.1	30.1	34.3	–	34.6	35.3	26.1	38.7
Neither has too much	9.0	9.5	8.5	11.5	7.4	–	6.6	6.7	7.4	33.6
Both have too much	47.8	40.4	47.0	42.9	43.0	–	48.6	49.4	51.4	11.9
Only business has too much	19.6	22.0	16.4	15.5	15.2	–	10.3	8.6	15.1	15.9
Total	100.0	100.0	100.0	100.0	100.0	–	100.0	100.0	100.0	100.0
Total unions have too much power	71.4	68.5	75.1	73.0	77.3	–	83.2	84.7	77.5	50.6
Total business has too much power	67.4	62.4	63.4	58.4	58.2	–	58.9	58.0	66.5	27.8
N. of respondents	713	639	705	399	688	–	1001	810	1685	1716

Table 8.3 *Perceptions of business and trade union power by age (%)*

	Aged under 25									
	1963	1964	1966	1969	1970	Feb. 1974	Oct. 1974	1979	1983	1987
Business and trade union power										
Only trade unions have too much	27.2	37.1	31.2	41.1	36.6	–	31.1	24.2	24.6	32.6
Neither has too much	8.7	17.3	15.5	14.4	16.7	–	8.4	22.3	14.9	42.5
Both have too much	42.4	24.6	33.8	26.7	30.8	–	43.3	40.1	42.5	6.5
Only business has too much	21.7	21.0	19.5	17.8	15.9	–	17.2	13.4	18.0	18.3
Total	100.0	100.0	100.0	100.0	100.0	–	100.0	100.0	100.0	100.0
Total unions have too much power	69.6	61.7	65.0	67.8	67.4	–	74.4	64.3	67.1	39.1
Total business has too much power	64.1	45.6	53.3	44.5	46.7	–	60.5	53.5	60.5	24.8
N. of respondents	92	87	116	90	217	–	238	157	457	427

Table 8.3 (*cont.*)

	Aged 25–34									
	1963	1964	1966	1969	1970	Feb. 1974	Oct. 1974	1979	1983	1987
Business and trade *union power*										
Only trade unions have too much	28.1	26.1	28.3	40.9	42.9	–	29.8	33.7	25.0	29.4
Neither has too much	9.8	11.4	15.8	9.8	7.8	–	7.7	8.2	11.4	41.3
Both have too much	36.3	38.7	36.6	29.5	29.6	–	48.3	45.8	44.9	9.4
Only business has too much	25.8	23.8	19.2	19.7	19.7	–	14.1	12.4	18.7	19.8
Total	100.0	100.0	100.0	100.0	100.0	–	100.0	100.0	100.0	100.0
Total unions have too much power	64.4	64.8	64.9	70.4	72.5	–	78.1	79.5	69.9	38.8
Total business has too much power	62.1	62.5	55.8	49.2	49.3	–	62.4	58.2	63.6	29.2
N. of respondents	256	240	256	132	246	–	439	380	641	601

	Aged 35–44									
	1963	1964	1966	1969	1970	Feb. 1974	Oct. 1974	1979	1983	1987
Business and trade *union power*										
Only trade unions have too much	17.4	21.5	28.1	32.1	33.1	–	31.3	33.0	24.6	30.3
Neither has too much	8.5	8.7	9.2	9.3	9.3	–	6.7	6.8	8.0	35.8
Both have too much	44.8	36.1	42.3	40.0	37.7	–	48.0	48.0	46.4	11.7
Only business has too much	29.3	33.7	20.4	18.6	19.9	–	14.0	12.2	20.9	22.3
Total	100.0	100.0	100.0	100.0	100.0	–	100.0	100.0	100.0	100.0
Total unions have too much power	62.2	57.6	70.4	72.1	70.8	–	79.3	81.0	71.0	42.0
Total business has too much power	74.1	69.8	62.7	58.6	57.6	–	62.0	60.2	67.3	34.0
N. of respondents	328	294	303	140	251	–	371	294	628	672

Table 8.3 (*cont.*)

Aged 45–54

	1963	1964	1966	1969	1970	Feb. 1974	Oct. 1974	1979	1983	1987
Business and trade union power										
Only trade unions have too much	17.2	22.2	23.2	31.1	36.0	–	33.5	30.2	22.5	35.2
Neither has too much	10.5	12.4	7.8	7.3	8.7	–	8.1	6.5	8.0	29.6
Both have too much	46.2	39.5	49.2	40.2	35.5	–	48.1	52.9	49.7	12.4
Only business has too much	26.1	25.8	19.8	21.3	19.9	–	10.3	10.4	19.9	22.8
Total	100.0	100.0	100.0	100.0	100.0	–	100.0	100.0	100.0	100.0
Total unions have too much power	63.4	61.7	72.4	71.3	71.5	–	81.6	83.1	72.2	47.6
Total business has too much power	72.3	65.3	69.0	61.5	55.4	–	58.4	63.3	69.6	35.2
N. of respondents	314	283	334	164	240	–	370	308	549	518

Aged 55–64

	1963	1964	1966	1969	1970	Feb. 1974	Oct. 1974	1979	1983	1987
Business and trade union power										
Only trade unions have too much	19.3	25.6	26.3	30.7	31.3	–	31.1	29.4	19.2	32.7
Neither has too much	9.6	10.0	7.2	13.1	9.1	–	4.8	3.5	4.7	29.8
Both have too much	43.7	39.1	48.4	40.5	43.9	–	52.7	54.5	56.9	15.2
Only business has too much	27.4	25.3	18.1	15.7	15.6	–	11.4	12.6	19.2	22.4
Total	100.0	100.0	100.0	100.0	100.0	–	100.0	100.0	100.0	100.0
Total unions have too much power	63.0	64.7	74.7	71.2	75.2	–	83.8	83.9	76.1	47.9
Total business has too much power	71.1	64.44	66.5	56.2	59.5	–	64.1	67.1	76.1	37.6
N. of respondents	270	259	279	153	269	–	334	231	526	539

Table 8.3 (*cont.*)

| | Aged 65–74 | | | | | | | | | |
	1963	1964	1966	1969	1970	Feb. 1974	Oct. 1974	1979	1983	1987
Business and trade union power										
Only trade unions have too much	17.1	21.0	27.9	25.3	36.0	–	32.7	37.9	21.4	41.6
Neither has too much	9.4	9.2	4.5	10.1	5.4	–	3.1	2.7	4.0	28.1
Both have too much	42.4	40.9	51.3	55.7	46.0	–	53.7	51.1	62.5	10.5
Only business has too much	31.2	28.8	16.3	8.9	12.7	–	10.5	8.2	12.1	19.8
Total	100.0	100.0	100.0	100.0	100.0	–	100.0	100.0	100.0	100.0
Total unions have too much power	59.5	61.9	79.2	81.0	82.0	–	86.4	89.0	83.9	52.1
Total business has too much power	73.6	69.7	67.6	64.6	58.7	–	64.2	59.3	74.6	30.3
N. of respondents	170	142	151	79	158	–	257	182	375	373

| | Aged over 74 | | | | | | | | | |
	1963	1964	1966	1969	1970	Feb. 1974	Oct. 1974	1979	1983	1987
Business and trade union power										
Only trade unions have too much	29.8	30.8	37.0	26.5	36.2	–	39.4	38.9	28.5	49.4
Neither has too much	3.5	4.9	6.9	5.9	3.5	–	5.5	5.3	4.2	25.7
Both have too much	45.6	41.2	38.8	52.9	49.6	–	48.6	47.4	53.7	16.2
Only business has too much	21.1	23.2	17.2	14.7	10.8	–	6.4	8.4	13.6	8.6
Total	100.0	100.0	100.0	100.0	100.0	–	100.0	100.0	100.0	100.0
Total unions have too much power	75.4	72.0	75.8	79.4	85.8	–	88.0	86.3	82.2	65.6
Total business has too much power	66.7	64.4	56.0	67.6	60.4	–	55.0	55.8	67.3	24.8
N. of respondents	57	62	64	34	61	–	109	95	191	196

Table 8.4 *Perceptions of business and trade union power by marital status (%)*

	Single									
	1963	1964	1966	1969	1970	Feb. 1974	Oct. 1974	1979	1983	1987
Business and trade union power										
Only trade unions have too much	20.6	38.2	33.2	41.3	40.4	–	–	30.0	24.3	30.6
Neither has too much	9.8	7.6	9.7	12.9	14.5	–	–	16.4	13.2	39.8
Both have too much	43.8	32.6	38.5	28.9	29.8	–	–	41.5	42.7	8.0
Only business has too much	25.8	21.7	18.6	16.9	15.3	–	–	12.1	19.8	21.6
Total	100.0	100.0	100.0	100.0	100.0	–	–	100.0	100.0	100.0
Total unions have too much power	64.4	70.8	71.7	70.2	70.2	–	–	71.5	67.0	38.6
Total business has too much power	69.6	54.3	57.1	45.8	45.1	–	–	53.6	62.5	29.6
N. of respondents	194	164	171	201	269	–	–	207	582	589

	Married									
	1963	1964	1966	1969	1970	Feb. 1974	Oct. 1974	1979	1983	1987
Business and trade union power										
Only trade unions have too much	20.4	22.4	26.0	30.8	34.9	–	33.2	32.2	23.2	34.1
Neither has too much	9.6	11.3	10.0	10.0	8.7	–	7.4	6.3	7.6	33.2
Both have too much	42.6	37.6	44.8	40.0	38.2	–	46.4	50.1	50.7	11.7
Only business has too much	27.5	28.7	19.2	19.2	18.2	–	13.0	11.4	18.4	21.0
Total	100.0	100.0	100.0	100.0	100.0	–	100.0	100.0	100.0	100.0
Total unions have too much power	63.0	60.0	70.8	70.8	73.1	–	79.6	82.3	73.9	45.8
Total business has too much power	70.1	66.3	64.0	59.2	56.4	–	59.4	61.5	69.1	32.7
N. of respondents	1149	1092	1193	578	1041	–	1720	1209	2391	2333

Table 8.4 (*cont.*)

	1963	1964	1966	1969	1970	Feb. 1974	Oct. 1974	1979	1983	1987
Widowed										
Business and trade union power										
Only trade unions have too much	–	–	28.3	–	–	–	–	36.1	22.3	40.9
Neither has too much	–	–	5.7	–	–	–	–	6.3	4.2	30.6
Both have too much	–	–	46.9	–	–	–	–	48.7	59.9	17.6
Only business has too much	–	–	19.1	–	–	–	–	8.9	13.6	10.9
Total	–	–	100.0	–	–	–	–	100.0	100.0	100.0
Total unions have too much power	–	–	75.2	–	–	–	–	84.8	82.2	58.5
Total business has too much power	–	–	66.0	–	–	–	–	57.6	73.5	28.5
N. of respondents	–	–	136	–	–	–	–	158	255	270

	1963	1964	1966	1969	1970	Feb. 1974	Oct. 1974	1979	1983	1987
Divorced and separated										
Business and trade union power										
Only trade unions have too much	–	–	(63.5)	–	–	–	–	29.9	22.9	33.4
Neither has too much	–	–	(6.3)	–	–	–	–	6.0	9.3	36.7
Both have too much	–	–	(23.8)	–	–	–	–	49.3	47.3	9.8
Only business has too much	–	–	(6.3)	–	–	–	–	14.9	20.5	20.1
Total	–	–	(100.0)	–	–	–	–	100.0	100.0	100.0
Total unions have too much power	–	–	(87.3)	–	–	–	–	79.2	70.2	43.2
Total business has too much power	–	–	(30.1)	–	–	–	–	64.2	67.8	29.9
N. of respondents	–	–	13	–	–	–	–	67	150	161

Table 8.5 *Perceptions of business and trade union power by political generation (%)*

	First voted 1918–1935									
	1963	1964	1966	1969	1970	Feb. 1974	Oct. 1974	1979	1983	1987
Business and trade union power										
Only trade unions have too much	18.0	24.1	27.5	26.8	32.7	–	34.2	38.7	27.3	47.5
Neither has too much	9.6	9.9	6.6	11.8	7.8	–	3.3	3.9	4.3	27.5
Both have too much	44.2	39.2	47.6	47.2	44.2	–	52.6	49.6	55.0	14.9
Only business has too much	28.2	26.8	18.4	14.2	15.2	–	9.8	7.8	13.4	10.2
Total	100.0	100.0	100.0	100.0	100.0	–	100.0	100.0	100.0	100.0
Total unions have too much power	62.2	63.3	75.1	74.0	76.9	–	86.8	88.3	82.3	62.4
Total business has too much power	72.4	66.0	66.0	61.4	59.4	–	62.4	57.4	68.4	25.1
N. of respondents	616	543	546	246	422	–	479	256	380	227

	First voted 1936–1950									
	1963	1964	1966	1969	1970	Feb. 1974	Oct. 1974	1979	1983	1987
Business and trade union power										
Only trade unions have too much	18.3	21.9	25.5	31.0	35.4	–	31.6	31.2	18.7	38.4
Neither has too much	9.3	10.7	8.0	8.3	8.1	–	7.2	3.8	4.4	28.0
Both have too much	45.3	38.2	46.5	40.1	37.7	–	50.6	53.5	59.9	13.5
Only business has too much	27.2	29.2	20.1	20.7	18.8	–	10.6	11.6	17.1	20.1
Total	100.0	100.0	100.0	100.0	100.0	–	100.0	100.0	100.0	100.0
Total unions have too much power	63.6	60.1	72.0	71.1	73.1	–	82.2	84.7	78.6	51.9
Total business has too much power	72.5	67.4	66.6	60.8	56.5	–	61.2	65.1	77.0	33.6
N. of respondents	497	447	478	242	408	–	538	372	716	676

Table 8.5 (*cont.*)

First voted 1951–1970

	1963	1964	1966	1969	1970	Feb. 1974	Oct. 1974	1979	1983	1987
Business and trade union power										
Only trade unions have too much	28.0	29.0	28.5	39.8	38.4	–	30.6	31.2	24.5	32.1
Neither has too much	9.7	12.3	14.9	11.1	10.5	–	7.6	6.9	8.1	33.1
Both have too much	37.1	34.3	38.0	30.7	32.6	–	47.6	49.1	47.7	12.0
Only business has too much	25.2	24.3	18.6	18.4	18.5	–	14.2	12.8	19.6	22.8
Total	100.0	100.0	100.0	100.0	100.0	–	100.0	100.0	100.0	100.0
Total unions have too much power	65.1	63.3	66.5	70.5	71.0	–	78.2	80.3	72.2	44.1
Total business has too much power	62.3	58.6	56.6	49.1	51.1	–	61.8	61.9	67.3	34.8
N. of respondents	361	353	473	342	590	–	929	764	1416	1327

First voted after 1970

	1963	1964	1966	1969	1970	Feb. 1974	Oct. 1974	1979	1983	1987
Business and trade union power										
Only trade unions have too much	–	–	–	–	–	–	32.3	30.2	22.0	30.7
Neither has too much	–	–	–	–	–	–	7.6	18.4	13.0	40.9
Both have too much	–	–	–	–	–	–	42.4	40.8	45.1	8.7
Only business has too much	–	–	–	–	–	–	17.7	10.6	19.8	19.6
Total	–	–	–	–	–	–	100.0	100.0	100.0	100.0
Total unions have too much power	–	–	–	–	–	–	74.7	71.0	67.1	39.4
Total business has too much power	–	–	–	–	–	–	60.1	51.4	64.9	28.3
N. of respondents	–	–	–	–	–	–	158	255	610	1097

Table 8.6 *Perceptions of business and trade union power: non voters (%)*

	1963	1964	1966	1969	1970	Feb. 1974	Oct. 1974	1979	1983	1987
Business and trade union power										
Only trade unions have too much	–	24.8	30.8	–	33.1	–	32.3	29.3	22.8	33.1
Neither has too much	–	15.1	11.9	–	12.8	–	5.4	8.7	10.4	39.2
Both have too much	–	39.5	44.3	–	35.9	–	52.9	49.3	50.0	10.6
Only business has too much	–	20.5	13.0	–	18.2	–	9.4	12.7	16.8	17.1
Total	–	100.0	100.0	–	100.0	–	100.0	100.0	100.0	100.0
Total unions have too much power	–	64.3	75.1	–	69.0	–	85.2	78.6	72.8	43.7
Total business has too much power	–	60.0	57.3	–	54.1	–	62.3	62.0	66.8	27.7
N. of respondents	–	137	217	–	267	–	297	229	538	433

Table 8.7 *Perceptions of business and trade union power by vote (%)*

Conservative voters										
	1963	1964	1966	1969	1970	Feb. 1974	Oct. 1974	1979	1983	1987
Business and trade union power										
Only trade unions have too much	36.4	41.2	45.5	44.7	52.2	–	53.2	49.6	38.1	57.0
Neither has too much	8.2	10.3	6.6	10.0	8.5	–	2.6	3.1	4.7	24.4
Both have too much	46.8	40.4	42.2	36.5	34.4	–	43.5	46.7	53.6	13.2
Only business has too much	8.6	8.1	5.7	8.7	5.0	–	0.8	0.6	3.6	5.4
Total	100.0	100.0	100.0	100.0	100.0	–	100.0	100.0	100.0	100.0
Total unions have too much power	83.2	81.6	87.7	81.2	86.6	–	96.7	96.3	91.7	70.2
Total business has too much power	65.4	48.5	47.9	45.2	39.4	–	44.3	47.3	57.2	18.6
N. of respondents	511	507	502	438	546	–	662	651	1249	1250

Table 8.7 (*cont.*)

	Labour voters									
	1963	1964	1966	1969	1970	Feb. 1974	Oct. 1974	1979	1983	1987
Business and trade union power										
Only trade unions have too much	9.4	9.5	13.1	18.4	20.0	–	14.3	14.6	7.2	8.4
Neither has too much	11.3	10.1	11.2	11.4	8.6	–	12.2	12.8	10.7	42.8
Both have too much	32.3	32.5	43.4	39.5	41.5	–	45.6	47.1	38.5	8.2
Only business has too much	46.9	48.0	32.3	30.7	29.8	–	27.9	25.5	43.6	40.6
Total	100.0	100.0	100.0	100.0	100.0	–	100.0	100.0	100.0	100.0
Total unions have too much power	41.7	42.0	56.5	57.9	61.5	–	59.9	61.7	45.7	16.6
Total business has too much power	79.2	80.5	75.7	70.2	71.3	–	73.5	72.6	82.1	48.8
N. of respondents	635	566	662	228	510	–	735	514	791	863

	Liberal voters									
	1963	1964	1966	1969	1970	Feb. 1974	Oct. 1974	1979	1983	1987
Business and trade union power										
Only trade unions have too much	21.8	21.3	24.2	29.1	30.0	–	27.5	26.0	16.8	24.9
Neither has too much	7.1	9.9	8.4	11.4	9.8	–	3.8	6.6	10.2	39.2
Both have too much	53.8	49.6	55.0	44.3	38.9	–	63.3	58.2	56.0	13.0
Only business has too much	17.3	19.2	12.4	15.2	21.4	–	5.4	9.2	17.1	22.9
Total	100.0	100.0	100.0	100.0	100.0	–	100.0	100.0	100.0	100.0
Total unions have too much power	75.6	70.9	79.2	73.4	68.9	–	90.8	84.2	72.8	37.9
Total business has too much power	71.1	68.8	67.4	59.5	60.3	–	68.7	67.4	73.1	35.9
N. of respondents	197	126	109	79	89	–	316	196	693	697

Table 8.7 (cont.)

				Voters for other parties						
	1963	1964	1966	1969	1970	Feb. 1974	Oct. 1974	1979	1983	1987
Business and trade union power										
Only trade unions have too much	(0.0)	(53.6)	(31.6)	(33.3)	48.4	–	28.1	19.0	19.4	16.8
Neither has too much	(0.0)	(0.0)	(0.0)	(6.7)	3.7	–	4.7	14.3	7.2	26.7
Both have too much	(50.0)	(34.5)	(52.6)	(33.3)	31.3	–	56.3	52.4	45.4	14.6
Only business has too much	(50.0)	(11.9)	(15.8)	(26.7)	16.6	–	10.9	14.3	28.0	41.9
Total	(100.0)	(100.0)	(100.0)	(100.0)	100.0	–	100.0	100.0	100.0	100.0
Total unions have too much power	(0.0)	(88.1)	(84.2)	(66.6)	79.7	–	84.4	71.4	64.8	31.4
Total business has too much power	(100.0)	(46.4)	(68.4)	(60.0)	47.9	–	67.2	66.7	73.4	56.5
N. of respondents	2	8	6	15	23	–	64	21	38	40

Table 8.8 *Perceptions of business and trade union power by strength and direction of partisanship (%)*

				Very strong Conservative identifiers						
	1963	1964	1966	1969	1970	Feb. 1974	Oct. 1974	1979	1983	1987
Business and trade union power										
Only trade unions have too much	40.5	45.2	51.0	46.9	57.0	–	59.8	60.5	50.6	68.3
Neither has too much	7.6	8.5	5.1	7.7	7.0	–	3.3	0.7	2.9	18.7
Both have too much	44.8	42.3	40.5	39.9	34.2	–	36.8	38.8	44.6	11.5
Only business has too much	7.1	4.0	3.5	5.6	1.8	–	0.0	0.0	1.9	1.4
Total	100.0	100.0	100.0	100.0	100.0	–	100.0	100.0	100.0	100.0
Total unions have too much power	85.3	87.5	91.5	86.8	91.2	–	96.6	99.3	95.2	79.8
Total business has too much power	51.9	46.3	44.0	45.5	36.0	–	36.8	38.8	46.5	12.9
N. of respondents	210	273	279	143	305	–	209	152	314	287

Table 8.8 (*cont.*)

	Fairly strong Conservative identifiers									
	1963	1964	1966	1969	1970	Feb. 1974	Oct. 1974	1979	1983	1987
Business and trade union power										
Only trade unions have too much	32.9	42.4	43.9	42.1	51.2	–	51.9	52.0	39.5	57.2
Neither has too much	9.0	9.8	10.2	14.6	9.6	–	2.8	2.3	5.6	24.4
Both have too much	48.7	36.7	40.8	32.6	32.8	–	44.4	44.6	51.7	12.2
Only business has too much	9.4	11.0	5.2	10.7	6.5	–	1.0	1.1	3.2	6.3
Total	100.0	100.0	100.0	100.0	100.0	–	100.0	100.0	100.0	100.0
Total unions have too much power	81.6	79.1	84.7	74.7	84.0	–	96.3	96.6	91.2	69.4
Total business has too much power	58.1	47.7	46.0	43.3	39.3	–	45.4	45.7	54.9	18.5
N. of respondents	234	205	209	178	230	–	399	354	590	642

	Not very strong Conservative identifiers									
	1963	1964	1966	1969	1970	Feb. 1974	Oct. 1974	1979	1983	1987
Business and trade union power										
Only trade unions have too much	26.6	32.3	32.9	48.8	43.8	–	42.9	38.2	26.9	44.3
Neither has too much	9.8	14.5	7.9	7.0	13.2	–	1.1	3.9	6.9	34.8
Both have too much	52.4	43.9	48.6	36.0	32.2	–	55.4	54.5	60.8	13.8
Only business has too much	11.2	9.2	10.6	8.1	10.8	–	0.6	3.4	5.3	7.1
Total	100.0	100.0	100.0	100.0	100.0	–	100.0	100.0	100.0	100.0
Total unions have too much power	79.0	76.2	81.5	84.8	76.0	–	98.3	92.7	87.7	58.1
Total business has too much power	63.6	53.1	59.2	44.1	43.0	–	56.0	57.9	66.1	20.9
N. of respondents	143	63	78	86	83	–	177	178	375	298

Table 8.8 (*cont.*)

	Very strong Liberal identifiers									
	1963	1964	1966	1969	1970	Feb. 1974	Oct. 1974	1979	1983	1987
Business and trade union power										
Only trade unions have too much	22.9	21.9	18.2	(7.7)	18.4	–	31.7	19.2	14.7	14.9
Neither has too much	6.3	9.4	0.0	(7.7)	5.3	–	2.4	7.7	8.8	47.3
Both have too much	60.4	43.4	69.4	(76.9)	49.4	–	63.4	61.5	61.8	4.4
Only business has too much	10.4	25.3	12.4	(7.7)	26.9	–	2.4	11.5	14.7	33.4
Total	100.0	100.0	100.0	(100.0)	100.0	–	100.0	100.0	100.0	100.0
Total unions have too much power	63.3	65.3	87.6	84.6	67.8	–	95.1	80.7	76.5	19.3
Total business has too much power	70.8	68.7	81.8	84.6	76.3	–	65.8	73.0	76.5	37.8
N. of respondents	48	57	58	13	32	–	41	26	68	61

	Fairly strong Liberal identifiers									
	1963	1964	1966	1969	1970	Feb. 1974	Oct. 1974	1979	1983	1987
Business and trade union power										
Only trade unions have too much	17.1	18.8	25.2	40.5	25.7	–	25.9	34.0	18.4	25.1
Neither has too much	10.0	8.6	9.7	5.4	7.0	–	2.9	4.1	8.1	39.2
Both have too much	55.7	57.2	51.4	40.5	45.4	–	65.5	55.7	59.6	13.9
Only business has too much	17.1	15.3	13.7	13.5	21.9	–	5.7	6.2	14.0	21.8
Total	100.0	100.0	100.0	100.0	100.0	–	100.0	100.0	100.0	100.0
Total unions have too much power	72.8	76.0	76.6	81.0	71.1	–	91.4	89.7	78.0	39.0
Total business has too much power	72.8	72.5	65.1	54.0	67.3	–	71.2	61.9	73.6	35.7
N. of respondents	70	78	82	37	61	–	174	97	272	251

Table 8.8 (*cont.*)

Not very strong Liberal identifiers

	1963	1964	1966	1969	1970	Feb. 1974	Oct. 1974	1979	1983	1987
Business and trade union power										
Only trade unions have too much	15.8	18.9	28.1	21.4	45.5	–	29.4	29.5	23.6	29.9
Neither has too much	3.5	11.1	16.1	10.7	7.8	–	5.9	6.4	9.1	38.1
Both have too much	54.4	45.5	37.9	50.0	38.9	–	60.8	57.7	54.2	13.0
Only business has too much	26.3	24.5	17.9	17.9	7.7	–	3.9	6.4	13.1	19.0
Total	100.0	100.0	100.0	100.0	100.0	–	100.0	100.0	100.0	100.0
Total unions have too much power	70.2	64.4	66.0	71.4	84.4	–	90.2	87.2	77.8	42.9
Total business has too much power	80.7	70.0	55.8	67.9	46.6	–	64.7	64.1	67.3	32.0
N. of respondents	57	40	22	28	27	–	102	78	275	292

Very strong Labour identifiers

	1963	1964	1966	1969	1970	Feb. 1974	Oct. 1974	1979	1983	1987
Business and trade union power										
Only trade unions have too much	5.2	4.7	9.0	10.9	15.6	–	11.7	12.0	4.1	9.5
Neither has too much	11.6	7.0	10.1	12.0	9.1	–	13.1	12.0	10.5	34.0
Both have too much	24.1	30.7	40.0	40.2	41.7	–	41.3	43.4	34.0	8.7
Only business has too much	59.0	57.6	40.9	37.0	33.6	–	33.9	32.6	51.4	47.8
Total	100.0	100.0	100.0	100.0	100.0	–	100.0	100.0	100.0	100.0
Total unions have too much power	29.3	35.4	49.0	51.1	57.3	–	53.0	55.4	38.1	18.2
Total business has too much power	83.1	88.3	80.9	77.2	75.3	–	75.2	76.0	85.4	56.5
N. of respondents	249	287	355	92	286	–	298	175	315	262

Table 8.8 (*cont.*)

	Fairly strong Labour identifiers									
	1963	1964	1966	1969	1970	Feb. 1974	Oct. 1974	1979	1983	1987
Business and trade union power										
Only trade unions have too much	12.3	10.4	14.8	15.0	23.1	–	14.2	13.5	7.9	5.6
Neither has too much	10.8	13.9	15.3	12.1	8.9	–	10.7	13.9	12.3	48.1
Both have too much	34.3	31.3	46.2	39.3	41.3	–	48.3	48.8	38.2	7.6
Only business has too much	42.6	44.4	23.6	33.6	26.7	–	26.9	23.8	41.7	38.6
Total	100.0	100.0	100.0	100.0	100.0	–	100.0	100.0	100.0	100.0
Total unions have too much power	46.6	41.7	61.0	54.3	64.4	–	62.5	62.3	46.1	13.2
Total business has too much power	76.9	75.7	69.8	72.9	68.0	–	75.2	72.6	79.9	46.2
N. of respondents	277	224	265	107	233	–	402	303	432	442

	Not very strong Labour identifiers									
	1963	1964	1966	1969	1970	Feb. 1974	Oct. 1974	1979	1983	1987
Business and trade union power										
Only trade unions have too much	15.3	23.5	22.5	35.7	31.2	–	24.2	15.9	13.0	17.8
Neither has too much	9.0	18.3	10.3	9.2	15.1	–	13.1	14.0	10.9	45.0
Both have too much	47.2	30.1	41.7	34.7	35.4	–	51.0	58.0	51.9	10.1
Only business has too much	28.5	28.1	25.5	20.4	18.4	–	11.8	12.1	24.2	27.1
Total	100.0	100.0	100.0	100.0	100.0	–	100.0	100.0	100.0	100.0
Total unions have too much power	62.5	53.6	64.2	70.4	66.6	–	75.2	73.9	64.9	27.9
Total business has too much power	75.7	58.2	67.2	55.1	53.8	–	62.8	70.1	76.1	37.2
N. of respondents	144	75	74	98	106	–	153	157	322	308

Table 8.9 *Perceptions of business and trade union power: non-partisans (%)*

	1963	1964	1966	1969	1970	Feb. 1974	Oct. 1974	1979	1983	1987
Business and trade *union power*										
Only trade unions have too much	13.8	31.9	36.7	20.0	32.2	–	34.2	30.4	21.2	32.6
Neither has too much	5.2	18.8	6.2	16.0	13.3	–	1.4	8.9	8.4	38.6
Both have too much	53.4	39.1	48.9	38.0	30.5	–	56.2	51.9	56.0	11.8
Only business has too much	27.6	10.2	8.2	26.0	24.0	–	8.2	8.9	14.4	17.0
Total	100.0	100.0	100.0	100.0	100.0	–	100.0	100.0	100.0	100.0
Total unions have too much power	67.2	71.0	85.6	58.0	62.7	–	90.4	82.3	77.2	44.4
Total business has too much power	81.0	49.3	57.1	64.0	54.5	–	64.4	60.8	70.4	28.8
N. of respondents	50	43	66	50	66	–	73	79	144	170

Table 8.10 *Perceptions of business and trade union power by political generation and partisanship (%)*

	Conservative identifiers: first voted 1918–1935									
	1963	1964	1966	1969	1970	Feb. 1974	Oct. 1974	1979	1983	1987
Business and trade *union power*										
Only trade unions have too much	31.2	41.6	44.3	40.3	50.9	–	54.2	53.4	42.7	65.6
Neither has too much	7.9	9.0	5.1	12.4	7.5	–	1.5	0.8	2.7	16.5
Both have too much	52.7	44.7	45.3	44.2	38.1	–	43.8	43.6	53.5	16.2
Only business has too much	8.2	4.7	5.3	3.1	3.5	–	0.5	2.3	1.1	1.7
Total	100.0	100.0	100.0	100.0	100.0	–	100.0	100.0	100.0	100.0
Total unions have too much power	83.9	86.3	89.6	84.5	89.0	–	98.0	97.0	96.2	81.8
Total business has too much power	60.9	49.4	50.6	47.3	41.6	–	44.3	45.9	54.6	17.9
N. of respondents	279	237	247	129	204	–	213	133	184	119

Table 8.10 (*cont.*)

Labour identifiers: first voted 1918–1935

	1963	1964	1966	1969	1970	Feb. 1974	Oct. 1974	1979	1983	1987
Business and trade union power										
Only trade unions have too much	5.5	5.4	11.7	12.9	11.6	–	14.8	18.8	6.8	11.9
Neither has too much	12.2	11.2	10.3	10.6	8.0	–	7.1	8.2	9.4	53.0
Both have too much	28.2	29.3	43.3	45.9	49.7	–	54.9	55.3	45.6	6.7
Only business has too much	54.2	54.0	34.7	30.6	30.7	–	23.1	17.6	38.2	28.4
Total	100.0	100.0	100.0	100.0	100.0	–	100.0	100.0	100.0	100.0
Total unions have too much power	33.7	34.7	55.0	58.8	61.3	–	69.7	74.1	52.4	18.6
Total business has too much power	82.4	83.3	78.0	76.5	80.4	–	78.0	72.9	83.8	35.1
N. of respondents	238	209	217	85	162	–	182	85	109	58

Conservative identifiers: first voted 1936–1950

	1963	1964	1966	1969	1970	Feb. 1974	Oct. 1974	1979	1983	1987
Business and trade union power										
Only trade unions have too much	32.9	39.0	47.7	42.7	53.8	–	49.1	49.3	32.0	58.3
Neither has too much	8.8	10.8	5.0	6.8	11.7	–	1.4	2.0	2.2	22.2
Both have too much	47.1	42.2	43.4	38.8	31.5	–	49.5	48.0	63.0	13.5
Only business has too much	11.2	8.0	4.0	11.7	3.0	–	0.0	0.7	2.9	5.9
Total	100.0	100.0	100.0	100.0	100.0	–	100.0	100.0	100.0	100.0
Total unions have too much power	80.0	81.2	91.1	81.5	85.3	–	98.6	97.3	95.0	71.8
Total business has too much power	58.3	50.2	47.4	50.5	34.5	–	49.5	48.7	65.9	19.4
N. of respondents	170	164	172	103	181	–	220	148	276	301

Table 8.10 (*cont.*)

Labour identifiers: first voted 1936–1950

	1963	1964	1966	1969	1970	Feb. 1974	Oct. 1974	1979	1983	1987
Business and trade union power										
Only trade unions have too much	10.5	10.0	9.2	19.4	17.9	–	15.0	15.4	7.1	13.0
Neither has too much	10.1	10.4	10.0	10.2	5.7	–	14.5	6.7	7.3	35.0
Both have too much	37.7	30.4	47.0	37.8	43.4	–	45.3	53.7	49.0	13.0
Only business has too much	41.7	49.2	33.9	32.7	33.0	–	25.2	24.2	36.5	39.0
Total	100.0	100.0	100.0	100.0	100.0	–	100.0	100.0	100.0	100.0
Total unions have too much power	48.2	40.4	56.2	57.2	61.3	–	60.3	69.1	56.1	26.0
Total business has too much power	79.4	79.6	80.9	70.5	76.4	–	70.5	77.9	85.5	52.0
N. of respondents	247	209	231	98	176	–	214	149	255	195

Conservative identifiers: first voted 1951–1970

	1963	1964	1966	1969	1970	Feb. 1974	Oct. 1974	1979	1983	1987
Business and trade union power										
Only trade unions have too much	40.6	50.3	45.0	51.9	54.9	–	52.1	48.6	41.2	54.3
Neither has too much	10.9	10.3	14.9	10.9	6.4	–	3.9	2.5	6.7	25.8
Both have too much	40.6	27.8	33.8	27.6	30.9	–	43.0	47.7	46.9	13.1
Only business has too much	7.8	11.6	6.2	9.6	7.8	–	1.0	1.2	5.1	6.8
Total	100.0	100.0	100.0	100.0	100.0	–	100.0	100.0	100.0	100.0
Total unions have too much power	81.2	78.1	78.8	79.5	85.8	–	95.1	96.3	88.1	67.4
Total business has too much power	48.4	39.4	40.0	37.2	38.7	–	44.0	48.9	52.0	19.9
N. of respondents	128	130	143	156	216	–	305	321	574	560

Table 8.10 (*cont.*)

Labour identifiers: first voted 1951–1970

	1963	1964	1966	1969	1970	Feb. 1974	Oct. 1974	1979	1983	1987
Business and trade union power										
Only trade unions have too much	16.4	13.2	16.3	25.0	28.4	–	15.4	13.8	8.4	9.3
Neither has too much	10.7	12.5	15.9	12.0	13.2	–	12.9	11.8	8.2	36.1
Both have too much	34.5	34.6	38.3	34.3	34.0	–	44.4	48.5	43.0	9.4
Only business has too much	38.4	39.7	29.5	28.7	24.4	–	27.3	25.9	40.5	45.2
Total	100.0	100.0	100.0	100.0	100.0	–	100.0	100.0	100.0	100.0
Total unions have too much power	50.9	47.8	54.6	59.3	62.4	–	59.8	62.3	51.4	18.7
Total business has too much power	72.9	74.3	67.8	63.0	58.4	–	71.7	74.4	83.5	54.6
N. of respondents	177	159	243	108	279	–	396	292	424	398

Conservative identifiers: first voted after 1970

	1963	1964	1966	1969	1970	Feb. 1974	Oct. 1974	1979	1983	1987
Business and trade union power										
Only trade unions have too much	–	–	–	–	–	–	59.1	53.7	33.2	54.9
Neither has too much	–	–	–	–	–	–	2.3	4.9	6.9	30.1
Both have too much	–	–	–	–	–	–	36.4	39.0	57.6	10.0
Only business has too much	–	–	–	–	–	–	2.3	2.4	2.3	5.0
Total	–	–	–	–	–	–	100.0	100.0	100.0	100.0
Total unions have too much power	–	–	–	–	–	–	95.5	92.7	90.8	64.9
Total business has too much power	–	–	–	–	–	–	38.7	41.4	59.9	15.0
N. of respondents	–	–	–	–	–	–	44	82	213	384

Table 8.10 (*cont.*)

	Labour identifiers: first voted after 1970									
	1963	1964	1966	1969	1970	Feb. 1974	Oct. 1974	1979	1983	1987
Business and trade union power										
Only trade unions have too much	–	–	–	–	–	–	14.8	7.5	10.0	10.4
Neither has too much	–	–	–	–	–	–	9.8	30.8	18.3	51.2
Both have too much	–	–	–	–	–	–	41.0	41.1	30.6	6.8
Only business has too much	–	–	–	–	–	–	34.4	20.6	41.1	31.6
Total	–	–	–	–	–	–	100.0	100.0	100.0	100.0
Total unions have too much power	–	–	–	–	–	–	55.8	48.6	40.6	17.2
Total business has too much power	–	–	–	–	–	–	75.4	61.7	71.7	38.4
N. of respondents	–	–	–	–	–	–	61	107	223	399

Table 8.11 *Perceptions of business and trade union power by party membership (%)*

	All political party members									
	1963	1964	1966	1969	1970	Feb. 1974	Oct. 1974	1979	1983	1987
Business and trade union power										
Only trade unions have too much	26.7	31.7	–	50.0	–	–	45.5	–	29.4	55.3
Neither has too much	6.8	8.6	–	9.6	–	–	6.5	–	8.1	16.6
Both have too much	42.5	40.1	–	26.9	–	–	37.7	–	44.6	8.0
Only business has too much	24.0	19.6	–	13.5	–	–	10.4	–	17.8	20.0
Total	100.0	100.0	–	100.0	–	–	100.0	–	100.0	100.0
Total unions have too much power	69.2	71.8	–	76.9	–	–	83.2	–	74.0	63.3
Total business has too much power	66.5	59.7	–	40.4	–	–	48.1	–	62.4	28.0
N. of respondents	146	150	–	52	–	–	154	–	232	175

Table 8.11 (*cont.*)

| Conservative party members | | | | | | | | | |
	1963	1964	1966	1969	1970	Feb. 1974	Oct. 1974	1979	1983	1987
Business and trade union power										
Only trade unions have too much	34.8	43.1	–	67.7	–	–	62.4	–	43.0	73.3
Neither has too much	7.6	8.9	–	9.7	–	–	4.0	–	5.1	16.1
Both have too much	52.2	43.6	–	22.6	–	–	32.7	–	51.3	9.1
Only business has too much	5.4	4.4	–	0.0	–	–	1.0	–	0.7	1.4
Total	100.0	100.0	–	100.0	–	–	100.0	–	100.0	100.0
Total unions have too much power	87.0	86.7	–	90.3	–	–	95.1	–	94.3	82.4
Total business has too much power	57.6	48.0	–	22.6	–	–	43.7	–	52.0	10.5
N. of respondents	92	93	–	31	–	–	101	–	101	138

| Labour party members | | | | | | | | | |
	1963	1964	1966	1969	1970	Feb. 1974	Oct. 1974	1979	1983	1987
Business and trade union power										
Only trade unions have too much	5.4	4.0	–	(20.0)	–	–	10.7	–	4.1	0.0
Neither has too much	5.4	6.1	–	(10.0)	–	–	14.3	–	14.4	18.1
Both have too much	18.9	25.2	–	(40.0)	–	–	32.1	–	14.3	4.6
Only business has too much	70.3	64.7	–	(30.0)	–	–	42.9	–	67.2	77.3
Total	100.0	100.0	–	(100.0)	–	–	100.0	–	100.0	100.0
Total unions have too much power	24.3	29.2	–	(60.0)	–	–	42.8	–	18.4	4.6
Total business has too much power	89.2	89.9	–	(70.0)	–	–	75.0	–	81.5	81.9
N. of respondents	37	33	–	10	–	–	28	–	48	43

Table 8.12 *Perceptions of business and trade union power by social class (%)*

	Professional and managerial classes									
	1963	1964	1966	1969	1970	Feb. 1974	Oct. 1974	1979	1983	1987
Business and trade union power										
Only trade unions have too much	30.3	31.7	42.1	46.2	53.1	–	39.0	38.9	28.0	37.4
Neither has too much	9.7	11.3	7.7	7.5	7.0	–	4.2	5.8	8.7	33.6
Both have too much	48.2	40.2	43.7	33.3	32.6	–	50.3	48.2	48.9	9.3
Only business has too much	11.8	16.7	6.5	12.9	7.3	–	6.5	7.0	14.4	19.7
Total	100.0	100.0	100.0	100.0	100.0	–	100.0	100.0	100.0	100.0
Total unions have too much power	78.5	71.9	85.8	79.5	85.7	–	89.3	87.1	76.9	46.7
Total business has too much power	60.0	56.9	50.2	46.2	39.9	–	56.8	55.2	63.3	29.0
N. of respondents	195	189	213	93	253	–	336	342	900	870

	Intermediate and routine non-manual classes									
	1963	1964	1966	1969	1970	Feb. 1974	Oct. 1974	1979	1983	1987
Business and trade union power										
Only trade unions have too much	27.3	30.9	37.1	38.1	41.9	–	36.9	38.8	26.3	40.7
Neither has too much	5.4	8.0	8.9	9.5	7.0	–	5.6	5.0	7.8	31.4
Both have too much	51.5	42.1	41.2	41.0	37.1	–	49.8	49.7	51.2	11.7
Only business has too much	15.8	19.0	12.8	11.4	14.1	–	7.8	6.5	14.7	16.2
Total	100.0	100.0	100.0	100.0	100.0	–	100.0	100.0	100.0	100.0
Total unions have too much power	78.8	73.0	78.3	79.1	79.0	–	86.7	88.5	77.5	52.4
Total business has too much power	67.3	61.1	54.0	52.4	51.2	–	57.6	56.2	65.9	27.9
N. of respondents	425	417	418	210	389	–	735	443	627	857

Table 8.12 (*cont.*)

		Manual working class								
	1963	1964	1966	1969	1970	Feb. 1974	Oct. 1974	1979	1983	1987
Business and trade union power										
Only trade unions have too much	15.3	19.3	19.2	28.8	28.4	–	25.0	25.6	18.9	28.0
Neither has too much	10.9	12.5	10.0	10.8	11.9	–	8.1	9.3	8.5	36.2
Both have too much	37.5	34.0	45.5	36.1	38.0	–	48.9	49.6	49.9	12.9
Only business has too much	36.3	34.3	25.3	24.3	21.7	–	17.9	15.5	22.7	23.0
Total	100.0	100.0	100.0	100.0	100.0	–	100.0	100.0	100.0	100.0
Total unions have too much power	52.8	53.3	64.7	64.9	66.4	–	73.9	75.2	68.8	40.9
Total business has too much power	73.8	68.3	70.8	60.4	59.7	–	66.8	65.1	72.6	35.9
N. of respondents	816	728	860	379	771	–	959	808	1627	1477

Table 8.13 *Perceptions of business and trade union power by subjective social class (%)*

		'Spontaneous' middle class identification								
	1963	1964	1966	1969	1970	Feb. 1974	Oct. 1974	1979	1983	1987
Business and trade union power										
Only trade unions have too much	32.0	35.4	40.4	44.4	44.5	–	37.6	42.5	29.8	41.6
Neither has too much	9.8	9.9	6.7	11.1	5.1	–	5.3	5.6	7.8	30.2
Both have too much	44.1	42.6	42.5	35.0	41.3	–	50.3	44.3	49.9	10.5
Only business has too much	14.1	12.1	10.4	9.4	9.1	–	6.8	7.7	12.4	17.7
Total	100.0	100.0	100.0	100.0	100.0	–	100.0	100.0	100.0	100.0
Total unions have too much power	76.1	78.0	82.9	79.4	85.8	–	87.9	86.8	79.7	52.1
Total business has too much power	58.2	54.7	52.9	44.4	50.4	–	57.1	52.0	62.3	28.2
N. of respondents	297	209	264	117	114	–	338	287	689	533

Table 8.13 (*cont.*)

'Forced' middle class identification										
	1963	1964	1966	1969	1970	Feb. 1974	Oct. 1974	1979	1983	1987
Business and trade union power										
Only trade unions have too much	29.1	30.2	43.0	46.5	39.4	–	43.0	40.7	32.2	42.7
Neither has too much	3.8	14.0	9.0	11.3	12.0	–	5.8	4.4	8.7	30.6
Both have too much	53.2	41.5	43.3	32.1	37.8	–	46.7	50.5	48.6	12.0
Only business has too much	13.9	14.3	4.8	10.1	10.8	–	4.5	4.4	10.5	14.6
Total	100.0	100.0	100.0	100.0	100.0	–	100.0	100.0	100.0	100.0
Total unions have too much power	82.3	71.7	86.3	78.6	77.2	–	89.7	91.2	8.0	54.7
Total business has too much power	67.1	55.8	48.1	42.2	48.6	–	51.2	54.9	59.1	26.6
N. of respondents	158	195	202	159	129	–	377	275	482	609

No class identification										
	1963	1964	1966	1969	1970	Feb. 1974	Oct. 1974	1979	1983	1987
Business and trade union power										
Only trade unions have too much	18.8	36.2	17.8	38.2	44.8	–	34.6	38.4	26.3	31.5
Neither has too much	7.5	8.8	11.9	10.3	7.5	–	6.5	5.8	8.8	36.9
Both have too much	48.8	38.5	42.3	29.4	26.2	–	46.7	50.0	51.0	12.4
Only business has too much	25.0	16.5	28.1	22.1	21.6	–	12.1	5.8	13.9	19.2
Total	100.0	100.0	100.0	100.0	100.0	–	100.0	100.0	100.0	100.0
Total unions have too much power	67.6	74.7	60.1	67.6	71.0	–	81.3	88.4	77.3	43.9
Total business has too much power	73.8	55.0	70.4	51.5	47.8	–	58.8	55.8	64.9	31.6
N. of respondents	80	72	51	68	52	–	107	86	200	132

Table 8.13 (*cont.*)

| | 'Forced' working class identification | | | | | | | | | |
	1963	1964	1966	1969	1970	Feb. 1974	Oct. 1974	1979	1983	1987
Business and trade union power										
Only trade unions have too much	19.2	22.8	23.0	28.0	29.1	–	31.8	29.9	22.7	34.9
Neither has too much	8.2	12.1	11.1	9.7	10.7	–	5.5	9.5	8.1	34.2
Both have too much	41.6	34.9	44.7	41.8	38.5	–	50.9	49.4	52.6	13.7
Only business has too much	31.0	30.1	21.2	20.5	21.7	–	11.8	11.3	16.6	17.2
Total	100.0	100.0	100.0	100.0	100.0	–	100.0	100.0	100.0	100.0
Total unions have too much power	61.8	57.7	67.7	69.8	67.6	–	82.7	79.3	75.3	48.6
Total business has too much power	72.6	65.0	65.9	62.3	60.2	–	62.7	60.7	69.2	30.9
N. of respondents	255	354	397	361	257	–	761	539	860	1044

| | 'Spontaneous' working class identification | | | | | | | | | |
	1963	1964	1966	1969	1970	Feb. 1974	Oct. 1974	1979	1983	1987
Business and trade union power										
Only trade unions have too much	14.7	17.1	19.5	24.1	21.9	–	20.1	22.2	15.3	24.1
Neither has too much	10.8	9.1	10.1	11.7	8.3	–	9.6	8.6	8.9	38.6
Both have too much	39.5	36.6	44.7	40.7	43.8	–	47.7	50.1	48.3	9.0
Only business has too much	35.0	37.3	25.6	23.5	26.0	–	22.6	19.0	27.6	28.3
Total	100.0	100.0	100.0	100.0	100.0	–	100.0	100.0	100.0	100.0
Total unions have too much power	54.2	53.7	64.2	64.8	65.7	–	67.8	72.3	63.6	33.1
Total business has too much power	74.5	73.9	70.3	64.2	69.8	–	70.3	69.1	75.9	37.3
N. of respondents	701	510	583	162	168	–	541	463	1101	1012

Table 8.14 *Perceptions of business and trade union power by employment status (%)*

Self-employed: with employees										
	1963	1964	1966	1969	1970	Feb. 1974	Oct. 1974	1979	1983	1987
Business and trade union power										
Only trade unions have too much	23.4	36.1	32.8	29.6	34.8	–	41.7	42.9	37.8	45.2
Neither has too much	9.4	6.2	3.3	0.0	4.4	–	1.4	0.0	7.1	23.6
Both have too much	53.1	41.2	58.4	59.3	54.5	–	54.2	57.1	47.7	17.6
Only business has too much	14.1	16.6	5.4	11.1	6.3	–	2.8	0.0	7.3	13.6
Total	100.0	100.0	100.0	100.0	100.0	–	100.0	100.0	100.0	100.0
Total unions have too much power	76.5	77.3	91.2	88.9	89.3	–	95.9	100.0	85.5	62.8
Total business has too much power	67.2	57.8	63.8	70.4	60.8	–	57.0	0.0	55.0	31.2
N. of respondents	64	63	55	27	59	–	72	49	152	148

Self-employed: no employees										
	1963	1964	1966	1969	1970	Feb. 1974	Oct. 1974	1979	1983	1987
Business and trade union power										
Only trade unions have too much	(22.2)	(42.2)	26.7	(45.0)	52.8	–	42.2	50.8	34.2	39.8
Neither has too much	(5.6)	(5.8)	12.8	(0.0)	8.5	–	3.6	1.5	4.6	28.7
Both have too much	(61.1)	(40.5)	39.9	(55.0)	31.8	–	49.4	43.1	50.4	14.7
Only business has too much	(11.1)	(11.6)	20.5	(0.0)	6.8	–	4.8	4.6	10.9	16.7
Total	(100.0)	(100.0)	100.0	(100.0)	100.0	–	100.0	100.0	100.0	100.0
Total unions have too much power	(83.3)	(82.7)	66.6	(100.0)	84.6	–	91.6	93.9	84.6	54.5
Total business has too much power	(72.2)	(52.1)	60.4	(55.0)	38.6	–	54.2	47.7	61.3	31.4
N. of respondents	18	17	27	20	25	–	83	65	114	147

Table 8.14 (*cont.*)

Managers

	1963	1964	1966	1969	1970	Feb. 1974	Oct. 1974	1979	1983	1987
Business and trade *union power*										
Only trade unions have too much	26.3	28.8	42.4	61.9	54.7	–	40.4	35.8	26.6	44.5
Neither has too much	13.2	10.1	6.4	4.8	10.1	–	5.8	5.8	9.4	30.9
Both have too much	44.7	42.2	44.2	21.4	27.6	–	48.5	49.6	48.2	8.6
Only business has too much	15.8	18.8	7.0	11.9	7.6	–	5.3	8.8	15.7	15.9
Total	100.0	100.0	100.0	100.0	100.0	–	100.0	100.0	100.0	100.0
Total unions have too much power	71.0	71.0	86.6	83.3	82.3	–	88.9	85.4	74.8	53.1
Total business has too much power	60.5	61.0	51.2	33.3	35.2	–	53.8	58.4	63.9	24.5
N. of respondents	76	72	82	42	90	–	171	137	527	310

Foremen and supervisors

	1963	1964	1966	1969	1970	Feb. 1974	Oct. 1974	1979	1983	1987
Business and trade *union power*										
Only trade unions have too much	17.6	23.4	24.9	39.3	32.6	–	33.6	34.3	20.1	36.5
Neither has too much	2.0	10.1	7.2	9.8	8.1	–	1.7	5.0	7.7	26.8
Both have too much	53.9	31.0	53.0	36.1	38.1	–	54.6	49.7	52.9	13.9
Only business has too much	26.5	35.5	15.0	14.8	21.3	–	10.1	11.0	19.3	22.8
Total	100.0	100.0	100.0	100.0	100.0	–	100.0	100.0	100.0	100.0
Total unions have too much power	71.5	54.4	77.9	75.4	70.7	–	88.2	84.0	73.0	50.4
Total business has too much power	80.4	66.5	68.0	50.9	59.4	–	64.7	60.7	72.2	36.7
N. of respondents	102	101	102	61	112	–	119	181	441	215

Table 8.14 (*cont.*)

	Rank and file employees									
	1963	1964	1966	1969	1970	Feb. 1974	Oct. 1974	1979	1983	1987
Business and trade union power										
Only trade unions have too much	18.4	23.1	25.6	31.0	33.5	–	28.9	28.5	21.5	31.4
Neither has too much	10.0	11.9	11.6	11.3	11.0	–	7.2	9.4	8.3	36.3
Both have too much	37.6	34.8	40.5	36.8	35.2	–	48.9	48.7	50.4	11.1
Only business has too much	34.0	30.1	22.3	20.9	20.3	–	15.0	13.4	19.9	21.2
Total	100.0	100.0	100.0	100.0	100.0	–	100.0	100.0	100.0	100.0
Total unions have too much power	56.0	57.9	66.1	67.8	68.7	–	77.8	77.2	71.9	42.5
Total business has too much power	71.6	64.9	62.8	57.7	55.5	–	63.9	62.1	70.3	32.3
N. of respondents	798	728	834	352	811	–	1383	831	1764	2405

Table 8.15 *Perceptions of business and trade union power: unemployed (%)*

	Unemployed									
	1963	1964	1966	1969	1970	Feb. 1974	Oct. 1974	1979	1983	1987
Business and trade union power										
Only trade unions have too much	–	(48.8)	(17.5)	(30.0)	(14.2)	–	31.6	17.6	19.4	17.0
Neither has too much	–	(0.0)	(21.4)	(10.0)	(4.4)	–	15.8	5.9	11.8	41.7
Both have too much	–	(51.2)	(35.0)	(50.0)	(62.6)	–	47.4	58.8	46.7	13.2
Only business has too much	–	(0.0)	(26.2)	(10.0)	(18.9)	–	5.3	17.6	22.2	28.1
Total	–	(100.0)	(100.0)	(100.0)	(100.0)	–	100.0	100.0	100.0	100.0
Total unions have too much power	–	(100.0)	(52.5)	(80.0)	(76.8)	–	79.0	76.4	66.1	30.2
Total business has too much power	–	(51.2)	(81.2)	(60.0)	(81.5)	–	52.7	76.4	68.9	41.3
N. of respondents	–	8	10	10	20	–	38	34	214	188

Table 8.16 *Perceptions of business and trade union power by class and employment status (%)*

| | Professional and managerial classes: self-employed | | | | | | | | | |
	1963	1964	1966	1969	1970	Feb. 1974	Oct. 1974	1979	1983	1987
Business and trade union power										
Only trade unions have too much	21.2	40.6	34.1	(45.0)	43.0	–	53.5	43.3	35.0	43.6
Neither has too much	15.2	5.5	6.0	(0.0)	0.0	–	0.0	0.0	5.7	23.6
Both have too much	54.5	35.4	50.7	(40.0)	48.3	–	46.5	53.3	51.2	15.7
Only business has too much	9.1	18.4	9.3	(15.0)	8.7	–	0.0	3.3	8.1	17.1
Total	100.0	100.0	100.0	(100.0)	100.0	–	100.0	100.0	100.0	100.0
Total unions have too much power	75.7	76.0	84.8	(85.0)	91.3	–	100.0	96.6	86.2	59.3
Total business has too much power	63.6	53.8	60.0	(55.0)	57.0	–	46.5	56.6	59.3	32.8
N. of respondents	33	35	30	20	23	–	43	30	123	140

| | Professional and managerial classes: employees | | | | | | | | | |
	1963	1964	1966	1969	1970	Feb. 1974	Oct. 1974	1979	1983	1987
Business and trade union power										
Only trade unions have too much	29.8	32.9	47.1	46.6	54.5	–	36.4	35.8	27.0	36.2
Neither has too much	11.5	13.5	10.4	9.6	7.4	–	4.7	7.1	9.2	35.6
Both have too much	42.3	37.9	35.8	31.5	30.3	–	50.6	49.2	48.3	8.2
Only business has too much	16.3	15.8	6.7	12.3	7.8	–	8.3	7.9	15.5	20.1
Total	100.0	100.0	100.0	100.0	100.0	–	100.0	100.0	100.0	100.0
Total unions have too much power	72.1	70.8	82.9	78.1	84.8	–	87.0	85.0	75.3	44.4
Total business has too much power	58.6	53.7	42.5	43.8	38.1	–	58.9	57.1	63.8	28.3
N. of respondents	104	98	112	73	154	–	253	240	753	730

Table 8.16 (*cont.*)

Intermediate and routine non-manual classes: self-employed

	1963	1964	1966	1969	1970	Feb. 1974	Oct. 1974	1979	1983	1987
Business and trade union power										
Only trade unions have too much	21.1	35.2	37.4	(26.3)	35.0	–	42.7	49.0	42.3	56.3
Neither has too much	2.6	7.5	4.5	(0.0)	9.8	–	2.7	0.0	11.5	21.9
Both have too much	57.9	44.6	54.8	(73.7)	51.7	–	50.7	51.0	42.3	18.8
Only business has too much	18.4	12.7	3.4	(0.0)	3.5	–	4.0	0.0	3.8	3.1
Total	100.0	100.0	100.0	(100.0)	100.0	–	100.0	100.0	100.0	100.0
Total unions have too much power	79.0	79.8	92.2	(100.0)	86.7	–	93.4	100.0	84.6	75.1
Total business has too much power	76.3	57.3	58.2	(73.7)	55.2	–	54.7	51.0	44.1	21.9
N. of respondents	38	40	36	19	48	–	75	49	26	32

Intermediate and routine non-manual classes: employees

	1963	1964	1966	1969	1970	Feb. 1974	Oct. 1974	1979	1983	1987
Business and trade union power										
Only trade unions have too much	26.7	31.0	36.1	39.3	42.9	–	35.3	36.5	25.3	40.1
Neither has too much	5.3	8.4	9.9	10.5	7.9	–	6.2	6.0	7.4	31.8
Both have too much	49.8	38.3	39.3	37.7	35.2	–	49.7	49.7	52.1	11.4
Only business has too much	18.2	22.4	14.6	12.5	14.1	–	8.8	7.8	15.2	16.7
Total	100.0	100.0	100.0	100.0	100.0	–	100.0	100.0	100.0	100.0
Total unions have too much power	76.5	69.3	75.4	77.0	78.1	–	85.0	86.2	77.4	51.5
Total business has too much power	68.0	60.7	53.9	50.2	49.3	–	58.5	57.5	67.3	28.1
N. of respondents	285	300	306	191	262	–	612	334	580	826

Table 8.16 (*cont.*)

Manual working class: self-employed

	1963	1964	1966	1969	1970	Feb. 1974	Oct. 1974	1979	1983	1987
Business and trade union power										
Only trade unions have too much	(30.0)	(40.8)	(11.6)	(37.5)	(55.3)	–	27.0	48.6	37.4	38.0
Neither has too much	(10.0)	(0.0)	(5.2)	(0.0)	(0.0)	–	5.4	2.9	5.1	29.8
Both have too much	(50.0)	(59.2)	(53.5)	(62.5)	(31.2)	–	59.5	42.9	49.5	15.7
Only business has too much	(10.0)	(0.0)	(29.7)	(0.0)	(13.5)	–	8.1	5.7	8.1	16.5
Total	(100.0)	(100.0)	(100.0)	(100.0)	(100.0)	–	100.0	100.0	100.0	100.0
Total unions have too much power	(80.0)	(100.0)	(64.9)	(100.0)	(86.5)	–	86.5	91.5	86.9	53.7
Total business has too much power	(60.0)	(59.2)	(83.2)	(62.5)	(44.7)	–	67.6	48.6	57.6	32.2
N. of respondents	10	5	16	8	13	–	37	35	99	120

Manual working class: employees

	1963	1964	1966	1969	1970	Feb. 1974	Oct. 1974	1979	1983	1987
Business and trade union power										
Only trade unions have too much	13.3	17.6	18.4	28.6	27.0	–	24.6	24.4	18.0	27.0
Neither has too much	11.1	13.2	11.2	11.1	12.7	–	7.7	10.1	8.8	36.8
Both have too much	34.6	32.1	44.6	35.6	35.8	–	48.7	48.5	49.9	12.6
Only business has too much	41.1	37.2	25.7	24.8	24.5	–	19.0	16.9	23.4	23.6
Total	100.0	100.0	100.0	100.0	100.0	–	100.0	100.0	100.0	100.0
Total unions have too much power	47.9	49.7	63.0	64.2	62.8	–	73.3	72.9	67.9	39.6
Total business has too much power	75.7	69.3	70.3	60.4	60.3	–	67.7	65.4	73.3	36.2
N. of respondents	587	500	599	371	597	–	801	573	1386	1354

Table 8.17 *Perceptions of business and trade union power by trade union membership (%)*

	Trade union members									
	1963	1964	1966	1969	1970	Feb. 1974	Oct. 1974	1979	1983	1987
Business and trade union power										
Only trade unions have too much	11.2	11.3	–	23.3	21.5	–	21.5	21.5	15.4	21.0
Neither has too much	12.0	16.2	–	13.2	16.5	–	14.3	12.1	11.0	40.7
Both have too much	28.5	33.7	–	26.0	30.1	–	39.0	47.9	41.6	8.9
Only business has too much	48.3	38.7	–	37.4	31.9	–	25.2	18.5	32.0	29.4
Total	100.0	100.0	–	100.0	100.0	–	100.0	100.0	100.0	100.0
Total unions have too much power	39.7	45.0	–	49.3	51.6	–	60.5	69.4	57.0	29.9
Total business has too much power	76.8	72.4	–	63.4	62.0	–	64.7	66.4	73.6	38.3
N. of respondents	383	377	–	219	386	–	540	520	931	773

	Married to a trade union member									
	1963	1964	1966	1969	1970	Feb. 1974	Oct. 1974	1979	1983	1987
Business and trade union power										
Only trade unions have too much	16.1	20.9	–	21.7	25.6	–	28.3	31.0	17.7	29.2
Neither has too much	13.4	8.8	–	15.2	9.6	–	7.7	6.6	7.3	38.6
Both have too much	39.2	34.3	–	43.5	44.5	–	46.0	48.8	55.7	11.5
Only business has too much	31.2	36.1	–	19.6	20.3	–	18.0	13.6	19.3	20.7
Total	100.0	100.0	–	100.0	100.0	–	100.0	100.0	100.0	100.0
Total unions have too much power	55.3	55.2	–	65.2	70.1	–	74.3	79.8	73.4	40.7
Total business has too much power	70.4	70.4	–	63.1	64.8	–	64.0	62.4	75.0	32.2
N. of respondents	186	114	–	46	85	–	236	242	376	324

Table 8.17 (*cont.*)

	\multicolumn{10}{c}{Neither respondent nor spouse belongs to a trade union}
	1963	1964	1966	1969	1970	Feb. 1974	Oct. 1974	1979	1983	1987
Business and trade union power										
Only trade unions have too much	25.3	31.0	–	38.4	42.4	–	40.5	38.7	27.8	39.6
Neither has too much	7.2	8.2	–	9.3	6.6	–	5.9	5.1	7.5	30.9
Both have too much	49.6	40.1	–	41.9	39.4	–	44.4	49.5	52.6	12.6
Only business has too much	17.9	20.6	–	10.5	11.6	–	9.2	6.6	12.0	16.9
Total	100.0	100.0	–	100.0	100.0	–	100.0	100.0	100.0	100.0
Total unions have too much power	74.9	71.1	–	80.3	81.8	–	84.9	88.2	80.4	52.2
Total business has too much power	67.5	60.7	–	52.4	51.0	–	53.6	56.1	64.6	19.5
N. of respondents	917	809	–	602	986	–	1420	888	2057	2083

Table 8.18 *Perceptions of business and trade union power by class and trade union membership (%)*

	\multicolumn{10}{c}{Professional and managerial classes: trade union members}
	1963	1964	1966	1969	1970	Feb. 1974	Oct. 1974	1979	1983	1987
Business and trade union power										
Only trade unions have too much	28.6	26.5	–	(13.3)	38.6	–	45.4	25.0	17.6	24.2
Neither has too much	23.8	16.0	–	(6.7)	15.7	–	11.8	8.0	11.7	40.0
Both have too much	28.6	42.4	–	(33.3)	27.2	–	36.1	53.0	41.8	8.4
Only business has too much	19.0	15.2	–	(46.7)	18.4	–	6.7	14.0	28.9	27.3
Total	100.0	100.0	–	(100.0)	100.0	–	100.0	100.0	100.0	100.0
Total unions have too much power	57.2	68.9	–	(60.0)	65.8	–	81.5	78.0	59.4	32.6
Total business has too much power	47.6	57.6	–	(80.0)	45.6	–	42.8	67.0	70.7	35.7
N. of respondents	21	26	–	(15)	35	–	103	100	239	219

Table 8.18 (*cont.*)

	Professional and managerial classes: non-members of trade unions									
	1963	1964	1966	1969	1970	Feb. 1974	Oct. 1974	1979	1983	1987
Business and trade union power										
Only trade unions have too much	30.5	34.2	–	52.6	55.3	–	49.4	44.6	34.0	42.1
Neither has too much	8.0	10.0	–	7.7	5.6	–	5.3	5.0	7.6	31.6
Both have too much	50.6	37.9	–	33.3	33.4	–	40.3	46.3	49.2	9.5
Only business has too much	10.9	17.8	–	6.4	5.6	–	5.0	4.1	9.2	16.8
Total	100.0	100.0	–	100.0	100.0	–	100.0	100.0	100.0	100.0
Total unions have too much power	81.1	72.1	–	85.9	88.7	–	89.7	90.9	83.2	51.6
Total business has too much power	61.5	55.7	–	39.7	39.0	–	45.3	50.4	58.4	26.3
N. of respondents	174	155	–	78	218	–	260	242	476	642

	Intermediate and routine non-manual classes: trade union members									
	1963	1964	1966	1969	1970	Feb. 1974	Oct. 1974	1979	1983	1987
Business and trade union power										
Only trade unions have too much	18.5	12.5	–	33.3	38.4	–	35.6	32.7	18.8	32.7
Neither has too much	3.1	10.7	–	14.8	14.6	–	10.5	7.5	13.9	38.4
Both have too much	43.1	39.1	–	29.6	26.9	–	35.9	48.6	39.6	6.4
Only business has too much	35.4	37.7	–	22.2	20.1	–	18.0	11.2	27.8	22.6
Total	100.0	100.0	–	100.0	100.0	–	100.0	100.0	100.0	100.0
Total unions have too much power	61.6	51.6	–	62.9	65.3	–	71.5	81.3	58.4	39.1
Total business has too much power	78.5	76.8	–	51.8	47.0	–	53.9	59.8	67.4	29.0
N. of respondents	65	85	–	27	62	–	108	107	144	128

Table 8.18 (*cont.*)

	Intermediate and routine non-manual classes: non-members of trade unions									
	1963	1964	1966	1969	1970	Feb. 1974	Oct. 1974	1979	1983	1987
Business and trade union power										
Only trade unions have too much	28.7	34.8	–	38.8	42.6	–	41.5	40.8	26.4	42.3
Neither has too much	5.9	7.7	–	8.7	5.5	–	4.9	4.2	4.8	29.6
Both have too much	53.1	44.0	–	42.5	39.0	–	44.0	50.0	58.5	12.8
Only business has too much	12.4	13.6	–	9.9	12.9	–	9.6	5.1	10.3	15.3
Total	100.0	100.0	–	100.0	100.0	–	100.0	100.0	100.0	100.0
Total unions have too much power	81.8	78.8	–	81.3	81.6	–	85.5	90.8	84.9	55.1
Total business has too much power	65.5	57.6	–	52.4	51.9	–	53.6	55.1	68.8	28.1
N. of respondents	356	315	–	206	327	–	354	336	483	719

	Manual working class: trade union members									
	1963	1964	1966	1969	1970	Feb. 1974	Oct. 1974	1979	1983	1987
Business and trade union power										
Only trade unions have too much	8.5	9.6	–	22.0	15.7	–	16.2	16.8	12.7	15.8
Neither has too much	12.9	17.4	–	12.7	17.3	–	16.7	15.2	9.9	41.8
Both have too much	25.2	29.6	–	25.4	30.8	–	36.8	45.8	42.0	9.9
Only business has too much	53.4	43.4	–	39.9	36.2	–	30.3	22.3	35.4	32.5
Total	100.0	100.0	–	100.0	100.0	–	100.0	100.0	100.0	100.0
Total unions have too much power	33.7	39.2	–	47.4	46.5	–	53.0	62.6	54.7	25.7
Total business has too much power	78.6	73.0	–	65.3	67.0	–	67.1	68.1	77.4	42.4
N. of respondents	294	251	–	173	285	–	319	310	536	425

Table 8.18 (*cont.*)

	1963	1964	1966	1969	1970	Feb. 1974	Oct. 1974	1979	1983	1987
Manual working class: non-members of trade unions										
Business and trade union power										
Only trade unions have too much	19.0	24.1	–	34.5	35.9	–	33.5	31.1	22.7	33.0
Neither has too much	9.4	9.8	–	9.2	8.7	–	7.1	5.6	7.1	33.7
Both have too much	44.6	36.7	–	45.1	42.2	–	47.1	52.0	53.5	14.1
Only business has too much	27.0	29.4	–	11.2	13.3	–	12.3	11.2	16.7	19.3
Total	100.0	100.0	–	100.0	100.0	–	100.0	100.0	100.0	100.0
Total unions have too much power	63.6	60.8	–	79.9	78.1	–	80.6	83.1	76.2	47.1
Total business has too much power	71.6	66.1	–	56.3	55.5	–	59.4	63.2	70.2	33.4
N. of respondents	511	465	–	206	486	–	632	498	705	944

Table 8.19 *Perceptions of business and trade union power by economic sector (%)*

	1963	1964	1966	1969	1970	Feb. 1974	Oct. 1974	1979	1983	1987
Works in private sector										
Business and trade union power										
Only trade unions have too much	–	–	–	–	–	–	32.9	31.5	23.2	35.1
Neither has too much	–	–	–	–	–	–	5.8	7.5	8.6	35.4
Both have too much	–	–	–	–	–	–	48.4	48.6	51.8	11.3
Only business has too much	–	–	–	–	–	–	12.9	12.3	16.4	18.2
Total	–	–	–	–	–	–	100.0	100.0	100.0	100.0
Total unions have too much power	–	–	–	–	–	–	81.3	80.1	75.0	46.4
Total business has too much power	–	–	–	–	–	–	61.3	60.9	68.2	29.5
N. of respondents	–	–	–	–	–	–	991	691	1801	1900

Table 8.19 (*cont.*)

							Feb.	Oct.			
	Works in public sector										
	1963	1964	1966	1969	1970	Feb. 1974	Oct. 1974	1979	1983	1987
Business and trade union power										
Only trade unions have too much	–	–	–	–	–	–	25.7	26.1	20.6	29.8
Neither has too much	–	–	–	–	–	–	7.6	9.8	8.6	34.2
Both have too much	–	–	–	–	–	–	51.2	49.9	47.7	10.5
Only business has too much	–	–	–	–	–	–	15.5	14.1	23.2	25.4
Total	–	–	–	–	–	–	100.0	100.0	100.0	100.0
Total unions have too much power	–	–	–	–	–	–	76.9	76.0	68.3	40.3
Total business has too much power	–	–	–	–	–	–	66.7	64.0	70.9	35.9
N. of respondents	–	–	–	–	–	–	490	417	1112	941

Table 8.20 *Perceptions of business and trade union power by class and economic sector (%)*

	Professional and managerial classes: private sector									
	1963	1964	1966	1969	1970	Feb. 1974	Oct. 1974	1979	1983	1987
Business and trade union power										
Only trade unions have too much	–	–	–	–	–	–	48.1	41.8	30.9	44.2
Neither has too much	–	–	–	–	–	–	2.8	7.3	9.3	32.9
Both have too much	–	–	–	–	–	–	46.2	46.4	49.9	9.6
Only business has too much	–	–	–	–	–	–	2.8	4.5	9.9	13.3
Total	–	–	–	–	–	–	100.0	100.0	100.0	100.0
Total unions have too much power	–	–	–	–	–	–	94.3	88.2	80.8	53.8
Total business has too much power	–	–	–	–	–	–	49.0	50.9	59.8	22.9
N. of respondents	–	–	–	–	–	–	106	110	375	341

Table 8.20 (*cont.*)

			Professional and managerial classes: public sector						
	1963	1964	1966	1969	1970	Feb. 1974	Oct. 1974	1979	1983	1987

	1963	1964	1966	1969	1970	Feb. 1974	Oct. 1974	1979	1983	1987
Business and trade										
union power										
Only trade unions										
have too much	–	–	–	–	–	–	27.3	28.9	23.8	29.1
Neither has too much	–	–	–	–	–	–	5.8	6.1	9.0	37.5
Both have too much	–	–	–	–	–	–	52.9	54.4	47.3	7.3
Only business has										
too much	–	–	–	–	–	–	14.0	10.5	19.9	26.1
Total	–	–	–	–	–	–	100.0	100.0	100.0	100.0
Total unions have										
too much power	–	–	–	–	–	–	80.2	83.3	71.1	36.4
Total business has										
too much power	–	–	–	–	–	–	66.9	64.9	67.2	33.4
N. of respondents	–	–	–	–	–	–	121	114	366	354

			Intermediate and routine non-manual classes: private sector						
	1963	1964	1966	1969	1970	Feb. 1974	Oct. 1974	1979	1983	1987

	1963	1964	1966	1969	1970	Feb. 1974	Oct. 1974	1979	1983	1987
Business and trade										
union power										
Only trade unions										
have too much	–	–	–	–	–	–	39.9	37.9	25.8	40.6
Neither has too much	–	–	–	–	–	–	4.4	5.6	7.5	32.5
Both have too much	–	–	–	–	–	–	47.9	48.1	54.3	12.0
Only business has										
too much	–	–	–	–	–	–	7.8	8.4	12.4	14.8
Total	–	–	–	–	–	–	100.0	100.0	100.0	100.0
Total unions have										
too much power	–	–	–	–	–	–	87.8	86.0	80.1	52.6
Total business has										
too much power	–	–	–	–	–	–	55.7	56.5	66.7	26.8
N. of respondents	–	–	–	–	–	–	361	214	387	589

Table 8.20 (*cont.*)

						Feb.	Oct.			
Intermediate and routine non-manual classes: public sector										
	1963	1964	1966	1969	1970	1974	1974	1979	1983	1987
Business and trade union power										
Only trade unions have too much	–	–	–	–	–	–	28.3	32.0	25.6	41.5
Neither has too much	–	–	–	–	–	–	5.9	7.8	7.7	28.1
Both have too much	–	–	–	–	–	–	56.6	52.4	46.7	9.4
Only business has too much	–	–	–	–	–	–	9.2	7.8	20.0	21.0
Total	–	–	–	–	–	–	100.0	100.0	100.0	100.0
Total unions have too much power	–	–	–	–	–	–	84.9	84.4	72.3	50.9
Total business has too much power	–	–	–	–	–	–	65.8	60.2	66.7	30.4
N. of respondents	–	–	–	–	–	–	152	103	195	218

						Feb.	Oct.			
Manual working class: private sector										
	1963	1964	1966	1969	1970	1974	1974	1979	1983	1987
Business and trade union power										
Only trade unions have too much	–	–	–	–	–	–	24.8	24.8	18.6	28.3
Neither has too much	–	–	–	–	–	–	7.3	8.7	8.9	38.2
Both have too much	–	–	–	–	–	–	49.3	49.6	50.8	11.6
Only business has too much	–	–	–	–	–	–	18.6	16.9	21.7	21.9
Total	–	–	–	–	–	–	100.0	100.0	100.0	100.0
Total unions have too much power	–	–	–	–	–	–	74.1	74.4	69.4	39.9
Total business has too much power	–	–	–	–	–	–	67.9	66.5	72.5	33.5
N. of respondents	–	–	–	–	–	–	521	367	971	958

Table 8.20 (*cont.*)

				Manual working class: public sector						
	1963	1964	1966	1969	1970	Feb. 1974	Oct. 1974	1979	1983	1987
Business and trade *union power*										
Only trade unions have too much	–	–	–	–	–	–	23.0	21.7	15.2	22.8
Neither has too much	–	–	–	–	–	–	9.9	13.1	9.2	34.5
Both have too much	–	–	–	–	–	–	46.9	46.0	48.1	14.6
Only business has too much	–	–	–	–	–	–	20.2	19.2	27.5	28.0
Total	–	–	–	–	–	–	100.0	100.0	100.0	100.0
Total unions have too much power	–	–	–	–	–	–	69.6	67.7	63.3	37.4
Total business has too much power	–	–	–	–	–	–	67.1	65.2	75.6	42.6
N. of respondents	–	–	–	–	–	–	213	198	513	361

Table 8.21 *Perceptions of business and trade union power by region (%)*

				Scotland						
	1963	1964	1966	1969	1970	Feb. 1974	Oct. 1974	1979	1983	1987
Business and trade *union power*										
Only trade unions have too much	21.5	22.4	26.8	41.0	27.7	–	30.0	27.7	15.3	30.9
Neither has too much	8.1	10.4	10.3	10.8	11.0	–	3.9	5.4	9.1	39.1
Both have too much	42.3	35.6	41.0	37.3	40.1	–	50.0	51.5	50.1	9.1
Only business has too much	28.2	31.6	21.9	10.8	21.3	–	16.1	15.4	25.5	20.8
Total	100.0	100.0	100.0	100.0	100.0	–	100.0	100.0	100.0	100.0
Total unions have too much power	63.8	58.0	67.8	78.3	67.8	–	80.0	79.2	65.4	40.0
Total business has too much power	70.5	67.2	62.9	48.1	61.4	–	66.1	66.9	75.6	29.9
N. of respondents	149	142	134	83	148	–	180	130	319	295

Table 8.21 (*cont.*)

Wales

	1963	1964	1966	1969	1970	Feb. 1974	Oct. 1974	1979	1983	1987
Business and trade union power										
Only trade unions have too much	14.7	29.7	25.3	23.7	28.1	–	20.9	29.1	16.1	23.7
Neither has too much	10.7	18.0	5.4	15.8	11.4	–	10.4	12.8	11.1	36.6
Both have too much	40.0	22.0	53.5	44.7	41.0	–	47.8	39.5	57.2	11.3
Only business has too much	34.7	30.3	15.7	15.8	19.4	–	20.9	18.6	15.6	28.5
Total	100.0	100.0	100.0	100.0	100.0	–	100.0	100.0	100.0	100.0
Total unions have too much power	54.7	51.7	78.8	68.4	69.1	–	68.7	68.6	73.3	35.0
Total business has too much power	74.7	52.3	69.2	60.5	60.4	–	68.7	58.1	72.8	39.8
N. of respondents	75	50	67	38	65	–	115	86	175	173

The North

	1963	1964	1966	1969	1970	Feb. 1974	Oct. 1974	1979	1983	1987
Business and trade union power										
Only trade unions have too much	16.9	18.6	22.7	25.6	34.0	–	27.1	29.1	22.7	30.3
Neither has too much	10.7	14.5	10.5	10.5	9.5	–	6.7	9.5	9.1	37.0
Both have too much	40.2	35.9	41.5	40.8	39.4	–	52.5	47.6	46.9	10.9
Only business has too much	32.2	31.0	25.2	23.1	17.1	–	13.6	13.9	21.3	21.8
Total	100.0	100.0	100.0	100.0	100.0	–	100.0	100.0	100.0	100.0
Total unions have too much power	57.1	54.5	64.2	66.4	73.4	–	79.6	76.7	69.6	41.2
Total business has too much power	72.4	66.9	66.7	63.9	56.5	–	66.1	61.5	68.2	32.7
N. of respondents	413	387	407	238	416	–	609	454	920	879

Table 8.21 (*cont.*)

The Midlands	1963	1964	1966	1969	1970	Feb. 1974	Oct. 1974	1979	1983	1987
Business and trade union power										
Only trade unions have too much	21.8	30.8	27.7	44.6	36.7	–	33.2	31.5	25.4	33.7
Neither has too much	12.5	9.0	8.5	6.4	9.6	–	8.2	7.7	9.0	37.0
Both have too much	37.1	33.3	43.8	28.7	34.2	–	47.0	47.0	46.7	10.3
Only business has too much	28.6	26.9	19.9	20.4	19.4	–	11.5	13.8	18.8	19.0
Total	100.0	100.0	100.0	100.0	100.0	–	100.0	100.0	100.0	100.0
Total unions have too much power	58.9	64.1	71.5	73.3	70.9	–	80.2	78.5	72.1	44.0
Total business has too much power	65.7	60.2	63.7	49.1	53.6	–	58.5	60.8	65.5	29.3
N. of respondents	248	253	294	157	270	–	355	298	537	578

Greater London	1963	1964	1966	1969	1970	Feb. 1974	Oct. 1974	1979	1983	1987
Business and trade union power										
Only trade unions have too much	26.1	31.2	32.0	34.1	38.4	–	33.2	34.7	21.3	30.5
Neither has too much	5.1	7.3	11.2	9.1	10.3	–	7.0	6.5	8.9	35.7
Both have too much	46.2	39.7	40.9	39.0	33.5	–	44.4	49.4	51.3	8.5
Only business has too much	22.5	21.8	15.9	17.7	17.8	–	15.4	9.4	18.4	25.3
Total	100.0	100.0	100.0	100.0	100.0	–	100.0	100.0	100.0	100.0
Total unions have too much power	72.3	70.4	72.9	73.1	71.9	–	77.6	84.1	72.6	39.0
Total business has too much power	68.7	61.5	56.8	56.7	51.3	–	59.8	58.8	69.7	33.8
N. of respondents	253	214	239	164	233	–	214	170	405	390

Table 8.21 (*cont.*)

The South

	1963	1964	1966	1969	1970	Feb. 1974	Oct. 1974	1979	1983	1987
Business and trade union power										
Only trade unions have too much	21.4	22.8	29.6	33.2	41.1	–	37.6	36.1	27.4	41.2
Neither has too much	8.8	8.5	8.8	14.4	7.4	–	5.7	5.7	6.5	28.4
Both have too much	47.9	45.7	48.5	40.1	37.6	–	48.2	52.0	52.3	14.2
Only business has too much	21.9	23.0	13.1	12.3	14.0	–	8.4	6.3	13.7	16.3
Total	100.0	100.0	100.0	100.0	100.0	–	100.0	100.0	100.0	100.0
Total unions have too much power	69.3	68.5	78.1	73.3	78.7	–	85.8	88.1	79.7	55.4
Total business has too much power	69.8	68.7	61.6	52.4	51.6	–	56.6	58.3	66.0	30.5
N. of respondents	365	321	372	187	324	–	651	512	1023	1037

Table 8.22 *Government's handling of strikes: all respondents (%)*

	Feb. 1974	Oct. 1974	1979	1983	1987
Government handled strikes					
Very well	12.0	15.2	7.3	2.5	–
Fairly well	39.0	40.1	30.3	24.6	–
Not very well	31.2	28.8	40.3	38.9	–
Not at all well	17.8	15.8	22.1	33.9	–
Total	100.0	100.0	100.0	100.0	–
N. of respondents	2395	2274	1857	3866	–

Table 8.23 *Government's handling of strikes by age and gender (%)*

	Men aged under 25				
	Feb. 1974	Oct. 1974	1979	1983	1987
Government handled strikes					
Very well	5.8	13.8	7.6	1.1	–
Fairly well	40.8	51.4	38.0	23.8	–
Not very well	30.8	23.2	38.0	42.2	–
Not at all well	22.5	11.6	16.5	32.9	–
Total	100.0	100.0	100.0	100.0	–
N. of respondents	120	138	79	284	–

	Women aged under 25				
	Feb. 1974	Oct. 1974	1979	1983	1987
Government handled strikes					
Very well	5.5	16.5	11.1	1.2	–
Fairly well	39.8	49.6	23.3	21.4	–
Not very well	41.4	23.6	44.4	44.5	–
Not at all well	13.3	10.2	21.1	33.0	–
Total	100.0	100.0	100.0	100.0	–
N. of respondents	128	127	90	267	–

	Men aged 25–44				
	Feb. 1974	Oct. 1974	1979	1983	1987
Government handled strikes					
Very well	10.3	14.1	7.1	1.9	–
Fairly well	35.6	40.7	35.4	22.3	–
Not very well	35.3	30.6	38.7	38.2	–
Not at all well	18.8	14.5	18.7	37.6	–
Total	100.0	100.0	100.0	100.0	–
N. of respondents	447	447	364	687	–

	Women aged 25–44				
	Feb. 1974	Oct. 1974	1979	1983	1987
Government handled strikes					
Very well	14.6	15.6	5.5	0.9	–
Fairly well	40.1	43.8	35.0	25.8	–
Not very well	29.6	28.1	43.3	41.9	–
Not at all well	15.7	12.5	16.2	31.4	–
Total	100.0	100.0	100.0	100.0	–
N. of respondents	426	409	383	755	–

Table 8.23 (*cont.*)

	Men aged 45–64				
	Feb. 1974	Oct. 1974	1979	1983	1987
Government handled strikes					
Very well	9.7	13.9	9.5	2.3	–
Fairly well	37.6	39.0	27.9	25.1	–
Not very well	32.2	28.1	37.4	36.3	–
Not at all well	20.5	19.0	25.2	36.3	–
Total	100.0	100.0	100.0	100.0	–
N. of respondents	391	374	305	572	–

	Women aged 45–64				
	Feb. 1974	Oct. 1974	1979	1983	1987
Government handled strikes					
Very well	13.7	15.6	4.0	3.4	–
Fairly well	40.4	39.5	26.5	22.5	–
Not very well	29.7	30.4	47.7	39.6	–
Not at all well	16.2	14.5	21.8	34.5	–
Total	100.0	100.0	100.0	100.0	–
N. of respondents	431	365	298	630	–

	Men aged over 64				
	Feb. 1974	Oct. 1974	1979	1983	1987
Government handled strikes					
Very well	14.3	15.2	12.9	6.4	–
Fairly well	39.0	27.5	23.8	28.7	–
Not very well	29.1	32.6	32.0	35.3	–
Not at all well	17.6	24.7	31.3	29.6	–
Total	100.0	100.0	100.0	100.0	–
N. of respondents	182	178	147	292	–

	Women aged over 64				
	Feb. 1974	Oct. 1974	1979	1983	1987
Government handled strikes					
Very well	17.0	18.9	6.5	5.1	–
Fairly well	41.7	32.2	25.6	29.6	–
Not very well	23.1	28.6	34.2	34.0	–
Not at all well	18.2	20.3	32.6	31.3	–
Total	100.0	100.0	100.0	100.0	–
N. of respondents	247	227	184	360	–

Table 8.24 *Government's handling of strikes by political generation (%)*

	First voted 1918–1935				
	Feb. 1974	Oct. 1974	1979	1983	1987
Government handled strikes					
Very well	15.1	18.5	8.4	6.7	–
Fairly well	39.5	32.4	24.0	31.4	–
Not very well	26.4	28.8	34.1	32.8	–
Not at all well	19.0	20.4	33.4	29.2	–
Total	100.0	100.0	100.0	100.0	–
N. of respondents	583	525	308	454	–
	First voted 1936–1950				
	Feb. 1974	Oct. 1974	1979	1983	1987
Government handled strikes					
Very well	11.9	13.5	6.5	3.3	–
Fairly well	39.9	39.3	27.3	23.6	–
Not very well	31.1	29.5	41.8	39.3	–
Not at all well	17.1	17.6	24.4	33.8	–
Total	100.0	100.0	100.0	100.0	–
N. of respondents	637	562	414	787	–
	First voted 1951–1970				
	Feb. 1974	Oct. 1974	1979	1983	1987
Government handled strikes					
Very well	11.5	14.9	6.8	2.0	–
Fairly well	37.7	43.1	33.6	24.5	–
Not very well	33.0	29.1	41.2	38.4	–
Not at all well	17.8	12.9	18.4	35.1	–
Total	100.0	100.0	100.0	100.0	–
N. of respondents	1024	983	848	1596	–
	First voted after 1970				
	Feb. 1974	Oct. 1974	1979	1983	1987
Government handled strikes					
Very well	3.8	14.4	8.2	1.0	–
Fairly well	43.1	50.0	32.3	23.1	–
Not very well	37.7	23.9	41.6	40.0	–
Not at all well	15.4	11.7	17.9	35.8	–
Total	100.0	100.0	100.0	100.0	–
N. of respondents	130	180	279	716	–

Table 8.25 *Government's handling of strikes by vote (%)*

	Conservative voters				
	Feb. 1974	Oct. 1974	1979	1983	1987
Government handled strikes					
Very well	24.7	2.5	1.4	5.4	–
Fairly well	56.5	20.6	15.8	50.1	–
Not very well	15.4	44.6	46.8	38.3	–
Not at all well	3.4	32.4	36.0	6.2	–
Total	100.0	100.0	100.0	100.0	–
N. of respondents	773	680	727	1405	–

	Labour voters				
	Feb. 1974	Oct. 1974	1979	1983	1987
Government handled strikes					
Very well	3.3	30.0	14.7	0.1	–
Fairly well	20.9	57.5	49.8	3.5	–
Not very well	43.3	10.5	28.4	30.2	–
Not at all well	32.5	2.0	7.1	66.3	–
Total	100.0	100.0	100.0	100.0	–
N. of respondents	822	800	578	903	–

	Liberal voters				
	Feb. 1974	Oct. 1974	1979	1983	1987
Government handled strikes					
Very well	9.3	8.6	7.1	0.4	–
Fairly well	41.2	39.5	33.0	8.4	–
Not very well	35.0	37.2	42.0	45.4	–
Not at all well	14.5	14.7	17.9	45.8	–
Total	100.0	100.0	100.0	100.0	–
N. of respondents	386	339	212	789	–

	Voters for other parties				
	Feb. 1974	Oct. 1974	1979	1983	1987
Government handled strikes					
Very well	6.4	13.8	4.0	2.1	–
Fairly well	42.6	33.8	28.0	2.2	–
Not very well	25.5	33.8	52.0	41.0	–
Not at all well	25.5	18.5	16.0	54.7	–
Total	100.0	100.0	100.0	100.0	–
N. of respondents	47	65	25	43	–

Table 8.26 *Government's handling of strikes by strength and direction of partisanship (%)*

	Very strong Conservative identifiers				
	Feb. 1974	Oct. 1974	1979	1983	1987
Government handled strikes					
Very well	38.4	2.8	0.6	50.3	–
Fairly well	50.7	13.3	11.8	44.9	–
Not very well	9.1	42.7	40.6	4.0	–
Not at all well	1.8	41.2	47.1	0.9	–
Total	100.0	100.0	100.0	100.0	–
N. of respondents	276	211	170	352	

	Fairly strong Conservative identifiers				
	Feb. 1974	Oct. 1974	1979	1983	1987
Government handled strikes					
Very well	20.3	4.1	0.3	35.1	–
Fairly well	60.4	22.5	16.3	60.1	–
Not very well	15.9	44.4	49.7	4.2	–
Not at all well	3.5	29.0	33.7	0.6	–
Total	100.0	100.0	100.0	100.0	–
N. of respondents	429	417	386	667	–

	Not very strong Conservative identifiers				
	Feb. 1974	Oct. 1974	1979	1983	1987
Government handled strikes					
Very well	12.4	4.9	2.1	27.6	–
Fairly well	57.5	29.0	19.5	61.0	–
Not very well	25.8	40.4	45.6	10.5	–
Not at all well	4.3	25.7	32.8	0.9	–
Total	100.0	100.0	100.0	100.0	–
N. of respondents	186	183	195	438	–

	Very strong Liberal identifiers				
	Feb. 1974	Oct. 1974	1979	1983	1987
Government handled strikes					
Very well	8.3	13.3	20.0	15.6	–
Fairly well	55.6	24.4	30.0	39.0	–
Not very well	22.2	42.2	30.0	35.1	–
Not at all well	13.9	20.0	20.0	10.4	–
Total	100.0	100.0	100.0	100.0	–
N. of respondents	36	45	30	77	–

Table 8.26 (*cont.*)

	Fairly strong Liberal identifiers				
	Feb. 1974	Oct. 1974	1979	1983	1987
Government handled strikes					
Very well	8.0	6.6	6.5	19.9	–
Fairly well	37.9	45.1	29.9	53.0	–
Not very well	38.5	34.1	42.1	22.5	–
Not at all well	15.5	14.3	21.5	4.6	–
Total	100.0	100.0	100.0	100.0	–
N. of respondents	174	182	107	302	–

	Not very strong Liberal identifiers				
	Feb. 1974	Oct. 1974	1979	1983	1987
Government handled strikes					
Very well	11.3	7.8	2.2	14.6	–
Fairly well	49.1	45.2	21.3	60.7	–
Not very well	28.3	31.3	49.4	18.5	–
Not at all well	11.3	15.7	27.0	6.2	–
Total	100.0	100.0	100.0	100.0	–
N. of respondents	106	115	89	308	–

	Very strong Labour identifiers				
	Feb. 1974	Oct. 1974	1979	1983	1987
Government handled strikes					
Very well	2.6	44.2	23.7	9.4	–
Fairly well	17.6	47.5	45.8	30.4	–
Not very well	37.5	6.7	24.2	32.8	–
Not at all well	42.3	1.5	6.3	27.4	–
Total	100.0	100.0	100.0	100.0	–
N. of respondents	392	326	190	329	–

	Fairly strong Labour identifiers				
	Feb. 1974	Oct. 1974	1979	1983	1987
Government handled strikes					
Very well	3.7	22.8	10.7	11.2	–
Fairly well	20.5	60.6	53.6	40.2	–
Not very well	47.9	14.3	30.1	35.2	–
Not at all well	27.9	2.3	5.5	13.5	–
Total	100.0	100.0	100.0	100.0	–
N. of respondents	430	434	345	483	–

Table 8.26 (*cont.*)

	Not very strong Labour identifiers				
	Feb. 1974	Oct. 1974	1979	1983	1987
Government handled strikes					
Very well	3.6	13.1	10.5	14.6	–
Fairly well	32.1	56.6	37.6	41.8	–
Not very well	46.1	24.6	40.3	34.8	–
Not at all well	18.1	5.7	11.6	8.9	–
Total	100.0	100.0	100.0	100.0	–
N. of respondents	193	175	181	371	–

Table 8.27 *Government's handling of strikes by social class (%)*

	Professional and managerial classes				
	Feb. 1974	Oct. 1974	1979	1983	1987
Government handled strikes					
Very well	12.1	6.1	3.5	26.5	–
Fairly well	49.5	31.9	26.4	54.5	–
Not very well	27.2	37.4	43.7	15.1	–
Not at all well	11.2	24.6	26.4	3.9	–
Total	100.0	100.0	100.0	100.0	–
N. of respondents	338	342	371	994	–

	Intermediate and routine non-manual classes				
	Feb. 1974	Oct. 1974	1979	1983	1987
Government handled strikes					
Very well	13.0	12.5	5.2	25.9	–
Fairly well	45.9	38.4	26.3	53.1	–
Not very well	27.1	30.3	43.4	16.3	–
Not at all well	13.9	18.7	25.1	4.7	–
Total	100.0	100.0	100.0	100.0	–
N. of respondents	823	781	502	725	–

	Manual working class				
	Feb. 1974	Oct. 1974	1979	1983	1987
Government handled strikes					
Very well	11.9	19.7	10.2	20.3	–
Fairly well	29.8	44.4	34.1	47.2	–
Not very well	35.1	25.2	36.8	22.7	–
Not at all well	23.2	10.7	19.0	9.8	–
Total	100.0	100.0	100.0	100.0	–
N. of respondents	1091	1033	906	1839	–

Table 8.28 *Government's handling of strikes by age and social class (%)*

	Professional and managerial classes: aged under 35				
	Feb. 1974	Oct. 1974	1979	1983	1987
Government handled strikes					
Very well	20.0	12.2	6.5	23.5	–
Fairly well	43.6	40.8	34.3	54.2	–
Not very well	29.8	29.6	38.9	17.6	–
Not at all well	10.6	17.3	20.4	4.6	–
Total	100.0	100.0	100.0	100.0	–
N. of respondents	94	98	108	306	

	Intermediate and routine non-manual classes: aged under 35				
	Feb. 1974	Oct. 1974	1979	1983	1987
Government handled strikes					
Very well	11.8	14.7	3.8	19.1	–
Fairly well	47.6	42.5	33.3	55.1	–
Not very well	27.2	26.6	45.4	20.2	–
Not at all well	13.4	16.2	17.5	5.5	–
Total	100.0	100.0	100.0	100.0	–
N. of respondents	254	259	183	272	–

	Manual working class: aged under 35				
	Feb. 1974	Oct. 1974	1979	1983	1987
Government handled strikes					
Very well	9.3	17.3	8.3	17.8	–
Fairly well	29.3	49.4	39.4	47.9	–
Not very well	37.9	25.0	38.3	24.9	–
Not at all well	23.5	8.3	14.0	9.3	–
Total	100.0	100.0	100.0	100.0	–
N. of respondents	311	336	264	578	–

	Professional and managerial classes: aged 35–54				
	Feb. 1974	Oct. 1974	1979	1983	1987
Government handled strikes					
Very well	7.3	3.2	2.5	27.5	–
Fairly well	53.3	28.6	25.9	55.0	–
Not very well	30.0	42.2	49.4	14.1	–
Not at all well	9.3	26.0	22.2	3.4	–
Total	100.0	100.0	100.0	100.0	–
N. of respondents	150	154	158	411	–

Table 8.28 (*cont.*)

	Intermediate and routine non-manual classes: aged 35–54				
	Feb. 1974	Oct. 1974	1979	1983	1987
Government handled strikes					
Very well	12.0	10.8	6.6	34.9	–
Fairly well	43.2	43.6	24.0	47.5	–
Not very well	31.2	30.7	45.5	12.2	–
Not at all well	13.6	15.0	24.0	5.5	–
Total	100.0	100.0	100.0	100.0	–
N. of respondents	317	287	167	255	–

	Manual working class: aged 35–54				
	Feb. 1974	Oct. 1974	1979	1983	1987
Government handled strikes					
Very well	12.8	21.0	10.2	23.5	–
Fairly well	29.7	45.6	34.9	48.6	–
Not very well	35.4	23.1	38.3	20.4	–
Not at all well	22.1	10.2	16.7	7.5	–
Total	100.0	100.0	100.0	100.0	–
N. of respondents	367	333	324	609	–

	Professional and managerial classes: aged over 54				
	Feb. 1974	Oct. 1974	1979	1983	1987
Government handled strikes					
Very well	17.8	4.5	1.9	28.0	–
Fairly well	48.9	28.1	19.0	54.2	–
Not very well	21.1	37.1	40.0	13.8	–
Not at all well	12.2	30.3	39.0	4.0	–
Total	100.0	100.0	100.0	100.0	–
N. of respondents	90	89	105	275	–

	Intermediate and routine non-manual classes: aged over 54				
	Feb. 1974	Oct. 1974	1979	1983	1987
Government handled strikes					
Very well	17.0	12.4	5.3	20.3	–
Fairly well	44.9	27.8	20.5	49.1	–
Not very well	22.7	33.8	39.1	13.4	–
Not at all well	15.4	26.1	35.1	2.2	–
Total	100.0	100.0	100.0	100.0	–
N. of respondents	247	234	151	232	–

Table 8.28 (*cont.*)

| | Manual working class: aged over 54 | | | | |
	Feb. 1974	Oct. 1974	1979	1983	1987
Government handled strikes					
Very well	13.2	20.9	11.6	19.6	–
Fairly well	30.2	38.0	28.9	45.7	–
Not very well	32.7	27.7	34.0	22.8	–
Not at all well	23.9	13.4	25.5	11.9	–
Total	100.0	100.0	100.0	100.0	–
N. of respondents	401	358	318	637	–

Table 8.29 *Government's handling of strikes by employment status (%)*

| | Self-employed with employees | | | | |
	Feb. 1974	Oct. 1974	1979	1983	1987
Government handled strikes					
Very well	17.8	2.7	0.0	2.6	–
Fairly well	53.3	21.9	14.0	43.9	–
Not very well	23.3	50.7	43.9	36.7	–
Not at all well	5.6	24.7	42.1	16.9	–
Total	100.0	100.0	100.0	100.0	–
N. of respondents	90	73	57	157	–
	Self employed, no employees				
	Feb. 1974	Oct. 1974	1979	1983	1987
Government handled strikes					
Very well	12.0	7.7	1.4	6.8	–
Fairly well	45.8	42.9	23.9	33.4	–
Not very well	33.7	23.1	43.7	37.6	–
Not at all well	8.4	26.4	31.0	22.2	–
Total	100.0	100.0	100.0	100.0	–
N. of respondents	83	91	71	132	–
	Managers				
	Feb. 1974	Oct. 1974	1979	1983	1987
Government handled strikes					
Very well	12.2	4.1	4.1	2.7	–
Fairly well	50.6	32.5	29.7	31.7	–
Not very well	20.7	36.1	44.1	38.4	–
Not at all well	16.5	27.2	22.1	27.2	–
Total	100.0	100.0	100.0	100.0	–
N. of respondents	164	169	145	577	–

Table 8.29 (*cont.*)

	Foremen and supervisors				
	Feb. 1974	Oct. 1974	1979	1983	1987
Government handled strikes					
Very well	15.3	9.3	7.8	3.3	–
Fairly well	38.8	44.9	27.6	25.9	–
Not very well	24.5	28.8	38.5	38.9	–
Not at all well	21.4	16.9	26.0	31.9	–
Total	100.0	100.0	100.0	100.0	–
N. of respondents	98	118	192	484	–
	Rank and file employees				
	Feb. 1974	Oct. 1974	1979	1983	1987
Government handled strikes					
Very well	11.7	17.2	9.4	2.1	–
Fairly well	35.0	41.9	31.0	21.3	–
Not very well	33.9	27.7	40.5	40.0	–
Not at all well	19.4	13.2	19.2	36.6	–
Total	100.0	100.0	100.0	100.0	–
N. of respondents	1636	1484	924	2066	–

Table 8.30 *Government's handling of strikes by trade union membership (%)*

	Trade union members				
	Feb. 1974	Oct. 1974	1979	1983	1987
Government handled strikes					
Very well	3.3	25.0	9.5	1.6	–
Fairly well	20.9	57.5	32.6	17.7	–
Not very well	43.5	15.5	40.7	36.5	–
Not at all well	32.3	2.0	17.2	44.1	–
Total	100.0	100.0	100.0	100.0	–
N. of respondents	540	530	558	1034	–
	Married to a trade union member				
	Feb. 1974	Oct. 1974	1979	1983	1987
Government handled strikes					
Very well	9.3	20.0	6.6	1.7	–
Fairly well	41.2	55.0	35.0	18.7	–
Not very well	30.0	12.5	40.5	41.9	–
Not at all well	19.5	12.5	17.9	37.7	–
Total	100.0	100.0	100.0	100.0	–
N. of respondents	230	226	274	427	–

Table 8.30 (*cont.*)

	Neither respondent nor spouse belongs to a trade union				
	Feb. 1974	Oct. 1974	1979	1983	1987
Government handled strikes					
Very well	15.5	9.8	6.2	3.1	–
Fairly well	42.0	24.2	27.7	28.5	–
Not very well	25.5	35.9	40.1	39.6	–
Not at all well	17.0	30.1	26.0	28.8	–
Total	100.0	100.0	100.0	100.0	–
N. of respondents	1307	1296	1025	2388	–

Table 8.31 *Government's handling of strikes by economic sector (%)*

	Works in private sector				
	Feb. 1974	Oct. 1974	1979	1983	1987
Government handled strikes					
Very well	–	14.9	9.4	2.7	–
Fairly well	–	40.3	32.2	23.9	–
Not very well	–	28.9	37.6	40.0	–
Not at all well	–	15.8	20.7	33.4	–
Total	–	100.0	100.0	100.0	–
N. of respondents	–	1031	752	2086	–

	Works in public sector				
	Feb. 1974	Oct. 1974	1979	1983	1987
Government handled strikes					
Very well	–	15.5	7.4	2.2	–
Fairly well	–	42.9	28.6	22.0	–
Not very well	–	28.5	43.9	37.7	–
Not at all well	–	13.0	20.1	38.1	–
Total	–	100.0	100.0	100.0	–
N. of respondents	–	515	458	1242	–

Table 8.32 *Government's handling of strikes by class and economic sector (%)*

	Professional and managerial classes: private sector				
	Feb. 1974	Oct. 1974	1979	1983	1987
Government handled strikes					
Very well	–	5.7	7.1	2.3	–
Fairly well	–	30.5	27.4	34.9	–
Not very well	–	38.1	38.9	42.1	–
Not at all well	–	25.7	26.5	20.7	–
Total	–	100.0	100.0	100.0	–
N. of respondents	–	105	113	396	–

	Professional and managerial classes: public sector				
	Feb. 1974	Oct. 1974	1979	1983	1987
Government handled strikes					
Very well	–	8.9	3.4	3.1	–
Fairly well	–	35.8	26.9	27.3	–
Not very well	–	39.0	47.9	38.2	–
Not at all well	–	16.3	21.8	31.5	–
Total	–	100.0	100.0	100.0	–
N. of respondents	–	123	119	448	–

	Intermediate and routine non-manual classes: private sector				
	Feb. 1974	Oct. 1974	1979	1983	1987
Government handled strikes					
Very well	–	13.0	5.8	2.4	–
Fairly well	–	37.2	29.2	25.5	–
Not very well	–	30.4	42.5	41.7	–
Not at all well	–	19.3	22.5	30.3	–
Total	–	100.0	100.0	100.0	–
N. of respondents	–	368	240	878	–

	Intermediate and routine non-manual classes: public sector				
	Feb. 1974	Oct. 1974	1979	1983	1987
Government handled strikes					
Very well	–	10.9	6.0	2.1	–
Fairly well	–	48.5	27.4	21.9	–
Not very well	–	26.7	46.2	40.9	–
Not at all well	–	13.9	20.5	35.1	–
Total	–	100.0	100.0	100.0	–
N. of respondents	–	165	117	441	–

Table 8.32 (*cont.*)

	Manual working class: private sector				
	Feb. 1974	Oct. 1974	1979	1983	1987
Government handled strikes					
Very well	–	18.0	12.3	3.1	–
Fairly well	–	44.3	35.3	16.5	–
Not very well	–	26.1	34.3	37.2	–
Not at all well	–	11.5	18.0	43.2	–
Total	–	100.0	100.0	100.0	–
N. of respondents	–	555	399	805	–
	Manual working class: public sector				
	Feb. 1974	Oct. 1974	1979	1983	1987
Government handled strikes					
Very well	–	22.5	10.0	1.1	–
Fairly well	–	42.8	30.5	15.2	–
Not very well	–	24.3	40.5	33.2	–
Not at all well	–	10.4	19.1	50.4	–
Total	–	100.0	100.0	100.0	–
N. of respondents	–	222	220	351	–

Table 8.33 *Government's handling of strikes by region (%)*

	Scotland				
	Feb. 1974	Oct. 1974	1979	1983	1987
Government handled strikes					
Very well	11.3	10.7	4.2	0.5	–
Fairly well	38.3	42.9	28.2	13.0	–
Not very well	31.7	30.6	42.3	35.5	–
Not at all well	18.7	15.8	25.4	51.0	–
Total	100.0	100.0	100.0	100.0	–
N. of respondents	230	196	142	355	
	Wales				
	Feb. 1974	Oct. 1974	1979	1983	1987
Government handled strikes					
Very well	7.8	30.1	10.7	2.4	–
Fairly well	33.3	45.5	35.0	18.8	–
Not very well	25.6	14.6	40.8	31.3	–
Not at all well	33.3	9.8	13.6	47.6	–
Total	100.0	100.0	100.0	100.0	–
N. of respondents	129	123	103	202	–

Table 8.33 (*cont.*)

	The North				
	Feb. 1974	Oct. 1974	1979	1983	1987
Government handled strikes					
Very well	11.3	15.7	7.1	2.3	–
Fairly well	37.7	38.4	30.0	30.0	–
Not very well	33.6	28.7	41.3	38.8	–
Not at all well	17.4	17.3	21.5	37.9	–
Total	100.0	100.0	100.0	100.0	–
N. of respondents	711	670	506	1037	–
	The Midlands				
	Feb. 1974	Oct. 1974	1979	1983	1987
Government handled strikes					
Very well	14.6	19.6	9.0	3.1	–
Fairly well	42.3	37.7	33.6	22.2	–
Not very well	28.7	27.5	34.3	44.7	–
Not at all well	14.4	15.2	23.1	30.0	–
Total	100.0	100.0	100.0	100.0	–
N. of respondents	376	382	324	619	–
	Greater London				
	Feb. 1974	Oct. 1974	1979	1983	1987
Government handled strikes					
Very well	7.7	14.9	7.2	3.6	–
Fairly well	38.7	41.4	25.6	27.0	–
Not very well	30.7	31.5	43.0	39.0	–
Not at all well	23.0	12.2	24.2	30.4	–
Total	100.0	100.0	100.0	100.0	–
N. of respondents	261	222	207	485	–
	The South				
	Feb. 1974	Oct. 1974	1979	1983	1987
Government handled strikes					
Very well	14.1	11.0	6.6	2.5	–
Fairly well	39.8	41.1	29.9	32.9	–
Not very well	31.1	30.8	41.4	38.2	–
Not at all well	14.9	17.0	22.1	26.4	–
Total	100.0	100.0	100.0	100.0	–
N. of respondents	689	681	575	1167	–

Chapter 9
<hr>

NATIONALISATION AND PRIVATISATIO.

1. A question on nationalisation has been asked in every year except 1969 and 1970 with only slight textual variations.

2. The question on the importance of the nationalisation issue was first asked in February 1974 and thereafter in October 1974, 1979 and 1983. The strongest category of importance is 'the most important single thing' in February and October 1974, and 'extremely important' in 1979 and 1983. These categories are treated as equivalent for the purposes of comparison.

See Appendix E, pp. 490–91 on the construction of the nationalisation variables.

Table 9.1 *Attitudes to nationalisation: all respondents (%)*

	1963	1964	1966	1969	1970	Feb. 1974	Oct. 1974	1979	1983	1987
Industries should be										
Nationalised:										
A lot more	12.2	8.7	8.8	–	–	10.0	9.6	6.0	6.9	6.8
A few more	17.0	19.8	20.1	–	–	18.4	22.6	10.9	10.6	10.3
No more	43.9	50.7	48.6	–	–	46.8	45.9	43.2	39.4	51.0
Privatised:										
Some/more	26.9	20.7	22.4	–	–	24.8	21.9	40.0	43.0	31.9
Total	100.0	100.0	100.0	–	–	100.0	100.0	100.0	100.0	100.0
N. of respondents	1646	1604	1628	–	–	2103	2109	1751	3491	3501

Table 9.2 *Attitudes to nationalisation by gender (%)*

Men										
	1963	1964	1966	1969	1970	Feb. 1974	Oct. 1974	1979	1983	1987
Industries should be										
Nationalised:										
A lot more	13.0	8.9	8.8	–	–	10.0	10.6	7.0	7.2	7.7
A few more	22.9	24.5	23.7	–	–	21.8	27.9	10.7	10.7	10.0
No more	38.9	47.7	47.7	–	–	44.9	42.5	40.5	36.0	45.5
Privatised:										
Some/more	25.2	18.9	19.8	–	–	23.3	19.0	41.8	46.0	36.8
Total	100.0	100.0	100.0	–	–	100.0	100.0	100.0	100.0	100.0
N. of respondents	813	788	844	–	–	1095	1105	882	1784	1723

Table 9.2 (*cont.*)

	Women									
	1963	1964	1966	1969	1970	Feb. 1974	Oct. 1974	1979	1983	1987
Industries should be										
Nationalised:										
A lot more	11.4	8.6	8.9	–	–	10.1	8.6	4.9	6.6	5.9
A few more	10.9	15.3	16.4	–	–	14.6	16.8	11.0	10.6	10.5
No more	49.1	53.6	49.4	–	–	48.9	49.5	45.9	42.9	56.4
Privatised:										
Some/more	28.5	22.5	25.3	–	–	26.4	25.1	38.1	39.9	27.2
Total	100.0	100.0	100.0	–	–	100.0	100.0	100.0	100.0	100.0
N. of respondents	813	817	787	–	–	1008	1004	869	1707	1779

Table 9.3 *Attitudes to nationalisation by age (%)*

	Aged under 25									
	1963	1964	1966	1969	1970	Feb. 1974	Oct. 1974	1979	1983	1987
Industries should be										
Nationalised:										
A lot more	18.8	10.5	13.2	–	–	12.0	11.8	8.0	11.3	12.1
A few more	25.0	14.7	24.0	–	–	23.9	30.0	21.6	16.2	14.6
No more	37.5	60.0	43.8	–	–	42.1	42.6	40.1	37.0	46.8
Privatised:										
Some/more	18.8	15.8	19.0	–	–	22.0	15.6	30.2	35.6	26.6
Total	100.0	100.0	100.0	–	–	100.0	100.0	100.0	100.0	100.0
N. of respondents	96	95	121	–	–	209	237	162	476	443

	Aged 25–34									
	1963	1964	1966	1969	1970	Feb. 1974	Oct. 1974	1979	1983	1987
Industries should be										
Nationalised:										
A lot more	11.2	9.2	8.8	–	–	11.9	10.5	5.5	6.7	5.3
A few more	19.2	25.0	23.2	–	–	22.2	24.5	12.0	12.5	13.0
No more	43.5	49.6	50.2	–	–	41.2	40.6	42.6	37.8	51.7
Privatised:										
Some/more	26.1	16.2	17.9	–	–	24.7	24.2	39.8	42.9	29.9
Total	100.0	100.0	100.0	–	–	100.0	100.0	100.0	100.0	100.0
N. of respondents	276	272	285	–	–	405	433	399	671	636

Table 9.3 (*cont.*)

	Aged 35–44									
	1963	1964	1966	1969	1970	Feb. 1974	Oct. 1974	1979	1983	1987
Industries should be										
Nationalised:										
A lot more	12.9	7.1	8.8	–	–	8.8	9.1	4.8	6.4	5.5
A few more	17.9	23.8	21.6	–	–	20.0	24.1	8.3	9.0	10.0
No more	49.3	51.8	51.3	–	–	48.2	46.0	41.0	37.4	50.4
Privatised:										
Some/more	19.9	17.3	18.4	–	–	23.0	20.8	45.8	47.2	34.0
Total	100.0	100.0	100.0	–	–	100.0	100.0	100.0	100.0	100.0
N. of respondents	357	533	320	–	–	365	361	312	644	695

	Aged 45–54									
	1963	1964	1966	1969	1970	Feb. 1974	Oct. 1974	1979	1983	1987
Industries should be										
Nationalised:										
A lot more	11.7	8.1	7.0	–	–	8.5	8.1	6.8	5.0	7.2
A few more	18.5	19.9	20.5	–	–	16.7	22.3	9.3	9.4	7.6
No more	43.3	53.9	51.1	–	–	50.0	48.1	45.0	41.4	48.6
Privatised:										
Some/more	26.5	18.1	21.3	–	–	24.9	21.5	38.8	44.2	36.6
Total	100.0	100.0	100.0	–	–	100.0	100.0	100.0	100.0	100.0
N. of respondents	351	367	356	–	–	390	372	322	562	545

	Aged 55–64									
	1963	1964	1966	1969	1970	Feb. 1974	Oct. 1974	1979	1983	1987
Industries should be										
Nationalised:										
A lot more	11.0	8.5	9.5	–	–	10.5	10.4	4.9	6.7	5.3
A few more	14.1	16.7	16.3	–	–	16.1	18.1	10.6	8.0	9.0
No more	43.3	47.3	48.1	–	–	48.8	52.5	49.0	43.4	53.6
Privatised:										
Some/more	31.6	27.6	26.1	–	–	24.6	19.0	35.5	41.9	32.1
Total	100.0	100.0	100.0	–	–	100.0	100.0	100.0	100.0	100.0
N. of respondents	291	294	295	–	–	342	337	245	535	551

Table 9.3 (*cont.*)

| | Aged 65–74 | | | | | | | | | |
	1963	1964	1966	1969	1970	Feb. 1974	Oct. 1974	1979	1983	1987
Industries should be										
Nationalised:										
A lot more	12.8	10.2	7.1	–	–	6.9	9.1	6.6	6.6	8.8
A few more	11.2	15.3	20.7	–	–	14.7	19.8	6.1	10.7	7.0
No more	40.4	46.6	41.4	–	–	49.0	45.2	41.8	38.7	54.7
Privatised:										
Some/more	35.6	27.8	30.8	–	–	29.3	25.8	45.4	44.0	29.5
Total	100.0	100.0	100.0	–	–	100.0	100.0	100.0	100.0	100.0
N. of respondents	188	175	169	–	–	259	252	196	385	383

| | Aged over 74 | | | | | | | | | |
	1963	1964	1966	1969	1970	Feb. 1974	Oct. 1974	1979	1983	1987
Industries should be										
Nationalised:										
A lot more	5.9	12.0	11.3	–	–	13.0	6.4	7.3	5.9	4.9
A few more	8.8	12.0	10.3	–	–	10.4	17.4	11.8	6.7	7.9
No more	48.5	48.2	46.2	–	–	51.3	45.9	40.0	42.1	53.6
Privatised:										
Some/more	36.8	27.7	32.1	–	–	25.2	30.3	40.9	45.4	33.6
Total	100.0	100.0	100.0	–	–	100.0	100.0	100.0	100.0	100.0
N. of respondents	68	83	78	–	–	115	109	110	203	220

Table 9.4 *Attitudes to nationalisation: new electors (%)*

	1963	1964	1966	1969	1970	Feb. 1974	Oct. 1974	1979	1983	1987
Industries should be										
Nationalised:										
A lot more	18.8	11.5	10.9	–	–	12.9	–	8.3	12.1	12.5
A few more	25.0	19.2	29.1	–	–	27.1	–	24.0	16.1	15.3
No more	37.5	55.4	45.5	–	–	42.9	–	37.2	37.0	48.0
Privatised:										
Some/more	18.8	13.8	14.5	–	–	17.1	–	30.6	34.7	24.3
Total	100.0	100.0	100.0	–	–	100.0	–	100.0	100.0	100.0
N. of respondents	96	130	55	–	–	70	–	121	264	241

Table 9.5 *Attitudes to nationalisation by political generation (%)*

| | First voted 1918–1935 | | | | | | | | | |
	1963	1964	1966	1969	1970	Feb. 1974	Oct. 1974	1979	1983	1987
Industries should be										
Nationalised:										
A lot more	10.8	8.6	8.7	–	–	10.6	9.8	6.7	5.6	5.2
A few more	13.9	16.3	17.5	–	–	13.0	19.1	7.7	8.0	7.2
No more	44.2	48.8	45.7	–	–	49.3	46.8	41.2	40.6	55.6
Privatised:										
Some/more	31.2	26.3	28.2	–	–	27.1	24.3	44.4	45.9	32.0
Total	100.0	100.0	100.0	–	–	100.0	100.0	100.0	100.0	100.0
N. of respondents	693	650	589	–	–	499	481	284	406	253

| | First voted 1936–1950 | | | | | | | | | |
	1963	1964	1966	1969	1970	Feb. 1974	Oct. 1974	1979	1983	1987
Industries should be										
Nationalised:										
A lot more	12.9	8.2	8.5	–	–	8.1	8.3	6.4	7.0	6.8
A few more	18.2	22.8	19.8	–	–	16.7	20.0	8.9	9.3	8.3
No more	46.1	52.0	52.4	–	–	49.2	49.9	47.4	41.9	54.5
Privatised:										
Some/more	22.8	17.1	19.3	–	–	26.0	21.7	37.2	41.9	30.4
Total	100.0	100.0	100.0	–	–	100.0	100.0	100.0	100.0	100.0
N. of respondents	534	527	519	–	–	569	539	392	726	690

| | First voted 1951–1970 | | | | | | | | | |
	1963	1964	1966	1969	1970	Feb. 1974	Oct. 1974	1979	1983	1987
Industries should be										
Nationalised:										
A lot more	13.9	9.3	9.6	–	–	10.6	9.7	5.2	5.5	6.0
A few more	21.1	22.9	24.1	–	–	21.4	25.3	10.3	9.7	8.9
No more	41.1	52.0	47.6	–	–	44.5	43.4	42.4	39.1	49.9
Privatised:										
Some/more	23.9	15.8	18.7	–	–	23.5	21.6	42.0	45.7	35.2
Total	100.0	100.0	100.0	–	–	100.0	100.0	100.0	100.0	100.0
N. of respondents	389	398	503	–	–	868	908	802	1452	1374

Table 9.5 (*cont.*)

	First voted after 1970									
	1963	1964	1966	1969	1970	Feb. 1974	Oct. 1974	1979	1983	1987
Industries should be										
Nationalised:										
A lot more	–	–	–	–	–	11.4	13.5	6.7	8.9	8.3
A few more	–	–	–	–	–	24.3	28.2	18.7	13.9	13.4
No more	–	–	–	–	–	44.3	42.3	41.6	37.3	49.4
Privatised:										
Some/more	–	–	–	–	–	20.0	16.0	33.0	39.8	28.9
Total	–	–	–	–	–	100.0	100.0	100.0	100.0	100.0
N. of respondents	–	–	–	–	–	140	163	267	636	1156

Table 9.6 *Attitudes to nationalisation by vote (%)*

	Conservative voters									
	1963	1964	1966	1969	1970	Feb. 1974	Oct. 1974	1979	1983	1987
Industries should be										
Nationalised:										
A lot more	2.1	1.1	1.2	–	–	2.8	0.5	1.1	1.9	1.4
A few more	9.6	4.0	5.5	–	–	4.2	5.0	3.2	5.2	3.8
No more	48.8	62.9	54.9	–	–	52.9	57.5	33.3	27.2	36.3
Privatised:										
Some/more	39.5	31.9	38.3	–	–	40.1	37.1	62.3	65.7	58.5
Total	100.0	100.0	100.0	–	–	100.0	100.0	100.0	100.0	100.0
N. of respondents	572	623	561	–	–	720	661	709	1352	1313

	Labour voters									
	1963	1964	1966	1969	1970	Feb. 1974	Oct. 1974	1979	1983	1987
Industries should be										
Nationalised:										
A lot more	24.9	18.0	16.2	–	–	19.4	20.6	12.5	18.3	17.5
A few more	24.9	38.4	32.9	–	–	32.8	40.4	20.4	21.7	20.1
No more	36.9	36.4	42.1	–	–	38.5	13.7	52.1	48.3	56.6
Privatised:										
Some/more	13.3	7.2	8.8	–	–	9.3	5.2	15.1	11.7	5.8
Total	100.0	100.0	100.0	–	–	100.0	100.0	100.0	100.0	100.0
N. of respondents	686	635	693	–	–	696	712	530	777	901

Table 9.6 (*cont.*)

						Feb.	Oct.			
Liberal voters										
	1963	1964	1966	1969	1970	1974	1974	1979	1983	1987
Industries should be										
Nationalised:										
A lot more	3.4	1.3	2.6	–	–	4.0	3.6	1.5	2.8	3.1
A few more	12.6	15.6	16.5	–	–	18.8	19.3	7.9	8.0	9.4
No more	50.2	57.8	57.4	–	–	52.6	52.7	55.2	53.2	68.0
Privatised:										
Some/more	33.8	25.3	23.5	–	–	24.7	24.4	35.5	36.0	19.5
Total	100.0	100.0	100.0	–	–	100.0	100.0	100.0	100.0	100.0
N. of respondents	207	154	115	–	–	352	332	203	712	699

						Feb.	Oct.			
Voters for other parties										
	1963	1964	1966	1969	1970	1974	1974	1979	1983	1987
Industries should be										
Nationalised:										
A lot more	(0.0)	(25.0)	(0.0)	–	–	5.0	8.5	4.2	12.3	7.2
A few more	(50.0)	(12.5)	(33.3)	–	–	22.5	16.9	4.2	13.3	9.5
No more	(0.0)	(25.0)	(55.6)	–	–	47.5	47.5	54.2	48.9	59.2
Privatised:										
Some/more	(50.0)	(37.5)	(11.1)	–	–	25.0	27.1	37.5	25.5	24.0
Total	(100.0)	(100.0)	(100.0)	–	–	100.0	100.0	100.0	100.0	100.0
N. of respondents	2	8	9	–	–	40	59	24	37	40

Table 9.7 *Attitudes to nationalisation by strength and direction of partisanship (%)*

						Feb.	Oct.			
Very strong Conservative identifiers										
	1963	1964	1966	1969	1970	1974	1974	1979	1983	1987
Industries should be										
Nationalised:										
A lot more	1.4	1.2	1.6	–	–	2.7	1.0	1.2	2.4	1.0
A few more	6.8	4.3	4.3	–	–	3.5	2.4	1.2	3.6	2.7
No more	44.3	52.2	45.9	–	–	50.4	50.0	22.2	20.5	30.4
Privatised:										
Some/more	47.5	42.3	48.2	–	–	43.4	46.7	75.3	73.6	65.9
Total	100.0	100.0	100.0	–	–	100.0	100.0	100.0	100.0	100.0
N. of respondents	221	324	305	–	–	258	210	162	337	307

Table 9.7 (*cont.*)

	1963	1964	1966	1969	1970	Feb. 1974	Oct. 1974	1979	1983	1987
Industries should be										
Nationalised:										
A lot more	3.6	0.0	1.7	–	–	1.3	1.3	1.6	2.2	1.5
A few more	9.5	4.5	6.7	–	–	3.8	5.3	3.7	4.0	2.3
No more	50.4	69.1	58.4	–	–	53.3	61.5	34.5	26.4	33.2
Privatised:										
Some/more	36.5	26.4	33.2	–	–	41.6	32.0	60.3	67.4	63.0
Total	100.0	100.0	100.0	–	–	100.0	100.0	100.0	100.0	100.0
N. of respondents	274	265	238	–	–	392	397	380	625	674

Not very strong Conservative identifiers

	1963	1964	1966	1969	1970	Feb. 1974	Oct. 1974	1979	1983	1987
Industries should be										
Nationalised:										
A lot more	1.3	2.4	1.1	–	–	4.1	2.2	1.0	2.4	2.2
A few more	12.2	4.8	15.4	–	–	9.4	10.6	5.8	7.7	5.4
No more	52.6	72.3	62.6	–	–	58.5	53.6	37.2	31.7	54.9
Privatised:										
Some/more	34.0	20.5	20.9	–	–	28.1	33.5	56.0	58.2	37.5
Total	100.0	100.0	100.0	–	–	100.0	100.0	100.0	100.0	100.0
N. of respondents	156	83	91	–	–	171	179	191	416	320

Very strong Liberal identifiers

	1963	1964	1966	1969	1970	Feb. 1974	Oct. 1974	1979	1983	1987
Industries should be										
Nationalised:										
A lot more	0.0	1.5	5.3	–	–	6.5	7.0	7.4	5.6	1.8
A few more	9.4	4.6	10.5	–	–	9.7	11.6	7.4	5.6	10.7
No more	52.8	64.6	57.9	–	–	41.9	51.2	51.9	53.5	73.8
Privatised:										
Some/more	37.7	29.2	26.3	–	–	41.9	30.2	33.3	35.2	13.8
Total	100.0	100.0	100.0	–	–	100.0	100.0	100.0	100.0	100.0
N. of respondents	53	65	57	–	–	31	43	27	71	55

Table 9.7 (*cont.*)

Fairly strong Liberal identifiers

	1963	1964	1966	1969	1970	Feb. 1974	Oct. 1974	1979	1983	1987
Industries should be										
Nationalised:										
A lot more	3.7	0.0	4.3	–	–	3.3	2.3	1.0	1.4	3.7
A few more	7.3	18.8	11.7	–	–	15.0	19.7	4.8	9.1	7.1
No more	52.4	58.3	64.9	–	–	56.2	56.1	57.7	52.3	65.8
Privatised:										
Some/more	36.6	22.9	19.1	–	–	25.5	22.0	36.5	37.2	23.4
Total	100.0	100.0	100.0	–	–	100.0	100.0	100.0	100.0	100.0
N. of respondents	82	96	94	–	–	153	173	104	285	249

Not very strong Liberal identifiers

	1963	1964	1966	1969	1970	Feb. 1974	Oct. 1974	1979	1983	1987
Industries should be										
Nationalised:										
A lot more	3.4	2.2	3.7	–	–	4.8	2.6	0.0	4.9	3.7
A few more	22.4	26.1	24.8	–	–	22.1	20.5	5.8	9.5	7.1
No more	51.7	50.0	41.5	–	–	46.2	53.0	57.0	48.2	65.8
Privatised:										
Some/more	22.4	21.7	30.0	–	–	26.9	23.9	37.2	37.3	23.4
Total	100.0	100.0	100.0	–	–	100.0	100.0	100.0	100.0	100.0
N. of respondents	58	46	27	–	–	104	117	86	284	249

Very strong Labour identifiers

	1963	1964	1966	1969	1970	Feb. 1974	Oct. 1974	1979	1983	1987
Industries should be										
Nationalised:										
A lot more	36.7	25.3	24.4	–	–	27.7	30.8	25.6	24.7	3.3
A few more	25.1	40.4	34.1	–	–	32.1	39.7	21.1	25.1	7.2
No more	27.7	28.9	33.3	–	–	34.2	25.1	44.4	41.0	65.8
Privatised:										
Some/more	10.5	5.4	8.1	–	–	6.0	4.4	8.9	9.2	23.7
Total	100.0	100.0	100.0	–	–	100.0	100.0	100.0	100.0	100.0
N. of respondents	267	332	369	–	–	336	295	180	295	293

Table 9.7 (*cont.*)

	| Fairly strong Labour identifiers									
	1963	1964	1966	1969	1970	Feb. 1974	Oct. 1974	1979	1983	1987
Industries should be										
Nationalised:										
A lot more	18.2	13.5	9.3	–	–	14.2	15.9	8.3	13.8	14.2
A few more	30.1	39.6	33.5	–	–	32.7	42.7	23.8	20.1	23.6
No more	39.2	40.8	49.4	–	–	43.5	36.7	52.1	51.9	55.0
Privatised:										
Some/more	12.6	6.1	7.8	–	–	9.7	4.7	15.9	14.3	7.2
Total	100.0	100.0	100.0	–	–	100.0	100.0	100.0	100.0	100.0
N. of respondents	286	245	269	–	–	352	384	315	428	459

	| Not very strong Labour identifiers									
	1963	1964	1966	1969	1970	Feb. 1974	Oct. 1974	1979	1983	1987
Industries should be										
Nationalised:										
A lot more	13.4	11.1	6.7	–	–	14.5	11.6	3.8	9.7	10.4
A few more	17.7	18.5	32.6	–	–	26.7	34.9	13.9	14.3	16.9
No more	47.6	56.8	42.7	–	–	41.8	38.4	55.1	52.3	62.2
Privatised:										
Some/more	21.3	13.6	18.0	–	–	17.0	15.1	27.2	23.7	10.5
Total	100.0	100.0	100.0	–	–	100.0	100.0	100.0	100.0	100.0
N. of respondents	164	81	89	–	–	165	146	158	321	330

Table 9.8 *Attitudes to nationalisation by political generation and partisanship (%)*

	| Conservative identifiers: first voted 1918–1935									
	1963	1964	1966	1969	1970	Feb. 1974	Oct. 1974	1979	1983	1987
Industries should be										
Nationalised:										
A lot more	1.3	2.2	0.4	–	–	2.4	1.4	2.1	1.5	2.5
A few more	7.3	4.2	7.1	–	–	3.7	3.8	3.5	4.3	1.7
No more	47.5	53.1	47.8	–	–	55.5	56.0	33.3	28.8	47.3
Privatised:										
Some/more	43.9	40.5	44.7	–	–	38.4	38.8	61.1	65.4	48.5
Total	100.0	100.0	100.0	–	–	100.0	100.0	100.0	100.0	100.0
N. of respondents	314	309	267	–	–	245	209	144	203	130

Table 9.8 (*cont.*)

Labour identifiers: first voted 1918–1935

	1963	1964	1966	1969	1970	Feb. 1974	Oct. 1974	1979	1983	1987
Industries should be										
Nationalised:										
A lot more	25.2	19.8	17.7	–	–	23.4	22.2	15.8	15.3	10.8
A few more	23.3	34.5	33.2	–	–	23.9	39.2	16.8	16.2	23.0
No more	38.3	37.9	39.2	–	–	41.1	33.3	49.5	46.8	58.4
Privatised:										
Some/more	13.2	7.8	9.9	–	–	11.7	5.3	17.9	21.6	7.8
Total	100.0	100.0	100.0	–	–	100.0	100.0	100.0	100.0	100.0
N. of respondents	266	232	232	–	–	197	171	95	107	66

Conservative identifiers: first voted 1936–1950

	1963	1964	1966	1969	1970	Feb. 1974	Oct. 1974	1979	1983	1987
Industries should be										
Nationalised:										
A lot more	2.2	0.0	3.2	–	–	1.7	0.9	1.3	1.7	0.4
A few more	8.7	4.8	5.8	–	–	4.7	6.0	1.9	2.5	2.7
No more	53.8	65.6	55.8	–	–	51.3	61.0	35.3	29.2	44.5
Privatised:										
Some/more	35.3	29.6	35.2	–	–	42.2	32.1	61.5	66.6	52.5
Total	100.0	100.0	100.0	–	–	100.0	100.0	100.0	100.0	100.0
N. of respondents	184	189	190	–	–	232	218	156	294	303

Labour identifiers: first voted 1936–1950

	1963	1964	1966	1969	1970	Feb. 1974	Oct. 1974	1979	1983	1987
Industries should be										
Nationalised:										
A lot more	23.3	17.1	14.9	–	–	17.8	19.6	13.7	16.4	18.3
A few more	25.3	39.8	31.7	–	–	29.8	35.0	19.0	20.7	20.7
No more	37.0	36.6	44.6	–	–	45.8	37.4	53.6	50.1	55.5
Privatised:										
Some/more	14.4	6.5	8.8	–	–	6.7	7.9	13.7	12.8	5.5
Total	100.0	100.0	100.0	–	–	100.0	100.0	100.0	100.0	100.0
N. of respondents	257	246	248	–	–	225	214	153	240	209

Table 9.8 (*cont.*)

Conservative identifiers: first voted 1951–1970

	1963	1964	1966	1969	1970	Feb. 1974	Oct. 1974	1979	1983	1987
Industries should be										
Nationalised:										
A lot more	5.6	0.0	2.3	–	–	3.0	1.7	0.6	1.5	1.0
A few more	13.9	4.4	6.4	–	–	4.0	5.6	4.0	4.5	2.5
No more	45.1	72.5	57.9	–	–	53.2	53.6	30.5	24.1	36.1
Privatised:										
Some/more	35.4	23.1	33.3	–	–	39.9	39.1	64.9	69.9	60.4
Total	100.0	100.0	100.0	–	–	100.0	100.0	100.0	100.0	100.0
N. of respondents	144	160	171	–	–	301	302	345	607	594

Labour identifiers: first voted 1951–1970

	1963	1964	1966	1969	1970	Feb. 1974	Oct. 1974	1979	1983	1987
Industries should be										
Nationalised:										
A lot more	22.8	19.6	16.9	–	–	18.9	18.8	10.6	13.2	16.6
A few more	27.7	39.9	36.4	–	–	35.0	43.4	19.1	19.2	18.4
No more	36.4	35.7	37.6	–	–	36.1	31.2	51.5	50.6	57.3
Privatised:										
Some/more	13.0	4.8	9.1	–	–	10.0	6.6	18.8	17.0	7.7
Total	100.0	100.0	100.0	–	–	100.0	100.0	100.0	100.0	100.0
N. of respondents	180	168	242	–	–	360	378	303	425	413

Conservative identifiers: first voted after 1970

	1963	1964	1966	1969	1970	Feb. 1974	Oct. 1974	1979	1983	1987
Industries should be										
Nationalised:										
A lot more	–	–	–	–	–	0.0	0.0	3.4	4.8	2.3
A few more	–	–	–	–	–	18.2	15.6	5.7	6.5	5.0
No more	–	–	–	–	–	60.6	55.6	33.3	24.6	36.0
Privatised:										
Some/more	–	–	–	–	–	21.2	28.9	57.5	64.1	56.6
Total	–	–	–	–	–	100.0	100.0	100.0	100.0	100.0
N. of respondents	–	–	–	–	–	33	45	87	236	408

Table 9.8 (*cont.*)

Labour identifiers: first voted after 1970

	1963	1964	1966	1969	1970	Feb. 1974	Oct. 1974	1979	1983	1987
Industries should be										
Nationalised:										
A lot more	–	–	–	–	–	15.6	26.6	9.5	15.8	15.6
A few more	–	–	–	–	–	37.5	43.8	30.5	20.1	22.0
No more	–	–	–	–	–	34.4	26.6	45.7	49.7	54.4
Privatised:										
Some/more	–	–	–	–	–	12.5	3.1	14.3	14.3	8.1
Total	–	–	–	–	–	100.0	100.0	100.0	100.0	100.0
N. of respondents	–	–	–	–	–	64	64	105	217	414

Table 9.9 *Attitudes to nationalisation by party membership (%)*

All party members

	1963	1964	1966	1969	1970	Feb. 1974	Oct. 1974	1979	1983	1987
Industries should be										
Nationalised:										
A lot more	10.4	7.0	–	–	–	–	5.8	–	8.6	–
A few more	15.3	13.4	–	–	–	–	18.7	–	8.6	–
No more	36.2	54.8	–	–	–	–	40.6	–	24.9	–
Privatised:										
Some/more	38.0	24.7	–	–	–	–	34.8	–	57.8	–
Total	100.0	100.0	–	–	–	–	100.0	–	100.0	–
N. of respondents	163	186	–	–	–	–	155	–	253	–

Conservative party members

	1963	1964	1966	1969	1970	Feb. 1974	Oct. 1974	1979	1983	1987
Industries should be										
Nationalised:										
A lot more	2.0	0.8	–	–	–	–	0.0	–	0.7	–
A few more	6.0	4.9	–	–	–	–	8.8	–	2.8	–
No more	41.0	63.4	–	–	–	–	43.1	–	15.6	–
Privatised:										
Some/more	51.0	30.9	–	–	–	–	48.0	–	80.9	–
Total	100.0	100.0	–	–	–	–	100.0	–	100.0	–
N. of respondents	100	123	–	–	–	–	102	–	158	–

Table 9.9 (*cont.*)

	Labour party members									
	1963	1964	1966	1969	1970	Feb. 1974	Oct. 1974	1979	1983	1987
Industries should be										
Nationalised:										
A lot more	29.5	23.7	–	–	–	–	24.1	–	35.8	–
A few more	34.1	44.7	–	–	–	–	55.2	–	31.1	–
No more	27.3	26.3	–	–	–	–	20.7	–	28.7	–
Privatised:										
Some/more	9.1	5.3	–	–	–	–	0.0	–	4.3	–
Total	100.0	100.0	–	–	–	–	100.0	–	100.0	–
N. of respondents	44	38	–	–	–	–	29	–	46	–

Table 9.10 *Attitudes to nationalisation by social class (%)*

	Professional and managerial classes									
	1963	1964	1966	1969	1970	Feb. 1974	Oct. 1974	1979	1983	1987
Industries should be										
Nationalised:										
A lot more	2.4	2.3	3.0	–	–	4.3	3.6	2.5	3.3	3.7
A few more	19.8	13.6	10.9	–	–	18.1	21.6	7.5	7.9	8.6
No more	50.2	63.2	53.9	–	–	46.0	53.0	39.6	36.4	46.5
Privatised:										
Some/more	27.5	20.9	32.2	–	–	31.6	21.9	50.4	52.4	41.2
Total	100.0	100.0	100.0	–	–	100.0	100.0	100.0	100.0	100.0
N. of respondents	207	220	230	–	–	326	338	361	967	914

	Intermediate and routine non-manual classes									
	1963	1964	1966	1969	1970	Feb. 1974	Oct. 1974	1979	1983	1987
Industries should be										
Nationalised:										
A lot more	6.9	6.2	7.4	–	–	7.0	6.8	4.4	3.9	4.1
A few more	13.8	15.2	16.3	–	–	15.0	19.9	8.0	8.5	9.0
No more	45.8	52.1	50.5	–	–	49.1	45.7	41.6	38.7	50.4
Privatised:										
Some/more	33.5	26.5	25.8	–	–	29.0	27.6	46.0	48.9	36.6
Total	100.0	100.0	100.0	–	–	100.0	100.0	100.0	100.0	100.0
N. of respondents	465	486	461	–	–	742	739	476	661	889

Table 9.10 (*cont.*)

| | Manual working class | | | | | | | | | |
	1963	1964	1966	1969	1970	Feb. 1974	Oct. 1974	1979	1983	1987
Industries should be										
Nationalised:										
A lot more	17.1	12.2	11.0	–	–	14.0	14.2	8.0	10.2	9.8
A few more	18.4	23.7	24.0	–	–	21.3	25.5	13.8	13.2	11.5
No more	40.7	46.9	46.7	–	–	45.4	43.3	46.1	42.3	54.4
Privatised:										
Some/more	23.7	17.2	18.3	–	–	19.2	17.1	32.1	34.3	24.4
Total	100.0	100.0	100.0	–	–	100.0	100.0	100.0	100.0	100.0
N. of respondents	900	851	915	–	–	920	938	850	1624	1538

Table 9.11 *Attitudes to nationalisation by employment status (%)*

| | Self-employed with employees | | | | | | | | | |
	1963	1964	1966	1969	1970	Feb. 1974	Oct. 1974	1979	1983	1987
Industries should be										
Nationalised:										
A lot more	1.5	0.0	0.0	–	–	4.6	6.9	0.0	2.7	3.3
A few more	10.3	11.8	13.1	–	–	5.7	15.3	1.8	5.1	5.7
No more	41.2	57.9	42.6	–	–	48.3	48.6	31.6	20.7	35.4
Privatised:										
Some/more	47.1	30.3	44.3	–	–	41.4	29.2	66.7	71.5	55.6
Total	100.0	100.0	100.0	–	–	100.0	100.0	100.0	100.0	100.0
N. of respondents	68	76	61	–	–	87	72	57	157	163

| | Self-employed, no employees | | | | | | | | | |
	1963	1964	1966	1969	1970	Feb. 1974	Oct. 1974	1979	1983	1987
Industries should be										
Nationalised:										
A lot more	(5.0)	(5.3)	0.0	–	–	0.0	3.3	2.9	2.6	5.9
A few more	(10.0)	(10.5)	12.5	–	–	10.5	15.6	1.5	7.2	6.6
No more	(45.0)	(47.4)	62.5	–	–	52.6	46.7	25.0	28.2	45.6
Privatised:										
Some/more	(40.0)	(36.9)	25.0	–	–	36.8	34.4	70.6	62.0	41.8
Total	(100.0)	(100.0)	100.0	–	–	100.0	100.0	100.0	100.0	100.0
N. of respondents	20	19	32	–	–	76	90	68	122	157

Table 9.11 (*cont.*)

Managers

	1963	1964	1966	1969	1970	Feb. 1974	Oct. 1974	1979	1983	1987
Industries should be										
Nationalised:										
A lot more	1.2	1.2	3.3	–	–	3.2	5.8	5.0	3.0	2.4
A few more	20.5	17.1	13.2	–	–	21.5	25.6	7.9	6.7	5.3
No more	51.8	58.5	58.2	–	–	46.8	49.4	39.3	37.9	41.1
Privatised:										
Some/more	26.5	23.2	25.3	–	–	28.5	19.2	47.9	52.4	51.2
Total	100.0	100.0	100.0	–	–	100.0	100.0	100.0	100.0	100.0
N. of respondents	83	82	91	–	–	158	172	140	362	336

Foremen and supervisors

	1963	1964	1966	1969	1970	Feb. 1974	Oct. 1974	1979	1983	1987
Industries should be										
Nationalised:										
A lot more	8.7	8.3	4.7	–	–	6.5	8.1	5.8	6.5	4.0
A few more	25.0	22.2	24.5	–	–	22.8	25.2	9.5	10.4	8.9
No more	43.3	46.3	48.1	–	–	51.1	44.1	40.0	38.7	49.6
Privatised:										
Some/more	23.1	23.1	22.6	–	–	19.6	22.5	44.7	44.5	37.5
Total	100.0	100.0	100.0	–	–	100.0	100.0	100.0	100.0	100.0
N. of respondents	110	113	106	–	–	92	111	190	217	214

Rank and file employees

	1963	1964	1966	1969	1970	Feb. 1974	Oct. 1974	1979	1983	1987
Industries should be										
Nationalised:										
A lot more	14.9	10.0	10.0	–	–	11.5	11.0	7.4	7.5	7.6
A few more	20.0	22.8	21.9	–	–	19.8	23.6	11.8	12.1	11.2
No more	40.5	49.0	48.2	–	–	46.0	44.9	45.6	43.1	53.8
Privatised:										
Some/more	24.7	18.2	19.9	–	–	22.6	20.5	35.3	37.2	27.3
Total	100.0	100.0	100.0	–	–	100.0	100.0	100.0	100.0	100.0
N. of respondents	860	826	869	–	–	1387	1379	868	2237	2495

Table 9.12 *Attitudes to nationalisation: unemployed (%)*

	1963	1964	1966	1969	1970	Feb. 1974	Oct. 1974	1979	1983	1987
Industries should be										
Nationalised:										
A lot more	(0.0)	(0.0)	(10.4)	–	–	20.9	16.7	8.3	17.2	11.7
A few more	(33.3)	(8.3)	(19.1)	–	–	25.6	30.6	16.7	14.7	16.0
No more	(33.3)	(50.0)	(46.5)	–	–	30.2	30.6	47.2	37.4	48.7
Privatised:										
Some/more	(33.3)	(41.7)	(23.9)	–	–	23.3	22.2	27.8	30.6	23.6
Total	(100.0)	(100.0)	(100.0)	–	–	100.0	100.0	100.0	100.0	100.0
N. of respondents	3	12	11	–	–	43	36	35	212	195

Table 9.13 *Attitudes to nationalisation by class and employment status (%)*

	Professional and managerial classes: self-employed									
	1963	1964	1966	1969	1970	Feb. 1974	Oct. 1974	1979	1983	1987
Industries should be										
Nationalised:										
A lot more	0.0	0.0	0.0	–	–	0.0	0.0	0.0	4.7	2.0
A few more	8.8	4.9	6.7	–	–	10.6	11.6	5.3	7.0	7.4
No more	52.9	63.4	33.3	–	–	51.1	65.1	28.9	21.0	39.9
Privatised:										
Some/more	38.2	31.7	60.0	–	–	38.3	23.3	65.8	67.2	50.7
Total	100.0	100.0	100.0	–	–	100.0	100.0	100.0	100.0	100.0
N. of respondents	37	43	29	–	–	47	43	38	128	148

	Professional and managerial classes: employees									
	1963	1964	1966	1969	1970	Feb. 1974	Oct. 1974	1979	1983	1987
Industries should be										
Nationalised:										
A lot more	3.8	1.9	2.1	–	–	5.4	4.7	2.5	3.1	4.0
A few more	32.1	19.8	13.9	–	–	21.9	24.7	8.3	8.3	8.7
No more	36.8	63.2	60.4	–	–	44.6	49.4	39.4	39.0	47.8
Privatised:										
Some/more	27.4	15.1	23.6	–	–	28.1	21.2	49.8	49.7	39.4
Total	100.0	100.0	100.0	–	–	100.0	100.0	100.0	100.0	100.0
N. of respondents	106	106	144	–	–	242	255	241	811	767

Table 9.13 (*cont.*)

Intermediate and routine non-manual classes: self-employed

	1963	1964	1966	1969	1970	Feb. 1974	Oct. 1974	1979	1983	1987
Industries should be										
Nationalised:										
A lot more	4.5	2.2	0.0	–	–	4.3	3.7	0.0	0.0	5.7
A few more	13.6	13.0	17.1	–	–	5.4	16.0	0.0	7.4	5.7
No more	31.8	52.1	56.1	–	–	49.5	43.2	32.1	22.2	31.4
Privatised:										
Some/more	50.0	32.6	28.8	–	–	40.9	37.0	67.9	70.4	57.1
Total	100.0	100.0	100.0	–	–	100.0	100.0	100.0	100.0	100.0
N. of respondents	44	51	41	–	–	93	81	53	27	35

Intermediate and routine non-manual classes: employees

	1963	1964	1966	1969	1970	Feb. 1974	Oct. 1974	1979	1983	1987
Industries should be										
Nationalised:										
A lot more	8.1	6.2	9.3	–	–	7.3	7.3	5.6	4.1	4.0
A few more	15.6	18.7	19.4	–	–	16.9	20.6	8.4	8.0	9.1
No more	45.8	51.9	46.4	–	–	49.0	45.9	41.0	39.8	51.2
Privatised:										
Some/more	30.5	23.1	25.0	–	–	26.8	26.1	44.9	48.1	35.7
Total	100.0	100.0	100.0	–	–	100.0	100.0	100.0	100.0	100.0
N. of respondents	308	337	248	–	–	604	616	356	613	855

Manual working class: self-employed

	1963	1964	1966	1969	1970	Feb. 1974	Oct. 1974	1979	1983	1987
Industries should be										
Nationalised:										
A lot more	(0.0)	(0.0)	0.0	–	–	0.0	13.2	5.9	0.9	6.7
A few more	(0.0)	(26.5)	13.6	–	–	13.6	18.4	0.0	6.5	4.4
No more	(44.4)	(47.1)	59.1	–	–	50.0	36.8	20.6	26.2	43.0
Privatised:										
Some/more	(55.6)	(26.5)	27.3	–	–	36.4	31.6	73.5	66.4	45.9
Total	(100.0)	(100.0)	100.0	–	–	100.0	100.0	100.0	100.0	100.0
N. of respondents	9	7	21	–	–	22	38	34	107	135

Table 9.13 (*cont.*)

	1963	1964	1966	1969	1970	Feb. 1974	Oct. 1974	1979	1983	1987
Manual working class: employees										
Industries should be										
Nationalised:										
A lot more	17.2	12.3	10.2	–	–	14.5	14.6	9.2	9.8	10.1
A few more	21.0	24.7	23.8	–	–	22.1	26.1	13.5	13.4	12.2
No more	40.4	45.5	47.8	–	–	45.0	43.7	47.7	44.0	55.4
Privatised:										
Some/more	21.3	17.5	18.1	–	–	18.4	15.7	29.6	32.8	22.3
Total	100.0	100.0	100.0	–	–	100.0	100.0	100.0	100.0	100.0
N. of respondents	633	567	667	–	–	778	783	598	1383	1404

Table 9.14 *Attitudes to nationalisation by trade union membership (%)*

	1963	1964	1966	1969	1970	Feb. 1974	Oct. 1974	1979	1983	1987
Trade union members										
Industries should be										
Nationalised:										
A lot more	18.8	12.6	–	–	–	13.3	13.1	7.6	8.8	8.5
A few more	25.9	29.6	–	–	–	24.3	26.4	14.9	13.5	12.0
No more	36.9	42.2	–	–	–	45.1	44.6	47.2	44.8	52.9
Privatised:										
Some/more	18.3	15.5	–	–	–	17.3	15.8	30.2	32.9	26.5
Total	100.0	100.0	–	–	–	100.0	100.0	100.0	100.0	100.0
N. of respondents	398	412	–	–	–	572	542	536	957	789
Respondent is married to a trade union member										
Industries should be										
Nationalised:										
A lot more	14.3	11.9	–	–	–	13.1	12.9	4.7	5.8	5.3
A few more	18.3	25.2	–	–	–	19.2	21.0	10.5	11.2	9.2
No more	44.2	48.9	–	–	–	46.5	45.6	49.2	45.6	55.7
Privatised:										
Some/more	23.2	14.1	–	–	–	21.2	20.5	35.7	37.4	29.8
Total	100.0	100.0	–	–	–	100.0	100.0	100.0	100.0	100.0
N. of respondents	224	135	–	–	–	245	237	258	379	340

Table 9.14 (*cont.*)

	1963	1964	1966	1969	1970	Feb. 1974	Oct. 1974	1979	1983	1987
Neither respondent nor spouse belongs to a trade union										
Industries should be										
Nationalised:										
A lot more	9.1	5.4	–	–	–	8.0	7.8	5.4	6.3	6.4
A few more	13.5	15.5	–	–	–	15.6	15.8	8.7	9.3	9.8
No more	46.4	55.2	–	–	–	47.7	47.8	39.3	36.0	49.7
Privatised:										
Some/more	31.1	23.8	–	–	–	28.8	28.6	46.6	48.4	34.0
Total	100.0	100.0	–	–	–	100.0	100.0	100.0	100.0	100.0
N. of respondents	1003	973	–	–	–	1286	1297	957	2138	2345

Table 9.15 *Attitudes to nationalisation by economic sector (%)*

	1963	1964	1966	1969	1970	Feb. 1974	Oct. 1974	1979	1983	1987
Works in private sector										
Industries should be										
Nationalised:										
A lot more	–	–	–	–	–	–	10.2	6.1	6.9	7.0
A few more	–	–	–	–	–	–	23.7	41.7	38.5	50.8
No more	–	–	–	–	–	–	45.2	41.7	44.1	32.2
Privatised:										
Some/more	–	–	–	–	–	–	20.9	40.9	44.1	32.2
Total	–	–	–	–	–	–	100.0	100.0	100.0	100.0
N. of respondents	–	–	–	–	–	–	973	717	1863	1986
Works in public sector										
Industries should be										
Nationalised:										
A lot more	–	–	–	–	–	–	11.2	8.7	8.1	6.4
A few more	–	–	–	–	–	–	27.7	10.0	11.5	11.4
No more	–	–	–	–	–	–	42.8	48.1	45.0	54.6
Privatised:										
Some/more	–	–	–	–	–	–	18.3	33.3	35.4	27.6
Total	–	–	–	–	–	–	100.0	100.0	100.0	100.0
N. of respondents	–	–	–	–	–	–	491	439	1134	972

Table 9.16 *Attitudes to nationalisation by school leaving age (%)*

	Left school aged under 15									
	1963	1964	1966	1969	1970	Feb. 1974	Oct. 1974	1979	1983	1987
Industries should be										
Nationalised:										
A lot more	13.3	10.0	10.7	–	–	11.1	11.7	7.5	8.1	8.1
A few more	15.8	21.9	20.5	–	–	17.2	22.5	10.6	10.9	9.1
No more	44.5	47.1	48.1	–	–	49.4	46.3	45.9	43.3	57.1
Privatised:										
Some/more	26.3	20.9	20.7	–	–	22.3	19.5	36.0	37.7	25.8
Total	100.0	100.0	100.0	–	–	100.0	100.0	100.0	100.0	100.0
N. of respondents	968	917	888	–	–	886	862	575	990	822

	Left school aged 15									
	1963	1964	1966	1969	1970	Feb. 1974	Oct. 1974	1979	1983	1987
Industries should be										
Nationalised:										
A lot more	14.2	11.0	7.8	–	–	12.1	10.7	7.4	7.3	7.9
A few more	19.6	18.6	23.5	–	–	20.7	24.8	9.8	9.5	10.0
No more	40.7	52.8	49.6	–	–	43.0	44.7	46.4	43.2	52.4
Privatised:										
Some/more	25.5	17.7	19.1	–	–	24.1	19.8	36.5	40.0	29.7
Total	100.0	100.0	100.0	–	–	100.0	100.0	100.0	100.0	100.0
N. of respondents	337	345	361	–	–	588	597	502	884	845

	Left school aged 16									
	1963	1964	1966	1969	1970	Feb. 1974	Oct. 1974	1979	1983	1987
Industries should be										
Nationalised:										
A lot more	7.9	1.8	5.2	–	–	6.3	5.4	4.8	8.2	6.3
A few more	19.9	14.6	18.2	–	–	18.9	22.1	13.2	11.8	11.6
No more	43.8	60.8	46.9	–	–	41.9	44.2	38.4	35.3	49.6
Privatised:										
Some/more	28.4	22.8	29.7	–	–	32.9	28.4	43.7	44.8	32.5
Total	100.0	100.0	100.0	–	–	100.0	100.0	100.0	100.0	100.0
N. of respondents	176	171	192	–	–	301	317	357	846	838

Table 9.16 (*cont.*)

			Left school aged 17							
	1963	1964	1966	1969	1970	Feb. 1974	Oct. 1974	1979	1983	1987
Industries should be										
Nationalised:										
A lot more	0.0	5.8	7.1	–	–	5.4	7.5	2.4	3.3	4.8
A few more	13.3	11.6	11.8	–	–	15.6	17.0	10.6	12.2	9.7
No more	50.7	56.5	54.1	–	–	51.7	44.9	35.8	34.7	40.7
Privatised:										
Some/more	36.0	26.1	27.1	–	–	27.2	30.6	51.2	49.8	44.7
Total	100.0	100.0	100.0	–	–	100.0	100.0	100.0	100.0	100.0
N. of respondents	75	69	85	–	–	147	147	123	306	286

			Left school aged over 17							
	1963	1964	1966	1969	1970	Feb. 1974	Oct. 1974	1979	1983	1987
Industries should be										
Nationalised:										
A lot more	11.1	3.4	4.5	–	–	8.1	4.7	2.2	3.7	4.8
A few more	18.5	22.5	15.9	–	–	17.4	21.8	11.1	8.8	7.8
No more	45.7	53.9	43.2	–	–	50.6	51.8	38.9	34.8	51.0
Privatised:										
Some/more	24.7	20.2	36.4	–	–	23.8	21.8	47.8	52.7	36.4
Total	100.0	100.0	100.0	–	–	100.0	100.0	100.0	100.0	100.0
N. of respondents	81	89	88	–	–	172	170	180	458	358

Table 9.17 *Attitudes to nationalisation: university or polytechnic educated (%)*

	1963	1964	1966	1969	1970	Feb. 1974	Oct. 1974	1979	1983	1987
Industries should be										
Nationalised:										
A lot more	9.4	7.9	–	–	–	–	–	2.1	5.4	–
A few more	40.6	26.3	–	–	–	–	–	16.7	8.2	–
No more	31.3	50.0	–	–	–	–	–	40.6	38.2	–
Privatised:										
Some/more	18.8	15.8	–	–	–	–	–	40.6	48.2	–
Total	100.0	100.0	–	–	–	–	–	100.0	100.0	–
N. of respondents	32	38	–	–	–	–	–	96	368	–

Table 9.18 *Attitudes to nationalisation by region (%)*

	Scotland									
	1963	1964	1966	1969	1970	Feb. 1974	Oct. 1974	1979	1983	1987
Industries should be										
Nationalised:										
A lot more	15.1	15.4	11.2	–	–	15.0	11.7	11.7	11.9	10.4
A few more	10.5	19.1	20.2	–	–	15.0	21.7	12.4	11.3	10.4
No more	42.8	42.6	44.1	–	–	48.0	49.4	42.3	52.2	56.0
Privatised:										
Some/more	31.6	22.8	24.5	–	–	22.0	17.2	33.6	24.7	23.3
Total	100.0	100.0	100.0	–	–	100.0	100.0	100.0	100.0	100.0
N. of respondents	152	162	143	–	–	200	180	137	290	309

	Wales									
	1963	1964	1966	1969	1970	Feb. 1974	Oct. 1974	1979	1983	1987
Industries should be										
Nationalised:										
A lot more	14.7	17.6	10.7	–	–	15.4	15.6	12.4	7.3	8.6
A few more	13.3	17.6	21.3	–	–	18.8	32.1	14.4	9.9	19.6
No more	48.0	45.2	42.7	–	–	42.7	34.9	46.4	46.1	52.1
Privatised:										
Some/more	24.0	22.6	25.3	–	–	23.1	17.4	26.8	36.6	19.6
Total	100.0	100.0	100.0	–	–	100.0	100.0	100.0	100.0	100.0
N. of respondents	75	62	75	–	–	117	109	97	185	163

	The North									
	1963	1964	1966	1969	1970	Feb. 1974	Oct. 1974	1979	1983	1987
Industries should be										
Nationalised:										
A lot more	13.6	9.9	10.7	–	–	10.2	10.2	5.0	9.2	7.4
A few more	19.7	19.3	19.6	–	–	19.7	22.2	11.0	12.4	11.8
No more	41.1	51.0	49.5	–	–	46.9	45.8	45.4	40.6	53.3
Privatised:										
Some/more	25.6	19.9	20.1	–	–	23.1	21.7	38.6	37.8	27.6
Total	100.0	100.0	100.0	–	–	100.0	100.0	100.0	100.0	100.0
N. of respondents	457	467	438	–	–	618	607	482	936	882

Table 9.18 (*cont.*)

The Midlands

	1963	1964	1966	1969	1970	Feb. 1974	Oct. 1974	1979	1983	1987
Industries should be										
Nationalised:										
A lot more	11.1	8.2	7.8	–	–	8.2	11.4	6.6	7.3	6.5
A few more	16.0	21.8	23.8	–	–	19.6	24.4	10.6	9.7	7.9
No more	44.3	54.9	48.8	–	–	48.3	45.3	43.0	39.3	54.0
Privatised:										
Some/more	28.6	15.0	19.7	–	–	23.9	18.9	39.7	43.6	31.7
Total	100.0	100.0	100.0	–	–	100.0	100.0	100.0	100.0	100.0
N. of respondents	287	293	320	–	–	331	360	302	560	556

Greater London

	1963	1964	1966	1969	1970	Feb. 1974	Oct. 1974	1979	1983	1987
Industries should be										
Nationalised:										
A lot more	12.2	7.2	6.7	–	–	12.6	14.1	8.3	7.1	8.1
A few more	18.9	19.8	17.8	–	–	16.7	18.9	12.5	11.1	11.2
No more	40.4	44.3	48.5	–	–	45.2	44.7	42.2	35.4	46.4
Privatised:										
Some/more	28.5	28.7	27.0	–	–	25.5	22.3	37.0	46.4	34.4
Total	100.0	100.0	100.0	–	–	100.0	100.0	100.0	100.0	100.0
N. of respondents	270	237	270	–	–	239	206	192	443	384

The South

	1963	1964	1966	1969	1970	Feb. 1974	Oct. 1974	1979	1983	1987
Industries should be										
Nationalised:										
A lot more	9.9	4.7	7.3	–	–	7.2	5.1	3.1	3.2	4.2
A few more	16.5	19.7	18.4	–	–	17.9	21.8	9.2	9.3	7.6
No more	48.9	55.4	50.9	–	–	47.0	47.4	41.2	35.6	47.9
Privatised:										
Some/more	24.7	20.2	23.3	–	–	27.9	25.7	46.4	51.8	40.3
Total	100.0	100.0	100.0	–	–	100.0	100.0	100.0	100.0	100.0
N. of respondents	405	386	369	–	–	598	647	541	1078	1050

Table 9.19 *Importance of nationalisation issue: all respondents (%)*

	Feb. 1974	Oct. 1974	1979	1983	1987
Nationalisation was					
Extremely important	8.4	12.8	19.1	20.8	–
Fairly important	39.5	49.9	33.0	29.5	–
Not very important	52.1	37.3	47.9	49.7	–
Total	100.0	100.0	100.0	100.0	–
More nationalisation: extremely important	0.8	0.8	1.5	2.4	–
More privatisation: extremely important	3.4	4.8	11.1	10.4	–
N. of respondents	2373	2253	1815	3926	–

Table 9.20 *Importance of nationalisation issue by gender (%)*

Men					
	Feb. 1974	Oct. 1974	1979	1983	1987
Nationalisation was					
Extremely important	8.9	14.9	22.3	22.0	–
Fairly important	46.8	55.1	37.9	28.0	–
Not very important	44.3	30.0	39.7	50.0	–
Total	100.0	100.0	100.0	100.0	–
More nationalisation: extremely important	1.2	0.9	2.2	2.6	–
More privatisation: extremely important	3.1	4.8	12.8	12.0	–
N. of respondents	1143	1141	891	1863	–

Women					
	Feb. 1974	Oct. 1974	1979	1983	1987
Nationalisation was					
Extremely important	7.9	10.7	16.0	19.8	–
Fairly important	32.8	44.7	28.2	30.9	–
Not very important	59.3	44.7	55.7	49.4	–
Total	100.0	100.0	100.0	100.0	–
More nationalisation: extremely important	0.4	0.8	1.0	1.6	–
More privatisation: extremely important	3.9	4.7	10.4	9.1	–
N. of respondents	1230	1122	924	2063	–

Table 9.21 *Importance of nationalisation issue by age (%)*

	Aged under 25				
	Feb. 1974	Oct. 1974	1979	1983	1987
Nationalisation was					
Extremely important	5.7	9.9	14.6	13.8	–
Fairly important	32.5	47.9	36.7	34.6	–
Not very important	61.8	42.2	48.7	51.6	–
Total	100.0	100.0	100.0	100.0	–
More nationalisation: extremely important	0.4	1.1	0.6	2.3	–
More privatisation: extremely important	1.6	2.9	8.2	5.0	–
N. of respondents	246	263	158	555	–

	Aged 25–34				
	Feb. 1974	Oct. 1974	1979	1983	1987
Nationalisation was					
Extremely important	6.2	11.6	16.0	18.8	–
Fairly important	39.8	53.5	30.4	30.1	–
Not very important	54.0	34.9	53.6	51.1	–
Total	100.0	100.0	100.0	100.0	–
More nationalisation: extremely important	0.4	1.3	1.9	1.9	–
More privatisation: extremely important	2.4	5.0	10.0	9.0	–
N. of respondents	452	467	418	743	–

	Aged 35–44				
	Feb. 1974	Oct. 1974	1979	1983	1987
Nationalisation was					
Extremely important	7.8	11.9	19.0	24.4	–
Fairly important	39.6	51.0	33.3	28.6	–
Not very important	52.6	37.0	47.7	46.9	–
Total	100.0	100.0	100.0	100.0	–
More nationalisation: extremely important	0.7	0.5	0.6	2.1	–
More privatisation: extremely important	2.9	5.5	14.6	13.9	–
N. of respondents	409	386	321	711	–

Table 9.21 (*cont.*)

	Aged 45–54				
	Feb. 1974	Oct. 1974	1979	1983	1987
Nationalisation was					
Extremely important	9.7	12.6	17.0	24.2	–
Fairly important	44.2	53.5	39.4	30.1	–
Not very important	46.1	33.8	43.6	45.7	–
Total	100.0	100.0	100.0	100.0	–
More nationalisation: extremely important	0.5	0.2	0.9	1.9	–
More privatisation: extremely important	5.1	4.4	9.3	12.5	–
N. of respondents	432	396	335	630	–

	Aged 55–64				
	Feb. 1974	Oct. 1974	1979	1983	1987
Nationalisation was					
Extremely important	10.0	18.0	23.1	24.0	–
Fairly important	42.0	48.3	32.7	27.3	–
Not very important	48.0	33.7	44.2	48.6	–
Total	100.0	100.0	100.0	100.0	–
More nationalisation: extremely important	1.3	1.1	1.5	2.7	–
More privatisation: extremely important	3.4	5.2	12.7	11.5	–
N. of respondents	379	350	260	590	–

	Aged 65–74				
	Feb. 1974	Oct. 1974	1979	1983	1987
Nationalisation was					
Extremely important	10.3	13.6	24.8	21.0	–
Fairly important	41.8	45.2	29.7	25.8	–
Not very important	47.9	41.2	45.5	53.2	–
Total	100.0	100.0	100.0	100.0	–
More nationalisation: extremely important	1.7	1.0	3.5	2.1	–
More privatisation: extremely important	5.1	5.7	15.8	10.0	–
N. of respondents	292	272	202	439	–

Table 9.21 (*cont.*)

| | Aged over 74 | | | | |
	Feb. 1974	Oct. 1974	1979	1983	1987
Nationalisation was					
Extremely important	8.5	10.8	24.1	16.3	–
Fairly important	27.5	42.5	25.0	27.6	–
Not very important	64.1	46.7	50.9	56.2	–
Total	100.0	100.0	100.0	100.0	–
More nationalisation: extremely important	0.0	0.7	3.5	1.7	–
More privatisation: extremely important	2.8	3.6	10.3	10.0	–
N. of respondents	142	120	116	240	–

Table 9.22 *Importance of nationalisation issue: new electors (%)*

	Feb. 1974	Oct. 1974	1979	1983	1987
Nationalisation was					
Extremely important	8.3	14.4	16.2	13.0	–
Fairly important	32.1	43.2	35.0	34.1	–
Not very important	59.5	42.4	48.7	52.9	–
Total	100.0	100.0	100.0	100.0	–
More nationalisation: extremely important	0.0	1.4	0.9	2.3	–
More privatisation: extremely important	2.3	2.9	9.4	5.2	–
N. of respondents	84	139	117	308	–

Table 9.23 *Importance of nationalisation issue by political generation (%)*

| | First voted 1918–1935 | | | | |
	Feb. 1974	Oct. 1974	1979	1983	1987
Nationalisation was					
Extremely important	9.0	14.1	25.1	19.9	–
Fairly important	37.6	44.4	27.5	25.6	–
Not very important	53.4	41.5	47.5	54.5	–
Total	100.0	100.0	100.0	100.0	–
More nationalisation: extremely important	1.3	1.4	3.4	1.7	–
More privatisation: extremely important	3.5	4.6	13.9	10.4	–
N. of respondents	569	518	295	472	–

Table 9.23 (*cont.*)

	First voted 1936–1950				
	Feb. 1974	Oct. 1974	1979	1983	1987
Nationalisation was					
Extremely important	10.7	15.4	20.7	22.3	–
Fairly important	45.0	52.3	35.6	27.7	–
Not very important	44.3	32.3	43.7	50.0	–
Total	100.0	100.0	100.0	100.0	–
More nationalisation: extremely important	0.6	0.4	1.2	2.6	–
More privatisation: extremely important	5.0	5.7	11.2	10.8	–
N. of respondents	627	566	410	807	–

	First voted 1951–1970				
	Feb. 1974	Oct. 1974	1979	1983	1987
Nationalisation was					
Extremely important	6.9	10.6	17.3	23.7	–
Fairly important	39.4	53.1	33.6	29.0	–
Not very important	53.7	36.3	49.1	47.3	–
Total	100.0	100.0	100.0	100.0	–
More nationalisation: extremely important	0.6	0.9	1.2	1.9	–
More privatisation: extremely important	2.4	4.9	12.0	13.1	–
N. of respondents	974	979	839	1607	–

	First voted after 1970				
	Feb. 1974	Oct. 1974	1979	1983	1987
Nationalisation was					
Extremely important	5.4	13.4	15.5	16.7	–
Fairly important	31.3	44.7	33.6	32.9	–
Not very important	63.3	41.9	50.9	50.4	–
Total	100.0	100.0	100.0	100.0	–
More nationalisation: extremely important	0.0	1.1	1.1	2.4	–
More privatisation: extremely important	1.8	3.9	8.3	6.8	–
N. of respondents	166	179	265	723	–

Table 9.24 *Importance of nationalisation issue by vote (%)*

	Conservative voters				
	Feb. 1974	Oct. 1974	1979	1983	1987
Nationalisation was					
Extremely important	14.5	25.5	28.9	27.8	–
Fairly important	51.0	56.0	39.3	29.6	–
Not very important	34.5	18.5	31.8	42.7	–
Total	100.0	100.0	100.0	100.0	–
More nationalisation: extremely important	0.1	0.0	0.3	0.6	–
More privatisation: extremely important	7.5	12.4	21.8	20.3	–
N. of respondents	768	686	717	1445	–

	Labour voters				
	Feb. 1974	Oct. 1974	1979	1983	1987
Nationalisation was					
Extremely important	5.4	5.3	11.2	18.6	–
Fairly important	31.3	46.2	28.0	33.3	–
Not very important	63.4	48.6	60.8	48.0	–
Total	100.0	100.0	100.0	100.0	–
More nationalisation: extremely important	1.9	2.1	3.7	6.1	–
More privatisation: extremely important	0.6	0.5	2.5	1.1	–
N. of respondents	816	795	571	911	–

	Liberal voters				
	Feb. 1974	Oct. 1974	1979	1983	1987
Nationalisation was					
Extremely important	7.0	11.2	16.6	14.6	–
Fairly important	39.0	53.4	32.2	30.3	–
Not very important	54.0	35.3	51.2	55.1	–
Total	100.0	100.0	100.0	100.0	–
More nationalisation: extremely important	0.2	0.0	0.0	0.0	–
More privatisation: extremely important	3.5	3.4	9.5	6.3	–
N. of respondents	387	348	211	793	–

Table 9.24 (*cont.*)

	Voters for other parties				
	Feb. 1974	Oct. 1974	1979	1983	1987
Nationalisation was					
Extremely important	2.1	3.1	20.0	21.7	–
Fairly important	40.4	49.2	28.0	26.9	–
Not very important	57.4	47.7	52.0	51.4	–
Total	100.0	100.0	100.0	100.0	–
More nationalisation: extremely important	0.0	1.5	4.0	2.3	–
More privatisation: extremely important	2.1	1.5	4.0	4.7	–
N. of respondents	47	65	25	43	–

Table 9.25 *Importance of nationalisation issue by strength and direction of partisanship (%)*

	Very strong Conservative identifiers				
	Feb. 1974	Oct. 1974	1979	1983	1987
Nationalisation was					
Extremely important	16.2	36.0	46.4	38.5	–
Fairly important	53.9	48.1	28.6	23.9	–
Not very important	29.9	15.9	25.0	37.6	–
Total	100.0	100.0	100.0	100.0	–
More nationalisation: extremely important	0.4	0.0	0.6	0.0	–
More privatisation: extremely important	7.1	19.6	40.5	32.6	–
N. of respondents	271	214	168	356	–

	Fairly strong Conservative identifiers				
	Feb. 1974	Oct. 1974	1979	1983	1987
Nationalisation was					
Extremely important	15.0	22.1	26.6	27.2	–
Fairly important	50.4	56.3	44.3	31.5	–
Not very important	34.6	21.6	29.0	41.3	–
Total	100.0	100.0	100.0	100.0	–
More nationalisation: extremely important	0.0	0.0	0.3	0.0	–
More privatisation: extremely important	8.9	8.2	19.5	19.3	–
N. of respondents	419	416	379	673	–

Table 9.25 (*cont.*)

	Not very strong Conservative identifiers				
	Feb. 1974	Oct. 1974	1979	1983	1987
Nationalisation was					
Extremely important	9.9	14.8	19.0	19.1	–
Fairly important	44.0	58.5	39.5	29.9	–
Not very important	46.1	26.8	41.5	51.0	–
Total	100.0	100.0	100.0	100.0	–
More nationalisation: extremely important	0.0	0.0	0.5	0.0	–
More privatisation: extremely important	3.6	7.7	13.3	13.1	–
N. of respondents	191	183	195	451	–

	Very strong Liberal identifiers				
	Feb. 1974	Oct. 1974	1979	1983	1987
Nationalisation was					
Extremely important	16.7	10.9	14.3	20.5	–
Fairly important	41.7	47.8	35.7	25.6	–
Not very important	41.7	41.3	50.0	53.8	–
Total	100.0	100.0	100.0	100.0	–
More nationalisation: extremely important	0.0	0.0	0.0	0.0	–
More privatisation: extremely important	8.3	2.2	7.1	5.3	–
N. of respondents	36	46	28	78	–

	Fairly strong Liberal identifiers				
	Feb. 1974	Oct. 1974	1979	1983	1987
Nationalisation was					
Extremely important	7.2	10.4	16.5	14.7	–
Fairly important	37.3	52.2	35.0	29.3	–
Not very important	55.4	37.4	48.5	56.0	–
Total	100.0	100.0	100.0	100.0	–
More nationalisation: extremely important	0.0	0.0	0.0	0.2	–
More privatisation: extremely important	2.9	2.7	10.7	6.1	–
N. of respondents	166	182	103	307	–

Table 9.25 (*cont.*)

	Not very strong Liberal identifiers				
	Feb. 1974	Oct. 1974	1979	1983	1987
Nationalisation was					
Extremely important	2.5	7.5	17.0	15.3	–
Fairly important	42.0	51.7	28.4	28.4	–
Not very important	55.5	40.8	54.5	56.3	–
Total	100.0	100.0	100.0	100.0	–
More nationalisation: extremely important	0.0	0.0	0.0	1.0	–
More privatisation: extremely important	1.7	1.7	10.2	8.3	–
N. of respondents	119	120	88	320	–

	Very strong Labour identifiers				
	Feb. 1974	Oct. 1974	1979	1983	1987
Nationalisation was					
Extremely important	6.2	6.2	19.9	24.0	–
Fairly important	37.4	50.6	33.5	32.0	–
Not very important	56.4	43.2	46.6	44.0	–
Total	100.0	100.0	100.0	100.0	–
More nationalisation: extremely important	3.0	3.4	8.4	12.2	–
More privatisation: extremely important	0.5	0.6	2.1	1.2	–
N. of respondents	388	324	191	341	–

	Fairly strong Labour identifiers				
	Feb. 1974	Oct. 1974	1979	1983	1987
Nationalisation was					
Extremely important	4.4	4.4	7.0	16.2	–
Fairly important	30.3	45.1	27.9	32.5	–
Not very important	65.3	50.5	65.1	51.3	–
Total	100.0	100.0	100.0	100.0	–
More nationalisation: extremely important	0.9	1.6	0.9	7.6	–
More privatisation: extremely important	0.5	0.2	1.8	1.1	–
N. of respondents	412	432	341	495	–

Table 9.25 (*cont.*)

	Not very strong Labour identifiers				
	Feb. 1974	Oct. 1974	1979	1983	1987
Nationalisation was					
Extremely important	1.0	5.3	9.4	12.1	–
Fairly important	22.2	38.0	18.8	29.5	–
Not very important	76.8	56.7	71.8	58.4	–
Total	100.0	100.0	100.0	100.0	–
More nationalisation: extremely important	0.5	0.6	1.8	4.0	–
More privatisation: extremely important	0.0	3.5	2.4	1.0	–
N. of respondents	203	171	170	380	–

Table 9.26 *Importance of nationalisation issue by political generation and partisanship (%)*

	Conservative identifiers: first voted 1918–1935				
	Feb. 1974	Oct. 1974	1979	1983	1987
Nationalisation was					
Extremely important	12.1	20.2	32.0	24.8	–
Fairly important	45.8	45.9	33.3	24.1	–
Not very important	42.0	33.9	34.7	51.0	–
Total	100.0	100.0	100.0	100.0	–
More nationalisation: extremely important	0.0	0.0	1.3	0.9	–
More privatisation: extremely important	5.8	7.9	22.4	16.8	–
N. of respondents	264	218	147	226	–

	Labour identifiers: first voted 1918–1935				
	Feb. 1974	Oct. 1974	1979	1983	1987
Nationalisation was					
Extremely important	5.6	9.7	18.2	18.8	–
Fairly important	27.4	41.8	22.2	28.0	–
Not very important	67.1	48.5	59.6	53.2	–
Total	100.0	100.0	100.0	100.0	–
More nationalisation: extremely important	3.3	3.6	7.1	4.5	–
More privatisation: extremely important	0.4	1.5	2.0	3.0	–
N. of respondents	234	196	99	134	–

Table 9.26 (*cont.*)

	Conservative identifiers: first voted 1936–1950				
	Feb. 1974	Oct. 1974	1979	1983	1987
Nationalisation was					
Extremely important	19.5	27.5	30.4	29.9	–
Fairly important	56.0	58.1	42.2	25.7	–
Not very important	24.5	14.4	27.3	44.4	–
Total	100.0	100.0	100.0	100.0	–
More nationalisation: extremely important	0.4	0.0	0.0	0.3	–
More privatisation: extremely important	10.2	11.5	21.7	20.6	–
N. of respondents	241	222	161	310	–

	Labour identifiers: first voted 1936–1950				
	Feb. 1974	Oct. 1974	1979	1983	1987
Nationalisation was					
Extremely important	5.7	6.0	13.3	17.3	–
Fairly important	36.2	46.6	27.7	33.0	–
Not very important	58.1	47.4	59.0	49.8	–
Total	100.0	100.0	100.0	100.0	–
More nationalisation: extremely important	1.1	0.9	3.0	6.0	–
More privatisation: extremely important	0.9	1.3	2.4	1.4	–
N. of respondents	265	232	166	283	–

	Conservative identifiers: first voted 1951–1970				
	Feb. 1974	Oct. 1974	1979	1983	1987
Nationalisation was					
Extremely important	12.3	23.6	28.0	32.9	–
Fairly important	51.4	61.0	40.9	27.9	–
Not very important	36.3	15.3	31.1	39.3	–
Total	100.0	100.0	100.0	100.0	–
More nationalisation: extremely important	0.0	0.0	0.3	0.6	–
More privatisation: extremely important	6.4	12.6	22.9	26.0	–
N. of respondents	325	313	350	647	–

Table 9.26 (*cont.*)

	Labour identifiers: first voted 1951–1970				
	Feb. 1974	Oct. 1974	1979	1983	1987
Nationalisation was					
Extremely important	3.4	2.3	7.9	16.9	–
Fairly important	31.8	47.9	29.5	30.5	–
Not very important	64.8	49.8	64.7	52.6	–
Total	100.0	100.0	100.0	100.0	–
More nationalisation: extremely important	1.2	1.9	2.4	4.3	–
More privatisation: extremely important	0.2	0.2	2.1	1.2	–
N. of respondents	415	426	331	487	–

	Conservative identifiers: first voted after 1970				
	Feb. 1974	Oct. 1974	1979	1983	1987
Nationalisation was					
Extremely important	16.2	31.9	26.7	19.3	–
Fairly important	40.5	44.7	40.7	36.9	–
Not very important	43.2	23.4	32.6	43.8	–
Total	100.0	100.0	100.0	100.0	–
More nationalisation: extremely important	0.0	0.0	0.0	0.8	–
More privatisation: extremely important	5.3	0.8	23.3	13.3	–
N. of respondents	37	47	86	255	–

	Labour identifiers: first voted after 1970				
	Feb. 1974	Oct. 1974	1979	1983	1987
Nationalisation was					
Extremely important	1.3	6.9	11.0	17.6	–
Fairly important	26.9	41.7	29.4	32.9	–
Not very important	71.8	51.4	59.6	49.5	–
Total	100.0	100.0	100.0	100.0	–
More nationalisation: extremely important	0.0	2.8	1.8	4.8	–
More privatisation: extremely important	0.0	2.8	0.9	0.4	–
N. of respondents	78	72	109	251	–

Table 9.27 *Importance of nationalisation issue by social class (%)*

	Professional and managerial classes				
	Feb. 1974	Oct. 1974	1979	1983	1987
Nationalisation was					
Extremely important	10.6	16.7	21.6	23.6	–
Fairly important	54.0	61.7	34.9	32.1	–
Not very important	35.5	21.6	43.5	44.3	–
Total	100.0	100.0	100.0	100.0	–
More nationalisation: extremely important	0.9	0.3	0.8	1.6	–
More privatisation: extremely important	5.2	5.8	15.7	15.0	–
N. of respondents	341	347	370	1012	–

	Intermediate and routine non-manual classes				
	Feb. 1974	Oct. 1974	1979	1983	1987
Nationalisation was					
Extremely important	10.0	14.3	22.4	21.9	–
Fairly important	42.7	53.4	30.9	30.8	–
Not very important	47.3	32.4	46.7	47.4	–
Total	100.0	100.0	100.0	100.0	–
More nationalisation: extremely important	0.4	0.6	0.4	1.2	–
More privatisation: extremely important	4.6	6.5	16.1	12.2	–
N. of respondents	810	785	492	741	–

	Manual working class				
	Feb. 1974	Oct. 1974	1979	1983	1987
Nationalisation was					
Extremely important	6.9	10.4	16.5	19.6	–
Fairly important	33.2	44.2	32.6	26.9	–
Not very important	59.8	45.3	50.9	53.5	–
Total	100.0	100.0	100.0	100.0	–
More nationalisation: extremely important	1.1	1.3	2.5	3.8	–
More privatisation: extremely important	2.0	3.7	7.6	5.1	–
N. of respondents	1080	1017	884	1882	–

Table 9.28 *Importance of nationalisation issue by employment status (%)*

	Self-employed with employees				
	Feb. 1974	Oct. 1974	1979	1983	1987
Nationalisation was					
Extremely important	18.0	25.0	36.8	37.6	–
Fairly important	57.3	59.7	31.6	20.3	–
Not very important	24.7	15.3	31.6	42.0	–
Total	100.0	100.0	100.0	100.0	–
More nationalisation: extremely important	2.2	0.0	0.0	1.2	–
More privatisation: extremely important	11.9	12.5	29.8	30.2	–
N. of respondents	89	72	57	162	–
	Self-employed, no employees				
	Feb. 1974	Oct. 1974	1979	1983	1987
Nationalisation was					
Extremely important	7.5	22.0	24.3	30.4	–
Fairly important	53.8	48.4	47.1	24.3	–
Not very important	38.8	29.7	28.6	45.3	–
Total	100.0	100.0	100.0	100.0	–
More nationalisation: extremely important	0.0	0.0	0.0	2.2	–
More privatisation: extremely important	1.2	11.0	22.8	20.1	–
N. of respondents	80	91	70	134	–
	Managers				
	Feb. 1974	Oct. 1974	1979	1983	1987
Nationalisation was					
Extremely important	9.7	23.3	28.8	24.2	–
Fairly important	56.4	52.3	34.2	30.5	–
Not very important	33.9	24.4	37.0	45.2	–
Total	100.0	100.0	100.0	100.0	–
More nationalisation: extremely important	0.0	1.7	2.1	1.4	–
More privatisation: extremely important	5.4	8.1	16.4	16.2	–
N. of respondents	165	172	146	585	–

Table 9.28 (*cont.*)

	Foremen and supervisors				
	Feb. 1974	Oct. 1974	1979	1983	1987
Nationalisation was					
Extremely important	13.4	16.9	26.6	21.3	–
Fairly important	34.0	50.8	33.3	30.1	–
Not very important	52.6	32.2	40.1	48.6	–
Total	100.0	100.0	100.0	100.0	–
More nationalisation: extremely important	0.0	2.4	1.6	1.2	–
More privatisation: extremely important	4.1	4.1	16.1	10.6	–
N. of respondents	97	118	192	490	–

	Rank and file employees				
	Feb. 1974	Oct. 1974	1979	1983	1987
Nationalisation was					
Extremely important	7.9	10.3	15.9	19.0	–
Fairly important	37.8	50.6	32.2	30.1	–
Not very important	54.4	39.0	51.8	51.0	–
Total	100.0	100.0	100.0	100.0	–
More nationalisation: extremely important	1.0	0.7	2.1	2.2	–
More privatisation: extremely important	2.9	4.0	8.9	7.4	–
N. of respondents	1573	1481	903	2099	–

Table 9.29 *Importance of nationalisation issue: unemployed (%)*

	Feb. 1974	Oct. 1974	1979	1983	1987
Nationalisation was					
Extremely important	2.2	10.3	10.8	16.9	–
Fairly important	46.7	43.6	27.0	29.6	–
Not very important	51.1	46.2	62.2	53.5	–
Total	100.0	100.0	100.0	100.0	–
More nationalisation: extremely important	0.0	2.6	2.7	5.4	–
More privatisation: extremely important	2.2	5.1	2.7	6.3	–
N. of respondents	45	39	37	240	–

Table 9.30 *Importance of nationalisation issue by class and employment status (%)*

	Professional and managerial classes: self-employed				
	Feb. 1974	Oct. 1974	1979	1983	1987
Nationalisation was					
Extremely important	10.4	20.9	28.9	31.3	–
Fairly important	70.8	62.8	34.2	25.4	–
Not very important	18.8	16.3	36.8	43.3	–
Total	100.0	100.0	100.0	100.0	–
More nationalisation: extremely important	0.0	0.0	0.0	0.0	–
More privatisation: extremely important	10.4	7.0	23.7	26.3	–
N. of respondents	48	43	38	134	–

	Professional and managerial classes: employees				
	Feb. 1974	Oct. 1974	1979	1983	1987
Nationalisation was					
Extremely important	10.3	16.9	21.5	22.6	–
Fairly important	53.8	60.5	35.5	33.6	–
Not very important	36.0	22.6	43.0	43.8	–
Total	100.0	100.0	100.0	100.0	–
More nationalisation: extremely important	1.2	0.4	1.2	1.4	–
More privatisation: extremely important	4.3	5.7	15.1	15.4	–
N. of respondents	253	261	251	849	–

	Intermediate and routine non-manual classes: self-employed				
	Feb. 1974	Oct. 1974	1979	1983	1987
Nationalisation was					
Extremely important	15.6	25.9	30.9	34.5	–
Fairly important	47.9	51.9	36.4	27.6	–
Not very important	36.5	22.2	32.7	37.9	–
Total	100.0	100.0	100.0	100.0	–
More nationalisation: extremely important	2.1	0.0	0.0	0.0	–
More privatisation: extremely important	1.3	14.8	27.3	30.5	–
N. of respondents	96	81	55	29	–

Table 9.30 (*cont.*)

	Intermediate and routine non-manual classes: employees				
	Feb. 1974	Oct. 1974	1979	1983	1987
Nationalisation was					
Extremely important	9.5	12.5	22.1	21.7	–
Fairly important	41.3	53.9	31.1	30.9	–
Not very important	49.2	33.6	46.9	47.4	–
Total	100.0	100.0	100.0	100.0	–
More nationalisation: extremely important	0.1	0.6	0.5	0.7	–
More privatisation: extremely important	4.7	5.3	15.5	14.9	–
N. of respondents	664	657	367	686	–
	Manual working class: self-employed				
	Feb. 1974	Oct. 1974	1979	1983	1987
Nationalisation was					
Extremely important	8.3	20.5	29.4	37.7	–
Fairly important	54.2	46.2	52.9	18.4	–
Not very important	37.5	33.3	17.6	43.9	–
Total	100.0	100.0	100.0	100.0	–
More nationalisation: extremely important	0.0	0.0	0.0	0.0	–
More privatisation: extremely important	0.0	10.3	26.5	34.8	–
N. of respondents	24	39	34	114	–
	Manual working class: employees				
	Feb. 1974	Oct. 1974	1979	1983	1987
Nationalisation was					
Extremely important	6.9	10.2	16.5	18.7	–
Fairly important	33.6	45.1	32.3	27.4	–
Not very important	59.6	44.7	51.3	53.9	–
Total	100.0	100.0	100.0	100.0	–
More nationalisation: extremely important	1.2	1.3	3.2	4.2	–
More privatisation: extremely important	2.0	3.2	6.5	6.9	–
N. of respondents	905	845	620	1612	–

Table 9.31 *Importance of nationalisation issue by trade union membership (%)*

	Trade union members				
	Feb. 1974	Oct. 1974	1979	1983	1987
Nationalisation was					
Extremely important	5.9	8.2	16.5	21.7	–
Fairly important	41.8	49.8	34.5	28.3	–
Not very important	52.4	42.0	48.9	50.0	–
Total	100.0	100.0	100.0	100.0	–
More nationalisation: extremely important	1.3	2.3	2.6	3.4	–
More privatisation: extremely important	1.6	2.1	6.8	7.4	–
N. of respondents	613	535	544	1039	–

	Respondent is married to a trade union member				
	Feb. 1974	Oct. 1974	1979	1983	1987
Nationalisation was					
Extremely important	7.6	8.0	14.7	19.2	–
Fairly important	33.0	36.7	33.8	30.7	–
Not very important	59.5	55.2	51.5	50.2	–
Total	100.0	100.0	100.0	100.0	–
More nationalisation: extremely important	0.7	0.8	0.4	1.2	–
More privatisation: extremely important	4.0	2.8	9.2	10.9	–
N. of respondents	291	263	272	431	–

	Neither respondent nor spouse belongs to a trade union				
	Feb. 1974	Oct. 1974	1979	1983	1987
Nationalisation was					
Extremely important	9.6	14.2	21.7	20.7	–
Fairly important	39.9	52.0	31.9	29.8	–
Not very important	50.5	33.9	51.5	50.2	–
Total	100.0	100.0	100.0	100.0	–
More nationalisation: extremely important	0.6	0.4	1.4	1.7	–
More privatisation: extremely important	4.0	5.6	14.8	11.6	–
N. of respondents	1469	1432	999	2440	–

Table 9.32 *Importance of nationalisation issue by economic sector (%)*

	Works in private sector				
	Feb. 1974	Oct. 1974	1979	1983	1987
Nationalisation was					
Extremely important	–	13.3	18.8	18.9	–
Fairly important	–	49.6	34.0	29.0	–
Not very important	–	37.1	47.2	52.1	–
Total	–	100.0	100.0	100.0	–
More nationalisation: extremely important	–	1.2	1.8	1.8	–
More privatisation: extremely important	–	5.3	11.7	10.3	–
N. of respondents	–	1035	738	2118	–
	Works in public sector				
	Feb. 1974	Oct. 1974	1979	1983	1987
Nationalisation was					
Extremely important	–	9.6	18.6	22.2	–
Fairly important	–	55.6	29.5	32.1	–
Not very important	–	34.8	51.9	45.7	–
Total	–	100.0	100.0	100.0	–
More nationalisation: extremely important	–	0.8	2.4	2.9	–
More privatisation: extremely important	–	2.9	9.0	8.0	–
N. of respondents	–	511	457	1255	–

Table 9.33 *Importance of nationalisation issue by school leaving age (%)*

	Left school aged under 15				
	Feb. 1974	Oct. 1974	1979	1983	1987
Nationalisation was					
Extremely important	9.0	12.7	19.9	19.1	–
Fairly important	36.2	45.9	30.6	26.6	–
Not very important	54.7	41.5	49.4	54.3	–
Total	100.0	100.0	100.0	100.0	–
More nationalisation: extremely important	1.1	1.2	1.8	2.3	–
More privatisation: extremely important	3.5	4.2	10.2	7.7	–
N. of respondents	1029	931	607	1153	–

Table 9.33 (*cont.*)

	Left school aged 15				
	Feb. 1974	Oct. 1974	1979	1983	1987
Nationalisation was					
Extremely important	5.8	11.4	16.9	22.2	–
Fairly important	36.7	45.1	31.9	27.8	–
Not very important	57.5	43.6	51.1	50.0	–
Total	100.0	100.0	100.0	100.0	–
More nationalisation: extremely important	0.4	0.9	2.5	2.6	–
More privatisation: extremely important	1.7	5.3	11.4	10.4	–
N. of respondents	673	659	526	1003	–

	Left school aged 16				
	Feb. 1974	Oct. 1974	1979	1983	1987
Nationalisation was					
Extremely important	9.6	13.8	19.2	19.9	–
Fairly important	42.9	62.0	33.6	31.6	–
Not very important	47.5	24.2	47.2	48.4	–
Total	100.0	100.0	100.0	100.0	–
More nationalisation: extremely important	0.0	0.3	0.3	2.1	–
More privatisation: extremely important	4.2	5.5	10.7	10.6	–
N. of respondents	324	326	354	951	–

	Left school aged 17				
	Feb. 1974	Oct. 1974	1979	1983	1987
Nationalisation was					
Extremely important	9.0	17.0	25.2	24.6	–
Fairly important	55.1	56.9	39.8	31.7	–
Not very important	35.9	26.1	35.0	43.7	–
Total	100.0	100.0	100.0	100.0	–
More nationalisation: extremely important	0.6	0.7	0.8	1.2	–
More privatisation: extremely important	3.2	7.8	17.9	14.6	–
N. of respondents	156	153	123	328	–

Table 9.33 (*cont.*)

	Left school aged over 17				
	Feb. 1974	Oct. 1974	1979	1983	1987
Nationalisation was					
Extremely important	11.9	14.1	18.2	21.2	–
Fairly important	49.7	62.1	39.0	33.5	–
Not very important	38.4	23.7	42.8	45.3	–
Total	100.0	100.0	100.0	100.0	–
More nationalisation: extremely important	1.6	1.1	1.6	1.0	–
More privatisation: extremely important	7.9	4.5	13.4	14.1	–
N. of respondents	177	177	187	481	–

Table 9.34 *Importance of nationalisation issue by region (%)*

	Scotland				
	Feb. 1974	Oct. 1974	1979	1983	1987
Nationalisation was					
Extremely important	5.2	4.6	15.7	18.7	–
Fairly important	34.8	47.4	31.3	28.4	–
Not very important	60.0	47.9	53.0	52.9	–
Total	100.0	100.0	100.0	100.0	–
More nationalisation: extremely important	0.9	0.5	3.7	3.0	–
More privatisation: extremely important	1.7	0.5	6.7	3.0	–
N. of respondents	230	194	134	363	–
	Wales				
	Feb. 1974	Oct. 1974	1979	1983	1987
Nationalisation was					
Extremely important	7.0	4.8	20.8	15.6	–
Fairly important	42.6	45.2	36.6	34.6	–
Not very important	50.4	50.0	42.6	49.8	–
Total	100.0	100.0	100.0	100.0	–
More nationalisation: extremely important	1.6	0.8	5.0	1.0	–
More privatisation: extremely important	2.3	1.6	7.0	6.8	–
N. of respondents	129	126	100	205	–

Table 9.34 (*cont.*)

	The North				
	Feb. 1974	Oct. 1974	1979	1983	1987
Nationalisation was					
Extremely important	7.4	12.6	18.4	20.5	–
Fairly important	38.5	50.1	34.4	28.9	–
Not very important	54.2	37.3	47.2	50.6	–
Total	100.0	100.0	100.0	100.0	–
More nationalisation: extremely important	0.7	1.2	1.6	2.7	–
More privatisation: extremely important	2.4	6.2	13.0	10.0	–
N. of respondents	707	659	500	1048	–

	The Midlands				
	Feb. 1974	Oct. 1974	1979	1983	1987
Nationalisation was					
Extremely important	8.4	10.3	17.9	22.3	–
Fairly important	33.3	50.3	34.8	25.3	–
Not very important	58.3	39.5	47.3	52.3	–
Total	100.0	100.0	100.0	100.0	–
More nationalisation: extremely important	0.5	0.5	1.3	2.2	–
More privatisation: extremely important	3.5	3.4	9.7	11.6	–
N. of respondents	369	380	319	629	–

	Greater London				
	Feb. 1974	Oct. 1974	1979	1983	1987
Nationalisation was					
Extremely important	9.2	14.4	18.0	20.0	–
Fairly important	44.4	51.8	32.5	31.0	–
Not very important	46.4	33.8	49.5	49.0	–
Total	100.0	100.0	100.0	100.0	–
More nationalisation: extremely important	1.5	1.8	2.0	3.3	–
More privatisation: extremely important	5.4	3.2	10.5	9.5	–
N. of respondents	261	222	200	486	–

Table 9.34 (*cont.*)

	The South				
	Feb. 1974	Oct. 1974	1979	1983	1987
Nationalisation was					
Extremely important	10.5	17.7	21.4	22.2	–
Fairly important	43.1	50.6	30.7	30.9	–
Not very important	46.4	31.7	48.0	46.9	–
Total	100.0	100.0	100.0	100.0	–
More nationalisation: extremely important	0.6	0.6	0.5	1.0	–
More privatisation: extremely important	4.7	7.2	13.7	13.6	–
N. of respondents	677	682	561	1196	–

Chapter 10

THE WELFARE STATE

1. The importance of the social services issue question was first asked in February 1974 and thereafter in October 1974, 1979 and 1983.
2. In February 1974, October 1974 and 1979 the question refers to 'social services and benefits'; in 1983 it refers to 'health and social services'. The strongest category of importance in February 1974 and October 1974 is 'the most important single thing', while in 1979 and 1983 it is 'extremely important'. These categories are treated as equivalent for the purposes of comparison.
3. The questions on government expenditure on poverty, economic redistribution and welfare benefits were first asked in October 1974 and in every election thereafter.

See Appendix E, pp. 488, 492, 494 and 495 on the construction of these variables.

Table 10.1 *Importance of social services as an issue: all respondents (%)*

	Feb. 1974	Oct. 1974	1979	1983	1987
Social services and benefits were					
Extremely important	6.7	7.4	23.0	62.4	–
Fairly important	48.5	52.2	41.4	32.0	–
Not very important	44.9	40.5	35.5	5.3	–
Total	100.0	100.0	100.0	100.0	–
N. of respondents	2390	2262	1837	3939	–

Table 10.2 *Importance of social services as an issue by gender (%)*

	Men				
	Feb. 1974	Oct. 1974	1979	1983	1987
Social services and benefits were					
Extremely important	5.2	6.8	21.4	56.8	–
Fairly important	49.7	49.8	41.7	36.3	–
Not very important	45.1	43.4	37.0	6.9	–
Total	100.0	100.0	100.0	100.0	–
N. of respondents	1143	1129	893	1865	–
	Women				
	Feb. 1974	Oct. 1974	1979	1983	1987
Social services and benefits were					
Extremely important	7.9	7.9	24.6	67.1	–
Fairly important	47.3	54.5	41.2	28.5	–
Not very important	44.7	37.5	34.2	4.3	–
Total	100.0	100.0	100.0	100.0	–
N. of respondents	1247	1133	944	2075	–

Table 10.3 *Importance of social services as an issue by age (%)*

	Age under 25				
	Feb. 1974	Oct. 1974	1979	1983	1987
Social services and benefits were					
Extremely important	4.4	5.4	17.8	52.1	–
Fairly important	44.0	44.4	44.2	39.6	–
Not very important	51.6	50.2	38.0	8.3	–
Total	100.0	100.0	100.0	100.0	–
N. of respondents	248	261	163	556	–
	Aged 25–34				
	Feb. 1974	Oct. 1974	1979	1983	1987
Social services and benefits were					
Extremely important	6.2	3.6	17.3	58.8	–
Fairly important	42.5	48.4	41.7	33.6	–
Not very important	51.3	48.0	41.0	7.6	–
Total	100.0	100.0	100.0	100.0	–
N. of respondents	454	469	422	743	–

Table 10.3 (*cont.*)

	Aged 35–44				
	Feb. 1974	Oct. 1974	1979	1983	1987
Social services and benefits were					
Extremely important	3.4	4.4	20.6	54.7	–
Fairly important	47.8	49.7	40.8	38.8	–
Not very important	48.8	45.9	38.7	6.5	–
Total	100.0	100.0	100.0	100.0	–
N. of respondents	414	386	326	715	–
	Aged 45–54				
	Feb. 1974	Oct. 1974	1979	1983	1987
Social services and benefits were					
Extremely important	5.5	5.6	23.4	66.9	–
Fairly important	49.3	56.1	42.9	29.5	–
Not very important	45.2	38.3	33.6	3.7	–
Total	100.0	100.0	100.0	100.0	–
N. of respondents	436	394	333	633	–
	Aged 55–64				
	Feb. 1974	Oct. 1974	1979	1983	1987
Social services and benefits were					
Extremely important	8.2	11.7	27.7	67.8	–
Fairly important	56.6	56.3	43.1	28.0	–
Not very important	35.3	32.0	29.2	4.2	–
Total	100.0	100.0	100.0	100.0	–
N. of respondents	380	350	260	593	–
	Aged 65–74				
	Feb. 1974	Oct. 1974	1979	1983	1987
Social services and benefits were					
Extremely important	13.5	15.5	31.9	72.7	–
Fairly important	53.4	58.7	37.7	24.3	–
Not very important	33.1	25.8	30.4	3.0	–
Total	100.0	100.0	100.0	100.0	–
N. of respondents	296	271	207	438	–

Table 10.3 (*cont.*)

	Aged over 75				
	Feb. 1974	Oct. 1974	1979	1983	1987
Social services and benefits were					
Extremely important	7.8	10.7	30.8	73.1	–
Fairly important	42.6	54.1	35.0	23.5	–
Not very important	49.6	35.2	34.2	3.3	–
Total	100.0	100.0	100.0	100.0	–
N. of respondents	141	122	120	244	–

Table 10.4 *Importance of social services as an issue by marital status (%)*

	Single				
	Feb. 1974	Oct. 1974	1979	1983	1987
Social services and benefits were					
Extremely important	5.6	–	20.5	51.4	–
Fairly important	46.8	–	45.7	39.5	–
Not very important	47.6	–	33.8	9.1	–
Total	100.0	–	100.0	100.0	–
N. of respondents	340	–	219	693	–
	Married				
	Feb. 1974	Oct. 1974	1979	1983	1987
Social services and benefits were					
Extremely important	6.2	6.3	22.0	63.5	–
Fairly important	48.6	52.1	41.5	31.6	–
Not very important	45.2	41.6	36.6	4.9	–
Total	100.0	100.0	100.0	100.0	–
N. of respondents	1761	1700	1324	2744	–
	Separated and divorced				
	Feb. 1974	Oct. 1974	1979	1983	1987
Social services and benefits were					
Extremely important	18.5	–	37.5	68.3	–
Fairly important	44.4	–	37.5	26.8	–
Not very important	37.0	–	25.0	4.9	–
Total	100.0	–	100.0	100.0	–
N. of respondents	27	–	80	181	–

Table 10.4 (*cont.*)

	Widowed				
	Feb. 1974	Oct. 1974	1979	1983	1987
Social services and benefits were					
Extremely important	9.9	–	25.9	71.5	–
Fairly important	50.0	–	37.8	24.4	–
Not very important	40.1	–	36.3	4.0	–
Total	100.0	–	100.0	100.0	–
N. of respondents	262	–	193	319	–

Table 10.5 *Importance of social services as an issue by marital status and gender (%)*

	Single men				
	Feb. 1974	Oct. 1974	1979	1983	1987
Social services and benefits were					
Extremely important	4.9	–	17.1	47.8	–
Fairly important	46.2	–	47.2	41.4	–
Not very important	48.9	–	35.8	10.9	–
Total	100.0	–	100.0	100.0	–
N. of respondents	184	–	123	397	–
	Single women				
	Feb. 1974	Oct. 1974	1979	1983	1987
Social services and benefits were					
Extremely important	6.4	–	25.0	56.2	–
Fairly important	47.4	–	43.8	37.0	–
Not very important	46.2	–	31.3	6.7	–
Total	100.0	–	100.0	100.0	–
N. of respondents	156	–	96	296	–
	Married men				
	Feb. 1974	Oct. 1974	1979	1983	1987
Social services and benefits were					
Extremely important	5.1	6.3	21.1	58.7	–
Fairly important	50.2	50.3	40.9	35.6	–
Not very important	44.8	43.4	38.1	5.8	–
Total	100.0	100.0	100.0	100.0	–
N. of respondents	889	890	678	1338	–

Table 10.5 (*cont.*)

	Married women				
	Feb. 1974	Oct. 1974	1979	1983	1987
Social services and benefits were					
Extremely important	7.3	6.3	22.9	68.1	–
Fairly important	47.0	54.0	42.1	27.9	–
Not very important	45.6	39.8	35.0	4.0	–
Total	100.0	100.0	100.0	100.0	–
N. of respondents	872	810	646	1406	–

	Divorced and separated men				
	Feb. 1974	Oct. 1974	1979	1983	1987
Social services and benefits were					
Extremely important	(0.0)	–	35.5	60.4	–
Fairly important	(50.0)	–	38.7	30.1	–
Not very important	(50.0)	–	25.8	9.5	–
Total	(100.0)	–	100.0	100.0	–
N. of respondents	8	–	31	63	–

	Divorced and separated women				
	Feb. 1974	Oct. 1974	1979	1983	1987
Social services and benefits were					
Extremely important	(26.3)	–	38.8	72.5	–
Fairly important	(42.1)	–	36.7	25.0	–
Not very important	(31.6)	–	24.5	2.5	–
Total	(100.0)	–	100.0	100.0	–
N. of respondents	19	–	49	118	–

	Widowed men				
	Feb. 1974	Oct. 1974	1979	1983	1987
Social services and benefits were					
Extremely important	9.7	–	28.0	69.3	–
Fairly important	53.2	–	38.0	27.7	–
Not very important	37.1	–	34.0	3.0	–
Total	100.0	–	100.0	100.0	–
N. of respondents	62	–	50	65	–

Table 10.5 (*cont.*)

	Widowed women				
	Feb. 1974	Oct. 1974	1979	1983	1987
Social services and benefits were					
Extremely important	10.0	–	25.2	72.1	–
Fairly important	49.0	–	37.8	23.6	–
Not very important	41.0	–	37.1	4.3	–
Total	100.0	–	100.0	100.0	–
N. of respondents	200	–	143	254	–

Table 10.6 *Importance of social services as an issue: new electors (%)*

	Feb. 1974	Oct. 1974	1979	1983	1987
Social services and benefits were					
Extremely important	4.2	–	19.7	48.6	–
Fairly important	43.1	–	42.6	41.6	–
Not very important	52.7	–	37.7	9.8	–
Total	100.0	–	100.0	100.0	–
N. of respondents	167	–	122	309	–

Table 10.7 *Importance of social services as an issue by political generation (%)*

	First voted 1918–1935				
	Feb. 1974	Oct. 1974	1979	1983	1987
Social services and benefits were					
Extremely important	10.5	14.7	30.9	72.0	–
Fairly important	51.4	55.0	36.2	25.5	–
Not very important	38.1	30.3	32.9	2.6	–
Total	100.0	100.0	100.0	100.0	–
N. of respondents	570	518	304	475	–
	First voted 1936–1950				
	Feb. 1974	Oct. 1974	1979	1983	1987
Social services and benefits were					
Extremely important	6.8	6.5	26.9	69.5	–
Fairly important	53.1	58.4	42.5	26.3	–
Not very important	40.1	35.0	30.6	4.2	–
Total	100.0	100.0	100.0	100.0	–
N. of respondents	633	565	409	810	–

Table 10.7 (*cont.*)

	First voted 1951–1970				
	Feb. 1974	Oct. 1974	1979	1983	1987
Social services and benefits were					
Extremely important	4.8	4.3	20.2	60.5	–
Fairly important	45.1	49.7	41.4	33.9	–
Not very important	50.1	46.0	38.3	5.7	–
Total	100.0	100.0	100.0	100.0	–
N. of respondents	982	981	845	1614	–
	First voted after 1970				
	Feb. 1974	Oct. 1974	1979	1983	1987
Social services and benefits were					
Extremely important	4.2	5.1	16.9	57.2	–
Fairly important	43.1	40.1	44.9	35.8	–
Not very important	52.7	54.8	38.2	6.9	–
Total	100.0	100.0	100.0	100.0	–
N. of respondents	167	177	272	723	–

Table 10.8 *Importance of social services as an issue by vote (%)*

	Conservative voters				
	Feb. 1974	Oct. 1974	1979	1983	1987
Social services and benefits were					
Extremely important	3.5	5.5	20.2	48.6	–
Fairly important	48.2	49.9	42.1	44.8	–
Not very important	48.3	44.6	37.7	6.6	–
Total	100.0	100.0	100.0	100.0	–
N. of respondents	772	686	724	1447	–
	Labour voters				
	Feb. 1974	Oct. 1974	1979	1983	1987
Social services and benefits were					
Extremely important	10.0	9.8	28.5	81.3	–
Fairly important	51.0	56.0	42.2	16.2	–
Not very important	39.0	34.2	29.3	2.4	–
Total	100.0	100.0	100.0	100.0	–
N. of respondents	826	795	576	917	–

Table 10.8 (*cont.*)

| | Liberal voters | | | | |
	Feb. 1974	Oct. 1974	1979	1983	1987
Social services and benefits were					
Extremely important	6.6	5.8	21.0	64.9	–
Fairly important	42.5	54.3	43.8	29.1	–
Not very important	50.9	39.9	35.2	5.9	–
Total	100.0	100.0	100.0	100.0	–
N. of respondents	391	346	210	794	–
	Voters for other parties				
	Feb. 1974	Oct. 1974	1979	1983	1987
Social services and benefits were					
Extremely important	2.1	4.6	20.0	76.0	–
Fairly important	57.4	26.2	28.0	14.8	–
Not very important	40.4	69.2	52.0	9.2	–
Total	100.0	100.0	100.0	100.0	–
N. of respondents	47	65	25	43	–

Table 10.9 *Importance of social services as an issue by strength and direction of partisanship (%)*

| | Very strong Conservative identifiers | | | | |
	Feb. 1974	Oct. 1974	1979	1983	1987
Social services and benefits were					
Extremely important	4.4	8.9	24.3	55.6	–
Fairly important	49.1	54.7	37.9	38.8	–
Not very important	46.5	36.4	37.9	5.6	–
Total	100.0	100.0	100.0	100.0	–
N. of respondents	271	214	169	356	–
	Fairly strong Conservative identifiers				
	Feb. 1974	Oct. 1974	1979	1983	1987
Social services and benefits were					
Extremely important	3.8	5.1	18.5	45.8	–
Fairly important	47.4	50.8	42.6	45.8	–
Not very important	48.8	44.1	38.9	8.3	–
Total	100.0	100.0	100.0	100.0	–
N. of respondents	422	415	383	674	–

Table 10.9 (*cont.*)

	Not very strong Conservative identifiers				
	Feb. 1974	Oct. 1974	1979	1983	1987
Social services and benefits were					
Extremely important	2.6	4.4	17.9	48.9	–
Fairly important	39.8	40.1	40.3	45.1	–
Not very important	57.6	55.5	41.8	6.0	–
Total	100.0	100.0	100.0	100.0	–
N. of respondents	191	182	196	452	–

	Very strong Liberal identifiers				
	Feb. 1974	Oct. 1974	1979	1983	1987
Social services and benefits were					
Extremely important	5.6	8.7	34.5	73.1	–
Fairly important	50.0	52.2	34.5	23.1	–
Not very important	44.4	39.1	31.0	3.8	–
Total	100.0	100.0	100.0	100.0	–
N. of respondents	36	46	29	78	–

	Fairly strong Liberal identifiers				
	Feb. 1974	Oct. 1974	1979	1983	1987
Social services and benefits were					
Extremely important	6.6	6.0	23.6	61.2	–
Fairly important	44.9	59.3	42.5	33.6	–
Not very important	48.5	34.6	34.0	5.2	–
Total	100.0	100.0	100.0	100.0	–
N. of respondents	167	182	106	307	–

	Not very strong Liberal identifiers				
	Feb. 1974	Oct. 1974	1979	1983	1987
Social services and benefits were					
Extremely important	5.0	2.5	13.8	62.8	–
Fairly important	43.3	47.9	42.5	31.6	–
Not very important	51.7	49.6	43.7	5.6	–
Total	100.0	100.0	100.0	100.0	–
N. of respondents	120	119	87	320	–

Table 10.9 (*cont.*)

	Very strong Labour identifiers				
	Feb. 1974	Oct. 1974	1979	1983	1987
Social services and benefits were					
Extremely important	13.7	14.9	40.5	88.4	–
Fairly important	55.2	57.5	37.4	9.9	–
Not very important	31.2	27.6	22.1	1.7	–
Total	100.0	100.0	100.0	100.0	–
N. of respondents	388	322	190	345	–

	Fairly strong Labour identifiers				
	Feb. 1974	Oct. 1974	1979	1983	1987
Social services and benefits were					
Extremely important	8.8	7.6	23.6	79.8	–
Fairly important	55.4	54.8	50.4	18.8	–
Not very important	35.8	37.6	25.9	1.4	–
Total	100.0	100.0	100.0	100.0	–
N. of respondents	419	436	343	495	–

	Not very strong Labour identifiers				
	Feb. 1974	Oct. 1974	1979	1983	1987
Social services and benefits were					
Extremely important	5.4	4.1	20.0	68.8	–
Fairly important	39.5	51.2	37.1	26.3	–
Not very important	55.1	44.8	42.9	4.9	–
Total	100.0	100.0	100.0	100.0	–
N. of respondents	205	172	175	384	–

Table 10.10 *Importance of social services as an issue: non-partisans (%)*

	Feb. 1974	Oct. 1974	1979	1983	1987
Social services and benefits were					
Extremely important	4.1	8.0	26.4	51.3	–
Fairly important	43.2	50.7	28.6	34.7	–
Not very important	52.7	41.3	45.1	14.0	–
Total	100.0	100.0	100.0	100.0	–
N. of respondents	74	75	91	193	–

Table 10.11 *Importance of social services as an issue by political generation and partisanship (%)*

	Conservative identifiers: first voted 1918–1935				
	Feb. 1974	Oct. 1974	1979	1983	1987
Social services and benefits were					
Extremely important	5.7	11.0	22.0	62.2	–
Fairly important	51.3	50.7	36.7	35.6	–
Not very important	43.0	38.4	41.3	2.2	–
Total	100.0	100.0	100.0	100.0	–
N. of respondents	263	219	150	226	–

	Labour identifiers: first voted 1918–1935				
	Feb. 1974	Oct. 1974	1979	1983	1987
Social services and benefits were					
Extremely important	15.0	19.3	41.7	85.3	–
Fairly important	52.4	56.3	39.8	12.4	–
Not very important	32.6	24.4	18.4	2.3	–
Total	100.0	100.0	100.0	100.0	–
N. of respondents	233	197	103	137	–

	Conservative identifiers: first voted 1936–1950				
	Feb. 1974	Oct. 1974	1979	1983	1987
Social services and benefits were					
Extremely important	5.0	6.8	25.2	56.0	–
Fairly important	48.8	54.3	37.4	37.8	–
Not very important	46.3	38.9	37.4	6.2	–
Total	100.0	100.0	100.0	100.0	–
N. of respondents	242	221	163	312	–

	Labour identifiers: first voted 1936–1950				
	Feb. 1974	Oct. 1974	1979	1983	1987
Social services and benefits were					
Extremely important	10.4	8.2	30.5	84.2	–
Fairly important	58.6	61.4	44.5	13.4	–
Not very important	31.0	30.5	25.0	2.5	–
Total	100.0	100.0	100.0	100.0	–
N. of respondents	268	233	164	283	–

Table 10.11 (*cont.*)

	Conservative identifiers: first voted 1951–1970				
	Feb. 1974	Oct. 1974	1979	1983	1987
Social services and benefits were					
Extremely important	1.2	1.9	18.5	45.9	–
Fairly important	43.4	49.5	42.7	45.9	–
Not very important	55.4	48.6	38.7	8.3	–
Total	100.0	100.0	100.0	100.0	–
N. of respondents	327	311	351	647	–

	Labour identifiers: first voted 1951–1970				
	Feb. 1974	Oct. 1974	1979	1983	1987
Social services and benefits were					
Extremely important	7.8	6.1	23.3	80.4	–
Fairly important	49.1	52.6	41.7	18.4	–
Not very important	43.1	41.4	35.0	1.2	–
Total	100.0	100.0	100.0	100.0	–
N. of respondents	422	428	331	492	–

	Conservative identifiers: first voted after 1970				
	Feb. 1974	Oct. 1974	1979	1983	1987
Social services and benefits were					
Extremely important	2.7	2.1	10.3	43.8	–
Fairly important	21.6	31.9	47.1	49.1	–
Not very important	75.7	66.0	42.5	7.1	–
Total	100.0	100.0	100.0	100.0	–
N. of respondents	39	47	87	255	–

	Labour identifiers: first voted after 1970				
	Feb. 1974	Oct. 1974	1979	1983	1987
Social services and benefits were					
Extremely important	5.1	7.0	20.4	74.0	–
Fairly important	51.9	46.5	51.3	22.0	–
Not very important	43.0	46.5	28.3	4.0	–
Total	100.0	100.0	100.0	100.0	–
N. of respondents	79	71	113	251	–

Table 10.12 *Importance of social services as an issue by social class (%)*

	Professional and managerial classes				
	Feb. 1974	Oct. 1974	1979	1983	1987
Social services and benefits were					
Extremely important	3.2	3.2	18.0	52.1	–
Fairly important	45.3	47.6	42.4	40.8	–
Not very important	51.5	49.3	39.7	7.1	–
Total	100.0	100.0	100.0	100.0	–
N. of respondents	342	347	373	1013	–
	Intermediate and routine non-manual classes				
	Feb. 1974	Oct. 1974	1979	1983	1987
Social services and benefits were					
Extremely important	5.4	7.3	19.1	61.0	–
Fairly important	47.5	53.6	43.6	33.5	–
Not very important	47.1	39.1	37.3	5.5	–
Total	100.0	100.0	100.0	100.0	–
N. of respondents	821	782	491	744	–
	Manual working class				
	Feb. 1974	Oct. 1974	1979	1983	1987
Social services and benefits were					
Extremely important	9.0	8.3	26.6	68.6	–
Fairly important	49.6	52.9	39.7	26.7	–
Not very important	41.3	38.9	33.7	4.7	–
Total	100.0	100.0	100.0	100.0	–
N. of respondents	1086	1016	896	1891	–

Table 10.13 *Importance of social services as an issue by employment status (%)*

	Self-employed with employees				
	Feb. 1974	Oct. 1974	1979	1983	1987
Social services and benefits were					
Extremely important	4.4	5.6	19.3	41.5	–
Fairly important	44.4	51.4	35.1	47.7	–
Not very important	51.1	43.1	45.6	10.9	–
Total	100.0	100.0	100.0	100.0	–
N. of respondents	90	72	57	161	–

Table 10.13 (*cont.*)

	Self-employed, no employees				
	Feb. 1974	Oct. 1974	1979	1983	1987
Social services and benefits were					
Extremely important	3.7	4.6	17.1	56.7	–
Fairly important	42.7	58.6	44.3	35.9	–
Not very important	53.7	36.8	38.6	7.4	–
Total	100.0	100.0	100.0	100.0	–
N. of respondents	82	87	70	134	–

	Managers				
	Feb. 1974	Oct. 1974	1979	1983	1987
Social services and benefits were					
Extremely important	1.8	6.4	20.0	53.0	–
Fairly important	50.3	40.9	44.1	39.7	–
Not very important	47.9	52.6	35.9	7.2	–
Total	100.0	100.0	100.0	100.0	–
N. of respondents	165	171	145	345	–

	Foremen and Supervisors				
	Feb. 1974	Oct. 1974	1979	1983	1987
Social services and benefits were					
Extremely important	7.2	2.6	19.5	65.6	–
Fairly important	48.5	59.0	37.4	31.6	–
Not very important	44.3	38.5	43.2	2.8	–
Total	100.0	100.0	100.0	100.0	–
N. of respondents	97	117	190	225	–

	Rank and file employees				
	Feb. 1974	Oct. 1974	1979	1983	1987
Social services and benefits were					
Extremely important	6.8	7.8	23.7	65.6	–
Fairly important	48.9	51.8	41.2	29.5	–
Not very important	44.3	40.4	35.1	4.9	–
Total	100.0	100.0	100.0	100.0	–
N. of respondents	1586	1482	915	2620	–

Table 10.14 *Importance of social services as an issue: unemployed (%)*

	Feb. 1974	Oct. 1974	1979	1983	1987
Social services and benefits were					
Extremely important	17.8	16.2	37.8	65.7	–
Fairly important	60.0	56.8	40.5	27.0	–
Not very important	22.2	27.0	21.6	7.3	–
Total	100.0	100.0	100.0	100.0	–
N. of respondents	45	37	37	240	–

Table 10.15 *Importance of social services as an issue by class and employment status (%)*

	Professional and managerial classes: self-employed				
	Feb. 1974	Oct. 1974	1979	1983	1987
Social services and benefits were					
Extremely important	6.3	2.3	23.1	45.9	–
Fairly important	33.3	53.5	35.9	44.4	–
Not very important	60.4	44.2	41.0	9.8	–
Total	100.0	100.0	100.0	100.0	–
N. of respondents	48	43	39	133	–
	Professional and managerial classes: employees				
	Feb. 1974	Oct. 1974	1979	1983	1987
Social services and benefits were					
Extremely important	2.8	3.8	18.0	53.1	–
Fairly important	46.6	44.8	42.4	40.2	–
Not very important	50.6	51.3	39.6	6.7	–
Total	100.0	100.0	100.0	100.0	–
N. of respondents	253	261	250	851	–
	Intermediate and routine non-manual classes: self-employed				
	Feb. 1974	Oct. 1974	1979	1983	1987
Social services and benefits were					
Extremely important	3.0	9.0	16.7	55.2	–
Fairly important	44.4	53.8	38.9	37.9	–
Not very important	52.5	37.2	44.4	6.9	–
Total	100.0	100.0	100.0	100.0	–
N. of respondents	99	78	54	29	–

Table 10.15 (*cont.*)

	Intermediate and routine non-manual classes: employees				
	Feb. 1974	Oct. 1974	1979	1983	1987
Social services and benefits were					
Extremely important	5.6	7.0	20.1	61.0	–
Fairly important	47.8	53.7	43.8	33.7	–
Not very important	46.5	39.3	36.1	5.4	–
Total	100.0	100.0	100.0	100.0	–
N. of respondents	673	656	368	689	–

	Manual working class: self-employed				
	Feb. 1974	Oct. 1974	1979	1983	1987
Social services and benefits were					
Extremely important	4.2	0.0	14.7	48.2	–
Fairly important	62.5	60.5	47.1	41.2	–
Not very important	33.3	39.5	38.2	10.5	–
Total	100.0	100.0	100.0	100.0	–
N. of respondents	24	38	34	114	–

	Manual working class: employees				
	Feb. 1974	Oct. 1974	1979	1983	1987
Social services and benefits were					
Extremely important	8.0	8.5	25.9	69.9	–
Fairly important	50.2	51.6	38.8	25.9	–
Not very important	41.8	39.9	35.3	4.2	–
Total	100.0	100.0	100.0	100.0	–
N. of respondents	909	845	629	1620	–

Table 10.16 *Importance of social services as an issue by economic sector (%)*

	Works in private sector				
	Feb. 1974	Oct. 1974	1979	1983	1987
Social services and benefits were					
Extremely important	–	6.9	21.2	62.5	–
Fairly important	–	48.9	41.9	32.5	–
Not very important	–	44.2	37.0	5.0	–
Total	–	100.0	100.0	100.0	–
N. of respondents	–	1032	744	2128	–

Table 10.16 (*cont.*)

	Works in public sector				
	Feb. 1974	Oct. 1974	1979	1983	1987
Social services and benefits were					
Extremely important	–	6.9	25.0	65.6	–
Fairly important	–	57.3	41.4	29.1	–
Not very important	–	35.9	33.6	5.3	–
Total	–	100.0	100.0	100.0	–
N. of respondents	–	510	456	1258	–

Table 10.17 *Importance of social services as an issue by school leaving age (%)*

	Left school aged under 15				
	Feb. 1974	Oct. 1974	1979	1983	1987
Social services and benefits were					
Extremely important	9.5	11.5	29.1	73.8	–
Fairly important	51.8	56.9	40.0	22.7	–
Not very important	38.8	31.6	30.9	3.5	–
Total	100.0	100.0	100.0	100.0	–
N. of respondents	1037	928	612	1160	–

	Left school aged 15				
	Feb. 1974	Oct. 1974	1979	1983	1987
Social services and benefits were					
Extremely important	5.9	5.0	22.9	66.3	–
Fairly important	46.6	50.6	38.6	29.4	–
Not very important	47.6	44.4	38.4	4.3	–
Total	100.0	100.0	100.0	100.0	–
N. of respondents	683	658	536	1007	–

	Left school aged 16				
	Feb. 1974	Oct. 1974	1979	1983	1987
Social services and benefits were					
Extremely important	4.0	5.2	19.0	55.5	–
Fairly important	46.9	46.6	42.0	37.4	–
Not very important	49.1	48.2	38.9	7.1	–
Total	100.0	100.0	100.0	100.0	–
N. of respondents	324	328	357	953	–

Table 10.17 (*cont.*)

| | Left school aged 17 | | | | |
	Feb. 1974	Oct. 1974	1979	1983	1987
Social services and benefits were					
Extremely important	0.6	3.2	19.7	48.8	–
Fairly important	45.5	45.5	44.3	43.2	–
Not very important	53.8	51.3	36.1	8.0	–
Total	100.0	100.0	100.0	100.0	–
N. of respondents	156	154	122	328	–
	Left school aged over 17				
	Feb. 1974	Oct. 1974	1979	1983	1987
Social services and benefits were					
Extremely important	4.0	2.3	11.7	48.1	–
Fairly important	41.2	49.2	50.5	43.4	–
Not very important	54.8	48.6	37.8	8.4	–
Total	100.0	100.0	100.0	100.0	–
N. of respondents	177	177	188	481	–

Table 10.18 *Importance of social services as an issue by region (%)*

| | Scotland | | | | |
	Feb. 1974	Oct. 1974	1979	1983	1987
Social services and benefits were					
Extremely important	6.9	7.2	26.6	71.8	–
Fairly important	49.6	40.5	34.5	24.2	–
Not very important	43.5	52.3	38.8	4.0	–
Total	100.0	100.0	100.0	100.0	–
N. of respondents	232	195	139	363	–
	Wales				
	Feb. 1974	Oct. 1974	1979	1983	1987
Social services and benefits were					
Extremely important	7.9	11.2	27.5	67.9	–
Fairly important	58.3	57.6	51.0	28.8	–
Not very important	33.9	31.2	21.6	3.3	–
Total	100.0	100.0	100.0	100.0	–
N. of respondents	127	125	102	206	–

Table 10.18 (*cont.*)

	The North				
	Feb. 1974	Oct. 1974	1979	1983	1987
Social services and benefits were					
Extremely important	8.3	6.6	22.6	62.9	–
Fairly important	49.7	54.2	44.0	31.5	–
Not very important	42.0	39.1	33.3	5.6	–
Total	100.0	100.0	100.0	100.0	–
N. of respondents	712	662	504	1054	–

	The Midlands				
	Feb. 1974	Oct. 1974	1979	1983	1987
Social services and benefits were					
Extremely important	5.3	4.5	23.0	61.9	–
Fairly important	49.5	58.0	39.7	32.5	–
Not very important	45.2	37.5	37.2	5.7	–
Total	100.0	100.0	100.0	100.0	–
N. of respondents	376	376	317	630	–

	Greater London				
	Feb. 1974	Oct. 1974	1979	1983	1987
Social services and benefits were					
Extremely important	6.6	8.1	24.0	61.6	–
Fairly important	45.2	52.7	41.2	33.8	–
Not very important	48.3	39.2	34.8	4.6	–
Total	100.0	100.0	100.0	100.0	–
N. of respondents	259	222	204	487	–

	The South				
	Feb. 1974	Oct. 1974	1979	1983	1987
Social services and benefits were					
Extremely important	5.4	8.8	21.4	58.1	–
Fairly important	45.6	49.1	40.1	35.2	–
Not very important	49.0	42.1	38.5	6.7	–
Total	100.0	100.0	100.0	100.0	–
N. of respondents	684	682	571	1199	–

Table 10.19 *Attitudes to: expenditure on poverty, economic redistribution and the availability of welfare benefits: all respondents (%)*

	Government expenditure to get rid of poverty . . .				Redistribution of income and wealth . . .				Welfare benefits have . . .			
	Oct. 1974	1979	1983	1987	Oct. 1974	1979	1983	1987	Oct. 1974	1979	1983	1987
All respondents												
Should be done	87.0	83.5	85.7	87.9	56.2	55.2	47.5	43.9	Gone too far 34.0	50.1	19.5	24.8
Does not matter	6.4	7.9	3.1	4.6	15.7	16.5	15.2	19.9	Are about right 43.1	32.9	51.1	40.3
Should not be done	6.6	8.6	11.2	7.5	28.1	28.3	37.3	36.2	Not gone far enough 23.0	17.0	29.4	34.9
Total	100.0	100.0	100.0	100.0	100.0	100.0	100.0	100.0	100.0	100.0	100.0	100.0
N. of respondents	2228	1775	3704	3711	2200	1745	3932	3347	2209	1812	3753	3643

Table 10.20 Attitudes to: expenditure on poverty, economic redistribution and the availability of welfare benefits: by gender (%)

Men

Government expenditure to get rid of poverty . . .	Oct. 1974	1979	1983	1987
Should be done	87.6	83.9	86.6	88.8
Does not matter	6.5	8.2	2.5	4.1
Should not be done	5.9	8.0	10.9	7.1
Total	100.0	100.0	100.0	100.0
N. of respondents	1123	867	1771	1808

Redistribution of income and wealth . . .	Oct. 1974	1979	1983	1987
Should be done	56.0	53.9	45.0	44.7
Does not matter	16.6	17.0	13.1	20.3
Should not be done	27.3	29.1	41.9	35.0
Total	100.0	100.0	100.0	100.0
N. of respondents	1112	865	1869	1642

Welfare benefits have . . .	Oct. 1974	1979	1983	1987
Gone too far	33.9	50.5	19.6	24.1
Are about right	42.1	32.5	51.7	41.5
Not gone far enough	24.0	17.0	28.7	34.3
Total	100.0	100.0	100.0	100.0
N. of respondents	1117	877	1798	1780

Women

Government expenditure to get rid of poverty . . .	Oct. 1974	1979	1983	1987
Should be done	86.3	83.3	84.9	87.1
Does not matter	6.3	7.6	3.6	5.1
Should not be done	7.3	9.1	11.5	7.8
Total	100.0	100.0	100.0	100.0
N. of respondents	1105	908	1933	1904

Redistribution of income and wealth . . .	Oct. 1974	1979	1983	1987
Should be done	56.4	56.6	49.7	43.0
Does not matter	14.7	16.0	17.1	19.6
Should not be done	28.9	27.4	33.2	37.3
Total	100.0	100.0	100.0	100.0
N. of respondents	1088	880	2063	1705

Welfare benefits have . . .	Oct. 1974	1979	1983	1987
Gone too far	34.1	49.6	19.3	25.4
Are about right	44.0	33.4	50.6	39.1
Not gone far enough	21.9	17.0	30.0	35.4
Total	100.0	100.0	100.0	100.0
N. of respondents	1092	935	1955	1865

Government expenditure to get rid of poverty . . .

	Oct. 1974	1979	1983	1987
Aged under 25				
Should be done	90.6	83.3	90.3	91.7
Does not matter	5.6	10.1	1.5	3.7
Should not be done	3.8	6.5	8.2	4.6
Total	100.0	100.0	100.0	100.0
N. of respondents	266	168	518	484
Aged 25–34				
Should be done	90.3	85.1	88.9	90.0
Does not matter	4.7	8.5	2.2	4.8
Should not be done	5.0	6.3	8.9	5.3
Total	100.0	100.0	100.0	100.0
N. of respondents	464	410	717	679
Aged 35–44				
Should be done	89.6	84.6	84.7	89.2
Does not matter	5.4	6.9	3.4	3.1
Should not be done	4.9	8.5	11.9	7.7
Total	100.0	100.0	100.0	100.0
N. of respondents	386	318	687	740
Aged 45–54				
Should be done	85.3	82.1	86.5	87.3
Does not matter	7.7	6.7	2.8	5.1
Should not be done	7.0	11.2	10.7	7.6
Total	100.0	100.0	100.0	100.0
N. of respondents	388	329	595	566

Redistribution of income and wealth . . .

	Oct. 1974	1979	1983	1987
Aged under 25				
Should be done	60.5	64.6	53.4	54.9
Does not matter	19.9	17.7	18.0	20.9
Should not be done	19.5	17.7	28.6	24.2
Total	100.0	100.0	100.0	100.0
N. of respondents	261	164	556	432
Aged 25–34				
Should be done	65.3	59.5	50.2	49.0
Does not matter	14.6	13.8	14.8	20.1
Should not be done	20.1	26.7	35.0	31.0
Total	100.0	100.0	100.0	100.0
N. of respondents	458	405	745	607
Aged 35–44				
Should be done	59.5	57.5	45.7	43.4
Does not matter	15.2	15.7	12.9	18.7
Should not be done	25.3	26.8	41.4	37.8
Total	100.0	100.0	100.0	100.0
N. of respondents	376	306	714	675
Aged 45–54				
Should be done	53.9	55.7	46.9	38.7
Does not matter	15.3	15.6	14.1	18.9
Should not be done	30.8	28.7	39.0	42.3
Total	100.0	100.0	100.0	100.0
N. of respondents	386	327	633	522

Welfare benefits have . . .

	Oct. 1974	1979	1983	1987
Aged under 25				
Gone too far	21.8	35.0	12.2	16.7
Are about right	41.6	42.7	51.8	38.9
Not gone far enough	36.6	22.3	36.0	44.4
Total	100.0	100.0	100.0	100.0
N. of respondents	262	167	531	476
Aged 25–34				
Gone too far	32.5	47.6	14.8	20.2
Are about right	40.7	32.8	49.3	39.5
Not gone far enough	26.8	19.6	35.9	40.3
Total	100.0	100.0	100.0	100.0
N. of respondents	452	419	718	669
Aged 35–44				
Gone too far	33.6	54.0	19.0	23.6
Are about right	44.5	27.9	53.3	40.0
Not gone far enough	21.9	18.6	27.7	36.5
Total	100.0	100.0	100.0	100.0
N. of respondents	375	319	679	720
Aged 45–54				
Gone too far	40.1	53.2	18.9	31.1
Are about right	40.1	31.7	52.3	36.6
Not gone far enough	19.8	15.1	28.9	32.3
Total	100.0	100.0	100.0	100.0
N. of respondents	384	331	610	562

Table 10.21 (cont.)

Government expenditure to get rid of poverty . . .

	Oct. 1974	1979	1983	1987
Aged 55–64				
Should be done	85.0	83.2	84.0	88.5
Does not matter	5.9	6.4	2.8	4.5
Should not be done	9.1	10.4	13.2	7.0
Total	100.0	100.0	100.0	100.0
N. of respondents	341	250	565	584
Aged 65–74				
Should be done	81.6	83.8	80.4	83.5
Does not matter	8.6	9.4	4.9	6.8
Should not be done	9.8	6.8	14.8	9.7
Total	100.0	100.0	100.0	100.0
N. of respondents	256	191	404	415
Aged over 74				
Should be done	80.7	79.0	79.5	78.1
Does not matter	10.9	9.5	6.9	6.6
Should not be done	8.4	11.4	13.6	15.3
Total	100.0	100.0	100.0	100.0
N. of respondents	119	105	202	244

Redistribution of income and wealth . . .

	Oct. 1974	1979	1983	1987
Aged 55–64				
Should be done	52.2	51.2	47.1	38.7
Does not matter	13.9	18.0	14.5	19.5
Should not be done	33.9	30.7	38.4	41.8
Total	100.0	100.0	100.0	100.0
N. of respondents	339	244	587	539
Aged 65–74				
Should be done	46.2	45.7	43.2	42.9
Does not matter	16.2	18.6	14.0	21.3
Should not be done	37.5	35.6	42.8	35.8
Total	100.0	100.0	100.0	100.0
N. of respondents	253	188	437	373
Aged over 74				
Should be done	42.9	42.5	41.9	34.5
Does not matter	16.8	22.6	21.8	21.6
Should not be done	40.3	34.9	36.3	43.9
Total	100.0	100.0	100.0	100.0
N. of respondents	119	106	240	199

Welfare benefits have . . .

	Oct. 1974	1979	1983	1987
Aged 55–64				
Gone too far	34.9	52.7	27.5	27.9
Are about right	42.0	31.6	48.2	42.7
Not gone far enough	23.1	17.6	24.3	29.4
Total	100.0	100.0	100.0	100.0
N. of respondents	338	259	556	575
Aged 65–74				
Gone too far	41.1	51.5	28.1	30.0
Are about right	45.7	35.0	47.3	39.4
Not gone far enough	13.2	12.5	24.6	30.6
Total	100.0	100.0	100.0	100.0
N. of respondents	265	201	423	402
Aged over 74				
Gone too far	29.8	50.8	19.8	26.6
Are about right	56.5	37.3	59.9	50.8
Not gone far enough	13.7	11.9	20.3	22.6
Total	100.0	100.0	100.0	100.0
N. of respondents	124	118	217	239

Table 9.22 *Attitudes to: expenditure on poverty, economic redistribution and the availability of welfare benefits by marital status (%)*

	Government expenditure to get rid of poverty . . .				Redistribution of income and wealth . . .					Welfare benefits have . . .			
	Oct. 1974	1979	1983	1987	Oct. 1974	1979	1983	1987		Oct. 1974	1979	1983	1987
Single													
Should be done	–	84.5	89.3	91.3	–	59.6	52.0	51.4	Gone too far	–	43.3	14.7	17.8
Does not matter	–	8.2	1.7	3.6	–	18.3	15.2	20.7	Are about right	–	36.0	51.1	42.0
Should not be done	–	7.3	9.0	5.1	–	22.0	32.8	27.9	Not gone far enough	–	20.7	34.3	40.1
Total	–	100.0	100.0	100.0	–	100.0	100.0	100.0		–	100.0	100.0	100.0
N. of respondents	–	219	632	683	–	218	690	596		–	217	648	667
Married													
Should be done	87.1	83.1	85.4	87.5	58.3	54.4	45.8	42.5	Gone too far	35.1	52.3	21.0	26.8
Does not matter	6.3	7.7	3.1	4.1	14.8	16.4	15.1	19.3	Are about right	42.7	32.1	51.2	40.3
Should not be done	6.6	9.1	11.5	7.8	27.0	29.0	39.0	38.2	Not gone far enough	22.2	15.6	27.8	32.9
Total	100.0	100.0	100.0	100.0	100.0	100.0	100.0	100.0		100.0	100.0	100.0	100.0
N. of respondents	1679	1295	2608	2550	1654	1268	2741	2345		1651	1317	2633	2510
Divorced and separated													
Should be done	–	88.3	86.7	87.8	–	68.9	55.4	45.7	Gone too far	–	32.5	16.5	26.4
Does not matter	–	10.4	2.5	4.1	–	9.5	12.8	20.5	Are about right	–	35.0	45.3	29.1
Should not be done	–	1.3	10.8	8.1	–	21.6	31.8	33.8	Not gone far enough	–	32.5	38.2	44.5
Total	–	100.0	100.0	100.0	–	100.0	100.0	100.0		–	100.0	100.0	100.0
N. of respondents	–	77	174	183	–	74	182	166		–	77	170	183
Widowed													
Should be done	–	82.3	80.0	83.8	–	47.4	47.6	37.9	Gone too far	–	46.8	18.0	23.0
Does not matter	–	8.0	6.5	6.5	–	18.5	17.3	23.5	Are about right	–	37.4	53.7	43.3
Should not be done	–	9.7	13.5	9.6	–	34.1	35.1	38.6	Not gone far enough	–	15.8	28.3	33.7
Total	–	100.0	100.0	100.0	–	100.0	100.0	100.0		–	100.0	100.0	100.0
N. of respondents	–	175	288	327	–	173	316	266		–	190	300	313

Table 10.23 *Attitudes to: expenditure on poverty, economic redistribution and the availability of welfare benefits by political generation (%)*

	Government expenditure to get rid of poverty . . .				Redistribution of income and wealth . . .					Welfare benefits have . . .			
	Oct. 1974	1979	1983	1987	Oct. 1974	1979	1983	1987		Oct. 1974	1979	1983	1987
First voted 1918–35													
Should be done	82.1	82.5	80.7	77.4	47.3	44.5	40.8	35.2	Gone too far	37.3	51.4	24.5	25.9
Does not matter	8.2	8.8	5.2	7.2	15.6	20.6	19.4	20.8	Are about right	45.8	35.8	54.6	49.4
Should not be done	9.7	8.8	14.1	15.1	37.1	34.9	39.8	44.0	Not gone far enough	16.9	12.5	20.8	24.7
Total	100.0	100.0	100.0	100.0	100.0	100.0	100.0	100.0		100.0	100.0	100.0	100.0
N. of respondents	497	274	414	279	493	272	473	230		509	296	432	272
First voted 1936–1950													
Should be done	85.5	83.6	82.5	85.9	52.7	53.2	46.6	40.3	Gone too far	38.6	50.2	27.4	29.5
Does not matter	7.6	6.8	3.8	5.7	15.1	17.4	13.9	21.0	Are about right	42.0	34.1	47.4	41.2
Should not be done	6.9	9.6	13.7	8.4	32.1	29.4	39.4	38.7	Not gone far enough	19.4	15.6	25.3	29.3
Total	100.0	100.0	100.0	100.0	100.0	100.0	100.0	100.0		100.0	100.0	100.0	100.0
N. of respondents	552	397	765	738	548	391	803	674		547	408	764	727
First voted 1951–1970													
Should be done	89.9	83.8	86.0	88.4	62.2	57.1	46.4	40.8	Gone too far	32.8	52.2	18.9	27.2
Does not matter	4.9	7.5	3.0	4.1	15.2	15.1	13.7	18.9	Are about right	41.7	29.9	52.7	39.2
Should not be done	5.2	8.6	11.0	7.5	22.7	27.8	39.9	40.2	Not gone far enough	25.5	17.6	28.4	33.7
Total	100.0	100.0	100.0	100.0	100.0	100.0	100.0	100.0		100.0	100.0	100.0	100.0
N. of respondents	978	822	1540	1453	962	808	1613	1333		952	835	1544	1423
First voted after 1970													
Should be done	90.6	83.4	89.5	90.8	61.4	63.6	51.6	51.3	Gone too far	17.4	40.1	12.4	19.0
Does not matter	6.1	9.7	1.8	4.1	21.0	15.2	15.1	20.1	Are about right	44.4	36.9	50.0	39.0
Should not be done	3.3	6.9	8.6	5.1	17.6	21.2	33.3	28.5	Not gone far enough	38.2	22.6	37.6	41.9
Total	100.0	100.0	100.0	100.0	100.0	100.0	100.0	100.0		100.0	100.0	100.0	100.0
N. of respondents	181	277	697	1242	176	269	724	1110		178	274	994	1221

Table 10.24 *Attitudes to: expenditure on poverty, economic redistribution and the availability of welfare benefits by vote (%)*

	Government expenditure to get rid of poverty . . .				Redistribution of income and wealth . . .				Welfare benefits have . . .			
	Oct. 1974	1979	1983	1987	Oct. 1974	1979	1983	1987	Oct. 1974	1979	1983	1987
Conservative voters												
Should be done / Gone too far	81.0	78.9	77.0	80.2	29.6	36.1	25.6	18.7	49.2	66.9	29.6	36.2
Does not matter / Are about right	8.7	9.6	3.3	7.0	16.7	17.6	15.0	19.8	38.5	24.2	57.5	47.5
Should not be done / Not gone far enough	10.3	11.4	19.7	12.8	53.7	46.3	59.4	61.5	12.4	8.8	12.9	16.4
Total	100.0	100.0	100.0	100.0	100.0	100.0	100.0	100.0	100.0	100.0	100.0	100.0
N. of respondents	658	684	1311	1366	659	682	1440	1246	663	713	1357	1355
Labour voters												
Should be done / Gone too far	92.9	90.1	95.9	96.1	79.2	76.5	75.4	73.3	21.3	32.2	10.3	12.0
Does not matter / Are about right	3.7	4.8	1.6	1.7	11.1	12.4	12.6	16.0	45.6	42.1	38.9	29.4
Should not be done / Not gone far enough	3.4	5.2	2.5	2.1	9.7	11.1	12.0	10.7	33.1	25.7	50.7	58.6
Total	100.0	100.0	100.0	100.0	100.0	100.0	100.0	100.0	100.0	100.0	100.0	100.0
N. of respondents	789	563	896	987	784	557	913	1246	780	568	891	961
Liberal voters												
Should be done / Gone too far	84.0	82.8	89.6	91.6	52.6	51.0	52.6	51.1	36.5	53.4	15.9	20.9
Does not matter / Are about right	7.4	9.1	3.7	3.5	20.3	25.3	15.3	23.0	43.0	32.0	55.6	40.3
Should not be done / Not gone far enough	8.6	8.1	6.7	4.9	27.1	23.7	32.2	26.0	20.5	14.6	28.5	38.8
Total	100.0	100.0	100.0	100.0	100.0	100.0	100.0	100.0	100.0	100.0	100.0	100.0
N. of respondents	338	209	760	743	325	198	792	700	337	206	755	726
Voters for other parties												
Should be done / Gone too far	86.2	79.2	93.2	94.9	49.2	50.0	57.4	60.5	31.7	52.2	14.6	29.2
Does not matter / Are about right	13.8	16.7	0.0	5.1	22.2	25.0	21.5	14.7	48.3	30.4	56.1	33.9
Should not be done / Not gone far enough	0.0	4.2	6.8	0.0	28.6	25.0	21.1	24.8	20.0	17.4	29.3	36.9
Total	100.0	100.0	100.0	100.0	100.0	100.0	100.0	100.0	100.0	100.0	100.0	100.0
N. of respondents	65	24	41	44	63	24	43	39	60	23	41	43

Table 10.25 *Attitudes to: expenditure on poverty, economic redistribution and the availability of welfare benefits by strength and direction of partisanship* (%)

	Government expenditure to get rid of poverty . . .				Redistribution of income and wealth . . .				Welfare benefits have . . .			
	Oct. 1974	1979	1983	1987	Oct. 1974	1979	1983	1987	Oct. 1974	1979	1983	1987
Very strong Conservative identifiers												
Should be done	80.1	71.5	67.2	72.9	18.5	27.2	18.5	10.7				
Does not matter	6.5	10.1	5.3	8.6	13.0	14.8	11.2	10.9				
Should not be done	13.4	18.4	27.5	18.5	68.5	58.0	70.2	78.4				
Gone too far									54.4	77.0	38.6	47.6
Are about right									35.3	18.0	52.3	41.8
Not gone far enough									10.3	5.0	9.1	10.6
Total	100.0	100.0	100.0	100.0	100.0	100.0	100.0	100.0	100.0	100.0	100.0	100.0
N. of respondents	201	158	320	314	200	162	356	283	204	161	329	314
Fairly strong Conservative identifiers												
Should be done	81.0	79.9	77.3	82.9	33.5	36.5	25.3	18.0				
Does not matter	9.4	9.8	2.8	5.9	19.6	17.0	15.0	21.6				
Should not be done	9.6	10.3	19.9	11.2	46.9	46.4	59.7	60.4				
Gone too far									44.7	64.2	28.1	36.3
Are about right									41.3	24.6	59.3	48.2
Not gone far enough									14.0	11.2	12.7	15.5
Total	100.0	100.0	100.0	100.0	100.0	100.0	100.0	100.0	100.0	100.0	100.0	100.0
N. of respondents	406	368	612	689	403	364	668	640	407	383	648	688
Not very strong Conservative identifiers												
Should be done	85.2	79.9	82.4	85.3	38.1	39.5	33.3	28.7				
Does not matter	7.4	9.5	3.8	6.2	18.8	19.5	18.8	25.3				
Should not be done	7.4	10.6	13.8	8.5	43.2	41.1	47.9	46.0				
Gone too far									46.3	61.2	21.9	30.5
Are about right									39.4	33.2	59.4	49.2
Not gone far enough									14.3	5.6	18.6	20.3
Total	100.0	100.0	100.0	100.0	100.0	100.0	100.0	100.0	100.0	100.0	100.0	100.0
N. of respondents	176	189	420	329	176	185	451	304	175	196	424	322

Very strong Liberal identifiers

Should be done	80.4	80.0	93.3	93.6	48.9	61.5	66.7	68.9
Does not matter	10.9	12.4	4.0	3.3	26.7	15.4	5.1	18.3
Should not be done	8.7	7.6	2.7	3.1	24.4	23.1	28.2	12.7
Total	100.0	100.0	100.0	100.0	100.0	100.0	100.0	100.0
N. of respondents	46	29	75	59	45	26	78	61
Gone too far	34.8	46.7	24.7	14.4				
Are about right	45.7	30.0	46.6	37.1				
Not gone far enough	19.6	23.3	28.8	48.5				
Total	100.0	100.0	100.0	100.0				
N. of respondents	46	30	73	61				

Fairly strong Liberal identifiers

Should be done	86.0	80.0	92.3	93.1	57.2	36.3	48.9	54.4
Does not matter	8.4	12.4	2.7	2.2	18.5	34.3	13.4	18.8
Should not be done	5.6	7.6	5.1	4.7	24.3	24.4	37.7	26.8
Total	100.0	100.0	100.0	100.0	100.0	100.0	100.0	100.0
N. of respondents	178	105	297	269	173	102	305	250
Gone too far	34.7	51.4	14.9	23.3				
Are about right	40.5	33.3	60.3	39.7				
Not gone far enough	24.9	15.2	24.7	37.0				
Total	100.0	100.0	100.0	100.0				
N. of respondents	173	105	295	259				

Not very strong Liberal identifiers

Should be done	77.6	80.0	83.6	90.0	49.5	53.1	50.3	47.6
Does not matter	11.2	12.9	4.6	4.2	17.1	21.0	15.9	23.4
Should not be done	11.2	7.1	11.8	5.0	33.3	25.9	33.8	29.0
Total	100.0	100.0	100.0	100.0	100.0	100.0	100.0	100.0
N. of respondents	116	85	305	313	111	81	320	291
Gone too far	48.3	60.5	19.0	19.6				
Are about right	37.9	27.9	53.9	43.0				
Not gone far enough	13.8	11.6	27.1	37.4				
Total	100.0	100.0	100.0	100.0				
N. of respondents	116	86	310	308				

Very strong Labour identifiers

Should be done	92.9	93.5	94.4	95.8	86.4	86.2	79.2	83.4
Does not matter	4.3	2.7	4.1	3.1	7.3	5.5	10.6	9.6
Should not be done	2.8	2.7	4.1	3.1	6.3	8.3	10.3	7.0
Total	100.0	100.0	100.0	100.0	100.0	100.0	100.0	100.0
N. of respondents	323	186	339	295	317	181	341	261
Gone too far	15.9	25.9	7.3	13.8				
Are about right	47.5	43.9	35.1	24.9				
Not gone far enough	36.6	30.2	57.6	61.3				
Total	100.0	100.0	100.0	100.0				
N. of respondents	320	189	328	290				

Table 10.25 (cont.)

Government expenditure to get rid of poverty . . .

	Oct. 1974	1979	1983	1987
Fairly strong Labour identifiers				
Should be done	93.7	90.8	95.5	96.3
Does not matter	2.8	3.3	1.9	1.5
Should not be done	3.5	5.9	2.7	2.2
Total	100.0	100.0	100.0	100.0
N. of respondents	429	338	484	494
Not very strong Labour identifiers				
Should be done	89.7	86.6	92.6	93.6
Does not matter	5.2	4.7	3.0	3.0
Should not be done	5.2	8.7	4.4	3.4
Total	100.0	100.0	100.0	100.0
N. of respondents	174	172	365	360

Redistribution of income and wealth . . .

	Oct. 1974	1979	1983	1987
Fairly strong Labour identifiers				
Should be done	77.8	78.9	76.2	71.4
Does not matter	12.2	13.7	11.9	16.6
Should not be done	10.1	7.4	11.9	12.0
Total	100.0	100.0	100.0	100.0
N. of respondents	427	336	496	447
Not very strong Labour identifiers				
Should be done	67.8	64.1	60.2	59.5
Does not matter	17.0	17.4	19.4	19.5
Should not be done	15.2	18.6	20.4	21.0
Total	100.0	100.0	100.0	100.0
N. of respondents	171	167	387	314

Welfare benefits have . . .

	Oct. 1974	1979	1983	1987
Fairly strong Labour identifiers				
Gone too far	24.9	32.5	9.4	12.9
Are about right	44.8	40.8	42.2	29.0
Not gone far enough	30.3	26.6	48.4	58.1
Total	100.0	100.0	100.0	100.0
N. of respondents	429	338	479	488
Not very strong Labour identifiers				
Gone too far	23.3	42.0	12.1	14.5
Are about right	47.2	37.4	26.4	35.6
Not gone far enough	29.4	20.7	41.6	49.9
Total	100.0	100.0	100.0	100.0
N. of respondents	163	174	373	349

Table 10.26 Attitudes to: expenditure on poverty, economic redistribution and the availability of welfare benefits by social class (%)

	Government expenditure to get rid of poverty . . .				Redistribution of income and wealth . . .				Welfare benefits have . . .			
	Oct. 1974	1979	1983	1987	Oct. 1974	1979	1983	1987	Oct. 1974	1979	1983	1987
Professional and managerial classes												
Should be done	84.5	75.9	80.4	85.1	37.8	36.0	32.3	35.3				
Does not matter	6.8	10.8	3.4	5.7	21.1	21.6	15.5	18.0				
Should not be done	8.6	13.3	16.2	9.3	41.2	42.4	52.2	46.8				
Gone too far									45.5	59.2	24.3	27.4
Are about right									37.2	28.7	56.5	43.0
Not gone far enough									17.3	12.1	19.2	29.5
Total	100.0	100.0	100.0	100.0	100.0	100.0	100.0	100.0	100.0	100.0	100.0	100.0
N. of respondents	336	353	933	952	323	356	1015	874	336	365	972	943
Intermediate and routine non-manual classes												
Should be done	85.0	82.7	84.2	87.5	49.1	49.5	43.3	37.7				
Does not matter	6.9	8.1	3.7	4.7	15.8	17.2	17.0	20.0				
Should not be done	8.1	9.1	12.2	7.8	35.0	33.3	39.8	42.3				
Gone too far									39.9	58.2	22.5	26.7
Are about right									40.0	29.9	54.1	43.0
Not gone far enough									20.1	11.8	23.5	30.3
Total	100.0	100.0	100.0	100.0	100.0	100.0	100.0	100.0	100.0	100.0	100.0	100.0
N. of respondents	769	481	707	931	759	471	737	861	765	491	712	909
Manual working class												
Should be done	89.9	87.1	89.3	89.8	68.2	65.9	57.5	52.0				
Does not matter	5.4	6.4	2.4	4.2	13.9	14.4	13.6	21.0				
Should not be done	4.6	6.5	8.3	6.0	17.9	19.7	28.9	26.9				
Gone too far									27.1	42.6	16.8	23.0
Are about right									46.1	36.6	46.8	37.0
Not gone far enough									26.8	20.8	36.4	40.1
Total	100.0	100.0	100.0	100.0	100.0	100.0	100.0	100.0	100.0	100.0	100.0	100.0
N. of respondents	1013	878	1905	1677	1010	859	1890	1488	996	891	1902	1648

Table 10.27 *Attitudes to: expenditure on poverty, economic redistribution and the availability of welfare benefits by class and gender (%)*

Professional and managerial classes: men

	Government expenditure to get rid of poverty...				Redistribution of income and wealth...				Welfare benefits have...			
	Oct. 1974	1979	1983	1987	Oct. 1974	1979	1983	1987	Oct. 1974	1979	1983	1987
Should be done / Gone too far	83.2	72.8	81.1	82.3	33.5	35.4	28.4	32.3	49.5	58.9	25.3	27.4
Does not matter / Are about right	7.7	13.6	2.8	6.6	23.6	22.4	14.6	17.0	35.6	28.1	57.5	48.0
Should not be done / Not gone far enough	9.1	13.6	16.0	11.1	42.9	42.2	57.0	50.7	14.9	13.0	17.2	24.6
Total	100.0	100.0	100.0	100.0	100.0	100.0	100.0	100.0	100.0	100.0	100.0	100.0
N. of respondents	208	191	493	563	205	192	535	521	208	192	513	552

Professional and managerial classes: women

	Government expenditure to get rid of poverty...				Redistribution of income and wealth...				Welfare benefits have...			
	Oct. 1974	1979	1983	1987	Oct. 1974	1979	1983	1987	Oct. 1974	1979	1983	1987
Should be done / Gone too far	86.7	79.6	79.5	89.1	45.0	36.6	36.7	39.6	39.1	59.5	23.1	27.5
Does not matter / Are about right	5.5	7.4	4.1	4.3	16.7	20.7	16.5	19.4	39.8	29.5	55.3	36.0
Should not be done / Not gone far enough	7.8	13.0	16.4	6.6	38.3	42.7	46.9	41.0	21.1	11.0	21.6	36.5
Total	100.0	100.0	100.0	100.0	100.0	100.0	100.0	100.0	100.0	100.0	100.0	100.0
N. of respondents	128	162	440	390	120	164	480	353	128	173	459	391

Intermediate and routine non-manual classes: men

	Government expenditure to get rid of poverty...				Redistribution of income and wealth...				Welfare benefits have...			
	Oct. 1974	1979	1983	1987	Oct. 1974	1979	1983	1987	Oct. 1974	1979	1983	1987
Should be done / Gone too far	84.2	85.9	86.8	92.3	46.6	43.6	41.0	42.4	41.2	58.4	23.0	24.7
Does not matter / Are about right	8.7	6.1	3.4	2.5	17.6	20.2	13.2	17.0	39.7	29.5	56.5	41.2
Should not be done / Not gone far enough	7.2	8.0	9.8	5.2	35.9	36.2	45.8	40.6	19.1	12.0	20.6	34.0
Total	100.0	100.0	100.0	100.0	100.0	100.0	100.0	100.0	100.0	100.0	100.0	100.0
N. of respondents	265	163	204	200	262	163	212	185	267	166	209	197

Intermediate and routine non-manual classes:

women

Should be done	85.5	81.1	83.1	86.2	50.5	52.6	44.2	36.4	—	—	—	—
Does not matter	6.0	9.1	3.8	5.3	14.9	15.6	18.5	20.8	—	—	—	—
Should not be done	8.5	9.7	13.1	8.6	34.6	31.8	37.3	42.8	—	—	—	—
Gone too far	—	—	—	—	—	—	—	—	39.2	58.2	22.3	27.3
Are about right	—	—	—	—	—	—	—	—	40.2	30.1	53.1	43.5
Not gone far enough	—	—	—	—	—	—	—	—	20.7	11.7	24.7	29.2
Total	100.0	100.0	100.0	100.0	100.0	100.0	100.0	100.0	100.0	100.0	100.0	100.0
N. of respondents	504	318	503	731	497	308	525	676	498	325	503	712

Manual working class

men

Should be done	90.9	87.4	89.9	91.8	68.2	63.6	54.9	52.0	—	—	—	—
Does not matter	4.9	6.7	2.0	3.2	14.0	14.3	12.0	23.0	—	—	—	—
Should not be done	4.2	5.9	8.0	5.0	17.8	22.1	33.1	25.0	—	—	—	—
Gone too far	—	—	—	—	—	—	—	—	26.4	44.6	16.8	22.5
Are about right	—	—	—	—	—	—	—	—	44.7	35.9	47.2	38.1
Not gone far enough	—	—	—	—	—	—	—	—	29.0	19.5	36.0	39.4
Total	100.0	100.0	100.0	100.0	100.0	100.0	100.0	100.0	100.0	100.0	100.0	100.0
N. of respondents	616	493	994	972	613	489	1035	874	611	498	995	963

Manual working class:

women

Should be done	88.4	86.8	88.5	87.1	68.3	69.0	60.7	52.0	—	—	—	—
Does not matter	6.3	6.0	3.0	5.5	13.6	14.5	15.6	18.2	—	—	—	—
Should not be done	5.3	7.3	8.5	7.4	18.1	16.4	23.7	29.7	—	—	—	—
Gone too far	—	—	—	—	—	—	—	—	28.3	40.2	16.7	23.7
Are about right	—	—	—	—	—	—	—	—	48.3	37.5	46.3	35.4
Not gone far enough	—	—	—	—	—	—	—	—	23.4	22.4	36.9	40.9
Total	100.0	100.0	100.0	100.0	100.0	100.0	100.0	100.0	100.0	100.0	100.0	100.0
N. of respondents	397	385	811	706	397	365	855	614	385	393	807	685

Table 10.28 *Attitudes to: expenditure on poverty, economic redistribution and the availability of welfare benefits by subjective and objective class (%)*

	Government expenditure to get rid of poverty . . .				Redistribution of income and wealth . . .				Welfare benefits have . . .			
	Oct. 1974	1979	1983	1987	Oct. 1974	1979	1983	1987	Oct. 1974	1979	1983	1987
Objectively middle class: subjectively middle class												
Should be done	83.4	74.4	78.9	84.2	35.1	29.7	30.5	30.9				
Does not matter	6.5	12.5	3.7	5.5	18.7	22.4	14.9	17.6				
Should not be done	10.1	13.1	17.5	10.3	46.2	47.9	54.6	51.5				
Gone too far									46.0	66.0	26.8	27.9
Are about right									36.7	27.4	57.3	45.9
Not gone far enough									17.3	6.5	15.9	26.2
Total	100.0	100.0	100.0	100.0	100.0	100.0	100.0	100.0	100.0	100.0	100.0	100.0
N. of respondents	356	313	767	856	353	313	817	807	365	321	790	846
Objectively middle class: subjectively no class identification												
Should be done	82.2	67.7	77.9	89.5	38.1	30.0	26.5	30.1				
Does not matter	2.2	12.9	4.9	4.2	28.6	16.7	26.5	20.5				
Should not be done	15.6	19.4	17.2	6.3	33.3	53.3	47.1	49.4				
Gone too far									45.0	66.7	22.2	21.3
Are about right									32.5	24.2	62.7	52.1
Not gone far enough									22.5	9.1	15.1	26.6
Total	100.0	100.0	100.0	100.0	100.0	100.0	100.0	100.0	100.0	100.0	100.0	100.0
N. of respondents	45	31	122	95	42	30	136	83	40	33	126	94
Objectively middle class: subjectively working class												
Should be done	85.8	82.2	86.2	87.9	51.1	49.3	46.3	42.4				
Does not matter	9.2	7.0	3.3	4.9	18.2	19.2	15.2	20.2				
Should not be done	5.0	10.7	10.5	7.2	30.7	31.5	38.5	37.4				
Gone too far									45.6	49.1	19.5	26.9
Are about right									37.2	31.8	52.8	39.4
Not gone far enough									17.2	19.1	27.8	33.7
Total	100.0	100.0	100.0	100.0	100.0	100.0	100.0	100.0	100.0	100.0	100.0	100.0
N. of respondents	239	214	717	919	231	213	764	837	239	220	735	902

Objectively working class: subjectively middle class

	1	2	3	4	5	6	7	8
Should be done	84.9	81.6	82.9	87.0	49.4	52.5	51.3	39.6
Does not matter	7.7	7.3	4.5	4.5	14.9	16.5	13.2	19.6
Should not be done	7.4	11.0	12.6	8.4	35.7	31.0	35.5	40.7
Total	100.0	100.0	100.0	100.0	100.0	100.0	100.0	100.0
N. of respondents	337	245	374	308	336	242	394	280

	1	2	3	4
Gone too far	33.3	53.4	23.5	28.5
Are about right	44.8	32.5	46.7	40.8
Not gone far enough	21.8	14.1	29.8	30.7
Total	100.0	100.0	100.0	100.0
N. of respondents	330	249	379	309

Objectively working class: subjectively no class identification

	1	2	3	4	5	6	7	8
Should be done	89.3	79.6	87.5	77.4	50.8	53.7	39.3	43.5
Does not matter	7.1	13.0	1.3	8.1	16.9	14.8	18.0	21.7
Should not be done	3.6	7.4	11.3	14.5	32.2	31.5	42.7	34.8
Total	100.0	100.0	100.0	100.0	100.0	100.0	100.0	100.0
N. of respondents	56	54	80	62	59	54	89	46

	1	2	3	4
Gone too far	22.6	54.1	11.3	15.0
Are about right	60.4	39.3	61.3	40.0
Not gone far enough	17.0	6.6	27.5	45.0
Total	100.0	100.0	100.0	100.0
N. of respondents	53	61	80	60

Objectively working class: subjectively working class

	1	2	3	4	5	6	7	8
Should be done	89.8	88.7	91.1	91.4	68.2	67.7	60.3	55.2
Does not matter	5.1	5.8	1.9	3.9	13.8	14.1	13.4	21.5
Should not be done	5.2	5.5	7.0	4.7	18.0	18.2	26.2	23.3
Total	100.0	100.0	100.0	100.0	100.0	100.0	100.0	100.0
N. of respondents	1085	855	1338	1296	1071	829	1392	1152

	1	2	3	4
Gone too far	29.1	43.3	15.2	21.9
Are about right	44.3	35.5	46.0	35.9
Not gone far enough	26.6	21.1	38.8	42.2
Total	100.0	100.0	100.0	100.0
N. of respondents	1070	863	1329	1270

Table 10.29 Attitudes to: expenditure on poverty, economic redistribution and the availability of welfare benefits by employment status (%)

Government expenditure to get rid of poverty . . .

	Oct. 1974	1979	1983	1987
Self employed with employees				
Should be done	77.9	70.4	78.1	77.8
Does not matter	8.8	14.8	2.9	5.2
Should not be done	13.2	14.8	19.0	17.0
Total	100.0	100.0	100.0	100.0
N. of respondents	68	54	143	169
Self employed; no employees				
Should be done	80.2	75.4	74.7	84.4
Does not matter	3.5	7.2	7.7	7.1
Should not be done	16.3	17.4	17.6	8.5
Total	100.0	100.0	100.0	100.0
N. of respondents	86	69	119	167
Managers				
Should be done	82.0	78.7	80.6	84.8
Does not matter	9.0	8.5	3.7	5.2
Should not be done	9.0	12.8	15.6	10.0
Total	100.0	100.0	100.0	100.0
N. of respondents	167	141	354	353

Redistribution of income and wealth . . .

	Oct. 1974	1979	1983	1987
Self employed with employees				
Should be done	20.6	23.2	24.2	23.2
Does not matter	20.6	21.4	9.5	18.1
Should not be done	58.8	55.4	66.3	58.7
Total	100.0	100.0	100.0	100.0
N. of respondents	68	56	163	148
Self employed; no employees				
Should be done	44.0	37.3	31.0	35.5
Does not matter	15.5	17.9	17.1	22.1
Should not be done	40.5	44.8	51.9	42.4
Total	100.0	100.0	100.0	100.0
N. of respondents	84	67	134	148
Managers				
Should be done	37.5	39.1	33.7	29.3
Does not matter	23.2	21.7	15.0	16.9
Should not be done	39.3	39.1	51.3	53.8
Total	100.0	100.0	100.0	100.0
N. of respondents	168	138	304	312

Welfare benefits have . . .

	Oct. 1974	1979	1983	1987
Self employed with employees				
Gone too far	63.9	64.9	29.6	34.3
Are about right	33.3	28.1	61.2	47.6
Not gone far enough	2.8	7.0	9.0	18.1
Total	100.0	100.0	100.0	100.0
N. of respondents	72	57	152	169
Self employed; no employees				
Gone too far	49.4	57.1	25.2	83.0
Are about right	32.9	28.5	56.3	36.6
Not gone far enough	14.6	14.3	18.5	30.4
Total	100.0	100.0	100.0	100.0
N. of respondents	85	70	119	165
Managers				
Gone too far	46.7	58.6	28.6	31.0
Are about right	34.9	27.9	53.6	41.3
Not gone far enough	18.3	13.6	17.9	27.6
Total	100.0	100.0	100.0	100.0
N. of respondents	169	140	308	348

Foremen and supervisors

Should be done	85.2	83.4	83.5	85.3	57.8	45.9	46.1	42.3
Does not matter	7.8	9.1	3.1	5.6	11.2	19.7	15.9	18.5
Should not be done	7.0	7.5	13.5	9.1	31.0	34.4	38.0	39.2
Total	100.0	100.0	100.0	100.0	100.0	100.0	100.0	100.0
N. of respondents	115	187	268	229	116	183	237	215

Gone too far	36.8	59.5	23.5	26.8
Are about right	37.6	30.6	47.9	41.2
Not gone far enough	25.6	10.0	28.6	32.0
Total	100.0	100.0	100.0	100.0
N. of respondents	117	190	238	225

Rank and file employees

Should be done	89.0	85.4	88.2	89.3	59.9	61.9	52.4	47.3
Does not matter	5.8	7.5	2.6	4.4	15.5	15.1	15.3	20.4
Should not be done	5.2	7.1	9.2	6.3	24.6	23.1	32.3	32.4
Total	100.0	100.0	100.0	100.0	100.0	100.0	100.0	100.0
N. of respondents	1464	892	2686	2668	1440	879	2603	2421

Gone too far	31.9	49.4	18.4	23.1
Are about right	44.7	32.4	51.1	39.7
Not gone far enough	23.5	18.1	30.5	37.2
Total	100.0	100.0	100.0	100.0
N. of respondents	1444	904	2602	2619

Table 10.30 *Attitudes to: expenditure on poverty, economic redistribution and the availability of welfare benefits: unemployed (%)*

	Government expenditure to get rid of poverty . . .				Redistribution of income and wealth . . .				Welfare benefits have . . .			
	Oct. 1974	1979	1983	1987	Oct. 1974	1979	1983	1987	Oct. 1974	1979	1983	1987
Unemployed												
Should be done	97.4	86.1	90.6	92.2								
Does not matter	2.6	8.3	3.8	4.7								
Should not be done	0.0	5.6	5.6	3.1								
Should be done					72.5	67.6	66.5	64.6				
Does not matter					10.0	17.6	13.9	17.8				
Should not be done					17.5	14.8	19.6	17.6				
Gone too far									10.5	23.7	4.0	9.5
Are about right									50.0	39.5	37.6	40.1
Not gone far enough									39.5	36.8	58.4	50.4
Total	100.0	100.0	100.0	100.0	100.0	100.0	100.0	100.0	100.0	100.0	100.0	100.0
N. of respondents	39	36	234	217	40	34	241	187	38	38	173	210

Table 10.31 *Attitudes to: expenditure on poverty, economic redistribution and the availability of welfare benefits by class and employment status (%)*

	Government expenditure to get rid of poverty . . .				Redistribution of income and wealth . . .				Welfare benefits have . . .			
	Oct. 1974	1979	1983	1987	Oct. 1974	1979	1983	1987	Oct. 1974	1979	1983	1987
Professional and managerial classes: self-employed												
Should be done	78.0	73.0	71.2	79.2								
Does not matter	7.3	13.5	6.3	5.2								
Should not be done	14.6	13.5	22.5	15.6								
Gone too far					21.1	25.0	22.2	25.7	61.9	61.5	28.3	34.6
Are about right					13.2	22.2	17.0	20.7	33.3	30.8	62.2	41.8
Not gone far enough					65.8	52.8	60.7	53.6	4.8	7.7	9.4	23.5
Total	100.0	100.0	100.0	100.0	100.0	100.0	100.0	100.0	100.0	100.0	100.0	100.0
N. of respondents	41	37	111	151	38	36	135	140	42	39	127	153
Professional and managerial classes: employees												
Should be done	86.1	76.0	82.1	86.2								
Does not matter	6.7	11.6	2.8	5.8								
Should not be done	7.1	12.4	15.1	8.0								
Gone too far					38.2	36.9	33.6	37.1	42.1	60.5	23.6	26.1
Are about right					23.2	22.0	15.3	17.4	38.2	26.3	55.9	43.3
Not gone far enough					38.6	41.1	51.1	45.5	19.7	13.2	20.5	30.6
Total	100.0	100.0	100.0	100.0	100.0	100.0	100.0	100.0	100.0	100.0	100.0	100.0
N. of respondents	252	242	795	799	246	241	851	734	254	243	821	790
Intermediate and routine non-manual classes: self-employed												
Should be done	77.3	71.2	78.6	79.5								
Does not matter	6.7	7.7	3.6	7.7								
Should not be done	16.0	21.2	17.5	12.8								
Gone too far					30.7	28.3	31.0	12.1	60.8	66.0	21.4	42.1
Are about right					17.3	24.5	17.2	18.2	31.6	24.5	57.1	42.1
Not gone far enough					52.0	47.2	51.7	69.7	7.6	9.4	21.4	15.8
Total	100.0	100.0	100.0	100.0	100.0	100.0	100.0	100.0	100.0	100.0	100.0	100.0
N. of respondents	75	52	28	39	75	53	29	33	79	53	28	38

Table 10.31 (cont.)

Government expenditure to get rid of poverty . . .

	Oct. 1974	1979	1983	1987
Intermediate and routine non-manual classes: employees				
Should be done	86.2	84.3	84.0	87.9
Does not matter	7.0	8.3	3.5	4.5
Should not be done	6.8	7.5	12.4	7.6
Total	100.0	100.0	100.0	100.0
N. of respondents	647	362	652	891
Manual working class: self employed				
Should be done	84.2	76.5	82.9	82.3
Does not matter	2.6	11.8	2.9	7.1
Should not be done	13.2	11.8	14.2	10.6
Total	100.0	100.0	100.0	100.0
N. of respondents	38	34	105	141
Manual working class: employed				
Should be done	90.0	87.6	89.4	90.4
Does not matter	5.6	6.2	2.5	3.9
Should not be done	4.4	6.2	8.1	5.7
Total	100.0	100.0	100.0	100.0
N. of respondents	839	614	1549	1537

Redistribution of income and wealth . . .

	Oct. 1974	1979	1983	1987
Intermediate and routine non-manual classes: employees				
Gone too far	51.3	53.4	42.6	38.6
Are about right	16.2	17.2	17.2	20.0
Not gone far enough	32.5	29.4	40.2	41.3
Total	100.0	100.0	100.0	100.0
N. of respondents	637	354	681	828
Manual working class: self employed				
Gone too far	51.3	41.2	31.6	36.7
Are about right	23.1	8.8	7.0	20.8
Not gone far enough	25.6	50.0	61.4	42.5
Total	100.0	100.0	100.0	100.0
N. of respondents	39	34	114	120
Manual working class: employed				
Gone too far	68.2	66.6	58.3	53.3
Are about right	13.8	14.1	14.0	21.1
Not gone far enough	18.0	19.3	27.6	25.5
Total	100.0	100.0	100.0	100.0
N. of respondents	833	602	1618	1368

Welfare benefits have . . .

	Oct. 1974	1979	1983	1987
Intermediate and routine non-manual classes: employees				
Gone too far	38.3	57.7	23.1	26.1
Are about right	40.3	29.8	54.0	43.1
Not gone far enough	21.4	12.5	22.9	30.9
Total	100.0	100.0	100.0	100.0
N. of respondents	640	369	658	871
Manual working class: self employed				
Gone too far	38.9	51.4	30.3	31.2
Are about right	36.1	31.4	54.1	42.8
Not gone far enough	25.0	17.1	15.6	26.1
Total	100.0	100.0	100.0	100.0
N. of respondents	36	35	109	138
Manual working class: employed				
Gone too far	27.4	45.4	16.7	22.3
Are about right	46.9	34.7	47.6	36.4
Not gone far enough	25.7	19.9	35.8	41.4
Total	100.0	100.0	100.0	100.0
N. of respondents	829	619	1543	1509

Table 10.32 *Attitudes to: expenditure on poverty, economic redistribution and the availability of welfare benefits by trade union membership (%)*

	Government expenditure to get rid of poverty . . .				Redistribution of income and wealth . . .				Welfare benefits have . . .			
	Oct. 1974	1979	1983	1987	Oct. 1974	1979	1983	1987	Oct. 1974	1979	1983	1987
Respondent is a member of a trade union												
Should be done / Gone too far	89.2	85.6	89.3	90.5	63.4	60.4	52.0	52.0	30.0	45.4	16.0	23.5
Does not matter / Are about right	5.3	6.6	2.4	3.9	18.1	17.5	14.2	19.2	47.5	33.6	49.9	37.3
Should not be done / Not gone far enough	5.6	7.7	8.3	5.6	18.5	22.0	33.8	28.7	22.5	21.1	34.1	39.2
Total	100.0	100.0	100.0	100.0	100.0	100.0	100.0	100.0	100.0	100.0	100.0	100.0
N. of respondents	536	543	1008	836	530	536	1042	780	545	549	1012	829
Respondent is married to a trade union member												
Should be done / Gone too far	86.3	84.5	88.4	88.7	65.4	64.9	55.5	43.1	31.2	51.1	20.0	24.8
Does not matter / Are about right	6.7	6.4	2.3	3.3	17.3	11.8	14.6	19.5	48.6	33.3	53.6	35.8
Should not be done / Not gone far enough	7.0	9.1	9.2	8.1	17.3	23.3	29.9	37.4	20.2	15.6	26.4	39.4
Total	100.0	100.0	100.0	100.0	100.0	100.0	100.0	100.0	100.0	100.0	100.0	100.0
N. of respondents	262	264	416	360	257	262	431	329	260	270	416	350
Neither is a member of a trade union												
Should be done / Gone too far	85.4	82.1	83.6	86.9	54.0	49.6	44.2	41.3	35.9	52.0	24.9	25.3
Does not matter / Are about right	7.4	9.0	3.5	5.1	14.3	17.2	15.6	20.2	43.1	33.0	50.0	41.8
Should not be done / Not gone far enough	7.2	8.9	12.8	8.0	31.7	33.2	40.2	38.5	21.0	15.0	25.1	32.8
Total	100.0	100.0	100.0	100.0	100.0	100.0	100.0	100.0	100.0	100.0	100.0	100.0
N. of respondents	1405	968	2266	2520	1398	947	2442	2238	1404	1000	2261	2468

Table 10.33 *Attitudes to: expenditure on poverty, economic redistribution and the availability of welfare benefits by economic sector (%)*

	Government expenditure to get rid of poverty . . .				Redistribution of income and wealth . . .					Welfare benefits have . . .			
	Oct. 1974	1979	1983	1987	Oct. 1974	1979	1983	1987		Oct. 1974	1979	1983	1987
Private sector													
Should be done	88.3	83.8	86.4	88.6	56.4	56.4	48.3	43.4	Gone too far	32.9	52.5	18.6	23.4
Does not matter	6.0	8.4	3.1	4.3	17.4	16.6	15.6	20.6	Are about right	43.2	30.1	50.2	40.1
Should not be done	5.7	7.8	10.6	7.1	26.2	27.0	36.1	36.0	Not gone far enough	23.9	17.4	31.2	36.5
Total	100.0	100.0	100.0	100.0	100.0	100.0	100.0	100.0		100.0	100.0	100.0	100.0
N. of respondents	1013	734	2011	2114	1007	716	2120	1904		1009	741	2023	2068
Public sector													
Should be done	88.3	84.6	86.6	88.5	60.3	59.5	50.6	47.3	Gone too far	35.1	49.2	20.0	26.3
Does not matter	6.2	7.5	2.4	5.4	14.2	15.3	14.6	18.7	Are about right	39.7	34.2	50.5	40.1
Should not be done	5.5	7.9	11.0	6.1	25.5	25.2	34.8	34.0	Not gone far enough	25.2	16.6	37.5	33.6
Total	100.0	100.0	100.0	100.0	100.0	100.0	100.0	100.0		100.0	100.0	100.0	100.0
N. of respondents	513	441	1192	1038	501	437	1256	953		496	447	1214	1028

Table 10.34 *Attitudes to: expenditure on poverty, economic redistribution and the availability of welfare benefits by class and economic sector (%)*

Government expenditure to get rid of poverty . . .

	Oct. 1974	1979	1983	1987
Professional and managerial classes: private sector				
Should be done	86.4	72.3	80.5	83.8
Does not matter	4.9	13.4	3.2	7.1
Should not be done	8.7	14.3	16.2	9.2
Total	100.0	100.0	100.0	100.0
N. of respondents	103	112	401	377
Professional and managerial classes: public sector				
Should be done	87.1	76.1	82.2	88.2
Does not matter	7.3	12.4	2.9	4.8
Should not be done	5.6	11.5	14.9	6.9
Total	100.0	100.0	100.0	100.0
N. of respondents	124	113	382	385
Intermediate and routine non-manual classes: private sector				
Should be done	86.1	84.7	84.6	87.9
Does not matter	6.3	8.7	3.6	3.9
Should not be done	7.6	6.6	11.8	8.1
Total	100.0	100.0	100.0	100.0
N. of respondents	367	229	441	639

Redistribution of income and wealth . . .

	Oct. 1974	1979	1983	1987
Professional and managerial classes: private sector				
Should be done	31.4	38.5	29.7	28.2
Does not matter	28.4	19.3	14.3	18.2
Should not be done	40.2	42.2	56.1	53.6
Total	100.0	100.0	100.0	100.0
N. of respondents	102	109	428	340
Professional and managerial classes: public sector				
Should be done	46.2	36.8	37.5	44.4
Does not matter	20.2	23.7	16.5	17.3
Should not be done	33.6	39.5	46.0	38.3
Total	100.0	100.0	100.0	100.0
N. of respondents	119	114	411	359
Intermediate and routine non-manual classes: private sector				
Should be done	47.4	49.8	41.8	36.9
Does not matter	18.2	17.5	19.0	20.3
Should not be done	34.4	32.7	39.2	42.8
Total	100.0	100.0	100.0	100.0
N. of respondents	363	223	462	593

Welfare benefits have . . .

	Oct. 1974	1979	1983	1987
Professional and managerial classes: private sector				
Gone too far	47.6	70.0	25.9	27.0
Are about right	35.2	20.9	57.1	47.4
Not gone far enough	17.1	9.1	17.1	25.5
Total	100.0	100.0	100.0	100.0
N. of respondents	105	110	410	365
Professional and managerial classes: public sector				
Gone too far	36.4	50.0	22.5	24.2
Are about right	39.7	34.5	53.4	41.0
Not gone far enough	24.0	15.5	24.1	34.8
Total	100.0	100.0	100.0	100.0
N. of respondents	121	116	395	386
Intermediate and routine non-manual classes: private sector				
Gone too far	38.6	59.2	21.0	24.6
Are about right	38.1	26.9	54.0	42.8
Not gone far enough	23.3	13.9	25.1	32.6
Total	100.0	100.0	100.0	100.0
N. of respondents	365	238	439	623

Table 10.34 (cont.)

Government expenditure to get rid of poverty . . .

	Oct. 1974	1979	1983	1987
Intermediate and routine non-manual classes: *public sector*				
Should be done	84.8	86.0	83.7	86.3
Does not matter	7.9	7.0	3.3	6.7
Should not be done	7.3	7.0	13.0	7.1
Total	100.0	100.0	100.0	100.0
N. of respondents	164	114	215	234
Manual working class: *private sector*				
Should be done	90.0	86.5	89.5	90.7
Does not matter	6.1	6.9	2.7	3.6
Should not be done	3.9	6.6	7.8	5.8
Total	100.0	100.0	100.0	100.0
N. of respondents	540	393	1093	1084
Manual working class: *public sector*				
Should be done	91.4	88.3	91.0	90.6
Does not matter	4.5	5.2	1.8	4.8
Should not be done	4.1	6.6	7.2	4.6
Total	100.0	100.0	100.0	100.0
N. of respondents	220	213	558	410

Redistribution of income and wealth . . .

	Oct. 1974	1979	1983	1987
Intermediate and routine non-manual classes: *public sector*				
Gone too far	58.0	61.3	46.2	41.3
Are about right	12.3	16.2	12.6	18.8
Not gone far enough	29.6	22.5	41.3	39.8
Total	100.0	100.0	100.0	100.0
N. of respondents	162	111	223	217
Manual working class: *private sector*				
Gone too far	67.3	65.4	58.2	53.0
Are about right	14.8	15.4	14.5	21.8
Not gone far enough	17.8	19.3	27.3	25.2
Total	100.0	100.0	100.0	100.0
N. of respondents	539	384	1143	958
Manual working class: *public sector*				
Gone too far	69.8	70.5	61.9	54.2
Are about right	12.6	10.5	13.7	20.0
Not gone far enough	17.7	19.0	24.4	25.9
Total	100.0	100.0	100.0	100.0
N. of respondents	215	210	577	369

Welfare benefits have . . .

	Oct. 1974	1979	1983	1987
Intermediate and routine non-manual classes: *public sector*				
Gone too far	44.3	54.9	25.6	31.2
Are about right	36.7	33.6	55.6	42.7
Not gone far enough	19.0	11.5	18.8	26.0
Total	100.0	100.0	100.0	100.0
N. of respondents	158	113	223	228
Manual working class: *private sector*				
Gone too far	25.9	43.5	15.3	21.3
Are about right	48.4	34.6	46.2	36.0
Not gone far enough	25.7	21.9	38.4	42.7
Total	100.0	100.0	100.0	100.0
N. of respondents	537	393	1088	1066
Manual working class: *public sector*				
Gone too far	27.8	45.8	16.1	25.4
Are about right	41.0	34.7	46.2	37.3
Not gone far enough	31.1	19.4	37.7	37.3
Total	100.0	100.0	100.0	100.0
N. of respondents	212	216	552	403

Table 10.35 Attitudes to: expenditure on poverty, economic redistribution and the availability of welfare benefits by school leaving age (%)

	Government expenditure to get rid of poverty . . .				Redistribution of income and wealth . . .				Welfare benefits have . . .			
	Oct. 1974	1979	1983	1987	Oct. 1974	1979	1983	1987	Oct. 1974	1979	1983	1987
Left school aged under 15												
Should be done / Gone too far	85.0	83.9	85.9	87.6	57.7	56.3	51.7	46.7	33.8	47.0	21.4	27.3
Does not matter / Are about right	6.8	7.0	3.5	4.3	13.6	17.5	16.2	21.5	46.7	35.8	48.4	38.9
Should not be done / Not gone far enough	8.2	9.1	10.6	8.0	28.7	26.2	32.1	31.8	19.5	17.2	30.1	33.8
Total	100.0	100.0	100.0	100.0	100.0	100.0	100.0	100.0	100.0	100.0	100.0	100.0
N. of respondents	911	585	1087	897	904	572	1155	775	910	609	1096	874
Left school aged 15												
Should be done / Gone too far	90.6	87.6	87.3	87.6	64.5	66.4	53.0	44.7	29.8	45.8	17.1	24.9
Does not matter / Are about right	5.6	5.9	2.9	4.5	16.1	13.7	14.4	19.7	42.1	33.2	50.0	38.6
Should not be done / Not gone far enough	3.8	6.5	9.8	7.8	19.4	19.9	32.6	35.6	28.1	20.9	32.9	36.5
Total	100.0	100.0	100.0	100.0	100.0	100.0	100.0	100.0	100.0	100.0	100.0	100.0
N. of respondents	657	525	963	898	651	512	1006	818	641	530	974	884
Left school aged 16												
Should be done / Gone too far	86.2	79.4	86.9	89.0	46.1	49.3	45.1	45.8	37.9	56.2	18.6	22.7
Does not matter / Are about right	5.9	9.4	2.3	4.7	17.7	17.0	15.4	20.3	38.2	30.2	51.3	41.4
Should not be done / Not gone far enough	7.8	11.1	10.8	6.3	36.3	33.7	39.5	33.9	23.8	13.6	30.2	35.9
Total	100.0	100.0	100.0	100.0	100.0	100.0	100.0	100.0	100.0	100.0	100.0	100.0
N. of respondents	320	350	889	891	317	347	953	807	319	354	905	879

Table 10.35 (cont.)

Government expenditure to get rid of poverty . . .

	Oct. 1974	1979	1983	1987
Left school aged 17				
Should be done	88.5	80.3	79.7	83.3
Does not matter	6.1	10.7	4.4	4.9
Should not be done	5.4	9.0	15.9	11.9
Total	100.0	100.0	100.0	100.0
N. of respondents	148	122	311	303
Left school aged over 17				
Should be done	84.6	80.9	83.5	89.4
Does not matter	8.0	11.5	2.9	4.6
Should not be done	7.4	7.7	13.6	6.0
Total	100.0	100.0	100.0	100.0
N. of respondents	175	183	445	373

Redistribution of income and wealth . . .

	Oct. 1974	1979	1983	1987
Left school aged 17				
Should be done	44.3	39.3	38.3	30.1
Does not matter	18.1	18.0	15.1	17.3
Should not be done	37.6	42.6	46.6	52.6
Total	100.0	100.0	100.0	100.0
N. of respondents	149	122	327	269
Left school aged over 17				
Should be done	44.4	41.4	36.6	38.3
Does not matter	19.1	19.9	14.2	23.0
Should not be done	36.4	38.7	49.2	38.8
Total	100.0	100.0	100.0	100.0
N. of respondents	162	181	480	349

Welfare benefits have . . .

	Oct. 1974	1979	1983	1987
Left school aged 17				
Gone too far	46.4	56.5	24.8	30.1
Are about right	36.6	31.4	52.9	42.9
Not gone far enough	17.0	12.1	22.3	27.0
Total	100.0	100.0	100.0	100.0
N. of respondents	153	124	314	297
Left school aged over 17				
Gone too far	32.0	55.2	18.1	27.3
Are about right	42.6	30.6	58.2	39.1
Not gone far enough	25.4	14.2	23.7	33.6
Total	100.0	100.0	100.0	100.0
N. of respondents	169	183	447	365

Table 10.36 *Attitudes to: expenditure on poverty, economic redistribution and the availability of welfare benefits by region (%)*

Government expenditure to get rid of poverty . . . .

	Oct. 1974	1979	1983	1987
Scotland				
Should be done	88.0	87.3	91.0	90.5
Does not matter	8.4	3.7	1.6	3.1
Should not be done	3.7	9.0	7.5	6.4
Total	100.0	100.0	100.0	100.0
N. of respondents	191	135	350	345
Wales				
Should be done	90.6	88.3	85.9	92.9
Does not matter	2.6	9.6	1.0	3.3
Should not be done	6.8	2.1	13.0	3.8
Total	100.0	100.0	100.0	100.0
N. of respondents	117	94	186	196
The North				
Should be done	89.0	83.8	86.0	89.2
Does not matter	4.2	7.7	3.6	4.1
Should not be done	6.8	8.5	10.4	6.6
Total	100.0	100.0	100.0	100.0
N. of respondents	647	482	1005	964

Redistribution of income and wealth . . . .

	Oct. 1974	1979	1983	1987
Scotland				
Should be done	59.2	60.7	63.5	55.5
Does not matter	15.2	17.0	12.1	15.2
Should not be done	25.7	22.2	24.4	29.4
Total	100.0	100.0	100.0	100.0
N. of respondents	191	135	359	298
Wales				
Should be done	70.1	78.9	51.7	53.7
Does not matter	12.8	14.4	22.3	22.9
Should not be done	17.1	6.7	26.1	23.4
Total	100.0	100.0	100.0	100.0
N. of respondents	117	90	205	175
The North				
Should be done	59.1	58.6	52.5	48.8
Does not matter	14.8	15.1	14.6	19.6
Should not be done	26.1	26.3	32.9	31.6
Total	100.0	100.0	100.0	100.0
N. of respondents	643	476	1052	875

Welfare benefits have . . .

	Oct. 1974	1979	1983	1987
Scotland				
Gone too far	32.8	43.5	16.0	22.3
Are about right	49.4	31.9	45.2	38.0
Not gone far enough	17.8	24.6	38.8	39.7
Total	100.0	100.0	100.0	100.0
N. of respondents	180	138	376	337
Wales				
Gone too far	26.8	36.4	15.7	20.7
Are about right	43.9	39.4	54.5	34.0
Not gone far enough	29.3	24.2	29.8	45.3
Total	100.0	100.0	100.0	100.0
N. of respondents	123	99	198	189
The North				
Gone too far	34.1	48.4	16.9	24.0
Are about right	43.7	34.9	50.7	37.1
Not gone far enough	22.2	16.7	32.4	38.9
Total	100.0	100.0	100.0	100.0
N. of respondents	645	498	1058	957

Table 10.36 (cont.)

The Midlands

Government expenditure to get rid of poverty . . .

	Oct. 1974	1979	1983	1987
Should be done	86.2	82.6	86.7	87.3
Does not matter	7.9	8.5	3.0	6.1
Should not be done	5.8	8.8	10.3	6.6
Total	100.0	100.0	100.0	100.0
N. of respondents	378	317	603	634

Redistribution of income and wealth . . .

	Oct. 1974	1979	1983	1987
Should be done	58.5	57.9	48.8	42.3
Does not matter	13.9	19.0	13.6	20.8
Should not be done	27.6	23.2	37.7	36.8
Total	100.0	100.0	100.0	100.0
N. of respondents	366	311	631	580

Welfare benefits have . . .

	Oct. 1974	1979	1983	1987
Gone too far	36.7	49.0	19.9	26.6
Are about right	39.4	33.7	51.6	40.1
Not gone far enough	23.9	17.2	28.5	33.3
Total	100.0	100.0	100.0	100.0
N. of respondents	373	314	649	625

Greater London

Government expenditure to get rid of poverty . . .

	Oct. 1974	1979	1983	1987
Should be done	86.0	82.2	85.7	85.0
Does not matter	7.5	9.6	5.1	4.2
Should not be done	6.5	8.1	9.2	10.8
Total	100.0	100.0	100.0	100.0
N. of respondents	214	197	458	452

Redistribution of income and wealth . . .

	Oct. 1974	1979	1983	1987
Should be done	56.3	51.6	39.9	43.4
Does not matter	16.0	12.9	17.2	17.7
Should not be done	27.7	35.5	43.0	38.9
Total	100.0	100.0	100.0	100.0
N. of respondents	213	186	489	397

Welfare benefits have . . .

	Oct. 1974	1979	1983	1987
Gone too far	30.7	51.5	21.5	22.6
Are about right	41.3	30.7	51.5	41.3
Not gone far enough	28.0	17.8	27.0	36.1
Total	100.0	100.0	100.0	100.0
N. of respondents	218	202		432

The South

Government expenditure to get rid of poverty . . .

	Oct. 1974	1979	1983	1987
Should be done	84.9	82.6	83.2	86.5
Does not matter	7.5	7.8	2.6	5.2
Should not be done	7.6	9.6	14.2	8.3
Total	100.0	100.0	100.0	100.0
N. of respondents	681	551	1102	1152

Redistribution of income and wealth . . .

	Oct. 1974	1979	1983	1987
Should be done	49.0	46.8	40.0	35.8
Does not matter	18.1	17.7	15.5	21.5
Should not be done	33.0	35.5	44.5	42.7
Total	100.0	100.0	100.0	100.0
N. of respondents	670	547	1196	1047

Welfare benefits have . . .

	Oct. 1974	1979	1983	1987
Gone too far	35.2	54.9	22.9	26.8
Are about right	43.1	31.0	52.6	44.4
Not gone far enough	21.8	13.6	24.4	28.8
Total	100.0	100.0	100.0	100.0
N. of respondents	670	568	1072	1137

Chapter 11

ISSUES OF CITIZENSHIP

1. A question on capital punishment was asked in 1963, 1966, 1969, 1970, 1979, 1983 and 1987. There are a number of differences of question wording and answer categories across the years. See Appendix E, p. 487.

2. The questions on racial equality, sexual equality, pornography and the availability of abortion were first asked in October 1974 and thereafter in every election study.

See Appendix E, pp. 487, 491, 492 and 493 on the construction of these variables.

Table 11.1 *Support for capital punishment: all respondents (%)*

	1963	1964	1966	1969	1970	Feb. 1974	Oct. 1974	1979	1983	1987
All respondents	77.5	–	81.9	79.3	80.8	–	–	74.6	63.1	81.3

Table 11.2 *Support for capital punishment by gender (%)*

	1963	1964	1966	1969	1970	Feb. 1974	Oct. 1974	1979	1983	1987
Men	77.2	–	80.6	77.3	79.1	–	–	75.7	64.2	81.8
Women	77.7	–	83.0	81.3	82.5	–	–	73.6	62.0	80.7

Table 11.3 *Support for capital punishment by age (%)*

	1963	1964	1966	1969	1970	Feb. 1974	Oct. 1974	1979	1983	1987
Aged under 25	67.2	–	80.4	71.0	71.1	–	–	67.1	59.7	77.1
Aged 25–34	74.3	–	76.3	73.2	78.1	–	–	70.8	59.1	79.1
Aged 35–44	76.5	–	77.9	78.8	81.1	–	–	74.8	60.9	79.3
Aged 45–54	77.6	–	82.7	80.3	78.7	–	–	70.8	61.2	80.5
Aged 55–64	83.3	–	87.4	89.9	86.7	–	–	77.0	66.6	84.4
Aged 65–74	79.8	–	85.3	86.7	91.0	–	–	81.5	70.5	87.3
Aged over 74	78.8	–	88.6	92.2	86.2	–	–	90.2	74.4	85.7

Table 11.4 *Support for capital punishment: new electors (%)*

	1963	1964	1966	1969	1970	Feb. 1974	Oct. 1974	1979	1983	1987
New electors	67.2	–	74.7	67.7	71.1	–	–	66.7	54.9	80.6

Table 11.5 *Support for capital punishment: non-voters (%)*

	1963	1964	1966	1969	1970	Feb. 1974	Oct. 1974	1979	1983	1987
Non-voters	–	–	78.7	–	82.0	–	–	78.3	67.2	80.6

Table 11.6 *Support for capital punishment by vote (%)*

	1963	1964	1966	1969	1970	Feb. 1974	Oct. 1974	1979	1983	1987
Conservative voters	81.4	–	87.6	84.2	88.9	–	–	81.5	69.6	88.6
Labour voters	75.6	–	79.4	72.2	74.5	–	–	67.0	56.4	73.7
Liberal voters	68.7	–	78.8	78.9	70.9	–	–	69.9	55.4	74.6
Other party voters	(100.0)	–	(75.3)	(76.5)	(74.9)	–	–	72.7	62.6	78.1

Table 11.7 *Support for capital punishment by strength and direction of partisanship (%)*

	1963	1964	1966	1969	1970	Feb. 1974	Oct. 1974	1979	1983	1987
Conservative identifiers										
very strong	86.3	–	92.1	88.9	93.6	–	–	85.2	76.8	88.6
fairly strong	81.7	–	86.4	84.2	86.7	–	–	84.1	65.6	89.9
not very strong	75.3	–	75.5	75.5	79.3	–	–	69.0	69.8	83.6
Liberal identifiers										
very strong	67.9	–	70.0	78.6	76.3	–	–	58.6	50.7	55.4
fairly strong	73.6	–	77.8	81.8	75.0	–	–	73.0	54.5	70.1
not very strong	68.9	–	87.7	65.8	70.0	–	–	75.0	55.8	77.4
Labour identifiers										
very strong	76.2	–	77.3	75.7	75.2	–	–	66.7	56.8	74.5
fairly strong	73.9	–	79.8	72.3	75.2	–	–	69.6	57.3	72.2
not very strong	78.0	–	76.6	75.6	74.0	–	–	73.1	63.6	84.2

Table 11.8 *Support for capital punishment by social class (%)*

	1963	1964	1966	1969	1970	Feb. 1974	Oct. 1974	1979	1983	1987
Professional and managerial classes	65.8	–	70.8	69.2	68.0	–	–	64.7	50.9	70.0
Intermediate and routine non-manual classes	77.5	–	81.1	76.8	76.5	–	–	75.4	64.0	81.6
Manual working class	79.5	–	84.8	83.7	86.1	–	–	79.7	70.5	88.1

Table 11.9 *Support for capital punishment by school leaving age (%)*

	1963	1964	1966	1969	1970	Feb. 1974	Oct. 1974	1979	1983	1987
Left school										
aged under 15	81.6	–	86.2	87.4	87.2	–	–	80.6	71.8	89.6
aged 15	75.5	–	82.5	79.2	84.6	–	–	80.5	70.8	88.6
aged 16	69.3	–	76.4	68.1	69.3	–	–	72.6	66.1	85.4
aged 17	77.0	–	75.9	65.0	62.2	–	–	61.0	47.5	80.9
aged over 17	50.6	–	51.3	52.3	52.4	–	–	50.0	32.6	66.3

Table 11.10 *Support for capital punishment: university or polytechnic educated (%)*

	1963	1964	1966	1969	1970	Feb. 1974	Oct. 1974	1979	1983	1987
Attended university or polytechnic	39.3	–	–	48.8	47.4	–	–	–	40.8	–

Table 11.11 *Support for capital punishment by religion (%)*

	1963	1964	1966	1969	1970	Feb. 1974	Oct. 1974	1979	1983	1987
Anglicans	80.3	–	83.4	83.3	86.5	–	–	80.7	67.8	85.6
Non-conformists	70.2	–	80.0	77.1	77.1	–	–	66.3	59.6	74.8
Roman Catholics	75.5	–	80.2	68.0	70.7	–	–	65.9	56.3	78.6
No religion	49.2	–	59.7	48.1	47.6	–	–	71.9	59.8	76.4

Table 11.12 *Support for capital punishment by religiosity (%)*

	1963	1964	1966	1969	1970	Feb. 1974	Oct. 1974	1979	1983	1987
Attend church										
regularly	73.8	–	78.9	74.9	72.8	–	–	65.5	46.4	69.5
occasionally	77.4	–	82.3	83.6	84.1	–	–	77.7	65.7	84.9
rarely	81.9	–	85.6	79.8	84.7	–	–	76.9	69.1	85.1
never	80.2	–	82.2	79.8	81.9	–	–	73.9	70.4	89.1

Table 11.13 *Support for capital punishment by region (%)*

	1963	1964	1966	1969	1970	Feb. 1974	Oct. 1974	1979	1983	1987
Scotland	81.1	–	87.7	84.2	77.6	–	–	77.9	66.7	82.3
Wales	76.5	–	74.0	82.2	80.9	–	–	73.9	63.1	77.0
The North	79.7	–	83.4	83.6	85.6	–	–	75.0	64.1	85.1
The Midlands	76.1	–	84.9	76.5	82.6	–	–	79.2	67.9	84.4
Greater London	72.8	–	77.6	74.2	73.2	–	–	67.0	63.6	73.5
The South	77.6	–	79.7	77.8	80.1	–	–	73.6	58.2	79.6

Table 11.14 *Attitudes to racial equality, sexual equality, pornography and the availability of abortion: all respondents* (%)

	Attempts to ensure racial equality . . .				Attempts to ensure sexual equality . . .				The availability of pornography . . .				The availability of abortion . . .			
	Oct. 1974	1979	1983	1987	Oct. 1974	1979	1983	1987	Oct. 1974	1979	1983	1987	Oct. 1974	1979	1983	1987
Gone too far	27.0	29.9	19.8	29.3	19.2	22.7	9.5	8.6	64.3	66.7	64.2	66.8	42.9	44.4	31.7	32.9
About right	44.3	41.0	52.9	41.9	46.0	47.8	58.2	48.5	30.1	28.9	31.4	29.8	42.6	44.0	55.4	56.8
Not gone far enough	28.7	29.1	27.3	28.8	34.8	29.5	32.3	42.9	5.6	4.5	4.4	3.5	14.6	11.6	12.9	10.3
Total	100.0	100.0	100.0	100.0	100.0	100.0	100.0	100.0	100.0	100.0	100.0	100.0	100.0	100.0	100.0	100.0
N. of respondents	2196	1762	3705	3670	2260	1783	3793	3718	2250	1814	3797	3723	2123	1714	3282	3267

Table 11.15 *Attitudes to racial equality, sexual equality, pornography and the availability of abortion by gender* (%)

Men

	Attempts to ensure racial equality . . .				Attempts to ensure sexual equality . . .				The availability of pornography . . .				The availability of abortion . . .			
	Oct. 1974	1979	1983	1987	Oct. 1974	1979	1983	1987	Oct. 1974	1979	1983	1987	Oct. 1974	1979	1983	1987
Gone too far	26.9	28.7	18.8	30.3	16.8	22.6	10.6	10.1	52.3	57.6	52.4	56.2	36.0	38.3	26.1	29.0
About right	44.0	42.0	52.4	40.7	46.4	48.5	60.4	49.5	39.0	35.7	41.8	38.7	47.0	48.2	59.2	58.9
Not gone far enough	29.1	29.3	28.7	29.0	36.8	29.0	29.0	40.4	8.7	6.7	5.8	5.1	17.0	13.5	14.7	12.1
Total	100.0	100.0	100.0	100.0	100.0	100.0	100.0	100.0	100.0	100.0	100.0	100.0	100.0	100.0	100.0	100.0
N. of respondents	1112	871	1812	1793	1137	873	1803	1799	1125	883	1807	1787	1049	824	1526	1552

Women

	Attempts to ensure racial equality . . .				Attempts to ensure sexual equality . . .				The availability of pornography . . .				The availability of abortion . . .			
	Oct. 1974	1979	1983	1987	Oct. 1974	1979	1983	1987	Oct. 1974	1979	1983	1987	Oct. 1974	1979	1983	1987
Gone too far	27.0	31.0	20.7	28.2	21.6	22.9	8.6	7.2	76.4	75.3	74.9	76.5	49.6	50.0	36.5	36.5
About right	44.6	40.1	53.3	43.1	45.5	47.1	56.2	47.4	21.1	22.3	22.0	21.6	38.4	40.1	52.1	54.9
Not gone far enough	28.3	29.0	26.0	28.8	32.9	30.0	35.2	45.3	2.5	2.4	3.1	2.0	12.0	9.9	11.4	8.6
Total	100.0	100.0	100.0	100.0	100.0	100.0	100.0	100.0	100.0	100.0	100.0	100.0	100.0	100.0	100.0	100.0
N. of respondents	1084	891	1893	1879	1123	910	1990	1919	1125	931	1990	1936	1074	890	1756	1715

Table 11.16 *Attitudes to racial equality, sexual equality, pornography and the availability of abortion by age (%)*

Aged under 25

	Attempts to ensure racial equality . . .				Attempts to ensure sexual equality . . .				The availability of pornography . . .				The availability of abortion . . .			
	Oct. 1974	1979	1983	1987	Oct. 1974	1979	1983	1987	Oct. 1974	1979	1983	1987	Oct. 1974	1979	1983	1987
Gone too far	19.2	23.8	16.7	22.1	18.0	20.4	8.3	7.5	34.0	38.3	37.2	44.5	26.1	32.5	22.2	28.9
About right	34.9	24.4	42.3	33.7	44.7	46.9	57.0	48.3	53.4	50.6	54.7	47.2	53.3	46.6	56.5	55.7
Not gone far enough	45.9	51.8	41.0	44.2	37.2	32.7	34.7	44.2	12.6	11.1	8.1	8.4	20.6	20.9	21.3	15.4
Total	100.0	100.0	100.0	100.0	100.0	100.0	100.0	100.0	100.0	100.0	100.0	100.0	100.0	100.0	100.0	100.0
N. of respondents	255	164	528	473	266	162	533	476	262	162	534	474	257	163	463	422

Aged 25–34

	Attempts to ensure racial equality . . .				Attempts to ensure sexual equality . . .				The availability of pornography . . .				The availability of abortion . . .			
	Oct. 1974	1979	1983	1987	Oct. 1974	1979	1983	1987	Oct. 1974	1979	1983	1987	Oct. 1974	1979	1983	1987
Gone too far	21.1	25.5	16.7	27.3	15.8	19.0	8.4	7.9	40.8	45.9	50.0	48.8	28.8	37.7	23.6	23.6
About right	41.2	37.9	48.4	38.6	45.3	44.3	55.6	47.6	47.7	45.9	44.9	47.0	47.6	46.7	60.8	62.3
Not gone far enough	37.7	36.7	34.8	34.1	38.9	36.7	36.1	44.5	11.5	8.2	5.1	4.1	23.6	15.6	15.7	14.1
Total	100.0	100.0	100.0	100.0	100.0	100.0	100.0	100.0	100.0	100.0	100.0	100.0	100.0	100.0	100.0	100.0
N. of respondents	456	412	710	669	468	411	738	676	461	416	720	671	445	403	649	607

Table 11.16 (*cont.*)

Aged 35–44

	Attempts to ensure racial equality . . .				Attempts to ensure sexual equality . . .				The availability of pornography . . .				The availability of abortion . . .			
	Oct. 1974	1979	1983	1987	Oct. 1974	1979	1983	1987	Oct. 1974	1979	1983	1987	Oct. 1974	1979	1983	1987
Gone too far	23.8	25.8	18.4	28.4	15.8	23.5	9.1	7.7	60.6	60.4	59.4	61.0	35.8	37.1	24.8	29.9
About right	49.6	44.8	52.6	39.3	45.7	48.6	56.9	46.1	34.5	34.2	36.1	35.3	47.0	49.0	63.4	60.2
Not gone far enough	26.6	29.4	29.0	32.3	38.4	27.9	34.0	46.2	5.0	5.4	4.5	3.7	17.2	13.9	11.8	9.9
Total	100.0	100.0	100.0	100.0	100.0	100.0	100.0	100.0	100.0	100.0	100.0	100.0	100.0	100.0	100.0	100.0
N. of respondents	369	306	671	733	385	319	697	740	383	316	699	739	366	302	613	647

Aged 45–54

	Attempts to ensure racial equality . . .				Attempts to ensure sexual equality . . .				The availability of pornography . . .				The availability of abortion . . .			
	Oct. 1974	1979	1983	1987	Oct. 1974	1979	1983	1987	Oct. 1974	1979	1983	1987	Oct. 1974	1979	1983	1987
Gone too far	27.3	31.3	19.2	36.0	16.7	19.8	7.9	9.4	73.8	77.3	70.2	73.5	41.7	48.3	30.3	32.8
About right	48.3	44.6	55.3	32.7	50.5	50.9	57.4	46.6	22.9	20.9	27.9	24.9	47.0	42.6	55.7	57.5
Not gone far enough	23.8	24.1	25.5	25.3	32.8	29.3	34.7	43.9	3.3	1.8	2.0	1.6	11.3	9.1	14.0	9.7
Total	100.0	100.0	100.0	100.0	100.0	100.0	100.0	100.0	100.0	100.0	100.0	100.0	100.0	100.0	100.0	100.0
N. of respondents	383	323	595	565	390	328	614	566	393	335	615	566	372	317	542	497

Aged 55–64

	Attempts to ensure racial equality . . .				Attempts to ensure sexual equality . . .				The availability of pornography . . .				The availability of abortion . . .			
	Oct. 1974	1979	1983	1987	Oct. 1974	1979	1983	1987	Oct. 1974	1979	1983	1987	Oct. 1974	1979	1983	1987
Gone too far	34.5	29.4	18.9	30.7	23.9	24.0	10.4	11.0	81.6	82.9	79.9	82.4	56.9	47.7	42.3	38.3
About right	45.0	44.1	61.2	46.8	42.8	45.2	57.4	46.3	16.9	16.4	17.6	16.2	35.2	46.4	49.7	54.2
Not gone far enough	20.5	26.5	19.9	22.5	33.3	30.8	32.3	42.7	1.5	0.8	2.5	1.3	8.0	9.0	8.0	7.5
Total	100.0	100.0	100.0	100.0	100.0	100.0	100.0	100.0	100.0	100.0	100.0	100.0	100.0	100.0	100.0	100.0
N. of respondents	342	245	558	575	348	250	575	583	343	257	565	584	327	235	484	514

Aged 65–74

	Attempts to ensure racial equality . . .				Attempts to ensure sexual equality . . .				The availability of pornography . . .				The availability of abortion . . .			
	Oct. 1974	1979	1983	1987	Oct. 1974	1979	1983	1987	Oct. 1974	1979	1983	1987	Oct. 1974	1979	1983	1987
Gone too far	36.2	40.3	26.9	27.7	24.7	27.6	12.3	7.4	90.4	87.7	88.0	88.4	66.9	62.2	46.1	39.7
About right	40.8	44.4	58.4	51.9	45.8	49.5	63.6	53.4	8.9	11.3	8.4	9.3	27.7	31.9	45.9	54.0
Not gone far enough	23.1	15.3	14.7	20.4	29.5	23.0	24.2	39.3	0.7	1.0	3.6	2.3	5.4	5.9	8.0	6.3
Total	100.0	100.0	100.0	100.0	100.0	100.0	100.0	100.0	100.0	100.0	100.0	100.0	100.0	100.0	100.0	100.0
N. of respondents	260	196	404	395	271	196	411	405	271	203	423	408	242	185	350	358

Table 11.16 (*cont.*)

Aged over 74

	Attempts to ensure racial equality . . .				Attempts to ensure sexual equality . . .				The availability of pornography . . .				The availability of abortion . . .			
	Oct. 1974	1979	1983	1987	Oct. 1974	1979	1983	1987	Oct. 1974	1979	1983	1987	Oct. 1974	1979	1983	1987
Gone too far	30.3	43.2	32.3	34.4	26.6	35.4	15.9	10.4	91.5	93.3	86.3	86.7	73.6	59.6	57.7	54.8
About right	52.5	44.1	54.2	55.1	47.6	53.1	67.3	59.0	7.8	5.0	8.7	10.2	21.7	34.6	38.0	42.8
Not gone far enough	17.2	12.6	13.5	10.6	25.8	11.5	16.9	30.6	0.8	1.7	5.1	3.1	4.7	5.8	4.3	2.5
Total	100.0	100.0	100.0	100.0	100.0	100.0	100.0	100.0	100.0	100.0	100.0	100.0	100.0	100.0	100.0	100.0
N. of respondents	122	111	221	231	124	113	207	240	129	120	222	248	106	104	167	192

Table 11.17 *Attitudes to racial equality, sexual equality, pornography and the availability of abortion by age and gender* (%)

Men aged under 25

	Attempts to ensure racial equality . . .				Attempts to ensure sexual equality . . .				The availability of pornography . . .				The availability of abortion . . .			
	Oct. 1974	1979	1983	1987	Oct. 1974	1979	1983	1987	Oct. 1974	1979	1983	1987	Oct. 1974	1979	1983	1987
Gone too far	20.9	28.2	17.6	23.2	19.4	25.0	8.9	8.3	24.3	28.2	24.7	36.2	23.3	20.0	20.8	27.1
About right	35.1	24.4	41.3	37.2	43.9	48.7	62.1	54.0	58.1	55.1	63.4	52.6	50.4	57.3	54.6	55.4
Not gone far enough	44.0	47.4	41.2	39.6	36.7	26.3	29.0	37.7	17.6	16.7	11.9	11.2	26.3	22.7	24.6	17.5
Total	100.0	100.0	100.0	100.0	100.0	100.0	100.0	100.0	100.0	100.0	100.0	100.0	100.0	100.0	100.0	100.0
N. of respondents	134	78	279	236	139	76	271	238	136	78	280	238	133	75	232	202

Women aged under 25

	Attempts to ensure racial equality . . .				Attempts to ensure sexual equality . . .				The availability of pornography . . .				The availability of abortion . . .			
	Oct. 1974	1979	1983	1987	Oct. 1974	1979	1983	1987	Oct. 1974	1979	1983	1987	Oct. 1974	1979	1983	1987
Gone too far	17.4	19.8	15.7	21.1	16.5	16.3	7.7	6.8	44.4	47.6	51.0	52.8	29.0	43.2	23.6	30.5
About right	34.7	24.4	43.5	30.2	45.7	45.3	51.8	42.6	48.4	46.4	45.1	41.7	56.5	37.5	58.4	56.0
Not gone far enough	47.9	55.8	40.8	48.7	37.8	38.4	40.5	50.6	7.1	6.0	3.9	5.5	14.5	19.3	18.0	13.5
Total	100.0	100.0	100.0	100.0	100.0	100.0	100.0	100.0	100.0	100.0	100.0	100.0	100.0	100.0	100.0	100.0
N. of respondents	121	86	249	237	127	86	262	238	126	84	254	237	124	88	231	219

Table 11.17 (cont.)

Men aged 25–44

	Attempts to ensure racial equality . . .				Attempts to ensure sexual equality . . .				The availability of pornography . . .				The availability of abortion . . .			
	Oct. 1974	1979	1983	1987	Oct. 1974	1979	1983	1987	Oct. 1974	1979	1983	1987	Oct. 1974	1979	1983	1987
Gone too far	23.8	24.6	17.6	29.9	16.4	23.9	10.5	9.7	34.6	39.7	40.6	42.9	25.0	33.8	21.1	22.3
About right	44.4	42.9	50.1	38.1	43.5	44.1	59.3	51.3	51.7	48.9	53.4	51.5	51.9	48.7	63.7	64.2
Not gone far enough	31.8	32.5	32.3	32.0	40.1	32.0	30.2	40.0	13.7	11.5	6.0	5.6	23.1	17.5	15.2	13.5
Total	100.0	100.0	100.0	100.0	100.0	100.0	100.0	100.0	100.0	100.0	100.0	100.0	100.0	100.0	100.0	100.0
N. of respondents	437	354	672	696	446	356	680	698	439	358	678	697	420	343	585	602

Women aged 25–44

	Attempts to ensure racial equality . . .				Attempts to ensure sexual equality . . .				The availability of pornography . . .				The availability of abortion . . .			
	Oct. 1974	1979	1983	1987	Oct. 1974	1979	1983	1987	Oct. 1974	1979	1983	1987	Oct. 1974	1979	1983	1987
Gone too far	20.6	26.6	17.6	25.8	15.2	18.2	7.1	5.8	66.2	64.2	67.5	67.3	39.4	40.9	26.9	31.0
About right	45.6	38.7	50.8	40.0	47.7	48.1	53.4	42.5	30.9	33.2	28.8	30.3	42.5	46.7	60.0	58.4
Not gone far enough	33.8	34.6	31.6	34.2	37.1	33.7	39.4	51.7	3.0	2.7	3.7	2.4	18.2	12.4	12.5	10.6
Total	100.0	100.0	100.0	100.0	100.0	100.0	100.0	100.0	100.0	100.0	100.0	100.0	100.0	100.0	100.0	100.0
N. of respondents	388	364	709	706	407	374	754	718	405	374	740	713	391	362	674	652

Men aged 45–64

	Attempts to ensure racial equality . . .				Attempts to ensure sexual equality . . .				The availability of pornography . . .				The availability of abortion . . .			
	Oct. 1974	1979	1983	1987	Oct. 1974	1979	1983	1987	Oct. 1974	1979	1983	1987	Oct. 1974	1979	1983	1987
Gone too far	31.7	27.6	17.7	33.8	15.8	18.8	11.5	11.9	68.8	74.1	66.1	69.0	44.5	43.3	30.7	33.6
About right	45.5	44.4	58.8	42.2	48.8	49.7	59.3	44.8	27.7	24.2	32.0	28.7	45.4	48.7	56.9	56.8
Not gone far enough	22.8	28.0	23.5	24.0	35.4	31.5	29.3	43.3	3.5	1.7	2.0	2.2	10.1	8.0	12.4	9.6
Total	100.0	100.0	100.0	100.0	100.0	100.0	100.0	100.0	100.0	100.0	100.0	100.0	100.0	100.0	100.0	100.0
N. of respondents	369	293	568	583	373	298	571	587	372	301	558	581	346	275	468	509

Women aged 45–64

	Attempts to ensure racial equality . . .				Attempts to ensure sexual equality . . .				The availability of pornography . . .				The availability of abortion . . .			
	Oct. 1974	1979	1983	1987	Oct. 1974	1979	1983	1987	Oct. 1974	1979	1983	1987	Oct. 1974	1979	1983	1987
Gone too far	30.3	33.5	20.4	32.9	24.4	24.6	6.9	8.5	86.3	85.6	82.7	87.3	53.0	52.7	40.4	37.6
About right	48.0	44.4	57.6	43.5	44.9	47.1	55.6	48.1	12.4	13.4	14.9	12.0	37.7	39.7	49.4	55.0
Not gone far enough	21.6	22.2	22.0	23.6	30.7	28.2	37.4	43.3	1.4	1.0	2.5	0.7	9.3	7.6	10.2	7.4
Total	100.0	100.0	100.0	100.0	100.0	100.0	100.0	100.0	100.0	100.0	100.0	100.0	100.0	100.0	100.0	100.0
N. of respondents	356	275	586	556	365	280	618	563	364	291	628	568	353	277	557	502

Table 11.17 (*cont.*)

Men aged over 64

	Attempts to ensure racial equality . . .				Attempts to ensure sexual equality . . .				The availability of pornography . . .				The availability of abortion . . .			
	Oct. 1974	1979	1983	1987	Oct. 1974	1979	1983	1987	Oct. 1974	1979	1983	1987	Oct. 1974	1979	1983	1987
Gone too far	29.3	41.0	25.6	30.8	17.7	26.1	11.1	9.2	83.9	83.3	80.4	81.5	59.6	50.4	35.1	36.4
About right	46.1	44.4	56.1	48.3	50.9	56.0	63.7	51.5	15.5	16.7	13.1	13.5	32.9	40.3	56.8	55.6
Not gone far enough	24.6	14.6	18.2	20.9	31.4	17.7	25.2	39.3	0.6	0.0	6.5	5.0	7.5	9.3	8.1	8.0
Total	100.0	100.0	100.0	100.0	100.0	100.0	100.0	100.0	100.0	100.0	100.0	100.0	100.0	100.0	100.0	100.0
N. of respondents	167	144	284	263	175	141	272	262	174	144	282	259	146	129	231	225

Women aged over 64

	Attempts to ensure racial equality . . .				Attempts to ensure sexual equality . . .				The availability of pornography . . .				The availability of abortion . . .			
	Oct. 1974	1979	1983	1987	Oct. 1974	1979	1983	1987	Oct. 1974	1979	1983	1987	Oct. 1974	1979	1983	1987
Gone too far	38.1	41.7	31.4	29.8	31.4	33.9	15.3	8.1	96.0	95.0	92.9	91.9	75.7	70.0	61.7	50.6
About right	43.3	44.2	57.6	56.5	42.7	46.4	65.7	58.2	3.1	2.8	4.9	7.1	20.8	26.9	32.5	46.6
Not gone far enough	18.6	14.1	11.0	13.8	25.9	19.6	19.0	33.8	0.9	2.2	2.3	1.0	3.5	3.1	5.5	2.8
Total	100.0	100.0	100.0	100.0	100.0	100.0	100.0	100.0	100.0	100.0	100.0	100.0	100.0	100.0	100.0	100.0
N. of respondents	215	163	342	363	220	168	347	385	226	179	363	397	202	160	286	324

Table 11.18 *Attitudes to racial equality, sexual equality, pornography and the availability of abortion by marital status (%)*

Single

	Attempts to ensure racial equality . . .				Attempts to ensure sexual equality . . .				The availability of pornography . . .				The availability of abortion . . .			
	Oct. 1974	1979	1983	1987	Oct. 1974	1979	1983	1987	Oct. 1974	1979	1983	1987	Oct. 1974	1979	1983	1987
Gone too far	–	24.0	17.7	22.4	–	21.6	7.9	7.5	–	46.7	42.9	50.6	–	34.5	25.5	28.7
About right	–	30.0	44.1	36.5	–	42.3	57.8	48.3	–	44.9	49.3	42.2	–	47.1	55.9	56.0
Not gone far enough	–	46.1	38.3	41.1	–	36.2	34.3	44.2	–	8.4	7.8	7.2	–	18.4	18.6	15.3
Total	–	100.0	100.0	100.0	–	100.0	100.0	100.0	–	100.0	100.0	100.0	–	100.0	100.0	100.0
N. of respondents	–	217	656	661	–	213	659	672	–	214	657	669	–	206	558	576

Married

	Attempts to ensure racial equality . . .				Attempts to ensure sexual equality . . .				The availability of pornography . . .				The availability of abortion . . .			
	Oct. 1974	1979	1983	1987	Oct. 1974	1979	1983	1987	Oct. 1974	1979	1983	1987	Oct. 1974	1979	1983	1987
Gone too far	26.6	30.3	19.1	30.2	17.8	22.4	9.5	8.8	64.3	66.6	66.7	68.3	41.6	44.4	31.3	32.4
About right	45.9	42.3	54.8	41.9	47.5	48.8	58.1	47.8	30.7	29.2	29.8	28.8	43.8	44.4	56.6	58.1
Not gone far enough	27.4	27.5	26.1	27.9	34.8	28.8	32.4	43.4	5.0	4.2	3.5	2.8	17.7	11.2	12.1	9.5
Total	100.0	100.0	100.0	100.0	100.0	100.0	100.0	100.0	100.0	100.0	100.0	100.0	100.0	100.0	100.0	100.0
N. of respondents	1641	1285	2603	2522	1694	1302	2669	2548	1684	1322	2667	2546	1597	1249	2333	2258

Table 11.18 (*cont.*)

Divorced and separated

	Attempts to ensure racial equality . . .				Attempts to ensure sexual equality . . .				The availability of pornography . . .				The availability of abortion . . .			
	Oct. 1974	1979	1983	1987	Oct. 1974	1979	1983	1987	Oct. 1974	1979	1983	1987	Oct. 1974	1979	1983	1987
Gone too far	–	27.8	22.4	32.6	–	20.0	8.7	7.2	–	62.7	65.8	69.5	–	42.9	24.9	26.2
About right	–	36.1	46.9	41.0	–	44.0	53.9	46.1	–	33.3	26.4	28.9	–	41.4	57.4	60.6
Not gone far enough	–	36.1	30.7	26.4	–	36.0	37.4	46.7	–	4.0	7.8	1.6	–	15.7	17.7	13.1
Total	–	100.0	100.0	100.0	–	100.0	100.0	100.0	–	100.0	100.0	100.0	–	100.0	100.0	100.0
N. of respondents	–	72	161	180	–	75	173	180	–	75	173	182	–	70	151	160

Widowed

	Attempts to ensure racial equality . . .				Attempts to ensure sexual equality . . .				The availability of pornography . . .				The availability of abortion . . .			
	Oct. 1974	1979	1983	1987	Oct. 1974	1979	1983	1987	Oct. 1974	1979	1983	1987	Oct. 1974	1979	1983	1987
Gone too far	–	35.1	29.8	33.8	–	27.9	14.1	9.8	–	90.4	87.1	86.5	–	57.1	54.4	50.2
About right	–	46.8	58.8	54.2	–	48.6	62.2	55.4	–	7.4	9.9	11.9	–	37.1	41.1	45.6
Not gone far enough	–	18.1	11.7	12.0	–	23.5	23.7	34.8	–	2.1	3.0	1.7	–	5.7	4.6	4.2
Total	–	100.0	100.0	100.0	–	100.0	100.0	100.0	–	100.0	100.0	100.0	–	100.0	100.0	100.0
N. of respondents	–	171	283	309	–	179	290	317	–	188	297	325	–	175	237	272

Table 11.19 *Attitudes to racial equality, sexual equality, pornography and the availability of abortion by marital status and gender* (%)

Single men

	Attempts to ensure racial equality . . .				Attempts to ensure sexual equality . . .				The availability of pornography . . .				The availability of abortion . . .			
	Oct. 1974	1979	1983	1987	Oct. 1974	1979	1983	1987	Oct. 1974	1979	1983	1987	Oct. 1974	1979	1983	1987
Gone too far	–	24.0	17.5	23.0	–	21.7	8.0	8.5	–	36.4	31.1	40.0	–	26.8	22.8	25.8
About right	–	33.9	45.5	39.0	–	45.8	63.5	51.2	–	52.9	59.8	50.0	–	52.7	58.0	58.3
Not gone far enough	–	42.1	37.0	38.0	–	32.5	28.5	40.3	–	10.7	9.1	10.0	–	20.5	19.2	15.9
Total	–	100.0	100.0	100.0	–	100.0	100.0	100.0	–	100.0	100.0	100.0	–	100.0	100.0	100.0
N. of respondents	–	121	382	374	–	120	376	377	–	121	381	375	–	112	313	312

Single women

	Attempts to ensure racial equality . . .				Attempts to ensure sexual equality . . .				The availability of pornography . . .				The availability of abortion . . .			
	Oct. 1974	1979	1983	1987	Oct. 1974	1979	1983	1987	Oct. 1974	1979	1983	1987	Oct. 1974	1979	1983	1987
Gone too far	–	24.0	18.0	21.7	–	21.5	7.7	6.2	–	60.2	59.2	64.0	–	43.6	29.1	32.1
About right	–	25.0	42.0	33.2	–	37.6	50.3	44.7	–	34.4	34.9	32.3	–	40.4	53.1	53.2
Not gone far enough	–	51.0	40.0	45.1	–	40.9	42.0	49.1	–	5.4	5.9	3.7	–	16.0	17.8	14.7
Total	–	100.0	100.0	100.0	–	100.0	100.0	100.0	–	100.0	100.0	100.0	–	100.0	100.0	100.0
N. of respondents	–	96	274	287	–	93	284	295	–	93	277	294	–	94	245	264

Table 11.19 (*cont.*)

Married men

	Attempts to ensure racial equality . . .				Attempts to ensure sexual equality . . .				The availability of pornography . . .				The availability of abortion . . .			
	Oct. 1974	1979	1983	1987	Oct. 1974	1979	1983	1987	Oct. 1974	1979	1983	1987	Oct. 1974	1979	1983	1987
Gone too far	27.8	28.9	18.7	32.4	16.0	22.3	11.2	10.5	55.1	60.2	57.2	59.8	37.4	40.0	27.8	29.4
About right	45.9	43.7	54.3	40.7	47.9	48.7	59.6	49.5	37.5	33.8	38.1	36.3	46.4	48.3	58.5	59.3
Not gone far enough	26.2	27.4	27.0	26.9	36.2	29.0	29.2	40.0	7.5	6.0	4.8	3.9	16.2	11.7	13.7	11.3
Total	100.0	100.0	100.0	100.0	100.0	100.0	100.0	100.0	100.0	100.0	100.0	100.0	100.0	100.0	100.0	100.0
N. of respondents	869	664	1306	1288	890	669	1305	1293	881	678	1300	1285	827	633	1109	1132

Married women

	Attempts to ensure racial equality . . .				Attempts to ensure sexual equality . . .				The availability of pornography . . .				The availability of abortion . . .			
	Oct. 1974	1979	1983	1987	Oct. 1974	1979	1983	1987	Oct. 1974	1979	1983	1987	Oct. 1974	1979	1983	1987
Gone too far	25.3	31.7	19.4	27.9	19.8	22.6	7.9	7.1	74.3	73.3	75.8	77.1	46.1	48.9	34.4	35.5
About right	46.0	40.7	55.4	43.2	47.0	48.8	56.7	46.0	23.3	24.4	21.9	21.2	40.9	40.4	54.9	56.8
Not gone far enough	28.8	27.5	25.1	29.0	33.2	28.6	35.4	46.9	2.4	2.3	2.2	1.7	13.0	10.7	10.6	7.7
Total	100.0	100.0	100.0	100.0	100.0	100.0	100.0	100.0	100.0	100.0	100.0	100.0	100.0	100.0	100.0	100.0
N. of respondents	772	621	1297	1233	804	633	1364	1255	803	644	1367	1261	770	616	1224	1126

Divorced and separated men

	Attempts to ensure racial equality . . .				Attempts to ensure sexual equality . . .				The availability of pornography . . .				The availability of abortion . . .			
	Oct. 1974	1979	1983	1987	Oct. 1974	1979	1983	1987	Oct. 1974	1979	1983	1987	Oct. 1974	1979	1983	1987
Gone too far	–	35.7	21.9	29.8	–	32.1	11.3	11.0	–	51.7	60.8	60.6	–	48.1	15.4	16.2
About right	–	28.6	48.9	46.8	–	39.3	55.1	52.2	–	37.9	31.4	33.0	–	22.2	68.2	70.0
Not gone far enough	–	35.7	29.3	23.4	–	28.6	33.6	36.8	–	10.3	7.8	3.4	–	29.6	16.9	13.8
Total	–	100.0	100.0	100.0	–	100.0	100.0	100.0	–	100.0	100.0	100.0	–	100.0	100.0	100.0
N. of respondents	–	28	58	47	–	28	60	76	–	29	62	74	–	27	50	55

Divorced and separated women

	Attempts to ensure racial equality . . .				Attempts to ensure sexual equality . . .				The availability of pornography . . .				The availability of abortion . . .			
	Oct. 1974	1979	1983	1987	Oct. 1974	1979	1983	1987	Oct. 1974	1979	1983	1987	Oct. 1974	1979	1983	1987
Gone too far	–	22.7	22.7	34.1	–	12.8	7.2	6.9	–	69.6	68.6	66.7	–	39.5	29.7	31.8
About right	–	40.9	45.8	50.8	–	46.8	53.3	51.7	–	30.4	23.6	26.4	–	53.5	52.0	55.8
Not gone far enough	–	36.4	31.5	15.2	–	40.4	39.5	41.4	–	0.0	7.8	6.9	–	7.0	18.3	12.4
Total	–	100.0	100.0	100.0	–	100.0	100.0	100.0	–	100.0	100.0	100.0	–	100.0	100.0	100.0
N. of respondents	–	44	102	132	–	47	112	104	–	46	111	108	–	43	101	105

Table 11.19 (cont.)

Widowed men

	Attempts to ensure racial equality . . .				Attempts to ensure sexual equality . . .				The availability of pornography . . .				The availability of abortion . . .			
	Oct. 1974	1979	1983	1987	Oct. 1974	1979	1983	1987	Oct. 1974	1979	1983	1987	Oct. 1974	1979	1983	1987
Gone too far	–	30.6	27.2	29.8	–	22.9	13.1	12.0	–	74.5	73.6	71.0	–	40.0	20.8	20.2
About right	–	46.9	58.5	46.4	–	56.3	63.9	61.3	–	21.3	21.9	24.3	–	46.7	71.9	72.8
Not gone far enough	–	22.4	14.3	23.9	–	20.8	23.0	26.7	–	4.3	4.5	4.7	–	13.3	7.2	7.0
Total	–	100.0	100.0	100.0	–	100.0	100.0	100.0	–	100.0	100.0	100.0	–	100.0	100.0	100.0
N. of respondents	–	49	63	84	–	48	60	77	–	47	62	77	–	45	51	58

Widowed women

	Attempts to ensure racial equality . . .				Attempts to ensure sexual equality . . .				The availability of pornography . . .				The availability of abortion . . .			
	Oct. 1974	1979	1983	1987	Oct. 1974	1979	1983	1987	Oct. 1974	1979	1983	1987	Oct. 1974	1979	1983	1987
Gone too far	–	36.9	30.6	34.7	–	29.8	14.4	10.3	–	95.7	90.7	90.3	–	63.1	63.6	61.5
About right	–	46.7	58.5	51.1	–	45.8	61.8	55.9	–	2.8	6.7	7.3	–	33.8	32.6	34.5
Not gone far enough	–	16.4	10.9	14.2	–	24.4	23.9	33.8	–	1.4	2.7	2.4	–	3.1	3.8	4.0
Total	–	100.0	100.0	100.0	–	100.0	100.0	100.0	–	100.0	100.0	100.0	–	100.0	100.0	100.0
N. of respondents	–	122	220	225	–	131	230	240	–	141	235	248	–	130	186	214

Table 11.20 Attitudes to racial equality, sexual equality, pornography and the availability of abortion by political generation (%)

First voted 1918–1935

	Attempts to ensure racial equality . . .				Attempts to ensure sexual equality . . .				The availability of pornography . . .				The availability of abortion . . .			
	Oct. 1974	1979	1983	1987	Oct. 1974	1979	1983	1987	Oct. 1974	1979	1983	1987	Oct. 1974	1979	1983	1987
Gone too far	35.9	42.7	28.4	34.4	25.4	30.2	13.5	10.4	89.0	90.7	88.5	88.1	66.8	63.1	49.8	54.4
About right	43.6	43.7	59.6	54.8	44.4	51.4	68.4	56.3	10.0	8.0	6.9	8.9	26.9	31.0	44.0	43.5
Not gone far enough	20.5	13.6	14.0	10.7	30.2	18.4	18.1	32.8	1.0	1.3	4.6	3.0	6.3	6.0	6.2	2.2
Total	100.0	100.0	100.0	100.0	100.0	100.0	100.0	100.0	100.0	100.0	100.0	100.0	100.0	100.0	100.0	100.0
N. of respondents	502	286	433	262	516	288	423	274	518	300	442	284	464	268	353	218

First voted 1936–1950

	Attempts to ensure racial equality . . .				Attempts to ensure sexual equality . . .				The availability of pornography . . .				The availability of abortion . . .			
	Oct. 1974	1979	1983	1987	Oct. 1974	1979	1983	1987	Oct. 1974	1979	1983	1987	Oct. 1974	1979	1983	1987
Gone too far	29.7	31.5	21.6	28.0	18.2	24.4	11.2	9.6	76.6	81.9	81.3	87.1	47.2	47.9	44.3	40.1
About right	46.7	44.9	60.0	50.8	49.2	45.7	57.6	50.6	20.9	17.1	15.9	11.7	43.8	44.5	47.1	53.3
Not gone far enough	23.5	23.6	18.4	21.2	32.6	29.9	31.2	39.8	2.5	1.0	2.8	1.3	9.1	7.6	8.0	6.6
Total	100.0	100.0	100.0	100.0	100.0	100.0	100.0	100.0	100.0	100.0	100.0	100.0	100.0	100.0	100.0	100.0
N. of respondents	548	390	759	719	559	398	779	730	560	409	778	734	530	380	653	647

Table 11.20 (*cont.*)

First voted 1951–1970

	Attempts to ensure racial equality . . .				Attempts to ensure sexual equality . . .				The availability of pornography . . .				The availability of abortion . . .			
	Oct. 1974	1979	1983	1987	Oct. 1974	1979	1983	1987	Oct. 1974	1979	1983	1987	Oct. 1974	1979	1983	1987
Gone too far	22.0	26.3	18.2	32.5	16.6	20.8	8.5	8.5	50.2	58.9	63.5	68.6	31.9	39.9	27.0	32.0
About right	44.8	42.2	53.2	39.6	45.5	47.9	56.9	46.3	41.4	35.6	33.1	28.5	48.1	47.4	60.2	58.4
Not gone far enough	33.1	31.5	28.7	27.9	37.9	31.3	34.5	45.2	8.5	5.5	3.5	2.9	20.0	12.7	12.8	9.7
Total	100.0	100.0	100.0	100.0	100.0	100.0	100.0	100.0	100.0	100.0	100.0	100.0	100.0	100.0	100.0	100.0
N. of respondents	948	809	1519	1442	979	824	1576	1452	969	830	1574	1450	934	794	1387	1271

First voted after 1970

	Attempts to ensure racial equality . . .				Attempts to ensure sexual equality . . .				The availability of pornography . . .				The availability of abortion . . .			
	Oct. 1974	1979	1983	1987	Oct. 1974	1979	1983	1987	Oct. 1974	1979	1983	1987	Oct. 1974	1979	1983	1987
Gone too far	18.9	24.0	17.6	24.9	17.6	18.7	8.6	7.8	28.1	40.9	42.6	47.4	22.7	34.2	22.1	25.6
About right	33.7	29.2	46.5	36.6	42.3	46.3	56.4	47.8	57.9	49.1	50.6	47.0	52.8	45.9	59.3	60.0
Not gone far enough	47.4	46.9	35.9	38.4	40.1	35.1	35.1	44.4	14.0	10.0	6.7	5.6	24.4	19.9	18.6	14.4
Total	100.0	100.0	100.0	100.0	100.0	100.0	100.0	100.0	100.0	100.0	100.0	100.0	100.0	100.0	100.0	100.0
N. of respondents	175	271	694	1219	182	268	713	1231	178	269	699	1223	176	266	623	1100

Table 11.21 Attitudes to racial equality, sexual equality, pornography and the availability of abortion by vote (%)

Conservative voters

	Attempts to ensure racial equality . . .				Attempts to ensure sexual equality . . .				The availability of pornography . . .				The availability of abortion . . .			
	Oct. 1974	1979	1983	1987	Oct. 1974	1979	1983	1987	Oct. 1974	1979	1983	1987	Oct. 1974	1979	1983	1987
Gone too far	31.8	35.8	22.7	34.5	21.6	27.1	11.2	10.1	71.4	71.3	66.9	70.0	47.6	44.2	32.3	31.6
About right	46.1	40.5	56.0	45.0	50.3	47.6	61.6	54.1	26.1	24.6	29.3	27.5	42.3	46.0	57.7	59.2
Not gone far enough	22.1	23.7	21.3	20.5	27.6	25.2	27.2	35.8	2.5	4.1	3.8	2.5	10.1	9.9	10.0	9.1
Total	100.0	100.0	100.0	100.0	100.0	100.0	100.0	100.0	100.0	100.0	100.0	100.0	100.0	100.0	100.0	100.0
N. of respondents	657	687	1369	1364	677	701	1404	1390	675	711	1404	1385	643	670	1200	1217

Labour voters

	Attempts to ensure racial equality . . .				Attempts to ensure sexual equality . . .				The availability of pornography . . .				The availability of abortion . . .			
	Oct. 1974	1979	1983	1987	Oct. 1974	1979	1983	1987	Oct. 1974	1979	1983	1987	Oct. 1974	1979	1983	1987
Gone too far	25.3	23.2	18.9	23.9	18.8	18.8	6.6	7.1	63.1	67.7	66.6	65.6	39.2	49.2	31.8	35.8
About right	45.8	43.3	48.5	37.4	44.0	50.4	53.2	41.2	30.3	28.5	28.7	31.1	44.9	39.4	49.2	53.2
Not gone far enough	30.9	33.5	32.8	38.7	37.2	30.8	40.2	51.7	6.6	3.7	4.6	3.4	15.9	11.4	19.0	11.1
Total	100.0	100.0	100.0	100.0	100.0	100.0	100.0	100.0	100.0	100.0	100.0	100.0	100.0	100.0	100.0	100.0
N. of respondents	780	556	857	955	793	559	865	961	788	561	870	967	737	535	762	858

Table 11.21 (*cont.*)

Liberal voters

	Attempts to ensure racial equality . . .				Attempts to ensure sexual equality . . .				The availability of pornography . . .				The availability of abortion . . .			
	Oct. 1974	1979	1983	1987	Oct. 1974	1979	1983	1987	Oct. 1974	1979	1983	1987	Oct. 1974	1979	1983	1987
Gone too far	23.7	27.6	15.2	24.3	15.1	18.6	9.9	6.3	63.3	61.1	61.9	63.1	40.9	35.7	29.3	31.9
About right	41.3	37.4	51.5	41.8	41.4	42.2	56.5	46.4	30.6	34.1	34.0	32.3	40.9	49.5	59.1	58.1
Not gone far enough	35.0	35.0	33.3	34.0	43.5	39.2	33.6	47.3	6.1	4.7	4.1	4.6	18.2	14.8	11.6	11.3
Total	100.0	100.0	100.0	100.0	100.0	100.0	100.0	100.0	100.0	100.0	100.0	100.0	100.0	100.0	100.0	100.0
N. of respondents	334	203	755	728	345	204	773	739	343	211	771	735	325	196	680	652

Voters for other parties

	Attempts to ensure racial equality . . .				Attempts to ensure sexual equality . . .				The availability of pornography . . .				The availability of abortion			
	Oct. 1974	1979	1983	1987	Oct. 1974	1979	1983	1987	Oct. 1974	1979	1983	1987	Oct. 1974	1979	1983	1987
Gone too far	33.3	30.4	21.7	22.1	14.1	16.0	5.0	6.6	48.4	54.2	53.2	64.8	40.7	55.0	30.0	31.4
About right	40.0	43.5	37.6	34.0	46.9	32.0	51.1	41.6	48.4	37.5	42.3	33.0	40.7	35.0	56.4	57.4
Not gone far enough	26.7	26.1	40.7	43.8	39.1	52.0	43.9	51.8	3.1	8.3	4.5	2.2	18.6	10.0	13.6	11.3
Total	100.0	100.0	100.0	100.0	100.0	100.0	100.0	100.0	100.0	100.0	100.0	100.0	100.0	100.0	100.0	100.0
N. of respondents	60	23	39	44	64	25	38	44	64	24	40	44	59	20	34	43

Table 11.22 *Attitudes to racial equality, sexual equality, pornography and the availability of abortion by strength and direction of partisanship (%)*

Very strong Conservative identifiers

	Attempts to ensure racial equality . . .				Attempts to ensure sexual equality . . .				The availability of pornography . . .				The availability of abortion . . .			
	Oct. 1974	1979	1983	1987	Oct. 1974	1979	1983	1987	Oct. 1974	1979	1983	1987	Oct. 1974	1979	1983	1987
Gone too far	37.7	45.5	25.5	39.2	28.8	29.9	13.1	12.5	76.4	76.4	79.0	74.4	54.4	49.0	38.0	34.2
About right	44.2	35.9	57.7	46.8	43.8	50.0	63.4	56.3	20.8	18.8	17.8	23.5	39.0	43.0	52.9	57.3
Not gone far enough	18.1	18.6	16.8	13.9	27.4	20.1	23.5	31.2	2.8	4.8	3.2	2.1	6.7	7.9	9.1	8.5
Total	100.0	100.0	100.0	100.0	100.0	100.0	100.0	100.0	100.0	100.0	100.0	100.0	100.0	100.0	100.0	100.0
N. of respondents	199	156	333	319	208	164	344	321	212	165	343	326	195	151	297	287

Fairly strong Conservative identifiers

	Attempts to ensure racial equality . . .				Attempts to ensure sexual equality . . .				The availability of pornography . . .				The availability of abortion . . .			
	Oct. 1974	1979	1983	1987	Oct. 1974	1979	1983	1987	Oct. 1974	1979	1983	1987	Oct. 1974	1979	1983	1987
Gone too far	32.1	33.2	20.3	34.5	21.1	27.1	10.5	10.3	67.1	70.3	63.8	72.7	46.9	43.0	31.1	33.1
About right	48.5	44.0	55.3	46.0	52.8	50.8	63.9	53.1	29.7	26.3	32.2	24.4	41.1	46.3	59.0	57.5
Not gone far enough	19.4	22.8	24.4	19.5	26.1	22.1	25.6	36.7	3.1	3.4	4.0	2.9	12.0	10.7	9.9	9.4
Total	100.0	100.0	100.0	100.0	100.0	100.0	100.0	100.0	100.0	100.0	100.0	100.0	100.0	100.0	100.0	100.0
N. of respondents	408	368	640	687	417	376	659	699	414	377	655	699	392	363	553	631

Table 11.22 (cont.)

Not very strong Conservative identifiers

	Attempts to ensure racial equality . . .				Attempts to ensure sexual equality . . .				The availability of pornography . . .				The availability of abortion . . .			
	Oct. 1974	1979	1983	1987	Oct. 1974	1979	1983	1987	Oct. 1974	1979	1983	1987	Oct. 1974	1979	1983	1987
Gone too far	28.1	32.4	21.1	31.4	15.9	33.0	10.0	8.6	66.7	62.4	55.9	62.2	40.6	37.4	25.6	33.3
About right	42.1	41.6	53.5	42.3	53.3	33.5	59.1	55.3	27.8	30.4	39.0	34.9	43.4	50.0	61.0	57.2
Not gone far enough	29.8	25.9	25.4	26.3	30.8	33.5	30.8	36.1	5.6	7.2	5.1	2.9	16.0	12.6	13.4	9.5
Total	100.0	100.0	100.0	100.0	100.0	100.0	100.0	100.0	100.0	100.0	100.0	100.0	100.0	100.0	100.0	100.0
N. of respondents	171	185	417	331	182	188	428	333	180	194	433	334	175	190	367	287

Very strong Liberal identifiers

	Attempts to ensure racial equality . . .				Attempts to ensure sexual equality . . .				The availability of pornography . . .				The availability of abortion . . .			
	Oct. 1974	1979	1983	1987	Oct. 1974	1979	1983	1987	Oct. 1974	1979	1983	1987	Oct. 1974	1979	1983	1987
Gone too far	25.0	14.8	23.0	15.3	17.4	22.2	8.0	2.9	68.9	70.0	72.7	64.8	43.2	50.0	47.1	32.0
About right	29.5	33.3	41.9	43.0	30.4	25.9	52.0	38.6	24.4	23.3	20.8	28.4	36.4	28.6	47.1	55.3
Not gone far enough	45.5	51.9	35.1	41.6	52.2	51.9	40.0	58.4	6.7	6.7	6.5	6.7	20.5	21.4	5.7	12.7
Total	100.0	100.0	100.0	100.0	100.0	100.0	100.0	100.0	100.0	100.0	100.0	100.0	100.0	100.0	100.0	100.0
N. of respondents	44	27	74	62	46	27	75	63	45	30	77	61	44	28	70	54

Fairly strong Liberal identifiers

	Attempts to ensure racial equality . . .				Attempts to ensure sexual equality . . .				The availability of pornography . . .				The availability of abortion . . .			
	Oct. 1974	1979	1983	1987	Oct. 1974	1979	1983	1987	Oct. 1974	1979	1983	1987	Oct. 1974	1979	1983	1987
Gone too far	19.0	24.8	11.5	22.2	17.1	18.3	9.6	4.6	64.8	61.3	64.4	63.4	37.8	38.4	28.3	28.0
About right	43.0	38.1	54.7	39.7	40.3	42.3	54.2	45.9	31.8	34.9	34.0	31.2	44.8	52.5	59.6	60.6
Not gone far enough	38.0	37.1	33.8	38.1	42.5	39.4	36.2	49.5	3.4	3.8	1.7	5.4	17.4	9.1	12.5	11.4
Total	100.0	100.0	100.0	100.0	100.0	100.0	100.0	100.0	100.0	100.0	100.0	100.0	100.0	100.0	100.0	100.0
N. of respondents	179	105	926	258	181	104	301	267	179	106	303	263	172	99	265	233

Not very strong Liberal identifiers

	Attempts to ensure racial equality . . .				Attempts to ensure sexual equality . . .				The availability of pornography . . .				The availability of abortion . . .			
	Oct. 1974	1979	1983	1987	Oct. 1974	1979	1983	1987	Oct. 1974	1979	1983	1987	Oct. 1974	1979	1983	1987
Gone too far	18.1	23.0	15.9	26.0	12.5	20.0	7.3	7.9	56.6	58.6	59.1	61.7	40.4	42.2	28.2	29.3
About right	49.1	37.9	55.1	43.5	45.0	43.5	64.2	49.4	37.8	35.6	36.7	34.8	40.4	42.2	60.7	60.3
Not gone far enough	32.8	39.1	28.9	30.5	42.5	36.5	28.4	42.7	7.6	5.7	4.2	3.5	19.3	15.7	11.1	10.3
Total	100.0	100.0	100.0	100.0	100.0	100.0	100.0	100.0	100.0	100.0	100.0	100.0	100.0	100.0	100.0	100.0
N. of respondents	116	87	301	312	120	85	313	315	119	87	308	311	114	83	262	283

Table 11.22 (*cont.*)

Very strong Labour identifiers

	Attempts to ensure racial equality . . .				Attempts to ensure sexual equality . . .				The availability of pornography . . .				The availability of abortion . . .			
	Oct. 1974	1979	1983	1987	Oct. 1974	1979	1983	1987	Oct. 1974	1979	1983	1987	Oct. 1974	1979	1983	1987
Gone too far	25.2	24.3	21.1	22.0	20.1	21.0	7.6	8.5	64.8	71.3	70.2	70.1	43.7	44.9	32.0	38.6
About right	42.9	40.3	46.0	37.5	38.6	46.4	51.4	37.5	28.6	26.1	24.9	27.5	43.7	42.0	49.3	49.2
Not gone far enough	31.9	35.4	32.9	40.5	41.4	32.6	41.0	53.9	6.6	2.7	4.9	2.4	12.6	13.1	18.7	12.2
Total	100.0	100.0	100.0	100.0	100.0	100.0	100.0	100.0	100.0	100.0	100.0	100.0	100.0	100.0	100.0	100.0
N. of respondents	317	181	322	286	324	181	327	288	318	188	329	285	302	176	294	262

Fairly strong Labour identifiers

	Attempts to ensure racial equality . . .				Attempts to ensure sexual equality . . .				The availability of pornography . . .				The availability of abortion . . .			
	Oct. 1974	1979	1983	1987	Oct. 1974	1979	1983	1987	Oct. 1974	1979	1983	1987	Oct. 1974	1979	1983	1987
Gone too far	25.4	23.6	17.0	27.1	17.4	15.5	7.0	8.0	62.3	62.3	65.2	65.4	37.8	46.5	32.4	33.1
About right	43.0	43.9	49.1	36.0	46.1	54.5	52.5	40.6	31.2	32.7	30.6	30.9	45.3	40.2	51.3	58.1
Not gone far enough	31.7	32.4	33.9	36.9	36.5	30.1	40.5	51.5	6.5	5.0	4.2	3.7	17.0	13.3	16.3	8.8
Total	100.0	100.0	100.0	100.0	100.0	100.0	100.0	100.0	100.0	100.0	100.0	100.0	100.0	100.0	100.0	100.0
N. of respondents	426	330	466	483	436	336	472	487	430	337	471	490	400	316	411	436

Not very strong Labour identifiers

	Attempts to ensure racial equality . . .				Attempts to ensure sexual equality . . .				The availability of pornography . . .				The availability of abortion . . .			
	Oct. 1974	1979	1983	1987	Oct. 1974	1979	1983	1987	Oct. 1974	1979	1983	1987	Oct. 1974	1979	1983	1987
Gone too far	23.4	34.9	19.8	29.6	13.5	17.1	10.1	8.0	54.6	68.0	55.4	62.0	38.4	46.6	33.2	36.5
About right	46.7	35.5	55.0	38.5	50.6	50.6	54.0	45.4	36.2	29.1	37.6	34.0	44.0	44.2	51.8	50.4
Not gone far enough	29.9	29.7	25.1	31.9	35.9	32.4	36.0	46.6	9.2	2.9	7.0	4.0	17.6	9.2	14.9	13.0
Total	100.0	100.0	100.0	100.0	100.0	100.0	100.0	100.0	100.0	100.0	100.0	100.0	100.0	100.0	100.0	100.0
N. of respondents	167	172	358	344	170	170	367	342	174	172	370	352	159	163	328	291

Table 11.23 *Attitudes to racial equality, sexual equality, pornography and the availability of abortion: non-partisans (%)*

	Attempts to ensure racial equality . . .				Attempts to ensure sexual equality . . .				The availability of pornography . . .				The availability of abortion . . .			
	Oct. 1974	1979	1983	1987	Oct. 1974	1979	1983	1987	Oct. 1974	1979	1983	1987	Oct. 1974	1979	1983	1987
Gone too far	21.6	25.8	23.0	30.0	28.2	20.9	9.2	7.2	66.7	63.5	62.4	64.5	42.3	46.2	33.2	34.1
About right	47.3	45.2	54.6	46.9	37.2	53.8	65.6	54.3	24.7	33.3	34.4	31.0	46.2	42.9	52.7	55.5
Not gone far enough	31.1	29.0	22.4	23.1	34.6	25.3	25.1	38.5	8.6	3.1	3.3	4.5	11.5	11.0	14.1	10.4
Total	100.0	100.0	100.0	100.0	100.0	100.0	100.0	100.0	100.0	100.0	100.0	100.0	100.0	100.0	100.0	100.0
N. of respondents	74	93	173	206	78	91	182	209	81	96	187	211	78	91	152	168

Table 11.24 *Attitudes to racial equality, sexual equality, pornography and the availability of abortion by social class (%)*

Professional and managerial classes

	Attempts to ensure racial equality . . .				Attempts to ensure sexual equality . . .				The availability of pornography . . .				The availability of abortion . . .			
	Oct. 1974	1979	1983	1987	Oct. 1974	1979	1983	1987	Oct. 1974	1979	1983	1987	Oct. 1974	1979	1983	1987
Gone too far	22.7	25.6	15.3	26.0	13.5	24.6	8.8	7.7	64.5	64.6	60.9	61.9	35.8	36.4	27.3	29.5
About right	45.1	42.5	50.4	39.4	49.0	45.9	58.2	46.8	30.5	30.1	34.8	34.7	49.7	50.3	61.1	60.1
Not gone far enough	32.2	31.9	34.4	34.6	37.5	29.5	33.1	45.5	5.0	5.2	4.3	3.3	14.5	13.4	11.6	10.4
Total	100.0	100.0	100.0	100.0	100.0	100.0	100.0	100.0	100.0	100.0	100.0	100.0	100.0	100.0	100.0	100.0
N. of respondents	339	360	963	957	347	366	992	964	341	362	982	958	332	352	846	840

Intermediate and routine non-manual classes

	Attempts to ensure racial equality . . .				Attempts to ensure sexual equality . . .				The availability of pornography . . .				The availability of abortion . . .			
	Oct. 1974	1979	1983	1987	Oct. 1974	1979	1983	1987	Oct. 1974	1979	1983	1987	Oct. 1974	1979	1983	1987
Gone too far	27.1	33.1	19.4	26.4	18.2	26.2	9.0	7.4	66.1	70.3	66.6	70.7	44.6	43.1	30.7	30.5
About right	46.1	39.9	53.8	45.2	46.5	43.9	56.8	49.1	30.1	27.5	29.7	26.9	41.1	46.6	56.3	60.5
Not gone far enough	26.8	27.0	26.8	28.5	35.3	29.9	34.2	43.5	3.9	2.2	3.7	2.5	14.2	10.2	13.0	9.0
Total	100.0	100.0	100.0	100.0	100.0	100.0	100.0	100.0	100.0	100.0	100.0	100.0	100.0	100.0	100.0	100.0
N. of respondents	757	471	701	919	782	481	723	934	772	491	725	936	744	459	631	831

Table 11.24 (cont.)

Manual working class

	Attempts to ensure racial equality . . .				Attempts to ensure sexual equality . . .				The availability of pornography . . .				The availability of abortion . . .			
	Oct. 1974	1979	1983	1987	Oct. 1974	1979	1983	1987	Oct. 1974	1979	1983	1987	Oct. 1974	1979	1983	1987
Gone too far	28.3	30.5	21.7	33.5	21.6	20.2	9.8	9.7	62.3	65.9	64.4	67.9	42.9	48.8	33.0	36.6
About right	43.5	41.6	54.8	42.7	44.8	50.9	59.3	49.7	30.6	29.3	30.9	28.1	42.6	40.0	53.1	53.3
Not gone far enough	28.3	27.9	23.5	23.8	33.6	28.9	30.9	40.6	7.1	4.8	4.7	4.0	14.6	11.1	13.9	10.2
Total	100.0	100.0	100.0	100.0	100.0	100.0	100.0	100.0	100.0	100.0	100.0	100.0	100.0	100.0	100.0	100.0
N. of respondents	987	865	1762	1622	1019	872	1808	1646	1021	894	1822	1654	940	844	1587	1445

Table 11.25 Attitudes to racial equality, sexual equality, pornography and the availability of abortion by school leaving age (%)

Left school aged under 15

	Attempts to ensure racial equality . . .				Attempts to ensure sexual equality . . .				The availability of pornography . . .				The availability of abortion . . .			
	Oct. 1974	1979	1983	1987	Oct. 1974	1979	1983	1987	Oct. 1974	1979	1983	1987	Oct. 1974	1979	1983	1987
Gone too far	32.1	36.4	23.8	34.0	22.6	24.5	11.2	9.7	80.7	84.4	82.3	83.9	56.2	54.8	42.6	42.7
About right	46.3	44.1	57.9	48.2	46.2	51.3	60.6	51.2	17.2	14.5	14.5	13.7	35.5	38.0	47.4	50.2
Not gone far enough	21.6	19.5	18.3	17.8	31.2	24.2	28.2	39.2	2.1	1.1	3.2	2.3	8.4	7.1	9.7	7.1
Total	100.0	100.0	100.0	100.0	100.0	100.0	100.0	100.0	100.0	100.0	100.0	100.0	100.0	100.0	100.0	100.0
N. of respondents	909	580	1076	861	929	59	1082	873	937	614	1096	886	849	560	936	756

Left school aged 15

	Attempts to ensure racial equality . . .				Attempts to ensure sexual equality . . .				The availability of pornography . . .				The availability of abortion . . .			
	Oct. 1974	1979	1983	1987	Oct. 1974	1979	1983	1987	Oct. 1974	1979	1983	1987	Oct. 1974	1979	1983	1987
Gone too far	25.7	29.4	21.5	37.6	19.3	19.9	8.8	9.3	50.7	58.1	62.7	66.4	33.4	39.7	30.3	33.1
About right	45.2	41.5	53.7	38.6	48.2	48.9	57.0	48.5	41.3	35.4	33.2	30.9	47.8	46.6	55.9	55.2
Not gone far enough	29.2	29.1	24.8	23.8	32.5	31.2	34.3	42.2	8.0	6.5	4.2	2.8	18.8	13.7	13.8	11.7
Total	100.0	100.0	100.0	100.0	100.0	100.0	100.0	100.0	100.0	100.0	100.0	100.0	100.0	100.0	100.0	100.0
N. of respondents	631	506	942	885	658	522	977	887	653	523	986	894	628	511	856	790

Table 11.25 (*cont.*)

Left school aged 16

	Attempts to ensure racial equality . . .				Attempts to ensure sexual equality . . .				The availability of pornography . . .				The availability of abortion . . .			
	Oct. 1974	1979	1983	1987	Oct. 1974	1979	1983	1987	Oct. 1974	1979	1983	1987	Oct. 1974	1979	1983	1987
Gone too far	25.2	29.3	20.5	29.0	15.5	21.7	10.1	9.4	58.2	57.8	53.1	59.3	34.4	39.2	25.9	31.2
About right	43.7	38.2	51.5	43.7	43.3	44.6	58.5	50.8	33.7	38.1	41.2	36.7	48.1	49.9	57.1	60.2
Not gone far enough	31.1	32.5	28.0	27.3	41.2	33.7	31.4	39.8	8.0	4.2	5.7	4.0	17.5	11.0	17.1	8.6
Total	100.0	100.0	100.0	100.0	100.0	100.0	100.0	100.0	100.0	100.0	100.0	100.0	100.0	100.0	100.0	100.0
N. of respondents	318	351	903	877	328	350	928	889	323	360	927	891	314	337	790	785

Left school aged 17

	Attempts to ensure racial equality . . .				Attempts to ensure sexual equality . . .				The availability of pornography . . .				The availability of abortion . . .			
	Oct. 1974	1979	1983	1987	Oct. 1974	1979	1983	1987	Oct. 1974	1979	1983	1987	Oct. 1974	1979	1983	1987
Gone too far	22.1	22.0	14.3	24.7	13.0	26.6	9.8	8.9	56.4	55.5	56.5	61.3	39.0	41.2	26.1	26.3
About right	40.3	41.5	52.2	44.4	48.7	45.2	55.9	47.6	36.2	37.8	38.2	32.1	44.5	41.2	60.8	59.6
Not gone far enough	37.7	36.6	33.5	30.9	38.3	28.2	34.3	43.4	7.4	6.7	5.2	6.6	16.4	17.6	13.1	14.1
Total	100.0	100.0	100.0	100.0	100.0	100.0	100.0	100.0	100.0	100.0	100.0	100.0	100.0	100.0	100.0	100.0
N. of respondents	154	123	313	300	154	124	322	304	149	119	314	299	146	119	280	274

Left school aged over 17

	Attempts to ensure racial equality . . .				Attempts to ensure sexual equality . . .				The availability of pornography . . .				The availability of abortion . . .			
	Oct. 1974	1979	1983	1987	Oct. 1974	1979	1983	1987	Oct. 1974	1979	1983	1987	Oct. 1974	1979	1983	1987
Gone too far	10.1	15.8	9.4	17.4	10.9	25.3	6.0	5.2	44.2	54.7	51.6	60.1	28.6	35.1	24.0	28.0
About right	35.1	34.4	42.2	40.4	41.7	40.1	55.8	47.1	46.5	35.9	44.1	36.1	49.4	47.1	65.5	61.4
Not gone far enough	54.8	49.7	48.3	42.2	47.4	34.6	38.3	47.7	9.3	9.4	4.4	3.8	22.0	17.8	10.5	10.5
Total	100.0	100.0	100.0	100.0	100.0	100.0	100.0	100.0	100.0	100.0	100.0	100.0	100.0	100.0	100.0	100.0
N. of respondents	168	183	459	367	175	182	475	375	172	181	465	376	168	174	412	326

Table 11.26 *Attitudes to racial equality, sexual equality, pornography and the availability of abortion by region* (%)

Scotland

	Attempts to ensure racial equality . . .				Attempts to ensure sexual equality . . .				The availability of pornography . . .				The availability of abortion . . .			
	Oct. 1974	1979	1983	1987	Oct. 1974	1979	1983	1987	Oct. 1974	1979	1983	1987	Oct. 1974	1979	1983	1987
Gone too far	18.5	18.7	15.1	25.7	17.4	17.3	7.8	6.0	60.7	69.3	65.4	65.4	47.4	47.7	38.2	30.4
About right	53.8	41.0	54.6	40.8	47.9	51.1	55.9	50.0	35.5	27.0	29.6	29.5	42.3	40.8	44.8	60.1
Not gone far enough	27.7	40.3	30.4	33.5	34.7	31.7	36.4	44.0	3.8	3.6	5.0	5.1	10.3	11.5	17.0	9.5
Total	100.0	100.0	100.0	100.0	100.0	100.0	100.0	100.0	100.0	100.0	100.0	100.0	100.0	100.0	100.0	100.0
N. of respondents	173	134	337	333	190	139	338	339	183	137	346	342	175	130	319	314

Wales

	Attempts to ensure racial equality . . .				Attempts to ensure sexual equality . . .				The availability of pornography . . .				The availability of abortion . . .			
	Oct. 1974	1979	1983	1987	Oct. 1974	1979	1983	1987	Oct. 1974	1979	1983	1987	Oct. 1974	1979	1983	1987
Gone too far	32.0	33.7	13.7	25.2	21.8	20.2	7.2	6.7	70.4	67.7	70.0	68.4	52.9	45.9	24.5	31.8
About right	35.2	38.8	58.3	38.8	43.5	53.2	66.5	45.7	25.6	26.3	27.1	28.2	36.1	42.9	62.3	59.9
Not gone far enough	32.8	27.6	28.0	35.9	34.7	26.6	26.3	47.6	4.0	6.1	3.0	3.4	10.9	11.2	13.2	8.3
Total	100.0	100.0	100.0	100.0	100.0	100.0	100.0	100.0	100.0	100.0	100.0	100.0	100.0	100.0	100.0	100.0
N. of respondents	122	98	170	192	124	94	188	193	125	99	197	192	119	98	154	179

The North

	Attempts to ensure racial equality . . .				Attempts to ensure sexual equality . . .				The availability of pornography . . .				The availability of abortion . . .			
	Oct. 1974	1979	1983	1987	Oct. 1974	1979	1983	1987	Oct. 1974	1979	1983	1987	Oct. 1974	1979	1983	1987
Gone too far	27.8	28.9'	17.6	31.4	17.9	20.4	8.7	9.7	68.5	67.5	63.4	68.4	46.1	48.6	31.4	38.4
About right	42.9	41.1	54.4	39.5	43.8	49.1	58.8	48.0	26.1	26.0	31.8	28.4	37.9	40.6	55.4	52.0
Not gone far enough	29.2	30.0	28.1	29.2	38.3	30.5	32.5	42.4	5.4	6.5	4.8	3.3	16.0	10.8	13.2	9.6
Total	100.0	100.0	100.0	100.0	100.0	100.0	100.0	100.0	100.0	100.0	100.0	100.0	100.0	100.0	100.0	100.0
N. of respondents	650	477	992	944	664	491	1015	961	667	492	1014	962	618	473	894	847

The Midlands

	Attempts to ensure racial equality . . .				Attempts to ensure sexual equality . . .				The availability of pornography . . .				The availability of abortion . . .			
	Oct. 1974	1979	1983	1987	Oct. 1974	1979	1983	1987	Oct. 1974	1979	1983	1987	Oct. 1974	1979	1983	1987
Gone too far	24.0	32.2	23.7	31.6	17.7	24.8	10.1	9.3	65.2	67.9	62.9	69.4	35.8	40.5	30.4	33.6
About right	47.8	40.5	52.9	44.7	47.4	47.6	57.5	47.2	28.6	28.6	34.0	27.2	48.6	44.8	55.8	52.4
Not gone far enough	28.1	27.3	23.5	23.6	34.9	27.7	32.4	43.4	6.1	3.5	3.1	3.4	15.6	14.7	13.8	14.1
Total	100.0	100.0	100.0	100.0	100.0	100.0	100.0	100.0	100.0	100.0	100.0	100.0	100.0	100.0	100.0	100.0
N. of respondents	366	311	599	620	378	307	609	625	374	315	618	630	360	306	538	557

Table 11.26 (*cont.*)

Greater London

	Attempts to ensure racial equality . . .				Attempts to ensure sexual equality . . .				The availability of pornography . . .				The availability of abortion . . .			
	Oct. 1974	1979	1983	1987	Oct. 1974	1979	1983	1987	Oct. 1974	1979	1983	1987	Oct. 1974	1979	1983	1987
Gone too far	33.8	35.8	26.0	23.3	15.7	23.1	9.6	7.4	63.1	65.5	65.4	65.5	37.3	45.5	28.9	30.4
About right	37.6	35.8	50.9	44.4	45.2	43.1	57.1	47.9	30.9	31.5	29.1	30.5	48.5	40.1	60.1	54.3
Not gone far enough	28.6	28.4	23.1	32.4	39.2	33.8	33.3	44.7	6.0	3.0	5.5	4.0	14.2	14.4	11.0	15.3
Total	100.0	100.0	100.0	100.0	100.0	100.0	100.0	100.0	100.0	100.0	100.0	100.0	100.0	100.0	100.0	100.0
N. of respondents	213	201	475	445	217	195	477	447	217	203	470	448	204	187	392	372

The South

	Attempts to ensure racial equality . . .				Attempts to ensure sexual equality . . .				The availability of pornography . . .				The availability of abortion . . .			
	Oct. 1974	1979	1983	1987	Oct. 1974	1979	1983	1987	Oct. 1974	1979	1983	1987	Oct. 1974	1979	1983	1987
Gone too far	26.8	29.2	19.3	30.1	22.4	25.3	10.8	8.8	59.9	65.0	63.7	64.6	42.5	41.3	32.8	29.9
About right	45.1	43.6	51.2	42.3	47.5	46.7	57.8	49.8	33.9	31.4	32.0	32.4	43.3	49.0	55.7	62.7
Not gone far enough	28.1	27.2	29.5	27.6	30.1	28.0	31.4	41.4	6.1	3.7	4.3	3.0	14.2	9.6	11.5	7.4
Total	100.0	100.0	100.0	100.0	100.0	100.0	100.0	100.0	100.0	100.0	100.0	100.0	100.0	100.0	100.0	100.0
N. of respondents	672	541	1132	1139	687	557	1166	1153	684	568	1153	1149	647	520	984	998

Chapter 12

NEWSPAPER READERSHIP

1. A question on newspaper readership was asked in every election study except 1979.
2. Respondents could mention more than one newspaper in all studies except 1983 and 1987. Readers of *The Financial Times, Morning Star* and regional daily newspapers are excluded from the variable.

See Appendix E, p. 496 on the construction of this variable.

Table 12.1   Newspaper readership: all respondents
Table 12.2   Newspaper readership: new electors
Table 12.3   Newspaper readership: non-voters
Table 12.4   Newspaper readership by vote
Table 12.5   Newspaper readership by strength and direction of partisanship

Table 12.1 *Newspaper readership: all respondents (%)*

Newspaper	1963	1964	1966	1969	1970	Feb. 1974	Oct. 1974	1979	1983	1987
Times	0.7	0.4	0.5	1.6	2.1	1.8	1.5	–	3.0	3.4
Guardian	2.2	2.6	2.6	2.6	3.0	3.2	3.5	–	7.2	6.6
Daily Telegraph	8.3	8.5	8.5	8.8	8.9	9.4	9.7	–	11.6	10.6
Daily Mail	14.1	13.8	14.1	11.1	12.4	10.2	10.4	–	15.5	15.1
Daily Express	32.1	28.8	28.3	24.0	25.8	22.8	21.8	–	13.9	12.9
Daily Mirror	33.1	34.9	37.2	42.7	37.2	31.8	32.4	–	24.9	24.2
Daily Herald	9.4	–	–	–	–	–	–	–	–	–
Sun	–	10.9	8.9	9.2	10.6	20.7	20.7	–	18.5	17.2
Star	–	–	–	–	–	–	–	–	5.2	3.9
Today	–	–	–	–	–	–	–	–	–	1.7
Independent	–	–	–	–	–	–	–	–	–	4.3
Total	100.0	100.0	100.0	100.0	100.0	100.0	100.0	–	100.0	100.0
N. of respondents	1345	1295	1297	693	1146	1804	1713	–	2332	2182

Table 12.2 *Newspaper readership: new electors (%)*

Newspaper	1963	1964	1966	1969	1970	Feb. 1974	Oct. 1974	1979	1983	1987
Times	1.3	0.0	0.0	6.7	4.1	2.8	–	–	2.8	4.2
Guardian	5.3	4.5	4.0	3.3	2.1	11.3	–	–	7.5	5.4
Daily Telegraph	7.9	12.2	4.0	6.7	3.5	5.6	–	–	9.8	7.3
Daily Mail	5.3	6.1	10.0	3.3	7.7	9.9	–	–	13.3	10.4
Daily Express	22.4	17.3	32.0	16.7	20.9	11.3	–	–	16.6	8.6
Daily Mirror	50.0	47.7	42.0	63.3	50.6	31.0	–	–	29.3	24.7
Daily Herald	7.9	–	–	–	–	–	–	–	–	–
Sun	–	12.1	8.0	0.0	11.1	28.2	–	–	15.6	22.0
Star	–	–	–	–	–	–	–	–	5.2	8.3
Today	–	–	–	–	–	–	–	–	–	2.4
Independent	–	–	–	–	–	–	–	–	–	6.6
Total	100.0	100.0	100.0	100.0	100.0	100.0	–	–	100.0	100.0
N. of respondents	76	101	40	30	161	71	–	–	146	125

Table 12.3 *Newspaper readership: non-voters (%)*

Newspaper	1963	1964	1966	1969	1970	Feb. 1974	Oct. 1974	1979	1983	1987
Times	–	0.0	0.0	–	2.8	2.0	1.7	–	1.9	6.1
Guardian	–	1.4	2.9	–	2.5	5.4	5.2	–	4.2	3.3
Daily Telegraph	–	8.1	6.9	–	5.1	3.5	8.2	–	9.2	7.4
Daily Mail	–	12.0	11.5	–	7.4	8.4	7.8	–	11.9	14.2
Daily Express	–	24.8	22.5	–	22.2	20.8	18.6	–	13.6	13.8
Daily Mirror	–	47.9	46.6	–	48.8	31.2	26.8	–	28.8	22.4
Sun	–	5.8	9.6	–	11.2	28.7	31.6	–	21.7	22.2
Star	–	–	–	–	–	–	–	–	8.6	3.5
Today	–	–	–	–	–	–	–	–	–	3.2
Independent	–	–	–	–	–	–	–	–	–	3.8
Total	–	100.0	100.0	–	100.0	100.0	100.0	–	100.0	100.0
N. of respondents	–	131	185	–	202	202	231	–	298	220

Table 12.4 *Newspaper readership by vote (%)*

| Conservative voters | | | | | | | | | |
Newspaper	1963	1964	1966	1969	1970	Feb. 1974	Oct. 1974	1979	1983	1987
Times	1.2	0.2	0.5	1.2	2.2	2.4	2.5	–	3.8	4.6
Guardian	0.5	1.3	1.2	0.6	1.2	1.0	1.3	–	2.2	1.6
Daily Telegraph	17.9	16.4	17.5	11.4	15.2	19.6	19.7	–	18.4	17.9
Daily Mail	20.4	20.0	21.7	12.0	18.6	16.1	16.9	–	24.2	22.7
Daily Express	43.6	40.1	39.0	31.0	33.5	35.0	34.1	–	20.8	19.4
Daily Mirror	14.6	19.0	18.5	40.6	24.1	16.3	14.4	–	11.4	8.0
Daily Herald	1.9	–	–	–	–	–	–	–	–	–
Sun	–	2.9	1.7	3.2	5.3	9.6	11.1	–	17.2	17.8
Star	–	–	–	–	–	–	–	–	2.1	2.8
Today	–	–	–	–	–	–	–	–	–	1.6
Independent	–	–	–	–	–	–	–	–	–	3.7
Total	100.0	100.0	100.0	100.0	100.0	100.0	100.0	–	100.0	100.0
N. of respondents	431	478	421	342	416	583	522	–	946	892

| Labour voters | | | | | | | | | |
Newspaper	1963	1964	1966	1969	1970	Feb. 1974	Oct. 1974	1979	1983	1987
Times	0.3	0.4	0.5	2.1	1.8	0.6	0.3	–	1.2	0.2
Guardian	2.1	2.3	2.5	4.2	3.9	2.8	3.9	–	10.4	14.8
Daily Telegraph	1.8	1.7	3.1	3.7	4.7	2.2	3.0	–	2.4	1.9
Daily Mail	7.8	8.6	8.6	9.0	8.8	6.3	6.9	–	5.2	4.4
Daily Express	25.4	21.2	22.3	15.9	20.1	15.5	14.2	–	5.4	4.5
Daily Mirror	45.5	45.6	48.8	43.4	44.8	44.9	43.5	–	42.9	49.7
Daily Herald	17.0	–	–	–	–	–	–	–	–	–
Sun	–	20.2	14.1	21.7	15.9	27.7	28.2	–	23.5	15.1
Star	–	–	–	–	–	–	–	–	9.1	6.3
Today	–	–	–	–	–	–	–	–	–	0.6
Independent	–	–	–	–	–	–	–	–	–	2.7
Total	100.0	100.0	100.0	100.0	100.0	100.0	100.0	–	100.0	100.0
N. of respondents	606	549	589	189	423	650	593	–	557	590

Table 12.4 (*cont.*)

Liberal voters

Newspaper	1963	1964	1966	1969	1970	Feb. 1974	Oct. 1974	1979	1983	1987
Times	0.6	1.5	1.1	0.0	1.5	2.8	2.1	–	4.1	3.9
Guardian	7.6	11.4	9.4	7.7	11.7	7.1	7.3	–	15.5	8.3
Daily Telegraph	4.5	7.9	5.3	6.2	8.8	10.3	8.5	–	10.3	8.5
Daily Mail	21.0	16.1	20.6	15.4	12.3	9.3	12.0	–	12.8	16.2
Daily Express	29.9	26.6	28.5	24.6	23.7	16.7	18.8	–	11.5	9.8
Daily Mirror	33.8	32.6	28.9	43.1	30.4	31.3	33.8	–	27.6	22.4
Daily Herald	2.5	–	–	–	–	–	–	–	–	–
Sun	–	4.0	6.2	3.1	11.6	22.4	17.5	–	13.5	15.7
Star	–	–	–	–	–	–	–	–	4.7	3.6
Today	–	–	–	–	–	–	–	–	–	3.2
Independent	–	–	–	–	–	–	–	–	–	8.4
Total	100.0	100.0	100.0	100.0	100.0	100.0	100.0	–	100.0	100.0
N. of respondents	157	108	84	65	68	281	134	–	459	434

Voters for other parties

Newspaper	1963	1964	1966	1969	1970	Feb. 1974	Oct. 1974	1979	1983	1987
Times	(0.0)	(0.0)	(0.0)	(0.0)	(0.0)	3.7	3.7	–	(0.0)	(0.0)
Guardian	(0.0)	(15.2)	(0.0)	(0.0)	(0.0)	0.0	3.7	–	(10.4)	(9.1)
Daily Telegraph	(0.0)	(15.2)	(0.0)	(0.0)	(6.7)	3.7	3.7	–	(15.5)	(9.8)
Daily Mail	(0.0)	(0.0)	(0.0)	(0.0)	(8.0)	3.7	0.0	–	(0.0)	(0.0)
Daily Express	(0.0)	(36.4)	(0.0)	(0.0)	(40.0)	25.9	48.1	–	(4.5)	(0.0)
Daily Mirror	(100.0)	(16.7)	(47.6)	(75.0)	(45.3)	48.1	11.1	–	(60.0)	(63.3)
Sun	–	(16.7)	(52.4)	(25.0)	(0.0)	14.8	29.6	–	(5.2)	(17.9)
Star	–	–	–	–	–	–	–	–	(4.5)	(0.0)
Total	(100.0)	(100.0)	(100.0)	(100.0)	(100.0)	100.0	100.0	–	(100.0)	(100.0)
N. of respondents	1	7	2	8	15	27	27	–	20	11

Table 12.5 *Newspaper readership by strength and direction of partisanship (%)*

	Very strong Conservative identifiers									
	1963	1964	1966	1969	1970	Feb. 1974	Oct. 1974	1979	1983	1987
Newspaper										
Times	1.7	0.0	0.4	0.0	2.5	3.3	1.2	–	3.6	3.5
Guardian	0.0	0.9	1.3	0.0	0.4	0.0	0.6	–	1.3	1.7
Daily Telegraph	16.9	19.5	20.2	15.0	16.8	20.0	20.4	–	25.0	25.2
Daily Mail	20.3	21.6	20.5	12.4	20.0	16.3	16.0	–	20.8	23.9
Daily Express	47.1	38.4	38.3	36.3	36.0	34.0	36.4	–	26.3	21.2
Daily Mirror	12.2	17.7	17.7	32.7	22.2	17.7	14.8	–	9.8	6.7
Daily Herald	1.7	–	–	–	–	–	–	–	–	–
Sun	–	1.9	1.5	3.5	2.1	8.8	10.5	–	11.7	15.7
Star	–	–	–	–	–	–	–	–	1.5	1.2
Today	–	–	–	–	–	–	–	–	–	0.4
Independent	–	–	–	–	–	–	–	–	–	0.4
Total	100.0	100.0	100.0	100.0	100.0	100.0	100.0	–	100.0	100.0
N. of respondents	171	244	225	113	237	215	162	–	240	241

	Fairly strong Conservative identifiers									
	1963	1964	1966	1969	1970	Feb. 1974	Oct. 1974	1979	1983	1987
Newspaper										
Times	1.5	0.9	0.5	1.5	2.0	1.9	2.9	–	2.6	3.6
Guardian	1.5	0.5	1.4	0.0	2.2	1.6	0.6	–	0.9	0.7
Daily Telegraph	16.3	15.7	14.4	9.9	11.5	18.2	16.5	–	18.5	18.2
Daily Mail	17.2	17.0	22.8	14.5	11.0	16.6	16.5	–	25.0	24.5
Daily Express	43.3	39.5	37.9	32.1	31.9	38.3	33.0	–	30.2	20.3
Daily Mirror	18.7	23.6	21.0	40.5	30.1	12.3	19.0	–	8.9	7.7
Daily Herald	1.5	–	–	–	–	–	–	–	–	–
Sun	–	2.8	2.0	1.5	11.4	11.0	11.4	–	12.6	16.9
Star	–	–	–	–	–	–	–	–	1.3	2.2
Today	–	–	–	–	–	–	–	–	–	1.5
Independent	–	–	–	–	–	–	–	–	–	4.4
Total	100.0	100.0	100.0	100.0	100.0	100.0	100.0	–	100.0	100.0
N. of respondents	203	206	177	131	175	308	315	–	448	450

Table 12.5 (*cont.*)

Not very strong Conservative identifiers

Newspaper	1963	1964	1966	1969	1970	Feb. 1974	Oct. 1974	1979	1983	1987
Times	0.0	0.0	1.2	1.7	4.9	4.3	2.2	–	4.3	7.3
Guardian	3.5	5.0	5.2	5.2	2.2	0.7	3.7	–	4.3	2.3
Daily Telegraph	21.1	9.4	22.0	10.3	8.1	13.5	22.8	–	9.8	8.8
Daily Mail	17.5	13.6	23.6	5.2	15.9	14.9	14.0	–	17.6	21.6
Daily Express	35.1	40.9	28.5	20.7	23.8	29.8	29.4	–	21.6	12.8
Daily Mirror	17.5	25.5	16.0	51.7	39.4	22.0	16.9	–	20.0	15.6
Daily Herald	5.3	–	–	–	–	–	–	–	–	–
Sun	–	5.5	3.6	5.2	5.7	14.9	11.0	–	18.7	21.5
Star	–	–	–	–	–	–	–	–	3.7	3.0
Today	–	–	–	–	–	–	–	–	–	3.0
Independent	–	–	–	–	–	–	–	–	–	4.2
Total	100.0	100.0	100.0	100.0	100.0	100.0	100.0	–	100.0	100.0
N. of respondents	114	62	70	58	57	141	136	–	300	173

Very strong Liberal identifiers

Newspaper	1963	1964	1966	1969	1970	Feb. 1974	Oct. 1974	1979	1983	1987
Times	0.0	0.0	0.0	(0.0)	0.0	0.0	0.0	–	1.8	2.8
Guardian	7.9	15.0	12.9	(13.3)	11.5	16.7	16.0	–	16.0	16.0
Daily Telegraph	5.3	5.4	1.8	(13.3)	3.5	12.5	12.0	–	10.3	9.3
Daily Mail	36.8	16.1	14.7	(0.0)	13.0	12.5	8.0	–	10.2	12.4
Daily Express	18.4	23.9	37.3	(33.3)	22.3	16.7	24.0	–	19.2	9.2
Daily Mirror	28.9	35.1	20.7	(33.3)	40.2	33.3	20.0	–	27.8	23.1
Daily Herald	2.6	–	–	–	–	–	–	–	–	–
Sun	–	4.5	12.7	(6.7)	9.4	8.3	20.0	–	13.0	11.9
Star	–	–	–	–	–	–	–	–	1.7	3.1
Today	–	–	–	–	–	–	–	–	–	3.3
Independent	–	–	–	–	–	–	–	–	–	9.0
Total	100.0	100.0	100.0	(100.0)	100.0	100.0	100.0	–	100.0	100.0
N. of respondents	38	52	45	15	24	24	25	–	47	32

Table 12.5 (*cont.*)

Fairly strong Liberal identifiers

Newspaper	1963	1964	1966	1969	1970	Feb. 1974	Oct. 1974	1979	1983	1987
Times	0.0	1.3	1.3	3.7	4.8	3.1	2.2	–	5.1	7.9
Guardian	4.7	2.0	4.6	0.0	8.9	4.7	5.9	–	9.3	9.6
Daily Telegraph	3.1	7.8	2.9	7.4	5.2	10.9	9.6	–	9.8	8.8
Daily Mail	21.9	22.3	14.2	22.2	20.6	6.3	11.1	–	11.7	13.5
Daily Express	31.3	35.2	32.7	25.9	24.2	22.7	17.0	–	15.2	7.6
Daily Mirror	37.5	29.8	36.1	37.0	30.6	28.9	31.1	–	29.9	21.7
Daily Herald	1.6	–	–	–	–	–	–	–	–	–
Sun	–	1.6	8.1	3.7	5.8	23.4	23.0	–	17.3	13.6
Star	–	–	–	–	–	–	–	–	1.7	3.5
Today	–	–	–	–	–	–	–	–	–	4.8
Independent	–	–	–	–	–	–	–	–	–	9.1
Total	100.0	100.0	100.0	100.0	100.0	100.0	100.0	–	100.0	100.0
N. of respondents	64	64	68	27	54	128	135	–	182	170

Not very strong Liberal identifiers

Newspaper	1963	1964	1966	1969	1970	Feb. 1974	Oct. 1974	1979	1983	1987
Times	2.2	4.2	(0.0)	4.0	(0.0)	4.1	2.7	–	3.1	3.7
Guardian	10.9	7.7	(0.0)	4.0	(0.0)	14.9	10.8	–	9.8	5.4
Daily Telegraph	6.5	7.9	(6.1)	4.0	(20.5)	12.2	12.2	–	8.8	10.8
Daily Mail	15.2	15.0	(16.5)	20.0	(4.6)	10.8	4.1	–	15.3	18.3
Daily Express	30.4	23.0	(40.2)	28.0	(53.4)	8.1	29.7	–	21.5	12.1
Daily Mirror	30.4	36.1	(30.5)	36.0	(11.3)	32.4	31.1	–	25.5	18.2
Daily Herald	4.3	–	–	–	–	–	–	–	–	–
Sun	–	6.1	(6.7)	4.0	(10.2)	17.6	9.5	–	13.3	14.5
Star	–	–	–	–	–	–	–	–	2.7	4.3
Today	–	–	–	–	–	–	–	–	1.8	1.8
Independent	–	–	–	–	–	–	–	–	11.0	11.0
Total	100.0	100.0	(100.0)	100.0	(100.0)	100.0	100.0	–	100.0	100.0
N. of respondents	46	38	16	25	19	74	74	–	188	165

Table 12.5 (*cont.*)

Very strong Labour identifiers

Newspaper	1963	1964	1966	1969	1970	Feb. 1974	Oct. 1974	1979	1983	1987
Times	0.0	0.7	0.0	2.6	0.8	0.3	0.7	–	0.3	0.0
Guardian	0.9	2.6	2.1	6.5	4.5	3.0	3.1	–	9.2	13.9
Daily Telegraph	0.4	0.7	1.6	2.6	3.4	2.6	1.6	–	3.1	0.9
Daily Mail	6.9	8.4	9.6	5.2	9.1	5.2	6.2	–	4.8	5.2
Daily Express	25.1	18.8	22.4	14.3	19.1	16.7	15.6	–	6.6	1.6
Daily Mirror	43.3	46.4	47.7	44.2	44.2	43.3	42.8	–	42.9	56.8
Daily Herald	23.4	–	–	–	–	–	–	–	–	–
Sun	–	22.5	16.7	24.7	18.8	28.9	30.0	–	24.4	15.6
Star	–	–	–	–	–	–	–	–	8.8	4.8
Today	–	–	–	–	–	–	–	–	–	1.0
Independent	–	–	–	–	–	–	–	–	–	0.5
Total	100.0	100.0	100.0	100.0	100.0	100.0	100.0	–	100.0	100.0
N. of respondents	231	292	304	77	238	305	257	–	212	187

Fairly strong Labour identifiers

Newspaper	1963	1964	1966	1969	1970	Feb. 1974	Oct. 1974	1979	1983	1987
Times	0.8	0.0	1.2	1.1	2.0	0.6	0.7	–	1.0	1.0
Guardian	1.9	3.3	2.8	4.5	3.1	3.2	3.7	–	11.3	15.7
Daily Telegraph	1.2	1.7	3.5	4.5	4.3	0.6	2.0	–	2.2	2.5
Daily Mail	6.6	9.2	7.7	8.0	8.2	7.7	7.4	–	8.6	4.4
Daily Express	23.3	20.9	16.7	18.2	19.2	12.7	12.8	–	9.9	5.2
Daily Mirror	51.2	43.0	56.3	43.2	51.3	45.4	41.6	–	37.9	44.2
Daily Herald	15.1	–	–	–	–	–	–	–	–	–
Sun	–	21.8	11.8	20.5	11.9	29.8	31.9	–	19.5	16.9
Star	–	–	–	–	–	–	–	–	9.6	6.2
Today	–	–	–	–	–	–	–	–	–	1.8
Independent	–	–	–	–	–	–	–	–	–	3.3
Total	100.0	100.0	100.0	100.0	100.0	100.0	100.0	–	100.0	100.0
N. of respondents	258	208	249	88	190	339	298	–	305	323

Table 12.5 (*cont.*)

Newspaper	Not very strong Labour identifiers									
	1963	1964	1966	1969	1970	Feb. 1974	Oct. 1974	1979	1983	1987
Times	0.0	0.0	0.0	2.4	2.5	1.4	0.8	–	0.0	0.6
Guardian	2.1	0.0	1.1	1.2	2.2	4.7	5.3	–	6.3	7.5
Daily Telegraph	4.1	1.4	3.9	6.0	6.0	3.4	4.5	–	1.4	1.2
Daily Mail	13.7	5.8	4.9	13.3	12.9	4.7	7.6	–	6.8	8.6
Daily Express	30.8	29.6	28.7	10.8	18.2	14.9	15.2	–	11.1	9.9
Daily Mirror	40.4	58.8	51.1	56.6	44.0	44.6	34.1	–	38.2	37.9
Daily Herald	8.9	–	–	–	–	–	–	–	–	–
Sun	–	4.3	10.2	9.6	14.1	26.4	32.6	–	32.0	19.5
Star	–	–	–	–	–	–	–	–	4.2	9.6
Today	–	–	–	–	–	–	–	–	–	1.7
Independent	–	–	–	–	–	–	–	–	–	3.5
Total	100.0	100.0	100.0	100.0	100.0	100.0	100.0	–	100.0	100.0
N. of respondents	146	69	70	83	79	148	132	–	239	167

APPENDIX A: THE FIELDWORK CHARACTERISTICS OF THE BRITISH ELECTION STUDY SAMPLES

Table A.1 *The fieldwork characteristics of the British Election Study samples*

Study[1]	Fieldwork dates[2]	Fieldwork organisation	Sample size[3]	Response rate (%)[4]	ESRC Data Archive id number	ICPSR Data Archive id number
1963	24 May – 30 June 1963	British Market Research Bureau Ltd	2009	79.4	044	7250
1964	18 Oct. – 7 Nov. 1964	British Market Research Bureau Ltd	1769	68.3	044	7232
1966	4 April – 2 May 1966	British Market Research Bureau Ltd	1877	70.0	044	7233
1969	9 June – 28 June 1969	British Market Research Bureau Ltd	1114	78.2	093	7004
1970	19 June – 21 July 1970	British Market Research Bureau Ltd	1845	69.8	044	7234
Feb. 1974	8 March – 18 May	British Market Research Bureau Ltd	2462	75.8	359	7868
Oct. 1974	15 Oct. – 7 Dec. 1974	Social & Community Planning Research	2365	73.7	666	7870
1979	7 May – 21 June	Research Services Ltd	1893	60.9	533	8196
1983	5 July – 18 Aug. 1983	Social & Community Planning Research	3955	72.4	005	8409
1987	22 June – 10 Aug. 1987	Social & Community Planning Research	3826	70.0[5]	–	–

1. None of the studies covers Northern Ireland.
2. Between 90 and 95 per cent of interviews were completed within this period. The remaining interviews took place over a further period of anything up to two months.
3. This is the unweighted total number of respondents included in the cross-sectional sample for the year in question. The total number given for 'all respondents' in the tables is the weighted number for those samples which were weighted, i.e., 1964, 1966, 1970, October 1974, 1979 and 1987, and therefore may differ from the figure given here.
4. The response rate is for the cross-sectional samples, not the panel samples.
5. If interviewees who failed to return the self-completion questionnaire are excluded, the response rate falls to 62.5%.

Further details about the sample design and fieldwork of these studies can be obtained from the following sources:
1963, 1964, 1966, 1969, 1970: David Butler and Donald Stokes, *Political Change in Britain*, 2nd edition (London: Macmillan, 1974), appendix A, pp. 425–39.
February 1974: *Technical Document*, obtainable from ESRC Data Archive, University of Essex.
October 1974: *Methodological Report*, obtainable from ESRC Data Archive, University of Essex.
1979: Neil Day, *Survey Design, Sample and Fieldwork*, obtainable from the ESRC Data Archive, University of Essex.
1983: Anthony Heath, Roger Jowell and John Curtice, *How Britain Votes* (Oxford: Pergamon Press, 1985), appendix I, pp. 177–84.
1987: Anthony Heath, Roger Jowell and John Curtice, *End of Award Report* (Economic and Social Research Council, 1988).

APPENDIX B: THE SOCIAL AND POLITICAL COMPOSITION OF THE BRITISH ELECTION STUDY SAMPLES

Table B.1 *The social and political composition of the British Election Study samples (%)*

Age

	1963	1964	1966	1969[1]	1970	Feb. 1974	Oct. 1974	1979	1983	1987
Under 25	6.5	6.0	7.4	11.4	14.7	10.2	11.7	9.3	12.7	12.9
25–34	16.8	16.5	17.5	16.2	16.4	19.1	20.4	22.7	17.8	17.9
35–44	21.1	21.2	19.5	18.3	17.1	17.3	17.1	17.6	19.1	20.0
45–54	20.6	20.3	20.6	18.7	16.4	18.2	17.5	18.3	16.9	15.3
55–64	17.7	18.4	17.8	18.7	18.1	16.0	15.4	14.0	15.9	15.8
65–74	12.0	11.5	11.3	10.7	11.9	12.6	12.0	11.2	11.2	11.1
Over 74	5.3	6.2	5.7	6.0	5.5	6.6	5.9	6.9	6.3	6.9
Total	100.0	100.0	100.0	100.0	100.0	100.0	100.0	100.0	100.0	100.0

1. The voting age was lowered from 21 to 18 in 1969.

Employment status

	1963	1964	1966	1969	1970	Feb. 1974	Oct. 1974	1979	1983	1987
Self-employed with employees	5.8	6.8	5.1	3.8	5.3	4.4	3.7	4.2	4.8	4.8
Self-employed no employees	2.1	1.7	2.5	3.0	2.3	4.0	4.6	5.1	4.0	4.6
Manager	6.9	6.9	7.2	5.6	7.9	8.0	8.8	10.4	17.7	9.8
Foreman/ supervisor	8.5	9.3	8.7	8.5	9.1	4.7	6.1	13.7	13.6	6.4
Rank and file employees	76.8	75.2	76.5	79.1	75.5	78.9	76.8	66.6	59.8	74.5
(Unemployed)	(0.3)	(1.1)	(1.1)	(1.2)	(3.1)	(2.1)	(1.6)	(2.2)	(6.3)	(5.7)
Total	100.0	100.0	100.0	100.0	100.0	100.0	100.0	100.0	100.0	100.0

Gender

	1963	1964	1966	1969	1970	Feb. 1974	Oct. 1974	1979	1983	1987
Men	44.9	45.2	46.9	47.8	47.1	47.5	49.8	48.3	47.3	48.0
Women	55.1	54.8	53.1	52.2	52.9	52.5	50.2	51.7	52.7	52.0
Total	100.0	100.0	100.0	100.0	100.0	100.0	100.0	100.0	100.0	100.0

Table B.1 (*cont.*)

Housing

	1963	1964	1966	1969	1970	Feb. 1974	Oct. 1974	1979	1983	1987
Owner-occupiers	44.8	47.9	–	46.5	51.3	53.8	53.8	57.1	65.7	68.1
Council tenants	29.5	29.2	–	29.6	29.3	30.9	29.7	31.4	26.2	21.2
Other renters	25.7	22.9	–	23.9	19.5	15.4	16.5	11.5	8.2	7.8
Total	100.0	100.0	–	100.0	100.0	100.0	100.0	100.0	100.0	100.0

Marital status: 2-category

	1963	1964	1966	1969[1]	1970	Feb. 1974	Oct. 1974	1979	1983	1987
Single	14.6	13.4	–	26.6	20.0	–	–	–	–	–
Married	85.4	86.6	–	73.4	80.0	–	74.5	–	–	–
Total	100.0	100.0	–	100.0	100.0	–	–	–	–	–

1.   The jump in the proportion of single people arises partly from the extension of the sample to 21 year olds, following the lowering of the voting age.

Marital status: 4-category

	1963	1964	1966	1969	1970	Feb. 1974	Oct. 1974	1979	1983	1987
Single	–	–	11.2	–	–	12.3	–	12.2	16.4	17.9
Married	–	–	77.3	–	–	76.4	–	72.7	71.0	68.1
Divorced/ separated	–	–	0.5	–	–	1.0	–	4.3	4.7	4.9
Widowed	–	–	11.0	–	–	10.3[1]	–	7.9	8.2	9.0
Total	–	–	100.0	–	–	100.0	–	100.0	100.0	100.0

1.   Includes separated respondents.

Non-voting

	1963	1964	1966	1969	1970	Feb. 1974	Oct. 1974	1979	1983	1987
Voted	–	88.9	84.0	–	81.1	87.9	85.3	85.6	83.3	86.1
Did not vote	–	11.1	16.0	–	18.9	12.1	14.7	14.4	16.7	13.9
Total	–	100.0	100.0	–	100.0	100.0	100.0	100.0	100.0	100.0

Partisanship: direction

	1963	1964	1966	1969	1970	Feb. 1974	Oct. 1974	1979	1983	1987
Conservative	37.7	40.6	37.2	45.1	40.4	36.9	35.6	40.8	39.8	41.2
Labour	46.5	43.7	47.8	35.2	42.9	42.5	41.4	38.9	33.2	32.8
Liberal[1]	11.1	12.4	10.4	9.6	7.8	13.3	15.3	12.2	18.9	18.2
Other	0.1	0.4	0.5	1.5	3.6	1.9	2.5	1.4	2.2	1.7
None	4.6	2.8	4.1	8.6	5.3	5.3	5.2	6.7	5.9	6.0
Total	100.0	100.0	100.0	100.0	100.0	100.0	100.0	100.0	100.0	100.0

1.   Includes SDP and 'Alliance' in 1983 and 1987.

Table B.1 (*cont.*)

Partisanship: strength and direction

	1963	1964	1966	1969	1970	Feb. 1974	Oct. 1974	1979	1983	1987
Very strong Conservative	13.6	19.9	18.4	17.1	21.5	12.3	10.2	10.0	11.5	10.3
Fairly strong Conservative	16.2	16.7	14.7	21.7	16.7	18.9	19.7	22.7	21.4	22.4
Not very strong Conservative	9.8	5.3	6.0	11.1	6.2	8.6	8.8	11.6	14.3	10.6
Very strong Liberal[1]	3.0	3.9	3.6	1.8	2.2	1.6	2.1	1.8	1.7	2.0
Fairly strong Liberal[1]	4.9	6.1	5.7	4.5	4.5	7.5	8.7	6.3	6.7	8.4
Not very strong Liberal[1]	3.8	2.9	1.5	4.4	1.9	5.3	5.6	5.3	6.3	10.0
Very strong Labour	17.5	22.4	24.2	11.1	21.1	17.6	15.7	11.4	10.7	9.4
Fairly strong Labour	19.8	16.9	19.9	14.4	18.0	18.8	20.8	20.3	15.4	15.6
Not very strong Labour	11.4	5.9	6.1	13.8	7.9	9.3	8.4	10.7	12.1	11.3
Total	100.0	100.0	100.0	100.0	100.0	100.0	100.0	100.0	100.0	100.0

1.   Includes SDP and 'Alliance' in 1983 and 1987.

Party membership

	1963	1964	1966	1969	1970	Feb. 1974	Oct. 1974	1979	1983	1987
Member of political party	9.4	10.0	–	6.2	–	–	6.8	–	6.5	5.8
Member of Conservative party	5.3	7.0	–	3.9	–	–	4.4	–	4.1	3.8
Member of Labour party	3.4	2.1	–	1.0	–	–	1.3	–	1.3	1.2

Political generation

	1963	1964	1966	1969	1970	Feb. 1974	Oct. 1974	1979	1983	1987
1918–35	43.8	42.9	38.0	30.7	31.0	25.0	23.5	16.9	13.1	7.9
1936–50	31.7	32.3	30.4	26.9	27.1	26.6	25.0	22.2	23.1	20.1
1951–70	24.5	24.8	31.6	42.5	41.9	41.4	43.4	45.7	45.7	39.3
1971 and after	–	–	–	–	–	8.0	8.0	15.1	18.1	32.8
Total	100.0	100.0	100.0	100.0	100.0	100.0	100.0	100.0	100.0	100.0

Table B.1 (*cont.*)

Region

	1963	1964	1966	1969	1970	Feb. 1974	Oct. 1974	1979	1983	1987
Scotland	9.6	9.8	9.0	9.6	9.3	9.5	8.8	7.9	9.1	9.2
Wales	4.9	4.0	4.6	4.8	5.3	5.3	5.6	5.4	5.5	5.2
The North	28.7	28.7	27.3	27.6	29.1	29.7	29.2	27.1	26.8	26.0
Midlands	17.6	18.3	19.7	17.3	18.4	15.9	16.7	17.3	15.0	16.8
Greater London	15.3	14.6	14.7	18.3	16.0	10.8	9.7	11.3	12.0	12.0
The South	23.9	24.6	24.6	22.3	21.9	28.8	30.1	31.0	31.6	30.8
Total	100.0	100.0	100.0	100.0	100.0	100.0	100.0	100.0	100.0	100.0

Religion

	1963	1964	1966	1969	1970	Feb. 1974	Oct. 1974	1979	1983	1987
Church of England	63.6	63.8	63.1	58.5	60.3	–	41.3	30.5	46.1	42.1
Non-Conformists	9.2	9.7	9.7	11.0	14.3	–	6.3	6.1	6.6	5.3
Catholic	8.5	7.6	8.5	9.8	10.5	–	9.0	9.7	11.6	9.8
None	3.2	3.0	3.1	5.1	4.2	–	33.6[1]	41.4[1]	24.3	32.4
Other	15.5	15.8	15.7	15.5	10.6	–	9.9	12.2	11.4	10.5
Total	100.0	100.0	100.0	100.0	100.0	–	100.0	100.0	100.0	100.0

1.   The substantial increase in the 'none' category, and decline in the 'Church of England' category is almost certainly due to the change of question wording between 1970 and later studies. The question up to 1970 asked 'What is your religion?'. The question after 1970 varied from study to study but always asked respondents whether they *belonged* to a religious denomination, church etc. For details, see appendix E, p. 475.

Religiosity: attendance

	1963	1964	1966	1969	1970	Feb. 1974	Oct. 1974	1979	1983	1987
Regular	22.1	22.0	20.9	18.3	21.1	–	–	17.7	20.7	21.6
Occasional	31.6	30.6	31.4	27.2	25.7	–	–	25.9	21.0	19.8
Rare	23.5	24.3	25.7	29.5	31.4	–	–	37.7	20.1	19.7
Never	22.8	23.0	21.9	25.0	21.8	–	–	18.7	38.2	38.9
Total	100.0	100.0	100.0	100.0	100.0	–	–	100.0	100.0	100.0

School leaving age

	1963	1964	1966	1969	1970	Feb. 1974	Oct. 1974	1979	1983	1987
Under 15	60.8	59.2	56.1	48.5	47.9	44.3	41.9	33.7	29.7	26.9
15	21.2	21.5	22.8	28.5	28.0	28.5	29.5	29.4	25.5	26.9
16	9.2	10.2	11.2	10.1	10.5	13.5	14.3	19.8	23.4	26.4
17	4.3	4.1	4.9	6.3	6.6	6.4	6.7	6.8	8.7	8.9
Over 17	4.6	5.1	5.0	6.7	6.9	7.2	7.6	10.2	12.7	11.0
Total	100.0	100.0	100.0	100.0	100.0	100.0	100.0	100.0	100.0	100.0

Table B.1 (*cont.*)

Occupational status

	1963	1964	1966	1969	1970	Feb. 1974	Oct. 1974	1979	1983[1]	1987[1]
A	4.7	5.5	5.4	3.5	5.6	5.6	5.6	6.3	–	–
B	8.0	8.2	7.2	8.9	10.7	8.4	9.4	13.5	–	–
C1a	14.0	14.1	13.6	11.3	12.1	14.3	13.7	11.3	–	–
C1b	9.5	8.8	13.3	18.2	13.4	19.8	20.6	15.1	–	–
C2	35.5	36.0	34.6	28.4	30.7	24.2	25.6	31.0	–	–
D	22.2	22.8	23.9	26.1	23.1	21.5	19.8	17.9	–	–
Other[2]	6.2	4.6	2.0	3.6	4.4	6.2	5.2	4.8	–	–
Total	100.0	100.0	100.0	100.0	100.0	100.0	100.0	100.0	–	–

1. From 1963 to 1979 occupational status was defined according to the Market Research Society's categories. In 1983 and 1987 it was defined according to the Registrar General's social classes and is not strictly comparable.
2. Includes category E, which is omitted from the tables in the book.

Social class

	1963	1964	1966	1969	1970	Feb. 1974	Oct. 1974	1979	1983[1]	1987[1]
Professional and managerial	12.7	13.7	12.6	12.4	16.3	14.0	15.0	19.8	–	–
Intermediate and routine non-manual	23.5	22.9	26.9	29.5	25.5	34.1	34.3	26.4	–	–
Manual	57.7	58.8	58.5	54.5	53.8	45.7	45.4	48.9	–	–
Other[2]	6.2	4.6	2.0	3.6	4.4	6.2	5.2	4.8	–	–
Total	100.0	100.0	100.0	100.0	100.0	100.0	100.0	100.0	–	–

1. See note 1 above.
2. See note 2 above.

Middle versus working class

	1963	1964	1966	1969	1970	Feb. 1974	Oct. 1974	1979	1983[1]	1987[1]
Middle class	26.7	27.8	26.2	23.7	28.4	28.3	28.7	31.1	–	–
Working class	67.2	67.6	71.8	72.7	67.2	65.5	66.0	64.0	–	–
Other[2]	6.2	4.6	2.0	3.6	4.4	6.2	5.2	4.8	–	–
Total	100.0	100.0	100.0	100.0	100.0	100.0	100.0	100.0	–	–

1. See note 1 above.
2. See note 2 above.

Table B.1 (*cont.*)

Subjective social class

	1963	1964	1966	1969	1970	Feb. 1974	Oct. 1974	1979	1983	1987
Spontaneous middle class	17.9[1]	14.9	16.9	12.5	16.6	15.2	15.6	16.5	20.9	16.0
Forced middle class	9.7	13.7	13.0	17.8	18.4	18.0	17.5	15.5	14.4	17.6
No class	5.9	5.6	3.3	9.2	8.2	4.7	5.4	7.1	6.2	4.7
Forced working class	18.1	27.1	27.3	41.2	30.0	38.2	36.1	32.9	25.8	31.4
Spontaneous working class	48.4[1]	38.7	39.5	19.3	26.9	23.8	25.5	28.1	32.6	30.2
Total	100.0	100.0	100.0	100.0	100.0	100.0	100.0	100.0	100.0	100.0

1. The markedly higher proportion in the two 'spontaneous' class categories in 1963 than in later studies is probably the result of a preamble to the question, which mentioned that 'most people say that they belong to the middle class or the working class'. In 1964 and 1966 the preamble was put to only half the sample. From 1969 onwards it was put only to respondents who answered 'no class' or 'don't know' to the question 'Do you ever think of yourself as belonging to a particular social class? Which class is that?'

Trade union membership

	1963	1964	1966	1969	1970	Feb. 1974	Oct. 1974	1979	1983	1987
Member	22.0	25.6	–	22.9	24.5	25.5	24.9	29.6	27.0	22.5
Spouse of member	14.5	10.0	–	6.1	6.8	12.1	12.2	14.6	11.4	9.5
Non-member	63.5	64.5	–	70.9	68.7	62.4	62.9	55.7	61.6	68.0
Total	100.0	100.0	–	100.0	100.0	100.0	100.0	100.0	100.0	100.0

Type of school

	1963	1964	1966	1969	1970	Feb. 1974	Oct. 1974	1979	1983	1987
State non-selective	81.3	80.0	80.4	78.2	78.8	73.1	72.8	69.7	73.2	73.4
State selective	14.1	14.9	14.0	17.1	16.3	20.8	21.6	25.0	22.6	21.1
Private fee-paying	4.6	5.1	5.6	4.6	4.8	6.1	5.6	5.3	4.2	5.5
Total	100.0	100.0	100.0	100.0	100.0	100.0	100.0	100.0	100.0	100.0

Table B.1 (*cont.*)

University/polytechnic educated

	1963	1964	1966	1969	1970	Feb. 1974	Oct. 1974	1979	1983	1987
	1.6	2.3	–	4.1	3.2	–	–	5.2	10.7	–

Vote

	1963	1964	1966	1969	1970	Feb. 1974	Oct. 1974	1979	1983	1987
Conservative	37.0	41.9	38.7	56.3	45.7	38.1	36.0	47.0	44.7	43.9
Labour	49.5	47.0	52.6	31.2	44.6	40.7	42.5	37.6	29.3	31.2
Liberal	13.4	10.7	8.2	10.6	7.4	19.1	18.0	13.8	24.6	23.5
Other	0.1	0.4	0.5	2.0	2.4	2.1	3.5	1.6	1.4	1.4
Total	100.0	100.0	100.0	100.0	100.0	100.0	100.0	100.0	100.0	100.0

APPENDIX C: A NOTE ON SAMPLING ERROR AND REPRESENTATIVENESS

Sampling errors

The percentage figures displayed in this book are *sample estimates*, i.e. they are based on samples that are not necessarily perfectly representative of the registered electorate from which they were drawn. Each percentage, and each comparison between percentages, is therefore subject to *sampling error*.

Estimating the reliability of a sample estimate is straightforward for a simple random sample, where each registered elector has an equal and independent chance of selection. However, for reasons of cost, simple random samples are very rarely used: what they gain in representativeness by dispensing with clustering they lose by requiring, through cost, a smaller sample size. All the British Election Studies therefore adopted a multi-stage, stratified and clustered sample design, for which calculations of the reliability of sample estimates are much more complex.

In a simple random sample the formula for calculating the sampling error for any percentage, p, is:

$$s.e.\ (p) = \frac{p\ (100-p)}{n}$$

where n is the number of respondents on which the percentage is based. In other words, the sampling error depends on the size of the sample (or sub-sample) and the size of the percentage. Having calculated the sampling error one can work out the true percentage for the actual electorate at different levels of confidence. For example, for a 95 per cent level of confidence, the formula is

$$p + 1.96 \times s.e.$$

In other words the probability that the true percentage for the electorate lies within this interval is 95 per cent.

In multi-stage, stratified, sample designs, however, the sampling error of a percentage depends not only on the sample size and the percentage size, but also on the degree to which the variable in question is clustered within and between the polling districts that make up the primary sampling units of the sample. The sampling errors in such complex sampling designs may be assessed in relation to simple random sampling by calculating some of the *design factors*, DFs, according to the formula.

$$DF = \frac{var\ (p)c}{var\ (p)s}$$

where var (p)c is the sampling variance of a percentage, p, in a complex design, with a sample size of n, and var (p)s is the sampling variance of a percentage, p, in a simple random design, with a sample size of n.

Thus DF is the multiplying factor to be applied to the simple random sampling error to produce its complex equivalent. If the design factor for a particular characteristic is known, a 95 per cent confidence interval for a percentage, p, may be calculated by using the formula.

$$p \pm 1.96 \times DF \times \frac{p\ (100-p)}{n}$$

A design factor of 1.0 means that the complex sample has achieved the same precision as a simple random sample of the same size. A design factor greater than 1.0 means that the complex design is less precise than its simple random equivalent. The design factor for the great majority of variables included in this book is between 1.0 and 1.5. The design factors for high-variance variables, i.e. those with a 'lumpy' distribution across polling districts, such as council housing and Labour voting, are relatively large. The design factors for low-variance variables, i.e. those with an even distribution across polling districts, such as gender, age and marital status, approximate to 1.0. Because most political attitudes and orientations other than those involving partisanship (vote, party identification etc.) are distributed fairly evenly, the design factor for such variables typically falls in the range 1.1 to 1.2. Thus the 95 per cent confidence limits to be placed around the percentages in this book *will usually be wider than those appropriate for a simple random sample.*

Two tables are provided to help the reader estimate the sampling error, at a 95 per cent probability level, for the percentage figures in this book. Table C.1 sets out the sampling errors for percentages of different sizes and samples of different sizes for a simple random sample. Table C.2 displays an estimate of the design factor for the high-variance and low-variance variables included in this book, in the light of the complex sample designs of the British Election Studies. These estimates are based on those provided by the principal investigators.[1]

Table C.1 *Sampling errors for simple random samples*

Sample size	Reported percentages											
	50 50	60 or 40	70 or 30	80 or 20	85 or 15	90 or 10	92 or 8	94 or 6	95 or 5	96 or 4	97 or 3	98 or 2
50	14.1	13.9	13.0	11.3	10.1	8.5	7.7	6.7	6.2	5.5	4.8	4.0
100	10.0	9.8	9.2	8.0	7.1	6.0	5.4	4.7	4.4	3.9	3.4	2.8
150	8.2	8.0	7.5	6.5	5.8	4.9	4.4	3.9	3.6	3.2	2.8	2.3
200	7.1	7.0	6.5	5.7	5.0	4.2	3.8	3.4	3.1	2.8	2.4	2.0
250	6.3	6.2	5.8	5.1	4.5	3.8	3.4	3.0	2.8	2.5	2.2	1.8
300	5.8	5.7	5.3	4.6	4.1	3.5	3.1	2.7	2.5	2.3	2.0	1.6
400	5.0	4.9	4.6	4.0	3.6	3.0	2.7	2.4	2.2	2.0	1.7	1.4
500	4.5	4.4	4.1	3.6	3.2	2.7	2.4	2.1	1.9	1.8	1.5	1.3
600	4.1	4.0	3.7	3.3	2.9	2.4	2.2	1.9	1.8	1.6	1.4	1.1
700	3.8	3.7	3.5	3.0	2.7	2.3	2.0	1.8	1.6	1.5	1.3	1.1
800	3.5	3.5	3.2	2.8	2.5	2.1	1.9	1.7	1.5	1.4	1.2	1.0
900	3.3	3.3	3.1	2.7	2.4	2.0	1.8	1.6	1.5	1.3	1.1	0.93
1000	3.2	3.1	2.9	2.5	2.3	1.9	1.7	1.5	1.4	1.2	1.1	0.89
1250	2.8	2.8	2.6	2.3	2.0	1.7	1.5	1.3	1.2	1.1	0.96	0.79
1500	2.6	2.5	2.4	2.1	1.8	1.5	1.4	1.2	1.1	1.0	0.88	0.72
1750	2.4	2.3	2.2	1.9	1.7	1.4	1.3	1.1	1.0	0.94	0.82	0.67
2000	2.2	2.2	2.0	1.8	1.6	1.3	1.2	1.1	1.0	0.88	0.76	0.63
3000	1.8	1.8	1.7	1.5	1.3	1.1	1.0	0.97	0.87	0.72	0.62	0.51
4000	1.6	1.5	1.4	1.3	1.1	0.95	0.86	0.75	0.69	0.62	0.54	0.44

Table C.2 *Estimated average design factors for variables with high or low variance across sampling units, British Election Studies, 1963–87*

Variable	Design Factor
Gender	1.0
Age groups	1.0
Marital status	1.0
Unemployed	1.1
Self-employed without employees	1.0
Owner-occupier	2.1
Council tenant	2.2
Other renter	1.6
Professional and managerial	1.1
Skilled manual workers	1.0
Voted Labour 1964–79	1.4
Voted Labour 1983–87	1.6
Voted Conservative	1.4
Conservative party identification	1.5
Labour party identification	1.6
Liberal (SDP/Alliance) identification	1.1
Political attitudes	1.1 to 1.2

1.   See David Butler and Donald Stokes, *Political Change in Britain*, 2nd edition (London: Macmillan, 1974), pp. 439–45; *The British Election Study of October 1974: Methodological Report* (London: Social & Community Planning Research, 1975), pp. 7–9; and Anthony Heath, Roger Jowell and John Curtice, *How Britain Votes* (Oxford: Pergamon Press, 1985), pp. 235–38.

APPENDIX D: YEAR BY YEAR CHART OF VARIABLES

In the following table variables available in a cross-sectional sample and included in this book are marked by an asterisk (*). Variables available in the panel sample but not the cross-sectional sample for that particular year are marked (†) and are excluded from the book. A blank space indicates that the variable was not available in any sample for that year.

Table D.1 *Year by year chart of variables*

	1963	1964	1966	1969	1970	Feb. 1974	Oct. 1974	1979	1983	1987
Category Variables										
Age	*	*	*	*	*	*	*	*	*	*
Economic sector							*	*	*	*
Employment status	*	*	*	*	*	*	*	*	*	*
Gender	*	*	*	*	*	*	*	*	*	*
Housing	*	*		*	*	*	*	*	*	*
Marital status: 2-category	*	*		*	*					
4-category			*			*		*	*	*
New electors	*	*	*	*	*	*		*	*	*
Non-partisanship	*	*	*	*	*	*	*	*	*	*
Non-voting		*	*		*	*	*	*	*	*
Partisanship										
Direction	*	*	*	*	*	*	*	*	*	*
Strength and direction	*	*	*	*	*	*	*	*	*	*
Party membership	*	*		*				*	*	*
Political generation	*	*	*	*	*	*	*	*	*	*
Region	*	*	*	*	*	*	*	*	*	*
Religion	*	*	*	*	*		*	*	*	*
Religiosity	*	*	*	*	*			*	*	*
School leaving age	*	*	*	*	*	*	*	*	*	*
Social class:										
Occupational status	*	*	*	*	*	*	*	*		
Social class	*	*	*	*	*	*	*	*	*	*
Middle vs working class	*	*	*	*	*	*	*	*	*	*
Subjective social class	*	*	*	*	*	*	*	*	*	*
Trade union membership	*	*		*	*	*	*	*	*	*
Type of school	*	*	*	*	*	*	*	*	*	*
Unemployed	*	*	*	*	*	*	*	*	*	*
University/polytechnic										
educated	*	*		*	*			*	*	
Vote	*	*	*	*	*	*	*	*	*	*
Combined category variables										
Age + Class	*	*	*	*	*	*	*	*	*	*
Age + Gender	*	*	*	*	*	*	*	*	*	*
Class + Economic sector							*	*	*	*
Class + Employment status	*	*	*	*	*	*	*	*	*	*
Class + Housing	*	*	*	*	*	*	*	*	*	*
Class + Trade union	*	*		*	*	*	*	*	*	*

Table D.1 (*cont.*)

	1963	1964	1966	1969	1970	Feb. 1974	Oct. 1974	1979	1983	1987
Combined category Variables (cont.)										
Gender + Class	*	*	*	*	*	*	*	*	*	*
Marital status (2-category) + Gender	*	*		*	*		*			
Marital status (4-category) + Gender			*			*		*	*	*
Political generation + Partisanship	*	*	*	*	*	*	*	*	*	*
Religion + Religiosity	*	*	*						*	*
Subjective + Objective class	*	*	*	*	*	*	*	*	*	*
Dependent variables										
Business power	*	*	*	*	*	†	*	*	*	*
Business + trade union power	*	*	*	*	*	†	*	*	*	*
Campaign wavering		*	*		*	*	*	*	*	*
Cares about election result	*	*	*	*	*	*	*		*	*
Interest in politics	*	*	*		*	*	*	*		
Issues:										
availability of abortion							*	*	*	*
capital punishment	*		*	*	*			*	*	
economic redistribution							*	*	*	*
inflation: government's handling						*	*	*	*	*
inflation: importance of issue						*	*	*	*	
nationalisation/privatisation	*	*	*		†	*	*	*	*	*
nationalisation/privatisation: importance of issue						*	*	*	*	
pornography						*	*		*	*
poverty						*	*		*	*
racial equality						*	*		*	*
sexual equality						*	*		*	*
social services: importance of issue						*	*	*	*	
strikes: government's handling						*	*	*	*	
welfare benefits						*	*		*	*
Liberal Party: closer to Conservatives or Labour?						*	*	*	*	*
Newspaper readership	*	*	*	*	*	*	*	*	*	*
Non-partisanship	*	*	*	*	*	*	*	*	*	*
Non-voters: preferred party		*	*		*	*	*		*	*
Partisanship: strength and direction	*	*	*	*	*	*	*	*	*	*
Party image of Conservatives or Labour										
extreme/moderate						*	*		*	*
good for one/good for all classes						*	*		*	*
Party membership	*	*		*		*			*	*
Perceived difference between parties	*	*	*	*	*	*	*	*	*	*
Standard of living:										
change in past year								*	*	*
change in coming year						*	*	*	*	
Time of voting decision		*	*		*	*	*	*		*
Trade union power	*	*	*	*	*	†	*	*	*	*
Vote	*	*	*	*	*	*	*	*	*	*

APPENDIX E: THE DEFINITION AND CONSTRUCTION OF THE VARIABLES

This appendix provides information about the definition and construction of each of the variables used in this book. For each variable it gives

    a) the question number in the original questionnaire;
    b) the variable identification number in the codebook;
    c) the question wording;
    d) notes on differences of wording and answer categories between surveys;
    e) additional information about definition and construction.

The codebooks for the 1969 and 1970 surveys do not assign variable numbers but specify the deck and column location of each variable. These are set out in the text with the deck number preceding the colon and the column number(s) following or below the colon. Thus, the age variable in 1969 is described as 78:

                                                           13–14

which means that it is in deck 78, columns 13 and 14.
    The variables appear in their order of listing in appendix C.

Age

	1963	1964	1966	1969	1970	Feb. 1974	Oct. 1974	1979	1983	1987
Question No.	face-sheet	face-sheet	face-sheet	face-sheet	face-sheet	138	93	105	56	58c
Variable No.	938	939	940	78: 13–14	98: 16–17	FEB191	OCT191	M191279	Q56	V58C

Question wording

1963 to 1970:
face: age was a facesheet variable. Interviewers were instructed to obtain information about the age of respondents and of members of households, but not required to use a standard question.

February 1974
'In what year were you born?'

October 1974
'Could you say in what year you were born?'

1979
'Would you say in which year you were born?'

1983, 1987
'What was your age last birthday?'

The voting age was reduced from 21 to 18 in 1969 and came into effect at the 1970 election. The 'under 25' category therefore consists of respondents aged 21 to 24 in the 1963, 1964, 1966 and 1969 studies, and of respondents aged 18 to 24 in the studies from 1970 onwards.

Twenty-one respondents in the 1963 study and four respondents in the 1966 study were interviewed even though they were aged 20 and too young to vote. They have been excluded from all tables in this book.

Economic sector

	1963	1964	1966	1969	1970	Feb. 1974	Oct. 1974	1979	1983	1987
Question No.	–	–	–	–	–	–	86	95a	53f	50f
Variable No.	–	–	–	–	–	–	OCT194A	M194A259	Q53F	V50F

Question wording

October 1974
'Do (did) you work for a private firm or for a public organisation like the Civil Service, local government, or a nationalised industry?'

1979
'Do (did) you work for a private firm or for a public organisation? By public organisation I mean central government, local government, nationalised industries and also public services such as health and education?'

1983
'Is (was) the organisation you work (worked) for a private firm, a nationalised industry, a local or central government organisation, a charity, or what?'

1987
'Which of the types of organisation on this card do (did) you work for?
[on card:] Private firm or company
            Nationalised industry/public corporation
            Local authority/local education authority
            Health authority/hospital
            Central government/civil service
            Charity or trust
            Other

The category 'public sector' includes central government, local government, nationalised industries and public corporations. It does not include charities or trusts.

Employment status

	1963	1964	1966	1969	1970	Feb. 1974	Oct. 1974	1979	1983	1987
Question No.	face-sheet	face-sheet	face-sheet	face-sheet	face-sheet	139a 141 143a 143b	84 85 87d	92 94a 94b 95b	52a 53d 53e 53h	49a 50d 50e 50h
Variable No.	975	976	977	78: 22	98: 33	FEB257 FEB260	OCT192 OCT194 OCT194B Q53E	M192253 M260292	Q52A Q53D Q53E	49A 50A2

Question wording

1963, 1964, 1966, 1969, 1970
The questions were part of the interviewer's facesheet and do not have an identification number. In the case of men, single women and widowed, separated and divorced women, interviewers were instructed to

establish whether the respondent was occupied, or temporarily out of work, or retired from an occupation, and to ask:

'What job does/did (respondent) actually do?'
IF IN CIVIL SERVICE, FORCES POLICE, ETC: 'What is his/her rank or grade?'
IF OTHER: 'Does/did (respondent) hold any particular position in the organisation? (e.g. foreman, typing supervisor, office manager, company secretary, etc.)?'
ASKED OF ALL: 'Roughly how many people work at the place where this person works?'

February 1974:
'Do you at present have a paid job?'
'Are/were you self-employed or do/did you work for someone else?'
'What exactly do/did you do in your job?'
'Are/were you in charge of any people where you work?'
IF YES: 'Are/were you in charge of a small group of workers and assistants, or do/did you have managerial responsibility over a large number of people?'

October 1974:
'Do you at present have a paid job?'
'Are/were you self-employed or do/did you work for someone else?'
'How many people would you say are (were) employed in the establishment where you work (worked)?'

1979:
'Do you at present have a full-time or part-time paid job?'
IF IN PAID JOB, OR TEMPORARILY UNEMPLOYED, OR RETIRED/DISABLED BUT USED TO WORK: 'Are/were you self-employed or do/did you work for someone else?'
IF SELF-EMPLOYED: 'Do/did you have any employees?'
IF EMPLOYED: 'Are/were you a supervisor of any kind?' IF YES: 'How many people do/did you supervise?'

1983 and 1987:
'Which of these descriptions applies to what you were doing last week, that is in the seven days ending last Sunday?' PROBE: 'Any others?'
IF IN PAID WORK (FOR AT LEAST 10 HOURS A WEEK), OR WAITING TO TAKE UP A JOB OFFER, OR UNEMPLOYED OR RETIRED: 'Do/did you supervise or are/were you responsible for the work of any other people?' IF YES: 'How many?'
'Are/were you an employee or self-employed?'
IF SELF-EMPLOYED: 'Including yourself, how many people are/were employed at the place you usually work/worked?'
[In 1987: IF SELF-EMPLOYED: 'Do you have any employees?' IF YES: 'How many?']

This variable consists of the respondent's employment status (or employment status before retirement), not that of the head of household.
'Self-employed without employees' does not count family members as employees.
'Managers' are employees with responsibility for 'a large number' of employees.
'Foremen/supervisors' are employees with responsibility for 'a small number' of employees.
The 'unemployed' are those in the 'economically active' age category seeking work but without a job; they exclude the retired.
From 1963 to 1970 married women with jobs were asked about their husband's job but not their own. They are therefore excluded from data about employment status for these years, but included thereafter.

Gender

	1963	1964	1966	1969	1970	Feb. 1974	Oct. 1974	1979	1983	1987
Variable No.	929	930	931	78: 11	98: 11	FEB199	OCT199	M199288	Q64B	V58B

Housing

	1963	1964	1966	1969	1970	Feb. 1974	Oct. 1974	1979	1983	1987
Question No.	82	75	–	85	88	132 133	78*	106a 106c	65a 65b	60a 60b
Variable No.	915	916	–	76: 27	96: 35	FEB187 FEB189	OCT187A	M187A280 M187A282	Q65AB	V60AB

* asked of newly sampled respondents only.

Question wording

1963, 1964, 1969, 1970
'Do you or your family rent or own your own home?'

Feb 1974
'Could you tell me whether this home is owned or rented?'
IF RENTED: 'Is it rented from the Council or from someone esle?'

1979
'Would you tell me whether your home is owned or rented?'
IF RENTED: 'Is it rented privately or from the Council?'

1983, 1987
'Do you – your household – own or rent this (house/flat/accommodation)?'
IF RENTED: 'From whom?'

Respondents renting from a New Town authority count as council tenants. Respondents renting from a private company count as private tenants. Tenants in tied accommodation and tenants of housing associations are not considered to belong to either category and are therefore excluded from the variable.

Marital Status

	1963	1964	1966	1969	1970	Feb. 1974	Oct. 1974	1979	1983	1987
Question No.	face-sheet	face-sheet	face-sheet	face-sheet	face-sheet	146a	–	97	54a	51a
Variable No.	933	934	935	78: 12	98: 13	FEB200	–	M200262	Q54A	V51A

Question wording

1963, 1964, 1966, 1969, 1970
Marital status was a facesheet variable. Interviewers were instructed to obtain information about the respondent's marital status, distinguishing between the categories single, married and widowed/divorced/separated, but were not issued with a specific question.

February 1974
As for 1963 to 1970, but interviewers were instructed to distinguish between four categories: single, married, divorced and widowed/separated.

October 1974
'Could you tell me whether you are currently married or single?'
[Interviewers were instructed to circle the words 'Divorced', 'Widowed' or 'Separated' if this was mentioned by the respondent but to code all such answers as 'single'.]

1979
'Could you tell me whether you are currently married, single, widowed, divorced, or separated?'

1983
'At present are you married (or living as married), widowed, divorced or separated, or single?'

1987
'At present are you married, or living as married, or widowed, divorced or separated, or not married?'

'Single' means never married.
'Married' excludes the widowed, separated and divorced; it includes those living as married.
Because different answer categories were adopted in different surveys, only two categories – single and married – are available for 1963, 1964 and 1970.
In the February 1974 study the widowed and separated were coded together. As only a small minority will have been separated, they are all counted as 'widowed'.

Middle class vs working class. *See* social class

New electors

	1963	1964	1966	1969	1970	Feb. 1974	Oct. 1974	1979	1983	1987
Question No.	face-sheet	face-sheet	face-sheet	face-sheet	face-sheet	138	–	105	56	58c
Variable No.	938	939	940	78: 13–14	98: 16–17	FEB191	–	M191279	Q56	V58C

Question wording

1963, 1964, 1966, 1969, 1970
Age, on which the 'new electors' variable is based, was a facesheet variable. Interviewers were instructed to obtain information about the age of respondents and of members of households, but were not required to use a standard question.

February 1974
'In what year were you born?'

October 1974
'Could you say in what year you were born?'

1979
'Would you say in which year you were born?'

1983, 1987
'What was your age last birthday?'

New electors are defined as those who were too young to vote at the previous *general* election, even if since that time they had in fact voted in local elections, by-elections, European elections or referendums.
The voting age was reduced from 21 to 18 in 1969 and came into effect at the 1970 election. Thus new electors from 1970 onwards were younger (roughly, 18 to 22) than new electors before 1970 (roughly, 21 to 25). The number of new electors in October 1974 and 1966 was too small to warrant inclusion in the book.
New electors in the 1963 and 1969 studies are defined as those respondents who would have been old enough to vote for the first time in a general election if a general election had been held on the first day of fieldwork. Twenty-one respondents in the 1963 study and four respondents in the 1966 study were interviewed even though they were aged 20 and too young to vote. They have been excluded from all tables in this book.

Non-partisanship. *See* partisanship

Non-voting

	1963	1964	1966	1969	1970	Feb. 1974	Oct. 1974	1979	1983	1987
Question No.	–	40a	44a	–	50	87a	30	39	7a	6a
Variable No.	–	356	357	–	94: 23	FEB114	OCT114	M114145	Q7A	V6A

Question wording

1964, 1966 and 1970
'We find many people around the country who have good reasons for not voting. How about you? Did you vote in the general election this year [1964, 1966: or did something prevent you from voting]?'

February 1974, October 1974
'Talking to people about the election, we have found that a lot of people were not able to vote this time, because they were away or ill on election day or found that they didn't have the time to vote. How about you? Did you vote in the recent election?'

1979
'Talking to people about the general election, we have found that a lot of people didn't vote. How about you? Did you vote in the general election?'

1983, 1987
'Talking to people about the general election, we have found that a lot of people didn't manage to vote. How about you? Did you manage to vote in the general election?'

Election surveys tend to under-sample non-voters, and under-estimate the number of non-voters in their sample. A small proportion of respondents will have wrongly informed interviewers that they voted at the general election. However, we may safely assume that the number of respondents who wrongly informed interviewers that they had not voted was tiny.

Occupational status. *See* social class

Partisanship: direction

	1963	1964	1966	1969	1970	Feb. 1974	Oct. 1974	1979	1983	1987
Question No.	37a 37f	49a 49f	48a 48f	44a 44f	57a 57f	98a 98b	43 44	48 49	13a 13b	12a 12b
Variable No.	1142	1143	1144	74: 24,31	94: 61,68	FEB129 FEB130	OCT129 OCT130	M129156 M130157	Q13A Q13B	V12A V12B

Question wording

1963, 1964, 1966, 1969, 1970
'Generally speaking, do you usually think of yourself as Conservative, Labour, Liberal or what?' [1963: '. . . as Conservative, Labour or Liberal?']
IF ANSWERS NONE/DON'T KNOW: 'Do you generally think of yourself as [1963: 'feel'] a little closer to one of the parties than the others?' IF YES: 'Which party is that?'

February 1974, October 1974, 1979
'Generally speaking, do you think of yourself as Conservative, Labour, Liberal (in Scotland: Scottish Nationalist; in Wales: Plaid Cymru) or what?'
IF ANSWERS NONE: as for 1963–70

1983, 1987
'Generally speaking, do you think of yourself as Conservative, Labour, Liberal, Social Democrat (Scotland: Nationalist; Wales: Plaid Cymru) or what?'
IF 'ALLIANCE', PROBE: 'Liberal or Social Democrat?'
IF ANSWERS NONE/DON'T KNOW: 'Do you generally think of yourself as [1963: 'feel'] a little closer to one of the parties than the others?' IF YES: 'Which party is that? IF ALLIANCE, PROBE: 'Liberal or Social Democrat?'

A Conservative (Labour, Liberal) identifier is someone who answered 'Conservative' ('Labour', 'Liberal') to either the first or the supplementary, question. The 'no partisan identification' category refers to respondents who answered 'none' or 'don't know' to the supplementary question.
In 1983 and 1987 respondents who answered SDP or Alliance were coded separately from those answering Liberal. For purposes of comparison with earlier studies they have been counted as Liberal identifiers.
Respondents identifying with the Scottish Nationalists, Plaid Cymru and other small parties are omitted from the classification.

Partisanship: strength and direction

	1963	1964	1966	1969	1970	Feb. 1974	Oct. 1974	1979	1983	1987
Question No.	37a	49a	48a	44a	57a	98a	43	48	13a	12a
	37b	49b	48b	44b	57b	98b	44	49	13b	12b
	37f	49f	48f	44f	57f	99	45a	50	13c	12c
						101	46a			
						103	47a			
Variable No.	1142	1143	1144	74:	94:	FEB129	OCT129	M129156	Q13A	V12A
	1146	1147	1148	24,25,	61,62	FEB130	OCT130	M130157	Q13B	V12B
				31	68	FEB131	OCT131	M131158	Q13C	V12C
						FEB133	OCT133			
						FEB135	OCT135			

Question wording

1963, 1964, 1966, 1969, 1970
'Generally speaking, do you usually think of yourself as Conservative, Labour, Liberal or what?' [1963: '. . . as Conservative, Labour or Liberal?']
IF RESPONDENT GIVES A PARTY AFFILIATION: 'How strongly (Conservative, Labour etc) do you generally feel – very strongly, fairly strongly, or not very strongly?'
IF ANSWERS NONE/DON'T KNOW: 'Do you generally think of yourself as [1963: 'feel'] a little closer to one of the parties than the others?' IF YES: 'Which party is that?'

February 1974, October 1974, 1979
'Generally speaking, do you think of yourself as Conservative, Labour, Liberal (in Scotland: Scottish Nationalist; in Wales: Plaid Cymru) or what?'
IF ANSWERS CONSERVATIVE/LABOUR/LIBERAL [in 1979: IF ANSWERS ANY PARTY]: 'Would you call yourself (a) very strong Conservative (Labour/Liberal), fairly strong, or not very strong?'
IF ANSWERS NONE/DON'T KNOW: as for 1963–70

1983
'Generally speaking, do you think of yourself as Conservative, Labour, Liberal, Social Democrat (Scotland: Nationalist; Wales: Plaid Cymru) or what?'
IF 'ALLIANCE', PROBE: 'Liberal or Social Democrat?'
IF RESPONDENT GIVES ANY PARTY AFFILIATION: 'Would you call yourself a very strong (name of party), fairly strong or not very strong?'
IF ANSWERS NONE/DON'T KNOW: 'Do you generally think of yourself as [1963: 'feel'] a little closer to one of the parties than the others?' IF YES: 'Which party is that?' IF ALLIANCE, PROBE: 'Liberal or Social Democrat?'

1987
As for 1983, except that the strength of identification question is also put to those respondents who, having answered 'none' or 'don't know' to the first question, say in answer to the supplementary question that they feel closer to one of the parties.

This variable excludes respondents who identified with the Scottish Nationalists, Plaid Cymru or other small parties; respondents who had no party identification; and respondents who identified with one of the main parties but were unable to say how strongly.

In 1983 and 1987 identifiers with the SDP and the Alliance are counted with Liberal identifiers.

Some but not all surveys asked respondents who felt 'closer' to one of the parties how strong their identification was; most answered 'not very strong'. For the sake of consistency, all respondents who felt 'closer' to one of the parties are categorised as having a 'not very strong' identification with that party, irrespective of whether they were asked the strength of identification question and, if they were, irrespective of their answer.

Party membership

	1963	1964	1966	1969	1970	Feb. 1974	Oct. 1974	1979	1983	1987
Question No.	52a 52b 52c	44a 44b 44c	–	82a 82b 82c	–	–	53a 53b	–	66a 66b	67a 67b
Variable No.	413 415 417	414 416 418	–	75: 75–77	–	–	OCT483 OCT484	–	Q66A Q66B	V67A V67B

Question wording

1963, 1964, 1969

'Have you paid a subscription to a [1969: any] political party in the last year? Which [1969: What] party was that?'

IF LABOUR: 'Was that as a member of the local party or through a trade union?'

October 1974

'Are you a paying member of any political party or some other political organisation? Which party or organisation is that?'

IF LABOUR: 'Did you pay a subscription as a member of the local party or through a trade union?'

1983, 1987

'Are you a member of a political party? Which one?'

IF LABOUR: 'Are you a member of the Labour party through a trade union or did you join as an individual member?'

The category 'member of a political party' excludes members of political organisations other than parties and those who belong to the Labour party through their trade union. It includes members of parties other than the Conservative and Labour parties.

The category 'member of the Labour party' excludes those who joined through their trade union.

Political generation

	1963	1964	1966	1969	1970	Feb. 1974	Oct. 1974	1979	1983	1987
Question No.	face-sheet	face-sheet	face-sheet	face-sheet	face-sheet	138	93	105	56	58c
Variable No.	938	939	940	78: 13–14	98: 16–17	FEB191	OCT191	M191279	Q56	V58C

Question wording

As for Age.

The definition of generations is as follows:

Generation	First general election at which respondent entitled to vote	Year of birth
1918–1935	1918, 1922, 1923, 1924, 1929, 1935	1890–1914
1936–1950	1945, 1950, 1951	1915–1929
1951–1970	1951, 1955, 1959, 1964 1966, 1970	1930–1949
1971 and after	Feb 1974, Oct 1974, 1979, 1983, 1987	1950 and later

Respondents born before 1890 will have been entitled to vote in elections before 1918 if they were male heads of household owning property of a certain value. As it is impossible to establish which male respondents born before 1890 were enfranchised before 1918, and as the numbers are small and decline with each successive survey, all male respondents born before 1890 are omitted from this variable.

Region

	1963	1964	1966	1969	1970	Feb. 1974	Oct. 1974	1979	1983	1987
Variable No.	31	32	33	71: 11–14	91: 15–19	FEB145	OCT145	M001001A	PA no.	PA no.

Region was coded according to the address at which respondents were interviewed, not their address on the electoral register. The definition of region in this book differs from the region variables (Nos. 35–38) in the studies for 1963 to 1970. The definition adopted in this book is:

Region	Registrar General's Standard Region	Counties*
SCOTLAND	Scotland	all counties in Scotland
WALES	Wales	all counties in Wales
GREATER LONDON	South East	Greater London
NORTH	North	Cleveland, Cumbria, Durham, Northumberland, Tyne & Wear (pre-1971: Cumberland)
	North West	Cheshire, Greater Manchester, Lancashire, Merseyside
	Yorkshire & Humberside	Humberside, North Yorkshire, South Yorkshire, West Yorkshire (pre-1971: East Riding, North Riding and West Riding of Yorkshire)
MIDLANDS	East Midlands	Derbyshire, Leicestershire, Lincolnshire, Northamptonshire, Nottinghamshire (pre-1971: Rutland)
	West Midlands	Hereford & Worcester, Shropshire, Staffordshire, Warwickshire, West Midlands (pre-1971: Herefordshire)

SOUTH	East Anglia	Cambridgeshire, Norfolk, Suffolk
	South East	Bedfordshire, Berkshire, Buckinghamshire, East Sussex, Essex, Hampshire, Hertfordshire, Isle of Wight, Kent, Oxfordshire, Surrey, West Sussex (pre-1971: Middlesex)
	South West	Avon, Cornwall, Devon, Dorset, Gloucestershire, Somerset, Wiltshire

* counties in parentheses were abolished in the 1971 reorganisation of local government.

Religion

	1963	1964	1966	1969	1970	Feb. 1974	Oct. 1974	1979	1983	1987
Question No.	83	L17*	N19*	98	103*	–	81a	82	63a	59a
Variable No.	920	920	920	76: 36	96: 55	–	OCT495	M495234	Q63A	V59A

* asked of newly sampled respondents only

Question wording

1963, 1964, 1966, 1969
'What is your religion?'

October 1974
'Do you belong to any religious denomination?'
IF YES: 'Which denomination?'

1979
'Do you belong to any church or religious group?' IF YES: 'Which denomination?'

1983, 1987
'Do you regard yourself as belonging to any particular religion?'
IF YES: 'Which one?'

'Church of England' includes Anglican, Episcopal and Church of Wales.
'Non-conformist' consists of Methodists, 'Chapel' and Baptists.
Because of the inconsistent coding of religions between surveys, respondents with the following denominations are excluded from the classification: Church of Scotland, Congregational Church, United Reform Church, and other Presbyterian sects in Scotland. Because of their small numbers Christian sects such as Jehovahs Witnesses, Mormons, Christian Scientists and Quakers and non-Christian respondents such as Jews, Moslems and Sikhs have been excluded from the classification.

Religiosity

	1963	1964	1966	1969	1970	Feb. 1974	Oct. 1974	1979	1983	1987
Question No.	85	L19*	N21*	100	105*	–	–	83	63b	59b
Variable No.	924	924	924	76: 40	96: 59	–	–	M000235	Q63B	V59B

* asked of newly sampled respondents only

Question wording

1963, 1964, 1966, 1969
'How often do you attend church (chapel) (synagogue)?'

1979
'How often do you attend church, chapel or other place of worship?'

1983, 1987
'Apart from special occasions, such as weddings, funerals, baptisms and so on, how often nowadays do you attend services or meetings connected with your religion?'

The four categories of religiosity are defined as follows:
'Regular': attends church (chapel, synagogue etc) at least several times a month.
'Occasional': attends church etc monthly or several times a year.
'Rare': attends church etc once a year or less.
'Never': never or practically never attends church etc
There is a slight non-equivalence between 1983/87 and earlier studies. Because of the difference in question wording a response of 'never' in 1983/87 might be the equivalent of 'rarely' in earlier years; a response of 'rarely' in 1983/87 the equivalent of 'occasionally' in earlier years.

School leaving age

	1963	1964	1966	1969	1970	Feb. 1974	Oct. 1974	1979	1983	1987
Question No.	74a	L11a*	N11a*	95b	107a,b* 108*	130	76*	87	59a	55
Variable No.	851	851	851	76: 31	96: 61,62 64	FEB184	OCT184	M184239	Q59A	V55

---

* asked of newly sampled respondents only

Question wording

1963, 1964, 1966, 1969, 1970
'[1963, 1964, 1966: Can you tell me] how old you were when you left school?'

1970
'Did you stay on at school after the minimum school leaving age?'
IF YES: 'How old were you when you left school?'

February 1974, 1979
'How old were you when you left school?'

1983
'How old were you when you left school (or 6th form college)?'

1987
'How old were you when you completed your continuous full-time education?'

The minimum school leaving age will have been under 14 for some older respondents in the surveys of the 1960s. Thus some older respondents in the 'lowest' school-leaving age category were in fact children who stayed on at school for longer than the law required.

Social class: occupational status
          social class
          middle vs working class

	1963	1964	1966	1969	1970	Feb. 1974	Oct. 1974	1979	1983	1987
Question No.	face-sheet	face-sheet	face-sheet	face-sheet	face-sheet	139a,b 140 141 142 143a,b 144a,b 146b,c 147 148 149 150a,b 151a,b 152	84 85 87a–d 89 90 92a–d	92 93a 94a–c 95b 96a–e 98 99a 100a–c 101b 102a–e	52a 53a–e 53g–i 54b 55a–e 55g–i	49a 50a–e 50g–i 51b 52a–e 52g–i
Variable No.	963 979	964 980	965 981	78: 23,30	98: 27,34 989	FEB262 FEB268 FEB274	OCT262 OCT268	M262295 M268299	Q52A Q53A–I Q54B Q55A–I	V50A4A V52A4

Question wording

1963, 1964, 1966, 1969, 1970
Interviewers were instructed to answer the following questions about the respondent or the 'senior breadwinner' in the respondent's household:
What type of firm or organisation does/did (this person) work for?
What job does/did (this person) actually do?
IF IN CIVIL SERVICE, ARMED FORCES, POLICE ETC: What is his/her rank or grade?
IF OTHER: Does/did (this person) hold any particular position in the organisation? (e.g. foreman, typing supervisor, office manager, company secretary etc)
[1963, 1964, 1966: IF PROPRIETOR OF BUSINESS OR MANAGER] [1969, 1970: ASKED OF ALL: About how big an organisation is this?
ASKED OF ALL: Has (this person) any qualification? (such as apprenticeships, professional qualifications, university degrees, diplomas, etc.)

February 1974
'Do you at present have a paid job?' (IF RETIRED, PENSIONER OR UNEMPLOYED, ESTABLISH NORMAL JOB WHEN WORKING)
'Does/did this job involve you mostly in manual working or labouring or do/did you spend most of your time at a desk or office?'
'Are/were you self-employed or do/did you work for someone else?'
'Did you have any special training for your job?'
'Are/were you in charge of any people where you work?'
'Are/were you in charge of a small group of workers and assistants or do/did you have managerial responsibility over a large number of people?'
IF MARRIED MAN: 'Does you wife have a paid job at present?'
IF NO/DON'T KNOW: 'Has she ever worked regularly since you were married?'
'Could you say exactly what her job is/was?'
[IF MARRIED WOMAN: the above questions were asked about the husband (substituting 'he' for 'you'). Married women without full-time paid jobs were given the occupational status of their husbands.]

October 1974
'Do you at present have a paid job?'
'Are (were) you self-employed or do (did) you work for someone else?'
'What exactly do (did) you do in your job?'
'In what industry do (did) you work?'

'Does (did) your job carry any rank, title or grade?'

'How many people would you say are (were) employed in the establishment where you work (worked)?'

[IF MARRIED WOMAN: the above questions were asked about the husband (substituting 'your husband' or 'he' for 'you'). Married women without full-time paid jobs were given the occupational status of their husbands.]

1979

'Do you at present have a full-time or part-time paid job?'

'Do (did) you work full-time or part-time?'

'Are (were) you self-employed or do (did) you work for someone else?'

SELF-EMPLOYED PEOPLE ONLY: 'Do (did) you have any employees?' IF YES: 'How many employees do (did) you have?'

'Are (were) you a supervisor of any kind?' IF YES: 'How many people do (did) you supervise?'

'What exactly do (did) you do in your job?'

'In what industry do (did) you work?'

'Does (did) your job carry any rank, title or grade?'

'How many people would you say are (were) employed in the establishment where you work(ed)?'

IF RESPONDENT IS/WAS FARMER OR SMALLHOLDER: 'How many acres do (did) you work on your farm/smallholding?'

[IF MARRIED, WIDOWED, OR CO-HABITING: the above questions were asked about the spouse (substituting 'your husband/wife' or 'he/she' for 'you'). Married women without full-time paid jobs were given the occupational status of their husbands.]

1983,1987

'Which of these descriptions applies to what you were doing last week, that is in the seven days ending last Sunday? PROBE: Any others?'

'Now I want to ask you about your (present/future/last) job?' [1987: 'What is your job?'] What is the name or title of that job?'

'What kind of work do you do most of the time? IF RELEVANT: 'What are the materials made of?' [1987: 'What materials/machinery do you use?']

'What training or qualifications [1983: do you have that] are needed for that job?'

'Do you supervise or are you responsible for the work of any other people?' IF YES: 'How many?'

'Are you an employee or self-employed?'

'What does your employer [IF SELF-EMPLOYED: you] make or do at the place where you usually work?' IF FARM GIVE NUMBER OF ACRES.

'Including yourself how many people are employed at the place you usually work from?'

[1987: IF SELF-EMPLOYED: 'do you have any employees?' IF YES: 'How many?']

'Is the job full-time (30 hours + per week) or part-time (10–29 hours per week)?'

[IF MARRIED, WIDOWED, OR CO-HABITING: the above questions were asked about the spouse (substituting 'your husband/wife' or 'he/she' for 'you'). Married women without full-time paid jobs were given the occupational status of their husbands.]

Respondents with a full-time paid job (or who have retired from one) are categorised according to the status of their occupation. Respondents without a *full-time* paid job at the time of the interview, or in the period recently preceding it, are categorised according to the status of the senior breadwinner's occupation.

In the eight studies from 1963 to 1979, all three social class variables are based on a schema of occupational grades that corresponds closely to that of the Market Research Society, as follows:

Occupational grade	Occupational status	Social class	Middle vs working class
Higher managerial or professional (A)	Class A	Professional and managerial classes	Middle class
Lower managerial or administrative (B)	Class B	Professional and managerial classes	Middle class
Skilled or supervisory non-manual (C1A)	Class C1A	Intermediate and routine non-manual classes	Working class
Lower non-manual (C1B)	Class C1B	Intermediate and routine non-manual classes	Working class
Skilled manual (C2)	Class C2	Manual working class	Working class
Unskilled manual (D)	Class D	Manual working class	Working class

Respondents in occupational grade E – most of whom are dependent on state benefits for their income – are omitted from the classification.

The 1983 and 1987 studies abandoned the Market Research Society's occupational grades for a new scheme which is not directly comparable. However, they also coded respondents according to the Registrar General's social classes, which are roughly comparable to the Market Research Society's categories, as follows:

Registrar–General's social class	*Market Research Society occupational grade*	*Social class*
Social class I	Higher managerial or professional (A)	Professional and managerial classes
Social class II	Lower managerial or administrative (B)	Professional and managerial classes
Social class III (non-manual)	Skilled or supervisory non-manual (C1A) Lower non-manual (C1B)	Intermediate and routine non-manual
Social class III (manual)	Skilled manual (C2)	Manual working class
Social class IV	Unskilled manual (D)	Manual working class
Social class V	Unskilled manual (D)	Manual working class

Readers may construct a manual vs non-manual dichotomy on the basis of occupational status. Occupational grades A, B, C1A and C1B (the Registrar-General's social classes I, II and III (non-manual)) consist of non-manual workers; classes C2 and D (the Registrar General's social classes III (manual), IV and V) of manual workers.

For information about the criteria and procedures for allocating respondents to their occupational grade, see: David Butler and Donald Stokes, *Political Change in Britain*, 2nd edition (London: Macmillan, 1974), pp. 70–3; Inter-university Consortium for Political Research, *Study of Political Change in Britain 1963–1970*, Volume II, pp. 173–81 (codebook for 1963, 1964, 1966 and 1970 studies); *The British Election Study of October 1974: Methodological Report*, pp. 30–4; Bo Sarlvik and Ivor Crewe, *Decade of Dealignment* (Cambridge: Cambridge University Press, 1983), p. 76. See also M. J. Kahan, D. Butler and D. Stokes, 'On the analytical division of social class', *British Journal of Sociology*, 17 (1966), 123–30, and D. Monk, *Social Grading on the National Readership Survey*, 4th edition (London: Joint Industry Committee for National Readership Surveys), 1978.

Subjective social class

	1963	1964	1966	1969	1970	Feb. 1974	Oct. 1974	1979	1983	1987
Question No.	65a–c	69–c† or 69a,b 69d,f	67a–c† or 67a,b 67d,f	67a,b 67d	79a–c	123a,b 124	70* 71*	73 74	49a,b	44a,b
Variable No.	800 805 810	803 808 816	819 820	75: 30–33	95: 45–47, 53–55	FEB175 FEB176 FEB177	OCT176 OCT177	M176225 M177226	Q49A Q49B	V44A V44B

† The two sets of questions were asked of random half samples.
* Asked of newly sampled respondents only.

Question wording

1963, 1964, 1966,
'There's quite a bit of talk these days about different social classes. Most people say they belong to either the middle class or the working class. Do you ever think of yourself as being in one of these classes?'
IF THINKS OF SELF IN THESE TERMS: 'Which class is that?'
IF DOES NOT THINK OF SELF IN THESE TERMS: 'Well, if you had to make a choice, would you call yourself middle class or working class?'
1964,1966 (random half samples)
'Do you ever think of yourself as belonging to a particular social class?'

IF YES: 'Which class is that?'
IF NO OR IF USES DESCRIPTION OTHER THAN MIDDLE CLASS OR WORKING CLASS: 'Most people say they belong either to the middle class or to the working class. If you had to make a choice, would you call yourself middle class or working class?'

1969, 1970
'Do you ever think of yourself as belonging to a particular social class?'
IF YES: 'Which class is that?'
IF NO OR IF USES DESCRIPTION OTHER THAN MIDDLE CLASS OR WORKING CLASS: 'Most people say they belong either to the middle class or to the working class. If you had to make a choice, would you call yourself middle class or working class?'

February 1974, October 1974, 1979, 1983, 1987
[Feb 1974, Oct 1974, 1979: 'One often hears talk about social classes.] Do you ever think of yourself as belonging to any particular class [Feb 1974, Oct 1974: of people]?'
IF YES: 'Which class is that?'
IF OTHER THAN MIDDLE CLASS/WORKING CLASS, NO OR DON'T KNOW: 'Most people say they belong either to the middle class or to the working class. If you had to make a choice, would you call yourself middle class or working class?'

Trade union membership

	1963	1964	1966	1969	1970	Feb. 1974	Oct. 1974	1979	1983	1987
Question No.	76a–c	73b,c	–	83c,d 83i–k	86c,d 86k–m	119a–c	68*	61 63	52c 54d	49c 51d
Variable No.	877 879 881	859 860 878 880 882	–	76: 13–16, 21–25	96: 19–22, 29–33	FEB245 FEB247 FEB247	OCT245 OCT247 OCT247	M245190 M000303 M000303 M000304 M000305	Q52C Q54D	V49C V51D

---

* asked of newly sampled respondents only.

Question wording

1963
'Does anyone in this household belong to a trade union?'
IF YES: 'Who is it that belongs?'
  'What trade union is that?'

1964, 1969, 1970
IF HAS PAID JOB: 'Are you a member of a trade union?'
IF YES: 'Which trade union is that?'
IF DOES NOT HAVE PAID JOB: 'Does anyone in this household belong to a trade union?'
IF YES: 'Who is it that belongs?'
  'Which trade union is that?'

February 1974
'Do you or anyone else in your household belong to a trade union?'
IF YES: 'Who is a member?'
  'Which union do you/does he/does she belong to?'

October 1974
'Do you belong to a trade union?'
IF YES: 'Which trade union is that?'
'Is anyone else in this household a member of trade union?'
IF YES: 'Who is that? Which trade union does he/she belong to?'

1979
'Are you a member of a trade union?' IF YES: 'Which union?'
'Is anybody else in your household a member of a trade union?'
IF YES: 'Could you tell me the name(s) of the union(s) and who in the household is a member?'

1983
'Are you now, or have you ever been, a member of a trade union?'
'Is your (husband/wife) now, or has (he/she) ever been, a member of a trade union?'

1987
'Are you now a member of a trade union or staff association?'
IF NO: 'Have you ever been a member of a trade union or staff association?'

The three categories are defined as follows:
MEMBER: respondent belongs to a trade union.
SPOUSE OF MEMBER: respondent does not belong to trade union but his/her spouse does.
NON-MEMBER: neither the respondent nor his/her spouse belongs to a trade union.
A 'trade union' is defined as a union or association affiliated to the Trade Union Congress. Most but not all are also affiliated to the Labour party.
The questions do not allow for precise comparability. The 1964, 1969 and 1970 studies ask only respondents in jobs whether they belong to a trade union and only respondents not in jobs whether anyone else in their household does. Thus an employed respondent who does not belong to a trade union but whose spouse does would be categorised as a non-member, not as a spouse of a member.
Respondents who belonged to a trade union in the past but are no longer members count as non-members.

Type of school

	1963	1964	1966	1969	1970	Feb. 1974	Oct. 1974	1979	1983	1987
Question No.	74B	L11B*	N11b*	94	106*	129	75*	85 86a,b	60a	26†
Variable No.	853	853	853	76: 29	96: 60	FEB183	OCT183	M183314	Q60A	V126

* asked of newly sampled respondents only.
† self-completion questionnaire

Question wording

1963, 1964, 1966
IF WENT TO SCHOOL: 'And what kind of school was that?'

1969, 1970, February 1974, October 1974
'What kind of school did you go to (i.e. last school)?'

1979
'What kind of school did you go to, that is the past school you attended? Was it, for example, an elementary school, a grammar school, a comprehensive, or what?'
'How did you get into that school? Did you have to pass an exam?'
'Did you go to a school where parents had to pay tuition fees?'

1983
'What kind of school was your last school: for instance, was it an elementary school, grammar school, comprehensive, or what?'
UNLESS PRIMARY ONLY OR SPECIAL SCHOOL: 'Did you have to pass any kind of exam to get into that school, or not?
'Did you go to any school where your parents or guardian had to pay tuition fees?' IF YES: 'At primary level, secondary level, or both?'

1987
'Which one of these types of school did you last attend full-time?'

1987
'Did you go to a private fee-paying primary or secondary school in Britain?' IF YES: 'At primary level, secondary level, or both?'

STATE NON-SELECTIVE: secondary modern, technical, comprehensive, elementary, church, junior secondary, central, intermediate, higher grade, council, all-age and advanced division schools.
STATE SELECTIVE: grammar, grammar-type, direct grant, county high, secondary grammar, senior secondary (Scotland), higher grade, grant-aided and voluntary-aided schools.
PRIVATE FEE-PAYING: independent fee-paying, 'public' and commercial private schools.
Respondents attending a school that fits into none of the three categories above were excluded from the variable.

Unemployed. *See* employment status

University/polytechnic education

	1963	1964	1966	1969	1970	Feb. 1974	Oct. 1974	1979	1983	1987
Question No.	75a	L12a*	–	96a,b	–	131b	77*	88 89	61a	–
Variable No.	857	857	–	76: 33	–	FEB186	OCT185A	M185A315	Q61A	–

* asked of newly sampled respondents only.

Question wording

1963, 1964
'Did you have any full-time or part-time education after leaving school?' IF YES: 'What was that?'

1969, 1970
'Did you have any further education after that?' IF YES: 'What was that?'

February 1974, October 1974
'Did you have any further education after that?' IF YES: 'What sort of further education was that?'

1979
'And did you have any further education or training, full-time or part-time, after leaving school?' IF YES: 'What sort of education or training was that?'

1983
'Have you had (or are you now in) any full-time higher or further education at any kind of college, university or polytechnic after leaving school or later?'
IF YES, PROBE: 'At a university or polytechnic, or at another kind of college?'

Because of inconsistent coding schemes across surveys, 'further education' is restricted to respondents who attended a university, polytechnic (or technical college before polytechnics were established in the mid-1960s). It does not include those who attended teacher training, commercial or nursing colleges. Because of inconsistent coding schemes part-time students are included until February 1974 but excluded thereafter.

Vote

	1963	1964	1966	1969	1970	Feb. 1974	Oct. 1974	1979	1983	1987
Question No.	47a	40d	44c	58a	50c	87b	34	41	9a	8a
Variable No.	551	363	364	74: 62	94: 25	FEB115	OCT115	M115147	Q9A	V8A

Question wording

1963
'If the general election were held tomorrow, which party would you vote for?'

1969
'If you were voting in a general election tomorrow, which party would you vote for?'

1964, 1966, 1970, February 1974, October 1974,
'Which party did you vote for?'

1979, 1983, 1987
'Which party did you vote for in the general election?'

In 1963 and 1969 party choice is *intended* vote 'if a general election were held tomorrow'; in all other years it is respondents' recall of their actual vote at the general election.
In 1983 and 1987 respondents answering 'Liberal', 'SDP' and 'Alliance' were coded separately. The small number answering 'Alliance' are included in the combined Alliance figure in the tables, but are not allocated to either the Liberal or SDP categories.

Age + Class

This variable combines a three-category version of the Age category with Social Class. The three age categories are 18 to 34, 35 to 54, and 55+. For information about question numbers, variable numbers and question wording see the entry for the separate variables.

Age + Gender

This variable combines a four-category version of Age and Gender. The four age categories are 24 and under, 25 to 44, 45 to 64 and 65+. For information about question numbers, variable numbers and question wording see the entry for the separate variables.

Class + Economic Sector

This variable combines Social class with Economic Sector. For information about question numbers, variable numbers and question wording see the entry for the separate variables.

Class + Employment Status

This variable combines Social Class with Employment Status. The latter is reduced to two categories:
'Self-employed with employees' + 'self-employed without employees' = Self-employed
'Manager' + 'Foreman/supervisor' + 'Employee' = Employee

'Unemployed' is omitted from the analysis
For information about question numbers, variable numbers and question wording see the entry for the separate variables.

Class + Housing

This variable combines Social Class with Housing. For information about question numbers, variable numbers and question wording see the entry for the separate variables.

Class + Trade Union

This variable combines Social Class with a two-category version of Trade Union Membership. The latter combines 'spouse of member' and 'non-member' to form a single category of 'non-member'. For information about question numbers, variable numbers and question wording see the entry for the separate variables.

Gender + Class

This variable combines Gender with a four-category version of Social Class: occupational status. The four categories of the latter are: A + B/C1A/C1B/C2 + D. For information about question numbers, variable numbers and question wording see the entry for the separate variables.

Marital Status (2-category) + Gender

This variable combines Marital Status (2-category) with Gender into a four-category combined variable. For information about question numbers, variable numbers and question wording see the entry for the separate variables.

Marital Status (4-category) + Gender

This variable combines Marital Status (4-category) with Gender into a eight-category combined variable. For information about question numbers, variable numbers and question wording see the entry for the separate variables.

Political Generation + Partisanship

This variable combines Political Generation with Partisanship to create an eight-category variable. It is restricted to Conservative and Labour identifiers only. For information about question numbers, variable numbers and question wording see the entry for the separate variables.

Religion + Religiosity

This variable combines Religion with Religiosity to create a three-category variable:
1. Regular Anglican
2. Regular Non-conformist
3. Regular Catholic
For information about question numbers, variable numbers and question wording see the entry for the separate variables.

Subjective and objective class

This variable combines Social Class: middle vs working class with Subjective Social Class. For information about question numbers, variable numbers and question wording see the entry for the separate variables.

In this combined variable, Subjective Social Class is reduced to three categories, as follows:

'Spontaneous middle class' + 'Forced middle class'	= Middle Class
'No class'	= No class
'Spontaneous working class' + 'Forced working class'	= Working class

Business power

	1963	1964	1966	1969	1970	Feb. 1974	Oct. 1974	1979	1983	1987
Question No.	23	26	25	28	26	–	60	56b	38b	11†
Variable No.	248	249	250	73: 54	93: 49	–	OCT491	M491180	Q38B	V111

† self-completion questionnaire.

Question wording

1963, 1964, 1966, 1969, 1970, October 1974, 1979
'Do you think that big business has too much power in this country or not? [1963: or do you think that it doesn't have too much power?]'

1983
'Thinking now of trade unions and big business in this country . . . do you think that big business in this country has too much power, or not?'

1987
'How about business and industry? Do they have too much power or too little power?'
[Respondents were invited to tick one of five boxes labelled 'Far too much power', 'Too much power', 'About the right amount of power', 'Too little power' and 'Far too little power'.]

The question in the 1987 study has five answer categories whereas in all previous studies it has two. For the purposes of comparability, the 1987 categories 'far too much power' and 'too much power' are combined into 'business has too much power' and respondents answering 'about the right amount of power' are omitted from the variable.

Business + Trade union power

This variable combines Business Power with Trade Union Power. For information about question numbers, variable numbers and question wording see the entry for the separate variables.

Campaign wavering

	1963	1964	1966	1969	1970	Feb. 1974	Oct. 1974	1979	1983	1987
Question No.	–	40h 40n 40t	44g 44m 44s	–	50g 50m 50s	92	35e 36d 37c	42	9b	8b
Variable No.	–	375	376	–	94: 31,40, 47	FEB122 FEB123	OCT115C OCT116C OCT119D	M119148	Q9B	V8B

Question wording

1964, 1966, 1970
ASKED OF THOSE WHO VOTED CONSERVATIVE, LABOUR OR LIBERAL: 'Did you think of voting for any other party?'
IF YES: 'Which party [1970: is] was that?'

February 1974, October 1974, 1979, 1983, 1987
'Was there any time during the election campaign when you seriously thought you might vote for another party?' IF YES: 'Which party?'

Respondents who thought of voting for two or more parties other than the one they eventually voted for are coded as 'other'.

Cares about election result

	1963	1964	1966	1969	1970	Feb. 1974	Oct. 1974	1979	1983	1987
Question No.	50	48	47	59	56	10	4	–	1a	1
Variable No.	440	441	442	74: 64	94: 60	FEB021	OCT021	–	Q1	V1

Question wording

1963, 1969

'Would you say that you usually care a good deal which party wins a general election or that you don't care very much which party wins?'

1964, 1966, 1970, February 1974, October 1974, 1983, 1987
'Would you say that you cared a good deal which party won the election or that you didn't care very much which party won?'

Interest in politics

	1963	1964	1966	1969	1970	Feb. 1974	Oct. 1974	1979	1983	1987
Question No.	31	7	6	–	6	14	13*	15	–	–
Variable No.	125	126	127	–	91: 47	FEB024	OCT024	M024061	–	–

* asked of newly sampled respondents only.

Question wording

1963
'How much interest do you generally have in what's going on in politics – a good deal, some or not much?'

1964, 1966, 1970
'How much interest did you have in the campaign – a good deal, some, or not much?'

February 1974, October 1974, 1979
'How much interest would you say you take in politics – a great deal, some, not much or none at all?'

Because of variations in question wording and answer categories across surveys, readers should interpret comparisons over time with care. The question in 1964, 1966 and 1970 refers to interest in the campaign; later surveys to interest in politics. The answer category 'none at all' was added to the question in February

1974, October 1974 and 1979. For purposes of comparison with earlier surveys it has been combined with the 'not much' category.

Issues: availability of abortion

	1963	1964	1966	1969	1970	Feb. 1974	Oct. 1974	1979	1983	1987
Question No.	–	–	–	–	–	–	26h	26g	451	43j
Variable No.	–	–	–	–	–	–	OCT457	M457101	Q45L	V43J

Question wording

October 1974, 1979
'Now we would like your views on some of the general changes that have been taking place in Britain over the last few years.
'How do you feel about the availability of abortion on the National Health Service?'
'Has it gone much too far, gone a little too far, is about right, not gone quite far enough, or not gone nearly far enough?'

1983
'Finally, on election issues. I want to ask about some changes that have been happening in Britain over the years. For each one I read out can you say whether you think it has gone too far or not gone far enough? [1983: or is it about right?]'
'The availability of abortion on the National Health Service?'
[In 1987 respondents were handed an answer card on which the answer categories were: gone much too far, gone too far, about right, not gone far enough, not gone nearly far enough, don't know.]

The October 1974, 1979 and 1987 question adopted a five-category answer format but the 1983 question a three-category answer format. For purposes of comparison, therefore, responses to the October 1974, 1979 and 1987 questions are collapsed into three categories, as follows:

'Gone much too far' + 'Gone a little too far' = Gone Too Far
'About right' = About Right
'Not gone quite far enough' + 'Not gone nearly far enough' = Not Gone Far Enough

Respondents answering 'don't know' are excluded from the variable. They are not included in the 'about right' category.

Issues: capital punishment

	1963	1964	1966	1969	1970	Feb. 1974	Oct. 1974	1979	1983	1987
Question No.	22	–	27	29	24 or	–	–	38f	42c	–
Variable No.	224	–	225	73: 55	93: 50	–	–	M000134	Q42C	–

Question wording

1963, 1966, 1969, 1970
'Did you want [1963: Would you like] to see the death penalty kept or abolished?'

1979

'I am going to read out a list of things that some people believe a Government should do. What is your view about bringing back the death penalty? Is it:

Very important that it should be done
Fairly important that it should be done
It doesn't matter either way
Fairly important that it should not be done
Very important that it should not be done?'

1983
'Please say whether you agree or disagree with each of these statements, or say if you are not sure either way:
"Britain should bring back the death penalty".'

The 1987 study did ask a question about capital punishment (Q. 21n of the self-completion questionnaire), but its wording is not comparable with the questions asked in previous studies.
Respondents coded 'in some cases' or 'it depends' are excluded from the variable.

Issues: economic redistribution

	1963	1964	1966	1969	1970	Feb. 1974	Oct. 1974	1979	1983	1987
Question No.	–	–	–	–	–	–	27k	38j	34b	21a†
Variable No.	–	–	–	–	–	–	OCT470	M470138	Q34B	V121A

---

† self-completion questionnaire

Question wording

October 1974, 1979
'I am going to read out a list of things that some people believe a Government should do. For each one can you say whether you feel it is:

1. Very important that it should be done
2. Fairly important that it should be done
3. It doesn't matter either way
4. Fairly important that it should not be done
5. Very important that it should not be done

Now, using one of the answers on this card, what is your view about redistributing income and wealth in favour of ordinary working people?'

1983
'Please say whether you agree or disagree with each of these statements, or say if you are not sure either way:
'Income and wealth should be redistributed towards ordinary working peopole?'

1987
'Please tick one box for each statement below to show how much you agree or disagree with it:
"Government should redistribute income from the better off to those who are less well-off".'
[The boxes were labelled 'Agree strongly', 'Agree', 'Neither agree nor disagree', 'Disagree', 'Disagree strongly'.]

The October 1974, 1979 and 1987 question adopted a five-category answer format but the 1983 question a three-category answer format. For purposes of comparison, therefore, responses to the October 1974, 1979 and 1987 questions are collapsed into three categories, as follows:
'Very important that it should be done'
'Fairly important that it should be done   = Should Be Done

'Does not matter either way'   = Does Not Matter

'Fairly important that it should not be done'
'Very important that it should not be done'   = Should Not Be Done

Respondents answering 'don't know' are excluded from the variable.

Issues: Inflation: government's handling

	1963	1964	1966	1969	1970	Feb. 1974	Oct. 1974	1979	1983	1987
Question No.	–	–	–	–	–	15	14a	16a	29a	13a*
Variable No.	–	–	–	–	–	FEB025	OCT025	M025062	Q29A	V113A

---

* self-completion questionnaire

Question wording

February 1974
'How well do you think the last Conservative government handled the problem of rising prices – very well, fairly well, not very well or not at all well?'

October 1974, 1979
'How well do you think the recent Labour government [October 1974: has] handled the problem of rising prices [October 1974: since taking over] – very well, fairly well, not very well or not at all well?'

1983
'On the whole, do you think the Conservative government over the last four years has handled the problem of inflation very well, fairly well, not very well or not at all well?'

1987
'Between 1983 and 1987, how well or badly do you think the Conservative government handled each of the following issues?

"Prices?"

[Respondents could tick one of four boxes marked 'very well', 'fairly well', 'not very well', 'not at all well']

The party complexion of the government referred to in the question was Conservative in February 1974, 1983 and 1987 and Labour in October 1974 and 1979.

Issues: Inflation: importance of issue

	1963	1964	1966	1969	1970	Feb. 1974	Oct. 1974	1979	1983	1987
Question No.	–	–	–	–	–	17	14c	16c	20a(iii)	–
Variable No.	–	–	–	–	–	FEB027	OCT027	M027064	Q2043	–

Question wording

February 1974, October 1974
'Think about when you were deciding about voting. How important to you when you were deciding about voting was the issue of rising prices – the most important single thing, fairly important or not very important?'

1979

'Think about when you were deciding about voting. How important to you then was the issue of rising prices – extremely important, fairly important, or not very important?'

1983

'Here is a list of six issues that were discussed during the election. When you were deciding about voting, how important was each of these issues to you? [Next, inflation.] Was it extremely important, quite important or not very important to you in deciding about voting?'

The February 1974, October 1974 and 1983 questions refer to 'rising prices', the 1987 question to 'inflation'. The strongest category of importance is 'the most important single thing' in February and October 1974, 'extremely important' in 1979 and 1983. These are treated as equivalent for the purposes of comparison.

Issues: nationalisation/privatisation

	1963	1964	1966	1969	1970	Feb. 1974	Oct. 1974	1979	1983	1987
Question No.	20	23a	20a	–	–	46	21a	24a	37	36a,b
Variable No.	214	215	216	–	–	FEB073	OCT073	M073086	Q37	V36A V36B

Question wording

1963, 1964, 1966

'There's also a lot of talk about nationalising industry. Which of these statements comes closest to what you yourself feel should be done? If you don't have an opinion about this, just say so.'

 a. A lot more industries should be nationalised.
 b. Only a few more industries, such as steel, should be nationalised.
 c. No more industries should be nationalised, but the industries that are nationalised now should stay nationalised.
 d. Some of the industries that are nationalised now should be de-nationalised.
 e. No opinion/don't know.

February 1974, October 1974, 1979

'There has been a lot of talk recently about nationalisation, that is, the government owning and running industries like steel and electricity. Which of these statements comes closest to what you yourself feel should be done. If you haven't a view on this, just say so.'

 1. A lot more industries should be nationalised.
 2. Only a few more industries should be nationalised.
 3. No more industries should be nationalised, but the industries that are nationalised now should stay nationalised.
 4. Some of the industries that are now nationalised should become private companies.
 5. No opinion/don't know.

1983

'Just to clarify your views on nationalisation, please tell me from this card which of the four statements comes closest to what you think should be done, or say if you can't choose any.'

[Card is identical to February 1974, October 1974 and 1979 except that category 5 is 'Can't choose/don't know.]

1987

'Just to make sure about your views, are you generally in favour of more nationalisation of companies by government, more privatisation of companies by government, or should things be left as they are now?'
IF MORE NATIONALISATION OR PRIVATISATION
'A lot more (nationalisation/privatisation) or a little more?'

Issues: Nationalisation/privatisation: importance of issue

	1963	1964	1966	1969	1970	Feb. 1974	Oct. 1974	1979	1983	1987
Question No.	–	–	–	–	–	50	21e	24d	20a(v)	–
Variable No.	–	–	–	–	–	FEB077	OCT077	M077089	Q20A5	–

Question wording

February 1974
'Think about when you were deciding about voting. How important to you when deciding about voting was the question of nationalisation – the most important single thing, fairly important or not very important?'

October 1974, 1979
'When you were deciding about voting, how important was the question of nationalisation – [October 1974: the most important single thing] [1979: extremely important], fairly important, or not very important?'

1983
'Here is a list of six issues that were discussed during the election. When you were deciding about voting, how important was each of these issues to you? [Next, nationalisation.] Was it extremely important, quite important or not very important to you in deciding about voting?'

The strongest category of importance is 'the most important single thing' in February and October 1974, 'extremely important' in 1979 and 1983. These are treated as equivalent for the purposes of comparison.

Issues: pornography

	1963	1964	1966	1969	1970	Feb. 1974	Oct. 1974	1979	1983	1987
Question No.	–	–	–	–	–	–	26c	26c	45c	43c
Variable No.	–	–	–	–	–	–	OCT452	M452097	Q45C	V43C

Question wording

October 1974, 1979
'Now we would like your views on some of the general changes that have been taking place in Britain over the last few years. How do you feel about the right to show nudity and sex in films and magazines? Has it gone much too far, gone a little too far, is about right, not gone quite far enough, or not gone nearly far enough?'

1983, 1987
'Finally, on election issues, I want to ask about some changes that have been happening in Britain over the years. For each one I read out can you say whether you think it has gone too far or not gone far enough? [1983: or is it about right?]'

"The right to show nudity and sex in films and magazines"

[In 1987 respondents were handed an answer card on which the answer categories were: gone much too far, gone too far, about right, not gone far enough, not gone nearly far enough, don't know.]

The October 1974, 1979 and 1987 question adopted a five-category answer format but the 1983 question a three-category answer format. For purposes of comparison, therefore, responses to the October 1974, 1979 and 1987 questions are collapsed into three categories, as follows:

'Gone much too far' + 'Gone a little too far'   = Gone Too Far

'About right'   = About Right

'Not gone quite far enough' + 'Not gone nearly far enough'   = Not Gone Far Enough

Respondents answering 'don't know' are excluded from the variable. They are not included in the 'about right' category.

Issues: poverty

	1963	1964	1966	1969	1970	Feb. 1974	Oct. 1974	1979	1983	1987
Question No.	–	–	–	–	–	–	27j	38i	35b	33b
Variable No.	–	–	–	–	–	–	OCT469	M469137	Q35B	V33B

Question wording

October 1974, 1979
'I am going to read out a list of things that some people believe a Government should do. For each one can you say whether you feel it is:

1. Very important that it should be done
2. Fairly important that it should be done
3. It doesn't matter either way
4. Fairly important that it should not be done
5. Very important that it should not be done

Now, using one of the answers on this card, what is your view about spending more money to get rid of poverty in Britain?'

1983
'Do you think the Government should or should not do each of the following things, or doesn't it matter either way:

"Spend more money to get rid of poverty"?

1987
'Please use this card to say whether you think the government should or should not do the following things, or doesn't it matter either way?

"Spend more money to get rid of poverty"?

[Respondents were handed a card on which the answer categories were: Definitely should, Probably should, Doesn't matter either way, Probably should not, Definitely should not, Don't know.]

Respondents answering 'don't know' are excluded from the variable. They are not included in the 'doesn't matter either way' category.

Issues: racial equality

	1963	1964	1966	1969	1970	Feb. 1974	Oct. 1974	1979	1983	1987
Question No.	–	–	–	–	–	–	26e	26e	45g	43f
Variable No.	–	–	–	–	–	–	OCT454	M454099	Q45G	V43F

Question wording

October 1974, 1979
'Now we would like your views on some of the general changes that have been taking place in Britain over the last few years. How do you feel about recent attempts to ensure equality for coloured people in Britain? Has it gone much too far, gone a little too far, is about right, not gone quite far enough, or not gone nearly far enough?'

1983, 1987
'Finally, on election issues, I want to ask about some changes that have been happening in Britain over the years. For each one I read out can you say whether you think it has gone too far or not gone far enough? [1983: or is it about right?]'

"Attempts to give equal opportunities to black people and Asians in Britain?"

[In 1987 respondents were handed a card on which the answer categories were: gone much too far, gone too far, about right, not gone far enough, not gone nearly far enough, don't know.]

The October 1974, 1979 and 1987 question adopted a five-category answer format but the 1983 question a three-category answer format. For purposes of comparison, therefore, responses to the October 1974, 1979 and 1987 questions are collapsed into three categories, as follows:

'Gone much too far' + 'Gone a little too far'	= Gone Too Far
'About right'	= About Right
'Not gone quite far enough' + 'Not gone nearly far enough'	= Not Gone Far Enough

Respondents answering 'don't know' are excluded from the variable. They are not included in the 'about right' category.

Issues: sexual equality

	1963	1964	1966	1969	1970	Feb. 1974	Oct. 1974	1979	1983	1987
Question No.	–	–	–	–	–	–	26a	26b	45b	43b
Variable No.	–	–	–	–	–	–	OCT450	M450096	Q45B	V43B

Question wording

October 1974, 1979
'Now we would like your views on some of the general changes that have been taking place in Britain over the last few years. How do you feel about the attempts to ensure equality for women? Has it gone much too far, gone a little too far, is about right, not gone quite far enough, not gone nearly far enough?'

1983, 1987
'Finally, on election issues.' I want to ask about some changes that have been happening in Britain over the years. For each one I read out can you say whether you think it has gone too far or not gone far enough? [1983: or is it about right?]'

"Attempts to give equal opportunities to women"

[In 1987 respondents were handed an answer card on which the answer categories were: gone much too far, gone too far, about right, not gone far enough, not gone nearly far enough, don't know.]

The October 1974, 1979 and 1987 question adopted a five-category answer format but the 1983 question a three-category answer format. For purposes of comparison, therefore, responses to the October 1974, 1979 and 1987 questions are collapsed into three categories, as follows:

'Gone much too far' + 'Gone a little too far'	= Gone Too Far

'About right'   = About Right

'Not gone quite far enough' + 'Not gone nearly far enough'   = Not Gone Far Enough

Respondents answering 'don't know' are excluded from the variable. They are not included in the 'about right' category.

Issues: Social services: importance of issue

	1963	1964	1966	1969	1970	Feb. 1974	Oct. 1974	1979	1983	1987
Question No.	–	–	–	–	–	57	22e	22d	20a(iv)	–
Variable No.	–	–	–	–	–	FEB084	OCT084	M084079	Q20A4	–

Question wording

February 1974
'Think about when you were deciding about voting. How important to you when you were deciding about voting was the question of social services and benefits – the most important single thing, fairly important or not very important?'

October 1974, 1979
'When you were deciding about voting, how important was the question of social services and benefits – [October 1974: the most important single thing] [1979: extremely important], fairly important, or not very important?'

1983
'Here is a list of six issues that were discussed during the election. When you were deciding about voting, how important was each of these issues to you? [Next, the health and social services.] Was it extremely important, quite important or not very important to you in deciding about voting?'

In February 1974, October 1974 and 1979 the question refers to 'social services and benefits'; in 1983 it refers to 'health and social services'. The strongest category of importance is 'the most important single thing' in February and October 1974, 'extremely important' in 1979 and 1983. These are treated as equivalent for the purposes of comparison.

Issues: Strikes: government's handling

	1963	1964	1966	1969	1970	Feb. 1974	Oct. 1974	1979	1983	1987
Question No.	–	–	–	–	–	24	16a	17a	39	–
Variable No.	–	–	–	–	–	FEB047	OCT047	M047065	Q39	–

Question wording

February 1974, October 1974, 1979
'How well do you think the recent Labour government [February 1974: the last Conservative government] generally handled the problem of strikes – very well, fairly well, not very well or not at all well?'

1983
'Do you think the Conservative government over the last four years has generally handled the problem of strikes very well, fairly well, not very well or not at all well?'

The party complexion of the government referred to in the question was Conservative in February 1974 and 1983 and Labour in October 1974 and 1979.

Issues: welfare benefits

	1963	1964	1966	1969	1970	Feb. 1974	Oct. 1974	1979	1983	1987
Question No.	–	–	–	–	–	–	26i	26a	45a	43a
Variable No.	–	–	–	–	–	–	OCT458	M458095	Q45A	V43A

Question wording

October 1974, 1979
'Now we would like your views on some of the general changes that have been taking place in Britain over the last few years. How do you feel about the welfare benefits that are available to people today? Have they gone much too far, gone a little too far, are they about right, not gone quite far enough, or not gone nearly far enough?'

1983
'Finally, on election issues, I want to ask about some changes that have been happening in Britain over the years. For each one I read out can you say whether you think it has gone too far or not gone far enough or is it about right? Thinking first about the welfare benefits that are available to people today, would you say they have gone too far, are they about right or have they gone far enough?'

1987
'And now I want to ask about some changes that have been happening in Britain over the years. For each one I read out, please use this card to say whether you think it has gone too far or not gone far enough. First, the welfare benefits that are available to people today?'

[Respondents were handed a card on which the answer categories were: gone much too far, gone too far, about right, not gone far enough, not gone nearly far enough, don't know.]

The October 1974, 1979 and 1987 question adopted a five-category answer format but the 1983 question a three-category answer format. For purposes of comparison, therefore, responses to the October 1974, 1979 and 1987 questions are collapsed into three categories, as follows:

'Gone much too far' + 'Gone a little too far'   = Gone Too Far

'About right'   = About Right

'Not gone quite far enough' + 'Not gone nearly far enough'   = Not Gone Far Enough

Respondents answering 'don't know' are excluded from the variable. They are not included in the 'about right' category.

Liberal Party: closer to Conservatives or Labour?

	1963	1964	1966	1969	1970	Feb. 1974	Oct. 1974	1979	1983	1987
Question No.	–	–	–	–	–	110	9e	53	6a	14a
Variable No.	–	–	–	–	–	FEB151	OCT151	M151166	Q6A	V14A

Question wording

February 1974, October 1974, 1979, 1983, 1987
'Generally speaking, do you regard [1983, 1987: think of] the Liberal party as [1983, 1987: being] closer to the Conservative Party or closer to the Labour Party?'

Newspaper readership

	1963	1964	1966	1969	1970	Feb. 1974	Oct. 1974	1979	1983	1987
Question No.	1a,b	2b	2b	1b	2b	1a	1*	–	2b,c	2b,c
Variable No.	74	75	76	71: 27–30	91: 36–39	FEB237	OCT237	–	Q2C	V2C

* asked of newly sampled respondents only

Question wording

1963, 1964, 1966, 1969, 1970
'[1963, 1969: First of all,] Do you read a morning newspaper regularly? IF YES: Which newspaper is that? Are there any other morning newspapers you read regularly?'

February 1974, October 1974
'Which, if any morning daily newspapers do you read regularly? (By regularly I mean 3 out of every 4 issues.) Any others?'

1983, 1987
'During the election campaign did you read any newspaper articles about the election campaign? IF YES: Which daily [1987: morning] newspaper did you read most? PROBE IF NECESSARY: Which one did you rely on most [1987: for news about the election campaign]?'

Respondents could mention more than one newspaper in all studies except 1983 and 1987. Readers of the *Financial Times, Morning Star* and regional daily newspapers are excluded from the variable.

Non-voters: preferred party

	1963	1964	1966	1969	1970	Feb. 1974	Oct. 1974	1979	1983	1987
Question No.	–	40x	44w	–	50w	93	38	–	7c	6c
Variable No.	–	393	394	–	94: 53	FEB124	OCT124	–	Q7C	V6C

Question wording

1964, 1966, 1970, February 1974, October 1974
'If you had voted, which party would you probably have voted for?'

1983, 1987
'Suppose you *had* voted: which party would you have been most likely to vote for?' DO NOT PROMPT.

Respondents answering 'don't know' or 'none' were prompted with a supplementary question in the 1964, 1966, 1970, 1983 and 1987 surveys (whose wording differs between the first three and latter two surveys). However, in this book all such respondents are categorised as 'don't know' whether or not they mentioned a party in response to the supplementary question.

In 1983 and 1987 the answer categories 'would not have voted/no party/none' and 'don't know' were not coded separately and are therefore treated as a single category in the tables.

Party image of Conservatives and Labour: extreme/moderate

	1963	1964	1966	1969	1970	Feb. 1974	Oct. 1974	1979	1983	1987
Question No.	–	–	–	–	–	9(v)	11E	–	18a	19a
Variable No.	–	–	–	–	–	FEB015 FEB016	OCT015 OCT016	–	Q18A1 Q18A2	V19A1 V19A2

Question wording

February 1974, October 1974
'On this card are listed some choices of opposite words or phrases, and I'd like you to say how much each one applies to a party [October 1974: different political parties]. [February 1974: I'm going to ask you about the Conservative party and the Labour party.] In which box would you put the Conservative party? In which box would you put the Labour party?'

		Very much	Somewhat	Neither	Somewhat	Very much	Don't know	
Extreme	Conservatives							Moderate
	Labour							

1983, 1987
'On the whole would you describe the Conservative party as extreme or moderate? And the Labour party nowadays, is it extreme or moderate?'

Party image of Conservatives and Labour: good for one/good for all classes

	1963	1964	1966	1969	1970	Feb. 1974	Oct. 1974	1979	1983	1987
Question No.	–	–	–	–	–	9(iv)	11D	–	18c	19c
Variable No.	–	–	–	–	–	FEB013 FEB014	OCT013 OCT014	–	Q18C1 Q18C2	V19C1 V19C2

Question wording

February 1974, October 1974
'On this card are listed some choices of opposite words or phrases, and I'd like you to say how much each one applies to a party [October 1974: different political parties.] [February 1974: I'm going to ask you about the Conservative party and the Labour party.] In which box would you put the Conservative party? In which box would you put the Labour party?'

		Very much	Somewhat	Neither	Somewhat	Very much	Don't know	
Good for one class	Conservatives							Good for all classes of people
	Labour							

1983, 1987
'On the whole would you describe the Conservative party as good for one class or good for all classes? And the Labour party nowadays, is it good for one class or good for all classes?'

Perceived difference between parties

	1963	1964	1966	1969	1970	Feb. 1974	Oct. 1974	1979	1983	1987
Question No.	9	13	11	9a	11a	8	8	5	6d	14d
Variable No.	149	150	151	71: 75	92: 31	FEB006	OCT006	M006028	Q6D	V14D

Question wording

1963, 1964, 1966, 1969, 1970, February 1974, October 1974
'Considering everything the parties stand for, would you say that there is a good deal of difference between the parties [February 1974, October 1974: between them], some difference or not much difference?'

1979, 1983, 1987
'Considering everything the Conservative and Labour parties stand for, would you say that there is a great [1979: deal of] difference between them, some difference, or not much difference?'

Standard of living: change in past year

	1963	1964	1966	1969	1970	Feb. 1974	Oct. 1974	1979	1983	1987
Question No.	–	–	–	–	–	–	63a	36a	50b	–
Variable No.	–	–	–	–	–	–	OCT154A	M154A125	Q50B	–

Question wording

October 1974, 1979, 1983
'Looking back over the last year or so, do you think that your [1983: would you say that your household's] income has fallen behind prices, kept up with prices or has gone up by more than prices?'

Standard of living: change in coming year

	1963	1964	1966	1969	1970	Feb. 1974	Oct. 1974	1979	1983	1987
Question No.	–	–	–	–	–	115	63b	36b	50c	–
Variable No.	–	–	–	–	–	FEB154	OCT154	M154126		–

Question wording

February 1974, October 1974, 1979
'Looking ahead to next year, do you think your income will fall behind prices, keep up with prices or go up by more than prices do?'

1983
'And looking forward to the year ahead, do you expect your household's income will fall behind prices, keep up with prices or go up by more than prices?'

Time of voting decision

	1963	1964	1966	1969	1970	Feb. 1974	Oct. 1974	1979	1983	1987
Question No.	–	40e 40k 40q	44d 44j 44p	–	48d	90	31	40	8a	7
Variable No.	–	366	367	–	368	FEB120	OCT120	M120146		V7

Question wording

1964, 1966, 1970
'How long ago did you decide to vote that way?'

February 1974, October 1974, 1979
'How long ago did you decide that you would definitely vote the way you did – a long time ago, sometime this year, or during the campaign?'

1983, 1987
'How long ago did you decide that you would definitely vote the way you did: was it a long time ago, sometime last year, sometime this year, or during the election campaign?'

The tables for 1983 and 1987 combine 'sometime last year' and 'sometime this year' into the single answer category 'sometime last year'.

Trade union power

	1963	1964	1966	1969	1970	Feb. 1974	Oct. 1974	1979	1983	1987
Question No.	26	24	21	25	21	–	59	56a	38a	10*
Variable No.	227	228	229	73: 48	93: 40	–	OCT490	M490179	Q38A	V110

* self-completion questionnaire

Question wording

1963, 1964, 1966, 1969, 1970
'Do you think that trade unions have too much power or not?'

October 1974
'Now I would like to talk about trade unions and [October 1974: big] business in this country. [1979: First, I would like to ask whether] [October 1974: Do] you think that the trade unions have too much power or not?'

1983
'Thinking now of trade unions and big business in this country . . . do you think that trade unions have too much power, or not?'

1987
'Do you think that trade unions in this country have too much power or too little power?'

[Respondents were invited to tick one of five boxes labelled 'Far too much power', 'Too much power', 'About the right amount of power', 'Too little power' and 'Far too little power'.]

The question in the 1987 study has five answer categories whereas in all previous studies it has two. For the purposes of comparability, the 1987 categories 'far too much power' and 'too much power' are combined into 'trade unions have too much power' and respondents answering 'about the right amount of power' are omitted from the variable.